A MAP of
EUROPE

J. Ellis sculpt

THE

MILITARY GUIDE

FOR

YOUNG OFFICERS,

CONTAINING

A SYSTEM of the ART of WAR;

PARADE, CAMP, FIELD DUTY; MANOEUVRES, STAND-
ING AND GENERAL ORDERS; WARRANTS, REGULA-
TIONS, RETURNS; TABLES, FORMS, EXTRACTS FROM
MILITARY ACTS; BATTLES, SIEGES, FORTS, PORTS,
MILITARY DICTIONARY, &c. WITH TWENTY-FIVE
MAPS AND COPPER PLATES.

By THOMAS SIMES, Efq.
Author of the MILITARY MEDLEY.

The SECOND EDITION, with the ADDITION of the
REGULATIONS of H. R. H. the late DUKE of CUMBER-
LAND, &c. in *Germany* and *Scotland.*

The Naval & Military Press Ltd

published in association with

ROYAL
ARMOURIES

Published by the
The Naval & Military Press
in association with the Royal Armouries

Unit 10 Ridgewood Industrial Park,
Uckfield, East Sussex, TN22 5QE
Tel: +44 (0) 1825 749494
Fax: +44 (0) 1825 765701

For a full listing of all N&MP titles, visit:
www.naval-military-press.com

MILITARY HISTORY AT YOUR FINGERTIPS

Online genealogy research:
www.military-genealogy.com

ROYAL
ARMOURIES

The Library & Archives Department at the
Royal Armouries Museum, Leeds, specialises
in the history and development of armour
and weapons from earliest times to the
present day. Material relating to the
development of artillery and modern
fortifications is held at the Royal
Armouries Museum, Fort Nelson.

For further information contact:
Royal Armouries Museum, Library, Armouries Drive,
Leeds, West Yorkshire LS10 1LT
Royal Armouries, Library, Fort Nelson, Down End Road, Fareham PO17 6AN

Or visit the Museum s website at
www.armouries.org.uk

*In reprinting in facsimile from the original, any imperfections are inevitably
reproduced and the quality may fall short of modern type and cartographic standards.*

Printed and bound by CPI Antony Rowe, Eastbourne

TO

THE KING.

WITH THE HIGHEST VENERATION FOR

YOUR MAJESTY's

MOST AUGUST PERSON AND FAMILY,

PERMIT ME

TO PRESENT THIS TREATISE TO

YOUR MAJESTY,

IN TESTIMONY OF MY ARDENT ZEAL

FOR YOUR MAJESTY's SERVICE.

THOMAS SIMES.

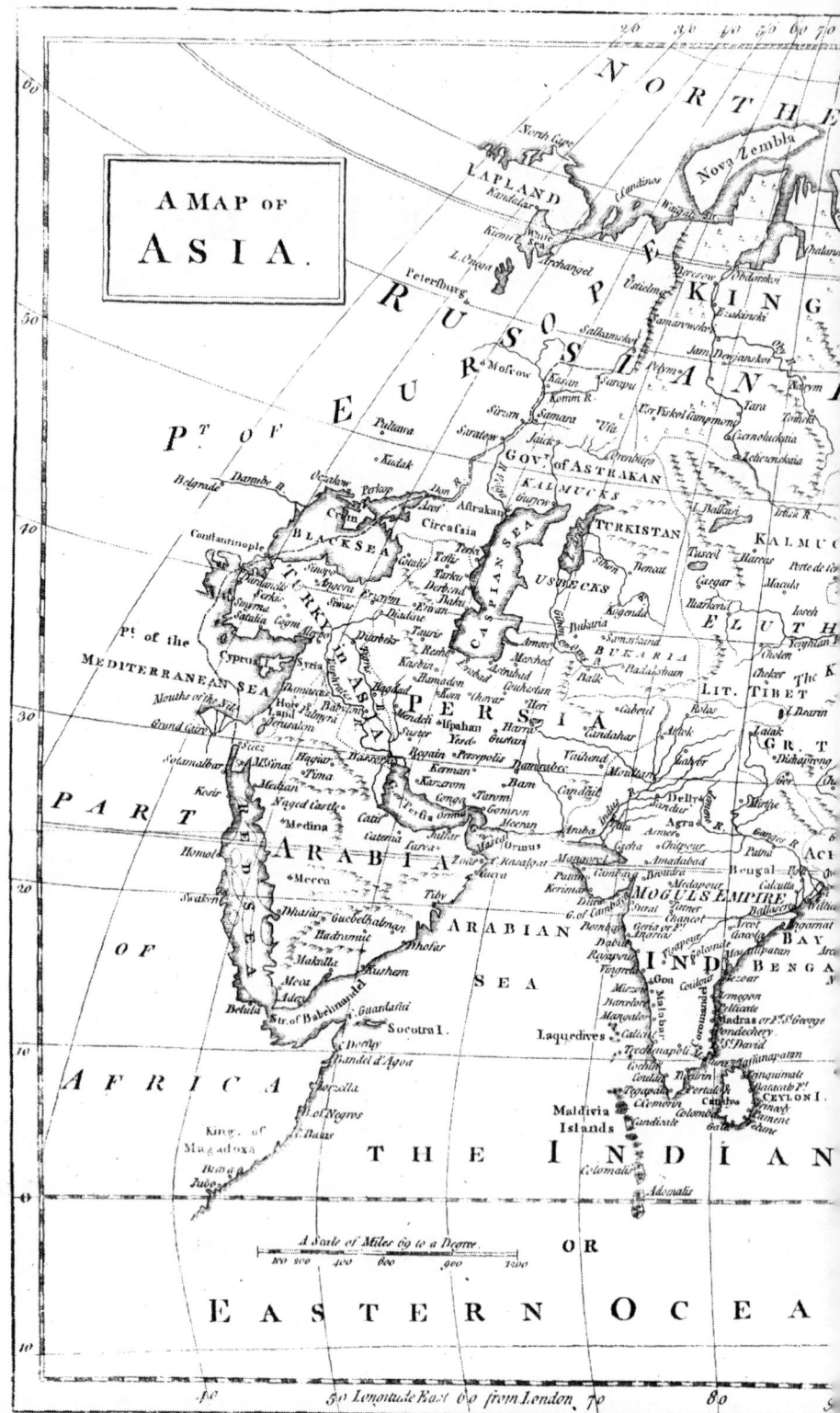

THE

MILITARY GUIDE.

MILITARY DISCIPLINE.

" NEXT to the forming of troops, military difcipline is the firft object that prefents itfelf to our notice. It is the foul of all armies; and unlefs it be eftablifhed amongft them with great prudence, and fupported with unfhaken refolution, they are no better than fo many contemptible heaps of rabble, which are more dangerous to the very ftate that maintains them, than even its declared enemies.

" It is a falfe notion, that fubordination, and a paffive obedience to fuperiors, is any debafement of a man's courage; fo far from it, that it is a general remark, that thofe armies which have been fubject to the fevereft difcipline, have always performed the greateft things.

" Many general officers imagine, that in giving out orders they do all that is expected from them; and therefore, as they are fure to find great abufes, enlarge their inftructions accordingly; in which they proceed upon a very erroneous principle, and take fuch meafures as can never be effectual in reftoring difcipline in an army wherein it has been loft or neglected.

" Few orders are beft; but they are to be executed with attention, and offences to be punifhed without refpect of either rank or extraction. All partiality and diftinction muft be utterly abolifhed, otherwife you expofe yourfelf to hate and refentment. By enforcing your authority with judgment, and fetting a proper example, you may render yourfelf at once both beloved and feared. Severity muft be accompanied with great tendernefs and moderation; fo difplayed upon every occafion as to appear void of all manner of defign, and totally the effect of a natural difpofition.

" Great punifhments are only to be inflicted for great crimes: but the more moderate they are in general, the more eafy it will be to reform abufes; becaufe all the world, concurring in the neceffity of them, will chearfully promote their effect.

" We

" We have, for example, one very pernicious custom ; which is, that of punishing marauders with certain death, so that a man is frequently hanged for a single offence ; in consequence of which they are rarely discovered ; because every one is unwilling to occasion the death of a poor wretch, for only having been seeking perhaps to gratify his hunger.

" If, instead of this method, we did but send them to the Provost's, there to be chained like galley-slaves ; and condemned to subsist upon bread and water for one, two, or three months ; or to be employed upon some of those works which are always carrying on in an army ; and not to be restored to their regiments, till the night before the engagement, or till the Commander in Chief shall think proper ; then all the world would join their endeavours to bring such delinquents to punishment : the officers upon grand guards and out-posts would not suffer one to escape ; by whose vigilance and activity the mischief would thus be soon put an entire stop to. Such as fall at present into the hands of justice, are very unfortunate indeed ; for the Provost and his party, when they discover any marauders, immediately turn their eyes another way, in order to give them an opportunity to escape : but as the Commander in Chief is perpetually complaining of the outrages which are committed, they are obliged to apprehend one now and then, who falls a sacrifice for the rest. Thus the examples that are made have no tendency towards removing the evil, or restoring discipline ; and hardly answer any other purpose, than to justify the common saying amongst the soldiers, That none but the unfortunate are hanged.—Perhaps it may be observed, that the officers likewise suffer marauders to pass by their posts unnoticed. But that is an abuse which may be easily remedied, by discovering from the prisoners what particular posts they passed by, and imprisoning the officers who commanded them, during the remainder of the campaign. This will render them careful, vigilant, and severe : nevertheless, when a man is to be punished with certain death for the offence, there are but few of them who would not risk two or three months imprisonment, rather than be instrumental to it.

" All other military punishments, when carried to extremes of severity, will be attended with the same consequences.— It is also very necessary to prevent those from being branded with the name of infamy, which should be regarded in a milder light ; as the gantlope, for instance, which in France

is

is reputed ignominious; but which, in the cafe of the foldier, deferves a different imputation, becaufe it is a punifhment which he receives from the hands of his comrades. The reafon of its being thus extravagantly vilified, proceeds from the cuftom of inflicting it in common upon whores, rogues, and fuch offenders as fall within the province of the hangman; the confequence of which is, that one is obliged to pafs the colours over a foldier's head, after he has received this punifhment, in order, by fuch an act of ceremony, to take off that idea of ignominy which is attached to it: a remedy worfe than the evil, and which is alfo productive of a much greater: for after a man has run the gantlope, his Captain immediately ftrips him, for fear he fhould defert, and then turns him out of the fervice; by which means this punifhment, how much foever neceffary, is never inflicted but for capital crimes; for when a foldier is confined for the commiffion of any trivial offence, the Commanding Officer always releafes him, upon the application of his Captain; becaufe the lofs of the man would be fome deduction from his perquifites.

" There are fome things of great importance towards the promotion of difcipline, that are altogether unattended to; which, as well as the perfons who practife them, are frequently laughed at and defpifed.—The French, for example, ridicule that law amongft the Germans, of not touching a dead horfe; which is a good inftitution, if not carried too far. Peftilential difeafes are, in a great meafure, prevented by it; for the foldiers frequently plunder dead carcaffes for their fkins, and thereby expofe themfelves to infection. It does not prevent the killing and eating of horfes during fieges, a fcarcity of provifions, or other exigencies. Let us from hence, therefore, judge, whether it is not rather ufeful than otherwife.

" The French alfo reproach the Germans for the baftinade, which is a military punifhment eftablifhed amongft them. If a German officer ftrikes, or otherwife abufes a private foldier, he is cafhiered, upon complaint made by the party injured; and is alfo compelled, on pain of forfeiting his honour, to give him fatisfaction, if he demands it, when he is no longer under his command. This obligation prevails alike through all ranks; and there are frequently inftances of general officers giving fatisfaction, at the point of the fword, to fubalterns who have quitted the fervice;

for

for there is no refufing to accept their challenge, without incurring ignominy.

" The French do not at all fcruple to ftrike a foldier with their hands; but they are hardly ever tempted to apply the ftick, becaufe that is a kind of chaftifement which has been exploded, as inconfiftent with that notion of liberty which prevails amongft them. Punifhments are certainly neceffary, provided they are not difhonourable.

" Let us compare thefe different cuftoms of the two nations, and judge which contributes moft to the good of the fervice, and the proper fupport of the point of honour. The punifhments for their officers are likewife of diftinct kinds. The French upbraid the Germans with their Provofts and their chains; the latter retort the reproach, by exclaiming againft the prifons and ropes of the French; for the German officers are never confined in the public prifons. They have a Provoft to every regiment; which poft is always given to an old Serjeant, in recompence for his fervice; but I have never heard of their officers being put in irons, unlefs for great crimes, and after they had been firft degraded.

" Thefe obfervations demonftrate the abfurdity of condemning particular cuftoms or prejudices, before one has examined their original caufes."

Nothing can be fo neceffary to the foldier as difcipline: without it, troops may become more dangerous than ufeful, more hurtful to ourfelves, than to our enemies. The means of difcipline are regulated by our military laws, and by the articles of war; which command obedience to fuperiors; and courage againft an enemy: in regard to private converfation, politenefs fhould exceed authority, and the Officer fubfide in the gentleman.

The nature of the fervice is fuch, that in actions, errors cannot be committed with impunity. The particulars neceffary to be obferved are many and various; but none more effential to victory, than a ftrict obedience to orders, and a juft obfervation of fignals: on this depends fuccefs and fafety of the troops.

GENERAL OFFICERS.

" THE inactivity of the greateft part of our General Officers, during a peace, is one of the moft prejudicial articles to the military ftate: the eafe and indolence which they enjoy at home, makes them infenfibly lofe all tafte for their profeffion; their genius is obfcured; their

under-

understanding weakened; and the excellent Officer is soon degenerated into an ordinary man.

"Suppose the peace lasts twelve years, many of our Generals, who used to distinguish themselves by their good conduct, are either dead, too old, or too infirm, to undergo the fatigues of war; yet we must have Generals, *Oh sad necessity!* which often obliges us to trust the safety of our troops, and the state itself, to officers without experience, and scarce acquainted with the occurrences of the late war. It is experience that makes the General; his capacity is not beheld in the force or number of his arms, but in the art of employing them, and in the methods he contrives to incline victory to his side. The more Generals there are at the head of our troops, capable of commanding, the more formidable they are." It was not the number of soldiers that gave us those laurels during the last war, under the commands of Ferdinand, Wolfe, Granby, Albemarle, Townshend, Amherst, Hodgson, Monckton, Murray, Draper, &c. It was owing to their military capacities to form, and resolution to execute, the greatest designs — their penetration to discover, and activity to defeat, the greatest machinations — and to the unshaken confidence of a few troops — that obtained those glorious, surprizing, and complete victories.

"The blood of the soldier and continual faults are the common steps by which some arrive in time to the reputation of excellent Generals. It is with many Generals as with Physicians, who become knowing and expert at the public expence of Peoples Lives. There might be an easy method (I imagine) to prevent the inconveniencies we speak of, by obliging the General Officers to a habitude of military exercises: the Prince might judge at leisure of the capacity of each one, and how much he is to be depended on in any emergency: they should divide the troops into brigades, who should lie as commodiously as possible, for their junction on the first order: a Lieutenant-general should command two, and each one have its Major-general. Being in this manner attached to particular corps, they would more easily discover the fort or foible of their respective commands.

"A General should be judicious and regular in his conduct; firm and resolute in his projects; vigilant, active, and alert to seize on all opportunities to bring those projects to a happy issue: his zeal for the service should furnish strength against fatigue, and intrepidity against obstacles: he should never be without a kind of diffidence, even where

there

there is no appearance of danger ; always careful for the eafe and fecurity of his own forces, and active in diftreffing the enemy. Now raifed by his merit to fo exalted a poft, let him regard the favours received as the price of his fervices ; let him efteem them in proportion to the pains and labours they have coft him ; employ thefe very favours to the glory of his Prince ; and ufe that opulence which fortune has beftowed on him, to foften the diftreffes of the inferior ftations."

M. Saxe, in his Reveries concerning the Art of War, makes thefe remarks refpecting a Commander in Chief.

" Of all the accomplifhments, therefore, that are required for the compofition of this exalted character, Courage is the firft ; without which, I make no account of the others, becaufe they then will be rendered ufelefs.—The fecond is Genius, which muft be ftrong and fertile in expeditions.— The third is Health.

" He ought to poffefs a talent for fudden and happy refources ; to have the art of penetrating into other men, and of remaining impenetrable himfelf. He fhould be endued with a capacity prepared for every thing ; with activity, accompanied by judgment ; with fkill, to make a proper choice upon all occafions ; and with an exactnefs of difcernment."

A i d s-d e-C a m p.

" AIDS-DE-CAMP are Officers attached to the perfon of a General Officer, to carry his orders. This employment is of greater importance than is generally believed ; it is, however, often intrufted to young men without experience, and often without capacity ; but in fome of the foreign fervices they give great attention to this article.

The Marefchal De Puyffegur fays, in his Art of War, on the fubject of Aids-de-Camp, " That in the time of the great Prince of Condé and Marefchal Turenne, the employment of Aid-de-camp was always filled with Officers of character. The reafon is, that in a battle, a moment may change the face of affairs ; infomuch that though an order fent by the General for an inferior Officer to act in fuch or fuch a manner, and which was properly given, with refpect to the fituation of the action at that moment, yet, before the Aid-de-camp arrives and delivers it, the actual ftate of the action may be fo far changed, as that the order becomes improper. It is therefore neceffary, that

he

he who carries it, has comprehended the fpirit in which the General meant it, and takes care not to deliver it in fuch a pofitive manner, as to oblige him who receives it to act up to the letter of the order, and not to leave him liberty to change it." The Marefchal fays, he faw a battle loft, becaufe an Aid-de-camp had, upon a falfe reprefentation of the local made to the General, been fent to him who commanded the right wing, to order him to change his ground; who, knowing the ftrength of it, tried to argue the matter, but to no purpofe; the Aid-de-camp delivered the pofitive order, and the Commander was obliged to obey: the enemy immediately poffeffed themfelves of his advantageous poft, and by that means won the battle.

STAFF OF THE ARMY.

" THE Staff properly exifts only in the time of war; the QUARTER-MASTER-GENERAL may be reckoned the firft perfon belonging to it: he works with the General on whatever regards the marches of the army; and the evening before they are to move, he gives to each General Officer, who is to conduct a column, a copy of what regards him; and to the General Officers of the day, a copy of the whole order of that day, that they may caufe every thing to be executed with his order by the General. He alfo keeps a roll of the General Officers, and makes them be advertifed when there is any thing new, which regards their tour to march. He marches to the new camp with the Major-general of the day, and diftributes the ground which the Major-general has marked out to be occupied by the army; he makes the Fourier mark the head-quarters, and the quarters of the General Officers; he vifits the avenues of the camp; reconnoitres the country round; makes the inhabitants give him exact information; and, on the report he makes the General, he receives his orders for regulating the marches of the army, in the manner the General intends they fhould be executed. It is he who delivers to each of the General Officers a copy of the order of battle; and he figns and diftributes all the orders for foraging, and commonly reconnoitres the quarters where the army can forage. In fhort, though he has no direct authority over the troops, yet he is continually with the General, whofe orders almoft always pafs through his hands; and as he necefjarily poffeffes the fecret of the movements of the army, this employment gives very great confideration to him who exercifes it,

and

and requires an intelligent Officer, well verfed in the great
parts of war : he has commonly 3 or 4 affiftants to eafe him
in his functions; and they are commonly gratified, at the
end of fome campaigns, with a Colonel's rank. The
Quarter-mafter-general, in a day of action, ftays clofe by
the General ; and, on every other day, he goes to receive
the parole from the Major-general of the day : but, when
neceffarily employed, he fends one of his affiftants to fetch
it to him.

" The ADJUTANT-GENERAL makes the detail of the
duty of the whole infantry of the army, with the Brigade-
majors. He keeps an exact ftate of the brigade, of each regiment in particular, and of the companies of grenadiers,
with a roll of the Colonels, Lieutenant-colonels, and Majors of the infantry. He is every day at the head-quarters
to take the orders which he receives from the Major-general
of the day ; he then diftributes them at his own quarters to
all the Majors of the Brigade, from whom he demands the
number of men they are to furnifh for the duty of the army, and informs them of any detail which may concern
them. In the morning, he is at the parade of the guards,
and fees them defile : he may, if he has time, vifit them at
their pofts, and always fee that the piquets are in good
order : he alfo accompanies and follows the General ; by
whofe orders he commands all the detachments of infantry,
and fees them march off from their rendezvous, or leave
this care to his affiftants.

On marching days, he follows the Major-general of the
day with the encampment, and diftributes to a Major of
each brigade the ground of the camp ; he makes a daily
report to the General, of the fituation of all the pofts of
the infantry, placed for the fafety of the army, and of any
changes made in their pofts. In a day of battle, the Adjutant-general fees the infantry drawn up, after which he
places himfelf by the General, to receive any orders which
may regard the body of which he has the detail. In a
fiege, he orders the number of workmen demanded ; he
counts them when they return from work, and figns the
billets for their payments : he receives the guards of the
trenches at their rendezvous, examines if they are in good
condition, and alfo gives and figns all the orders for fkirmifhing parties. As he is charged with all the duty of the
whole infantry, he has orderly men for that body ; that is
to fay, a Serjeant and Corporal from each brigade of infantry

fantry in the line, to carry them the orders which he may have occasion to send from the General.

N. B. To avoid repetition, the duty of the Adjutants-general of the cavalry and dragoons, *mutatis mutandis*, is the same with the infantry.

In France, the Major of the oldest regiment of each brigade, is the Major of Brigade ; in England, Holland, and elsewhere, he is a particular officer appointed for that purpose ; and towards the end of the late war, the Prince of Orange gave them a Lieutenant-colonel's rank, that the Majors of the regiments of each brigade might receive the parole and orders from them.

The MAJORS OF BRIGADE go every day to receive the orders from the Adjutant-general ; there they write exactly whatever is dictated to them ; from thence they go and give the orders, at the place appointed for that purpose, to the different Majors or Adjutants of the regiments which compose that brigade ; regulate with them the number of men and Officers which each are to furnish for the duty of the army, taking care to keep an exact roster, that one may not report more than another, and each march in their tour : in short, the Major of Brigade is charged with the particular detail in his own brigade, in much the same way as the Adjutant-general is charged with the general detail of the army. The Major of Brigade sends every morning to the Adjutant-general an exact return, by battalion and company, of the men of his brigade missing at the retreat; or a report expressing that none are absent : he also mentions the officers absent with or without leave.

As all the orders pass through the hands of the Majors of Brigade, they have infinite occasions of making known their talents and exactness."

The

Compliment due to General Officers, &c. with the Detail of Officers and Men they are intitled to.							
G U A R D S.	Captains.	Lieutenants.	Ensigns.	Serjeants.	Drummers.	Fifers.	Priv. men.
The General in Chief has — —	1	1	1	2	2	2	50
General of horse and foot — —	1	1	1	2	2	2	50
Lieutenant-general of horse and foot	—	1	—	1	1	1	30
Major-general of horse and foot —	—	—	1	1	1	1	20
Brigadier — — — —	—	—	—	1	—	—	12
Quarter-master-general (as such only)	—	—	—	1	—	—	12
The Majors of Brigade, incamped together — — — }				1			2
Judge Advocate — — —				1			7
Provost-marshal, as such, a Serjeant and eighteen men; but when he has prisoners, there is added a Subaltern, Serjeant, drummer, fifer, and thirty men. }		1		2	1	1	48

The Train of Artillery, according to the number they shall require.

The guard which mounts on the General in Chief has always colours.

SPIES AND GUIDES.

" ONE cannot bestow too much attention in the procuring of spies and guides: M. de Monticuculli says, that they serve as eyes to the head, and are equally as essential to a Commander; which observation of his is certainly very just; money, therefore, should not be wanting upon a proper occasion; for the acquisition of such as are good, is cheap at any price. They are to be taken out of the country in which the war is carried on, selecting those only who are active and intelligent, and dispersing them every where amongst the General Officers of the enemy; amongst his suttlers; and, above all, amongst the purveyors of provisions; because their stores, magazines, and other preparations, furnish the best intelligence concerning his real design.

" The

" The fpies are not to know one another ; and are to confift of various ranks or orders ; fome to affociate with the foldiers, others to follow the army, under the difguife of pedlars ; but it is neceffary that all of them fhould be admitted to the knowledge of fome one belonging to the firft order of their fraternity, from whom they may occafionally receive any thing that is to be conveyed to the General who pays them : this charge muft be committed to one who is both faithful and ingenious, obliging him to render an account of himfelf every day, and guarding as much as poffible againft his being corrupted.

" I fhall not infift any longer upon this fubject, which, upon the whole, is a detail that depends upon a great variety of circumftances, from which a General, by his prudence and intrigues, will be able to reap great advantage."

RENDEZVOUS OF AN ARMY.

WHEN the army is ordered to affemble, it is generally near the frontiers of the country where the General intends to open the fcene of war : in which cafe, the firft confideration fhould be the convenience of a navigable river, for the more ready conveyance of provifions, cannon, &c.

Great care muft be taken in the marching of troops, that they are not liable to be flanked or intercepted ; for of all operations none is more difficult, becaufe they muft not only be directed in the objects they have in view, but according to the movements the enemy may have made : therefore every neceffary precaution muft be taken ; fuch as fcouting parties of *light cavalry*, and flanking ones of *light infantry*.

The order of the march of the troops muft be fo difpofed, that each fhould arrive at their rendezvous, if poffible, on the fame day. The Quarter-mafter-general, or his deputy, with an able engineer, fhould fufficiently reconnoitre the country, to obtain a perfect knowledge of it and the enemy, before he forms his routs. When the encampment is to be formed, the General Officers, Brigade-majors, Aid-de-camps, &c. are appointed in public orders to their feveral pofts and ftations ; and the army divided into brigades, columns, wings, lines, fquadrons, &c.

MARCHING OF AN ARMY.

THE army to receive two days bread at 8 at night ; the Quarter-mafter's camp colour-men and poineers are to parade at 11, at the head of A. B. tent, and march
imme-

immediately after, commanded by the Quarter-master-general, or his deputy : they are to clear the ways, level roads, make preparations for the march of the army, and mark out the ground of encampment.

The army marches to-morrow : the general beats at 2 ; the assemblé at 3 ; and the march in 20 minutes after. Upon beating the general, the village and General Officer's guards, quarter and rear guards, must join their respective corps; and the army pack up their baggage. Upon beating the assemblé the tents are to be struck, and sent with the baggage to the place appointed for the assembling the bâs, horses, &c.

The companies are to draw up in their several streets, and the rolls to be called. At the time appointed, the drummers are to beat a march, and fifers play at the head of the line : upon which the companies will march out from their several streets, form battalions as they advance to the head of the line, and then halt.

The several battalions will be formed into columns by the Adjutant-general or his deputy, and the order of the march, &c. be given to the General Officers who lead the columns.

The cavalry will march by regiments or squadrons, which the General commanding the cavalry will direct according to the roads and country they are to march through.

The heavy artillery in general keeps the great road, in the centre of the columns, escorted by a strong party of infantry and cavalry : the field-pieces march with the column.

Each soldier is to march with 36 rounds of powder and ball, and 2 good flints, 1 of which is to be fixed in the cock of his firelock, so as to procure the most fire. If you are apprehensive of the enemy's wanting to attack you, the grenadiers and light company should be advanced at the head of each column, and small parties of light cavalry to scour the flanks.

If the enemy should appear to be near you, these parties are to post themselves on rising grounds, that they may be able to discover their approach, and give immediate notice —— Small parties should also be posted at all avenues to woods, openings to roads, villages, or towns; and remain there till the whole army-rear-guard, baggage, &c. have passed.

N. B. The routes must be so formed, that no column cross another on the march.

ROSTER

ROSTER for detaching BATTALIONS.

NATIONS.	No. of Battalions of each Nation.	1	2	3	4	5	6	7	8	9	10	11	12	13	14	15	16	17	18	19	20	21	22	23	24	25	26	27	28	29	30	31	32
English.	32	1	6	8	11	12	16	18	21	22	27	29	32	33	37	39	42	43	48	50	53	54	58	60	64	69	71	74	75	79	81	84	
Hanoverians.	24	2	7	9	19	23	28	31	34	38	40	44	49	51	55	59	61	65	70	72	76	80	82										
Prussians.	16	3	10	14	17	20	24	31	35	41	45	52	56	62	66	73	77	83															
Dutch.	8	4	15	25	36	46	57	67	78																								
Danes.	4	5	26	47	68																												
Total	**84**																																

EXPLANATION OF THE PRECEDING TABLE.

IN the firſt column are the names of nations ; in the ſecond the number of battalions each had ; and, the higheſt number being 32, there are 32 ſquares oppoſite to each nation : but, as the Danes have but 4 battalions, and only give in proportion to that number, all the ſquares except 4 are blanks : the ſame is obſerved in proportion to the Hanoverians, Pruſſians, and Dutch. The reaſon for dividing them will appear very plain : as 4 to 32, ſo is 1 to 8. The dividing of the blank ſquares oppoſite to the Danes will appear very regular and eaſy ; as 8 to 32, ſo is 1 to 4 ; which is the Dutch. The Pruſſians and Hanoverians are proportioned in the ſame manner.

All the columns are numbered on the top, from 1 to 32 ; and, as the columns, with the figures in them, are ſuppoſed to be battalions, I have numbered them from 1 to 84, that being the whole number of battalions : 10 of which I ſhall ſuppoſe ordered upon duty : in this caſe you begin column 1, number 1, and carry it on to the Pruſſians in colum 3, number 10, that being the endings of ſuch order. If 2 battalions more are ordered after, the endings will be with the Engliſh in column 5, number 12 ; and ſo on according to the demand of future orders. Thus, I preſume, I have made the nature and form of a roſter to be underſtood by the youngeſt Officer in the ſervice, and ſhall therefore ſpare myſelf the trouble of adding any ſimilar plans.

S I G N S.

" THERE are certain ſigns in war, which it is neceſſary to ſtudy, and by which you may form judgments with a kind of certainty. The knowledge you have of the enemy, and of his cuſtoms, will contribute a great deal to this. But there are ſome, at the ſame time, which are common to all nations.

" When your encampment is near that of the enemy, and you hear much firing in it, you may expect an engagement the day following, becauſe the men are diſcharging and cleaning their arms.

" When there is any great motion in the enemy's army, it may be diſcerned by the clouds of duſt raiſed by it : which is, at the ſame time, a certain indication of ſomething extraordinary being in agitation. The duſt occaſioned by foraging-parties is not the ſame as that of columns

in

in march; but then it is neceſſary that you ſhould be able to diſtinguiſh the difference.

"You may judge likewiſe which way the enemy directs his courſe, by the brightneſs of the arms when the ſun ſhines upon them: if the rays are perpendicular, he marches towards you; if they are varied and unfrequent, he retreats; if they dart from the right to the left, he is moving towards the left; and if, on the contrary, from the left to the right, his march is to the right: if there is a great quantity of duſt in his camp, which appears to be general, and is not raiſed by foraging-parties, he is ſending off his ſuttlers and baggage, and you may be aſſured that he will march himſelf preſently after. This diſcovery furniſhes you with an opportunity of making your diſpoſitions to attack him on his march; becauſe you ſhould know how far it is practicable for him to come to you, as alſo whether that is his intention, and what way is moſt probable he will march; of which you are to judge from his poſition, his magazines, his preparations, the ſituation, and, in ſhort, from his conduct in general. It is ſometimes uſual for him to erect his ovens upon the right or left of his army: in which caſe, if you happen to be covered by a ſmall river, and, in that ſituation, can diſcover the time of his baking any conſiderable quantity of bread, you can make ſome movement towards the ſide which is remote from his ovens, in order to amuſe him; after which you may ſuddenly return again, and ſend 10 or 12 thouſand men to attack them, ſupporting that detachment with your whole army, as faſt as it arrives. This enterprize muſt be executed with ſo much expedition as not to allow him time to prevent its ſucceſs, becauſe you will have the advantage of ſome hours before your firſt movement can arrive at his knowledge, excluſive of what more time may elapſe between his intelligence and the confirmation of it; for which he will undoubtedly wait, before he puts his army in motion; ſo that, in all probability, he may receive information of the attack of his magazine, before he has even given orders for his march.

"There are an infinite number of ſuch ſtratagems in war, which a ſkilful Commander may put in practice with little, or even no riſk, and whoſe conſequences are equally as beneficial as thoſe which attend a complete victory, by obliging the enemy either to attack him with a diſadvantage, or ſhamefully to retreat from him, with an army even ſuperior in ſtrength."

An Army decamping before, or invested by, another.

WHEN a General is under the difagreeable neceffity of decamping from before the enemy, it is neceffary that the utmoft fecrecy and filence fhould be obferved. The lefs public orders are given on this occafion, the more favourable and certain is fuccefs.

" When a General obferves that the enemy have a very great foraging-day, foon after their march for that purpofe, he fhould make a feint, as if he intended to do the fame, by fhewing a difpofition to move from the left; while in reality he is marching off from the right or centre. If the army is greatly his fuperior, and abfolutely cuts off the provifions, (an inconvenience a General fhould avoid); in fuch a cafe, if he occupies a poft the enemy dares not attack, and he finds that he cannot fubfift without rifking a battle, he fhould try it; but with the greateft brifknefs and vigour, after having informed his troops that this is the only means left, and that they muft *conquer or die.* A brifk and determined refolution often fucceeds; and it may happen that this army will not quit their poft with advantage, or that they may receive a convoy which will put them in a condition to maintain it. To fucceed in this, the convoy muft be brought about by that fide of the country which they believe to be the eafieft, and when they are informed it is near, the General fhould go to meet it with all his forces, and rifk the lofs of fome of his troops to receive it: for nothing fhould be fpared, if the fafety of the army depends on this convoy.

" If you judge it as difficult to procure the arrival of this convoy, as to quit your poft; or even, tho' it can be brought, you forefee you will be obliged to quit your poft foon, and that the delay will be of no advantage to you; it is then better to make a brave effort to get out of this difficulty, than to delay it; becaufe an army, fhut up in this manner, is always ruined by ficknefs and difeafes, and for want of proper means of treating the fick. You fhould then have the precaution to leave all your equipage in the poft you quit, with fome troops to guard it, if that can be done with a few: for if it is neceffary to leave many, you fhould rather carry all along with you, for fear of weakening yourfelf too much. If you apprehend the equipage may incumber or hinder the retreat, which otherwife might be performed, you fhould make no hefitation in burning a part of them, and keeping only the beft, or what will in-

cumber

cumber you leaft. When the General has taken all the neceſſary meaſures, and made all the proper difpofitions for his
retreat, he ſhould begin it at night, after having well obferved the eafieſt place he can paſs at, and having given the
alarm at ſeveral different places, that the enemy may be uncertain by which he intends to retire. If the baggage is
carried with you, the troops muſt cover it: that is to fay, if
the enemy is before you, the baggage muſt march behind the
troops; if, on the contrary, the enemy is in your rear, it
muſt march before you, efcorted: it muſt be placed on the
left, if the enemy are on the right; and if they are on the
left, it muſt be on the right. If the enemy are in your
front, your beſt troops ſhould form the van-guard; for fuc-
ceſs in ſuch an enterprize often depends upon the firſt ſtroke.
You ſhould uſe the fame precautions for your flanks or rear,
if you forefee that it is there they will make their chief efforts. It may happen, that, being in the night-time, the
enemy will only make feeble attacks to retard your march
till day, or till all their forces, which may be difperfed, are
joined. In this cafe the General ought not to ſtop, but defend himfelf retiring, without infiſting too much on fuſtain-
ing ſuch of the troops as may be attacked, even if he ſhould
fuffer the loſs of fome of them. There are occafions where
it is neceſſary to facrifice a part to fave the reſt: but as it is
a difagreeable alternative, it is only refolved on in the laſt
extremity. It may alfo happen, that the enemy hath fo divided his forces, that, when one part harraſſes your army,
the other is detached to feize a certain poſt: you have then
no other part to chufe, but that of attacking thofe who harrafs you. In ſuch a cafe, the principles for the difpofition
of the attack are regulated by the nature of the ground on
which the enemy is, and the kind of troops proper for it."

If one or two battalions are ordered to fupport and conduct the baggage, and they have reafon to expect the enemy will attack them in front, rear, and flanks, form the oblong fquare, and march the baggage in it. See Plan 1.

Cannon are very ufeful to a retreating army, in cafe you
pafs a defile or river. They may be placed at the entry of the
former, or an eminence, if there is one that commands the
defile thro' which the enemy muſt pafs to attack the rear.

Difpofition of Forces marching through an Enemy's Country.

" IF the General's defign is to relieve fome place befieged, to convey fupplies to it, and force fome quarter

C

of it, he contracts the wings of his army in marching, and
keeps himself in close order.

" If battle is designed to be given by the enemy (the occasion offering and country suiting) he sufficiently extends
the front of his army ; yet not so much, but that it shall be
strong enough in depth to sustain the enemy's charge, to
have the van, centre, and rear deep, and strong enough to
hinder a surprize on the flanks, that every man may fight ;
which is one of the most important considerations. And
this with a farther view of enclosing the enemy in a cres-
cent, so as to charge him in front, flanks, and rear.

" If the General's design is to traverse, or march thro'
an enemy's country, he keeps his army together in one body, without disuniting of any part ; and moves by columns,
chusing open and level plains, and avoiding woods and hills,
as much as possible ; securing quarters, and carrying provisions sufficient for the time of the passage. It is known to
be difficult to lead an army through an enemy's country, divided by rivers, covered with woods, and withal mountainous : for if, in such a situation, it has any places of strength,
and but a small army to defend it, the superior army may
easily be molested or hindered in its march ; the passage
of its provisions cut off, that be attacked on the flanks or
rear, or surprized by an ambuscade, and several occasions
sought to annoy it."

Measures to be taken for the Junction of two Armies.

" A General finds himself sometimes under the necessity
of fighting, when it is his interest to join an army
separated from his, and that the enemy's army has got between the 2, to prevent their junction. To succeed on
these important occasions, the chiefs of the two armies appoint a rendezvous at a proper place, and at the same hour,
on the right or left of the enemy, in order to endeavour to
join before he has intelligence of their march. Or, if it
cannot absolutely be done without fighting the enemy in
the post he occupies, they take their measures so justly, that
both armies arrive and attack him at the same time. To
this purpose they advertise each other of the day and hour
each will arrive at the place appointed, and agree on the
signals to be seen or heard ; to which the one and the other
should answer, to be the more certain that they are in condition to begin the attack. If this is well concerted and
well executed, it is almost impossible for the enemy's army

not

not to be defeated, who are commonly seized with a panic, when they find themselves attacked in front and rear.

' " If they find they can make the junction by either side, and that there is a river or a defile, which 1 of the 2 armies must pass to join the other ; that which is not to pass should march first, and construct, at the place appointed, redoubts or retrenchments, and guard them with infantry, to be masters of the passage. In case the enemy march to engage the other, the first shall then pass the river or the defile to succour it.

" If the enemy marches to 1 of the 2, that which he marches against shall endeavour to avoid the action till the others come up, which may be done by taking an advantageous post."

Precautions to be taken when obliged to establish your Quarters in a woody or mountainous Country.

" A Perfect knowledge of the country is always necessary, but more particularly when you establish your quarters in a woody or mountainous country.

" The more it appears difficult or impracticable to turn them and separate them, the more precaution is required on your part. A gorge or opening which you have not founded and examined, a road whose turnings you do not know, a valley whose bottom you are not perfectly acquainted with, heights which appear inaccessible, and which you have neglected to occupy, will sometimes furnish an opportunity to the enemy to penetrate by the rear of your quarters, and to attack and carry them.

" With this knowledge a General will not only keep his quarters in security, but he will spare his troops from much fatigue, by placing no unnecessary guards, and not multiplying the patrols ; which he will be obliged to do, if he has only a superficial knowledge of the country.

" After he has taken his first precautions, he will place all his infantry in a first line, in the most considerable places ; such as small towns or large villages. To this infantry he will join hussars, to be able to push detachments forward, whether for the security of the quarters, for carrying off the forage between him and the enemy, or for establishing contributions, if he finds means so to do. The dragoons can, according to the circumstances, do duty either on foot or on horseback : he will therefore place them on the flanks of the cavalry, to cover them.

" Besides

" Befides the retrenchments with which he fhould fortify every little town or village, he fhould alfo cut a trench at the head of all the gorges or roads leading to the quarters, placing barriers on them for the paffage of the detachments of huffars or dragoons : and thefe trenches muft be exactly guarded by infantry.

" In a mountainous country, the detachments fhould not advance fo far as in a plain country, becaufe it will be eafy for the enemy to get between them, and cut them off from the quarters, by fending infantry by bye-paths, where the huffars cannot penetrate. Thefe troops will place themfelves between the quarters and the detachment, after it has paffed, as we have faid ; and when it is attacked in front, they will attack it in rear, and fo place it between two fires.

" You muft place centinels on the heights, with orders to advertife you if they fee any troops coming, but pofitively not to fire ; that the enemy may believe the quarters are not on their guard, and fo be drawn into a fort of ambufcade, which will give a diflike of coming to attack your quarters, or even of approaching to examine them ; and this is neceffary in the beginning, becaufe the troops are there to repofe, and to fubfift during the winter, that they may be in a condition to take the field early in the fpring. However, if the enemy fhould attempt to attack fome of the quarters, as, by the precautions mentioned, he will find the troops under arms ready to receive him, he may probably be defeated, or at leaft be obliged to retire : and it is very likely fuch a check may difguft him, and he will leave the quarters in tranquility for the future. This tranquility, true or fuppofed, fhould not prevent the Commandant from fending out detachments to reconnoitre and examine the country exactly. For fuch detachments, fome Non commiffioned Officers, with 6 men each, fent out on different fides will be fufficient. Thofe detachments which are fent for foraging, or for eftablifhing contributions, muft be more confiderable, but not too numerous : they fhould be compofed of infantry, huffars, or dragoons, according to the nature of the country.

" If the gorges leading to the quarters are croffed by different roads, or if thefe roads all lead to the high road which conducts to the quarters, you muft, during the night, place a guard of huffars or dragoons where thefe crofs-roads meet, and centinels or vedettes along all the roads.

" This

" This guard will retire at fun-rifing : it will be ufelefs in the day-time, as the enemy feldom chufe to attack then ; and, even in that cafe, the firft attack muft be made at the trenches and barriers which are before the quarters, at the entry of the roads or gorges : and confequently the troops will have time enough to take arms, and occupy the poft ordered.

" If, for want of forage, the General cannot keep his cavalry, as they are of no ufe among the mountains, he may fend them behind him, to places where they can be in fafety, and where they can find forage, unlefs his project is to quit that country, and carry on the war in another, where they can act more eafily.

" But if the circumftance obliges him to remain in the mountains, and that forage is wanting, he will only keep the huffars and dragoons ; the firft will ferve for the advanced detachments, and the other will be ufeful on foot as infantry.

" Though cavalry are ill placed in the mountains, fometimes it is neceffary to eftablifh them there, when the plains have been laid wafte; but they fhould never be placed but in a fecond line, and in that part of the country the leaft mountainous, moft open, and moft abundant in forage. Care efpecially fhould be taken to remove them the fartheft from any danger of being attacked, both becaufe they cannot act, and even as it is impoffible for them to defend themfelves againft infantry, which the enemy certainly will employ in fuch a country.

" It would be needlefs to fpeak of the precautions to be taken by cavalry in a moutainous country, becaufe it cannot be fuppofed that cavalry alone are placed there. Thefe precautions can only ferve to facilitate their retreat, but never for their defence : and the enemy will foon be mafter of the country, if you have nothing but cavalry to oppofe him with."

Precautions for fecuring the Cavalry's Quarters in a plain covered Country.

" IT will be fufficient to mention here the means *George Bafta* (a *Spanifh* General of note, in the beginning of the feventeenth century) made ufe of for fecuring his quarters of cavalry : they appear to be the better, as they are very fimple ; befide, the authority of a man fo converfant in the military art, and fo generally approved of, fhould be regarded as a refpectable law.

C 3 " *George*

" *George Baſta* ſuppoſes a village in the middle of a plain ; he eſtabliſhes his guards, great and ſmall, on all the roads which lead to the quarters ; he ſends out his detachments as far as they poſſibly can go without the riſk of being cut off : he places guards 150 paces from the quarters, the ſmall advanced guards in proportion, and the vedettes 50 paces before the ſmall advanced guards.

" In the night-time, the vedettes formed a kind of circle round the quarters, near enough to hear each other : they were continually marching towards each other, as if they intended to change place. By this perpetual movement no perſon could come from or go to the quarters without being ſeen or ſtopped : the detachments which were advanced, ſecured the exterior part of the quarters to a great diſtance. Beſides all this there were patrols of 3 or 4 men, who kept on the roads 300 or 400 paces from the vedettes, in caſe the enemy ſhould eſcape the detachments. Theſe patrols, as well as the detachments, ſtopped from time to time, and liſtened attentively to hear if any troops were coming towards them. If the enemy had garriſons near, the detachments had orders to advance as near them as poſſible ; firſt to ſecure the tranquility of the quarters, and then to keep the enemy in awe, and prevent their coming to diſquiet them, by ſhewing them they were always on their guard.

" Theſe precautions appear to be excellent ; but if ſuch a quarter is attacked by infantry, what can cavalry do in a village ? All it can do, is to profit by the intelligence given them by the advanced parties, to ſend off their baggage, and then make their retreat ; for it is impoſſible to defend a town or village with cavalry againſt infantry. Whatever precautions are taken, by retrenching the village, making loop-holes through the walls of the houſes, and advancing detachments, the cavalry, when attacked by infantry, have no reſource but getting into a plain, in order to act : ramparts are not made for cavalry ; it is from their ſwords they are to expect victory or ſafety. Such quarters of cavalry alone, invented by *George Baſta*, ſerve only to prove the neceſſity of vigilance in war ; but this ſort of conduct in quarters of cavalry ſhould not be followed but when they are greatly expoſed. It is always a bad poſition for cavalry to place them alone in any country, however open it may be : it is even very ſeldom that the circumſtances oblige you to do ſo ; but if the ſituation of affairs, or the want of fo-

rage,

rage, require it, the precautions of *George Basta* are excellent, and should be employed for the preventing all surprize."

Of securing a Retreat of a large Detachment in Presence of an Enemy, by Cavalry.

" IT will be necessary to form into 2 lines, at the distance of 200 yards asunder; the first line is to wheel by fours by squadrons, retreat through the intervals of the second, and march 200 or 300 yards in the rear, according as it may be more or less pressed by the enemy, and then face about again.

" After the first line has thus moved into the rear of the second, the second is to wheel about, and march through the first, and so on, both lines continuing to retreat in this manner, as long as it may be necessary.

" During the retreat, a few small parties, composed of the bravest men, are to be advanced towards the enemy, in order to skirmish with them, and thereby to facilitate the movements of the main body.

" N. B. This is what may frequently be necessary for the rear-guard to put in practice, when the enemy makes attempts either to obstruct or to reconnoitre the march of the enemy."

Manœuvres to be opposed to the Enemy's false Alarms.

" A Vigilant enemy does not fail to give an alarm to the quarters, true or false, as often as he can ; and he can as often as he will. He has frequently no other view but to disturb and fatigue them, and, by keeping them always alert, to prevent their re-establishment during the winter ; or to abate the General's vigilance against true alarms, by often deceiving him with false ones. A negligence which will soon communicate itself among the troops, and the particular Commandants, if great care is not taken to prevent it, and will afford an easy opportunity of surprising and carrying off, at least, some of the quarters.

" But a wise and prudent General knows how to prevent these inconveniences, by preserving order in the quarters, by taking the necessary precautions for their security, by making the infantry take arms without beat of drum, and the cavalry mount without sound of trumpet : in order that the enemy, deceived by this silence, and believing them asleep, may advance into the quarters to fall upon them. When he finds them under arms, his surprize alone will oc-

casion

cafion his defeat; or, at leaft, will make him abandon his enterprize, and begin his retreat; but which he cannot perform without being greatly harraffed. It is on fuch occafions a General's genius appears. It is not fufficient to know how to fecure his quarters; he muft turn to the enemy's difadvantage the very manœuvres they intend to be his. This particular way of doing it feems very favourable; and, if it fucceeds, they will have no more caufe to fear falfe alarms, becaufe the enemy will be convinced of the vigilance of the troops. However, you muft not purfue your advantage too far, for fear of an ambufcade; but, fo long as you fee the country clear before you, you fhould profit by the enemy's furprize, and charge him with vivacity.

" It is always neceffary to bring the troops under arms without a noife. It is a general rule that, on all occafions, filence is favourable in war: the orders of the Commandant are then better underftood, and executed with more promptitude. This filence, which does not prevent your being on your guard, prevents the enemy, troubled and difpirited by feeing himfelf deceived in his project, from continuing to give you falfe alarms, and reftores tranquility to the quarters. The enemy himfelf will begin to think or allowing his troops repofe, after the fruitlefs fatigues they have fuffered in thefe attempts.

" As to the cavalry, they fhould alfo faddle and mount without any found of trumpet; for whatever good order there may be in the quarters, the trumpets on one hand, the cries on another, the hurry to faddle their horfes, and to find their arms, occafion confufion, and make the orders to be ill underftood. Quarters in fuch confufion may be eafily defeated by inferior numbers, who, perhaps, only came to give a falfe alarm, or to reconnoitre.

" In general, good order in the quarter depends on the knowledge and underftanding of him who commands, and on the vigilance and good difcipline he caufes to be obferved. It is by fuch conduct that he not only has nothing to fear from the enemy, but even draws from their attempts his own certain fuccefs. The reputation he will acquire among the enemy by his vigilance, will procure him advantages beyond his expectation."

GRAND MANOEUVRE.

" I AM perfuaded, that unlefs troops are properly fupported in an action, they muft be defeated; and that
the

the principles which *M. de Montecuculli* has laid down in his Memoirs, are founded upon certainties. He says that infantry and cavalry should be always reciprocally sustained by each other; yet we, in direct opposition to his measures, post all our cavalry upon the wings, and our infantry in the centre, each to be sustained by itself only; which disposition, as the interval between our lines is usually five or six hundred paces, is in itself sufficient to intimidate the troops; because it is natural for every man, who sees danger before him, and no relief behind, to be discouraged; and this is the reason why even the second line has sometimes given ground, while the first was engaging; which is what many others, probably, as well as myself, have seen happen more than once; and although it seems hitherto to have escaped the reflection of any, it cannot, as I have already observed, be imputed to any other cause than the frailty of the human heart. The following is a transcript of what the abovementioned illustrious author says upon this subject.

" In the armies of the antients every regiment of foot had a certain proportion of horse and artillery; the horse were divided into two sorts, under the appellation of heavy armed and light armed; the former of which wore breastplates : why, therefore, would they incorporate these distinct bodies together, unless it was on account of the absolute necessity of such a connection, and the mutual service they would be capable of rendering each other by acting in concert? According to the modern practice, where all the infantry is posted in the center, and the cavalry upon the flanks, at the extent of several thousand paces, how is it possible they can support each other? If the cavalry are defeated, it is evident that the infantry, becoming abandoned, and their flanks exposed, must unavoidably share the same fate, from the enemy's cannon at least, if not by other means, which happened to the *Swedes* in the year 1614. When their cavalry had been driven off the field of battle, they perceived the error of their disposition, and, in order to remedy it, posted some platoons of musqueteers between the squadrons; but all efforts were then ineffectual, for the squadrons were totally disordered; and the platoons, not having any body of troops at hand to retire to, nor pikemen to cover them, were put to the sword; for how could they possibly retreat to their infantry, which was at so great a distance ?"

" It

" It is for thefe reafons I would poft fmall bodies of cavalry at the diftance of 30 paces, in the rear of my infantry;
and battalions of pikemen formed in the fquare in the interval between my two wings of cavaly; in the rear of which,
likewife, it will be able to rally, if broken or repulfed *.
My fecond line of cavalry will never fly, fo long as they fee
the fquare battalions in their front, and their countenance
will alfo animate the firft. The battalions will maintain
their ground, from the perfuafion of being foon fuccoured
by the cavalry, who, under the cover of their fire, and a
vigorous refiftance, will prefently form again and renew the
charge with frefh courage, in order to retrieve their honour,
and wipe out the difgrace of their late difcomfiture: the
battalions will moreover ferve to cover the flanks of the infantry. Some, very improperly, poft fmall bodies of infantry between the intervals in their line of cavalry: the
weaknefs of this difpofition is alone fufficient to intimidate
them; for the foot fee that if the cavalry are defeated, they
muft inevitably be cut to pieces; and if the cavalry, who
have alfo a dependance upon them, make but a brifk movement, they leave them behind; fo that, perceiving they have
loft their affiftance, they foon fall into confufion, and, being put to flight, leave the flanks of your army open to
the enemy.

" Others again poft fquadrons of cavalry amongft their
infantry, which is equally abfurd; for the deftruction of
horfes from the enemy's fire occafions diforder; and if the
cavalry give way, the infantry will prefently do the fame.

" But I would afk, in what manner fquadrons in this difpofition are to act? Are they to ftand faft, fword in hand,
and wait the attack of the enemy's infantry, firing and advancing upon them with fixed bayonets; or muft they make
the charge themfelves? If they do the laft, and are repulfed, which will moft probably be the cafe, they muft break
their own infantry in the retreat, becaufe it will be difficult
for them to find their former pofts again; and the intervals
allowed them being fmall, will certainly have been filled
up; for the battalions are fubject to fuch great inconvenien-

---

* Perhaps it may be objected, that this cavalry, if repulfed by the enemy,
will fall into diforder upon the fquare battalions; but it fhould be obferved, that the Marfhal furnifhes them with pikes, on purpofe to render them
capable of oppofing the fhock of cavalry; befides, the intervals between
them are fo large, that, however precipitate the horfe might be in their
retreat, it is improbable they could fall upon them; but for a farther fecurity, they might be covered with *chevaux-de-frife*.

ces,

ces, from their prefent method of forming, that the diforder of a few files, whether occafioned by their own movement, the doubling of the ranks, or the enemy's cannon,
is fufficient to throw the whole into irretrievable confufion.
It is far otherwife with my centuries ; they follow each their
refpective ftandard, and keep in a body together : all diforders among them are eafily remedied, and if not, fo long
as they as they are guided by their ftandards, which are to
range in a line with that of the legion, no fatal confequence
can enfue, becaufe the Officers will be able to keep the ranks
ftraight, which it is impoffible for them to do in the battalions ; and this being alfo one great defect in *M. de Folard*'s column, I fhall take the prefent opportunity to give
my fentiments of it.

The COLUMN.

NOtwithftanding the very great regard I have for
the Chevalier *Folard*, and the high efteem I entertain of his ingenious writings, yet I cannot agree with him
in opinion concerning the column. It is ftriking, indeed,
and formidable in appearance ; and the idea of it, which
firft prefented itfelf to my imagination, feduced for a while
my judgment, till, by trying it in execution, I became convinced of my error.   The following analyfis, or calculation,
will be neceffary to difcover the defects of it.

In action, every man is to be allowed eighteen inches
diftance, and the flanks of the column are to face outwards ;
which flanks, in whatfoever order they are formed, muft be
always compofed of at leaft 40 files in depth, upon 24 ranks
in breadth ; and thus, when faced, it confequently takes
up 60 feet for its flank front : in marching, it requires
120, which is double its former diftance ; becaufe a man
will not be able to move, without kicking his leader, if confined within the fpace of 18 inches : but to march with celerity, he muft be allowed 3 feet ; fo that when the front of
the column marches firft off its ground, the rear will be obliged to wait till it has gained 60 paces ; and likewife to
march the fame diftance, after the front has halted ; as it
muft make intervals in the flanks, which will expofe them
to great danger.   This defect will naturally be increafed, in
proportion to the number of files which are added ; fo that
a column, confifting of 240, will occupy, in its ftanding
order, 360 feet in length, and, of courfe, 270, marching.
After having pierced the enemy, its flanks are to face to the
right

right and left outwards, in order to change their broken
ranks : but as it takes up double its proper allowance of
ground, its files will remain open, and large intervals be
left, especially if the charge is to be made with speed and
impetuosity, which should be the property of the column.

" The Chevalier is very much deceived in imagining it
to be a body capable of moving with ease ; infomuch that I
do not know any one fo unweildly, particularly when it is
formed in the manner above described. If it happens that
the files are once disordered, either by marching, the un-
evennefs of the ground, or the enemy's cannon, which laft
muft make a dreadful havock amongft them, it will be impoffible to reftore them to good order : thus it becomes a
huge, inactive mafs, divefted of all regularity, and totally
involved in confufion. I do not think, that the weight of
it can be of any great confequence ; for the men do not pufh
one another forwards, in the manner which he defcribes ;
neither is it poffible they fhould, while they take up 3 paces
diftance, which they are obliged to do in marching.

" In retreating, it has the advantage of battalions formed in the fquare ; not that it is capable of marching with
more celerity, but becaufe every part moves together ; and
though it be even pierced by the enemy's cavalry in purfuit,
yet the injury it will thereby fuftain is confiderable, for they
muft be expofed to a fire from behind, and the interval they
make will be prefently clofed up.

" Two battalions, formed back to back, will anfwer the
fame purpofe, marching by files, and facing to the right and
left outwards, when neceffary. This method of retreating
muft be performed very flowly, for otherwife the rear will
foon be feparated from the main body, by reafon of that
diftance of 3 feet, which every man will take up in marching. But to believe that the column is an active and light
body, is an error of which I am thoroughly convinced ; infomuch that I am even induced to think it a dangerous difpofition when compofed of but 24 by 16, on account of
the difficulty of forming it again, when once broken or dif-
ordered. Properly, it fhould never confift, in breadth, of
more than 2 battalions, formed each 4 deep, which does not
at all confound their natural order.

" What I have been faying concerning the room which
every man muft neceffarily take up, fhews the danger of
marching by files. If you do it in the prefence of an enemy, in order to fill up any interval, you muft inevitably
be

be undone ; for your battalion will then occupy double its former ground, and you will alſo require double the proper time to form it again : as, for inſtance, ſuppoſing your battalion conſiſts of 600 men, with files cloſed, it will cover 225 feet ; if it is to gain ground to the right, the right hand man will have marched that diſtance before tho left hand man has moved ; and after the former has halted, the latter will have the ſame number of feet to march, before the battalion can be in its proper order, to face to the front again ; which together takes up as much time as would be neceſſary to march the diſtance of 450 feet, or 180 paces. If then the enemy is 100 paces off, and ſeizes this opportunity to charge you, he will have the advantage of as much time, before you can be formed, as is required to march 80 paces ; the danger of this movement naturally increaſes in proportion as you augment the number of troops that are to make it ; for if you have 4 battalions, and the enemy is at the diſtance of 800 paces, you are expoſed to as great a diſadvantage. In this I proceed upon geometrical principles, to which it is neceſſary to have recourſe on many occaſions in war.

" The tact, or cadence, is the only effectual remedy for theſe defects, on which the event of all engagements totally depends. It is what I have dwelt upon the longer, on purpoſe to demonſtrate the great efficacy of it, and, at the ſame time, to expoſe the ignorance of our modern diſciplinarians ; who, though they concur with me in regard to the reality of theſe errors, remain yet unacquainted with any other method of avoiding them in practice, than by marching ſlow.

" We cannot even bring a ſingle battalion drawn up but 4 deep to the charge, without being ſubject to the inconvenience of which I have been ſpeaking : unleſs we march at a ſnail's pace, our ranks and files when we approach the enemy are open. This monſtrous defect in our diſcipline is what gave riſe to the preſent method of firing ; for to charge otherwiſe, it is neceſſary to move briſkly and together, which cannot be done, allowing only 18 inches to a man, without the tactic.

" It is alſo impoſſible that the Romans and Macedonians, as their manner of forming was in cloſe and deep order, could engage without it ; it is a term which is very familiarly uſed, but has hitherto been totally miſapplied.

" I have frequently been ſurprized, that the column is not made uſe of againſt the enemy, on a march ; for it is
certain,

certain, that a large army always takes up, then, 3 or 4 times more ground than is neceſſary to form it. If, therefore, you get intelligence of the enemy's route, and the hour at which he is to begin his march, though he is at the diſtance of 6 leagues from you, you would have very ſufficient time to intercept him ; for his front uſually arrives in the new camp before his rear has quitted the old. It is impoſſible to form troops that take up ſo much more than their proper quantity of ground without making large intervals, and a dreadful confuſion. Yet I have often ſeen the enemy ſuffer it to be done without moleſtation, when one would have imagined, that nothing leſs than faſcination could have prevented his taking advantage of an opportunity ſo favourable.

" The preſent ſubject might furniſh a very uſeful chapter ; for how many countries will occaſion ſuch ſtraggling marches, and in how many places may one make an attack without riſking any thing ? How frequently does it happen to an army, to be divided on its march by bad roads, rivers, difficult paſſes, &c. and how many ſituations will enable you to ſurprize any part of it ? How oft do opportunities preſent of ſeparating it, ſo as to be able, though inferior, to attack one part with advantage ; and, at the ſame time, by the proper diſpoſition of a ſmall number of troops only, prevent its being relieved by the other ? But all theſe circumſtances being as various and indeterminate as the ſituations which produce them, nothing more is required, than to keep good intelligence, to acquire a knowledge of the country, and to aſſume the courage to execute; for as theſe affairs are never deciſive on your ſide, and may be ſo on that of the enemy, the riſk you run is inconſiderable, when compared with the advantages you may gain. The manner of attack is with the heads of your columns, which are to charge as faſt as they arrive, and to be ſuſtained by the others which follow ; ſo that your diſpoſition is made in a manner ſpontaneouſly, and you attack an enemy without either order or ſupport, and totally unprepared to make any defence."

Advantages of the COLUMN.

" THE impetuoſity and violence of the ſhock of the column is generally allowed, even by thoſe who have been leaſt ſparing of their criticiſm on this regulation.

" The

" The refiftance of the phalanx has in like manner been always acknowledged, and every body is ready enough to admit this difpofition or arrangement to be the moft effectual defence in an open plain, where the efforts of men can only be oppofed by power derived from others of their fpecies, and where only the form of the troops, their goodnefs, the abilities of the Officers, and the manner of drawing up, determine the victory.

" If it be admitted that the column may act equally as a column or phalanx, the acknowledged qualities of thofe methods of ranging troops (that is to fay, the fhock of the one, and refiftance of the other) decides the queftion, and confirms the fuperiority of the column over all other *orders known.*

" But the phyfical ftrength refulting from the depths of its files, which the Chevalier Folard calls the weight of its fhock, cannot proceed from the order of the column; for then it fhould confift in the product of the bulk or mafs, multiplied by its celerity, and which in phyfics is defined quantity of motion. But men are not capable of uniting in a mafs, in the literal fenfe, as conftituent parts of a phyfical body; and confequently any order in which they might form, could never produce fuch effects.

" Let us not then be deceived by this illufion, but look upon the violence of the fhock of the column to proceed from the human heart, which is always fufceptible of impreffions arifing from circumftances: apparent danger difcourages a man, and flackens his actions; when affiftance is near, he fhews more ardour and courage; he acts upon the *offenfive or defenfive* more chearfully when followed by 20 men than 2; and his attack will ever be in proportion to the degree of *courage* that determines or accelerates his motion."

Defects *of the* COLUMN.

" THE defects of the column are, firft, the flaughter that an enemy's artillery would make in files that are fo deep; fecondly, the difficulty of maintaining order in the interior of fo deep a body; thirdly, the lengthening of its files, when the column is to advance or retreat, which hinders the rear from ftopping at the fame time, or with the fame expedition, as the head; from turning to right or left, and marching without confufion on either of its flanks. The other imperfections to which the column are liable, in

common

common with all other figures of tactics, cannot be an object of censure or argument.

" Having thus duly weighed the advantages and disadvantages of the column, and finding the balance appears in
its favour, it seems unnecessary to use more words in dis-
playing its advantages, or lessening its inconveniencies."

The Density, or Closeness of a Body of Troops.

" THE more closely united and compact the consti-
tuent parts of a physical body are, the more solid
and dense that body is said to be. This term has been applied to the troops, and many persons take it to be literally
true. From hence it has been imagined the closeness or
density of a body of troops cannot be too great, and that
its strength increases in proportion to its density.

" This mistake arises from an expression foreign to the
object, and which implies more than was first intended;
for were soldiers so closely united in ranks and files as to
form but one lump or mass, the troops would become a
mere lifeless passive body, incapable of performing any action. A body of forces should be then more or less closely
united, according to the weapons they are to use: but whatever the nature of their weapons may be, they should have
their bodies and hands free, that nothing may lessen their
quantity of action."

An Army within Lines.

" IF ever an army is so weak as to be within lines, you
take care to have communications between village and
village; and are sure to have small parties of light-horse
patrolling towards the enemy, and have videts and sentries,
posted so near one another, that you may have intelligence.
If the enemy, or any parties appear, you make your head-
quarters, if possible, in the centre, and you have a line of
battle marked out, for the rendezvous, upon an alarm,
where you may wait for the enemy, or march to attack
them before they are informed of your intention. As they
pass, you cover your flanks, by a fortified town, village,
river, or morass, and your field of battle is as near to your
works as possible. The Generals of each wing constantly
visit the out-guards, and see that the patroles, videts, and
sentries do their duty, and are alert, which is the means of
preventing surprize. Though the General in chief has
made all the preparations for the attack, if he sees it convenient,

venient, he fuddenly files or marches off, from the right or left; by which means he deceives his enemy, and may poffibly enter his works without lofs. This was done by the Duke of Marlborough."

Advantages to be taken in Lines.

" IF any villages, or woods, are in the front, and not at a great diftance from your lines, you are fure to keep them in poffeffion (efpecially if they flank your field of battle;) you fortify them, and place batteries there, whereby you are able to deftroy numbers of your enemy by putting them between crofs fires."

M. Saxe fays, " he is averfe to lines and retrenchments, from a perfuafion, that the only good lines are thofe which nature has made ; and that the beft retrenchments are, in other words, the beft difpofitions, and the beft difciplined troops.

" I fcarce remember a fingle inftance of lines of retrenchments having been affaulted and not carried. If you are inferior to the enemy in numbers, you will not be able to defend them, when they are attacked with all his forces, in 2 or 3 different places at once : the fame will be the confequence, if you are upon an equality with him: and, with a fuperiority, you have no occafion for them.

" What fufficient reafon can you therefore affign for beftowing fo much labour in the conftruction of works which appear to anfwer your purpofe fo little ?"

The perfuafion of the enemy, that you will never dare to leave them, renders him bold. He trifles with you even before your face, and hazards feveral movements, which he would be afraid to make, if you was in any other fituation. And this courage is equally diffufed among both Officers and foldiers ; becaufe a man always dreads danger itfelf lefs than he does the confequences of it ; which is an argument that I could fupport by a number of examples.

" Suppofe a retrenchment to be attacked by a column, the head of which is arrived upon the brink of the ditch : if, at that time, only a handful of men fhould make their appearance, at the diftance of 100 paces without the retrenchment, *nothing is more certain*, than that the front of this column would inftantly halt; or, at leaft, would not be followed by the rear : the reafon for which can be deduced from no other fource, than the *human heart*. If only 10 men get footing upon a retrenchment, whole battalions that

D

have

have been pofted behind for its defence will abandon it They no fooner fee a troop of horfe enter within half a league of them, than they give themfelves totally up to flight.

" As oft therefore as one is obliged to defend retrench-ments, one muft take particular care to poft all the troops behind the parapet : becaufe, if once the enemy fets foot upon that, the defendants will no longer think of any thing but their own fecurity ; which proceeds from that confternation which is the unavoidable effect of fudden and unexpected events.

" This is a general rule in war, and is what determines the fate of the day in all actions.   It is the irrefiftible im-pulfe of the human heart, which, on account of its confe-quences, was the principal motive that induced me to at-tempt this work; becaufe I am apt to imagine, it would never have occurred to any other perfon to afcribe the greateft part of the bad fuccefs of armies to this caufe, although the true one.

" If then you ftation your troops behind the parapet, their only hopes and expectations are, to prevent the ene-my by their fire from paffing the ditch, and forcing it ; which, if he is once able to accomplifh, they inftantly give themfelves up for loft, and in confequence take to flight. Inftead of this method, it will be much more prudent to poft a fingle rank there, armed with pikes, whofe bufinefs will be to pufh the affailants back therewith, as faft as they attempt to mount.   This the men will certainly execute ; becaufe it is what they expect and are prepared for.   If, moreover, you poft bodies of light infantry, at the diftance of 30 paces, in the front of the retrenchment, they will not be confounded at the approach of the enemy, from a confcioufnefs of being ftationed there for no other purpofe than to oppofe him, which, for that reafon, they will do with proper vigour and refolution : while, on the contrary, had they all been pofted behind it, they would have fled at his appearance.   Thus we fee upon what nice diftinctions every thing in war depends, and how irrefiftibly weak mortals are governed by mere momentary caprice and opinion."

If I had a retrenchment to maintain, I fhould poft fen-tries of light infantry all along the parapet, in 2 ranks : the firft armed with firelocks upon the banquette, and the fecond with pikes at the foot of it, together with the Officers and Non-commiffioned Officers.   The light infantry I fhould alfo poft upon the banquette.

As

" As I erect my parapet 6 feet high, the affailants, who would otherwife take poft upon the berm, in order to fire over it, will be deprived of their ufual refource, and find themfelves obliged to mount; in attempting which, they muft be pufhed back, and deftroyed by the pikes. The Officers and Non-commiffioned Officers muft be equally divided among the men, taking care that they make a proper ufe of that weapon."

The men fhould be encouraged and informed that they are by no means to depend upon the effect of their fmall arms, or imagine their firing only will be fufficient to repel the enemy; but that the top of the parapet is the place where they will be required to exert themfelves. Thefe precautions will prevent their being furprized or terrified to fee them enter the ditch: for as it cannot be doubted, but that they will take a firm refolution to ftand their fire, which it is as certain that they will be able to go through, one ought therefore to expect, and be prepared for the confequence. If they endeavour to take poft upon the berm of the retrenchment, in order to diflodge them from the banquette, which is frequently the cafe, I fhall be able to reach them with my pikes, to pufh them back, *man by man*, as faft as they approach; but if at length they force the retrenchments, and attempt to form, I fhall charge them *en détail*, by fentries or light infantry; and as my troops have been properly prepared for all extremities, they will for that reafon be fubject to no furprize, but will make their affault with vigour.

" Different referves muft be in readinefs to reinforce occafionally, thofe pofts againft which the enemy's principal ftrength appears directed: a circumftance not always eafy to accomplifh, becaufe it is what a fkilful adverfary will prevent your being able to difcover: they muft therefore be ftationed as much at hand, and as advantageoufly as poffible; which is to be determined by the nature of the fituation, as well without as within the retrenchment. You need be under no apprehenfion of being attacked in places where the ground is level to any confiderable diftance; for in fuch it will be fufficient for the enemy to difguife his real purpofe: but whenever thefe happen to be on an eminence, hollow, or other piece of ground that covers his approach, there you may expect him to make all his efforts, becaufe he will thereby hope to conceal his difpofition and real numbers.

" If

" If you can contrive some passages in your retrenchment for a sally or two, just as the head of the enemies columns arrives upon the brink of the ditch, that will certainly make them halt the same instant, even though they have forced the retrenchment, and though some part of them have already entered : for, as they are unprepared for such an event, they will be alarmed for their flanks and rear, and in all probability take to flight."

Cæsar, being desirous to relieve Amiens when besieged by the Gauls, arrived with his army, which consisted only of 7000 men, upon the borders of a rivulet ; where immediately after he threw up a retrenchment with so much precipitation, that the barbarians, imagining he was afraid of them, attacked it, although in reality he had no manner of intention to defend it ; for on the contrary, while they were employed in filling up the ditch, and rendering themselves masters of the parapet, he sallied out with his cohorts, and thereby threw them into so great a consternation, that they all turned their backs and fled, without so much as a single person attempting to defend himself.

Alesia being besieged by the Romans, the Gauls, who were infinitely superior in numbers, marched to attack them in their lines. Cæsar, instead of defending them, gave orders to his troops to make a sally, and to fall upon the enemy on one side, while he attacked them on the other : in which he succeeded so remarkably well, that the Gauls were routed with a considerable loss, exclusive of above 20,000 taken prisoners, together with their General.

M. Saxe, in recommendation of his method of forming troops (which I readily allow to be different from all others) says, " although the first battalion should be driven back, that which follows it, will, notwithstanding, be able to charge in the same instant, by moving up in quick succession, and renewing the attack with fresh vigour. I am moreover formed 8 deep *, have no sort of embarrassment to apprehend, my march is rapid, and yet free from all manner of disorder ; my charge is violent, and I shall always outflank the enemy, though equal in numbers. This order is far from being new, *for it is that of the Romans, that by which they conquered the Universe.* The Greeks had great knowledge in the art of war, and were well disciplined, yet their large phalanx was never able to contend with the small bodies of the Romans, disposed in this order ; in which

---

* Battalions form in 4 ranks each.

which opinion I am supported by Polybius, who concurs with me in giving them the preference.

"What then can be expected from our battalions, when oppofed againſt them, which have neither ſtrength or principle to vindicate their difpoſition? Let the fentries be poſted, or light infantry, in what ſituation you pleaſe, in a plain, or in a rough ground; make them fally out of a narrow pafs, or any other place, and you will fee with what furprizing celerity they will perform: or order them to run at full ſpeed, in order to take poſſeſſion of a defile, hedge, or eminence, and the inſtant in which ſtandards or colours arrive, they will draw up and dreſs. This is what is abſolutely impracticable with our battalions; for to form them in their natural difpoſition, will require too much time, and likewiſe a piece of ground almoſt made on purpoſe; which are things fo incompatible with the nature of that fervice, that it is impoſſible to fee them put in execution, without the greateſt difguſt and impatience."

¶ The reader will be pleaſed to obferve, that what I have cited, is not an exact copy, or the whole of what was laid down by M. Saxe; for that it would be quite foreign to the prefent art of war; but yet it is as nearly kept to as poſſible.

Paſſing Rivers.

"IT is juſtly confidered as one of the moſt delicate and dangerous movements in war; and yet it has oft fucceeded from a want of its opponents being perfectly acquainted with them, and from a want of their diligence, activity, and refolution to oppofe it; otherwiſe it could not fucceed; for though an enemy cannot prevent your making ufe of a bridge, under the protection of your artillery, if properly placed; yet he can hinder you from occupying fuch an extent of ground, as is neceſſary to develope your army, without expoſing himſelf to your artillery.

"One method of paſſing, is with a flank prefented to the enemy: which is what Prince Eugene was fuffered to do 3 times in 2 days in the prefence of the Duke of Orleans before the battle of Turin. The ground between the 2 armies was level, and there was an advantageous opportunity of attacking the enemy even with fuperior numbers: notwithſtanding which, it was neglected, and the fiege of Turin, in confequence, obliged to be raifed.

D 3 "With

" With regard to the paffing of rivers by open force, I look upon it as a thing hardly poffible to prevent, efpecially when fuftained by a large fire of artillery, to gain time for the van to intrench itfelf, and to throw up a work to cover the bridge. There is nothing effectual to be done in the day. Yet, during the night, this work may be attacked with great advantage; and if it happens that the enemy has begun his paffage at that time, he muft be thrown into a general confufion, attended with the certain lofs of thofe who may have already paffed. But an attack of this kind muft be made with a large force: and if the opportunity of the night is fuffered to pafs unimproved, his whole army will have got over before morning; after which, it is no longer practicable to make any attempt upon him, without drawing on a general engagement; which fituation and circumftance renders fometimes very imprudent to hazard."

Paffing Caufeways, or large Defiles, where there is Danger of being obftructed by the Enemy.

" A Body of men in paffing a large defile, or caufeway, is only to march in regular order, and form with a front fo narrow, as to leave room on the right flank for 1 man to move either forwards or backwards with eafe: fo that in cafe the enemy fhould attack it in the paffage, it may be able to make its retreat, without being diforderd by the fireings, which are to be performed as follows: *The front rank fires,* then faces to the right, marches one after the other along the flank, and falls into the rear of its divifion again: after that, the centre rank fires, and laftly the rear; both ranks facing to the right after they have fired, and marching to the rear in the fame manner as the front did, which muft be continued till they have retreated out of the defile.

' When a body of troops in a defile is to fire advancing, the above defcribed difpofition muft be obferved; namely, the centre rank, as foon as the front has fired, is to advance before it and fire, and fo on fucceffively till they paffed through the defile; nothing further being required, than to keep up an alternate and brifk fire, and to leave a fufficient fpace upon the flank, for a horfe to pafs by without obftruction."

Night

Night Marches.

" AS it may very eafily happen, that in marching of a large detachment in the night, fome troops or fquadrons may lofe themfelves, efpecially where there are any crofs-roads, or difficult paffes; to prevent fuch an accident, 2 or 3 guides muft be procured, if poffible; and, after they have fatisfied each concerning the rout, by a previous confultation together, be diftributed in the detachment.

" The Commanding Officer at the head of the detachment muft march flow, provided the nature of his expedition will admit of it: and wherever he finds any bye-roads on the march, he muft poft a few men there, to direct the fucceeding fquadron; which fquadron is to repeat the fame caution; and fo on throughout the whole.

" As it is almoft impoffible for fquadrons to keep conftantly clofe to one another; and as it likewife frequently happens, that, in order to conceal a march from the enemy, no trumpet muft be founded (which would otherwife ferve for a direction in the night-time); a good Non-commiffioned Officer with 4 or 6 men, muft be appointed to the rear of every fquadron, who are to divide themfelves, and form a chain in the interval, between it and the one fucceeding, in order to prevent any miftake of the road.

" Before the detachment marches off, the Officer commanding muft be careful to exhort the Officers leading troops or fquadrons, ftrictly to obferve all the above directions: he muft alfo have feveral orderly men to attend him, and, if poffible, more than 1 guide in front.

" The advance guard is to be ftrengthened in the night-time, march and at a fmall diftance from the main body, and, whenever it fhall happen unexpectedly to meet the enemy, it muft inftantly charge with all poffible vigour; on which account, and in order to be in continual readinefs, it is always to march with advanced arms.

" ¶ In the day-time, the advance-guard is ufually to march at a confiderable diftance from the main body, but not out of fight; and muft have a few good men, or a fmall party, advanced before it, to give timely intelligence to the Commanding Officer.

Making a Retreat.

" IN order to fecure the retreat of a *large detachment* in the prefence of an enemy, it will be neceffary to
form

form it into two lines, at the diftance of 200 large paces afunder : the firft line is to wheel by fours, by fquadrons, and, retreating through the intervals of the fecond, march about 2 or 300 paces in its rear, according as it may be more or lefs preffed by the enemy, and then face about again.

" After the firft line has moved in the rear of the fecond, the fecond is to wheel about, and march through the firft ; and fo on, both lines continuing to retreat in this manner, as long as it may be neceffary.

" During the retreat, a few fmall parties, compofed of the braveft men, are to be advanced towards the enemy, in order to fkirmifh with them, and thereby to facilitate the movements of the main body.

N. B. This is what may frequently be neceffary for the rear-guard to put in practice, when the enemy either attempts to obftruct or reconnoitre the march of an army.

PARTIES.

AN Officer who commands one, fhould be acquainted with roads, defiles, &c. If deficient in that refpect, an able guide fhould be provided.

An Officer fhould avoid being feen or heard in the night or day, till he has executed his orders; after which he fhould return by a different road from that he took, left the enemy lay wait to intercept him.

An Officer muft keep clear of all towns, of villages, and even of fingle houfes. If obliged to pafs through or near them, he fhould do it in the night, in a fmart regular run, to prevent his number from being known ; yet he muft always guard againft furprize, and never fuffer a fingle man to remain behind, left he fhould betray the party.

When the men are to be refrefhed, it fhould be under fome hedge, or in a ditch, copfe, &c. that they may be fecret and concealed.

An Officer fhould always (if the party will admit of it) have an advance-guard, at fuch a diftance before him, as, after firing upon a party of the enemy, it may give him fufficient time for his retreat to the body, in a flow and re-gular manner ; but if he perceives the enemy inclined to retreat, he then remains upon his ground, till joined by his Commander ; for did he purfue, the enemy might have a referve in ambufh that would deftroy the whole party.

But

But parties in general fhould be commanded by a partizan, " who is capable of forming ftratagems, by marches and counter-marches, to arrive at, and return from, the place he has in view: he fhould be capable of refolving quickly, and to determine at a glance on the time and occafion to engage or retreat. When weak, he fhould know how to poft to advantage ; how to drefs his ambufcades, and avoid thofe of the enemy : he muft preferve his ammunition, and take particular care that his arms are always in perfect order ; he muft, in fhort, keep his troops in the moft exact difcipline, and, above all, obferve the *ftricteft filence*, which is abfolutely neceffary for parties.

" Let him ever be mindful of the danger of halting in villages, farm-houfes, gentlemens feats, &c. If his foldiers need refrefhment (their provifions being out) let him fend an intelligent fagacious foldier to the neareft village, and, when brought out, detach 1 or 2 to fetch them to a place fo concealed, that the peafants may be prevented from counting his numbers, and even, if poffible, from feeing his men ; but yet fo fit for his defence, that he may inftantly be able to act, if then attacked ; to which he ever will be liable, as no caution may hinder the enemy's knowledge of what his troops are then about."

" If 2 equal parties engage in an open field or plain, it is the courage and hardinefs of the Partizan that obtains him a conqueft ; but if, by forming an ambufcade in a clofe covered country, he furprizes the enemy, who, for want of proper precautions, have fallen into it, he then owes his fuccefs to his judgment and fagacity. If he takes any booty, let him diftribute it with the utmoft equality. No other rules for the conduct of a Partizan and a party can be formed ; if any thing more is needful, it will readily occur to capacity and experience."

Directions for the Conduct of Officers on Grand-Guards, Out-Pofts, and Parties.

In cafe of an Attack.

" THE Commanding Officer of the grand-guard, when any alarm happens, is immediately to fend an Officer with fome men to the place, to gain information of the particulars.

" When a guard difcovers any body of the enemy in motion, an Officer muft immediately be fent with the intelligence,

telligence, particularizing as much as possible their numbers, and every other material circumstance : if afterwards they should approach very near the guard, the Commanding Officer must retreat slowly, and in good order, towards the camp.

" When the Commanding Officer perceives the enemy will attack him, he must sally out upon them, provided they are not too strong for him, when they are at the distance of 60 yards ; but if their numbers are much superior, he must retire before they approach so near.

" The videts are to carry their arms advanced before them, with the buts planted on the right knee."

" When General Officers come to visit the grand-guard, whether they be of the cavalry or infantry, the Officer must receive them with his guard mounted ; but he is not to sound his trumpet, *not even to the Commander in Chief*, because that is never to be done, but at the relief of this guard.

" Nor must any Officer, as his reputation and honour are at stake, take off his sword, pull off his boots, or have a chair to sleep upon, &c. but must keep on all his cloathes and accoutrements, together with the Non-commissioned Officers and men, both day and night ; nor presume to sleep as long as he continues on the guard.

" All inferior posts, detached from the grand-guard, and commanded by Non-commissioned Officers or Subalterns, depend upon the Commanding Officer of the grand-guard, and are to make their reports to him, and receive the patrol from him.

" One half of the grand-guard may, in the day-time, be suffered to dismount ; the other half to be drawn up 3 deep, and alternately relieved.

" Every Officer, as soon as he has relieved the guard, and his sentries are posted, is to visit them, to see whether they cover the ground sufficiently, or not; and if he thinks any part too open and exposed, he is at liberty to plant new sentries there: *but he must not remove, or alter any of the old posts*, because they were appointed by the Generals, and will be visited by them frequently, to prevent *surprizes and neglect of duty*.

" An hour before night, the Commanding Officer of the grand-guard is to give out the patrol, to all the Officers depending upon him, together with the counter-sign, or signal, that when the posts are visited in the night-time, they

may

may be able to diftinguifh with certainty their own rounds, and the enemy be prevented from impofing upon them.

" So foon as it is dark, all pofts belonging to the grand-guard, are to mount their horfes, and to continue on horfe-back during the whole night; particularly where there is any probability of their being attempted by the enemy : but at other times in camp, when there is no reafon to be ap-prehenfive of any danger, one half only of the guard muft conftantly remain mounted, and the other keep their horfes bridled, and ftand by them.

" Every Officer muft be careful to give proper in-ftru\u00e9tions to his fentries, and muft often patrol himfelf, as well as fend out patrols, to fee whether they be alert and watchful on their pofts : a Non-commiffioned Officer, with a fmall party, muft be alfo frequently detached to re-connoitre the intermediate country, between them and the enemy; in order to prevent any fentry, or fmall guard, being furprized : when the Non-commiffioned Officer, with a few men is fent to him from the guard, who is to demand the patrol from him, with his piftol in his hand ; and when he finds it right, he is then to take him to the Command-ing Officer, that he may make his report to him.

" The fentries are to challenge in proper time, and to demand the counter-fign before they permit any one to ap-proach within the diftance of fifty paces ; nor muft they on any account fuffer perfons to pafs till they are become per-fe\u00e9tly well convinced, they don't belong to the enemy.

" The fentries, when they have challenged any perfon, but receive no anfwer, are immediately to demand the counter-fign ; and if they ftill receive no anfwer, they are dire\u00e9tly to fire : for which reafon, the Officers are to ex-amine the arms of every relief, fee that they are in proper order, well primed, the powder dry, and the hammer-ftalls taken off.

" The Officers muft inform their fentries, that when-ever they perceive more then 2 men with arms, whether on horfe-back, or on foot, advancing towards them, notwith-ftanding they can give the counter-fign, they are not, after they have firft challenged, to fuffer them to advance one pace further ; but muft give the word to the next fentry, who is to pafs it to the guard ; the Commanding Officer is then to fend a good Non-commiffioned Officer, with a party of men, to make examinations : if the Non-commiffioned Officer finds them to be a detachment from the army, he

muft

muſt order it to ſtand faſt, and then return with the Officer
commanding it, to the Officer of his guard, who, in caſe
he be unacquainted with his perſon, and is afraid to con-
fide, either in his clothing, or his knowledge of the counter-
ſign, muſt ſcrutinize him ſtrictly, require his orders and
paſſports, and if he finds them authentic, permit his command to paſs.

    " When they happen to be a few men only, the Non-
    commiſſioned Officer muſt bring them to the guard ;
    from whence the Officer, in caſe he has no perſonal
    knowledge of them, muſt not diſmiſs them, before day-
    light ; nay, even in the day-time, if a body of men
    ſhould approach an Officer's guard, who give out that
    they are friends, he is to prevent them from advancing
    too near, unleſs he has a perſonal knowledge of the
    Officers ; nor is he then to let his guard diſmount, till
    they have marched by.

    " All Officers, when on out-poſts, or other parties out
of camp, muſt take the ſame precautions ; that whenever
they ſhall happen to be attacked by the enemy, they may
have their men mounted, in readineſs to receive them ; nor
remain at any time expoſed, even to a poſſibility of being
ſurpriſed ; every Officer ſhould keep his men always together, and take care that not one can find any opportunity
to quit his guard, ſteal away to *maraude, or do any other miſ-
chief.* He muſt likewiſe poſt his ſentries round in ſuch a
manner, as to render it impoſſible for any to eſcape their
obſervation, either by day or night.

    " When an Officer commands an out-poſt, it is highly
neceſſary that he ſhould become a judge of the ground : he
muſt therefore make himſelf perfectly acquainted with the
country round him, ſo as to be able to know from what
part the enemy can beſt make an attempt upon him : after
which he can poſt himſelf *behind a defile, bridge, hollow-way,
or bank* ; becauſe that when he preſents his guard, drawn
up in good order, in a ſituation ſo advantageous, he may
reſt aſſured no enemy will venture to paſs : an eminence is
alſo another defenſible poſt for a body of cavalry, where there
is a valley lying before it, and the flanks can be well covered ; for it is a very eſſential precaution for Officers in all
ſituations to render, as much as poſſible, their flanks and
rear ſecure.

    " When an Officer, poſted in ſuch a manner, diſcovers
the approaches of any party, he muſt immediately mount

his

his guard, and detach a corporal and 2 men, with their arms advanced, to reconnoitre them, who are to fire in cafe they find them enemies, and afterwards retire to their poft with the utmoft fpeed.

" When an Officer, notwithftanding his utmoft vigilance and precaution, is attacked on his poft, he fhall not abandon it, without firft having made all poffible refiftance ; nor retire, unlefs compelled thereto by abfolute neceffity : namely, the being overpowered by numbers, without any probability of receiving fuccours ; the reality of which he is, on an enquiry, to produce fufficient proof of : if, on the contrary, it fhall in the leaft degree appear, that he might either have maintained his poft, or made a better defence ; or, that he did not behave, in every refpect, as became a prudent and brave Officer, he fhall be cafhiered with infamy, or, according to the nature of his offence, be punifhed with death, and forfeiture of his effects.

" When an Officer is detached with a command to any confiderable diftance from the army, where it will be impoffible for him to receive any reinforcement, and perceives a much ftronger body of the enemy advancing towards him, he is to make his retreat in good order, and march back the fafeft way, through woods, villages, or defiles, to the army."

Inftructions concerning Foraging and Foraging Parties.

" THE Quarter-mafter-general is firft to reconnoitre the ground where the army is to forage ; after which he will be much better able to fix the difpofition of the covering party.

" When the foragers arrive at their ground, they muft be all drawn up together, to receive fuch orders on the fpot as circumftances may render neceffary ; after which every regiment is to march off, and forage in its appointed place.

" The foragers of the firft regiment in the front muft march flow, to prevent thofe that follow being obliged to run.

" When the army is to forage near an enemy, and where there are copfes and villages contiguous, in which they may have planted ambufcades, no man muft be fuffered either to wander from his party, or venture to go into them : and if they can forage in the copfes, the horfes muft be left at fome diftance from them in the open fields, and the truffes when made up be brought out to them on foot.

" The truffes are to be bound with 4 forage-cords, to prevent the horfes backs being galled ; the men taught how

to

to make them up, to load their horfes, and in what manner to mount afterwards, and ride with them.

" N. B. As great uneafinefs may arife from a bad manner of receiving forage, and from the orders for paying it, attention muft be ufed to fee that it is good, and the weight of the ration be mentioned in public orders ; fo that if any tricks are played, the Contractors and Quarter-mafters may be called to an account for them, and punifhed accordingly.

" When cavalry are to forage, (if the numbers will allow) they will do it by wings, or, at leaft, by brigades, at a time. No Officer fhall be fuffered to forage for himfelf alone, particularly when it is obliged to be fought for beyond the advanced pofts.

" The night before any grand forage, a ftrong covering-party muft be ordered out, fufficient for the fecurity of the foragers, the Commanding Officer of which muft difpofe the pofts in fuch manner, as entirely to cover the ground towards an enemy ; nor fhall any of the foragers be permitted to pafs them. After proper difpofition has been made, the Quarter-mafter-general muft well reconnoitre the ground, and affign to every regiment a limited proportion; or, when the forage is fupplied out of barns, or by fome particular village, the Quarter-mafters from every corps are to attend him, and afterwards conduct it for their refpective regiments to the places feverally appointed for them.

" The Officer commanding the covering-party, fo foon as he has made his difpofition, muft fend an Officer to camp, to conduct the foragers the neareft way to the place."

" When the army marches into a new camp, the forage happening to be upon the ground where any regiment encamps, it is to become the property of that regiment, provided the army is not in want ; if it is, it muft be fent away by the direction of the Quarter-mafter-general, and diftributed among the army.

" Every brigade fhall furnifh a party, who are to keep the foragers in proper order, taking care that thofe of one regiment don't mix with thofe of another ; to prevent which, when they march out of camp, one Officer is to be pofted in the front of every troop or fquadron, and another in the rear.

" When the foragers arrive at the place appointed to forage in, every regiment is to take poffeffion of, and to confine itfelf within, the ground refpectively allotted it ; nor fhall
any

any foldier or fervant prefume of his own accord, and without orders from an Officer, to quit his own troop or fquadron, and forage elfewhere."

No foragers muft advance beyond the pofts; " and if, contrary to all orders, any foldier or fervant fhall be guilty of this offence, it muft be reported to his regiment, that he may be punifhed in an exemplary manner; becaufe from fuch diforders it happens, that fo many horfes are carried off by the enemy, to the great detriment of the regiments they belong to, and expence of the Captains, who cannot upon their proportion of ftock-purfe well fupply their places.

" The feparate parties, furnifhed by each brigade, as well as each regiment, are to take all poffible pains to keep their refpective foragers together, and to prevent their marauding, or paffing their bounds; they therefore muft form a chain of fentries round them, and continue in that difpofition, till the foraging is over.

" When any alarm happens during the foraging, and there is a profpect of danger, the foragers are to quit their forage, and retire to camp.

" So foon as a regiment has done foraging, and is ready, it is to be marched back in good order to camp, the Officers of every troop or fquadron being pofted one in the front, and one in the rear, as before directed: its feparate party is likewife to march in the rear, but the brigade-parties are to remain in their pofts till all their refpective regiments have done foraging.

" The Officers, when out upon foraging-parties, either in the field or villages, muft always march their men, in a regular foldier-like manner, to the places in which they are to forage; and, after the foraging is over, they muft draw them up, have the roll called, and march them back in the fame order to camp.

" Every Officer, ordered out on thefe parties, fhall be anfwerable that he brings all his men back to the regiment; he muft therefore take his precautions accordingly."

Inftructions concerning the Baggage on a March.

" ON the march, the baggage muft be placed according to the difpofition ordered; the waggons are to be numbered, and follow regularly, in numerical order, by its regiment.

" A co-

" A covering-party over the baggage is to be appointed by order of the Commander in Chief, the strength of which is discretional, and to be determined by circumstances.

" When the Commanding Officer of the party has reason to apprehend himself in any danger, he must take every precaution to frustrate his enemies designs, and deprive them of all opportunities to surprize him, or attack his baggage; for which purpose it will be absolutely requisite to have patrols, not only in front, but also in rear, and upon the flanks, that he may discover their ambuscades in time, so as to take the proper measures effectually to counteract and disappoint them: and this vigilance and attention is in a more particular manner necessary in the passage of hollow ways, woods, thickets, &c.

" N. B. In marching through hollow ways, which are difficult to pass, a small detachment is to be posted upon both flanks, and in the front and rear, there to remain till the baggage has got through: the same must be done in the passage of all woods and thickets.

" These precautions are not only necessary for covering-parties appointed over baggage, but are likewise to be put in practice by all escorts or detachments on march.

" An Officer on a march, particularly if he has a large body under his command, must always have an advanced and rear-guard, and take care to reconnoitre well the country, and scour all villages, woods, defiles, and hollow ways, before he passes them: the Officers commanding the advance and rear-guards must likewise take the same precaution before they march through such places, to secure a passage, without subjecting themselves to any apprehension of being obstructed."

CONVOYS.

" AN Officer, having the command of one, must take all possible precautions for its security; and endeavour, before his march, to procure some good intelligence concerning the enemies out-posts: and as the Commanding Officer of the place, from which the convoy is to march, and those of such other places as it is to pass by, are the most proper persons to apply to for assistance; he must therefore take such measures as will enable him to keep up a constant intercourse with them.

" The time appointed for the march must be kept a secret: some particular day may first be given out for it, in

order

order to deceive the enemy; after which the convoy may depart sooner : but the gate of the town, if possible, must be kept shut both before and after its march. Patrols must be posted not only in the front of the convoy but on the flanks and in the rear, to prevent the enemy from falling upon them unexpectedly.

" Light cavalry or dragoons must be divided upon the flanks of the carriages, to see that they all follow close and regular, not permitting one to halt under pretence of forage or water, left the march should be hindered, and the train lengthened; to prevent which, they are not to be overloaded.

" The Officer having the command of a small escorte must conduct the waggons, or whatever he may have to escort, in the centre of it; and never march through coppices, woods, or villages, till he has previously reconnoitred them by a party proportionable to his command, which he is to advance before him for that purpose. If he be attacked, he must endeavour as much as possible to preserve his rear free and secure; and draw up his carriages on the most commodious ground, till, by an obstinate resistance, he may have dispersed the enemy, and can pursue his march.

" An Officer commanding a large escort is to have a van-guard to reconnoitre the way before him, and likewise a rear-guard, both composed of light-horse or dragoons : he must also detach small parties upon the flanks, with orders carefully to examine all suspected places contiguous to the road, march up to the top of every adjacent hill or eminence, and take a view of the country, to give intelligence of any danger.

" N. B. An Officer having the command of a detachment of infantry, shall never divide them into small platoons, on pain of being cashiered; but when his escort consists of a whole battalion, he shall post 1 division in the front of the carriages, 2 in the centre of them, and the fourth in the rear. If he has cavalry, they must be divided, in proportion to their numbers, between the divisions. He is moreover to take particular care that the waggons follow in close succession.

" When there is any hollow way to pass, an advanced guard is to march through it first; and some platoons or divisions, according to the strength of the detachment, must be ordered to take possession of the eminences on each side, before the carriages with the escort is to pass.

E

" The

" The platoons or divifions are to remain upon the eminences, till the efcort has paffed the hollow way, to
deter the enemy from making any attempts to obftruct
it ; and, after the whole has marched through, they
are to fall into the rear of their command again.

" The utmoft care and precaution muft be taken in the
conducting of powder-waggons: no perfon be fuffered to
fmoke, and the carriages be driven gently over ftone pave-
ments, left the powder fhould take fire. If at any time a
powder, corn, bread, or forage waggon fhould happen to
be broke down, the train is not to be ftopped by it, but to
keep on regular. In the mean time, the Waggon-mafter-
general, and his affiftants, are to take care that it be immediately repaired, and afterwards drove up to its former place;
but if it be fo damaged, as not to admit of being repaired,
the moft valuable things muft then be diftributed upon the
other waggons, and the broken carriage left.

" Whenever an efcort halts at night, the waggons muft
always be fecured from fire : and the defile, village, or town,
fo effectually guarded, as to remain expofed to no danger
from the enemy. The Commanding Officer is to poft a
detachment of his cavalry towards the enemy, by way of
grand guard, and keep patrols going conftantly all night,
that, in cafe the enemy fhould make any difpofition to attack
him, he may be able to receive timely intelligence.

" When the Commanding Officer of a convoy has certain intelligence that the enemy are in motion, he muft, if
circumftances require it, immediately fend advice to the
Commander in Chief, and to the garrifon moft contiguous :
and when it happens, that he has undoubted reafon to expect
being attacked, it will then become moft prudent for him,
though the enemy fhould be fuperior to him in numbers, to
march againft them himfelf, and begin the attack, rather
than wait to receive it : upon emergencies of which kind, it
is always incumbent upon the Commanding Officer to take
the advantage of ground.

" If the enemy are much too powerful, and it is abfolutely impoffible for the convoy to maintain its ground againft
them, and the Officer expects relief by fome means or other,
he muft, in that cafe, provided the circumftances of time
and ground admit of it, *form a barricade with the carriages,*
and fend intelligence of his fituation to all places from
whence he can expect a ready affiftance.

" In

" In general, let it be obferved, that it becomes a good Officer to take all imaginable precautions; to deny himfelf, during the whole march, all manner of eafe and indulgence; and ftudy, in a particular manner, to render himfelf confpicuous for diligence and attention to his duty."

Particular Duties on which Light Cavalry are to be employed.

" THEY are to be employed in reconnoitring the enemy, and difcovering his motions: and as oft as Officers are detached on fuch commands, all that will be required of them, is, to make their obfervations with certainty, fo as not to deceive the Commanding Officer by falfe intelligence: they are, alfo, on fuch parties, to avoid engaging with the enemy, as being fent out for a different purpofe.

" Light cavalry are alfo to be made ufe of for diftant advanced pofts, to prevent the army from being falfely alarmed or furprized.

" The Officers on fuch pofts are in a particular manner required to render themfelves judges of their fituation, and to poft their fentries in the moft proper places.

" Small patrols are to be kept going round the army, to prevent defertion; particular care being taken, that one patrol conftantly fucceeds another, fo as to render it impoffible for any thing to efcape them.

" Parties are alfo to be fent out to diftrefs the enemy, by depriving them of forage and provifions; by furprifing their convoys, attacking their baggage, harraffing them on their march, cutting off fmall detachments, and fometimes carrying off foraging-parties; in fhort, of feizing all opportunities to do them as much damage as they poffibly can.

" Light cavalry are moveover to be employed in raifing contributions: and, when the army marches, they may compofe the advance-guard; reconnoitring the front and flanks carefully, and fending intelligence to the Commander in Chief with expedition, whenever they difcover the enemy, or any kind of danger; and, when other troops cannot be fpared, they may form the rear-guard, or cover the baggage."

N. B. As the fervice of the light cavalry is attended with more fatigue and danger than the heavy, all vacancies fhould go regular in thofe corps, and indeed in all others, left the brave and deferving Officer, for want of money or friends, may lofe his juft promotion.

AMBUS-

AMBUSCADES.

" AMBUSCADES are snares set for the enemy, either to surprize them when marching without precaution, or by posting yourself advantageously, and drawing them there, by different stratagems, to attack them with superior force.

" An active and vigilant General oftener employs stratagem than open force in war ; and, by multiplying small advantages, procures, at length, a decisive one. Ambuscades are the surest means of procuring these small successes. They are of two kinds, great and small. It is very seldom the first kind can be practised against an able, cautious General : they may even be extremely dangerous, if discovered by the enemy ; and therefore, though we speak of the manner of employing them successfully, we insist less on the necessity of them than of small ambuscades, which are frequently employed, and with little risk. These small ambuscades have different objects in view : they serve to carry off magistrates or hostages for the payment of contributions, merchants who transport provisions to the enemy, &c.

" A Partizan may also form an ambuscade when he is well assured, by good spies, of the day and road one of the enemy's convoys is to pass ; whether with young horses to remount the cavalry, recruits, provisions, or ammunition, and that the escort is weaker than his party. The advice he receives from spies or friends, who give him intelligence, gives him often the facility of taking, by an ambuscade, one of the enemy's Generals, detached to reconnoitre some particular place, to be cured of his wounds, to receive some person of distinction, or otherwise.

" When you have a spy intriguing enough to be instructed, and to give advice of the day and road the enemy are to go a foraging, an ambuscade may be formed near the road to carry off some of the horses or foragers : you may also lie in ambuscade within the chain of forage, and fall on the foragers when dispersed ; but you must observe to plant your ambuscade, in both these cases, in a place distant from the enemy's troops, who form the chain ; that is to say, behind the centre of the foragers ; and have a sure retreat so soon as you have struck your stroke.

" You may also plant small parties of light-troops in ambuscade in different places, without the chain of escort ;

who,

who, fo foon as the foragers difband, give the alarm at
the different pofts; fo that the enemy, not knowing on
what fide the real attack is, are obliged to re-affemble the
efcort; and, as much time is loft in this way, night comes
on before the foraging is compleated, and the cavalry are
fatigued, weakened, and infenfibly deftroyed. Ambufcades
may alfo be placed to carry off the men or equipages who
remain behind when the army difperfes to go to quarters,
or when the troops, which are to compofe it, are affembling
in the fpring.

"Ambufcades are dreffed to carry off prifoners or inhabitants of the country, to gain intelligence. In this cafe,
the prifoners fhould not be allowed to remain or talk together, left they concert fome falfe intelligence to deceive you.

"In fhort, ambufcades may be employed to carry off
couriers, or fmall convoys of the enemy, who pafs between
their army and their great towns; but in all thefe cafes the
parties who form them muft be attended by good guides,
who know all the bridges, rivulets, fords, paffes, marfhes,
foot-paths through woods or over mountains, &c. that they
may retire through roads unknown to the enemy.

"It is not neceffary that thefe kind of ambufcades fhould
be compofed of greater numbers than the efcorts of the enemy, efpecially if thefe efcorts muft march thro' defiles.

"If you form an ambufcade, where the fafety of your retreat does not depend on your numbers, but entirely on their
addrefs and celerity, it fhould be compofed of light cavalry,
and of no more than are judged neceffary to defeat that part
of the enemy's corps againft whom they are intended.

"When your retreat is fhort, but through a rough covered road, the ambufcades fhould confift of more infantry
than cavalry; but if the retreat is to be long, and by a broad
open road, you muft have no more infantry than what the
half of your cavalry can carry behind them; while the other
half, having nothing to embarrafs them, form the front or
rear-guard, and make head againft the enemy. If you would
difquiet and harrafs the enemy by fmall but frequent ambufcades you muft, from time to time, form a great ambufcade, to over-awe the enemy, and prevent their fending out
detachments againft your fmall parties.

"Ambufcades fhould march with great fecrecy, and generally in the night; they ought never to carry dogs with
them, becaufe they bark; nor mares with ftone-horfes, becaufe of their neighing: they fhould take as few fervants

E 3   with

with them as poffible, and ftrictly forbid them, or the party,
to fire at game, if it fhould fpring.

" They fhould endeavour to enter the place of ambufh,
fo as to leave no trace behind them ; and for this purpofe they
may turn the fhoes of the horfes of the rear-guard, or throw
down their cloaks for the reft to walk along.

" They fhould not arrive at the place of ambufh long before they expect the enemy, becaufe accidents may happen
to difcover them ; or their men, if fatigued, may fall fleep.

" It is needlefs to mention the places fit for parties to
lay in ambufh ; every place is proper ; a hollow way, a fmall
wood, a dry ditch, the grotto of a mountain, a garden, a
court-yard, a field of corn, a thick hedge; in fhort, every
place covered by art or nature. It is the perfon that commands who muft chufe the fpot where he is not expofed to
be difcovered, and at hand to carry off his intended prize.

" Great ambufcades have fo immediate a connection with
marches, furprizes of armies, and battles, that, to have a
juft notion of the manner of employing them with fome
hopes of fuccefs, it is neceffary to combine what will be faid
hereafter on thefe three fubjects.

" The object of great ambufcades is to carry off a corps
of the enemy left to their own ftrength ; to furprize a convoy, or the equipages of the army ; the attack of an army
on march ; the carrying off a part of a garrifon ; or taking
a town by efcalade.

" Great ambufcades are formed in woods or vallies,
where care muft be taken to place fmall parties in ambufh
all round, or on the neighbouring eminences, to ftop and
arreft hunters, travellers, or other paffengers, who might
difcover your main body.

" Great ambufcades may alfo be formed in a village or
town, whofe inhabitants favour you ; where, for fear of
being betrayed by fome fpy, you leave fentries all round,
publifhing a ftrict order, on pain of death, not to pafs beyond your fentries. On a fteeple, or the higheft place,
there you appoint an Officer for fentry, who, with good
glaffes, difcovers the approach of the enemy, their numbers,
and the road they keep ; and informs you of thefe particulars, that you may have your troops in order of battle in the
ftreets : but if the Officer on the fteeple informs you that
the enemy is fuperior, and that you have not time to retire,
you muft draw up your troops in an oppofite ftreet, or in a
church, placing only a few of your men, difguifed and dreffed

fed like townſmen, in the ſtreet through which the enemy
are to march, to try to prevent any inhabitant informing
them. This precaution ſuppoſes you have taken all others
proper for your defence ; for, if the enemy has the leaſt experience, he will not enter the village till he has ſearched
and examined it.

" Plains covered with corn or bruſh-wood are very commodious for placing infantry in ambuſcade, becauſe from
thence you can ſee at ſome diſtance the number of the enemy, and the manner in which they approach ; you can march
out in order of battle to attack them ; or, if you find them
ſuperior, you have a free retreat on all ſides.

" When you know the enemy's army is to march through
a country which produces little water, eſpecially if the ſeaſon is hot, you may, if the ground permits, dreſs a ſtrong
ambuſcade near ſome fountain or rivulet by the road. The
ſucceſs in this caſe is more certain, becauſe the ſoldiers, fatigued with the march, never fail to diſperſe, 'each trying
to be the firſt to quench his thirſt before the water is troubled by the reſt ; and as the current of the water has dug a
courſe for itſelf, and has formed a hollow way where the
corps are obliged to defile, this renders it the more eaſy to
attack one part of them, before or after they have paſſed,
with great advantage.

" If it is neceſſary to keep in ambuſcade more than one
day, it is ſuppoſed they have brought proviſions with them,
and they muſt chuſe a place where there is water ; left, if at
a diſtance, the ſoldiers are diſcovered going to fetch it.

" The troops in ambuſcade muſt be placed without confuſion, ſo as to be able to make their ſally in order.

" So ſoon as they have arrived at the place where they
are to form the ambuſcade, the Commanding Officer of
each troop muſt review them : if any ſoldiers, ſervants, or
others, are miſſing, he is immediately to inform the Commander in Chief ; who ſhould, in that caſe, retire with
the party.

" He muſt place his ſentries where they can ſee fartheſt
on all ſides : but, that they may not themſelves be perceived at a diſtance, by the colour of their regimentals, or
the ſhining of their arms, the ſentries ſhould place their
firelocks on the ground, and lay themſelves amongſt the
leaves or buſhes on the eminence where they are placed ;
for, from the ſummit of a little hill or riſing ground, a man
ſees more than a mile : if there is no riſing ground, they

E 4   can

can place the fentries towards the top of thick bufhy trees, behind branches, or cover them by fome fmall brufh-wood they may have carried with them for the purpofe.

" If the fentries poft is fo far from the ambufcade that they cannot be heard, or come, or fend another with their intelligence, without the rifk of being perceived by the enemy, in walking over fome open field betwixt the ambufcade and the firft or fartheft off fentries, other fentries muft be placed at fmaller diftances, under the cover of fome hollow way, rock, or bufh, that the intelligence may pafs by word of mouth from one to the other.

" But, left thefe advices fhould not be clear, or to the purpofe, and may throw you into confufion, thefe fentries fhould be Officers, Serjeants, or intelligent Corporals. This is particularly neceffary with regard to the fentry the moft advanced on each fide; that is to fay, he who has the fartheft view.

" It is neceffary to have, on the right, the centre and left of the ambufcade, 3 fmall parties of cavalry; who, on the firft advice from the fentries, are ready to ride after and arreft deferters, or peafants, who may difcover your ambufcade.

" If you know the road a detachment of the enemy intends to take, and that this march is through your country, place at the fide oppofite to your fentries fome flocks or herds of cattle fcattered along the hills, within fight of your ambufcade; the defire of carrying them off will make the enemy difperfe, or at leaft weaken themfelves by fending parties to carry them off. Inftead of fhepherds, place foldiers difguifed to tend thefe flocks; who, feeing the enemy advance, fhall feem to retire with their flocks; and, when the enemy have got very near, thefe foldiers fhall make their efcape, the beft way they can, on horfes given them for that purpofe.

" You may alfo draw the enemy into your ambufcade, by bribing their guides; who, in concert with you, may propofe a road where you fhall be in ambufh; or may draw them there by giving falfe advice of the force of your party, or of your project. They may alfo be drawn into an ambufcade, by detaching a party to carry off cattle, or by making fome prifoners near the enemy: in fuch a cafe, this party muft be fent out before any of the foldiers who compofe it can fufpect your defign; fo that if any one fhould defert, he can never inform the enemy of your intended enterprize;

terprize; the Officers of the party muſt alone be informed of your intentions, and you muſt mention the exact hour at which they ſhall begin to ſhew themſelves, leſt the enemy following them ſhould arrive at the place of ambuſcade before you are poſted.

" But this party muſt not retire ſo near the ambuſcade that the enemy's patrols may diſcover it before their main body is engaged in it. The ſentries placed near the road, by which the enemy march, who are purſuing your ſmall party, ſhall retire before they are diſcovered, and the party ſhall continue their feigned flight, till they are got conſiderably beyond the ambuſcade, to oblige the enemy to advance the farther; for the troops which compoſe the ambuſcade ſhould not begin to charge the enemy till their main body is oppoſite to your front, in order to attack their flanks, that the action may be complete and leſs dangerous.

" To prevent your ambuſcade being diſcovered too ſoon, you muſt caution your men to remain quiet and concealed till they get a certain ſignal, even though they ſhould hear ſome ſhots fired by their troops in ambuſcade, which may happen either by ſome firelocks going off by accident, or by ſome one firing at game which may ſpring.

" The ſignal may be made by planting a ſtandard on ſome eminence within ſight of your troops, by ſounding a charge with ſeveral trumpets or drums united, or ſome other warlike ſound different from what the enemy uſe on their march, and which may be eaſily diſtinguiſhed by your troops. You may alſo place ſome ſtraw, ſo as to be ſeen by all your troops, and, by ſetting fire to it, give the ſignal for the attack; or by firing a certain number of ſhots, or throwing one or more ſky-rockets from an eminence, which may be ſeen by the whole. But in all theſe caſes, the perſons deſtined to give the ſignals muſt be people of intelligence, who give them exactly at the proper time, when the enemy are thoroughly engaged in your ambuſcade.

" When the troops of your ambuſcade are greatly ſuperior in number to thoſe of the enemy whom you expect, divide them into 2 corps, which you may place at greater or ſmaller diſtance from each other, in proportion to the breadth of the road or the ground the enemy may occupy from his van-guard to his rear-guard; ſo that theſe 2 corps may ſally out at once from their ambuſcade, and charge the enemy when juſt between the 2.

" Even

" Even if the troops are not numerous enough to be divided into 2 equal bodies, each of which are superior in number to the enemy, the defeat will still be greater, if you charge their van-guard with your main body, and their rear-guard with a detachment; but if the nature of the ground makes it easy for the ambuscade to attack the whole flank of the enemy's troops when defiling, it will be needless to divide the troops, it being more advantageous to charge them in flank.

" If the enemy have in the rear a considerable party at hand, to sustain their rear-guard so soon as engaged, it is necessary to preserve a detachment of your troops, to oppose this party, in case they should advance to charge your troops who have attacked the enemy's rear.

" When the ground (because of its inequality, it being covered with woods, or any other obstacle) prevents your seeing whether the enemy have in their rear such a party as is just mentioned; in such a case, you must have the precaution to keep in ambuscade a small corps de reserve; and your troops the farthest advanced in the ambuscade must use the same precautions, if the front of the enemy's main body is preceded by a detachment; without which, there would be great danger that this detachment, by wheeling to right or left, might take your troops in flank, when engaged by the enemy's main body.

" In an ambuscade, the best marksmen should be placed in the front line, and desired to fire at those whom they can distinguish to be Officers; for small resistance can be expected from troops surprized and thrown into confusion and disorder by an unexpected attack, if the loss of their Officers is added to it. The grenadier Officers, or such as carry fuzees, should have the same orders.

" If the Officers who have been placed as sentries report that they have discovered a more considerable body of the enemy than you expected, and more than you are able to defeat, let the Commanding Officer repair to that post; and if by the help of good glasses he is convinced of the truth of the report, he should hasten his retreat; for it is then to be presumed, that the enemy, informed of your dedesign, comes with a strong detachment to surprize you in your ambuscade.

" If the enemy have a superior body of troops near you, and you have reason to believe your ambuscade has been discovered, either by any of your people deserting, or that your

march

march has been feen by any of the enemy's parties, who will
difcover it to their camp or garrifons ; in any of thefe cafes
you fhould alfo immediately form your retreat.

" If, in fpite of retiring with all promptitude, you fhall
be overtaken and attacked by the enemy with fuperior numbers, you muft then take fuch neceffary precautions as prudence requires, to affure your retreat ; or, if you are near
enough to hope for fuccours, make a vigorous and gallant
defence till they fhall arrive.

" If you have made any detachments who are in ambufh
at a certain diftance, that they may not be abandoned and
loft, you fhould immediately fend 5 or 6 horfemen, who
fhould take the moft favourable road, and inform them of
your retreat ; having taken care to mark to thefe Officers
with the detachments, the route they are to purfue ; either
to join you, or form their own retreat.

" If you want to draw a part of the troops of one of
the enemy's garrifons into an ambufcade, you fhould conceal beyond your ambufcade, and as near the garrifon as
poffible, a fmall party of cavalry, who muft endeavour to
carry off the herds of cattle, flocks of fheep, or Officers
horfes belonging to the place, which come out to feed or
water in the morning ; or, in the evening, try to carry off
the Governor, the Officers, principal citizens, or ladies,
who then come out to take the air.

" In this laft fort of expedition, you fhould wait for a
fair or a holiday, when many walk out ; becaufe the more
people of diftinction you can furprize, the more will their
friends and relations endeavour to prevail with the Governor, and engage him to fend out a detachment againft your
party, which fhould not retire precipitately, left the enemy
fhould abandon the purfuit ; but draw them on by degrees
towards the ambufcade.

" You fhould not place the main body of your ambufcade too near the town, to render the retreat of the enemy's
detachment more difficult after you have put them in diforder.

" You may alfo, if the ground allows of it, place in
ambufcade a corps of cavalry, a little beyond the principal
ambufcade, towards the town, to cut off the enemy's retreat
when defeated. We fuppofe, however, that thefe two ambufcades are not fo far diftant from each other, but that the
principal one, which is the fartheft from the town, can eafily come to the other's affiftance, in cafe they have by any
accident been difcovered and are attacked by the enemy.

" If

" If the environs of a garrifon are fo entirely open, that it is not impoffible to place a proper number of troops in ambufcade, the cavalry, in that cafe, may ferve to conceal the infantry.

" If you have plenty of troops, and have reafon to be-lieve the Commandant of the town or poft is weak enough, or fo ill-advifed, as to allow himfelf to fend out fo great a number of troops on a fally, as to leave his garrifon unpro-vided, you may place an ambufcade on the oppofite fide of the town, provided with the neceffaries for a furprize-efcalade, or by applying the petard, who fhall make their attack when the enemy are at fome diftance in purfuit of your other party.

" The fame ftratagem may be employed againft a town where there are no regular troops, and whofe unexperienced inhabitants are eafily deceived by all the common ftrata-gems of war.

" Before you try a great ambufcade, it is very proper to have oft formed fmall or to have made excurfions into the country with fmall parties ; fo that the Governor or Com-mandant of the poft being accuftomed to believe you have but a few troops, is the more eafily determined to detach a part of his garrifon.

" If you want to draw the enemy's army, or a great part of it, into an ambufcade, you muft march with your army towards the enemy, fo long as you are not afraid of being difcovered by their parties, or grand advanced guards : there you muft halt with all poffible filence, and detach a good part of your cavalry ; which, without halting, fhall charge that flank of the enemy neareft your ambufcade ; the firft charge being over, without giving the enemy time to attack them with too many troops, they muft retire to their main body ; fo that, if the enemy fhall inconfiderately purfue them, they fall into the ambufcade.

" Having given our ideas on this fubject, we fhall conclude with obferving, that, with the quantity of light troops now in ufe, and who are continually patrolling the country, it is very difficult to furprize an enemy with a great ambufcade ; the fmall only can fucceed ; and fuch particularly as are conducted by an able Partifan, who has good intelligence, and who underftands the *petit guerre.*"

ORDERS

O R D E R S proper for Troops on Board Transports in Time of War.

PAROLE, KING GEORGE; Counterfign, QUEEN CHARLOTTE. (Parole and Counterfign may be changed.)

In cafe of dark nights or fogs, when you hear or fee a veffel come near you, fhe muft be hailed, to prevent your being deceived by an enemy. The fhip hailed, if of the convoy, will return her name ; then afk the other her's, and exchange with each other the parole and counterfign, that you may not be furprized by a fhip of war or privateer lurking near you by night or in hazy weather. A Subaltern-officer of the day to be appointed, who is to be on deck, upon all fuch occafions ; and a guard, to confift of 1 Serjeant, 1 Corporal, and 12 private men, to keep ftrict order and to prevent fire. As it may poffibly happen that the tranfports may be feparated from the convoy, the Commanding-officer on board each tranfport is to poft his men to their particular quarters, and turn them out with their arms, at leaft once a day, whilft they continue at anchor, if the weather is fair, that they may know how to do it readily, and without confufion, in cafe of neceffity. The men are to turn out with their waift-belts flung, as on the march, and not fix their bayonets, unlefs the enemy attempt to board them. All the recruits who have not fired ball, muft be pofted at the cannon, and as many more of the foldiers as are acquainted with that fervice, and will be fufficient to work the guns. The cartridges are to be taken from thofe men and diftributed among fuch as have diftinguifhed themfelves in firing at the mark. The firelocks belonging to the recruits, and the men ordered to the guns, muft be kept on deck loaded, and carefully put up in an arm-cheft, ready for an emergency. The fame number of cartouch-boxes, filled with cartridges, likewife muft be put up in a fafe place, to be ready on the fhorteft notice. If you fhould be attacked by a privateer, your expedient will be a clofe engagement; the foldiers therefore are not to be fuffered to fhew themfelves on deck till the enemy is very near, and quite under the command of your fmall arms; and, even then, they are not to prefume to fire till they are ordered. It is not expected, that, in fuch a confined fituation, they fhould fire by divifion, but fingly, as they can take aim : they are not to be in too great a hurry in loading,
but

but to be careful to ſhake all the powder out of the cartridge before they ram it down. If the Commanding-officer
on board finds it neceſſary to hold a Regimental Court-martial, he may (a ſufficient number of Officers being preſent)
and likewiſe put the ſentence in execution. No women
muſt be ſuffered to remain on board, but ſuch as are lawful
wives of the ſoldiers. A return from each tranſport muſt be
made to the Commanding-officer every *Monday* morning,
that the weather permits.

Regulations for debarking Troops on an Hoſtile Shore.

EVERY Officer knows that a regiment is generally drawn
up 3 deep, with arms loaded, and bayonets fixed ; told
off into wings, grand and ſub-diviſions, platoons, &c.

A regiment thus formed, is prepared to receive an enemy,
charge bayonets, or fire upon them.

My deſign is to ſhew how to debark a *regiment*, by which
we may have an idea, how a landing may be made with
many.

To do this, we muſt debark one ſub-diviſion in each
boat from the ſhip : the boats being regimented, there will
be, by this plan, for the 8 ſub-diviſions, grenadiers, and
light company, ten boats to a regiment; and for 4 regiments, it will take 40. Having now formed the boats into
ſeparate bodies, to throw them into as many regiments, I
muſt diſtinguiſh each 10, by ſome particular colour, viz.
the firſt a ſmall blue colour, to fly on a ſtaff at the prow,
like a jack, and a ſtreamer of the ſame colour at the ſtern ;
the 2d may have red at their ſterns, &c. the 3d yellow on
the larboard quarter, &c. the 4th on the ſtarboard, &c.
Theſe colours, placed as deſcribed, will diſtinguiſh the 10
boats, which are named for each regiment.

By this method, nothing but ſtormy weather, too bad for
embarkation, can diſperſe them, or make them interfere
with one another, ſo as to occaſion diſorder.

Care muſt be taken, that the boats of each regiment preſerve their proper places; as different corps do their intervals when encamped ; or diſtances upon the march ; that
a ſub-diviſion boat upon the right, may not fall into the
centre, or get upon the left ; nor one of the left into the
right ; and ſo of the reſt. This is as eaſy to be avoided,
as it is for a blue boat to ſteer clear of the red, yellow, &c.

I ſhall ſuppoſe each ſub-diviſion a company, and that
each company, rank and file, conſiſts of 100 men ; but by
death,

death, &c. are reduced to 96, which I fhall difpofe of in a flat broad-bottom boat, in the following manner.

The fub divifion is divided into 2 platoons, of 14 half files each, which makes 84 men, rank and file. The remaining 4 half files, are to be ftationed to the two pound gun, at each end, which will amount to 96.

Each boat fhould have 25 failors, but in cafe that number cannot be had, a file or two more muft be taken from the platoons, and employed at the oars. In the centre of the boat, eight rowers, 4 on each fide: in the front and rear of thefe centre rowers, 1 platoon at each: on each of thefe flanks are 8 more rowers, difpofed of in the fame manner, as thofe in centre, and 1 able man is appointed to the rudder.

The foldiers allotted to the guns, fhould be men who have been trained to the field pieces.

Being drawn up 3 deep, the 2 parts of the boat the platoons cover, are raifed a little higher than the reft of the floor of the boat: fo that when the front and rear rank of the platoons fit down eafy on the edge of this raifed part, there may be fpace enough between them, to have about 8 inches breadth of the whole length of the raifed part about 8 or 10 inches higher than the other raifed part; which will be a little bench for the centre rank to fit on: by this plan, as in the degrees of a play-houfe, they overlook thofe before them. What the front and the rear ranks, as they fet, reft their feet on, may be funk a few inches. This is the pofition whilft out of reach of the enemy.

The front and centre ranks *of all the platoons* muft fet one way, with either their right or left fide towards the prow of the boat: and the rear rank of the whole, when fetting, will confequently be reverfed: but when they draw near the fhore or enemy, *they ftand up*, and face with the reft. By which means, they will be about as much higher than the centre rank, as they are than the front, and confequently may fire together.

Before they are ordered to make ready to fire, the front and rear ranks reft the buts of their firelocks on the floor of the boat; the centre rank refts on the floor the front fets upon, when they are to make ready to fire, they then reft them on their knees, and the rear rifes with recovered arms: and when the rear rank ftands up, and are not in their firing pofition, they are to be fhouldered.

If

If ordered to load again, the whole ftand up : the front and rear ranks move a ftep to the front and rear, to give themfelves and the centre rank room to load.

Order of Embarking into the Boats.

THE boats being ready, the rowers enter firft, and feat themfelves : then the perfon who guides the rudder, with the men appointed for the guns ; then the right hand platoon ; the left following : all being properly fixed, they fail when ordered, obferving filence and attention, as falfe alarms are hurtful to an army, and a difgrace to thofe that occafion them.

The grenadiers and light companies will be ordered to land, when and where the enemy feem leaft to expect it, and drive their advance parties from little pofts they may occupy : the Officers muft be careful that the next body, by any miftake, does not fire upon them. The fub-divifions, as faft as they land, muft form into battalions, and be ready to charge whatever prefents itfelf. The artillery, &c. will be landed with the utmoft expedition, and a body left to fecure their landing. Should the army penetrate into the country ; the 8 battalion companies of each regiment, are never to purfue the enemy without orders ; but will be ordered to advance and fupport the grenadiers and light companies.

N. B. I apprehend it may be the bufinefs of the Officer commanding the fleet, at an embarkation (being beft acquainted with coafts, tides, currents, fhoals, &c.) to point out the time to order boats, &c. and to be aiding and affifting as much as he can to cover the landing with his fhipping : a Lieutenant of the navy, with a man of war's boat, fhould be directed to lead each 10 boats, dreffed as defcribed, with colours flying and jack.

A writer obferves, " the tranfport fervice is a matter of the higheft importance, and requires much confideration. The lofs of brave troops, and the failure of many military operations, have totally been occafioned by the impolitic expenfive ill method of hiring tranfport-veffels : fhips not formed for military fervice, are detrimental to the health of the troops ; always improperly equipped, and frequently commanded by men under no order or controul, who conftantly make it their ambition to difguft the troops, and who generally diftrefs, but never affift, the public fervice."

Attack

Attack of the Covert-way, Sword in Hand.

" WHEN a town is not ſtrongly garriſoned, the attack may be made as follows:

" The third parallel, in this caſe, ſhould be made at leaſt as forward as the mid-way of the glacis, having its parapet made ſtep faſhion, that the troops deſigned for the attack may paſs eaſily over it, without any confuſion ; a great quantity of faſcines, gabions, and other materials, muſt be got ready and placed at the back of this parallel ; a ſtrong party of grenadiers and light infantry is ordered, and placed in this parallel, 5 or 6 deep, and the workmen behind them, on the reverſe of the parallel, having their tools and materials by them : all the adjacent parts of the trenches muſt be well furniſhed with troops to ſupport the grenadiers and light infantry, if there is occaſion, and fire wherever the enemy appears. The grenadiers and light infantry muſt be provided with hatchets to cut the palliſades, in caſe the guns ſhould not have broke them.

" Before the attack is made, the guns and mortars are to fire briſkly for ſome time, at all the defences of and into the covert-way, to drive the beſieged from thence, to break the palliſades, if poſſible, and plough the ridge of the glacis in ſuch a manner, as the troops may enter the covert-way without much difficulty ; then the guns ceaſe in order to cool : when this is done, the ſignal is given for the attack ; upon which all the troops begin to move together, and, paſſing quickly over the parapet of the parallel, march directly to the covert-way, which they enter either through the ſally-ports or paſſages made by the guns ; or elſe the grenadiers and light infantry cut down the palliſades with their hatchets ; and, being entered, charge the enemy ſo vigorouſly as to oblige them to retire : then the engineers ſet the workmen about making a lodgment on the ridge of the glacis, oppoſite to that part of the covert-way which the beſieged have abandoned.

" Theſe lodgements are made with gabions and faſcines, in the ſame manner as the ſaps ; and traverſes are made every where to prevent the enfilades. The troops keep behind the workmen, and kneel down till the lodgement is ſo far advanced, that they may retire into it. Whilſt this is doing, the batteries fire continually upon all the defences of the covert-way, either to ſilence or abate the fire of the ene-

F   my,

my, as much as poſſible, and to oblige them to think more of their own ſafety, than oppoſing the beſiegers.

" If the beſieged ſhould return to the charge, as probably they will, and overthrow the work and maintain their ground, nothing but a ſuperior force can make the beſiegers maſters of the place.

" When the beſieged find that they cannot poſſibly hold out longer, they will ſet fire to their mines and retire ; upon which workmen are immediately ſent to make a lodgement in their ruins, which is afterwards joined to the reſt of the trenches.

" This was the manner of attacking the covert-way formerly ; but ſince M. Vauban, by great experience and knowledge, has brought the art of attack and defence to ſo great a perfection as it now is, the covert-way has very ſeldom been taken ſword in hand. His chief ſtudy was ever to preſerve the troops as much as poſſible, and never to expoſe them to any danger, without the utmoſt neceſſity.

" Yet, when a garriſon is but weak, and the army of the beſiegers very ſtrong, the guns of the beſieged may be ſilenced, and paliſades torn to pieces by the batteries a ricochet. In ſuch a caſe the covert-way may be attacked with open force, ſword in hand, and that without much danger ; but if the garriſon is ſtrong, and commanded by a Governor who knows his buſineſs, it would be imprudent to make ſuch an attack ; for it would prove one of the moſt bloody actions of the whole ſiege."

The taking a Place by Eſcalade.

" THE manner of taking a place by eſcalade, is much the ſame as that of ſurpriſing it by any other ſtratagem ; the only difference is, in paſſing the ditch and mounting the rampart by means of ladders. The ſcaling-ladders uſed upon theſe occaſions, are of various ſorts : ſome are of ropes, and ſome of wood ; ſome are made of ſeveral joints, ſo as, when put together, to make a ladder of any length ; which, in my opinion, are the beſt ſort ; for the height of the walls are ſeldom known till you come upon the ſpot ; and therefore no proper length can be given to the ladders before-hand. There is another ſort uſed here in *England*, much of the ſame make as the common ladder, only ſteps turn about wooden pegs, ſo that the poles may be brought near each other, or ſhut like a parallel ruler. This ladder

is

is very convenient for carriage; but as they are of certain lengths they are not so useful as those with joints.

" Being arrived before the place in the night, the first thing to be considered is, where and in what manner to pass the ditch. When it is dry and deep, there needs no other confideration than how to get into it; if it is muddy, boards, hurdles, or fascines, are to be thrown in; but if it is full of water, the passage is like to be troublesome. It often happens that a Governor, because the town seems to be in no immediate danger of surprize, grows careless in his duty, and negligent in military discipline, and by that means may be more easily surprized.

" When a river passes by or through a town, a great number of boats must be provided in as private a manner as possible, and brought in the dark, so as to be ready to carry the troops over, in the middle of the night or early in the morning, about an hour before day.

" But if there is a deep wet ditch which has no communication with any river, small boats made of tin should be provided, each to hold one man only. Sometimes baskets covered with skins or oiled cloth, have been used on such occafions. These kind of boats being very light, are easily carried by the detachment; and when the first have passed the ditch, they push the boats back again for others to get over, and so till all are passed.

" Suppoling then the troops prepared to pass the ditch, by some means or other a party must first be placed on the counterscarp opposite to the landing-place, ready to fire at the garrison, in case they have taken the alarm, and come to oppose their mounting the rampart. If the ditch is dry, the ladders are fixed in some place fartheft diftant from any fentry; and so soon as they are got upon the rampart, they put themselves in order, to be ready to receive the enemy if they should appear. Then the Commanding-officer, or some trusty man, who speaks the language of the garrison, advances some diftance before the rest, towards the gate: if he meets with a fentry he goes up to him, under some pretence or other, as if he belonged to the garrison; and if the fentry suffers himself to be thus surprised, claps a piftol to his breaft, to keep him quiet: but should the fentry, knowing his duty, offer to keep him at a diftance, he muft endeavour to kill him with as little noife as poffible, and then advance quickly with the detachment towards the gate, and either surprize or kill all who oppose them. Immediately upon this they fall to work, break open the gate, let in the rest of the party, and then proceed in the manner described before.

" If the ditch is wet, the rampart high, and has a revetement, it will be a hard matter to surprize the town that way ; but if there is no revetement, the troops may hide themselves along the outside slope of the rampart, till all are over, and then proceed as before."

Remarks upon the Undertaking of a Siege.

" TO undertake a siege (if considerable) is to engage in one of the most serious operations of war, and is, next to a general battle, of the utmost consequence to a state ; for should a siege be undertaken, and not succeed, a whole campaign will probably be thrown away, the treasure of a kingdom exhausted, and the lives of its subjects fruitlessly sacrificed.

" A General undertakes a siege, when, by a knowledge of the fortifications, garrison, and state of a particular place, he is sure of being able to take it ; and when, by a covering army, or his own intrenchments, he shall be certain that, the siege once begun, he shall not be obliged to raise it.

" It may sometimes be a proper stratagem, to let an enemy waste his strength in a siege, and attack him at the latter end of it. But the Governor of the town should, in such case, be a man of experienced abilities.

" Whether a siege should be the object of a campaign, circumstances alone must determine. History abounds with various examples."

Investing Places.

" BEFORE a place can be invested with success, the General must use various stratagems to deceive the enemy, and to prevent him from guessing his real design. Sometimes the deception may be carried so far as to invest another place ; at other times, it may be made by marching with the army, as if the General had a mind to attack the enemy, to drive him some distance from the place, and then return quickly to invest it. Therefore, no opportunity should be neglected to arrive before the place, ere the enemy has time to throw in their troops, ammunition or provision, since the success of the siege depends chiefly on this precaution.

" The

" The place is properly to be invelted in the following manner.

" A body of 4 or 5000 horfe is to be detached from the army, if the country is open ; or a body of horfe and foot, if it be full of defiles or woods ; commanded by a Lieutenant-general and two or three Major-generals, who muft march with all poffible fpeed, day and night, till they come within 4 or 5 miles of the place; where they muft halt, to con-fult and divide into as many parties as there are principal avenues leading to it; then march on, fo as to arrive in the dufk of the evening at their feveral appointed pofts, much about the fame time ; which pofts fhould be juft out of the reach of cannot-fhot from the place.

" This done, fmall parties of light infantry are fent to the very gates to carry off men, cattle, and whatever may be ferviceable to the garrifon. The parties are to be fup-ported by fome fquadrons of horfe, and it would be proper to receive fome cannot-fhot, to difcover the reach of the guns. In the mean time, the reft of the detachments take their pofts in the moft convenient places, fo as to prevent any fuccours being thrown into the town.

" In the day-time they keep without cannon-fhot; but fo foon as it is dark, the feveral parties approach the place as near as poffible, fo as to leave but fmall intervals between them ; then turning their backs upon the town, and placing guards before and behind them, to prevent any furprize, half the troops are to keep always mounted, whilft the reft refresh.

" So foon as day-light appears, they retire by degrees, obferving the fituation of the place, and the nature of the works, as likewife that of its environs, till they come to their former pofts, where they place proper guards towards the town, and in all the principal avenues towards the coun-try ; the reft repofe themfelves, keeping their horfes ready faddled for mounting at a minute's warning.

" Parties are fent to reconnoitre the enemy, while the Commanding-officer and Engineers pitch upon a proper place for encamping the army, as foon as it arrives, and obferve where the line of circumvallation is to be made.

" The day the place is invefted, the train of artillery begins to march, with all the ftores and ammunition necef-fary for a fiege ; whilft, on the other hand, the army makes forced marches, and arrives commonly within 3 or 4 days after the invefting.

F 3   The

The Commander of the detachment goes about 2 or 3 miles to meeet the General, to give an account of his proceedings ; on which the General settles the difposition of the camp.

" The next day he rectifies any miftakes that may have happened, and goes to reconnoitre the place ; attended by the reft of the General-officers and chief Engineers, fo that the fituation of the line of circumvallation may be determined.

" This done, the encampment regulated, and the troops placed in the order agreed on, the General affigns to the other General-officers their quarters ; the chief or head quarter is fixed upon, as alfo thofe for provifion, and the park of artillery. All thefe particulars are to be rectified, fo foon as the place for opening the trenches is determined.

" In the mean time, fmall guards are pofted near the town, in the moft convenient places, fuftained by larger, to ftrengthen the camp as much as poffible, and the Engineers roughly trace the line of circumvallation, with rods and pickets only, to regulate the encampment."

The Preparations which are generally made for an Affault on a confiderable Out-Work, or the Body of the Place.

" THE number of troops which are commanded on thefe occafions, muft depend on the ftrength of the place to be attacked, and the number of men who can be brought to defend it.

" A detachment from every company of grenadiers at the fiege, with a proper number of battalions, are ordered to join the guard of the trenches ; but to prevent any difpute about precedency or right, in making the attack, the battalions thus ordered fhould be thofe who are next on command for the trenches.

" A detachment of hatchet-men, with their large axes, are likewife ordered ; that, if the paffage of the grenadiers and light infantry is obftructed, by meeting with large palifades, either in the covert-way, or in the intrenchments behind the breach, they may be ready to cut them down ; becaufe, though the bombs and cannon from the batteries generally break them down, yet they cannot always reach them ; for which reafon there fhould be hatchet-men ordered, left they may be wanted for that purpofe.

" There are likewife a fufficient number of work-men ordered with tools, and others to carry the proper materials ;

rials ; fuch as wool-packs, fand-bags, gabions, fafcines, and pickets, for the making of a lodgement on the breach, if fo ordered, or an intrenchment in the body of the out-work, to cover you from the fire of the town, and fo fecure you againft any attempt which the befieged fhall make to regain it.

" Engineers are commanded with the workmen to direct them in making the proper lodgements, that no time may be loft in forming them.

" There are always more battalions ordered than are ne-ceffary for the attack, that fome may remain as a referve in the trenches ; which, in my opinion, fhould be thofe out of the additional number ordered, whofe turn of mounting the trenches is fartheft off.

" The battalions which compofe the guard of the trenches, always march after and fuftain the grenadiers and light infantry, and the additional battalions only fuftain them.

" The General-officers then on duty in the trenches, command the attack, unlefs the number of troops fo or-dered may require a greater number of Generals than are then on duty, or one of a fuperior rank ; in which cafe the command always falls to the eldeft ; but, unlefs for the rea-fon juft mentioned, the command is never taken from the Generals of the trenches.

" The difpofition of the troops for the attack is gene-rally made as follows.

" The grenadiers and light infantry defigned for the attack, are to be pofted at the head of the trenches, or that part of them which lies neareft the work to be attacked ; the particular difpofition of whom is as follows.

" 1. A Serjeant and 12 or 16 grenadiers or light infantry are drawn out for the forlorn hope ; they are not taken from one company, but one from each ; or, if they confift of the troops of different nations, they are taken in proportion to the number of the battalions of each nation.

" 2. A Lieutenant, and 30 or 40 grenadiers and light infantry, formed by detachment in the fame manner, to fuftain the forlorn hope.

" 3. A Captain, 2 or 3 Lieutenants, with 80 or 100 grenadiers or light infantry, formed alfo by detachment, to fuftain the Lieutenant.

" 4. A detachment of 200 grenadiers or light infantry, commanded by a Major, to fuftain the Captain.

F 4. " 5. The

" 5. The whole body of grenadiers or light infantry, according to feniority of companies, or nations, under the command of Field-officers, in proportion to their numbers. They fhould march as many in front as the ground they are to pafs will admit, or the breach contain.

" 6. The hatchet-men are to be pofted next to the grenadiers or light infantry, and to march immediately after them.

" 7. The battalions, which compofe the guard of the trenches are pofted, according to feniority, next to the hatchet-men, to fuftain the grenadiers.

" 8. The additional battalions that are to go upon the attack, are pofted next to the guard of the trenches, to fuftain them.

" 9. After the troops defigned for the attack, the detachments of workmen commanded by their Officers, are pofted, that they may be ready to march, when ordered to make the lodgements, with whom the Engineers are to march to inftruct them.

" 10. The battalions appointed for the referve, are pofted next to the workmen ; and when the others march out to the attack, they are to move up to the head of the trenches, that, if the troops which make the attack require any affiftance, they may be ready to march out and fuftain them, when they fhall be fo ordered by the General who commands the attack.

" That thofe who make the attack may be as little expofed to the fire of the befieged as poffible, all the cannon on the batteries are pointed againft the feveral works of the town which defend the breach ; on which they are to fire inceffantly, during the attack, to keep the enemy from the walls.

" The fignal ufually given for an attack, is the throwing of a certain number of bombs into the town at the fame time ; but if they are thrown into the work which is to be attacked, or towards the gorge of the baftion in which the breach is made, (that being the place where the befieged entrench themfelves for the defence of it) it will be of great fervice to thofe who make the attack : for, as the enemy will be obliged either to quit their pofts, or lie flat on the ground till the bombs have broke, it will give the grenadiers or light infantry (if they have not far to march) fufficient time to mount the breach, and attack the entrenchment without meeting with much oppofition till they come there,

provided

provided the batteries fire at the fame time on the defences of the town.

" Where there are more attacks than one to be made at the fame time (which, if the breaches are ready, would be exceeding proper, to divide the force of the garrifon ; each muft have the fame preparation and difpofition made for it, unlefs a greater oppofition is expected from the one than the other ; in which cafe, the difference then lies in the numbers ordered for each, but not in the difpofition or order of the attack.

" Sham attacks are fometimes made at the fame time with the real ; but as they are intended to amufe the befieged, to oblige them to divide their troops, that thofe who make the real attack may meet with lefs oppofition, the workmen are generally omitted.

" When an attack is to be made on the covert-ways, the troops which are appointed for that fervice are generally divided into feveral bodies, to attack at different parts at the fame time. The number of workmen, with the feveral materials before-mentioned, particularly wool-packs, are greater on thefe occafions ; becaufe an attack on the covert-way is generally defigned to force the enemy from thence, till a lodgement is made on the glacis, or, as commonly, though erroneoufly, called the counterfcarp ; for as the counterfcarp is the wall of the ditch which fupports the covert-way, to be lodged on the counterfcarp, properly fpeaking, is to be lodged on the brink of the ditch ; but, at prefent, that term is generally abufed, by faying, that they are on the counterfcarp, when they are only at the beginning of the glacis.

" The moft favourable time for the making of an attack, is in the day : for as the actions of every man will appear in full view, the brave, through a laudable emulation, will endeavour, at the expence of their lives, to out-do each other ; and even the timid exert, by performing their duty, rather than bear the infamous name of coward ; the fear of fhame acting generally more powerful than that of death. The batteries will be likewife of great fervice, by their firing with more certainty on the defences of the town and the top of the breach, to keep the enemy from oppofing the grenadiers in mounting it : befides, in the night, thofe who go on firft will run great danger from the fire of thofe who fuftain them ; therefore an attack on an out-work, or the covert-way, is generally a little after fun-fet, that

night

night may come on by the time the attack is finifhed, to favour them in making the neceffary lodgements. But this rule will not hold good in an attack on the body of the place : for if night fhould come on before the town is entirely reduced to your obedience, great inconvenience would attend both your own troops and the poor inhabitants ; to avoid which, it is generally made in the forenoon.

" I do not pretend, by what is mentioned in this article, to lay down certain rules ; but only to give a general idea of attacks, with the ufual preparations of workmen, &c. the neceffary difpofition of the troops, and the general time of making them.

Return

Return of the Troops under the Command of
at the Surrender of   with a Lift of the
Ships in the Harbour taken, burnt, funk, and deftroyed ;
and the Number of Officers, Non-commiffioned Officers, &c.
killed, wounded, miffing, and taken Prifoners.

	Officers prefent.																Effectives, Rank and File.					
	Commiffion.								Staff.													
	Generals.	Colonels.	Lieutenant-Colonels.	Majors.	Captains.	Lieutenants.	Second Lieutenants.	Enfigns.	Chaplain.	Adjutant.	Quarter Mafter.	Surgeon.	Mate.	Serjeants.	Drummers and Fifers.	Fit for Duty.	Sick at prefent.	Sick in Hofpital.	Recruiting.	On Furlough.	On Command.
Total—																					

Lift of Ships in the Harbour of taken, burnt, funk, and deftroyed.

Number of Officers, Non-commiffioned Officers, and private Men, killed, wounded, miffing, and taken Prifoners, during the Siege.

Ships.	Guns.			Generals.	Colonels.	Lieutenant-Colonels.	Majors.	Captains.	Lieutenants.	2d Lieutenants.	Enfigns.	Serjeants.	Corporals.	Drummers and Fifers.	Private Men.
		} taken.													
		} burnt.													
		} funk.	Killed. —												
			Wounded.												
			Miffing. —												
		} deftroyed.	Taken Prifoners }												
			Total.												

Obfervations to be made before the Ground of Encampment is marked out.

THE greateſt precaution muſt be taken that the ſituation is ſtrong ; that there is plenty of forage, water, &c.

A particular attention muſt be had as to the ſalubrity of the ground, and that it is not commanded by any eminence.

It is the duty and intereſt of every Officer who commands, frequently to conſult the moſt prudent and experienced Officers under his Command ; and hear their opinions reſpecting the ſtate and condition of his and the enemy's forces, forage, &c. He muſt then conſider and examine which has the ſuperiority of troops ; which are in beſt condition, beſt diſciplined, and moſt reſolute on emergencies.

" He muſt then reconnoitre the ground for action, and judge whether it is more advantageous for himſelf than the enemy.

" If ſtrongeſt in cavalry, he ſhould prefer plains and open ground : if ſuperior in infantry, chuſe a ſituation full of encloſures, woods, ditches, moraſſes, and ſometimes mountainous places.

" Plenty or ſcarcity in either army, are objects of attention ; for famine is an internal enemy, that makes more havock than the ſword : but the moſt eſſential article, is to determine, whether it is moſt proper to avoid coming to action ; or to bring it to a ſpeedy deciſion."

Camp for a Battalion of Foot, 10 *Companies, with* 2 *Field Pieces.*

The front, containing 175 yards, is divided as follows :

	Yards
For pitching { 8 double rows of tents at 5 yards each	40
2 ſingle rows at 2½ yards each, for grenadiers company	5
Ditto for light infantry	5
The breadth of { Grand ſtreet	21
8 leſſer ſtreets at 13 yards each	104

Total Front 175

Situation of the Battalion Guns.	Yards
From the ſide of the Serjeant's tent to the centre of the { 1ſt gun	4
{ 2d gun	6
Left of next regiment	20
Interval 30	30
Front and interval	200

N. B.

N. B. The muzzles of the battalion guns, are in a line with the front of the Serjeants tents.

The rearmoft of the Gunners tents, are in a line with the rear of the battalion tents.

The Subalterns of the artillery are in a line with the Subaltern of the battalion.

Depth 320 Yards.

	Yards
From the front pole of the Officer's tent of quarter guard to the centre of the bells of arms to ditto	8
To the parade of quarter guard	4
To the firſt line of parade of battalion	50
To the centre of the bells of arms	30
From the centre of the bells of arms to front pole of Serjeants tents	4
For pitching 10 tents with their intervals at 3 yards each	30
From the rear of battalions tents to the front of Subalterns	20

From front of	to the front of	Yards
Subalterns	Captains	24
Captains	Field Officers	24
Field Officers	Colonels	12
Colonels	Staff Officers	16
Staff Officers	1 row of Batmens tents	18

Front row of Batmens tents	To		Yards
	Firſt	Row pickets	2
	Secd	for horfes	12
1	2d row Batmens tents		2
2 Row	Pickets		
3	Ditto		
	Batmens		

1	Pickets	To	2d row Batmens tents	2
2 Row	Ditto		Front of Grand Sutler	14
3	Batmens		Kitchens	20

Front of	Grand Sutler	to	Centre	Petit Sutlers	5
Centre	Kitchens		Front of	Bells of arms	10
Front	Petit Sutlers		Centre	Of rear guard	15

Total depth 320

The front poles of the quarter-guard tents are in a line with the poles of the centre company, and in a line with the centre of their bells of arms.

The bells of arms front the poles of Serjeants tents.

The colours and efpontoons are planted, and the drums placed, in the centre of the grand ſtreet, in a line with the bells of arms.

Each company pitches 20 tents, of 10 in a row.

The

The Lieutenant-colonel's and Majors' tents front the centre of the fecond ftreets from right and left of the battalion.

The Colonel's tent is in the line of the grand ftreet fronting the colours.

The Staff-officers front the centre of the fecond ftreet on the right and left of the grand ftreet.

The Bàtmens tents front towards their horfes; and the Grand Suttler's is in the rear of the Colonel's.

Inner diameter of the kitchens 16 Feet, furrounded with a trench 3 feet broad, and the earth thrown inwards: the centres of the kitchens front the centre of the ftreets of their company.

The front poles of the Petit-futlers tents are in a line with the centres of the kitchens, allowing to each Petit-futler 6 yards in front, and 8 in depth, enclofed with a trench of 1 foot in breadth, and the earth thrown inwards.

The rear-guard front outwards; the front poles are in a line with the centre of their bells of arms, and each 6 yards diftance.

The parade of the rear-guard is 4 yards from their bells of arms.

Battalion Field-Pieces and Horfes.

EACH battalion encamps with 2 field-pieces. A Serjeant and 12 men of the battalion, who have been taught the artillery exercife, are to attend each gun in the field, on the march and in quarters, and are exempted from all other duties.

Six men will draw a light 6 pounder in the field.

A				requires but 1 horfe
A 3				
A 6		pounder		2
A 12				3
A 24				6

The light 3, 6, and 12 pounders, are commonly charged with a quarter of the fhot's weight, and the light 24 is loaded with 5 pounds of powder.

I fhall now fuppofe an encampment formed of a number of battalions, and that it is neceffary to make preparations for the attack. For this purpofe, gabions, fafcines, and picquets, are to be brought in great abundance, and laid in front of the camp, with pick-axes, fhovels, and fpades in plenty, hooks and forks with long poles fixed to them, for placing and fettling the gabions; wheel-barrows, hand-
bafkets,

balkets, mallets, and fand-bags in great numbers; likewife mantlets, ftuffed gabions, and fauciffons. The cannon are alfo to be mounted, the mortars on their beds, and the neceffaries for making the batteries and platforms in readinefs.

AMMUNITION.

CARE muft be taken that the camp is well fupplied with ammunition; as that want has not only been the lofs of an army, but the means of not taking advantages of an enemy, when worfted and retiring.

The tumbrils muft be ever well fupplied with cartridges, and always move with the field-pieces.

Turning out of the Line.

THE line turn out without Arms whenever the General commanding in Chief comes along the front of the camp.

When the lines turn out, the private men are to be drawn up in a line with the bells of arms; the Corporals on the right and left of their refpective companies; the picquet forms behind the colours, their accoutrements on, but without arms.

The Serjeants draw up one pace in the front of the men, dividing themfelves equally.

The Officers to be drawn up in ranks, according to their commiffions, in the front of the colours; 2 Enfigns taking hold of the colours.

The Field-officers advance before the Captains.

When the Commander in Chief comes along the line, the camp-colours on the flanks of the parade are to be ftruck, and planted oppofite to the bells of arms; efpontoons are to be planted between the colours, and the drums piled up behind them; the halberts are to be planted between, and on each fide the bells of arms, the hatchets turned from the colours.

Forming and returning the Picquet of the Infantry.

THE Officers and men for the picquet being ready dreffed and accoutred, fo foon as the drummer's call is beat, the men take their arms and form in the ftreets before the tents. The orderly Serjeants and Corporals having likewife their arms, are then to examine the men, and form thofe of

their

their refpective companies into ranks, and drefs with the line of tents.

When the retreat begins, they are to march them forward, the front rank even with the bells of arms, each Orderly Serjeant and Corporal advancing 3 paces and remaining at the head of his men. The Officers, Serjeants, drummers, and fifers, for the picquet, go to the head of the colours; and, taking their arms and drums, wait there. So foon as the retreat is ended, the Adjutant orders, *advance to form the picquet:* upon which the whole march forward in 3 ranks to the lines of parade; the Officers, Serjeants, drummers and fifers of the picquets, as well as the Orderly Serjeants and Corporals, advancing 12 paces before the front rank; and when they are come to the ground, the Adjutant orders *halt*; upon which the Officers, Serjeants, drummers and fifers, face to the right about. He then orders *form the picquets*, at which command, the whole, except the Officers, Serjeants, drummers and fifers of the picquets, face to the right and left inwards to the centre *March*; they march together, clofing to the centre; and the Officers, Serjeants, drummers and fifers, take their pofts; the Orderly Serjeants and Corporals clofe likewife, but fo as to be oppofite to the men of their refpective companies, to anfwer for what may be wanting or amifs. *Halt*; the picquet faces to the front, and the Orderly Serjeants and Corporals to the picquet.

The Adjutant is then to go through the ranks; and, after having examined the whole, and found all complete, he orders all the Orderly Serjeants and Corporals to their refpective companies to call the rolls. They are to face to the right and left outwards, and march regularly with halberts and firelocks recovered. The Adjutant is then to acquaint the Captain that his picquet is ready.

The Captain and his Officers are then to examine the mens arms and ammunition; which being done, he orders *prime and load.*

So foon as the Colonel or Field-officer of the picquet has acquainted the Captain that he may return the picquet, the Captain, having cautioned the men to be ready to turn out at a moment's warning, orders, *picquet to the right and left to your companies;* upon which the Officers, Serjeants, drummers and fifers, move 3 paces to the front, and the men face to the right and left outwards. *March*; they march until they come oppofite to the bells of arms of their

refpective

respective companies, waiting for the next word of command, *halt* ; upon which they face to the bells of arms, and the Officers, Serjeants, drummers and fifers, face to the colours. *Lodge your arms*; they march together, and having carefully lodged their arms, return to their tents ; the Officers, Serjeants, drummers and fifers, doing the same.

Method of giving and receiving the Rounds in Camp.

THE Field-officer is to be escorted by a Serjeant and 4 men, with a drummer to carry the lanthorn. Every sentry is to challenge the rounds, who are to answer, *grand round*, whereupon he is to rest his firelock. When the grand rounds are challenged near the quarter or rear-guards, the sentry, upon being answered *grand rounds*, is to reply *stand grand rounds*, and call the guard to turn out, before he suffers the rounds to advance.

The Officer commanding the quarter-guard is to order a Serjeant and a file of men to advance within 6 paces of the rounds, and there to halt and challenge again. When answered *grand rounds*, he replies, *stand grand rounds, advance Serjeant with the parole*, and then orders his file of men to rest their firelocks : the Serjeant of the grand rounds then advances unattended and gives the parole to the Serjeant of the guard, who at the same time is to hold the spear of his halbert at the other's breast.

The Serjeant of the rounds returns ; and the Serjeant of the guard, leaving his escort to prevent the rounds advancing, goes to the Officer of the guard and delivers to him the parole he received from the Serjeant of the rounds.

The Officer, finding the parole to be right, orders his Serjeant back to his escort, and says, *advance grand rounds*, commanding his guard to rest their firelocks. At the same time the Serjeant orders his men to wheel back from the centre, and make a lane for the rounds to go through : the Field-officer goes along the front of the guard ; and when he comes to the Officer, he receives the parole from him.

He may count the number of men under arms ; and, when he has asked such questions, and given such orders, as he judges necessary, he passes on, and the Officers of the guard order his men to lodge their arms.

PATROLES.

" AS the patroles usually consist of a few men, and are always detached in the night, generally to dangerous places, and more than once to the fame, they are therefore, as much as poffible, to avoid going at certain hours, and not to keep conftantly one way, either in their march out, or return.

" The patroles are always to march at fome diftance behind one another, efpecially in paffing defiles ; and are not to enter any village, without having firft detached 1 man or 2 to reconnoitre it, and to examine either the prieft, conftable, or fome inhabitant, concerning the enemy.

" The men who are fartheft advanced in the front of the patroles are frequently to halt, and liften whether they can hear any thing: to do which, they muft difmount, and lay their ears clofe to the ground. On horfeback, they are to move as gently as poffible ; are not to fing, to fpeak loud, or to fmoke tobacco without a ftopper over the pipe to prevent the fire from being feen. The horfes muft be likewife prevented, as much as poffible, from neighing, or making a noife.

Directions for the Care and Prefervation of the Horfe, in Time of War.

" AN Officer muft always go with the horfes to water, and never more than 1 troop or half-fquadron be fuffered to water at a time.

" The Officers to take particular care, that the men fodder their horfes regularly ; that they rub down, and curry them well ; and further, that they imbibe a regard for them, and learn to be fenfible of the many advantages accruing to themfelves, in confequence of the pains they beftow upon them ; for which reafon it is neceffary to be inculcated as much as poffible by all Officers, that for the horfe to be in good condition, whether in an engagement, or on a march, is of the higheft utility.

" If a regiment or party is pofted near the enemy, the horfe will receive no damage, though kept faddled for the fpace of 24 hours, provided that the Commanding-officer only takes care that the men loofen the girths a few times in the day, and wipe their backs.

" As it does not require much art to keep the horfes in good order, after every thing that is neceffary for that purpofe has been firft provided ; the Officers, therefore, in the cavalry, muft make it their duty, though it fhould be fometimes attended with fome trouble and expence, to preferve them conftantly in that ftate ; and, by their application and

diligence,

diligence, endeavour to have them, even in the worst of times, in fit condition for service.

" It is the duty of every Officer to acquire a knowledge of the diseases which horses are subject to, and the medicines proper to be applied ; such acquirements being essential for their preservation.

" Officers should instruct their men in what manner to load them, so as not to gall their backs ; taking care, at the same time, that the baggage is always well packed up, and as much as possible of an equal weight on both sides ; and that the saddles and every other part of the furniture is in complete order.

" It is not only the interest of his Majesty, for a squadron to be kept complete and in good condition ; but, in a particular manner, that of the Officers belonging to it ; because they will then always have it in their power to out-flank the enemy ; and, with horse robust and full of vigour, they must certainly overpower them : every Officer, therefore, as his life, honour, and reputation, are depending, is required to discharge his duty with the utmost diligence, and take all possible care to keep them as well as the men in constant good order."

Directions for Picquets and Village Guards.

ALL posts stationed behind ramparts, walls, hedges or ditches, are to be drawn up 2 deep in close order ; if behind a river, trench, or chevaux-de-frize, 3 deep ; with the ranks also in close order. The Officers are to be posted according to situation and circumstances.

If you should be attacked by a superior body, and are obliged to retire, they should file off in 1 or 2 ranks in a straight line, that the object may be as small as possible, lest the enemy fire at you through a hedge, or from a copse.

Vigilance of each Commandant in his own Quarter.

" SO soon as the troops are entered and established in a quarter, he who commands should narrowly inspect all the environs, and, upon his own knowledge, decide the places where posts are most necessary, and fix them there. He will then mark out a place of parade, or general rendezvous, where the troops shall assemble on the first intelligence of the enemy, to be ready to march immediately on the first order from the General.

G 2

" No

" No perfon whatever fhall quit the quarter, on any pretence, without permiffion from the Commandant. If the Officer gives the example of this exactnefs, the foldier will not murmur againft the feverity of the difcipline. The troops in quarters fhall, as in camp, be in meffes ; and the Commandant fhall daily, morning and evening, receive the report from the Officers of each troop.

A Field-officer fhall be daily appointed to vifit the meffes, befides the Vifiting-officer of each company, of which he fhall make his report to the Commandant, who fhall him-felf, every day, vifit the pofts on foot or on horfeback, that he may be well affured that every thing is in order : fo foon as he has examined every thing, and rectified what he finds wanting or amifs, he fhall go and make his report to the General ; or if, by the proximity of the enemy, or the diftance of the head-quarters, there may be fome rifque in abfenting himfelf, it will be fufficient to fend a Field-officer to the General, to inform him of what paffes in the quarter. The Commandant at each quarter fhall obferve the fame order, as well as thofe in the rear as thofe the moft expofed.

" It is abfolutely neceffary to have always advanced de-tachments : this is a general rule, without any exception. It is by this the quarters are fecured, or at leaft put beyond all furprize. This detail does not belong to the particular Commandant of each quarter ; it is the province of the Ge-neral who orders it ; they only obey : yet, as they may be attacked, they fhould ufe every precaution not to be fur-prized. The duty of the particular Commandant is to watch over the interior fecurity of the quarter ; and that of the General is to provide for its exterior fecurity, without neg-lecting the interior. Indolent minds, whom this multipli-city of precautions drag from floth and repofe, fometimes murmur againft the General, and accufe him of apprehen-fions and uneafinefs. The Officers fhould reprove and fup-prefs fuch reproaches among the foldiers, which only dif-honour thofe who make them : but the General or Com-mandant fhould take no other notice of them but to punifh them where they appear. The glory of fuccefs ever attend-ing fuch precautions, is a fufficient recompence for fuch mean, wretched imputations.

" It is not the multiplicity of guards, nor their force, which rather embarraffes them, that gives fecurity to one or many quarters ; it is the manner of difpofing and adapt-
ing

ing them to the fituation of the place. In fact, of what ufe are very ftrong guards, when, by their diftance from others, they cannot be fecured ? Whereas, guards, placed at a reafonable diftance, can affemble on the firft fignal, and compofe a little army, which appears to increafe in proportion as it is attacked. The advanced detachments, the exact difcipline of the troops, and vigilance of the Chiefs, are the fources of the moft glorious victories.

" The more the enemy appears to be tranquil, or the greater diftance you are from him, the more fhould you be on your guard : fecurity founded on the diftance of the enemy, is very dangerous : often the enemy's feigned tranquility is only a ftratagem to furprize you, to defeat you with more certainty, and which may draw along with it the defeat of feveral other quarters."

Military Honours due to Crowned Heads.

" ALL armies falute crowned heads with the utmoft refpect; drums beating a march, colours and ftandards dropping, and Officers faluting : their guards pay no compliment, except to Princes of the Blood, and even that by courtefy, in the abfence of the crowned head.

Due to the Captain-General of Great-Britain, Field-Marfhal, General of the Empire, or of the Dutch.

" All thofe denominations, meaning almoft the fame, are treated in the army with equal ceremony : their guards give them all the honours due to the reprefentatives of Sovereigns; the army in which they command fhew them, conjunctly and feparately, the fame refpect, except when any of the Royal Family are prefent."

" Regulations of Honours to be paid by his Majefty's Forces to the General Officers of the Army.

" GEORGE R.

" OUR will and pleafure is that the following rules be duly obferved and put in execution.

" Generals of horfe and foot, upon all occafions, to have the march beat to them, and faluted by all officers, the colours excepted : they are likewife entitled to a guard of a Captain, Lieutenant, Enfign, and 50 men, with colours and ftandards. Lieutenant-generals of horfe and foot upon

all

all occasions, to be saluted by all Officers ; they are to have 3 ruffles given them, and are entitled to a guard of a Lieutenant and 30 men.   Major-generals are to have 2 ruffles, and not saluted by any Officer, are entitled to a guard of an Ensign and 20 men.   Brigadiers 1 ruffle, are entitled to a guard of a Serjeant and 12 men.

" A Lieutenant-general, who is a Commander in Chief, by virtue of a commission from Us, is to have the same respect paid him, on all occasions, as a General of horse and foot ; a Major-general as a Lieutenant-general, and a Brigadier as a Major-general.

" All Governors, that are no General-officers, shall, in all places where they are Governors, have 1 ruffle given them, with rested arms; but for those that have no commission as Governors, no drum shall beat.

" A Lieutenant-governor, or the Officer who commands in his absence, shall have the main-guard turned out to him with shouldered arms.

" A Town or Fort-major, in a Garrison, is to command according to the rank he now has, or has had, in the army; and if he never had any other but that of Town or Fort-major, he is to command as youngest Captain.

" A General of horse or foot to be received with swords drawn, kettle-drums beating, trumpets sounding, and all the officers to salute, except the Cornet bearing the standard.

" A Lieutenant-general to be received with swords drawn, trumpets sounding, and all the officers to salute, except the Cornet who bears the standard, and the kettle-drums not to beat.

" A Major-general to be received with swords drawn, 1 trumpet of each squadron sounding ; no officers to salute, nor kettle-drums to beat.

" A Brigadier-general to be received with swords drawn, no trumpet to sound, nor any Officer to salute, nor kettle-drums to beat.

" As to the dragoons, they are to pay the same respect, according to the nature of their service.

" And Our further will and pleasure is, that Our several troops of horse and grenadier guards, and Our several regiments of foot guards, be exempted paying any honours to the Generals, unless when they shall be in line with other troops, or mixed with them in detachments, or
when

when they fhall be reviewed by any General, by Our fpecial Orders.

" *Honours to be paid to the Generals by the Horfe and Grenadier Guards, when mixed with other Troops.*

" A General of horfe or foot is to be received with fwords drawn, trumpets founding; all the Officers to falute, except the Cornet bearing the ftandard; the kettledrum not to beat.

" A Lieutenant-general to be received with fwords drawn; 1 trumpet of each fquadron founding; no Officer to falute, nor kettle-drum beat.

" A Major-general to be received with fwords drawn, no trumpets founding; no Officer to falute, nor kettledrum to beat.

" N. B. The troops of horfe-grenadier guards to beat a march to a General, but bayonets not to be fixed; 3 ruffles to a Lieutenant-general; 2 ruffles to a Major-General, &c.

" *Honours to be paid to the Generals by the Foot-Guards.*

" A General of horfe or foot to be faluted by all the Officers, except the Enfigns with the colours: a march is to be beat to him as he paffes, but bayonets not to be fixed.

" A Lieutenant-general to have 3 ruffles, and to be faluted by all the Officers, except the Enfigns with the colours.

" A Major-general 2 ruffles, and not to be faluted by the Officers.

" *Regulations for the Duty of Our Horfe and Foot-Guards, when joined with other of Our Troops.*

" That Our foot-guards are to give no guard to any General-officer, only to the General commanding in Chief, fuppofing him to be of the degree of a General or Lieutenant-general; in which cafe they are to furnifh, for a General's guard, a Lieutenant, Enfign, and 50 men: for a Lieutenant-general's guard, fo commanding in Chief, an Enfign and 40 men.

" That the quarter-guard be commanded by an Enfign, who is to do no honours, but to the Commander in Chief; but is to turn out his guard to all the Generals above the degree of a Major-general, and to ftand at the head of his guard, with his efpontoon in his hand, and the guard

fhouldered;

fhouldered; that the horfe-guards are never to mount any General's guard.

" That their ftandard-guard do turn out only to the General commanding in Chief, fuppofing him to be of the rank of a General or Lieutenant-general.

" That both horfe and foot are to turn out at the head of their camp, when the General, commanding in Chief, paffes along the line.

" That, in all cafes, when they fhall be detached in the manner above-mentioned, both Officer and foldier, as well horfe as foot, do equal duty, in proportion with other troops with whom they fhall be joined.

Colours.

" The firft ftandard, guidon, or colours of a regiment, is not to be carried on any guard but that of his Majefty, the Queen, Prince of Wales, or Captain-general; and, except in thefe cafes, fhall remain always with the regiment.

Honours to the Mafter-General of Ordnance.

" The Mafter-general of the Ordnance fhall have the fame refpects from the troops with Generals of horfe or foot; that is, upon all occafions, to have the march beat to him, and is to be faluted by all Officers, the colours excepted."

REMARKS proper to be made by the REVIEWING OFFICER.

OFFICERS.

PROPERLY armed, ready in their exercife, falute well, in good time, and with a good air; their uniform genteel. A good corps, that makes a very handfome appearance.

MEN.

A very good body, well limbed, but fome of them old and wounded. Clean and well dreffed; accoutrements well put on; very well fized in the ranks; the Serjeants expert in their duty, drummers perfect in their beatings, and fifers play correct.

EXERCISE.

In very good time, and with life; carry their arms well; march, wheel, and form well.

MA-

MANOEUVRES.

Performed with great exactnefs, in quick and flow time.

FIRINGS.

36 rounds, clofe and well.

By companies from the right and left to the centre 2 rounds; twice from the centre to the right and left, by companies; once by grand divifions, from the right and left to the centre; by 4 right-hand companies, and light company, and the 4 left-hand companies, and the grenadiers, 1 round; right wing of the battalion, and left wing, 1 round; battalion obliquely to the right and to the left, 1 round each; battalion to the front 1 round by the above firings, advancing and retreating. Left-hand companies, and the right divifion of grenadiers, before they retreat by files; and the 4 right-hand companies, and the light company; when marched up to their intervals, 1 round each: in the fquare by the faces and companies, 1 round each: ftreet firing, advancing, and retreating, 1 round each: a volly.

RECRUITS.

Such as will mend the regiment.

ARMS.

Good, and kept clean; halberds bad; drums good; a few fwords wanting, and fome bad.

ACCOUTREMENTS.

Good.

CLOTHING.

Of   year, but ftill pretty good and clean.

ACCOUNTS.

Kept regular.

COMPLAINTS.

None.

UNIFORM.

Red, lapelled and faced with
waiftcoats and breeches,   buttons.

A very fine regiment, well appointed, well difciplined, compleat, and fit for fervice.

Of

Of HOSPITALS.

" A General Officer fhould be appointed in the neareſt town, to which the fick men of every corps are to be fent.

" The hofpitals require infinite care and attention. The chief perfons employed are Phyficians and Surgeons, who are men eminent for their fkill in their profeffions, alfo for their credit and humanity : becaufe the lives of thoufands depend upon their wifdom and fkill. The choice of all fubordinate Officers being from their recommendation, therefore, as their reputation is at ftake, they take care to chufe good and careful ones. They infpect nicely into the feveral drugs and medicines provided for the ufe of the feveral hofpitals ; and fee likewife that they are fit for ufe ; by which means many lives are preferved.

" The chief and moft ufeful Officer, among thefe, is the Director, who has the principal management of the houfe : the providing the furniture, utenfils, fervants, nurfes, and likewife the provifions, of all kinds, are under his direction.

" As he allots the quantity, he therefore takes care of the quality, that each fpecies is wholefome and good ; that there is no purloining in the houfe, and that each patient has every thing he is ordered. As all the money goes through his hands, he is not one in mean circumſtances, who accepts his office as a mercenary jobb ; but is a man of credit and confcientious ; who fees juftice done to the fick in the ftricteft manner ; and is ambitious to ferve his King and Country.

" Over thefe, the Commander in Chief fhould appoint a General Officer, to be Infpector General. To him all complaints, if any, are to be fent ; and the Officer or Officers, who are appointed as a guard to the Hofpital, together with the Director, fend him their reports. As cft as he can, conveniently, he fhould vifit the hofpitals, and fee that the Phyficians and Surgeons do their duty ; infpect the provifions, examine the accompts, hear any complaints the patients may have to make, and order every thing he thinks proper for the good of the fervice."

Hofpital Books.

Names of each man, regiment, and company, &c. to be
entered agreeable to form.

Names.	Regiments.	Companies	When Entered.	Difcharged.	Dead.

The Commanding Officer of the hofpital, is anfwerable
for the arms, cloaths, accoutrements, and linen, of the
fick : for which, he may have a Serjeant from each brigade,
to carry them to a ftore-houfe ; where they are to be laid
and taken care of, till their owners recover.

Thofe belonging to the men that die, are to be fent to the
regiment they ferved in ; or kept in the ftore-houfe till the
army marches into winter-quarters.

Marauding and Oppreffion.

" NOT to murder or fteal, is a precept as binding in
the field, or winter quarters, as it is in the camp
or city. Marauders are a difgrace to the camp, to the military profeffion, and deferve no better quarter from their
Officers than they give to poor peafants ; nor fhould they
find more mercy, than they fhew in rifling of villages.
The rapes and violences of foldiers, rebound on their in-
dulging Commanders. Licentious armies, fpread a plague,
inftead of giving protection ; and where terror and defolation
march before the camp, a thoufand imprecations of undone
peafants follow. More purfes are plundered than towns
ftormed ; hen-roofts and fheep-cotes are affaulted, more
than counter-fcarps ; and where the lawlefs foldier fcatters
ruin with fire and fword, there Commanders fpread defolation with fafe-guards. Protection from thefe, is more expenfive than the avarice of thofe; and kindnefs and fury
prove equally cruel. The remedy is applied, when the
country

country can lofe, and the army gain no more. Yet thefe are the pranks fometimes played among friends and allies. Friendfhip fo expenfive, is unworthy of purchafe; and it may be more tolerable to be at the mercy of a foe, than thus to fuffer by the avarice of a friend; fince to be hug'd or piftol'd to death, are equally deftructive. We read, that mortality, for thefe offences, has fwept off whole companies without remedy, and buried, in oblivion, regiments without honour."

The common Order of Battle, or general Difpofition, ordered by the King of Pruffia, to be inviolably obferved by all Generals, Commandants of Regiments, and Subalterns in his Service; iffued after the battle of Molwitz.

1. THE van-guard fhall not advance above 2 miles before the army, but fhall take all imaginable precautions continually to reconnoitre the enemy.

2. The army marching in columns fhall halt 3 miles from the enemy, and form in order of battle.

3. When the army has advanced far enough, the regiments fhall range in the manner which fhall then be commanded them.

4. The firft line, 3 deep, fhall take great care to keep in clofe order, their ranks ftraight and equal.

5. The Colonels, Commandants, and Subalterns, who command platoons, fhould exhort the foldiers to do their duty, and make the affair appear as eafy to them as poffible.

6. The Non-commiffioned Officers, who are in the rear of the battalions, fhould beware of bringing the foldiers into confufion by ufelefs words, but to keep a watchful eye over them.

7. If it fhall happen that a foldier endeavours to run away, and goes one foot out of his rank for that purpofe, the Officer or Non-commiffioned Officer in the rear fhall kill him on the fpot, under the pain of being broke with infamy.

8. The King obferving, that at the laft battle the beft foldiers were with the baggage, he abfolutely hereby forbids it for the future; and the Commandants of regiments fhall anfwer for the fame, under pain of being cafhiered.

9. To this effect each regiment fhall employ only 3 Captains at arms with the worft foldiers, the fick, or others unfit for action.

10. The field-pieces, and fuch heavy artillery as the King may have along with him, fhall be advanced 80 paces before the firft line.　　　　　　　　　　　11. The

11. The grenadiers fhall be pofted behind the firft line on the right, left, and centre.

12. Three brigades of dragoons, of 400 each, fhall fuftain the right wing of the cavalry ; the reft fhall be pofted at the centre behind the firft line, where they fhall wait his Majefty's orders.

13. If the cavalry commanded for the attack fhall be repulfed, as at Molwitz, without having done their duty, the grenadiers fhall fire on them, even to exterminating them entirely.

14. The Majors and Adjutants fhall take care that their battalions do not fall into confufion, and for that purpofe fhall be continually riding along the front.

15. The corps de referve, confifting of 18 fquadrons and 6 battalions, fhall be pofted 20 paces behind the firft line, equally divided on right and left, and there wait orders.

16. The huffars fhall fuftain the left wing, fhall obferve the enemy's attacks, and act in confequence.

17. If the battle is well difputed, and many are killed, a regiment from the right, and another from the left, fhall complete the firft line, where the General judges it moft neceffary : and the fecond line fhall advance towards the firft.

18. The fecond line fhall be pofted 800 paces behind the firft, their firelocks fhouldered ; and the Officers fhall prevent, under pain of being broke, any foldier quitting his rank.

19. The Officers who command platoons fhall carefully vifit the foldiers arms, fee that the pan holds the priming, and that every thing is in good order : if any thing is wanting it muft be inftantly repaired.

20. The foldiers fhould be exhorted to take their aim well, to adjuft their fhot, and not fire too high : to all thefe points the Officers fhould give particular attention.

21. So foon as his Majefty fhall chufe the fignal to be given by 3 cannon-fhot at the centre, the artillery fhall, by a brifk fire, throw the enemy into confufion, and fhall continue their fire till the King fends them orders to ceafe, by one of his Adjutant-generals.

22. The Captains and Lieutenants of artillery fhall point the guns themfelves, and not truft it to the gunners.

23. After the cannonade, the fignal for the attack fhall be given by 3 cannon-fhot.

24. When the army in clofe order fhall come within 600 paces of the enemy, then, in order to familiarize the fol-

diers

diers to the fire, and to blind them with regard to danger, they fhall begin to fire regularly by platoons.

25. The firft line, continuing to advance charging, fhall take great care that no regiment breaks the line.

26. The Officers in advancing fhall give the word of command diftinct and loud, and place themfelves 1 pace before their platoons, that the men may hear them, and they, feeing the men better, may prevent their hurting each other by an irregular fire.

27. In cafe the enemy's cavalry or huffars fhall pierce the firft line, then the regiment where they have pierced fhall face about, and charge them in the rear.

28. If victory declares for his Majefty, and that the enemy have been obliged to yield, the platoon firing fhall ceafe.

29. The cavalry and huffars fhall then march out, and the King himfelf will chufe fuch of the infantry as, jointly with the cavalry, fhall purfue the enemy.

30. During the purfuit, no foldier fhall, under pain of death, quit his rank, to plunder or take booty : the Officers fhall anfwer for this.

31. The regiments who are not fent on the purfuit, fhall remain with fhouldered firelocks, until they are com-manded to order them : but even then no one fhould quit his rank.

32. His Majefty's pleafure is, that this difpofition fhall on all occafion be invariably followed.

Marfhal Contades *Orders,* *the Day before the Battle of Minden.*

General Difpofition for the Attack of the Army of the Enemy.

" THE Marfhal being determined to attack the enemy the firft of Auguft, 1759, in the difpofition it is about to take, and weakened by fending a detachment under the command of the Hereditary Prince, on the road to Bra-back, has judged that the beft form of inftructions he could give to the General Officers who command the principal divifions of the army, was to give them a plan of the general difpofition ; which would inftruct them of the whole of the firft difpofition ordered, and put them in a condition to ex-ecute, by a reciprocal harmony between thofe gentlemen equally informed of their pofitions, and of their refpective operations. The Marfhal reckons to attack the enemy to-morrow at day-break : he intends putting the army under

march

march this evening, at retreat beating, in the manner here-
after. The General Officers of the day, are the Count de
Noailles, Lieutenant General ; and the Count de Rougrave,
Major General.

The reserve of the Duke de Broglio, will form the right
of the whole, at the village of Jonhanfen ; and march from
thence againſt the camp of the Prince of Bevern, on the
road to Peterſhagen. The attack which this reſerve will
make, ſhould be quick and rapid, to overcome the Prince
of Bevern at once, to hinder him from returning to the army
of the enemy ; or at leaſt that he may retire in confuſion,
and carry diſorder with him. To inſure the ſucceſs of this
attack, it is neceſſary that it be ſtrong in the number of its
troops, particularly infantry and artillery. Theſe will be
joined to the infantry, the grenadiers of France, and the
royals ; and to the artillery of this reſerve, 6 12 pounders,
and four howitzers. The Duke de Broglio will point out
the place of rendevouz for this artillery, and will alſo ſend
his orders to the grenadiers of France, and the royals. It
is impoſſible to employ too many means on this attack ; the
ſucceſs of which uncovers the left flank of the enemy, and
inſures general ſucceſs.

" The reſerve will leave its camp as it grows dark, the
retreat ſerving for the general ; they will paſs the river by
the town bridge, and will go out at the port which leads to
the camp of the grenadiers of France, and the royals. The
Duke de Broglio will ſend his heavy baggage to remain
where that of the army is already ; he will cauſe them to
paſs the Weſer by the higher bridge of boats, to ſhun the
engagement. The army will remain compoſed of 14 brigades of infantry ; viz. Picardie, Bellzunce, Tourine,
Rouvergne, Condé, Aquitaine, du Roy, Champagne,
making 8 brigades, 33 battalions of the firſt line ; the brigades of Navarre, Anhault, Lowendahl, 2 brigades of
Saxons and Auvergne, making 6 brigades, 29 battalions,
of the ſecond line. It is to be underſtood that the 2 brigades of Saxons, make 13 battalions.

" The army has 6 brigades of cavalry, viz. Colonel,
General Cravaltes, Maitre de Camp, and Bourgognes,
making 29 ſquadrons of the firſt line, part upon the right,
and part upon the left wings. The brigade Du Roy, and
that of Royals Etranges, making 16 ſquadrons of the ſecond line, in all, 45 ſquadrons ; to which, adding 8 of
the gens d'armes, and 10 of the carabiniers, which are the
reſerve,

reſerve, makes the total of the cavalry, 63 ſquadrons. The nature of the country where the army is to form, being covered with extremities, and open in the centre, not per-mitting to form it in the uſual manner ; the right of the firſt line will be compoſed of the brigades ; of infantry of the right, which are, Picardie, Bellzunce, Tourine, and Rouvergne ; under the command of Lieutenant Generals de Reauper and Chevalier de Nicolai ; and of Major Ge-nerals de Planteau and Monley. 34 pieces of cannon, of different calibres, ſhall be placed at the head of thoſe 4 bri-gades ; and the ſtate of their diſpoſition ſhall be ſent to Che-valier de Nicolai. The centre of the army will be formed of the brigades of cavalry : Colonel General Cravaltes, and Maitre de Camp, under the command of Duke Fitz James, Monſieur de Pogue, and de Caſtres, Lieutenant Generals ; and of Monſieur de Lutzelbourg, de St. Chamont, de Lil-lebonne, and de Coutmainville, Major Generals. The left of the firſt line will be compoſed of 4 brigades of in-fantry ; which are, Condé, Aquitaine, du Roy, and Cham-pagne, under the command of Lieutenant General Mon-ſieur de Guerchy, and Major Generals Lovall, and Man-gereau. 30 cannon of different calibres, will be diſtributed at the head of thoſe brigades ; and Monſieur de Guerchy will have the ſtate of the diſpoſition of the artillery. The Chevalier de Pelatier will obſerve that this artillery be placed at the head of theſe 4 brigades, on the left, and make a croſs fire on the front of the centre of the cavalry ; he will therefore give the neceſſary orders for that purpoſe, to the Commanding Officers of thoſe brigades of artillery.

" Each brigade of infantry of the firſt line, will form its firſt battalion in column ; and the other in order of battle : the brigade of Rouvergne, which forms the left of the right, will be firſt in order ; that its firſt battalion, which is in column, may incline to the Maitre de Camp : ſuch is the diſpoſition ordered for the firſt line.

" The ſecond line will be formed in the ſame order as the firſt ; the right will be compoſed of the brigades of Auvergne and Anhault, under the command of Monſieur de St. Germaine, Lieutenant General and Major Ge-nerals Monſieur de Leyde and Glaubitz : the left will be compoſed of the Saxon brigades, under the command of the count de Luſace, and the other Saxon Officers ; the ſecond line, though leſs numerous than the firſt, will never-theleſs occupy the ſame front as the firſt, having intervals
between

between their corps; ſuch is the diſpoſition of the ſecond
line: the reſerve, compoſed of the gens d'armes and the
carabiniers, under the command of Monſieur de Pyanne,
Lieutenant General, and Meſſieurs Belfonds and Biſſey,
Major-Generals, will form a third line in the centre behind the cavalry: the brigades of Navarre and Lowendahl,
will have the deſtination hereafter mentioned. The army
being formed in the aforementioned manner, will be placed
as follows: the firſt line of the army, in its firſt diſpoſition,
juſt mentioned, will incline its left to the moraſs, at the
higheſt of the firſt hedges of the village of Hahlen: and the
right paſſing behind the red houſes, which are upon the
plain, will extend itſelf towards the wood.

" The ſecond line will form at 400 paces behind the
firſt: the reſerve of the Duke de Broglio will have its right
at the bank of the Weſer, and will fire upon the village of
Tonhauſen; and its left will extend ſo far as the right of
the army: its infantry will form the firſt line, and the cavalry its ſecond.

" All the troops of this reſerve, as well as the grenadiers
of France, and the royals, will conform themſelves, during
the action, to whatever orders the Duke de Broglio ſhall
think proper to give. It being neceſſary that the Buſineſs
of this reſerve be done ſpeedily, they will firſt march down
on the village of Tonhauſen; from whence they will drive
the advanced poſts of the enemy; and afterwards againſt
the camp of the Prince of Beverns, placed on the road from
Tonhauſen to Peterſhagen: during the time the reſerve
ſhall be employed on this object, the army will endeavour
to form itſelf; and afterwards march in line of battle; or
at leaſt, each brigade of cavalry will march by battalion
and ſquadron, in column, obſerving the proper diſtances
from one brigade to another, to have it in their power to
form again in line of battle: the firſt battalion of each brigade, which is ordered to form in column, will keep that
diſpoſition, whether on the march, or in the line of battle.
Every brigade of infantry will have 100 workmen; as alſo
waggons of utenſils, planks, &c. The army of the enemy
is incamped with its right behind the village of Hylla; and
its left behind that of Holtzhauſen; ſo that it is almoſt
upon the left flank of the enemy, that the army marches;
and if the reſerve of Broglio ſucceeds, it will ſurround the
left flank of the enemy. The reſt of the Manœuvres of
the day, depend entirely upon thoſe the enemy may make,

H which

which cannot be forefeen ; therefore the Marſhal will give his orders according to circumſtances. The brigade of Navarre, with the volunteers of Hannau, thoſe of Dauphin and Murett, and the 8 pounders of the park, will make a falſe attack upon the enemy's right, by the village of Eikhorſt, which is upon the moraſs ; and they will afterwards come round upon the village of Hylla : theſe troops will be under the command of the Duke of Havre, Lieutenant-General ; he will keep a briſk cannonade with the cannon he will have from the park, upon the redoubts, which the enemy have made upon the village of Hylla : but he will not venture to paſs the moraſs, except he finds that the left of the army, has reached the village of Hylla ; and that he can join himſelf to it : till this time his only objeĉt ſhould be to employ the enemy, and to hinder his inclining his right to the moraſs ; this is only to be done by a briſk cannonade. The Duke of Havre is to take upon him the care of covering the retreat of the army, in caſe of a misfortune ; for this reaſon he ſhould carefully guard the right, to hinder the enemy from penetrating : he will alſo take care to guard the heights of the mountains ; where he will place poſts of infantry, and light troops, againſt the chaſſeurs of the enemy ; who might from Lulke, endeavour to come in : this objeĉt is extremely eſſential : the Duke of Havre ſhould have notice, that the Duke of Briſſac is behind the rivulet of Elſe, and that he is obſerving the motions of the corps, under the Hereditary Prince.

" The Duke of Havre is to endeavour to communicate with the Duke of Briſſac, by the paſs of Birgkirken : and a part of cavalry of the volunteers of Dauphin may be employed on this ſervice, as knowing the roads. The Duke of Havre muſt be acquainted that the poſts of the army, placed along the moraſs, from the village of Eickhorſt, as far as the Caſtle of Hartenhauſen, are to remain in the ſame poſition, and to obſerve the moraſs. The brigade of Lowendahl, under the command of Major-General de Rezon, will enter this evening after the retreat beating into the town of Minden, to guard the ramparts, and heads of the bridges ; the largeſt, and beſt part of the iron cannon of the town, will be placed upon the cavaliers of the fortifications, to proteĉt the retreat of the army, in caſe of ill ſucceſs : he will alſo place cannon of this ſort, at the work which is at the head of the ſtone bridge of the town, to keep off the light troops of the enemy, who might approach

the

the bridges. The retreat will beat this evening, at the ufual hour, and will ferve for the general; the army and the referve will put themfelves under arms at the head of their encampment; and the referve will march over the ftone bridge before mentioned. The army will march in 8 columns; the firft column of the left, under the command of the Count de Guerchy, will be compofed of the brigades of Champagne and Du Roy; they will pafs the rivulet over the bridge, on the left; they will have on their left, the wood of Hulmbeck, which is in the midft of the Morafs, near the centre of the camp; they will halt at the hedges of the village of Hahlen, where they will wait in column till day-break; when they will form in line of battle, inclining their left to the fame hedges; and their right drawing in a line with the red houfes. 8 pieces of cannon fhall march in the evening to the head of the camp of Champagne and Du Roy; and have all things in order, ready to march at the head of thefe brigades, and to remain attached to them, during the action. Monfieur de Tourleville, Major-General to the army, conducts this column.

" The fecond column of the left, compofed of the brigades of Aquitaine and Condé, under Major-general de Mangenau, will pafs the rivulet, by the bridge which will be fhewn them by Monfieur de Bodevin, A. Q. M. G. who will alfo fhew them, where they are to wait in column till day, and afterward the line of battle. Six fix-pounders will be fent, before retreat beating, to the head of the camp of Aquitaine and Condé, and march at the head, and remain attached to them.

" The third column of the left, under the Count de Luzafe, will be compofed of the 2 Saxon brigades, which are to pafs the rivulet, which will be fhewn them by Monfieur de Monteau, A. Q. M. G. who will alfo fhew them where they are to halt in column till day-break, and afterwards form in line of battle, in the fecond line behind the brigades of Champagne du Roy, Aquitaine, and Condé, at the diftance of 400 paces, and parallel to thofe brigades.

" The 4th column of the left, under the Duke de Fitz James, will be compofed of the brigades of cavalry, Maitre de Camp, Cravaltes, and Royals Etranges, and they will pafs the rivulet by the bridge, which will be fhewn them by Monfieur Dangé, A. Q. M. G. who will alfo fhew them, where they are to halt in column, till day-break: and when the brigades of Maitre de Camp and Cravaltes, will form

the

the line, inclining the left of the Maitre de Camp, to the right of Condé : the right of the Cravaltes forming in a line with the Red Houfes : the brigade of Royals Etranges, will form themfelves at the fame time, in a fecond line, in the rear of the Maitre de Camp, at 400 paces diftance.

" The 5th column, under the Marquis Dumevail, Lieutenant-general, will be compofed of the brigades of cavalry ; Colonel General du Roy, and Bourgogne : they will pafs the rivulet over a bridge, which will be fhewn them by Monfieur de May, A. Q. M. G. who will fhew them where they are to halt in column, till day-break ; when the Colonel General will form himfelf in a line of battle, to the right of the Cravaltes, in a line with the Red Houfes : the brigades of Bourgogne and du Roy, will form themfelves in a line behind the Colonel General of Cravaltes.

" The 6th column of the left, under Monfieur de Beaupré, Lieutenant General, will be compofed of the brigades of Tourraine and Rouvergne: they will pafs the rivulet by a bridge, which will be fhewn them by Monfieur de Germain ; whence they will march to the redoubt of Picardie, where they will halt till day-break ; when they will form the line on the right of the Colonel General, having their right to the redoubt ; 8 cannon will be fent before retreat beating, to thefe brigades, to march at their head, and to be attached to them during the action.

" The 7th column of the left, under the command of Monfieur de St. Germain, Lieutenant General, will be compofed of the brigades of Auvergne and Anhault ; the brigade of Auvergne will pafs the rivulet over the bridge, which will be fhewn them by Monfieur Domell, belonging to the ftaff; this brigade will halt in column, before the prefent camp of the brigade of Anhault, which is in the gardens of the town. The brigade of Anhault will make no other movement, than the putting itfelf under arms, at the head of its camp, to wait till day-break ; when it and Auvergne will march and form in line of battle, in a fecond line, behind Picardie and Bellzunce.

" The 8th column of the left, under the Chevalier de Nicolai, will be compofed of the brigades of Picardie and Bellzunce ; they will march through the appertures which are in the front of their camp, and then ftretch out in colum, till day-break ; when they will form the line, by ftretching their right towards the wood ; and joining by this movement, the left of the Duke de Broglio's referve. Monfieur

fieur de Grand Pré, A. Q. M. G. will conduct these two brigades; 8 cannon will be sent to the head of these brigades to remain with them, during the action.

" The reserve of the Duke de Broglio forms the grand column; the intention of which has been already shewn.

" The gen d'arms and carabiniers, will mount their horses at the head of their camp, at day-break; and wait for an order to form a third line, in the rear of the cavalry. There will be 9 brigades on the rivulet, from the wood of Hameltbeck, which is the centre of the camp, as far as the town; these brigades will serve to facilitate the retreat of the army, in case of a defeat; should this occur, the left and centre will make their retreat, by the bridges of the present camp; and the troops on the right of the Duke de Broglio, will make theirs by the town; furnishing the hedges of the gardens with troops, and placing cannon behind them, to detain the enemy.

" The baggage of the General-officers, escorted by 200 infantry, and 50 cavalry, and two companies of chasseurs, attached particularly to the treasure; and will go off at day-break, to get behind the village of Berghausen, under the command of Monsieur de Lausen, Lieutenant General. The camp shall be struck, and the companies horses will be sent to the above-mentioned rendezvous. The principal part of the flying hospital will be in the town of Minden; a considerable part will be at the village of Outern, which is near the present incampment, of the brigade of Rouvergne; a detachment of the same hospital will be sent to the village of Afflan, for the brigade of Navarre, and light troops; the General-officers and troops will be acquainted where the Chevalier de Palatier intends putting his magazine of ammunition; which he will form for the right, left, and centre, the park of artillery will remain were it is,

H 3

Return

Return of Officers, Non-commissioned Officers, Private Men, Horses, &c. killed, wounded, missing, and taken Prisoners, at the Battle of   near

	Generals.	Colonels.	Lt. Colonels.	Majors.	Captains.	Lieutenants.	2d Lieutenants.	Ensigns or Cornets.	Chaplains.	Adjutants.	Qr.-Masters.	Surgeons.	Mates.	Serjeants.	Corporals.	Drums & Fifes.	Private.	Trumpeters.	Standards.	Colours.	Kettle-Drums.	Cannon.	Horses.	Tumbrils.	Baggage.
Cavalry. Killed																									
Wounded																									
Missing																									
Taken																									
Total																									
Infantry. Killed																									
Wounded																									
Missing																									
Taken																									
Total																									
Remarks upon the Battle.																									

Changing an Order of Battle on a Plain.

" A Movement made by any of the wings is, of all things, the moſt dangerous, and the moſt delicate, if performed in the preſence of the enemy. The greateſt man among the antients in this way was Scipio. I do not ſpeak here of the Greeks : they were, no doubt, greater tacïtians, and had more ability for general movements, than the Romans.

" Our preſent manner of ranging the troops is more favourable ; becauſe the firſt line covering the ſecond, which, by extending its wings, marching at firſt by its flank, and afterwards in front, may, by a converſion, form on the flanks of the firſt line : but for theſe movements there muſt be excellent troops and intelligent chiefs ; the time muſt be well choſen, and the movement performed with all dexterity and rapidity. That of the Mareſchal de Luxembourg, at Fleurus, is worthy of a great Captain.

" If you are the weakeſt, fortify as much as poſſible the firſt line, refuſe the combat, and keep back your centre, while you make your wings advance. In ſuch a ſtate, in order to fortify your wings, you divide the ſecond line in 2 corps towards the wings : it is theſe 2 corps who partly ſhould extend to the right and left, and ſurround the enemy with all their vigour : for, if the wings are defeated, the centre cannot hold out. The movements of the wings are not ſo difficult as thoſe of the centre : but theſe again being leſs common, and requiring more knowledge, are alſo more capable of deceiving the enemy." Vegetius ſays, in his general rules, " that a warlike and well-diſciplined army ſhould engage by their wings."

Precautions, &c. a Governor or Commandant of a Garriſon ſhould take in Time of War.

" BEFORE an enemy appears, the Governor or Commandant ſhould examine the works, repair thoſe that want, paliſade the covert way, and, if it has not been done before, he ſhould alſo lay ſome horizontally on the middle of the parapets, which have no revetement ; clear the ditches from the mud, ſee that the gates or entrances are ſecure and well defended from being broken up ; keep a ſtrict diſcipline and good order in the town, prevent the garriſon from moleſting and abuſing the inhabitants, and

watch

watch narrowly that no correspondence is kept with the enemy to betray the place : for which purpose he should send some people, whom he can trust, to get into companie; unsuspected, hear what passes, and give him notice of what they say. If there are any old aqueducts, or under-ground passages, they should be stopped up, and sentries placed at their entrances. If there is any river passing through or near the town, parties must be put into boats in the night, both above and below the place, to watch that the enemy do not enter that way. In frosty weather, the ice in the ditches should be broke daily, and the shoals laid on the top of one another towards the place ; which will make, in time, a kind of wall, so slippery as to be impassable.

" Parties should be sent out daily, both of horse and foot, to range about the country, and in all the principal avenues, for 2 or 3 miles distance from the place, to see if any enemy is approaching, or concealed ; and, in the night, he should take care that the several guards keep strict to their duty, watch carefully at their several posts, and let none approach the walls, not even the sentries, without the forms that are usual in such cases. The patrol should walk all night about the several posts, to see that the sentries do not sleep, that they continually listen to hear if any enemy approaches, and, on the least noise or suspicion, that they give notice to the guards, and they to the Governor.

" It is proper, on fair or market-days, that the gates should be strictly guarded : the horse and foot must be ready to assemble and march upon the first notice ; no people should be suffered to pass through the gates, but such as have some visible business in the town, or can give a good account of themselves. The sentries should not let any coaches, waggons, carts, &c. enter too close behind one another ; and when they are loaded with hay, straw, or with any thing, wherein people may be concealed, they should be well examined before they are permitted to pass ; and never let any carriage stop upon a draw-bridge, on any pretence, to prevent their being drawn up, if necessary.

" On holidays, festivals, or rejoicing days, military dif-cipline must be observed with the utmost rigour, the guards strictly watched, and no assemblies suffered after dark.

" When the town is besieged, or there is any apprehen-sion of the enemy's attempting to surprize the garrison, it is customary for the sentries posted on the ramparts to call out, every half hour, with a loud voice, *All is well.* When
this

this is ordered, the Town-major is to affign the post it shall begin at, and which way it shall go round. Upon the first faying, *All is well*, the next to him is to fay the fame ; and so on from one to another, till it comes quite round to him who began it. The defign of this is to keep the fentries alert on their posts, and to prevent their falling afleep. The fentries at the guard-room doors are to be very attentive to the word *(All is well)* coming round ; and when they find that it does not come punctually to the time, they are to acquaint their Officers with it, who are to fend a Corporal with a file of men round their fentries, left any of them should be afleep, or have quitted their posts, to find out where it stopped, that the offender may be brought to punishment.

" When the enemy approaches, and you discover towards the horizon, and upon the eminences, bodies of men affembled, unemployed, with their front facing the town, you may take it for granted, that preparations are making for fome confiderable attack : upon fuch occafions, every different corps will furnish grenadiers and light infantry, to be formed into one or more bodies ; by which their intentions will be known.

" The clergy being as apt to betray a place, and often more, than others, as experience has evinced, the Governor should examine the churches and religious houfes, in the night, to fee whether any men are concealed there, or if they have any under-ground paffages leading out of the town, as there fometimes are. Had the Governor of Cremona taken thefe precautions, he would not have been furprized by Prince Eugene, who held private correfpondence with a priest, who concealed a strong body of men in a chapel, which, together with others that were let in by treachery, furprifed the Governor in his bed."

The Governor's Command in his own Town, and the Refpect and Obedience due to him from the Troops which compofe its Garrifon.

ARTICLE I.

" WHOEVER is Governor of a town, has the entire command of the troops which compofe the garrifon, though Officers of a fuperior rank may be with them ; for the town being committed to his charge, he is anfwerable
able

able for it; and, confequently, cannot give up the command, without exprefs orders.

" In the abfence of the Governor, the command devolves on the Lieutenant-governor; in the abfence of both, on the eldeft Officer in the garrifon, whether he is of the horfe, foot, dragoons, or artillery, who is called, during the time, Commandant of the garrifon. This is the general rule; but as it may be neceffary, on particular occafions, to throw a confiderable body of troops into the garrifon (either for its defence, or to annoy the enemy) and that a General-officer of a confiderable rank may be ordered in with them, it is ufual to give him a commiffion of Commandant of the troops, in the body of which is particularly fpecified how far his power over them is to extend, to avoid all difputes that might happen betwixt him and the Governor about it; and though this may, in a great meafure, leffen and divide the Governor's power, yet the outward marks of diftinction are generally left with him; fuch as giving the parole, the adminiftration of the civil affairs, keeping the keys of the town, &c. as alfo the figning of a capitulation, jointly with the Commander of the troops, in cafe of a furrender.

" The reafon for appointing a Commandant of the troops, I fuppofe, may arife from the Governor's not being of a rank in the army fufficient to give him a due authority over them; or, that he may not be thought equal to the command; fuppofing him equal to it, both from his experience and ability, unlefs he is diftinguifhed with titles of dignity, his orders will not be fo readily executed as if he was; and though a commiffion of Governor creates him, in a manner, Captain-general in his own town, yet, when Officers of an equal rank to him in the army are ordered into the garrifon, it is difficult for him to keep up his command as it fhould be, or get them to obey him with the fame deference as they would one of a fuperior rank; and if it proves fo, when only thofe of an equal rank are commanded into the garrifon, it will be much more difficult for him to exert his authority over thofe who are his fuperiors, as well as fhocking to them to be commanded by an inferior; the truth of which, with the detriment that arifes from it to the fervice, is fo well known in France, that when it happens there, and they have no mind to fupercede the Governor, they always appoint an Officer of rank and ability (in proportion to the number of men, which, in cafe of danger, fhall be or-

dered

dered into the garrison) Commandant of the troops; in which care is generally taken, that the person so appointed, be of such a rank in the army, that not only all disputes about command in relation to him, are out of the question; but, likewise, all contests of this kind, may arise in the garrison, are immediately terminated, and his decisions more readily submitted to, than if they came from one of an inferior character.

" I shall now proceed to the command of a Governor, when there is no Commandant of the troops appointed.

" How far the Governor's power extends over the civil must be determined by the laws and constitutions of the country; however, all persons in the town, ecclesiastical or civil, are subject to his jurisdiction, as far as it relates to the order and preservation of the town; and whoever offends therein, though he may not have the power of punishing, yet he may secure their persons till they can be tried regularly for the crimes they have committed.

" His power over the military is very extensive; for all the Officers and soldiers in the Garrison are obliged implicitly to obey him.

" He may order the troops under arms as oft as he shall think proper; either to review them, or upon any other occasion.

" He may send out detachments or parties, without assigning a reason to the Officers for it, or come to an explanation with them on that head; neither have they a power to demand it: but if they think themselves aggrieved, they may represent it to him in a respectful manner; that is, singly, by way of request; but not in a riotous way, and in numbers; since that may be deemed mutiny, which, by the articles of war, is death.

" Neither Officer nor soldier must lie a night out of the garrison, without the Governor's leave; but, that the Colonels, or those who command regiments, may have a proper authority over their own corps, a Governor seldom grants his leave of absence to either Officer or soldier, but at their request. A Governor who forms a just idea of the service, will act invariably to this rule; and it appears to me reasonable that he should do so; otherwise how can they answer for their regiments, if their Officers and soldiers have leave of absence without their knowledge? Besides, as the Colonels are supposed to know those under their command, they must be proper judges who may have leave given them; and, therefore, will not importune the Governor, but when

it

it is proper; which will not only eafe him of infinite trouble, but prevent him from being impofed upon, by their
pretending that bufinefs, when, perhaps, pleafure, or indolence, is their chief motive; the truth of which cannot
fo eafily be entered into by the Governor as the Colonels;
who, in juftice to their regiments, will limit the number,
that the duty may not fall too hard on thofe who remain.

"What is above mentioned, without entering into the
deference due to Colonels, when it relates to thofe immediately under their command, is fo equitable, that it is
generally followed; yet, however juft this rule may appear,
a Governor has an undoubted right to deviate from it
when he fhall think proper, by granting his leave of abfence
to either Officers or foldiers without the confent of their
Colonels; and though particular regiments may fometimes
fuffer by fuch proceedings, yet that evil is of lefs confequence to the fervice, than what the limiting of the Governor's power might produce, viz. the lofs of fubordination; which is of fuch weight, that it is the very life and
foul (if I may be allowed the expreffion) of difcipline, without a due obfervance of which, the fervice can never be
carried on; for whoever endeavours to weaken it, by making the Officers or foldiers independent of the principal
perfons who are placed over them, whether Governors or
Generals, muft do it, either through evil defign or ignorance, fince each produce the fame effect, diforder and
confufion; a ftate which foldiers may be eafily brought into
(from that natural love of independency which reigns in all
mankind) but not fo foon reclaimed from; for, when a
licentious independent humour has prevailed amongft
troops, it will not only take time, but infinite pains, and
great feverity, to reduce them to their proper obedience;
the want of which may prove as prejudicial to the ftate, as
the want of troops; fince the lofs of fubordination produces not only the neglect of orders, but, in a great meafure, the power, or at leaft an imaginary one, to difpute
them; the confequence of which is too well known to be
further enlarged upon.

"The practice of the army in this cafe, is, that when
an Officer has bufinefs that may require his abfence from the
garrifon, he is to make his firft application to his Colonel,
and defire him to intercede with the Governor for leave. If
the Colonel complies with the Officer's requeft, he fhould
wait upon the Governor in his behalf; but, if the Colonel
refufes

refufes the Officer, he may then, no doubt, apply to the Governor; though such a step should not be taken without he is neceffitated fo to do, either from extraordinary bufinefs, or becaufe he finds himfelf harfhly ufed by his Colonel; fince the doing of it is, in a manner, putting him at defiance, and therefore not to be rafhly undertaken.

" When any of the private men want leave, they are to apply to their Captains firft, the Captains to the Colonel; and, if he agrees to it, he is to fend their names by the Adjutant to the Town-major, that he may acquaint the Governor that they have his confent, and defire he would be pleafed to grant them his leave of abfence.

" When the foldiers have applied to their Captains, and are refufed by them, they may then apply to their Colonels; but they fhould not do it till they have been with their Captains, for the fame reafon that an Officer fhould not apply to the Governor till he has been with his Colonel.

ARTICLE II.

" All foldiers who have leave to go out of the garrifon muft have paffports, figned by the Governor, fpecifying the regiment to which they belong, the place they are to go to, and the time they have leave to be abfent; the particulars of which muft be given in by the Adjutant to the Town-major. Whoever goes without one of thefe paffports, or is found taking a contrary road to that which is expreffed in it, will be looked upon as a deferter, and, when taken, tried accordingly. It is therefore the duty of the Officers on the port-guards, to examine all foldiers who fhall come into the town, and do not belong to the garrifon; when they find any of them without a pafs, or that they have taken a wrong route, or have any reafon to fufpeẟt it forged, they are to fend them to the main-guard, to be examnied by the Governor, or thofe whom he fhall appoint for that purpofe; and if they are found to be deferters, they fhould be fecured till they can be fent to their regiments to be tried as fuch.

" When Officers on party meet any foldiers, they muft examine their paffports; and if they have any reafon to fufpeẟt them, they muft take them prifoners, deliver them over to the main guard when they return to their garrifon, and acquaint the Governor with it.

" No

" No regiment can hold a Court-martial, or punish any of their men, without first obtaining the Governor's leave, or that of the Commandant, in his absence : however, it is customary, upon the first application which the Colonel makes of this kind to the Governor, to give him a discretionary power to hold regimental Courts-martial, as oft as he shall have occasion ; and to put the sentence in execution, provided the regiment is not to be under arms at the performing it ; because no Colonel can order his regiment under arms, either for exercise, punishing offenders, or otherwise, without leave of the Governor ; therefore it is usual to punish the soldiers on the regimental parade, in the presence of the men who mount the guard in the morning, unless the sentence directs otherwise.

" When the Colonel or Commanding-officer would have the regiment under arms for exercise, review, or to punish any of his men, he may send the Adjutant to the Town-major, that he may acquaint the Governor when he goes to receive the night orders ; and, if granted, the Town-major is to give out in public orders, that such a regiment is to be under arms, &c. to-morrow morning.

" The ceremony of giving out in public orders, when regiments are to be under arms, has an appearance as if it was only to keep up the authority of the Governor, and to shew his command over the troops in his garrison ; and, indeed, I never heard any reason given for it, but that it was the custom : however, it cannot be doubted but that a better reason than custom can be given ; but since it has not come to my knowledge, I beg leave to offer my opinion on that head.

" Should a part of the garrison draw out in the morning, without the rest being apprized of it, they might imagine that it proceeded from some attempt of the enemy, who were going to surprize the town ; and, consequently, occasion their beating to arms ; therefore, to prevent these false alarms, which would not only fatigue the troops, but, by their being too oft repeated, make them dilatory in repairing to their alarm-posts upon a real occasion, and also cause a bustle and disturbance in the town, it is therefore necessary that it should be given out in orders by the Town-major, the night before, when any of the troops are to be under arms, that all may know it : besides, the assembling of troops, without the Governor's leave, must put the town in the power of those Officers who command them ;
especially

especially if we will suspect them of any ill intention or corresponding with the enemy: for, though it is to be presumed that Officers of their rank are above temptation, yet instances of the contrary may be given; and, in war particularly, we should not rely on what they will not, but on what they cannot do.

ARTICLE III.

" In case of an alarm, the Officers and soldiers not on guard are to repair, with their arms, immediately to their alarm-posts.

" Upon these occasions, the Colonel's company may be ordered to assemble where the colours are lodged, which is generally at the Colonel's quarters, to guard them from thence to the alarm-post of the regiment.

" Sometimes all the Field-officer's companies are ordered to assemble there; but, unless the garrison is very numerous, they will be of more service with the regiment; one company being sufficient to guard them: and the Ensigns who are to carry the colours are to assemble there at the same time. The reason for the troops being ordered to their alarm-posts, may proceed from 1 of the 3 following causes.

" First, Upon the appearance of the enemy before the town, or intelligence being brought that a body of their troops are marching towards it.

" Secondly, Upon any considerable rising of the inhabitants, or a tumult in the town.

" Thirdly, Upon a fire breaking out in the town, it is extremely necessary to have the troops at their alarm-posts; for, by their being assembled, they may be sent, under the command of their Officers, to assist in extinguishing it; to keep the streets open, that the engines may be brought to play; and also, to prevent the mob from stealing such goods as may be saved from the flames. Besides, as the town may be set on fire by a stratagem of the enemy, they, by lodging a body of troops at some distance from the town, may endeavour to seize one of the gates, during the consternation; which, by the assistance of the inhabitants, might be easily effected, were the precaution of assembling the troops and shutting the gates omitted.

" But, on whatever occasion the alarm may be given, when the troops are assembled, no Officer commanding a corps must dismiss his regiment, though it should prove a
false

falfe alarm, till he receives the Governor's or Commandant's order for it.

" Every Officer commanding in any of our forts, caftles, barracks, or elfewhere, where the corps under his command confifts of detachments from different regiments, or of independent companies, may affemble courts-martial for the trial of offenders in the fame manner as if they were regimental ; but his fentence is not to be executed till it fhall be confirmed by the faid Commanding Officer.

" No Commiffioned Officer fhall be cafhiered or difmiffed from Our fervice, except by an Order from Us, or by the fentence of a general court-martial, approved by Us, or by fome perfon having authority from Us, under Our fign manual ; but Non-commiffioned Officers may be difcharged as private foldiers, and, by the order of the Colonel of the regiment, or by the fentence of a regimental court-martial, be reduced to private fentries."

Inftructions to the Officers on Guard, from the Time of Mounting, till they are relieved ; with the Manner of going and receiving the Rounds, and fending Pattrols ; with the Defign of them.

A R T I C L E I.

" NO Officer muft leave his guard during the time he is on duty.

" He muft not fuffer above 2 men at a time to leave the guard, and then only for their victuals and drink ; when they return, he may allow 2 more to go off on the fame account ; but he fhould allow them no farther time than what is abfolutely neceffary, that each may have his turn ; which, if they tranfgrefs, he fhould punifh them for it at their return. But left fome of the men fhould afk leave juft before it is their turn to ftand fentry, in order to efcape or avoid their duty, the Officer of the guard fhould always fend for the Corporal before he gives a man leave, that he may inform him when the man will be wanted ; as alfo to order the Serjeant or Corporal to fet down his name, with the hour he went, and the time allowed him : when he returns, he is to acquaint his Officer with it, that he may know whether he is punctual or not.

" The Officers of the port-guards are to examine all ftrangers who come into the garrifon, take their names in writing, with the place where they are to lodge, and the
time

time they intend to ftay ; which they are to mention in the next report they fend to the Captain of the main-guard ; but when a perfon of diftinction comes into the town, the Officer of the port-guard is to fend an account of it in writing immediately to the Captain of the main-guard, who is to acquaint the Governor, or Commandant, with it fo foon as he can. When any fufpected perfon, from his not being able to give a good account of himfelf, comes into the town, the Officer is to fend him to the Captain of the main-guard, who is to fecure him, till he can acquaint the Governor with it, in order to his being further examined."

ARTICLE II.

" THE Officers of the port-guards are to fend a report, night and morning, in writing, to the Captain of the main-guard, in which they are to infert the names of all ftrangers who have come into the town, the place where they lodge, and the time they intend to remain ; they muft alfo inform him of thofe who go out of the town, and likewife of every thing remarkable that fhall happen on their guard : each of which reports is to be figned by the Officers, fpecifying the day of the month, the port it came from, and be fent by the Serjeants who go for the keys to fhut and open the gates.

" All the other guards, except the referve, are to fend their reports in the fame manner, and at the fame time, to the Captain of the main-guard.

" So foon as the Captain of the main-guard receives the night-reports, he is to write them over fair in a fheet of paper, or more, if requifite, putting the report of each guard diftinctly by itfelf, with the Officer's name who commands it : after which he is to fign it ; and when the gates are fhut, and the orders are given out, he is to wait on the Governor, give him the parole, and deliver him the report of the whole.

" The Captain of the main-guard is to enter the morning reports in the fame manner, with every thing that has occurred during the night, either relating to the feveral rounds or patrols, with the time each went and finifhed, that it may be known whether the Officers have complied with their orders, or not; as alfo what prifoners are on the main-guard, with the reafons for their being committed ; and whether foldiers, townfmen, or ftrangers. In fhort, he is to put down every thing of confequence which has

I   happened

happened between the evening report and the time of relief, in order to give a faithful and exact report to the Governor, which he is to do fo foon as he is relieved, by giving him the parole firft in his ear, and then deliver him the report.

" When any thing happens on any of the guards between the morning report and the time of relief, fuch as ftrangers coming into town, &c. the Officers are to fend an account of it to the Captain of the main-guard, that it may be entered with the reft, before he delivers it to the Governor.

" When any of the rounds neglect going, or do not perform them at the hour appointed, the Officers of thofe guards to which the round or rounds have not gone, or gone after the time directed, are to mention it in their morning report to the Captain of the main-guard, who is to enter it in that which he gives to the Governor, that the reafon for fuch neglect may be enquired into.

" The referve-guard being only a number of men kept in readinefs to act either in the town or to march out of it, as the Governor fhall have an occafion for their fervice, the Officer who commands it is therefore to receive no orders but from the Governor, or the Town-major, by his directions; which he is to be ready to execute at a minute's warning. He is therefore to keep no more fentries than what are neceffary for the fecurity of his guard, and only patrol near his own guard-room; neither is he under the direction of the Captain of the main-guard, nor to make any report to him : but when he is relieved, he is to wait on the Governor, give him the parole, and deliver him a report of his guard in writing, figned.

A R T I C L E   III.

" THE Officers of the port-guards are to keep the barriers fhut, and the draw-bridges up, on Sundays and holidays, during the time of divine fervice.

" They are likewife to fhut the barriers, and draw up the draw-bridges, at the approach of any party of armed men, though it fhould be detachments of their own garrifon, and acquaint the Captain of the main-guard with it immediately, that he may wait on the Governor to receive his orders for their admittance, without which they muft not be permitted to come into the town. One Officer, or a Serjeant, may be allowed entrance, to fhew the order or route, that the Governor may have an exact account of them.

" When

" When any detachment, or a number of armed men, enter the town, the Officer of the port-guard is to have his men under arms; and if it is a detachment commanded by an Officer, the men of the port-guard are to reft their arms, the drummer beat, and the fifer play, a march; provided the party which enters beats a march: but if it is only a Serjeant's party, the guard is to remain fhouldered, and the Officer at the head of it without his efpontoon in his hand. This may be looked upon, by fome, as too great a compliment from an Officer's guard to a Serjeant's party; but they muft know that it is not done by way of refpect to thofe who enter, but for the fecurity of the town; left the enemy, by having forged or procured a route or order, fhould fend fuch a party to feize the gate, while his body lay concealed at fome little diftance, in readinefs to advance on the firft fignal. It is therefore a ftanding rule in all garrifons, for the port-guards to be under arms, when any number of armed men march into the town, though they belong to the garrifon.

" When a fire breaks out in a garrifon, the Officers of the port-guards are to put their men immediately under arms, order the barriers to be fhut, the draw-bridges drawn up, and keep them fo till the fire is extinguifhed.

" This precaution is abfolutely neceffary in frontier garrifons; for a town might eafily be furprized, if their gates were left open on fuch an occafion; it being natural for every body to run to that part which is flaming; nay, a fire may be contrived on purpofe by the enemy's emiffaries, that he, by lodging his troops at the time appointed, within a proper diftance of the town, may, during the confternation which always attends fuch accidents, feize one of the gates, and by that means poffefs himfelf of the town. But by fhutting the barriers, and raifing the draw-bridges, that danger will be effectually prevented, and leave no room for fuch an undertaking with any hopes of fuccefs.

" When a riot, or a tumultuous affembly, happens near a port, the Officer of that guard is to ufe the fame precautions, in fhutting of the barrier, drawing up the bridges, and keeping his men under arms till it is over, for the reafons abovementioned: but when thefe things happen to be only fome fmall diforder, occafioned by a quarrel, he may fend a Serjeant and a file of men to quell it.

" When a riot happens in thofe parts of the town which are at a diftance from the ports, the Captain of the main-

I 2   guard

guard is to fend parties, both from his own and the horfe-guard, to difperfe the mob, and feize the offenders.

" In all frontier garrifons, it is neceffary to double the guards on market-days, and to examine ftrictly all covered waggons, or thofe loaded with hay or ftraw ; as alfo boats, barges, or fhips, and every thing in which men, arms, or ammunition, may lie concealed ; and when any thing of that nature is difcovered, they are to ftop it, and acquaint the Captain of the main-guard, that he may inform the Go-vernor, and receive his directions."

ARTICLE IV.

" HALF an hour before the gates are to be fhut, which is generally at the fetting of the fun, a Serjeant and 4 men muft be fent from each port to the main-guard for the keys ; at which time, the drummers, &c. of the port-guards are to go upon the ramparts, and beat a retreat, to give notice to thofe without, that the gates are going to be fhut, that they may have time to come in. As foon as the drummers and fifers have finifhed the retreat, which they fhould not do in lefs than a quarter of an hour, the Officers muft order the barriers and gates to be fhut, leaving only the wickets open ; after which, no foldier fhould be fuffered to go out of the town, though port-liberty fhould be allowed them in the day-time.

" The town-major, or, in his abfence, one of the Town-adjutants, muft take a Serjeant and 12 men from the main-guard, and go to the Governor for the keys of the town, bring them from thence to the main-guard, and deliver them to the Serjeants of the feveral ports, who are to carry them to their guards, efcorted by the men they brought with them. As foon as the fentries at the ports perceive the Serjeants coming with the keys, they are to give notice of it; on which the Officers are to turn out their guards, ranging the men under the vault or arch of the port, in two ranks, facing one another, that the keys may pafs between them. He muft order a corporal and 4 men more with arms to efcort the keys to the outermoft barrier, and to place 2 men with refted arms, on every draw-bridge, till they return from locking the barriers. He muft fend likewife a fufficient number of men without arms to affift in the locking of the gates and drawing up the bridges.

" When

" When there are any guards to be pofted in the out-works duing the night, the Town-major, or the Town-adjutant, fhould go along with the keys of that port from whence they are to be detached, in order to fee them pofted, and to give the Officer or Serjeant who commands them, the word, counter-fign, and the neceffary orders relating to the care of the poft or pofts to be guarded, and then fee the gates of that port immediately locked.

" When there are guards to be placed in the out-works, at different parts of the town, if the Town-major and his Aids cannot fee them all pofted themfelves, without keeping the gates open beyond the ufual time, the Town-major may fend directions to the Officers of the port-guards, from whence they are to be detached, to go and poft them, with the orders, parole, and counter-fign, in writing, fealed up, to leave with thofe who command them, and directions not to open them till the gates are fhut. As cafes of this nature feldom happen, I do not know that the above method was ever practifed; and therefore will not recommend it; but when it cannot be avoided, by the night-pofts in the out-works being too numerous for the proper Officers to fee them all pofted themfelves, I believe this expedient will not be thought improper.

" When the gates are fhut, which the Officers on the port-guards are always to fee done, the keys are to be carried back to the main-guard, by the Serjeants and efcorts who brought them, and delivered to the Town-major, or Adjutant, who, when they are all returned, is to carry them to the Governor's, efcorted by a Serjeant and 12 men from the main-guard.

" As foon as the gates are fhut, all the additional night-fentries within the walls are to be pofted, and to take pof-feffion of all other night-pofts which fhall be ordered; after which the Officers are to order their men to recover their arms, and lodge them in the guard-room; taking care to place them in fuch order, that every man may take his own firelock, when commanded, without any buftle or confufion.

" The Serjeants who carried the keys back to the main-guard, are to remain there till they have received the night-orders from the Town-major, and the tickets for the rounds from the Captain of the main-guard: after which they are to return to their guards, and deliver the orders, parole,

and

and counter-fign, with the tickets, to their Officers, and then to the Corporals of the guards.

" So foon as the gates are fhut, and the keys returned to the Governor, the Town-major fhould come to the main-guard, and deliver out the night-orders to the Adjutants of the garrifon, and to the Serjeants from the port-guards, and others.

" The Captain of the main-guard is to deliver to the Serjeants from the port-guard, as many tickets as there are rounds ordered to go; taking care that the names of the Officers guards are named on the tickets, one of which is to be delivered to every round as they pafs.

" In frontier garrifons, they commonly order fo many rounds as to have an Officer always walking on the ram-parts in the night. When this is neceffary, they compute the time that the firft will be going round the town; and when that has almoft finifhed, the fecond is to begin, and fo one after another, till the reveille beats. Thefe are called the Vifiting rounds. The Officers who difmount in the morning, are always appointed to go thefe rounds, becaufe they have had the longeft reft. They are to affemble at the main-guard at the time of delivering the night-orders, to draw by lot for the hour each is to go his round; after which, the Town-major is to enter their names, the regi-ments they belong to, and the time of going their rounds, in his book; that the Governor, if he fhould find by the morning's report, that no round went fuch an hour, or ftayed beyond the ufual time, he may inform him who fhould have gone then, that the reafon may be enquired into.

" The tat-too is generally beat at 9 in fummer, and at 8 in winter. It is performed by the Drum-major, and all the drummers and fifers of that regiment which gives a Captain to the main-guard that day.

" They are to begin at the main-guard, beat round the grand-parade, and return back, and finifh where they began. They are to be efcorted by a Serjeant and a file of men from the main-guard.

" They are to be anfwered by the drummers and fifers of all the other guards; as alfo by 4 drummers and 4 fifers of each regiment in their refpective quarters, if the town is very large.

" The tat-too is the fignal given for the foldiers to retire to their barracks or quarters, to put out their fire and candle,

and

and go to bed. The public houfes are, at the fame time, to fhut their doors, and fell no more liquor that night.

" In frontier garrifons, the burghers are conftantly obliged, when they go out after tat-too, to carry a light with them. Thofe who do not, are taken up by the patrols, and kept prifoners all night upon the guard, to be punifhed next morning by the Governor, for difobeying the orders of the garrifon."

A R T I C L E V.

" The patrols are to go every hour in the night, from the beating of the tat-too till the reveille. The patrols are commonly compofed of a Serjeant and 6 or 12 men from each guard. They are to walk in the ftreets to prevent diforders, or any number of people affembling together, and oblige all thofe who keep public houfes to fend away their guefts, and fhut their doors. When they fee any light in their foldiers caferns or barracks, they muft oblige them to put it out, or acquaint the guard of thofe quarters with it, that they may fee it done. They are to take up all the foldiers they find out of their quarters; as alfo all the inhabitants who go without lights, if the orders of the garrifon are fuch, and carry them prifoners to the guard. When any of the public houfes entertain company after the patrol has forbid them, they are to carry the landlords to the guard, that the Governor may punifh them the next day for their difobedience.

" The Town-major is to affign a proper diftrict for each guard to patrol in, by dividing the town in fuch a manner, that every ftreet may be included in one patrol or another. The diftricts fhould lie contiguous to the feveral guards, that the patrols may not interfere with one another. The middle of the town belongs to the main-guard, and the ftreets near the ramparts to the port-guards.

" It is the cuftom, in fome garrifons, for the horfe-guard to perform thefe patrols on horfeback. When the town is large, it will be very proper to order them to patrol through the principal ftreets of the town, and the great fquares and market-places, to prevent any tumultuous affembly, or rifing of the inhabitants. But as to the performing of the other parts, for which patrols are defigned, as above-mentioned, how is it poffible for them to comply with it ? While the noife of the horfes feet are to be heard at a confiderable diftance, it will be eafy for thofe who difobey the orders of

I 4

the

the garrifon to avoid the patrol, and thereby efcape due punifhment.   For which reafon, patrols of horfe, in towns,
are generally laid afide, except in the cafe above-mentioned,
and thofe of foot appointed in their room ; which, as being
more ufeful, are infinitely more proper.

  " When the patrols are challenged by the fentries, they
are to anfwer *patrol* ; upon which the fentry replies, *pafs
patrol*.

  " When they return from patroling, and are challenged
by the fentry at the guard-room door, they are to anfwer,
patrol of the guard ; and name it ; as, main-guard, referve,
or from fuch a port ; upon which the fentry permits them
to go into the guard-room, and lodge their arms.

  " So foon as the patrol returns, the Serjeant is to make
a report to his Officer of every thing that happened during
his patrol, and what prifoners he has brought to the guard ;
that he may examine them himfelf, and fet down their
names in writing ; the time and reafon for their being taken
up ; their place of abode, if townfmen ; or, if foldiers,
the regiment and company they belong to ; all which muft
be inferted in the morning report to the Captain of the
main-guard ; at which time the prifoners muft be conducted
there alfo."

Method of going and receiving the Rounds in a Garrifon.

WHEN the Town-major goes his round, he comes to
the main-guard and demands a Serjeant and 4 men
to efcort him to the next guard ; 1 of the men carrying
a lanthorn.   He may go to which gate he pleafes firft ; but
all the other rounds, except the Governor's or Commandant's, are to go according to the method prefcribed them.
So foon as the fentry at the guard-room door perceives the
round coming, he fhould give notice to the guard, that
they may be ready to turn out.   When the round comes
within 20 paces of the guard, he is to challenge ; and,
when he is anfwered by the Serjeant who attends the Town-
major's round, he is to fay, *ftand round* ; after which he is
to call out immediately, *Serjeant, turn out your guard* ;
Town-major's round.   No round is to advance after the fentry has challenged and ordered them to ftand.   Upon the
fentry's calling, the Serjeant is to turn out the guard immediately, with fhouldered arms, and the Officer is to poft
himfelf at the head of it.   After this, he is to order the
Serjeant, and 4 men, to advance towards the round,
                                                        and

and challenge. When the Serjeant of the guard comes within 6 paces of the Serjeant who escorted the round, he is to halt and challenge briskly : the Serjeant of the escort answering, *Town-major's round* ; he replies, *advance Serjeant with the parole* ; and then orders his men to rest their firelocks. The Serjeant of the escort advancing alone, gives the Serjeant of the guard the parole in his ear; he then returns to his escort ; and, leaving the men he brought with him to keep the round from advancing, goes to his Officer, and gives him the parole he received from the Serjeant. The Officer, finding the parole to be right, orders his Serjeant to return to his men, and says, *advance Town-major's round—rest your firelocks* ; upon which the Serjeant of the guard orders his men to wheel back from the centre and make a lane, through which the round is to pass. The escort remaining where they were, he goes up to the Officer, and laying his mouth to his ear, gives him the parole. The Town-major then examines if the gates are locked and well secured ; whether they have taken possession of their night-posts, and placed the additional night-sentries ; counts the men who are under arms, to see if they are all on guard ; and, if any are missing, enquires into the reason of their absence. He may likewise examine the night-orders, as also all others relating to the guard, and rectify any mistakes. After these things are done, he should send back the Serjeant and men, who attended him, to the main-guard, and take the same number from this guard to escort him to the next; and so from one to another, till he has finished his round.

As the Town-major's round is designed to see if the gates are locked, the night-posts fixed, and the orders delivered right ; I presume he may go either along the ramparts or through the streets, from one guard to another, as he shall think proper ; but all other rounds, except the Governor's, must go along the ramparts.

So soon as the round is gone, the Officer is to order his men to lodge their arms.

The Town-major is at liberty to take what time he pleases for going his round, so that it is completed between the time of shutting the gates and 12 ; but it would be as well if he went at uncertain hours, and changed his way of going, to keep the guards alert ; however, he should always go the first round, to verify the night-orders.

" The

" The Town-major having finished his round, he is to wait on the Governor early next morning, and make him a report of the state of all the posts, and the condition he found them in.

All other rounds must be received in the same manner as is directed for the Town-major's, only with this difference, that the Officers on guard are to give the parole to the grand round; but all other rounds are to give it to them: and though the Governor should go his round, after the grand round is made by the Captain of the main guard, he is to give the parole to the Officers on guard: but, in this case, the Governor may carry an Officer to give the parole for him.

The Captain of the main-guard is to go the grand round; the Lieutenant, the visiting.

When the Governor, or Field-officer of the day, intends to go the grand round, notice of it must be sent to the Captain of the main-guard, to prevent his going, that he may be prepared to receive him; it being usual for the Governor, or Field-officer, to come to the main-guard first, and take an escort along with him from thence to the next guard, or to conduct him quite round, if he thinks proper. The Governor may order what number of men for his escort he pleases.

When the Governor, or Field-officer of the day, goes the grand, the Captain of the main-guard is to go the visiting round.

The grand round, or any round which the Governor or Field-officer of the day, shall make, may begin where he pleases; because, whatever round he meets, is to give him the parole; whereas, when 2 other rounds meet, that which challenges first has a right to demand the parole of the other; but as this might occasion disputes in giving the parole, should both challenge together, or imagine they did, the place where they are to begin, and the hour which each round is to go at, must be particularly mentioned; by which method they cannot possibly meet, but will follow one another in a regular manner, provided they are punctual to their orders.

N. B. All rounds should be reported by the several guards, the Officers names, at what hours they went, and every thing that happened extraordinary on them; such as Officers being absent from their guards, or negligent in their duty; sentries drunk, asleep, not alert, or off their posts;

polts; if they difcovered any thing of confequence, heard any noife in the country, faw any number of people affembled together, or met with any difturbance.

The ordinary rounds are three; the Town major's round, the grand round, and vifiting round: the extraordinary rounds are appointed to go every night, or every 2 hours, as the Governor fhall think proper; which rounds are performed by the Officers who difmount the guard that morning, and are called vifiting rounds.

So foon as the gates are fhut, and the night orders delivered to the garrifon, the Town-major may begin his round; the defign of which is, that he may fee whether all the gates are fhut, the additional night pofts and fentries pofted, and the Officers and foldiers all on guard.

Ceremony at the Barrier, before they enter, and how conducted to the Parade.

SO foon as the Town-major, or the Officer appointed to act for him, has notice from the fentries that a regiment or party is in view, he fhould take a Serjeant and file of men, go to the outermoft barrier, and order one of the drawbridges to be drawn up after him, till he has examined the original orders or route of the regiment, &c. left the enemy, by having notice of their march, fhould, under that pretence, endeavour to furprize the town.

The Town-major, and the party from the guard, are to remain within the barrier; and when the regiment approaches near it, he is to order the gate to be fhut; upon which the Commanding-officer, acting as fuch, fhall halt the regiment, and fend the Major with the original order for his marching to that garrifon, to be perufed by the Town-major, who is to receive it over the barrier; and when he finds it authentic, and has difcovered the regiment to be friends, he muft order the gate of the barrier to be opened, the draw-bridge let down, and the regiment to march in.

When the Commanding-officer comes up to the barrier, the Town-major is to return him the route or order, and then conduct the regiment to the grand-parade, where they are to draw up in battalion; after which, the Commanding-officer, attended by the Town-major, is to wait upon the Governor, or Commanding-officer, to whom he is to deliver the original order for his marching to that garrifon;

acquaint

acquaint him with the ftate of the regiment or party, and deliver him a return of it.

During the time the Commanding-officer is at the Governor's, or Commandant's of the garrifon, they may order their arms; but no man muft be fuffeied to ftir out of the ranks.

After the Governor, or Commandant, has perufed the route, and the return of the regiment, &c. and afked fuch further queftions concerning it, as he fhall think proper, he then orders the Town-major to wait upon the Commanding-officer back to the regiment, and read the garrifon-orders to the Officers and foldiers, that they may not be criminal through ignorance : he is then to conduct the regiment to the alarm-poft affigned them, and afterwards to their caferns, barracks, or cantonments, where he is to difmifs them.

Honours paid to Governors, General-Officers, Colonels, Lieutenant-Colonels, &c. in Garrifon.

THE guards fhall turn out with refted arms, and beat one ruffle to all Governors, in their own garrifons, whofe commiffions in the army are under the degree of General-officer ; but though the main-guards turns out with refted arms, every time he paffes, yet they give him the compliment of the drum but once a day : all the other guards beat as oft as he appears near them.

A Lieutenant-governor, or the Officer commanding, fhall have the main-guard turned out to him, with fhouldered arms.

If they are General-officers likewife, they are then to have the further compliment paid them by the feveral beatings of the drum, as is practifed in the army, and are as follows :

To Generals of the horfe and foot, the guards turn out, reft their arms, beat a march, and the Officers falute.

To Lieutenant-generals they turn out, reft their arms, beat 3 ruffles, and the Officers falute.

To a Major-general they turn out, reft their arms, and beat 2 ruffles, but not falute.

To Brigadier-generals they turn out with refted arms only, but of late they have added one ruffle to the compliment.

To

To Colonels, their own quarter-guards turn out, and rest their arms once a day; after which they only turn out with ordered arms.

To Lieutenant-colonels, their own quarter-guard turn out with shouldered arms once a day; at other times, they only turn out, and stand by their arms,

To Majors, their own guard turn out with ordered arms once a day; at all other times, they stand by their arms.

When a Lieutenant-colonel, or a Major, commands a regiment, his own quarter-guard pays him the same compliment as is ordered for the Colonel.

All sentries rest their arms to Generals, Colonels, Lieutenant-colonels, and Majors; which ceremony is the same both in camp and garrison.

The main-guard are to rest their arms to the Governor, and pay him a compliment with the drum, as before directed: if he continues to walk on the parade, or before the guard, they may lay down their arms.

All sentries are to rest their arms as he passes them, or comes near their posts.

A General of the horse and foot, when in garrison, has a Serjeant and 2 sentries at his door.

All Lieutenant-generals have the same.

A Major-general is to have 2 sentries at his door, and the same compliment paid him by the guards as in camp.

A Brigadier is to have 1 sentry at his door, and 1 ruffle from all the guards in the garrison.

All Colonels or Officers who command battalions, are to have 1 sentry, which they are to take from their own regiment; but those Colonels, who have no regiments in the town, are to have their sentries from the main-guard, or 1 of the port-guards, if their lodgings lie more convenient for them.

The main-guard is to turn out and stand by their arms once a day to all Colonels; but all other guards must order their arms for them as oft as they pass.

The main-guard is to pay no compliment to the Lieutenant-colonels or Majors; but the other guards are to stand by their arms for them.

Lieutenant-colonels are to be treated in their own garrisons as Colonels; and the Majors Commandant as Lieutenant-colonels, unless their rank in the army entitles them to a greater compliment; but when either of them command
mand

mand the garrison, they are then to be treated in all respects as the Governor.

When the Governor and Lieutenant-governor are absent, or by sickness rendered incapable of acting, the eldest Officer in the garrison is to take the command upon him, with the title of Commandant of the garrison; and all that respect shall be paid him by the guards as to the Governor, even that of the drum, if his rank in the army entitled him to it before.

A TABLE for the several Duties in a Garrison, to be kept by the Town-Major, Town-Adjutants, and the Adjutants of the Corps.

Regiments.		Total —
Town-Guards.	Captains.	
	Subalterns.	
	Serjeants.	
Picquet, or Relieve.	Captains.	
	Subalterns.	
	Serjeants.	
Detachments.	Captains.	
	Subalterns.	
	Serjeants.	
General Courts-Martial.	Captains.	
	Subalterns.	
Garrison Courts-Martial.	Captains.	
	Subalterns.	
Visiting of the Hospital.	Captains.	
	Subalterns.	

Town-Major and Town-Adjutant.

THE Town-major and Town-adjutant are to vifit all the guard-rooms, caferns, and barracks, pretty oft, to fee that they are kept in good order, and that the furniture and utenfils belonging to them are neither loft or more damaged than what may be reafonably expected. They are likewife to view all the parts of the fortifications, the fentry-boxes, platforms, batteries of cannon, fpare carriages, &c. fee that the palifades are not ftolen or decayed, and make a report of the fame to the Governor, that thofe things, which are out of order, may be repaired in due time.

In frontier garrifons, thofe who keep public houfes muft fend an account in writing every night of all their lodgers to the Town-major, fpecifying their names, quality, and country, when they came into the town, and from whence; that he may fhew it to the Governor or Commanding-officer, in order to compare it with the night-report from the Captain of the main-guard; by which he will know whether the Officers on the port-guards do their duty, in examining all ftrangers who come into town, or the inn-keepers conceal any of their lodgers; whether thofe who came in gave a wrong account of the place they would lodge at, to conceal fome evil defign they had to manage: from which he will be able to take proper meafures for finding them out, and punifhing them accordingly. In time of war, all private houfes are obliged to give an account to the Town-major of fuch ftrangers as lodge with them.

Where the towns are large, they have commiffaries appointed to take an account of the ftrangers from the public and private houfes, it being impoffible for a Town-major to perform this and all the other parts of his duty.

When the Town-major or Town-adjutant are ordered to put an Officer under an arreft for high-treafon, befides the ufual fentries pofted at the doors and windows, a Serjeant fhould always be kept in the fame room, and relieved every fix hours.

If an Officer is put under an arreft for a fmall crime, it is unneceffary to poft any fentries; as, by the articles of war, "If any Officer under an arreft fhould leave his confinement, before he is fet at liberty by the Officer who confined him, *he fhall be cafhiered for it.*"

Standing

Standing Orders in a Garrison for a Guard who mounts over the Prisoners of War.

THE Officer of the guard shall have a counter-part of the muster-roll of the prisoners of war, and the said roll shall be called over at the setting of the watch, or relief of the guard, or both, as the Officer of the guard shall direct. No prisoner is to be received, or admitted to liberty on parole, without previously acquainting the Commanding-officer. No person shall enter into the prison, or converse with the prisoners, without permission of the Officer of the guard, who, on such occasions, is to direct the necessary attendance. Sentries posted within-side of the prison are to be relieved every hour during the day, and every half-hour after dark; those without as customary, and not obey any orders but those of the Officer of the guard, Field-officer of the day, and Officer commanding. Patrols are alternately to go by a Serjeant or Corporal of the guard, during the night, to keep the sentries alert. The guard is to be mustered often, and the name of every absentee returned to the Commanding-officer. It is to be expected that the Commissary's œconomy of the prisoners of war, regarding victuals and place of confinement, should be such as humanity, security, and the credit of government require.

The sentry who misbehaves on his post should be severely punished: he is neither to quit it or his arms on any pretence whatever; he must not sit down, whistle, sing, or smoke tobacco; nor suffer any body to come into his sentry-box, except the Officer and Non-commissioned Officers of the guard: he must be very vigilant on his duty, and exact in passing the word, *all's well*; suffer no people to assemble on his post, nor hold the least conversation with any one; but be perfectly attentive to what he is planted for; of which the Corporal, at posting, is fully to instruct him.

During the time the retreat is beating, the guard must be under arms; when the Officer is to examine the mens arms and ammunition; and see that the number of prisoners committed to his charge are properly secured; for the escape of a prisoner implies a remissness of duty. After tat-too beating, patrols must frequently be sent to make prisoners such soldiers as they find out of their barracks or quarters.

No

No Officer muſt quit his poſt, during the time the guards are relieving, to walk or talk with another, except at the time the Officer of the old guard is giving up his charge to the new. The men muſt ſtand ſteady and ſilent, while the guards are relieving. If any perſon comes near, who is intitled to a compliment, the eldeſt Officer of both guards are to give the words of command. The Diſmounting-officer is to give a report to the Governor, Lieutenant-governor, or Officer commanding, and at the ſame time whiſper the parole in his ear.

K   **A Report**

A Report of a Guard where the Shipping are hailed by the Sentries before they pass, &c. &c.

A Report of the   Guard   Day of   17   Parole GLOUCESTER.

Prisoners Names.	Regiment.	Company	Confined by	Crimes	Nights confined.	Where confined.	Tried by what Court-Martial.	Sentence.	Punishment received.	Released by	Ships arrived	From whence	Where bound.	What laden with.	What Nation	By Day.	By Night.

Sentries.

Detail of the Guard.

Subalt.	Serjnt.	Corpl.	Drum.	Fifer.	Gunner	Private

I went my rounds at   found

guards and sentries   I received the

rounds at

Stores.

" THE quantity of each kind of ſtores required for a ſiege cannot be preciſely determined, becauſe of the various conſiderations on which it depends ; as, the ſtrength of the place and garriſon; the capacity of the Governor and Engineers; the quantity of artillery, ammunition, ſtores, and proviſion; and, laſtly, the time, place, ſituation, &c. But as it is neceſſary to give ſome idea to the unexperienced Officer, I ſhall here ſet down the quantity of each kind, for a month's ſiege, as eſtimated by Marſhal Vauban, whom I chuſe to follow, on account of his great experience and undoubted judgment.

Stores required for a Month's Siege.

Powder, according as the garriſon is more or leſs ſtrong, - -	8 or 900,000 lb.
Shot for battering pieces, - -	6,000 lb.
Shot of a leſſer ſort, - -	20,000 lb.
Battering cannons, - - -	80
Cannons of a leſſer ſort, - - -	40
Small field-pieces for defending the lines,	12
Mortars for throwing { ſhells, - -	24
ſtones, - -	24
Shells for mortars, - -	15 or 16,000
Hand-granades, - - -	40,000
Leaden bullets, - - -	180,000 lb.
Matches, - - -	10,000 braces.
Flints for muſkets, of the beſt ſort, -	10,000
Platforms complete for guns, - -	100
Platforms for mortars, - -	60
Spare { carriages for guns, - -	60
mortar beds, - - -	30
ſpunges, rammers, and ladles, -	40 ſets.
Tools for working in the trenches, -	40,000

" Several hand-jacks, gins, ſling-carts, travelling-forges, and other engines proper to raiſe and carry heavy burdens; as likewiſe ſome to carry water to extinguiſh fire.

" Several parcels of ſpare timber for bridges, wheel-wrights, carpenters, &c.

" There are, beſides, ſeveral other things neceſſary; as Miner's tools, mantlets, ſtuffed gabions, faſcines, pickets and gabions, in great quantities; tools for ſmiths, car-

penters

penters and wheelwrights; a number of horfes for the artillery ; carts and waggons. Such as can be procured in
the country, are alfo ufed upon occafion.

Attack of a Barrack.

TRIAL fhould be made to take it by efcalade, by paffing
the ditch and mounting over the wall with ladders.

The troops, by a ftolen and quick march, the better to
facilitate their intended furprize, being unfufpectedly arrived
before the barrack in the night, the firft thing to be confidered is, where, and in what manner, to pafs the ditch,
and efcalade the wall ; for the enemy's guards and fentries,
from a fenfe of being fecure, perhaps are negligent of their
duty, and may be eafily furprifed by a vigorous attack :
but if, on the other hand, they have taken an alarm, and
are prepared for the attack, the beft markfmen fhould be
ordered to fire fingly into the loop-holes, and to the top
of the wall : hand-grenades and a quantity of dry fafcines
dipped in refin fhould alfo be thrown over it. The markfmen fhould then immediately run up and endeavour to ftop
the loop-holes, while the reft of the party efcalade the wall.
This being effected, they are to form in one body and
charge the enemy, or break open the gate. If there fhould
be any houfes or eminences which command the barracks,
they muft be poffeffed as foon as poffible, to fire from them
on the enemy, whenever they prefent themfelves.

Defence of a Barrack.

I WILL fuppofe the barrack encompaffed by a wall, that
may ferve you for a parapet. Round the out-fide of this
a ditch fhould, at all hazards, be dug with the utmoft expedition, the earth of it thrown over the wall, and well
rammed down, to form part of a banquette, which the barrack bedfteads, by being placed upon it, will complete.

Upon every bedftead place a quantity of ftones, and
each of fuch weight as a man can but juft throw it over
the wall, in cafe the enemy fhould attempt to take fhelter
beneath it.

Directly oppofite to every bedftead, where the wall is
too high to fire over it, you muft break 2 holes, by way
of loop-holes, at 3 feet afunder; each loop-hole is to be
8 inches long, 2 inches wide within, and 6 without, if the
thicknefs of the wall will allow of it.

To

To fortify the gate, to fire upon the enemy, raife a femi-circular intrenchment, and dig a fmall ditch within fide it ; the earth of which ditch, together with boughs of trees, and fpare lumber in the barracks, muft form a parapet, 6 feet high.

If there are any houfes which command the barrack, they fhould be pulled down ; and if you have men fufficient to defend the windows of the firft floors, and are obliged to take fhelter, the windows fhould be barricaded, to prevent the enemy from firing upon thofe within : large openings fhould be made oppofite each window, wider than the width of it, which muft ferve by way of ditch, into which you may throw thofe that attempt to come in.

If you apprehend the enemy are determined and refolute, take off the tiles and flates from the roofs, and the walls down to breaft high, that the men may fire over them. The bricks and ftones will ferve to throw upon their men ; and the timber upon fuch of their ladders, as may happen to be placed againft the barrack, to efcalade it.

But endeavour to poft your men in fuch a manner in the night, as to prevent an efcalade ; and provide poles, pitch-forks, &c. to over-fet the ladders, in cafe the enemy fhould attempt it.

The fide towards a morafs, if a deep one, requires but a fmall defence ; but it muft not be neglected.

The number of men to be lodged in a barrack, what provifions you can lay in, their quantity and quality, how many barrels of beer, water, &c. are matters of nice con-fideration. If you fhould have a ftream of water in your barrack-yard, it is likely the enemy would find means to cut it off ; therefore, nothing fhould be left to chance. No perfons fhould be fuffered to remain in the barrack, except fuch as are able to oppofe the enemy, and are acquainted with the ufe of fire-arms ; left you may have too many mouths for your provifion.

N. B. The Officer commanding, has here an opportunity to acquire the greateft honour ; it not depending fo much upon the numbers that defend it, as their Commandant's capacity.

It is on his judgment, that the ftrength of the place de-pends. He fhould inform his men, that the plan laid by their enemy, is worfe than death ; and therefore that he is determined to defend it to the laft extremity.

CAPI-

CAPITULATIONS.

" WHEN a Governor, who defends a place, fees himself reduced to the laft extremity, or ordered by
his Prince to furrender, to get better conditions from the
enemy, and a more advantageous capitulation, both for the
inhabitants and the garrifon, he beats the chemade; for
which one or more drummers and fifers are ordered to the
rampart that is next to the attack, to give notice to the befiegers, that the Governor has fome propofals to make
them. One or more white colours are likewife to be placed
upon the breaches or ramparts for the fame purpofe; and
one of them at leaft, is to fly during the time of negocia-
tion. The fame thing is done upon afking a fufpenfion of
arms, to bury the dead, or carry off the wounded after a
violent attack.

" The chemade being beat, the fire ceafes on both fides,
and the Governor fends fome Officers of diftinction to the
Commander in Chief of the befiegers, who deliver to him
the conditions on which the Governor propofes to furrender
the town. But, as a fecurity for the Officers fent from
the garrifon, the befiegers fend a like number into the
town. When the Governor's propofals are not fatisfactory
to the General of the befiegers, he prefcribes the conditions on which the town is to furrender; he commonly
threatens the Governor to allow him no conditions at all,
in cafe he refufes thofe propofed, within a certain time,
or when fuch or fuch a work is finifhed; if the Governor
finds the condition of the befiegers too hard, the Officers
return to their homes, the fifes play, and the drums beat upon
the rampart, to make every body retire before that hoftility,
which immediately commences. It is to be obferved, that
during the fufpenfion of arms, no work fhould be done
on either fide; but it is neverthelefs neceffary to be upon
the watch, for fear of furprize, which is now looked upon
as lawful.

" But let us fuppofe, that the articles of capitulation are
agreed upon. In that cafe the Governor fends 2 or 3 of his
principal Officers into the camp, and the General fends the
fame number, of the fame rank, into the town, as a fecurity for its accomplifhment. When the befieged have performed every thing according to agreement, their hoftages
are fent back; and when the befiegers have performed every
thing

thing agreeable to the articles, their hoftages are likewife
fent to them.

" The conditions of the befieged may be of various
kinds, according to the different circumftances or fituations
in which they are; but thofe the moft common are as
follow:

" 1. That the garrifon fhall march out through the breach,
with their arms, baggage, fpare carriages, horfes, drums
beating, fifes playing, matches lighted on both ends, flying colours, fome cannons and mortars, with their appur-
tenances; and ammunition for a certain number of charges;
to be conducted in fafety to the town agreed on, which is
ufually the next in poffeffion of the befieged. It muft be
obferved to infert, *by the fhorteft road*, or, that the road is
fpecified in words, which the garrifon is to march. When
the garrifon has feveral days to march, before it can
reach the town agreed on, it is required that the troops
fhould be provided with provifion and lodgement during
that time.

" 2. One of the gates fhall be delivered up to the befiegers, either the fame evening, or at a certain hour next
day; and the garrifon fhall march out in a day or two
after, according to agreement.

" 3. The befiegers fhall furnifh a certain number of covered waggons; that is, fuch as are not to be fearched;
befides others to carry off the wounded and fick, which are
in a condition to be tranfported; and, in general, all the
carriages neceffary to convey the garrifon's baggage and artillery allowed by the capitulation.

4. " That the fick and wounded, which cannot be carried
off, and are obliged to remain in the place, fhall have free
liberty to go away with every thing that belongs to them,
when they are in a condition to do it; and they fhall be
furnifhed, in the mean time, with lodgings and provifion,
gratis, or otherwife.

" 5. There fhall be no indemnification required from
the befieged, for horfes taken from the inhabitants, or for
houfes burned or deftroyed during the fiege.

" 6. That the Governor, the reft of the Officers under
him, and thofe belonging to the garrifon, the garrifon itfelf, and, in general, every body in the King's fervice,
fhall freely go out of the place, without fuffering reprifals
of any nature whatfoever.

" 7. If

" 7. If thofe who take poffeffion of the town are of a different religion from that of the inhabitants, it muft be inferted in the capitulation, that the inhabitants fhall exercife their religion without any moleftation.

" 8. That the inhabitants, and thofe depending on the place, fhall be maintained in all their rights, privileges, and prerogatives.

" 9. It fhall be at the choice of thofe who have a mind to leave the place, to go where they pleafe, with all their effects. It is fometimes, and always fhould be ftipulated, that thofe of the inhabitants who have fhewn any partiality to the garrifon, fhall not be molefted on that account; which they might have been before and during the fiege.

" 10. It is alfo mentioned in the capitulation, that all the powder and ammunition remaining fhall be delivered to the befiegers; that the places where mines are ready loaded fhall likewife be fhewn; and,

" 11. That all the prifoners made on both fides, during the fiege, fhall be releafed.

" It muft be obferved, that a garrifon muft have provifions and ammunition, at leaft for 3 days, in order to be entitled to a compofition; without which they will be obliged to be made prifoners of war: but if the befiegers have not enquired into it before the capitulation is figned, it would be injuftice to make the garrifon prifoners of war, after having found the want of ammunition and provifion.

" When the befiegers will agree to no other compofition than that the garrifon fhall be made prifoners of war, and the garrifon is not in a condition to hold out any longer, it is a general endeavour to make the conditions as little onerous as poffible; and commonly agreed,

" 1. That the Governor, and the reft of the principal Officers, fhall keep their fwords, piftols, baggage, &c.

" 2. That the Subalterns, under the Captains, fhall keep their fwords only, with their baggage:

" 3. That the common men fhall not be rifled nor difperfed from their regiments:

" 4. That the garrifon fhall be conducted to a certain place, by the fhorteft road, where they are to remain prifoners of war:

" 5. That the principal Officers fhall have leave for 2 or 3 days to go where they pleafe, to fettle their affairs: and,

" 6. When

" 6. When the garrifon quits the place, it fhall not be permitted to decoy the foldiers, in order to make them defert from their regiments.

" When the capitulation is fettled, an Officer of artillery from the befiegers comes into the place, who, together with an Officer of artillery from the garrifon, takes an inventory of all the artillery and ammunition remaining in it ; and a Commiffary of provifion enters likewife, to take an account of thofe which remain.

" When it is found neceffary to furrender, and there are confiderable magazines ftored with ammunitions and provifions, as much of them as poffible fhould be deftroyed, before any mention is made of capitulating ; that fo there may remain no more than what is neceffary for capitulating, in order that the enemy may reap no benefit by them.   If this fhould be done after the capitulation is mentioned, the befiegers may infift on a recompence ; but what is done beforehand cannot be helped.

" Soon as the befieged have delivered the gate of the place to the befiegers, the eldeft regiment of the army enters and mounts guard.

" The day on which the garrifon is to leave the place being come, the befieger's army is put under arms, and ranged into 2 files, between which the garrifon paffes. The time of marching being come, the General, and the reft of the principal Officers, head the 2 files, to fee the garrifon defile before them.

" The Governor marches at the head, followed by the principal Officers, who make the garrifon march in the beft order poffible.   The eldeft regiment march commonly the firft and laft, and the reft in the centre, together with the baggage. When there is any horfe, it is alfo divided into 3 bodies, to march at the head, centre, and rear. Small detachments of horfe and foot are made, to march at the fides of the baggage, and take care of its not being rifled.

" The artillery, allowed by the capitulation, marches after the firft battalion.

" When the garrifon is arrived at the place agreed on, the Governor remits the hoftages of the befiegers to the efcorte ; and, when the efcorte is arrived at the army, the hoftages which the befieged have left for the fecurity of the efcorte, carriages, and other things allowed by the army, for efcorting the garrifon, are releafed.

" When

" When the garrifon is made prifoners of war, it is likewife efcorted to the place agreed on in the capitulation.

" Every thing agreed on in the capitulation ought to be looked upon as facred and inviolable ; and every word fhould be underftood in its plain and genuine fenfe, without any forced conftruction being put on it : yet, as this is not always the cafe, the governor fhould be very cautious that no words are inferted but fuch as are clear and plain, without admitting of any other fenfe than that for which they were ufed. There are abundance of examples which prove the neceffity of this precaution.

" In the capitulation of a garrifon, where there is a citadel, into which the garrifon retires, fome fuch particular conditions fhould be requefted as follow :

" That the citadel fhall not be attacked at that fide next to the place ; that the fick and wounded, which cannot be tranfported, fhall remain in the place, and in the lodgings where they are ; and, after being cured, they fhall be provided with carriages and paffports, to retire to the place agreed on in the capitulation.

" No perfons fhould be let into the citadel but fuch as are ufeful for its defence. It muft be mentioned in the capitulation, that thofe who are not fo, fhall be conducted to a neighbouring place belonging to their Sovereign, which place is to be named.

" Certain time fhould be allowed for the garrifon to march into the citadel ; and the befiegers abfolutely prohibited from making any works whatfoever for carrying on the approaches towards the reduction of the citadel, during the time prefcribed.

" A maritime town requires likewife fome particular conditions, relating to the fhips which may happen to be in harbour. It fhould be agreed, that they fhall leave it the fame day that the garrifon leaves the place, or fo foon after as the weather will permit them to fail for the port agreed on. They fhould keep all their artillery, ammunition, provifion, &c. and, left bad weather fhould oblige them to enter another harbour belonging to the befiegers, it fhould be mentioned in the capitulation, that they fhall be received there, and furnifhed with neceffaries to continue their voyage. They fhould alfo be provided with paffports ; and, in fhort, all the fecurity poffible, to avoid any infult from the enemy's fhips, during their voyage to the port fpecified.

" A great

" A great many other things might be faid on this fubject ; but it would require too great a volume to enter into
all the particulars of which this work is fufceptible. All
that has been faid fhould be looked upon as only a fummary
account of the principal attention which it requires, and that
which is moft generally obferved.

" Befides, as a late author, with reafon obferves, places
have different defences, according to their fituations, and to
their being defended with more or lefs forces. The experience and courage of a Governor fhould fuggeft to him the
beft defence, to furnifh him with refources to repair any accidents that may happen, and to make the beft advantage
of the befiegers miftakes and negligence.

" It is not fufficient to have courage enough to defend
the place well ; for it alfo requires a great deal of fagacity
and knowledge, not only in the art of war, but likewife in
fortification.

" The defence is attended with a great many more difficulties than the attack, and it may confequently do more
honour to a General who diftinguifhes himfelf in it. The
fuperiority over an enemy in an attack, the conveniences
there are in receiving frefh forces and ammunition, whenever they are wanted, and all other neceffaries, which may
be had from the neighbouring country ; all this may ferve
to repair any accidents that can happen during the fiege.
It is not fo in the defence ; no faults are committed with
impunity, in the face of an underftanding enemy. Attention muft be equally extended to the foldiers and inhabitants, in keeping a ftrict watch both within and without ;
the troops fhould not be expofed but on imergent neceffities,
and only on fuch occafions as are vifibly ufeful. In fhort,
the Governor muft create a refpect from the enemy, by his
conduct and fagacity ; and never part with the leaft of his
works, till after he hath exhaufted all poffible means for
maintaining it. All this requires the greateft capacity.

Commandant commanding a Corps.

" DISCIPLINE and fubordination (infeparable from
each other) can never fubfift in a corps, but where
the capacity of the Commandant is fufficient to maintain it,
by a ftrict and exact attention to every circumftance."

Conduct, on many occafions, is as neceffary as courage ;
an Officer can never have too many virtues, too much
knowledge or experience : he fhould have affability to gain

the

the affections of his corps; and, by the influence of example, occasion a perfect harmony to subsist among them : he must have sufficient address to acquire their good opinion ; and confidence and resolution, to support discipline, with unshaken firmness ; but if, on the other hand, the young or unexperienced Officer, inadvertently commits a fault, he, as his superior, should reprimand him, in private, with calmness and solidity ; which, in general, will have its proper effect ; *for the severity of an arrest,* is a thing of so serious a nature, as nothing but the severity of the service can justify.

A good Commandant will exert himself in administering strict justice to every one with the greatest disinterestedness : for which purpose, when vacancies happen, his interest, as their patron and benefactor, should be used to promote the succcession of all his Officers in rotation, except those whose incapacity or misconduct may render unworthy of his favour : such he must, at all events, endeavour to get rid of, by obliging them to sell or retire on half pay.

He should be well acquainted with the strength and detail of his corps, and thoroughly master of all manœuvres and principles of the military art. The despising of foes, the want of intelligence, and of reconnoitring and flanking parties, have been the sole cause of many a defeat, and often occasions a shameful, precipitate retreat, even from an inferior force.

The Commandant should have a particular attention to the arms, accoutrements, clothing, and all other appointments of his corps ; that the accounts are kept regular, complaints immediately redressed, the sick well attended, and particular care taken of them. He should never put his Captains to a superfluous expence for the ornaments of a soldier ; but content himself with what is proper and has a military appearance ; nor permit the Officer commanding in his absence to change the Officers uniform, or spare the stock-purse to raise men to mend the corps.

He should drum out, with infamy, by sentence of a court-martial, such men as are of a dishonest, quarrelsome, or mutiuous disposition ; and give marks of his liberality to those who distinguish themselves in the time of danger ; for rewards are as needful as punishments ; by the one they are led on to glorious actions, by the other they are deterred from committing base ones.

When

When the corps is under arms, or where the good of the fervice is concerned, the Commandant fhould remember, that he is anfwerable for the good order and difcipline of it, and therefore fhould oblige every Officer to a ftrict performance of his duty.

" What might we not expect from a Commandant, who is in himfelf a man of zeal for the fervice, and a man of vigilance, worth and fortitude ? " He is uncontroulable in his command of the regiment, efpecially where he makes a good ufe of it. The Officers (at leaft thofe worthy of that name) will regard him as their brother, and the foldiers look on him as their father ; he will be obeyed with pleafure and refignation by both, and the bufinefs of the regiment will be done with eafe and regularity ; he will gain more credit by politely infifting on a proper performance of duty, than by winking at idlenefs or crimes.

" Subordination in a great meafure depends on the difpofition of the Commandant. The military laws have authority enough to inveft him with all the feverity of German difcipline ; but the fpirit of equality, *in which Britifh youth are brought up*, makes it difagreeable for the one to exert, or the other to fubmit to, fo much fervility : yet where the Commandant is a man of fenfe and fpirit, and will give himfelf the trouble, he will certainly fucceed in forming his corps. He may meet with fome intractable difpofitions, but in general, he may manage to have little occafion for feverity.

" It is a difficult character to fupport, *if he means to pleafe* ; but I believe, that by avoiding all partialities, and exacting a ftrict attention to the duties of the regiment, with an eafy gentleman-like familiarity, he will find an eafy method to eftablifh harmony and unanimity, without which, the fervice can never be well carried on."

MAJOR.

THE Major of a corps, " requires many accomplifhments, and happy is that man (indebted both to nature and application) who is poffeffed of them." An Officer might make but an indifferent Major, and yet fhine in fome other character.

He fhould be active, vigilant, and well acquainted with the ftrength of the battalion and details of the army ; attentive that his regiment is not detached out of rofter ;
and

and have a perfect knowledge of the exercife, and all manœuvres.

He muft draw up the battalion and conduct it wherever
he is ordered.

He is to be mounted, with his fword drawn, at the head of
the grenadiers, when the regiment is marching by files, companies, fub, or grand divifions: when the battalion is prepared for the charge, his poft is then in the rear of the firft
right hand grand divifion.

The multiplicity of details which he is charged with, requires the utmoft attention, to keep them clear and free from
confufion: he fhould be mafter of the attack and defence of
fortified places, as fometimes a command of that nature may
fall upon him.

" This poft fhould be filled with men who are able to command and attract refpect; and the more he fhews to his fuperiors, the more he will receive from his inferiors; fo that the
Major who would implant the refpect due to him in the breaft
of his Officer, cannot proceed on a better method to eftablifh
fubordination, than by fhewing a proper deference to his Co-
lonel-commandant, or thofe in rank above him."

A CAPTAIN.

THE firft object of a Captain, is to gain the love and
affection of the foldiers of his company, by being prefent
when the Non-commiffioned Officers and private men are accounted with for their arrears and ftoppages; vifiting them
often, either in barracks, camp, quarters, infirmary, or hofpital; to fee them properly taken care of when fick, and reward fuch as are exact and well behaved. He fhould know
every man of his company, by name and character; and infpect his company's arms, accoutrements, ammunition, cloths
and neceffaries, once a week.

" If he is in garrifon, he fhould be punctual in executing
all the orders he fhall receive; if in the field, he fhould apply himfelf to the well difpofing of any command he may be
entrufted with; a fmall poft advantageoufly occupied, or an
entrenchment judicioufly thrown up, will make him appear
capable of more important matters. If employed in a fiege,
he fhould command a party of workmen, endeavour to infpire them by his *example*, and always appear at their head.
The more exalted the ftation, the more requifite the example
to infpire the irrefolute with firmnefs, and the timorous with
fortitude. In the day of battle, his calm intrepidity fhould
excite a confidence in his company. An intrepid courage,
con-

conducted by reason, is the moſt faithful companion of a ſoldier among the dangers which his profeſſion expoſes him to."

A LIEUTENANT.

THE Lieutenant, in the Captain's abſence, commands the company, and is not only anſwerable to the ſervice, *but to him alſo,* for the care and management of it; nor is it at his choice to exchange any man from the company, but by the leave of the commanding-officer of the corps, or his Captain.

He muſt pay a particular attention to the arms, accoutrements, ammunition, cloths, neceſſaries, *and dreſs of the ſoldiers,* in ſhort, to every circumſtance which may contribute to their health, &c. oblige the Non-commiſſioned Officers, commanding ſquads, to give him a return every market-day, ſpecifying the quantity, quality, and coſts of proviſions they have laid in; all which he is then to examine, and ſee if they anſwer their returns.

He ſhould viſit the ſick, to have them properly attended, and well taken care of; attend roll-calling at leaſt once a day, and oblige the Non-commiſſioned Officers to give him an exact account every morning, wherein they are to inſert all occurrences which happened during the preceding twenty-four hours; that he may redreſs all complaints with readineſs and exactneſs.

When on guard-party, or other duty, he muſt obſerve the precautions taken by his Captain, that he may be able to execute the ſame, when he comes to command.

" There is nothing ſo neceſſary or juſt, as, that the Lieutenant ſhould act his own part, and endeavour to acquire a knowledge of the commiſſion above him. But that prying diſpoſition, common to all mankind, is apt to occaſion ſome omiſſion in what he ought to do, while he employs himſelf in examining the conduct of his ſuperior; and, at laſt, by playing the General, to forget he is Lieutenant. This is not meant to check any Officer's genius, even of the moſt inferior rank; or to hinder his ſearches into the ſcientific parts of war; but only to prevent his attention being diverted from the moſt ſtrict execution of his duty, *by entertaining an opinion, that it is trifling and inſignificant."*

ENSIGN.

HE *ſhould conſider the truſt and confidence repoſed in him;* and, when he has the honour of carrying the colours

in

in action, *resolve rather to die, than lose them:* for courage is admired, and cowardice detested.

By the articles of war, " whatsoever Officer shall misbehave before the enemy, shall suffer death." Pay the same attention to your duty in time of profound peace, as when on the theatre of war : reward and punish where due ; *but on no account be too familiar with the soldiers, or suffer them to take liberties with you:* treat them as soldiers, with humanity and respect ; and they, as their Officer, will obey and esteem you.

Be attentive that the Serjeants and Corporals support a proper authority ; but let it be done with decency and good order.

Above all things, avoid the company of those who are given to slander, scandal, personal or national reflections, *as the pests of society.*

Honour is the peculiar characteristic of an Officer ; consequently, all your actions should be guided by it ; a man of true honour would rather exert his patience than his courage, except in defence of his King or his country ; for he that acts on principles of religion and justice, establishes his character, and recommends himself to the favour of his Prince, who rewards the deserving.

Sobriety is very becoming in all Officers, but I would in particular recommend it to you ; it will preserve your health and understanding, and intitle you to a respectful regard from your superiors. On the other hand, drunkenness will weaken the mind, and ruin the constitution.—By the articles of war, " whatever Commissioned-officer shall be found drunk on his guard, party, or other duty, under arms, shall be cashiered for it."

Attention in duty, is both proper and commendable ; it will improve your mind, and cultivate your understanding: though, at first, it may seem severe ; yet, if you do it calmly and cheerfully, a little perseverance will conquer what seemed so difficult.

" The respect you owe to superiors, demands particular attention ; you can never receive their advice with too much politeness and docility. A young Officer should always behave with politeness, and put a kind of restraint on his words and actions ; he should endeavour to oblige every body to the utmost of his power, but without a mean studied affectation, or cringing: he should avoid a fault which young people are often guilty of, viz. telling stories to their own

advantage,

advantage, or to the hurt of others, not always confiftent with truth : the mentioning of fortune or family is difagreeable in company ; and he fhould know, that the greater he is by thefe, the more it is incumbent to be filent on that head : but, above all, let him be careful of forfeiting *his word of honour, or breaking his promife, even in trifles.*"

Nothing will recommend you fooner to the favour of a General than having gained preferment by merit ; time, experience, and a proper attention, are the fure paths to honour. By fuch a conduct you will add to your reputation, and confirm your character.

ADJUTANT

IS to do no other duty than that of Adjutant. He is to fee all detachments before they are fent to the general parade ; that their arms are clean ; their ammunition, accoutrements, &c. in good order; and that a Serjeant be fent with them to the parade. He is alfo to keep an exact detail of the duty of every one in the regiment ; viz. of all detachments, court-martials, fick gone to or returned from the hofpital; foldiers deferted, dead, entertained from year to year, difcharged, or abfent by leave ; that a return be given in every morning to the Commanding-officer, in the ufual method, and to the Major of Brigade (if in camp) once a week, to be delivered to the General ; that they always take care to fend their fick to the infirmary or general-hofpital ; and that their arms and accoutrements are taken care of. He muft keep an exact lift of duties with the Majors of Brigade, that they may fee juftice performed ; and be able to tell every one when he is near duty, that he may keep in camp, and provide accordingly.

An Adjutant muft keep conftantly to the rules and forms of difcipline now in ufe, and on no pretence whatever change or let fall any of the faid cuftoms, till farther orders.

When a detachment is fent out, a Serjeant may accompany any number under 20, and a Subaltern may head any between 10 and 30. As the number of men encreafe, fo muft the Officers. A Captain may command from 50 to an 100. One Captain, 3 Subalterns, and 4 Serjeants, accompany 100 men; and fo in proportion to greater numbers.

" To be able to command men properly, we fhould firft know them, to have feen them in different ftations, to watch the moft minute movement of their fouls, to diftinguifh their talents, to form and employ them apropos. There is no

L   profefprofeſſion in which all this is ſo abſolutely neceſſary, as that of arms ; it is impoſſible for a man who fails in theſe reſpects to command a diſcipline ; that is to ſay, to form ſoldiers for the moſt laborious and fatiguing exerciſes, to wean them from any kind of will or opinion, to reduce them to an obedience the moſt exact and implicit, and from ſtubborn clowns to form machines only animated by the voice of their Officers," beats of the drum, or ſounds of the fife. Every one certainly has not theſe talents ; a man may be alert in his buſineſs and expert in conducting a march, commanding a company, or even a regiment, but yet very far from being able to make a perfect Adjutant. It is therefore evident, that the diſcipline of men ſhould not be truſted but to ſenſible and experienced Officers.

QUARTER-MASTER.

THE Quarter-maſter, though he ſhould have another commiſſion, is to do no duty but that of Quarter-maſter. He " ſhould be an honeſt careful man, exact at his pen, and a good accomptant ; very well ſkilled in the detail of a regiment; and perfectly acquainted with every individual circumſtance of its duty and finances.

" In garriſon, he is always to be employed in ſeeing the quarters kept clean, and receive all things belonging to the vivres, infirmary, or hoſpital ; provide all the camp equipage ; and, on all diſtributions of carriages, proviſions, and materials for work, receive and diſtribute them according to order. He muſt keep exact accounts, and return what is neceſſary or ordered, that the regiment may not be anſwerable for what is miſſing. He muſt be very careful in inſpecting the bread and proviſions, that no unwholeſome food be received, and no deliveries made but in juſt time. Beſide which, there are a great many things belonging to this employ that cannot be recited here, and happen without rule ; in which caſe, ancient cuſtoms, and the rules of war, muſt be followed.

SOLDIERS.

" A SOLDIER ſhould be brave, vigorous, careful, and obedient to all his Officers, from the General to the Corporal ; and obey the orders of the latter as if coming from the mouth of the former, as in reality they do ; the Corporal being the only means by which they are conveyed. He ſhould take care that his uniform, as well as other

apparel,

apparel, be neat and clean; his arms and accoutrements bright and in good order, the use of which he ought diligently to study, and also all his different duties: he should be master of all the beats of the drum and tunes of the fife, and instantly obey them: he should diligently attend his colours on all occasions: the limitation of his furlough should be religiously observed: his time for food and sleep regulated, not by his will, but by his leisure. When sentry, he should be alert, and observe his orders exactly and inviolably; ask no reasons for them, or dare to think them of little importance. The excuse of a soldier, convicted of quitting, or sleeping on his post, frequently is, that he thought no accident or bad consequence could attend it. How absurd! The necessity of his being posted there, is evident by his being ordered there. Suppose it in time of peace, there might (though unknown to him) be a large quantity of gunpowder, the money, arms, or accoutrements of the regiment, and many other things that perhaps his Officer might not think proper to inform him of.—It was in his orders, let them be his guide.

" The Officer should instil into the heart of a soldier, that obedience is the foundation of regularity and order; that, by this, discipline is maintained; by this, great designs are executed; and, without it, all is confusion and disorder."

The first thing that soldiers are to be taught is the military step; which can only be acquired by a constant practice of marching quick or slow together. It is of consequence on the march, or in the line, that they keep their ranks well dressed; for men who march in an irregular manner, are in disorder; and, if fallen upon by the enemy, must be defeated.

Nothing is more essential; for a man may be attacked in 4 parts; in the front, in the rear, and on both flanks; but he can defend himself, and annoy the enemy, only when his face is turned towards them.

Marching is reduced to 3 points; front, and both sides; (because it is impossible to do it regular, or for any time, backwards) and by this means you may face the enemy wherever it presents itself. The different steps to be used are 3; slow, fast, and oblique; which may be termed traversing.

The first is proper in advancing upon the enemy, when the ground is unequal, that the line may not be broken:

the

the fecond is chiefly neceffary, when you want to antici-
pate the enemy in occupying fome poft, or paffing a defile;
or, above all, in attacking a retrenchment, to avoid being
a long while expofed to the fire of the artillery and fmall
arms: and, laftly, when you come near the enemy, you
muft then advance with a bold faft ftep, have your bayonets
fixed, and charge with vigour and vivacity.

For other particulars, I refer the reader to the inftructions which the recruit receives at the drill, and the duty
of a Serjeant and Corporal, in the regulations and orders
to be given by the Colonel of a regiment of foot, &c.

Cautions, Directions, and Obfervations, for young Officers.

"YOUNG Officers are but too apt to commit miftakes, by exceeding their orders. Through a heat
and impetuofity of temper, they often attempt to do fome-
thing that is great and noble, without confidering the confequence that may attend it. I own it is an error on the
right fide; but ftill it is an error: for orders are for the
moft part pofitive; and, admitting of no conftruction,
leave nothing to inclination: a reftraint that proves rather
indulgent than hard in cafes of danger, into which youth
would precipitate themfelves and others, were it not checked
by the cool reafon of men of experience: they fhould, therefore, moft willingly fubmit to the commands of their fuperiors, and cheerfully conform to their judgment in all
things relating to the fervice. They will gain honour and
reputation enough, if they adhere ftrictly to their orders;
but difgrace is as liable to attend the exceeding, as well as
the falling fhort of them: the one, however, is more ex-
cufable than the other, though the confequences may prove
as fatal; fince this proceeds from a miftaken zeal, but
that from want of courage: but to blame a man for wanting what Nature has not given him, is not only hard, but
unjuft. The man, however, who continues in the fervice,
when he knows himfelf defective in that point, betrays
both his King and country; and, therefore, merits the
fevereft punifhment.

An Officer fhould be very circumfpect in his examination of fuch intelligence as he may receive from deferters,
and never undertake any thing by their advice before he
hath made himfelf fecure of their perfons; for though they
fhould leave even their wives and children as hoftages for
their fidelity, yet they are ever to be fufpected. He muft
alfo

alſo take great care of his guides, and never let them ſleep on the march ; *leſt the horſes, being left to their will, take a different road.*

When an Officer is ſent on a party or detachment, if he receives intelligence of an enemy being ſuperior to him, and that he is marching to intercept him, I would have the Officer ſend a drummer and fifer, to beat and play the long march, a different road from that he intends to take, with orders to conceal themſelves from the enemy; by which means the enemy may be induced to follow their ſounds, and give time for an ambuſcade.

All attacks in the night are to be made with bayonets, unleſs when troops are poſted with no other deſign than to alarm, harraſs or fatigue the enemy, by firing at their out-poſts, or into their camp.

If you are ſent with a party or detachment to occupy a poſt, and find the enemy lurking about, to intercept you, it would be adviſeable to march off in the darkneſs of night; for, if you ſhould not ſucceed in your attack, it will ſave the lives of many in the retreat. If you meet the enemy, ruſh on them with your bayonets; for the courage, ſtrength, and activity of *Britiſh troops* will add greatly to your ſucceſs : but you muſt not fire on any account, leſt you ſhould thereby alarm more of the enemy.

When you are to march through woods, encloſures, near houſes, or by croſs-roads, you ſhould never halt or encamp in the little openings of the woods, nor ever paſs through them without carefully examining their ſkirts. You ſhould always have ſcouts, whom you can depend upon, to reconnoitre, and prevent the danger of an am-buſcade ; for the avoiding of which you cannot be too much upon your guard, particularly when near a pond or rivulet ; for the enemy, ſuppoſing you fatigued and dry, and taking for granted that the ſoldiers will ſtrive who ſhall be firſt to drink, may take that opportunity to attack you, and throw all into confuſion, if the ſtricteſt diſcipline is not duly obſerved.

When the battalion is marching in order of battle on a plain, and meets with a hollow way, hedge, pond, or moraſs ; it muſt immediately form a column from the centre.

If one battalion attacks another of nearly equal extent, whoſe flanks are not covered, the grenadiers and light com-pany may be ordered to detach themſelves, and ſurround

L 3   the

the enemy, by attacking their flank and rear, while the 8 companies charge them in front.

If the enemy is marching to your front, you should beat a preparative, and fire by companies till they advance within 40 yards, when the general must be beat, and the battalion halted : then fire the centre and rear ranks ; the front referving their fire, and dropping their muzzles, till they can count 10 after the centre and rear ranks have fired : when the enemy is within 20 yards, fire your front rank, and rush on with bayonets.

Should the enemy recover their order, and be fuftained by a fuperior number of troops, your only expedient is a good retreat. If the enemy purfues, the grenadiers and light company muft keep up a conftant fire upon the enemy; the other 8 companies retreating till you can occupy fome ground to advantage, where you may be able to make a ftand : this is, however, difficult to put in practice, without a knowledge of the country.

Should the enemy be thrown into diforder in the purfuit (which has oft happened) bring the battalion to its proper front ; prepare for the attack, and advance with a quick pace, till you come within 20 yards of them ; then give a general difcharge, and rush on with bayonets.

If the battalion fhould be crouded at any time, or confined in their ground, the Captain, or Officer commanding a grand divifion, may order his centre platoon to fall back till the battalion can extend itfelf again.

If the battalion is attacked by column, the wings muft be extremely careful to fire obliquely ; that part of the battalion againft which the column marches referving their fire, and, if time will permit, they fhould put 2 or 3 bullets in their pieces.

If the enemy is in an enclofed country, village, or behind a defile neceffary to be fo.ced, the regiment muft form one or more columns.

But if the enemy, after gaining a champaign ground, offer battle, the regiment reduces its column, forms battalion, and fires by fub or grand divifions.

Should a regiment of cavalry be hardy enough to march up againft a regiment of infantry, the latter muft immediately form a fquare; the grenadiers and light company fupporting that part upon which the enemy feems inclined to make their ftrongeft effort. If the former attempt to force

it,

it, the infantry is to fire a volley and charge bayonets; which, againſt cavalry, is preferable to fire.

If the cavalry are thus repulſed and retire, the infantry reduce their ſquare, form battalion, and purſue with a quick pace, keeping their ranks well dreſſed.

But if the cavalry are able to form again, and attempt to return to the charge, it will then be adviſable for the infantry to form a ſquare, leſt the former ſhould move down in columns.

A column that receives an enemy's fire, and maintains good order till a well levelled one is returned, by then ruſhing in upon them with bayonets, muſt certainly defeat them.

The Pruſſian cavalry execute 3 manner of charges: one directly ſtraight before it, without deflecting either to the right or left; in the ſecond, it turns off to the right, for outſtretching the enemy's line by a ſquadron or two; and, in the third, it bears to the left, for outſtretching the enemy's right flank.

All theſe charges are performed at full gallop. At the firſt word of command, *march*, the line immediately moves in a trot; at the ſecond, it puts on a gallop; and thus it proceeds 5 or 600 paces, till, at the command, the whole body ſtops and dreſſes.

A regiment of foot, which conſiſted of about 600 men, being ordered to march from one quarter to another, the Commanding-officer imagined, from the diſtance of the enemy's frontier garriſons, which was at leaſt 10 leagues, that he had nothing to apprehend, and therefore neglected the common precautions uſually taken, in ordering his vanguard to examine all ſuſpected places, where horſe might lie concealed; beſides which, he took no care in keeping up the diviſions, but ſuffered the regiment to run into a train of near a mile long.

A little wood ſtood cloſe to the road through which the regiment was to march; and in this a famous partizan, with 80 horſes, lay concealed: the van-guard paſſed through this wood, without examining it; and as ſoon as the centre of the regiment came oppoſite to the wood, the partizan with the 80 horſe, ruſhed out upon them, and after killing about 50 men, and wounding as many more, the reſt threw down their arms, and ſurrendered themſelves priſoners; for the men having tent poles faſtened to their firelocks, could make little or no reſiſtance; and by march-

L 4

ing

ing in this straggling manner, they made his conquest the more easy, by giving infinitely superior strength to the partizan's numbers, by thus weakening their own.

The Officer who commanded the rear-guard, hearing the fire in front, and being about half a mile in the rear, had time to put his men in order (who, with those he had picked up, amounted to 50) and stand upon his defence: by which, notwithstanding the disaster that had happened to the regiment, and some attempts to take him, he saved both himself and his party, and retired back to the town in good order.

" Keiserslautern was surprized by the French in the following manner : A German deserter told the French Commander, that if he entrusted a party with him, he would engage to surprize the place: accordingly a detachment was sent, which marched through the woods, till within half a league of the place, where they stopped till it was dark, and provided themselves with as many sheep and horse racks as they could get, to serve them for ladders. The ditch was dry, and the wall low. In the dusk of the evening they approached the town, got into the ditch, and fixed their ladders : 400 grenadiers, provided with hatchets, mounted the rampart, with the German at their head : so soon as they were got up, he advanced, at some distance before the rest, to the sentry ; told him he went the round, that his light was out, and desired him to strike one : the sentry not suspecting his design, went to strike a light ; and whilst he was about it, the other gave him a blow with an iron bar, which he had ready for that purpose, by which he threw him into the ditch : the grenadiers upon this immediately advanced to the gate, surprized the guard, and opened it. The garrison finding how things went, withdrew into the castle ; and when the inhabitants had ransomed the town from plunder, the French retired."

" Charles the Twelfth of Sweden, in 1713, with 7 or 8 Officers and some domestics, defended himself in a house of wood near Bender, against 20,000 Turks and Tartars. Several historians mention the defence of this house, because it was done by a crowned head ; but brave actions, whoever are the authors, should never be buried in oblivion, as they excite emulation, and are full of instruction."

" Henry the Fourth of France, lost Amiens, in Picardy, by a waggoner letting fall a sack of nuts, as if by accident ; for while the soldiers of the guard were picking them up,

the

the Spaniards, who had difguifed themfelves like peafants, on purpofe, rufhed out of a houfe near the gate, where they had been in ambufh, put them to the fword, and carried the town."

"In 1676, Loo, a town on the river Dender, was furprized by the French: the ditch was wet, and the rampart without a revetement; half the detachment paffed the ditch in fmall bafkets covered with oil-cloths, while the other half ftood ready to fire upon thofe who fhould oppofe their paffage; then followed the reft in the fame boats, and took the place."

"In 1708, M. de Schower furprized Benevarri, in Spain, by the Spaniards neglecting the guard of an old caftle, at the entrance of the place; which he feized by a march in the night, and then detached feveral parties to attack the town. The garrifon, confufed by fuch a vifit, fought for fafety in flight, and ran to take fhelter in the citadel; but were fcarcely entered, before they were made prifoners. The enemy fucceeded, by the garrifon's fufpecting no danger."

"Prince Eugene having formed the defign of furprizing Cremona, in 1702, which was defended by a garrifon of French and Irifh, he got fome thoufands of Auftrian foldiers admitted at a fecret paffage by a prieft. Thefe troops fiezed the two gates, and killed the fentries that guarded them. The garrifon, buried in a fleep, were awakened by the affault to fight in their fhirts.

"By this excellent manœuvre of the Officers, and refolute bravery of the men, the Imperialifts were repulfed, from fquare to fquare, from ftreet to ftreet; and Prince Eugene was obliged to abandon that part of the town and ramparts, of which he had taken poffeffion."

"Nicholas Calviere, called Captain St. Cofme, having refolved to make himfelf mafter of Nifmes, engaged a miller, whofe mill was fituated within the walls, at the fide of the gate, to file the bars of a grate which fhut up the entry of an aqueduct, through which the water paffed into the town, and for feveral nights to put wax on the filed places, to conceal them in the day. He was then to be received with 100 armed men into the mill; while a more confiderable body of cavalry and infantry fhould arrive from different places to fuftain the enterprize. The day being fixed for the 16th of November, 156c, and orders given for the rendezvous of the troops, St. Cofme came out of

the

the mill with his party, at 3 in the morning, advanced to
the guard at the gate, put them to the fword, opened it,
and let in 200 horfe-men, with each a foot foldier behind
him. Having entered the town, he formed feveral detachments immediately; fent one of them to block up the citadel, while the reft fcattered over the fquares of the place,
and founding their trumpets, inftantly made themfelves
mafters of the town.

N. B. The founding of trumpets in the different ftreets
at the fame time, made the inhabitants imagine they were
very numerous."

Captain Vedel was once detached to a village, where the
curate of the parifh had obtained leave from the Commanding-officer, to make a proceffion of the penitents of a
neighbouring convent, to a chapel in the village which he
named; alledging that it was an annual cuftom: but the
Captain being aftonifhed to fee that fuch a numerous proceffion could be compofed of devotees, beat to arms, and
having drawn up his party of 56 men, difconcerted their
fcheme; for many in the proceffion, which he ftopped, were
found to be peafants, armed with piftols and fwords, whom
the Commanding-officer, upon being informed of his difcovery, caufed immediately to be hanged with the curate
and feveral of the penitents."

" In the campaign of 1760, that excellent General and
true genius of a partizan, the Prince of Brunfwick, was
fituated at fome diftance from Zerenberg, then in poffeffion
of the French; and being informed by two Hanoverian
Officers, who had been in the town difguifed like peafants,
that the garrifon were very remifs in their duty, trufting to
the vicinity of their army, and the diftance of ours; the
Prince was refolved to furprize them; therefore, after appointing a corps to fuftain him, he advanced in the night
with Major Macléan, of the 88th regiment; 200 highlanders, with bayonets fixed, and their arms not loaded,
following at a little diftance. Upon the firft fentry's challenging, the Prince anfwered in French; and the fentry feeing but 2 perfons advance (whom he believed to be
French) had no diftruft; fo that the Major getting up to
him, ftabbed him, and thus prevented his giving the alarm.
The highlanders immediately rufhed in, attacked the guard
with their bayonets, carried the town, and killed or took
prifoners the whole garrifon of 800 men.

" The French Officer who commanded at that time in
Zerenberg, concerted a fcheme for being amply revenged,
which

which failed only by a moſt trivial accident. When almoſt
every houſe in Bremen was filled with corn, being the
grand magazine and grand hoſpital of our army, this Officer
held a ſecret correſpondence in the town, which informed
him of the ſtate of the garriſon; and that there was a general order to let courriers, going to the army, paſs out at all
hours. He therefore diſpatched about 20 huſſars to ſcamper
over the country, who were all that were heard of his
party; while he marched 1500 infantry from Duſsledorp to
Bremen (about 200 miles) concealing them in the woods
by day, and marching in the night. Thus arriving to the
gate at the hour appointed, his ſpy on horſe-back, blowing
a horn, came along the ſtreet, and deſired to paſs out to
the army; but the Officer of the guard, who had the keys,
happened to be out of the way; and while a meſſenger
went for him, the people without grew impatient, and
beginning to break down the outer barrier, the ſentry fired
at the place where he heard the noiſe, which alarming the
guard, they got upon the rampart, and fired likewiſe at the
ſame place; upon which, the pretended courrier galloped
back, and the French, believing that they were diſcovered,
relinquiſhed their ſcheme and retired.".

In 1761, when Prince Ferdinand beat up the quarters
of the French, they retired a great way without being able
to reſiſt; however, when they came to collect their force,
and to recoil upon our army, Sir William Erſkine, with
the 5th regiment of light dragoons, was poſted in a village
in our front. In a very foggy morning, ſoon after the
patrols reported *all was well*, Sir William was alarmed by
his vedettes having ſeen a large body of cavalry coming to
ſurprize him; he inſtantly mounted his horſe, and ſallied
out at the head of the piquet, of only 50 men; leaving orders for the regiment to mount and follow with ſpeed,
without beating a drum, or making any noiſe: he attacked
their advanced guard in the curſory way of light cavalry,
and continued ſo to do, while his men were joining by fives
and tens, and the French cavalry were forming to reſiſt his
attack; before which, he collected the whole of his men,
and then retired; the ſurgeon of the regiment in the mean
time having carried off the baggage.

" Among many ſimilar inſtances of ſucceſs, in the courſe
of the war, is that of this Officer on another occaſion, where
he diſplayed the moſt ſingular addreſs, and which therefore
demands both applauſe and attention. After a repulſe, and
a march of about 70 miles in one day, when the men were
fatigued,

fatigued, and scarcely a horse able to walk, he saw a regiment of French infantry, drawn up with a morass in the
rear; he left his own corps, and advancing to the French,
desired to speak with the Commanding-officer, whom he
entreated to surrender, to prevent his men being cut to
pieces, by a large body of cavalry, that were then advancing. The French Officer desired leave to consult with his
Officers; which having done, they refused to submit; but
upon Sir William telling them that their blood must be on
their own heads, and turning to move off towards his own
corps, they called to him, and laying down their arms,
surrendered prisoners of war."

"A General of an army finding himself under very great
difficulties, by being obliged to engage a superior force; and
being apprehensive that the battle would go against him,
without some extraordinary means could be thought on to
prevent it, at last came to the following resolution. So
soon as he drew near the enemy, he ordered all the baggage
of his army to be placed in their full view; after which he
gave orders, that upon the making such a signal, they should
immediately retreat; which, however, would not be given
till he found that the battle was likely to go against him;
and as he conjectured, so it happened, from the superiority
of the enemy: upon which he ordered the signal to be made;
and his army retired in pretty good order, leaving the enemy masters of the field of battle, and all his baggage; the
temptation of which, and their apprehending that they had
nothing to fear from a beaten army, made them quit the pursuit, and fall to plunder. The General finding that the bate
which he had laid had taken effect, returned with his troops,
fell upon them in the height of their plundering, and by that
means gained a complete victory.

"Whether the above story is true or false is of no great
consequence. The carrying an air of probability in it is
sufficient to my purpose; and, I believe, if the same stratagem was to be made use of, even in this age, it might have
a very good effect in saving a great part of a broken army,
by taking the enemy off from the pursuit; for such is the love
of plunder in private soldiers, that were they not restrained
by their Officers, no hazard would deter them from it."

"Marshal Belleisle, when blocked up in Prague, having
his communication entirely cut off from all supplies, and his
garrison in all probability on the verge of being reduced to
the last extremity, was obliged to have recourse to politics,
to extricate himself out of that dangerous labyrinth, and

took

took his meafures accordingly with great prudence and dexterity. And, as the fuccefs of his enterprize depended on fecrecy, he took care to conceal it, not only from the townf-men, but even from his own troops; and to amufe them, he gave out that he intended a general fally, ordering a certain quantity of ammunition to be delivered to the foldiers, and all the horfes in town to be feized and diftributed to the re-fpective corps.

" When his defign was ripe for execution, he ordered the gates, on the 15th of December, at night, to be fhut, and that none fhould pafs or repafs on any account whatfoever, without firft acquainting him; and gave private orders to his troops to be in readinefs to march on the 17th, in the morning. He then put in practice two ftratagems; the one to prevent the enemy's getting immediate intelligence; and the other to diftract their councils, when they fhall have advice of his march. With the firft view he detached, early on the 16th, fome fquadrons of horfe to reconnoitre the country, as if a general forage was intended: and to accomplifh the latter, he difpatched a courier, with a letter to M. Defalleurs, the French minifter at Drefden, to inform him that he had marched with part of his forces, and left Count Baviere, with a garrifon of fix thoufand men; who he doubted not would be able to maintain the place till May. This courier was difpatched by fuch a rout, as to have the letter fall into the Auftrian General's hands.

" The 16th, at night, the Marfhal detached 900 men from the different corps, who were left under the command of Marfhal Chevert, to amufe the Auftrians with the appearance of a garrifon, and take care of the fick; and at one next morning, fet out with 15000 foot 3250, horfe, 30 cannon, and ammunition proportionable, with provifions for 12 days. He marched with fuch diligence, that he gained the defiles of the mountains before the Auftrians could overtake him; and carried off fome of the principal citizens, as hoftages for the fafety of the garrifon, and levied large contributions.

" This march was fo clofely concealed, that Prince Lobko-witz had no certain intelligence of it, till the enfuing day; when he detached General Nadafti with the Hungarian cavalry, and a body of Huffars, to purfue them, whilft he followed with the reft of his army. The horfe and Huffars often attacked them in their rout; but as the main army could not come up to fupport them, they were obliged to content

themfelves

themfelves with fkirmifhing; in which they picked up a confiderable number of prifoners, and fome baggage-waggons.

The French arrived on the 29th at Egra, after a march of 13 days, incumbered with inexpreffible hardfhips and fatigues, having loft near 3000 men by the enemy, fatigue, and inclemency of weather, fome hundreds having perifhed in the fnow; fo that they had not only Auftrian Huffars to ftruggle with in front, centre, and rear; but bad roads, and exceffive cold weather, which produced a general mortality amongft the troops, on their arrival at winter quarters, in Alface. However, it muft be allowed, on this occafion, that the French Marfhal performed the part of a brave and experienced Commander; though fo tortured with the hip-gout, that he was incapable of mounting his horfe; yet, on every emergency, he changed his coach for a horfe-litter, and appeared wherever he thought his prefence neceffary to encourage or affift his men. He repaired from Alface to Court; where, as the reward of his zeal and fatigue, he met fo cool a reception, that he retired to his country feat."

Lieutenant Governor Home, when Major of the 25th foot, was ordered, with 460 men and Officers of the Britifh picquets, to pafs the river Fulder, near Caffel, a peninfula, and poffefs himfelf of a pafs; which, with the greateft difficulty, he effected; the river running fo rapid, breaft high, as to oblige the files to link together, to ftem the current.

The Major then reconnoitred the fituation of the place, made an excellent difpofition of his advanced guards, and remained himfelf with his main body. Having procured fome pioneers, he raifed a fmall breaft-work of earth and limbs of trees; from whence, though attacked by 200 infantry and 70 cavalry, at 10 at night, he foon obliged them to retire.

At break of day, the enemy moved down, in brigade of infantry, to the number of 1800 men, and began to attack, expecting to deftroy this handful of brave men.

Surprized at their unexpected reception, defpairing of fuccefs, and finding the Major would neither abandon or give up an inch of ground, they retreated to the grand army, after fuftaining the lofs of a great many men, killed and wounded.

Prince Ferdinand complimented the Major and detachment with a public return of thanks; and Lord Granby (that ever-lamented friend to a foldier) gave 200 ducats to the men.

What

What is very remarkable, the action lasted near an hour; each side fired at least 60 rounds of powder and ball; and so close was their engagement at one time, that their bayonets clashed over the breast-work.

From hence we may see, that the Officer who has studied to make use of his talents, may, with 460 men and Officers, defend a pass against an army; and this will remain a proof to posterity of what determined bravery can do.

Polybius, in his seventh book, gives the following account of an attack, full of instruction for Officers.

" The blockade of Sardis by Antiochus the Great," says he, " had lasted two years, when Lagoras of Crete, a man of extensive knowledge, put an end to it in the following manner. He considered that the strongest fortifications are oft taken with the greatest ease; for the besieged in such places are generally negligent, and, trusting to the natural or artificial defences of their town, are at no pains to guard it. He knew likewise that they are oft taken at the strongest places, from the besieged being persuaded that their enemy will not attempt to attack them where they think themselves impregnable. Upon these considerations, though he knew it universally believed that Sardis could not be taken by assault, and that hunger only could induce its defenders to open the gates, yet he hoped to succeed; for the knowledge of his difficulties but encreased his zeal.

" Having perceived that a part of the wall, which joined the citadel of the town, was built upon a rock extremely high and steep; and that from thence, as into an abyss, the people of the town threw down the carcasses of dead horses, on which great numbers of carnivorous birds assembled daily to feed, and after having filled themselves, never failed to rest upon the top of the rock or wall; our Cretan concluded that no guard could be near it.

" He went to this place, examined carefully its approach, and where to fix his ladders. Having found a proper spot for his purpose, he informed the king of his discovery, and acquainted him with his design. Antiochus, delighted with the project, advised Lagoras to pursue it, and granted him two Officers, whom he asked for as people possessed of qualities necessary for assisting him.

" These 3, on consultation, resolved to execute their project the next night, at the end of which there was no moon: that being come, they chose 15 of their stoutest and bravest men to carry ladders, scale the walls, and run the
same

same risk that they did. They likewise took 30 others,
and placed them in ambush in the ditch, to assist those who
scaled the wall in breaking down a gate; at which, 2000
more from the king were to enter. Antiochus favoured
their enterprize by marching the rest of his army to the
opposite side. Lagoras and his people approached softly
with their ladders, and having scaled the rock, they broke
open the gate, let in the 2000, cut the throats of all they
met, and set fire to the houses; so that the town was pillaged and ruined in an instant."

Young officers who read this account, should reflect on
this attack. The penetration of Lagoras, in making his
discovery; his attention, in going himself to examine the
proper places for fixing his ladders; his discernment in the
choice of Officers and soldiers to support him; and the harmony of the whole means which were employed on that occasion, afford very excellent lessons for any Officers who
may attempt such attacks.

Though stupendous rocks may be thought inaccessible by
the besieged, yet this is a proof that none are insurmountable
to such penetrating geniuses as Antiochus's engineer.

That part of the military science which comprehends the
taking of posts, is little capable of being treated methodically.
The understanding of a great Officer, and the occasions which
chance produce, will find frequent opportunity for the execution of surprising actions. War is a business of schemes
and projects; and there are numberless precautions, which
escape the foresight of many employed in it, though a skilful
enemy may soon, perhaps, observe them, and artfully take
occasions for making some fine strokes. History contains
many such examples, which are only rare now-a-days because we do not study them sufficiently. But an elevated
genius, from a combination of ideas, depending on a thorough knowledge of the enemy's situation, which he should
always reconnoitre himself, will soon find his advantage
in perfectly understanding them.

REFLECTION.

WOULD it not be a disgrace, to see either an Officer
or soldier shrink back, or hesitate in the least, to obey
the orders of embarking or debarking upon any expedition,
especially where the service of his King and the welfare of
his country require it, though danger should appear inevi-
table? Can the Officer, who owes his preferment to the

King's

King's bounty, imagine it an annuity, given for his eafe
and pleafure only? Or can he who purchafes his commiffion
look upon the army as a convenient fituation to lay out his
money at intereft to the beft advantage? Who can think
that a country would maintain fuch a burden in time of
peace, but with the reafonable expectation of enjoying that
benefit, which even gratitude fhould compel from the army,
when occafion demands its fervice? And where is gratitude
fo highly due as from the vaffal to the patron, whofe favours
and bounty have enabled him to live, for a length of time
before, in pleafure, quiet, and tranquility? How defpicable
would that man appear in the eyes of the good and brave,
who, being young, *a foldier of fortune*, without any vifible
connection at home, fhould publicly declare his want of inclination to go abroad for his country's fervice; where he
might in fome meafure make a return for its favours; fhew
himfelf not unworthy of his Majefty's commiffion; and by
his courage, conduct, and knowledge of his profeffion, dif-
play thofe talents which otherwife muft lie in perpetual ob-
fcurity, and he be deemed an unprofitable fervant; an in-
folvent debtor to the grace that fo long fuftained him? Of
what weight will even 20 years fervice be to intitle fuch
a man to preferment? None; it will rather paint him as un-
grateful to his country, unworthy his Prince's favour, and
below the dignity of an Officer. How will his confcience
difturb him, not only when he reflects on the honours beftowed upon his former companions, but whenever the topic
of converfation is relative to the fervice? What muft be the
confequence? The death he feared abroad will find him foon
at home; or, what is worfe, an everlafting remorfe and internal conviction of unmanly behaviour.

But what fhall we fay to the man, who, without confulting his own courage and fortitude, runs blindly into dangers
which his foul cannot fupport? When once he has taken the
field, it is then too late to recede; it is then obedience to his
orders muft be his only confideration; that obedience may be
terrible, but ftill it is indifpenfable; to be expofed to all the
fire of an enemy, without daring to ftir, even to defend himfelf, is moft terrible; but every one muft then obey his
orders and maintain his poft; nay, even though at a fiege
he fhould hear from beneath his feet the hollow noife which
proclaims his death and burial in the felf-fame moment,
yet, even in this alarming fituation, the duty which has
placed him there, demands his obedience to remain: ne-

ceffity

ceffity fometimes requires the lofs of individuals for the prefervation of a multitude.

Victory.

" A Victory that intoxicates the conqueror is more dangerous than a defeat; it difarms him of caution,
introduces negligence, and lulls him to fleep with a treacherous fecurity. He who is afflicted with this weaknefs, is
ever at the mercy of his enemy; and, even if he lead an
army of lions, it would be routed by one of flags.

" Victorius loft himfelf by winning a battle, and its
confequence, applaufe; his reafon being difmounted, he
left the General behind. His prudence forfook him; and
the *ignus fatuus* of exulting in his late fuccefs, led him be-
yound the bounds of either council or caution; fo that
at the next battle he loft his laurels before the attack was
begun. Never were men difpofed of with lefs judgment,
or took up more difadvantageous ground; one wing had no
fuccour; the horfe were no fupport to the foot, or the foot
to the horfe; one might imagine he played booty, by refolving to try the chagrin of a defeat."

Rafhnefs and Prudence.

" RASHNESS is known to be the ruin of many weak
Officers, who are eafily drawn into it, becaufe it
has the appearance, and borrows the name of Courage;
though it is of quite another race, and not in the leaft
allied to that noble Britifh family. The one defcends in a
right line from Caution and Prudence; the other, directly
from Folly and Prefumption. Succefs feldom waits on rafhnefs, though twice profperous and triumphant; in Afia,
under the Macedonian Conqueror; and in Greece, beneath Aurelius the Firft; who, by his rafhnefs, won an
empire in nearly the fame manner as Aurelius the Second
loft one. But thefe examples are rare; and the Officer
who fteers his conduct by rafhnefs, muft go on by hazard,
and will feldom meet fuccefs. Prudence leaves nothing
unthought of, or unfought, which wifdom can fuggeft;
and fo, if poffible, leaves nothing to chance, or hazard.
And though an Officer, directed by prudence, will not engage fo oft, yet he will the feldomer be beat: fince it is
wifer to keep poffeffion of his ground, or what he has got,
than, out of prefumption and eagernefs, to lofe it. In
coming to action, he fights as if he trufted to his arms
more

more than to his courage, which may be trepanned; but, seconded by caution and prudence, he is for the moſt part invincible. Yet, if numbers ſhould over-top merit, chance over-rule prudence, and bear down conduct and valour, the Officer (though thus obliged to abandon his poſt, and leave victory behind) may keep honour in his retreat.

" Fortune is known to be never ſteady to her friends, nor implacable to her enemies; never conſtant to the ſame ſituation, nor true to the ſame intereſt; ſhe is now on this ſide, now on that, but ſtedfaſt to neither; and alike ſuſpected by all. A mixture of good and bad events uſually ſucceed. Now victory perches on your ſtandard, anon it flies over to the enemy; ſometimes you will conquer, and ſometimes be overcome; ſo that ſuch an Officer moves on in a circle of proſperity and adverſity; but his regulated confidence is not elated by the one, nor is his wary courage depreſſed by the other. He is neither preſuming nor deſponding; but, in the one ſtate, apprehenſive of a check; and in the other, in hope of an advantage."

Regulations and Orders for a Regiment of Foot.

NO Officer ſhall appear, when with the regiment, in any other dreſs but his uniform.

When the Colonel is abſent from his regiment, the Commanding Officer is to ſend him, on the firſt day of every month, a monthly return, with a ſtate of the regiment.

The Lieutenant-colonel, or Officer commanding the regiment, is to make choice of a Subaltern, who has the character of a diligent obedient good Officer, that when the Adjutant's or Quarter-maſter's commiſſion becomes vacant, he may recommend him to his Colonel, as entitled to preferment.

A Captain or Officer commanding a company, ſhould have a watchful eye over the behaviour and conduct of his private men; that when a halbert or knot falls, he may be able to recommend the deſerving.

The Pay-maſter of the regiment ſhould ſettle the non-effective account with the Agent, by letter, every two months; and the Agent tranſmit an account of what reimburſements have been made out of the ſtock-purſe during that time, and what balance remains, that the accounts may be compared together and ſettled, agreeable to the King's warrant, for regulating the non-effective account.

Abſtract

Abstract of the non-effective and recruiting account from to 17								
Dr. A.{B.------------------------Account to----------17-------Cr.--								
17	To	l.	s.	d.	17 By		l.	s.	d.

The Chaplain of the regiment is conftantly to attend, or
act by deputy, and vifit the fick conftantly in barracks,
quarters, or infirmary; and the Commanding Officer of the
regiment is to be anfwerable that the duty of the Chaplain
be executed with becoming regularity.

An infirmary-board muft fit the firft Monday in every
month, compofed of three Captains, and examine into the
ftate of the infirmary.

A Serjeant, or Corporal, whofe fobriety, honefty, and
good conduct, can be depended upon, and who is capable
to teach writing, reading, and arithmetic, fhould be employed to act in the capacity of fchool-mafter, by whom foldiers and their children may be carefully inftructed: a
room or tent fhould be appointed for that ufe; and it would
be highly commendable if the Chaplain, or his deputy,
would pay fome attention to the conduct of the fchool.

The Commanding Officers of companies fhould be defired
to prevent, as much as poffible, the inconveniencies and ill
confequences produced, by having too many foldiers married; for their wives are in general fo abandoned, as frequently to occafion quarrels, drunkennefs, difeafes, and defertions; they involve their hufbands in debt; and too oft
are the ruin and deftruction of a foldier: it is therefore recommended, that the Non-commiffioned Officers avoid entering into fuch engagements, without confulting their
Commanding Officer; and that they ufe their utmoft endeavours with the private men to prevent all fuch marriages
as they think are detrimental to his Majefty's fervice.

The Commanding Officer muft be ftrict in putting in
execution the Articles of War againft fwearing; the penalty
for

for which is one shilling, beside further punishment for the second offence: the soldiers should be cautioned to break themselves of a custom which is wicked, unsoldier like, and contrary to the Articles of War.

An Officer of a company should march the men to church every Sunday, and remain there during the time of divine service: if any Non-commissioned Officer or soldier absents himself from church, or leaves it before service is over, he should pay and suffer the penalties expressed in the Articles of War.

The Non-commissioned Officers should instil into the heart of a soldier, that obedience is the foundation of regularity and order; that by this, discipline is maintained, and great designs are executed; but that without it all is confusion.

If a Non-commissioned Officer will not behave himself conformable to orders, he should be considered as unworthy of his preferment, and accordingly reduced.

The Serjeants should be brave and prudent, as absolute in their commands to inferiors, as subordinate to their superiors: they should apply themselves to their duty, and be equitable and just in their accounts, write a good hand and understand accounts. The Corporals must inform the recruits of all kinds of military duties that are needful for them to learn; teach them the respect they are to pay to their superiors; and that when sentry the security of their post depends upon their vigilance: acquaint them with the method of challenging rounds, patrols, &c. and be careful, while planting a sentry, that he receives the full orders.

If a private soldier should think himself aggrieved, or ill used, by any Serjeant or Corporal, he must not only restrain from abusing him; but, on the contrary, in the first place obey, and then lay his complaint before the Commander of his company, who will apply to get him justice: but the greatest care is to be taken for preventing all frivolous and ill-grounded complaints; for misplaced indulgence will retort upon himself.

The Articles of War should be read every two months; after which, the Non-commissioned Officers and private men are to be accounted with for stoppages and arrears, and the balance due to them paid by the Commanding Officers of companies, after deducting the sums advanced them for necessaries. Each man is to sign his own account.

If the commanding Officer of a company goes from the

regiment,

regiment, his accounts fhould be left with the next Officer in rank; but if there happens to be no Commiffion-officer, they fhould be fealed up, left with the Serjeant, and given to the next Officer that comes.

The Non-commiffioned Officers and private men fhould, at leaft once a week, receive their pay.

A WEEKLY PAY-NOTE.				
One Week's Pay and Arrears for the of 17 to the			Company, from both Days inclufive.	

To	Serjeants ——— ——— ———	*l.*	*s.*	*d.*
	Corporals ——— ——— —			
	Mufic ——— ——— —			
	Drummers ——— — — —			
	Fifers ——— ——— —			
	Private Men — — —			

		l.	*s.*	*d.*
To	flints — —			—
	cartridge paper — { } —			
	repair of arms — { } Total —			

Received the above fum, in full of all demands, to the day of 17

 A. B. Pay-mafter Serjeant.

Encouragement fhould be given to all country people for bringing provifions to the market; and a Non-commiffioned Officer of each company muft go to market with the men, to prevent their quarrelling with them, or others, upon any occafion. If the price of provifions is exorbitant, application muft be made to the Chief Magiftrate or Provoft, who will regulate it. A foldier guilty of any infolence, or of ufing harfh words to any perfons, fhall, upon proof, be punifhed, according to the nature of the offence, by a Court-martial. A black-hole fhould be provided, free from damp, as dark and difmal as poffible, but fupplied with clean and dry ftraw once a week. To this, foldiers for offences are to be fent; and confined in proportion to the heinoufnefs of their crimes; for abfenting from the drill 24 hours

hours for the firſt offence ; for the ſecond, 48 ; but for the third they ſhould be ſent priſoners to the guard, and tried by a Court-martial.

Care muſt be taken that no man under ſentence of a Court-martial drinks any ſpirits before or after puniſhment. I once knew an inſtance of a priſoner, who, to damp the pain of his puniſhment, was brought intoxicated to the halberts; he was returned back to the guard-room ; but in a ſhort time after he died, from the violent effect of drams. Had he received his puniſhment, which he juſtly deſerved, it is probable, deſigning perſons might have imputed his death to that.

Compliment of Neceſſaries to be furniſhed each Soldier.

THREE ſhirts ; 2 white ſtocks ; 1 black hair ſtock ; 1 pair of braſs claſps for ditto ; 3 pair of white yarn ſtockings ; 2 pair of linen ſocks, dipped in oil, to be worn on the march, under ſpatterdaſhes, when neceſſary ; 2 pair of white linen gaiters, if belonging to the guards ; 1 pair of black long garters, with black tops for ditto ; 1 pair of half ſpatterdaſhes ; 1 pair of linen drawers ; 1 pair of red ſkirt breeches ; 1 red cap ; 1 cockade ; 1 knapſack ; 1 haverſack ; 1 pair of ſhoe-buckles ; 1 pair of garter-buckles ; black leather garters ; 2 pair of ſhoes ; 1 oil bottle ; 1 bruſh and picker ; 1 worm ; 1 turnkey ; 1 hammer-cap, and 1 ſtopper.

The company's ammunition, arms, accoutrements, cloths, and neceſſaries, muſt be inſpected weekly, by an Officer of a company, and a report made to the Commanding Officer of their ſtate.

INSPECTION REPORT.

I have inſpected   company's ammunition, arms, accoutrements, cloths, and neceſſaries.

Ammunition in	——	——	
Arms in	——	——	——
Accoutrements in	——	——	
Cloths in	——	——	——
Neceſſaries in	——	——	

To   the Officer commanding   [*Sign name* the   regiment of foot.   *and rank.*

N. B. If it is a report of the light company, after *Accoutrements in,* the Inſpector ſhould inſert

Powder-horns in	——	——
Bags for ball in	——	——

     Men

Men lofing their arms are to be charged for each firelock, 1l. 10s. each bayonet, 5s. each ramrod 2s. The price of a fword cannot be afcertained, as the charge muft be according to the goodnefs of thofe ufed in the corps. The above articles muft be charged to each man's account; alfo all repairs of arms and accoutrements, which can be made appear, before a Regimental Court-martial, to have been damaged or fpoiled by negleĉt. Whenever any of the above compliment of neceffaries are loft or worn out, the foldier is immediately to be fupplied with others. No man, properly provided with neceffaries, fhould be ftopped more than his arrears, except his neceffaries are much worn, and he alfo in debt to his Officer; in which cafe he is to be ftopped fixpence weekly befides his arrears. If it is neceffary to ftop more, it muft be by order of a Court-martial; and then it is not to exceed half of his pay, though the foldier fhould have made away with all his neceffaries, which is too oft the cafe; and, to avoid punifhment, fuch men are fometimes fo abandoned as to defert their colours.

In grenadier and battalion companies, each man fhould be provided with, and carry what follows: 1 ammunition-box, to contain 24 rounds of powder and ball, with 2 flints, which are not to be ufed but in cafes of neceffity; a machine to cut and cock hats; a powder-bag; a ream of whited brown paper; 3 locks; 1 dozen of fcrew-pins; 3 fpare pans; 6 iron ramrods; a mould to caft bullets; a ladle to melt lead, and a former to make cartridges. The caliber of his barrel muft be particularly attended to.

Each man in a light company fhould carry 12 rounds of powder and ball, made into cartridges; 4 pounds of lead and 1 quart of gun-powder, which will make about 58 cartridges.

Befides the ufual fmall articles, each Serjeant and Corporal muft carry a mould to caft bullets, and a ladle to melt lead in, with 3 fpare powder-horns, and 12 bags for ball.

The companies muft be formed into fquads; the firft of which fhould confift of the eldeft Serjeant, with the front rank; the fecond, of 2 Corporals, with the centre, and the third, of the youngeft Serjeant, with the rear rank. If any Serjeant or Corporal is fick, on party, or furlough, then the care of a fquad muft be given to the youngeft Corporal. The Serjeants and Corporals of fquads muft take pains with their recruits, in making them drefs with a foldier-like air, inftruĉt them in cleaning their arms and accoutrements, and

how

how to mount and difmount their firelocks, as no man fhould be fuffered to do it for another.

S Q U A D R O L L.		
FRONT RANK.	CENTER RANK.	REAR RANK.
Eldeft Serjeant. *A. B.* Drummer.	Eldeft Corporal. Youngeft Corporal.	Youngeft Serjeant. *C. D.* Fifer.

When the regiment is in barracks, a Subaltern Officer is daily to vifit them, the meffes, and regimental infirmary, between 10 and 12, and make his report to the Commanding Officer of the condition they are in ; if the rooms, galleries and ftairs are clean fwept, and the beds rolled up ; what number of meffes are in each company, and how fupplied with provifions ; the number of patients in the infirmary, and how they are attended.

Report

Reports of the barracks, meſſes, infirmary, &c. of the
regiment of foot.

I viſited the barracks, found them   beds
galleries and ſtairs   infirmary
attended. N° of patients.

Meſſes ſupplied with	Beef.	Mutton.	Pork.	Broth.	Fiſh.	Potatoes, or Bread.	N° of Meſſes.
Colonel's - - -							
Lieutenant-colonel's							
Major's - -							
Captain's {							
Total							

To
The Officer commanding   [*To ſign name and*
regiment of foot.   *rank here.*]

If billeted in Britain, an Officer of a company ſhould
viſit the mens quarters every pay-day, and aſk their landlords if the men behave well.

An Officer, when dreſſed for guard, ſhould have his
hair queued, his faſh, gorget, and eſpontoon, (except in
fuzileer corps, where they are to carry fuzees) buff-coloured
gloves, black linen gaiters, with black buttons and ſmall
ſtiff tops, black garters, and uniform buckles. The guards
ſhould be exerciſed every morning, by an Officer of the
guard, before they march off the parade, Sundays and field-
days excepted. Whilſt the retreat is beating, all guards
are to be under arms, when the Officers ſhould examine
their mens arms and ammunition, and ſee that the number
of priſoners committed to their charge are properly ſecured;
for the eſcape of a priſoner implies a remiſſneſs of duty.
After tat-too beating, patrols are frequently to be ſent to
make all ſoldiers priſoners they find out of their barracks
or quarters.   No

No Officer is to change his guard, or other duty, but by leave of the Commanding-officer; and even then he muft fend information to the Adjutant.

All Officers, commanding detachments, are, upon arrival at their deftined poft, to make a report to the Commanding Officer of all extraordinary accidents or deficiencies on the march.

When an Officer defires leave of abfence, if he has not the command of a company, he muft firft apply to the Officer commanding it, and then to the Commanding-Officer: when he has obtained leave, he muft acquaint the Adjutant for what time; and leave directions with him in writing, how he may be wrote to. If any Officer has leave of abfence from the regiment, he is not to take any foldier with him, without leave from the Commanding Officer; and no foldier attending upon any Officer fhould be excufed from his duty on field-days. Officers are defired to be very ftrict in confining and reporting all men, of any company whatever, whom they fee either drunk or difor-derly.

The young Officers fhould be kept at head-quarters till acquainted with their duty; and attend all Court-martials, for the fpace of 6 months, to obtain a thorough knowledge of their inftitutions, their laws, their power, and bufinefs,

Form of a Regimental Court-Martial.

Proceedings of a regimental Court-martial of the regiment of foot, commanded by held at this day of 17 By order of

Captain *A. B.* Prefident.

Lieutenant *C.* }
Enfign *E.* } Members. { Lieutenant *D.*
{ Enfign *F.*

Prifoner's Crime.] *G. H.* of the above regiment, and Captain *J*'s Company, confined by *K. L.* . . . . for . . . .
. . . .

Evidence.] *M. N.* informs the Court . . . .
. . . .

Prifoner's Defence.] *G. H.* . . . .
. . . .
. . . .

Sentence.]

Sentence.] The Court having duly confidered the evidence for and againft the prifoner, are of opinion, that he is guilty of a breach of the   article of the   fection; and alfo a breach of the article of the   fection of the Articles of War; and do fentence him to receive   lafhes, with a cat-o'-nine-tails, on his bare back.

A. B. Capt. and Prefident.

If the delinquent is to be drummed out of the regiment, it is proper to annex, That it is the further opinion of the Court, that the prifoner *G. H.* is, and he is hereby adjudged, unfit to have the honour of being a foldier; and, therefore, it doth order, that he fhall be drummed out of the regiment, with a halter about his neck, and a label pinned on his breaft and back, upon which is to be wrote, in large charaĉters, the crime for which he is brought to public infamy: and, to prevent his being entertained in another corps, the fentence of the Court-martial is to be inferted in his difcharge.

A. B. Capt. and Prefident.

I approve of the above proceedings, this
day of   17

[*The Commanding Officer to
fign his name and rank.*

When it happens that one company fhall receive a private man from another, to be promoted, the company that receives him fhall give him the choice of their company; grenadiers, light company, Gunners, and two private men, excepted: when they have no Gunners, four private men are to be excepted.

The grenadiers and light company fhould be kept complete with men, whofe health, ftrength, and aĉtivity, can be depended on.

No man fhall be difcharged who is fit for fervice, but upon procuring 2 good men in his place, or paying 10 guineas to the ftock-purfe.

D I S C H A R G E.

By   of his Majefty's   regiment of
foot, commanded by
Thefe are to certify, that the bearer hereof
private foldier, has ferved in the above-faid regiment, and
                    company, for the fpace of   years;
                                                             and

and is, for the reason below-mentioned, discharged from the said regiment, he having received his pay, arrears of pay, clothing of all sorts, and all other just demands, from the time of his inlisting in the said regiment to this day of his discharge, as appears by his receipt on the back of his discharge; he is discharged, having

And to prevent any ill use that may be made of his discharge, by its falling into the hands of any other person whatsoever, here follows the description of the above-said

aged   years,   feet   inches high,   complection,   hair, eyes, born in the parish of   in the county of   by trade

Given under my hand and regimental seal, at this   day of   17
[*Seal.*]

To all whom it may concern, civil and military.

I   do acknowledge to have received all my pay, arrears of pay, clothing of all sorts, and all other just demands, from the day of my inlisting into the said regiment to this day of my discharge.

[*Signed by the discharged man on the back of the receipt.*

Witness present,

N. B. If the person discharged is intitled to his Majesty's royal bounty, it is to be mentioned in the discharge.

Form of Advertising.

Deserted from the   regiment of commanded by A. B. and company, quartered at   C. D.   years of age,   feet   inches high, complection,   hair,   eyes; had on, when deserted,   coat,   waistcoat, breeches; born at   in the county of by trade a   inlisted by at   the   day of

17

Whoever

Whoever fecures the faid deferter, fo as he may be brought to juftice, for having been guilty of perjury, &c. fhall receive from the Commanding Officer of the faid regiment, at head-quarters, or of the Agent to the faid regiment, at his houfe   the fum of
                                over and above what is allowed
by act of parliament.

It is requefted of all well-wifhers to his Majefty's arms, that they caufe a copy of this advertifement to be pofted up at the moft public place.

All returns demanded from the companies, muft be figned by the Commanding Officer of each company, with his rank.
Proceedings of all regimental Courts-martial are to be entered in a regimental book, which is kept at head-quarters for that purpofe.

Orderly hour at   at the orderly room, where the Serjeant-major, Quarter-mafter Serjeant, with a Serjeant and Corporal from each company, Drum.-major, Fife-major, and the Mafter of the band of mufic, attend for orders.
An Orderly-ferjeant muft daily attend on the Commanding Officer of the regiment.

Of a Field-day.

TO keep the regiment perfect, they muft have 2 field-days a week, at leaft, and the manœuvres oft varied; which will improve and direct the Officers, inftead of tiring their patience with repetitions of the manual exercife.
The Officers, on fuch days, fhould have their hair queued, and appear in regimental frock fuits, with their fafhes, gorgets, and efpontoons or fufees. The Non-commiffioned Officers and private men muft plat and tuck up their hair; be fully accoutred; put on their black linen gaiters, tops and uniform buckles.

Method of fending for the Colours.

THE Officers having taken their pofts, the colours are thus to be fent for: viz.
The Major orders the grenadier drummers and fifers to beat and play the drummer's call; which is a warning for the Officers who carry the colours, the drummers and fifers. He then orders a flam; upon which the Officers, drummers,

mers, and fifers, face to the right, the Officers advancing
their efpontoons at the fame time; and, on the immediate
found of another flam, they march to the head of the grenadiers, and turn to their proper front. The Captain then
orders the company to advance their arms, and marches off
in the following order.

Captain.

Lieutenants.

Enfigns.

Fife-major.

Fifers.

Drum- major.

Drummers.

Firft divifion of grenadiers.

* * * * * * * Serjeants.

* * * * * * *

Serjeant * * * * * * *

Second divifion of grenadiers.

* * * * * * *

* * * * * * *

* * * * * * * Serjeant.

So foon as the Captain comes to the place where the colours are lodged, he muft draw up his company 3 deep,
with the Serjeants in the rear; and then give the following
words of command.

Fix your bayonets.

Shoulder your firelocks.

When the Enfigns receive the colours, the Captain gives
the word;

Prefent your arms.

Upon which the grenadiers prefent their arms, the Serjeants charge their halberts, and drummers and fifers beat
and play a point of war: after which the Captain orders;

Shoulder your firelocks.

Advance your arms.

To the right (or left) *wheel.*

March.

They march back to the battalion, beating and playing the
grenadiers march.

When the colours approach the left flank of the battalion, the Commanding Officer orders, *Prefent your arms,*
and *face the battalion to the left,* the drummers and fifers
beating and playing a point of war, and the mufic " God
fave

save great George our King." The Captain of grenadiers
makes 2 wheels to the left; the second division of grenadiers moves up to dress with the first: and both open their
ranks in the second wheel, so as to be in a direct line with
the ranks of the battalion. When the grenadiers halt, the
music, drummers, and fifers, cease; on which the Commanding Officer gives the word,

To the right, as you were.

The whole face to the right; the Captain of grenadiers
followed by his Lieutenants; behind whom the Ensigns,
with the colours, move briskly to the right: the Officers
and colours march in front of the line of Officers; the
fifers and drummers between the Officers and front rank of
the battalion : the front rank of grenadiers between the front
and centre of the battalion ; the centre rank of grenadiers
between the centre and rear rank; and the rear rank of
grenadiers along the rear rank of the battalion. When the
Ensigns come to the centre of the battalion, they are to fall
in, and dress with the line of Officers. The grenadiers,
having returned to their post on the right, get the words of
command from their Captain,

Turn to the Front.
Halt.
Shoulder your firelocks.
Unfix your bayonets.
Shoulder.

N. B. The Ensigns have their arms advanced in going
for the colours, as well as the grenadier Officers and Serjeants ; but in returning they display flying colours instead
of their arms.

Every Officer should, upon the colours passing by, take
off his hat; this being a respect due to the colours. The
Officers who carry them are not to take off their hats in
return, except when they salute with them.

FIELD

FIELD RETURN.

	Commissioned officers present						Staff-Officers.					Non-commissioned Officers and private men				Detail of Officers and Men on Duty.						
	Colonel	Lieut. Colonel	Major	Captains	Lieutenants	Ensigns	Chaplain	Adjutant	Quarter-Master	Surgeon	Mate	Serjeants	Corporals	Drumrs. & Fifes	Private Men	Places where.	Captains	Subalterns	Serjeants	Corporals	Drumrs. & Fifes	Private men
Under arms																						
On duty																						
Sick in quarters																						
Sick in barracks																						
Sick in infirmary																						
Sick in hospital																						
Prisoners																						
Absent by leave																						
Total Effectives																						
Wanting to compleat the Allowance.																						
Total																						

Manual Exercise.

THE manual exercise is certainly a branch of military discipline, necessary to render the soldier steady, adroit, &c. but as it is not of sufficient importance to engage his whole attention, *and is subject to frequent alterations,* I shall give no farther directions about it, than assist the young Officer and drill in fixing.

The

The Pofition of a Soldier under Arms.

Every foldier muft be perfectly attentive, remaining totally filent and fteady, and not make the leaft motion with
head, feet, body or hands, but as directed. He muft ftand
ftraight and firm upon his legs, incline his head to the right,
keep his heels clofe, turn his toes a little out, and draw the
belly a little in, but without conftraint; his breaft muft be
a little projected; his fhoulders fquare to the front and kept
back; the right hand hanging ftraight down the fide, with
its palm clofe to the thigh, and the left elbow not turned
from the body. The firelock muft be carried on the left
fhoulder, as low as can be admitted without conftraint; the
3 laft fingers under the butt, the fore-finger and thumb before the fwell, the flat of the butt fupported againft the hip-
bone, and fo preffed, that the firelock may be felt againft
the left fide, and ftand before the hollow of the fhoulder,
without leaning either towards the head or from it; the
barrel muft be almoft perpendicular.

Manœuvres, &c. and Explanations.

A Manœuvre or movement fhould be diftinct, fimple, natural, and executed by the fhorteft means; for troops
may be taught to perform them, at a fingle word or fign.

To render a manœuvre ferviceable, befides celerity, there
fhould be a connection between each company, divifion and
battalion, fo that they may be able to fupport one another,
in cafe of accidents, that the ftrength of the troops may encreafe every moment, and be continually in readinefs for re-
pulfing the enemy at thefe critical moments, where they
fuddenly ftop with defign to attack.

WORDS OF COMMAND.

*By Battalions, Wings, or Grand Divifions,——Form Column
from the Centre.*

THE 6 centre files move forward, the wings face inwards, and, marching by files to the front, follow the
centre files. If the column is formed by battalions, the
grenadiers and light companies face with the wings, and
follow them; if by the wings, the grenadiers and light companies, marching obliquely to the right and left, poft themfelves at the head of each column; if by grand divifions, the
grenadiers and light companies will poft at the head of the
right and left columns of the battalion.

Reduce

Reduce the Column.

EXCEPT the centre files, the whole column faces outward; when each wing wheeling to the right and left to the front, they form battalion. If the column was formed by battalion, the grenadiers and light company wheel with the wings; if by wings, or grand divisions, they face outwards, and march by files to their former posts on the flanks.

By Companies—Form Column from the Centre.

THE 2 centre companies move on slowly forward; the grenadiers and light company, with those on the right and left, face to the centre and march by files. When the Officers see their companies joined they give the word of command, To the front, turn, on which the column is formed.

Form Battalion.

THE 2 centre companies keep in motion, without gaining ground; the other 6, with the grenadiers and light company, face outwards, and march by files. So soon as they have got ground enough to march in front, the Officers of companies will give the word, To the front, turn. When the whole have got up, a signal is given from the centre for the battalion to move forward.

Grand Divisions to the Centre form Column by Files to the Front——March.

EACH grand division leads out by files, marches obliquely towards the centre and forms in one body on the march. The column is then formed.

Take Care to form Battalion.

THE divisions turn to their front, and gain their proper distance.

Form Battalion.

THEY wheel and form——N. B. The grenadiers and light company are to be disposed of in such manner as the Commanding-officer shall direct.

Grand Divisions by Files form Column to the Rear—March.

BY files they lead out to the rear, marching obliquely towards the centre and form in one body on the march. The column is then formed.

Take

Take Care to form Battalion.

THE grand divifions turn to their fronts, and gain their proper diftance.

Form Battalion.

THEY wheel and form——*N. B.* The difpofition of the grenadiers and light infantry muft be agreeable to the direction of the Commanding-officer.

By Grand Divifions form Column to the Right—March.

THE battalion are now fuppofed to be in 1 line: the grand divifion on the right marches 12 paces, the fecond 8 paces, the third 4 paces, and the 4th on the left ftands faft. When the divifions have made the number of paces ordered, the 3 divifions on the left, with the light company, face to the right, and march by files, till they cover the right-hand grand divifion; which then receives the word from the Officer, *To the front, turn.* The grenadiers march obliquely to the left, till they come oppofite the centre of the firft grand divifion; and the light company cover the rear of the column.

March to Clofe Order.

THEY clofe up to the front, and complete the column.

Form Battalion.

THE grenadiers turn to the right, and march by files to their former poft: the firft grand divifion ftands faft; and the other 3, with the light company in the rear, turning to the left, keep marching by files. When the Officer, commanding the fecond divifion, fees he has ground enough to form on the left of the firft grand divifion, he gives the word, *To the front, turn;* on which it marches up, and joins the firft grand divifion. 2 divifions, and that of the light company, form in the fame manner.

A column, by receiving the enemy's fire, and falling in immediately among them, muft neceffarily defeat them and diforder their troops.

Grand Divifion march to Half Diftance.

IF the battalion is marching in grand divifions, the grand divifions clofe to half diftance.

Form the Square.

THE front and rear divifions keep moving on very flow; and the right hand companies of the other 2 wheel to the right.

right. So foon as they have performed their wheelings, they
turn to the left, and form the right face of the fquare: while
the left companies move contrarywife, and form the left.
The grenadiers, being fubdivided, march obliquely to the
right and left, and leave an interval for the front of the
fquare, with which they drefs. The light company alfo
marches obliquely to its right and left, and dreffes with the
rear face of the fquare, which then is formed: if halted, the
grenadiers and light company cover the angles.

Reduce the Square.

THE front and rear faces continue marching; the right-
hand companies of the 2 other divifions wheel to the left by
files, and the left-hand companies to the right. When the
Commanding-officers of companies fee them joined, they
will each give the word, *To the front, turn*: on which the
divifions of grenadiers will advance brifkly by the oblique
ftep, and join oppofite the centre of the firft grand divifion;
while the divifions of the light companies march by files, till
they join in the rear of the fourth grand divifion; when the
Officer will order, *To the front, turn.*

Companies march to Half Diftance.

IF the battalion is marching by companies, they clofe to
half diftance with a quick pace.

Form the Oblong Square.

THE companies being told off, in 2 platoons, they wheel
to the right and left, proceeding in every refpect as already
directed for forming the fquare, the grenadiers making the
front face, and light company the rear.

Halt.

THE fquare ftands faft.

Reduce the Square.

THE platoons wheel, as before directed for the companies
in reducing the fquare.

March to clofe Order.

THE companies clofe up.

Form Battalion.

THE grenadiers turn to the right, and march by files to
their poft on the right: the firft company on the right ftands

N 3   faft;

faſt; the other 7 companies, and the light company, turning to the left, march by files. When the Officer, commanding the ſecond company, ſees he has ground enough to
form on the left of the right-hand company, he gives the
word, *To the front, turn:* upon which it marches up and
joins; when the Officer orders them to halt. In like manner do the other 6 companies and light company.

Second Method of forming the Oblong Square.
Form the Oblong Square——March.

THE left wing of the battalion, and the light company
on the left, face to the right; the whole ſtep off; the right
wing advances 8 paces in front, then turns to the left, both
wings marching as faced, till they double as far as the ſecond
company on the right and left of the battalion.

To the Front, turn.

EXCEPT the right and left hand companies of the battalion and the grenadiers and light company, both wings turn
to the front; the right wing forms the front face, and the
left wing the rear; the right hand company of the battalion
wheeling to the right by files, form the right face; while
the grenadiers do the ſame, to cover it; the left-hand company wheels contrarywiſe, and forms the left face; while the
light company do the ſame, and covers it.

Reduce the Square.

THE right wing of the battalion turning to the right,
and the left wing to the left, each marches as faced till they
have room to form battalion.

To the Front, turn.

THE grenadiers and flank companies wheeling up, while
the battalion turns to the front, the left wing march up eight
paces, and form the battalion.——*Halt.*

Third Method of forming the oblong Square.
Form the oblong Square.

THE 2 centre platoons and the grenadiers ſtand faſt; the
wings and light company facing inwards.

March.

THE centre platoons march forward; and the grenadiers
obliquely to the left, till they cover the centre platoons; the
                                                            wings

wings wheel into the right and left by files, following in the rear the flanks of the centre platoons, till the wheel comes to the flank platoons, which platoons join in the rear, turn to their front, and form the rear face; the light company marching on till it covers the rear face, turns to the front.

Form Battalion.

THE grenadiers turn to the right, and march by files to their former poft; the centre platoons ftand faft, the wings keep marching till the front file of each platoon comes clofe to the rear of the centre platoons, at which time each platoon has the word of command from its own Officer, *To the front, turn*; they then march to the right and left, and wheel up to their refpective places in battalion, and fo on to the 2 flank platoons, who face to the right and left, march by files, and form on the flanks; the light company faces to the left, and marches by files to its poft on the left of the battalion.

Battalion pafs the Bridge.—March.

THE grenadiers and light company advancing brifkly to the river, fire obliquely at the head of the bridge, till the front of the battalion comes up to it, when they fhould march and follow the battalion by files; the 2 centre platoons of the battalion moving forward, the wings face to the centre and wheel by files in the rear of the centre platoons. When the battalion has paffed the bridge, the Commanding Officer fhould give the word of command.

Form Battalions.

ON which the 2 centre platoons are to ftand faft, and begin to fire by word of command from their refpective Officers; the other platoons marching on till the front file of each platoon comes clofe to the centre platoons; then the Officer commanding gives the word, *To the front, turn*; when, marching to the right or left, they wheel up to their proper places in battalion, and begin to fire fo foon as formed : the battalion keeps a continued fire from the centre to the flanks (including the grenadiers and light company) till the Commanding Officer orders them to ceafe.

Battalion repafs the Bridge.

THE grenadiers and light company, with the 2 centre platoons, make ready, and the battalion faces outwards. Upon the word *march* to the battalion, the grenadiers, light

com-

company, and centre platoons, will begin firing. When the grenadiers and light company have fired, they will march obliquely to the centre, halt, and fire, at leaft once, before they join in the front of the centre platoons, who will have fired as oft as poffible.

March.

THE right and left wing of the battalion countre-march in the rear, wheeling by files on the ground they ftand on, until the head files of each meet in the rear of the centre platoons ; at which time they wheel up and continue their march for the bridge. When the laft files of the wings have wheeled, the 2 centre platoons get the word of command from their own Officers, *to the right about, march*—and march in the rear till the battalion have repaffed the bridge. When the head files have paffed, they wheel to the right and left outwards, taking care to obferve the proper diftance for the battalion to form. The centre platoons will march 4 paces beyond the battalion, where they turn to the right and left outwards. The grenadiers and light company will fire once after the centre platoons go to the right about ; they then recover their arms, and go likewife to the right about. When they have paffed the bridge, and come clofe to the centre platoons, they will turn to the right and left outward, and march by files along the rear of the battalion to their pofts on the flanks. The Commanding Officer then gives the word of command,

Turn to the Front—Halt.

WHICH done, the centre platoons march up into their interval, and form battalion.

N. B. A bridge may fometimes be made over rivulets, or large wet ditches, by cutting down the trees that grow frequently on the banks, and throwing them parallel to each other acrofs the ftream ; fafcines may be made of the boughs, to crofs them again ; and the whole covered with turf, &c.

Take care to pafs the Defile.

To pafs a defile where only two men can march in front, the 2 centre files muft ftand faft, while the grenadiers, light company, and wings of the battalion, face inwards.

March.

March.

THE 2 centre files march forward, the wings move to the centre, and, when they join, a file from each wing will turn to the front and follow them.

Form Battalion.

THE 2 centre files ſtand faſt, while the others run up and dreſs with the centre ones : the files on the right wing form on the right of each other ; and thoſe of the left wing form on the left.

Battalions, *Wings, or Grand Diviſions, advance by Files from the Right, or Left.*

THE whole turn to the right or left, and each wing or grand diviſion leads out by files from the right or left, while the grenadiers and light company do the ſame, and keep dreſſed with the front files of the battalion.

Form Battalion.

THE front file of each wing, or grand diviſion, the grenadiers, and light company, wheel to the right or left.

Turn to the Front.

THE whole turn to the front.

Battalions, *Wings, Grand Diviſions, or Companies, retreat by Files from the Right or Left.*

THE whole face to the right or left.

March.

EACH battalion, wing, grand diviſion, or company, wheels off by files to the right or left ; and the grenadiers and light company do the ſame.

By Files to the Right, or Left, Wheel—To the Front, turn— Halt.

THIS forms the battalion.

Battalions, *Wings, Grand Diviſions, or Companies, form Ranks intire.*

ALL, except the right hand file, turn to the right.

March

March.

THE right hand file march forward, while the others move on till they come to their ground ; they then turn to the front and follow the front file.

Form Battalion.

THE 3 firſt men ſtand faſt, the reſt march up in files upon the left of them, and form the battalion.

Battalion, advance from the Right by Files.

THE battalion turns to the right, and wheels to the left by files.

From 3 deep, form 2 deep.

EVERY ſecond and third file being told off from the right, opens an interval ſufficient for a file to march into.

March.

THE men in the rear of each file face to the left and come up with a quick pace into the interval.—They are then formed 2 deep.

From 2 deep, form 3 deep.

THE men that moved up, fall back again into their for-mer file.

Spring to the Centre.

THE right and left wing of the battalion ſprings to the centre, and the battalion is formed 3 deep again.

From Grand Diviſions, form Companies.

THE right hand company of each grand diviſion conti-nues marching forward, the left hand companies turning to their right and marching by files. When the Officers ſee that they cover the right hand companies, they will turn them to the front ; while the grenadiers and light company inclining to their right, cover the front and rear.

In this manner the battalion is to be formed into wings, grand diviſions, companies, and platoons. The ſignal is the pioneers' march. To form large bodies from ſmall, the ſignal is the troop ; on beating of which, if the battalion is marching in platoons, the right hand one of each company will keep in motion, without gaining any ground ; the left hand platoons will march obliquely to their left, and form on the left of the right hand ones. The grand diviſions, in
like

like manner, will be formed from companies, the wings from divifions, and battalions from wings.

In marching by the oblique ftep, in ranks, companies, fub or grand divifions, wings, battalion or column, a particular attention muft be paid by the Officers, Non-commiffioned Officers and foldiers, that they are parallel to their front.

To complete files in action, the battalion is to incline from the right and left to the centre of the battalion; which the Officers and Non-commiffioned Officers in the rear are to make them do with expedition.

If the battalion fhould at any time be crouded, or confined in their ground, the Captain, or Officer commanding a grand divifion, may order his centre platoon to fall back till the battalion can extend itfelf again.

To form a difperfed Regiment.

THE great advantage of this confifts in a regiment being able to form in a moment; therefore every Officer, Non-commiffioned Officer, and private man, muft know his right hand man, file, leader, and company, that he may, with the utmoft agility, be formed ready for whatever may prefent itfelf. When a regiment is fuddenly alarmed, repulfed by the enemy, or has performed this evolution, it may thus be formed again with the utmoft celerity. Commanding-officers fhould therefore accuftom their regiments to this evolution, that they may know how to form in the inftant they are ordered.

Take care to difperfe—March.

THE Officers, with the colours, march 6 paces forward.

A long Roll.

BY the 2 orderly drummers, difperfes the regiment.

To Arms.

THE battalion form, and the Officers, Non-commiffioned Officers, and private men, fall into their own files and drefs by the colours.

N. B. The Commanding-Officer fhould be careful of informing his men that their difperfion by an enemy is the greateft misfortune which can attend a battalion; yet, even in this cafe, they are not to look upon the action as loft;

for,

for, by their being accuftomed to rally, he may foon be able to form them again, and retrieve their honour.

FIRINGS.

THREE VOLLIES IN THE AIR.

THE ranks are to ftand at half diftance, and make ready as centre rank.

Preparative.
Make ready.
Prefent.

They prefent in the air.

Fire.

They fire, come to the priming pofture, and proceed to load and fhoulder.

Preparative.
Make ready.
Prefent.
Fire.

Go on as before.

Preparative.
Make ready.
Prefent.
Fire.

They fire and recover.

Flam.

They half cock.

Flam.

They fhoulder.

Flam.

They fhut pans.

After this they are to give 3 huzzas, firft taking off their hats with the 2 following motions.

Take the right fide of the fore-cock in the right-hand; tell 1, 2, lift it off, and hold it above the head. After the huzzas, they put them on at 2 motions; bring the hats to their heads, fix them; tell 1, 2, and let their hands fall down gracefully by their fides.

A FEU DE JOY.

THE ranks are to be clofed to half diftance; and, when they prefent, they are to raife their muzzles pretty high to fire in the air. The men of each file are to fire together; that is, each file diftinctly by itfelf; and fo run quick, from one file to another, from right to left.

STREET

Street Firing.

This method of firing is only used when troops are under the necessity of engaging in a street, defile, or highway, where many men cannot march in front. In whatever manner you fire in front, it must not be equal to the breadth of the place. An interval must be left on each flank, through which those who have fired, may have room to march by files to form in the rear.

Take Care to perform the Street-firing.

March.

The fifers and drummers play and beat a march. The whole step on with their left feet; and, upon the preparative, the first company receive a command from their own Officer to

Halt.
Make ready.
Present.
Fire.

After which the men recover their arms, and face outwards from their centre.

March.

They go down the flanks by files, form in the rear, load, shoulder, and keep marching to the front, till they are ordered to fire again.

When 1 company has fired, the next takes up its ground, fires and files off in the same manner. When the general beats, the firing ceases.

N. B. This firing is to be performed by each company retreating; when the first has fired it immediately divides in the centre and faces outwards, and marches by files to the rear, while the next presents to fire, without advancing to the ground of that which fired before them. The usual notice for this fire is a preparative, and the retreat beating immediately after.

Parapet Firing.

When a breast-work, or parapet, is to be defended, I would draw up my men 2 deep; not only to extend my front, but to prevent disorder in going through the intervals.

Upon the Preparative.

The front rank, with the Officers, march up to the breast-work, or parapet; the men with recovered arms, and the Officers with theirs advanced, who then give the word of command.

Present.

Prefent.
Fire.

After which they recover their arms, go to the right about; and, upon the word

March,

they go to the rear; the other rank marching up through intervals open for them to pafs.

OBLIQUE FIRING.

WHEN a battalion is ordered to fire obliquely to the right, the front rank turns on the left heel, throwing the right leg back to the left of the centre rank men in that file; the centre rank face on both heels; the rear rank turns on the right heel, ftepping forward with the left toe to the centre rank men of that file.

Prefent.
Fire.

The whole come to their proper front, load and fhoulder.

OBLIQUE FIRING TO THE LEFT.

THE front rank turns on the left heel, ftepping back with the right foot to the right of the centre rank men of that file; the centre rank turns on both heels to the left; the rear rank turns on the left heel, ftepping forward, with the right toe to the centre rank heels of the fame file.

Prefent.
Fire.

The whole come to their proper front, load and fhoulder.

N. B. In both the above firings, the Officers go in the rear of the intervals.

For other firings, fee page 105.

Method of lodging the Colours.

SO foon as the colours are ordered to be lodged, the grenadier drummers and fifers beat and play the drummer's call; on which the enfigns, with the colours, drummers, and fifers, except thofe ordered to remain with the battalion, repair immediately thither, and draw up as before. The Captain of grenadiers is then to order his men to fix their bayonets and advance their arms; and, when the Commanding Officer has ordered the battalion to prefent their arms, he is to march back the colours to the place where they are to be lodged, the drummers beating and fifers playing the troop as before. The colours are to be carried advanced and flying; but, fo

foon

foon as they arrive at the place, and the company is drawn up, they are to furl them ; and, at the time of lodging, pay the fame compliments as at the time of receiving them: when this is done, the Captain orders the men to unfix their bayonets and advance their arms; after which he is to march back in the fame manner he conducted the colours to the battalion, unlefs ordered to difmifs them there.

The Enfigns return with their fwords drawn, and refted over the left arm.

Roll-Calling, Morning Reports, Regulations for Duty, &c.

AN Officer of a company is to attend the morning roll-calling. When the troop beats, the companies will turn out ; and then the Serjeants or Corporals of the different fquads muft make an exact infpection ; after which an Officer is to infpect them, and, if he finds the Serjeant or Corporal has not made him an exact report, he is then immediately to confine him. After the Officers have made their infpection, the oldeft Officer on the fpot fhould review them ; and, if he finds any foldier not according to the order of the regiment, the Officer who makes the report muft be anfwerable for it, as it is expected that he examined every man particularly. A morning report muft be figned by each Officer of the company who infpected the men ; and all extraordinaries that happened in the preceding 24 hours muft be inferted.

Morning Report of		Company	of	17
Serjeants.	Prefent fit for duty — On duty		N A M E S.	
	Total			
Drummers.	Prefent fit for duty — On duty			
	Total			
Fifers.	Prefent fit for duty — On duty			
	Total			
Rank and file.	Prefent { fit for duty - { not fit			
	On duty —			
	Sick in { quarters — { barracks — { infirmary — { hofpital —			
	Recruiting —			
	On { furlough — { command —			
	Prifoners —			
	Abfent { by leave — { without —			
	Total			

One Captain and 2 Subalterns fhould attend at retreat beating, and report thofe that are abfent without leave, drunk, or improperly dreffed.

A Major fhould be active, vigilant, and well acquainted with the ftrength of the battalion and detail of the corps, as that duty and knowledge is effentially requifite in him; he fhould alfo be well inftructed in the exercife, and every kind of manœuvre. When the Major is abfent, the oldeft Captain fupplies that poft.

The Adjutant fhould do no duty but that of the Adjutant. When a young Officer joins the regiment, he fhould give him a copy of thefe orders, and acquaint him that he muft immedi-

ately

ately prepare an orderly book, wherein all orders relative to exercise, and other duties, are to be correctly inferted. The Adjutant fhould be very exact in reading the orders of the day to the men at roll-calling, and to keep his rofter and rolls for duties very clear; that no Officer may be fent on party, or put on duty, out of turn.

The Serjeant-major muft keep a rofter and role of duties of the Non-commiffion Officers and private men.

The Serjeants and Corporals muft keep the fize and duty rolls of their particular company, and the Drum and Fife-Major take care of thofe for their drums and fifes.

Regulation for doing Duty.

IN all duties, whether with or without arms, piquets or court-martials, the tour of duty fhall begin with the eldeft downwards.

1ft, Duties of honour.

The King's guard, the Queen's guard, the Prince of Wales's, and the Captain-General's, or Field-marfhal's, commanding the army.

2d, Detachments of the army and out-pofts.

3d, General Officers guards.

4th, The ordinary guards, either in camp or garrifon.

5th, The picquets.

6th, General courts-martial.

7th, Without arms, or of fatigues.

An Officer who is upon duty, cannot be ordered for any other before that duty is finifhed, except he be on the picquet.

If an Officer's tour for duty happens when he is on the picquet, he fhall be immediately relieved, and go upon that duty. The tour of the picquet fhall pafs him, though he fhould not have been on it a quarter of an hour.

If an Officer's tour for the picquet, general court-martial, or duty of fatigue, happens when he is on duty, he fhall not make good that picquet, court-martial, or fatigue, when he comes off, but his tour fhall pafs; and the fame if he be on a general court-martial, or duty of fatigue; for if his tour for guard or detachment fhould then happen, his guard or detachment fhall pafs, and he fhall not be obliged to make them up.

Guards or detachments, which have not marched off from the place of parade or rendezvous are not to be reckoned as a duty done; but, if they fhould have marched from the place

O of

of parade, it ſhall be reckoned as a duty, though they ſhould be diſmiſſed immediately.

General courts-martial that have aſſembled, and the members ſworn in, ſhall be reckoned a duty, though they ſhould be diſmiſſed without trying any perſon.

The King's ſtandard, in the guards, is never to be carried on any guard but that of his Majeſty's.

The firſt colour of regiments is not to be carried on any guard but the King's, Queen's, Prince of Wales's, or Captain general's, he being of the Royal Family: except in thoſe caſes, it ſhall always remain with the regiment. The union is the firſt colour.

The Quarter-maſter, though he ſhould have another commiſſion is to do no duty but that of Quarter-maſter. While the regiment is on actual ſervice, he is to take care of the ammunition and ſtores of the regiment; attend on all days, that coals, forage, &c. is delivered to the regiment; and prevent carriers, or any idle perſons uſually attending at ſuch times, from committing any fraud.

The Surgeon muſt keep a book, and enter therein the name and diſtemper of each man under his care, ſpecifying the day he was ſent, and whether to the regimental or other infirmary.

The Surgeon and his Mate are to viſit the infirmary every morning, and as often as occaſion requires. Every Saturday they are to make a return of the ſick, inſerting every man's name, his diſorder, and the company he belongs to.

Return

Return of the fick in the _____ Regiment of _____ commanded by _____ at _____ of _____ to _____ with an Account of the Pay of each fick Soldier in the Regimental Infirmary, from the _____ of _____ following, inclufive.

Companies.	Men's Names.	Difeafes.	When admitted.	Subfiftce. l. s. d.	Expences. l. s. d.	Ballance. l. s. d.	Difcharged from the Infirmary.	Where fick.
In quarters In barracks In infirmary In hofpital								

The Surgeon fhould lay a ftate of the expences of the infirmary, and other matters relating to it, before the Infirmary Board, the firft Monday in every month, for their infpection.

When the regiment is ordered under arms for exercife, the Surgeon, or his Mate, is to fign a return of the fick and lame of each company, which is to be given in with the field-return.

The Surgeon, or his Mate, muft attend morning and evening roll callings, at all times when the regiment is under arms; and be prefent at all punifhments, to judge if the delinquent's life is in danger, that no punifhment may extend to life or limb.

Drill Serjeants and Corporals are to take particular care of their fquads, teach the recruits how to fix their flints fo as to procure the moft fire, (for where fire is certain, it generally kills) caufe them to be fteady and filent under arms, to hold up their heads, and carry their arms well. Great attention muft be had in the inftructing of recruits how to take aim, and that they properly adjuft their ball. No recruit fhould be difmiffed from the drill, till fo expert with his firelock, as to load and fire 15 times in 3 minutes and three quarters.

Sounds of the Drum.

It is neceffary that recruits fhould be inftructed to know the founds and beatings of the drum before they are difmiffed from the drill, as, whether it be the general, affemblé, march, reveille, troop, retreat, tat-too, to arms, parley, chamade, &c. as they are thereby taught to march and perform their exercife, manœuvres, &c. It is alfo very proper to teach them every other found and fignal.

To beat the general, is an order for the whole to make ready to march; the affemblé to repair to their colours; and the march commands them to move: the reveille, at daybreak, warns the foldiers to rife, and the fentries to ceafe challenging; the troop affembles them together, to call over the roll and infpect the men for duty: the retreat is beat at fun-fet, for calling over the roll again, to warn the men for duty, and read the orders of the day: the tat-too beats at ten every night in fummer, nine in the winter; the foldiers muft then repair to their quarters or barracks, when the Non-commiffioned Officers of each fquad call over their rolls, and every man muft remain there till reveille-beating next morning. A beat to arms, is to advertife them to ftand to their

arms,

arms, or to repair to their alarm pofts; and a parley, or chamade, is to defire a conference with the enemy.

S I G N A L S.

Turn or face to the right	1 fingle ftroke and flam
Turn or face to the left	2 fingle ftrokes and flam
To the right about - - -	3 fingle ftrokes and flam
To the left about - - -	4 fingle ftrokes and flam
To wheel to the right - -	Roll, 1
To wheel to the left - - -	Roll, 2 (fingle ftrokes and
To wheel to the right about	Roll, 3 flam
To wheel to the left about -	Roll, 4
To front - - - - - -	Strong double flam
To make ready - - - -	Preparative
To ceafe firing - - - -	General
To march - - - - -	March
Quick pace - - - -	Quick march
To charge bayonets - - -	Point of war
To form battalion - - -	To arms
To eafe	Tow-row-dow
To fecure your arms -	Firft part of the tat-too
To fhoulder	Laft part of ditto
To call the Adjutant - -	Firft part of the troop
To call a Serjeant and Cor- poral of each company	3 rolls, 6 flams
To call all the Serjeants and Corporals	3 rolls, 9 flams.
To affemble the pioneers -	Pioneer's march
To affemble the drummers and fifers	Drummer's call.

If a Non-commiffioned Officer or private man is miffing after an engagement, and joins his company unhurt, he will be tried for his life.

If any Serjeant or Corporal drinks, or keeps company with the foldiers, drummers, or fifers, or conceals from his Officer any indecent or unfoldier-like behaviour among them, he will be reduced for it.

No Serjeant employed to buy neceffaries for the men fhall receive any advantage thereby, except that of employing his wife to make up the linen; and even that fhall be abfolutely at the choice of the men, for whom it is bought, who fhall be prefent at the buying, and fee the money paid; nor fhall he extort from the men, under pretence of money advanced, fince the Officer who commands the company will fupply

O 3   what

what is wanting; the more effectually to stop all proceedings of this kind, if any soldier, drummer, or fifer, should make full and clear proof of the above-mentioned fraud, he shall receive 1 guinea reward, and be put in any other company he desires, provided the complaint be lodged within 2 months after the fact is committed.

No Serjeant shall presume to go on party, or furlough, without leaving whatever accounts of the company he may have by him, either with an Officer or a Serjeant.

Any Serjeant, Corporal, drummer, fifer, or soldier, who goes on furlough, and does not return at the expiration of it, must expect to be punished for disobedience of orders, unless it is occasioned by sickness; then he is to get his furlough properly certified by an Officer of the army; if none be there, by the Chief Magistrate; and a letter must be wrote to the Commanding-officer of the regiment, acquainting him of his sickness and place he is at.

F U R L O U G H.

By . commanding his Majesty's
regiment of whereof
is Colonel.

Permit the bearer hereof private
soldier in the above regiment, and
company, aged years, size feet
inches high without shoes, born in the
parish of in the town of
in the county of by occupation a
to pass and repass from his present
quarters at in to
in he having leave of absence for the
space of days, to which time he is subsisted,
and at the expiration of which he is to repair to the quarters of the company he belongs to, wherever it may happen to be (sickness and contrary winds excepted) on pain of being treated as a deserter, should he not punctually comply with the terms of this furlough.

Given under my hand and seal of the regiment, this
day of 17

(*Seal.*) to the
above regiment of

N, B

N. B. It is requefted, that no Officer, either civil or military, will renew this furlough, except for the reafons before-mentioned.

Form to renew a Furlough, when detained by contrary Winds.

THESE are to certify, that   private foldier in the   regiment, and company now quartered at   in   came and acquainted me, that he waited for a paffage to   being wind-bound. I therefore renew this furlough for the fpace of   days, he behaving as becometh. Given under my hand, this   day of   17
A. B.   of the   regiment.

Form of a P A S S.

By   regiment of foot.
    Permit the bearer   private foldier in the above regiment, and   company, to pafs from hence to   for the fpace of   days, to join his colours or company, be behaving as becometh a foldier.

A. B.

                        in the   regiment.
To all concerned.

Serjeants and Corporals, fent on command, are ftrictly ordered, on their arrival in town, after the men have received their billets, and refrefhed themfelves, to fee that they pull off their gaiters, and appear, in ever refpect, as at their quarters.

No Serjeants, Corporals, drummers, fifers, or private foldiers, are to appear in the barrack-yard, or ftreet, without their hair being well platted and tucked under their hats; their fhoes well blacked, ftockings clean, black garters, black ftocks, buckles bright, and cloaths in thorough repair.

If any man be flothful, or not dreffed according to order, the Serjeant, or Corporal of the fquad, muft affift in making him obedient to it, and report the behaviour of fuch a man to his Officer.

A Serjeant or Corporal of each company muft be conftantly in the way to receive any orders that may be given,

and

and to attend the parade at the difmounting of guards, take their ammunition from the men, and fee them draw their arms if loaded.

A Serjeant or Corporal of each company muft attend the recruits and aukward men, when they parade for exercife, to fee they are properly dreffed, their arms and accoutrements well put on, and in perfect order.

A Serjeant or Corporal of each company muft go round the barracks or quarters of their companies, fo foon as the tat-too has beat, and report any men that are abfent. Every morning, before troop beating, one of them is to fee that the mens arms and accoutrements are properly placed, their beds well turned up, and the rooms, ftairs, and galleri s clean fwept.

All Serjeants and Corporals are to confine any drummer, fifer, or foldier, whom they fee gaming; which they are ordered never to be guilty of, as they will be punifhed for difobedience.

All Serjeants and Corporals are to confine any drummer, fifer, or foldier, they meet drunk or diforderly.

No Serjeant or Corporal fhall fell any kind of liquors.

When any cafualties happen in a company, the Pay-mafter-ferjeant muft take care to preferve the regimentals, that the fucceeding recruit may be clothed in like manner with his brother foldier, provided the foldier had not worn them 1 year; if he had, his wife or child fhould have them.

RETURN

RETURN of the Casualties of a Company,

Company.	Mens Names.	Dead.	Deserted.	Draughted.	Discharged.	Drumm'd out.	Cloths.				Necessaries.					Remarks.
							Coat.	Waistcoat.	Breeches.	Hat.	Shirts.	Stockings.	Rollers or Stocks.	Spatterdashes.	Shoes.	

The Serjeant of a guard is to infpect every relief of fentries, before the Corporal marches them off; and no man, who appears the leaft intoxicated, fhould be fuffered to ftand fentry.

The Pay-mafter-ferjeant of each company fhould keep by him a wig, which will drefs in the regimental form, left any man by ficknefs lofe his hair.

All ammunition delivered out for the ufe of each company muft be kept by the eldeft Serjeant of the company.

RETURN of Ammunition, Flints, &c. in each Company of the Regiment of commanded by	Companies.	Cartridges with ball.	Cartridges withoutball.	Loofe ball	Loofe powder.	Loft and damaged.	Quires of Cartridge Paper.	Flints.	Ammunition, &c.
17									

A Corporal

A Corporal, when he pofts a fentry, fhould carefully inftruct him in his duty ; and the fentry muft endeavour to know thofe who are intitled to refted arms ; a young recruit fhould be pofted fentry the neareft to the main-guard's protection.

If a Corporal either pofts or relieves a fentry irregularly, he fhould be broke.

A Corporal at relieving is not to fuffer any fentry to wear a watch-coat, or take fhelter in his fentry-box, except in very bad weather, to prevent his arms being wet; and this indulgence is only to be given, when no enemy is near.

A return of the fick and lame muft be given every morning to the Surgeon or his mate, by the Corporal of each company.

Return of the fick, &c. of morning	company 17			
Lame in { quarters, A. B. Serjeant	—	—	—	I
{ barracks, C. D. Corporal	—	—	—	I
Sick in { infirmary, E. F. drummer	—	—	—	I
{ hofpital, G. H. fifer	—	—	—	I
			Total	4
To The Surgeon.				
			J. K. Corporal.	

The Corporal fhould always have a brufh on the parade, that the foldiers cloths may be clean brufhed.

The Drum and Fife-majors, with all the drummers and fifers off duty, are to beat the troop, retreat, and tattoo beatings every day.

The Drum and Fife-majors muft take particular care that the drummers and fifers are properly dreffed, their drums and fifes in good order, and that they practife together twice a week. No drummer or fifer to beat or play after tattoo, or before reveille beating, on pain of fevere punifhment, except by order of the Commanding-officer. The Drum-major to be anfwerable that no cat has more than 9 tails.

All

All the muficians, drummers and fifers in action, except the 2 orderly drummers and fifers, are to ftay with their refpective companies, and affift the wounded.

The Muficians muft attend roll callings, and at all times when the regiment is on march or under arms; the moft fkilful fhould be appointed to act as mafter of the band; to his care and infpection the others fhould be fubjected, and he fhould be anfwerable for their clean and uniform appearance; but they are not to play except by order of the Commanding Officer.

The Non-commiffioned Officers and foldiers when they meet an Officer, either of the army or navy, in his Majefty's fervice, fhall pull off their hats, and be careful of their carriage, that they may not contract an unfoldier-like air.

No foldiers muft carry coals, or any other thing, on their heads, when they have their regimental cloths or hat on; nor muft they carry any children about the barrack-yard or ftreet. No man fhould be allowed to work who does not produce to his Officer a coat and hat for that purpofe; or excufed from being under arms, with the regiment or company, under pretence of working, or any other reafon, but that of being included in the Surgeon's lift.

The Pioneers, in clearing away a country for the paffage of the corps, are to fet up branches of trees from 50 to 100 paces, with leaves, furze, ftraw, grafs or hay, faftened to them; and where alterations have been made to the detriment of any adjacent villages, a proper detachment muft be pofted all night, that the inhabitants may not deftroy the work. Where there are any hollow ways which are very narrow, the pioneers muft widen them, and make a ditch on each fide.

The pioneers are to have an ax, a faw, and an apron, a cap with a leather crown, and a black bear fkin front.

No man, returned in the fick lift, muft go out of his barracks or quarters, without leave from the Surgeon or his Mate; if recovered, he is expected to conform in every refpect, to the order of his regiment.

Any man prefuming to cut off his hair, except thought neceffary by the Surgeon or his Mate, fhall be confined for difobedience.

If the accoutrements want cleaning, the men are to rub off the dirty fpots, with a wet woollen cloth, put fome colouring-ball upon the place, and, when dry, rub it off with

a hard

a hard brufh; but never fcrape them with knives, fciffars, or any thing that may cut them.

No foldier muft make ufe of his bayonet to turn the cock-fcrew of his firelock, or otherwife damage that ufeful weapon.

As the men's arms are properly numbered, fo that each may know his own, therefore no man is allowed to put any private mark upon his firelock.

No man fhall take his arms or accoutrements out of his barracks or quarters, unlefs for duty, or to learn his ex-ercife, without leave from a Commiffion or Non-commif-fioned Officer.

Whatever man's firelock fhall mifs fire twice, or be de-fective in any part, the man to whom it belongs, if he neglects to report it to his Officer, fhould be fent to the drill for a month, and make good the duty he miffes dur-ing that time.

Any men who fire their pieces without orders, or occa-fion falfe alarms by drawing their fwords, beating of drums, or any other means, if in Great Britain or Ireland, fhall be moft feverely punifhed; but if in foreign parts, they fhall be tried by a General Court-martial.

Any man convicted of felling his ammunition, clothing, or other neceffaries provided for him, on any pretence what-ever, without leave from his Officer, fhall be punifhed with the utmoft feverity.

No man, upon any pretence, muft be above 1 mile from quarters, without leave from the Commanding Officer; neither fhall they drain ponds, fifh, fhoot, deftroy rabbits, fearch for game, cut trees, climb over hedges, ditches, break down fences, or give the leaft offence. The man who dif-obeys any part of the above order, fhall be confined and tried for difobedience.

Every man muft retire to his barracks or quarters, whenever there is any mob, bull-baiting, or foot-ball matches, on pain of being confined for difobedience of orders.

No man being drunk on guard, party, duty, or under arms, is to expect the leaft lenity.

The man who fhall ufe any infolent fpeeches, or geftures, to provoke another, fhall be fent to the black-hole for 14 days, and then afk his pardon in prefence of the Com-manding-officer.

All recruiting-parties fhould confift of 1 Commiffion-offi-cer, 1 Serjeant, 1 Corporal, 1 drummer, and 2 private men.

RE-

RECRUITING-INSTRUCTIONS *for A. B. of the*
Regiment of Foot, commanded by   *the*
            Day of   17

1. You are to enlift no man who is not a Proteftant and a native of Great Britain ; if any Irifhman, or foreigner, through miftake, fhould happen to be approved of, and, within 3 months after joining the regiment, fhall be difcovered to be fo, he will be difcharged at your lofs ; provided it can be made appear, the Officer had reafon to fufpect him.

2. You are to enlift no man under the age of nor above   unlefs he has ferved in the army ; in which cafe he will be accepted of, provided he does not exceed   years of age. No man who has been whipped or drummed out of any regiment, will be approved of ; if any fuch is found out, within 3 months after joining the regiment, he will be difcharged at your lofs.

3. You muft inlift no man under the fize of 5 feet   without fhoes, or who has not ftraight limbs, broad fhoulders, a good face, and every way well made. Neither muft you enlift any man who cannot wear his hair, who is thin, or has the leaft defect in his knees.

4. You will take particular care to have all your recruits carefully examined by a Surgeon ; for a man who is fubject to fits, or has any appearance of a rupture, broken bones, fore legs, fcald head, ulcers, or running fores, on any part of his body, old wounds ill cured, or any infirmity in body or limb, will not be approved of, but will be difcharged at your lofs, if difcovered within 3 months after joining the regiment. Should you difcover that your Serjeant, Corporal, or other man of your party, knew that any of your recruits was afflicted as above, and concealed it from you, he or they fhall be brought to a Court-martial, and feverely punifhed.

5. All recruits muft be duly attefted before a magiftrate ; a receipt taken on the back of their atteftations, and witneffed, for the bounty-money agreed on. If any of your party inlift a man for you, you muft allow him 5 fhillings as an encouragement.

The atteftations of inlifted men are to be fent to the regiment by the Serjeant or Corporal who brings the recruits to quarters, who is to deliver them to the Commanding
                              Officer,

Officer, and he give them to the Adjutant, that recourse may be had to them, if neceſſary.

6. You muſt inliſt no ſtrollers, vagabonds, tinkers, chimney-ſweepers, colliers, or ſailors; but endeavour to get men born and bred in the neighbourhood of the country you are recruiting in.

7. For every recruit, approved of at the regiment, you will be allowed   out of which ſum no more than   ſhall be given to each recruit as bounty-money.

8. The non-effective fund ſhall be charged with the real expences of all the recruits who may die before they join the regiment, provided the day of their death, and the exact bounty-money given them, be certified on the back of the atteſtation.

9. Not leſs than   recruits ſhall be ſent at a time; they are to go under the care of a Serjeant or Corporal to the regiment, with money to ſubſiſt them.

10. You muſt take great care that the recruits furniſh out of their bounty-money, with linen, ſhoes, ſtockings, &c.

A return of their neceſſaries muſt be ſent with them to the regiment, ſigned by you, and alſo a return of the ſir-name, age, ſize, country, and deſcription of each recruit, &c.

11. All ſubſiſtence given to the recruits before they join their regiments, ſhall be charged ſeparately from the levy-money.

When you arrive at the place where you are to recruit, you will write to the Commanding-officer at head quarters, to acquaint him of it; and alſo if you change your place of recruiting.

No Serjeant, Corporal, drummer, fifer, or private man, once inliſted in this regiment, muſt be diſcharged, but as the Articles of War direct.

When you ſend any recruits to the regiment, you muſt give notice of it to the Agent by letter, incloſing a ſtate of your account.

N. B. When directions are given to inliſt lads for drummers or fifers, they are to be inſerted in the certificates; when the Commanding-officer ſhall think proper, they ſhall be put into the ranks, and ſerve as private ſoldiers, without being intitled to any further bounty-money.

Form

Form of a Beating Order.

G. R.

THESE are to authorize you, by beat of drum or otherwife, to raife fo many volunteers in any county or part
of our kingdom of Great Britain, as are or fhall be wanting
to recruit and fill up the refpective companies of our
regiment of foot, under your command, to the number allowed upon the eftablifhment; and you are to caufe the
faid volunteers, to be raifed and levied as aforefaid, to march
under the command of fuch Commiffion or Non-commiffioned Officer, in fuch numbers and at fuch times, to any
place or port you fhall think proper: and all Magiftrates,
Juftices of the Peace, Conftables, and all other Our civil
Officers whom it may concern, are hereby required to be
affifting unto you in providing quarters, impreffing carriages,
and otherwife as there fhall be occafion; and for fo doing,
this Our order fhall remain in force for 12 months from the
date hereof, and no longer.

Given at Our Court at St. James's, this
day of   17   in the
year of Our reign.

By his Majefty's command,

The S P E E C H.

To all afpiring heroes bold, who have fpirits above flavery
and trade, and inclinations to become gentlemen, by bearing arms in his Majefty's   regiment, commanded
by the magnanimous   let them repair to
the drum head [*Tow-row-dow*] where each gentleman volunteer fhall be kindly and honourably entertained, and enter
into prefent pay and good quarters: befides which, gentlemen, for your further and better encouragement, you fhall
receive   advance; a crown to drink his Majefty King GEORGE's health; and when you come to
join your refpective regiment, fhall have new hats, caps,
arms, cloths, and accoutrements, and every thing that is
neceffary and fitting to complete a gentleman foldier.

God fave their Majefties, and fuccefs to their arms.

Form of an Atteftation.

I *A. B.* do make oath, that I am a proteftant, and born
of proteftant parents; that I am no apprentice, nor belong
to

to any regiment of militia, or to any other regiment in his Majefty's fervice; that I am by trade a   and, to the beft of my information and belief, was born in the parifh of   in the county of and kingdom of   and that I have no rupture, nor was ever troubled with fits; that I am no way difabled by lamenefs or otherwife; but have the perfect ufe of my limbs, and that I voluntarily inlifted myfelf to ferve his Majefty King George, as a private foldier, in the   regiment of   commanded by   and that I have received all the inlifting money which I agreed for. As witnefs my hand this   day of   17

Witnefs prefent,

C. D. of the above   A. B. Recruit.

Regiment.

These are to certify, that the aforefaid
aged   years   feet   inches high,
                  complexion,   hair,   eyes,
                  made,   came before me, one of his
Majefty's   for the   and maketh
oath (as above) that he had voluntarily inlifted himfelf to ferve his Majefty King George, in the above-mentioned re-giment: he alfo acknowledged, that he had heard the 2d and 6th fections of the Articles of War read unto him, againft mutiny and defertion, and took the oath of fidelity, accord-ing to the directions of the third fection of the Articles of War, as follows:

E. F. Mayor.

I A. B. fwear to be true to our Sovereign Lord King George, and to ferve him honeftly and faithfully in the de-fence of his perfon, crown and dignity, againft all his ene-mies and oppofers whatfoever, and to obferve and obey his Majefty's orders, and the orders of the Generals and Officers fet over me by his Majefty.

So help me God.

A. B. Recruit.

Sworn before me the   day of
in the year of our Lord, 17
at   E. F.

P   Return

Return of Recruits raifed by ⸻ for ⸻ Regiment ⸻ 17

Names.	Age.		Size.		Born.		Defcription.			Inlifted		Former Service.			Neceffaries.		
	Years.	Months.	Feet.	Inches.	Town.	County.	Hair.	Byes.	Complexion.	When.	Where.	In what corps.	Years.	Months.	Shirts.	Shoes.	Stockings.

The Lieutenant-colonel, or Officer commanding the regiment, is not to make any alteration in its clothing, without further orders.

The mens new coats muſt be dipped in clean water, and dried in the ſun; after which each man muſt be fitted with a ſuit. A foraging-Cap and ſtopper, conformable to a pattern-one, muſt be made out of a part of the old coat; but the ſkirts muſt be taken into ſtore, and made into breeches, when the ammunition-breeches are near worn out.

Directions for making the Skirt-Breeches.

Each man muſt be meaſured, and care taken that they are lined with ſtrong new linen, are full in the ſeat, come well over the hips, and low under the knee, with a ſtrap for the buckle, and four buttons and button-holes.

No taylor muſt preſume to purloin or ſteal any part of the cloth; nor are the waiſtcoats to be worked upon, till the coats and breeches are well finiſhed, and fitted to the ſoldier. The offender if found out, will be ſeverely puniſhed.

REGULATIONS and ORDERS for a REGIMENTAL INFIRMARY.

EVERY ſoldier, when taken ſick, muſt be ſent to the infirmary, a portable chair ſhould always be in readineſs at the main-guard, to carry ſuch as are very ill; but, if not ſo, a Corporal and 2 men ſhould aſſiſt them.

The Orderly Corporal of the company muſt bring the pay, with the ſick man; and take care that the patient has a cap and a ſhirt, and ſearch him, that he may not carry into the infirmary, money, cards, dice, ſpirits or tobacco: nor is any clean linen to be brought, or foul fetched away, except by a Serjeant or Corporal. If the ſick man's meſs is put in, his meſs-mates muſt allow him his proportion in money, for the remainder of the week; and what is deficient muſt be advanced to make good his pay to the pay-day following.—

_s._   _d._ _per_ week is to be the infirmary allowance, till further orders: Serjeants, Corporals, drummers, muſicians and fifers, to pay the ſame. A Serjeant or Corporal of the Companies, who have any men in the regimental infirmary, are ordered to carry their linen every   and   ; on which laſt day they muſt alſo carry their ſubſiſtence, and pay it to the Serjeant attending the infirmary. If any ſoldier, while a patient in the infirmary, does not quietly ſubmit to the rules of the houſe, and directions of the doctor, he is to be

confined

confined in the black-hole, as foon as cured, for 24 hours; if notorioufly refractory, he fhould be tried by a regimental Court-martial. If a patient in the infirmary fhould break out from thence, he fhall, when recovered, be fent to the black-hole for 10 days.

A Serjeant or Corporal of a company muft vifit the fick in the infirmary twice every week, to know what linen they want; and he muft bring nothing to any patient but wearing apparel, without the Surgeon's or his Mate's permiffion. If any foldier fhould be detected in conveying fpirituous liquors to the fick in the infirmary, or is aiding or affifting thereto, he fhall be punifhed by the fentence of a Court-martial. If any Serjeant or Corporal is a patient in the infirmary, he muft be aiding and affifting to the Doctor, in keeping order and decency among the patients, and in detecting any mean practices committed in the infirmary: for if either Serjeant or Corporal connives at any thing improper to be brought in, or does not difcover it to the Surgeon, he will be reduced to the pay and duty of a private foldier.

The Serjeant attending the infirmary muft keep an exact account of the pay of each ward; fee it properly expended by the nurfe, according to the Doctor's directions; give receipts for coals, candles, and fheeting, and clofe the account every half week; that any man, who is to be difcharged on   , may have his overplus divided when he is difmiffed.

A Corporal of a company muft attend every and   afternoon, to receive the recovered men; and every man difcharged the infirmary muft be duty-free for 3 days, or more, at the difcretion of the Surgeon.

The account of money difburfed, and the dividend for each man, muft be given every   morning to the Surgeon, that the Commanding Officer may infpect it when he pleafes; and the Serjeant muft give a diftinct copy of that account to the Serjeant or Corporal who relieves him: which relief muft be weekly.

No fick foldier can have his wife employed as one of the nurfes; and if any of the nurfes hufbands are taken ill, fuch nurfe muft be difmiffed, or her pay difcontinued till the recovery of her hufband; but married men of good character, who live near the infirmary, and who have careful wives, if they are taken ill, may be allowed to remain in their lodgings, at the difcretion of the Surgeon.

When

When any man is taken ill of the fmall-pox, or any other peftilential diforder, he fhould immediately, upon the difco-very of the difeafe, be fent to as private and remote lodgings as can be had ; and all foldiers prevented from vifiting him, left the vifitors catch fuch diftempers, and communicate the infection. The fentry pofted at an infirmary muft fuffer no one to enter, unlefs accompanied by a Corporal or the peo-ple attending it : he is alfo to prevent the fick from coming out, or leaving their wards to trouble the kitchens. The fentry may be taken off every night at 10 (except any thing extraordinary requires his being continued) and planted again at day-break. Any of the men who have flight com-plaints, may attend the Surgeon at a place appointed, in the morning, when the Corporals are to give in their reports of the fick. The Surgeon muft make a report to the Com-manding Officer whenever any of thefe orders are not com-plied with, that the offenders may be punifhed for neglect.

REGULA-

REGULATIONS OF DIET FOR THE INFIRMARY.

Day of the week.	Meals.	FULL DIET.	HALF DIET.
Sunday and Thurfday.	Breakfaft, Dinner, Supper,	A pint of water-gruel. Eight ounces of boiled beef. One pint of broth.	A pint of water-gruel. Four ounces of beef, and a pint of broth. A pint of broth.
Tuefday and Saturday.	Breakfaft, Dinner, Supper,	A pint of water-gruel. Eight ounces of boiled mutton. A pint of broth.	A pint of water-gruel. Four ounces of mutton, and a pint of broth. A pint of broth.
Monday.	Breakfaft, Dinner, Supper,	A pint of water-gruel. A pint of rice-milk. Two ounces of cheefe, or one of butter.	A pint of water-gruel. A pint of rice-milk. A pint of water-gruel.
Wednefday.	Breakfaft, Dinner, Supper,	A pint of water-gruel. Twelve ounces of pudding. Two ounces of cheefe, or one of butter.	A pint of water-gruel. Six ounces of pudding. A pint of water-gruel.
Friday.	Breakfaft, Dinner, Supper,	A pint of water-gruel. A pint of barley-gruel. Two ounces of cheefe, or one of butter.	A pint of water-gruel. A pint of barley-gruel. A pint of water-gruel.

N. B. The men on full diet have a pound of bread and a pint of fmall beer daily.
The men on half diet have half a pound of bread and a pint of fmall beer daily.

When the regiment is entire, a picquet guard, confifting of 1 Captain, 2 Subalterns, 2 Serjeants, 2 Corporals, 2 Drummers, 2 fifers, and 50 private men, befides all other ufual guards, is to mount. The Subalterns are to be fent on vifiting rounds. Where no lefs that 4 companies are quartered, a guard of 1 Serjeant, 1 Corporal, and 12 private men, muft be mounted, with a picquet of 1 Subaltern, 1 Serjeant, 1 Corporal, 1 Drummer, 1 fifer, and 24 private men : where 3 companies are quartered, the guard muft confift of 1 Serjeant, 1 Corporal, 12 private men, and an orderly Officer for the day : but, where lefs than 3 companies are in quarters, a guard of 1 Serjeant, 1 Corporal, and 12 private men, and an Officer to ftay in garrifon or quarters. When any of the above guards are mounted, they are to hold in readinefs for all requifite occafions, and not only keep good order and regularity, but grant fuch affiftance to authorized magiftrates as demand military aid ; the magiftrates, however, remaining with the party. The demand muft be in writing, and figned.

When the regiment is ordered into cantonments, the Commanding Officer will difpofe of the companies in fuch manner as he fhall judge moft beneficial to his Majefty's fervice, paying a particular attention to appoint an Officer for each whofe conduct may be depended upon. The colours, Chaplain, Pay-mafter, Surgeon, Adjutant, Quarter-mafter, Serjeant-major, Quarter-mafter Serjeant, Drill-ferjeant, Corporal, and all the recruits, Drum-major, Fife-major, the Serjeant or Corporal appointed to act as School-mafter, with the mufic and fifers, are all to be kept at head-quarters. When 7 companies are ordered to march, the Lieutenant-colonel, with the colours, Staff-officers, mufic, &c. fhould march with them. A Major fhould command 4 companies ; and a Captain may march with either 3 companies or 1. A Lieutenant, with 1 Serjeant, 1 Corporal, 1 drummer, 1 fifer, and 27 private ; an Enfign, with 1 Serjeant, 1 Corporal, 1 drummer, 1 fifer, and 21 men ; a Serjeant, from 12 to 15, and a Corporal from 4 to 9 men. Surgeon muft attend the Field-officer's march ; and his Mate attend that of 1 or more companies. But, notwith-ftanding the foregoing regulations, Officers and Non-com-miffioned Officers, are obliged to march fometimes with more, and fometimes with lefs, as occafion requires.

The day before a regiment begins to march, the Quarter-mafter, or an Officer as fuch, is to be fent forward to pre-

pare

pare quarters againſt its arrival. Each man ſhould be provided with 24 rounds of powder and ball, have 2 flints,
and carry all his neceſſaries. The reveille muſt not be beat
in the morning that the regiment marches. When the
whole troops march off at once, the firſt beat is the general;
the ſecond, the aſſemblé; the third, a march; but if only
a part march off, the firſt beat is an aſſemblé; the ſecond,
a troop; and the third, a march. In Great Britain and
Ireland, I would have the regiment march by files, to prevent Interruption by narrow roads, carriages, or droves of
cattle. The Officer who commands the grenadiers, leads
the centre of the front file; and the Officer commanding the
battalion, leads the centre of the front file of the battalion:
the Lieutenant-colonel, when the Colonel is preſent, brings
up the centre of the laſt file of the battalion; and the Officer commanding the light company, covers him at the
head of its laſt file. The reſt of the Officers march upon
the outward flank of the front rank.

The drummers and fifers march in the ſame line; the
Serjeants, upon the outward flank of the rear rank; the
muſic, in a line by the colours; and the Major, Adjutant,
and Serjeant-major, upon the flanks. An advance rear,
and baggage-guard, ſhould be appointed in proportion to
the ſtrength of the regiment. No Officer, Non-commiſſioned Officer, or ſoldier, may leave his poſt, or quit his
file, without leave; the Officer that ſuffers it will be anſwerable for neglect. The regiment muſt behave with great
regularity upon the march; and before it enters any village,
town, or garriſon, an Officer muſt be ſent forward; that,
if troops are already there, he may wait on their Commanding-Officer for his permiſſion to march in. When
they arrive at their quarters, the credit of the regiment
ſhould be cried down, a place of parade appointed, the
guards mounted, the colours lodged in form at the Commanding Officer's quarters, and a ſentry poſted over them;
the alarm poſts muſt be fixed, and inſtructions given to the
men againſt whoring, drinking, gaming, and rioting.
Upon beating to arms, all Officers and ſoldiers who are not
upon duty, muſt repair with their arms to the alarm-poſts;
and the picquet-guard aſſemble where the colours are
lodged. If the alarm is occaſioned by fire, the pioneers are
alſo to aſſemble, but with their axes and ſaws only. The
Commanding Officers will give ſuch neceſſary orders as

the

the exigency requires for fecuring the effects of unhappy fufferers.

The regiment muft not march from its alarm-poft till difmiffed, except by order of the Commanding Officer.

Advance-guard.

IN a champaign country they may march as far as 400 yards in front ; but where it is interfperfed with woods, inclofures, defiles, &c. they are not to advance above 200.

This guard muft not only reconnoitre in front but on the flanks, to prevent their being unexpectedly attacked ; all ftraggling houfes or villages, through which the regiment is to march or pafs near, muft alfo be reconnoitred, that it may not be impeded.

When the Commanding Officer thinks it neceffary to view any woods or villages, he muft halt, at about the diftance of 50 yards, and fend a Serjeant with a few files to reconnoitre and fend him proper intelligence ; after which he continues the march. If they difcover any troops, he is to halt, and fend immediately to the Commanding Officer an account of fuch difcoveries. But if the enemy endeavours to fall upon him before the meffenger returns, he muft perform the ftreet-firing retreat till he joins his corps; if the ground he is forced to retreat on be very narrow, he muft reduce his guard, if numbers allow of it, into 2 platoons.

Baggage-Guard.

THE waggons are, if poffible, to be numbered by companies, and follow one another regularly. A covering party muft be appointed ; which, if the battalion is not ftrong, may, through neceffity, be the rear-guard. When the Officer has reafon to apprehend danger, he muft take every neceffary ftep to fruftrate the enemy's defigns, and deprive them of all opportunities to furprize him, or attack his baggage: for which purpofe it will be abfolutely requifite to have patroles upon the flanks, to difcover their ambufcade in time, fo as to take proper meafures effectually to counteract and difappoint them ; vigilance and attention in the paffage of hollow ways, woods, and thickets, muft be ftrictly obferved.

Rear-guard.

THE rear-guard is to march 100 yards in the rear of the baggage, and to make prifoners all foldiers who fhall have

stayed

ftayed behind the regiment, which many do to defert, maraud, or plunder. Therefore, the Officer muft be careful in having every place examined where they can be fufpected of concealing.

If any man is taken ill, and incapable of marching, 2 careful men of this guard muft be left with him, till 1 can be fpared to inform the Commanding Officer where fuch man is left, and what is his diforder.

This guard is alfo a fecurity for the battalion, and a protection to the baggage : for the inftant that any troops appear in the rear, or on the flanks, its Officer muft fend off intelligence to acquaint the Commanding Officer ; and, if attacked in the mean time, oppofe them in the beft manner he can, by retreating in a regular manner, and making a ftand at every fpot he can difpute. If the enemy fhould cut off his communication, he muft endeavour to gain the neareft place of fecurity; but he muft not attempt that while the fmalleft hope remains of being able to maintain his diftance, or while the baggage is in danger.

Directions for making up of the contingent Bill.

War-Office, Nov. 26, 1765.

" I AM to fignify to you his Majefty's pleafure, that for the future all demands for marches, and other contingent charges of the regiment under your command, fhall be fent, at Midfummer and Chriftmas, to the War-office directly. You will at the fame time tranfmit to your Agent a duplicate of the faid account.

" It is likewife his Majefty's pleafure that in the faid accounts, all expences fhall be entered under their true heads ; and no more charged on any head whatever than what was really and truly paid.

" That in the contingent bills there fhall be a column for the dates of the orders upon which the marches were made.

" That the marches fhall be fet down in the order of time in which they happened.

" That none but the ufual and cuftomary charges fhall be made, and no extraordinary charges fet down, unlefs vouched by a particular order from the Secretary at War, the date of which order muft be fpecified.

" And, for the more perfect exactnefs in ftating and vouching the aforefaid accounts, you will be pleafed to take

care,

care, that each Captain fhall give into the regimental Paymafter an account of what he has expended, figned by him, which accounts, certified by the Paymafter of the regiment likewife under his hand, fhall be delivered to the Commanding Officer for the time being ; to be fent, after examination by him as aforefaid, to the War-office and Agent with the following declaration figned by him.

" I certify upon honour, as directed by a letter from the Secretary at War, that the exact fums which are charged in this bill for the feveral contingent expences therein mentioned, are the actual fums which have been advanced, and no more, according to the beft of my knowledge and belief, after the moft careful examination."

" I am alfo to acquaint you, that all the declarations aforefaid, made refpectively by the Captains, Pay-mafter, and by yourfelf, will be regarded in the fame light as returns upon honour."

" *Warrant for regulating the non-effective Fund of the feveral Regiments of Infantry.*

" GEORGE R.

" WHEREAS We have judged it neceffary for Our fervice to afcertain the articles which may be charged againft the non-effective fund of Our marching rements of foot, excluding at the fame time all other articles whatever; that the faid fund may be kept apart for the purpofe of recruiting, and that the ballance which fhall remain (after fatisfying the charges hereby admitted) may be applied to other public military ufes : We have therefore thought fit to order and direct, that for the future no charge fhall be made againft the faid non-effective fund, but what comes fairly and evidently under the following heads, viz.

" The levy-money and expence of each recruit, and alfo his fubfiftence till he joins the regiment.

" Bounty-money to difcharged men, to carry them home.

" The fubfiftence of invalids difcharged, and recommended to Our royal bounty of Chelfea-hofpital, from the day to which they are fubfifted by the regiment, to that on which they are admitted on the penfion, or rejected by the board.

" Expences of beating-orders, and attefted copies thereof.
" Expences

" Expences of debenture warrants.

" Expences relating to deferters.

" Expences of the paffage of recruiting parties, and recruits, by fea, from and to the regiment.

" And whereas Our late Royal Grandfather, of glorious
memory, was pleafed to direct, by a regulation in 1743,
that the non-effective accounts of the feveral regiments of
infantry fhould be annually ftated on the 24th of June,
and that whatever ballance remained (after deducting £5
for every man wanting, to compleat, to be carried to the
credit of the fucceeding account) fhould be divided among
the Captains ; partly in aid of their extraordinary expences,
and partly as a reward of their care and diligence in compleating their companies ; which regulation Our faid late
Royal Grandfather was pleafed to fufpend during the late
war : And whereas We have judged that it will be more
for the benefit of Our fervice, that the allowance made to
the Captains fhould be limited ; We are pleafed to direct,
that, for the future, the non-effective accounts fhall continue to be fettled annually to the 24th of June, when £5
fhall be fet apart for each man wanting to compleat, at the
preceding fpring-review, and carried to the fucceeding accounts ; after which the ballance which fhall remain fhall
be divided among the Captains, provided it fhould not
exceed £20 to each Captain. And We are pleafed to
direct, that the fums fo paid to the Captains fhall be entered
as the laft charge in the non-effective account of each regiment. And Our further will and pleafure is, that in cafe
any furplus fhall remain on ballance of the non-effective
fund, annually ftated on the 24th of June, after deducting
£5 for every man wanting to compleat, (which muft be
carried to the credit of the fucceeding accounts, as aforefaid) and after paying to each Captain their entire allowance of £20 that ballance fhall be carried to the credit of
the fucceeding year's account. And the feveral Agents are
hereby directed to acquaint Our Secretary at War, upon
the fettling each year's accounts, with the amount of this
furplus or ballance for Our information.

" And We do further direct, that all other charges and
expences whatever, incurred by Our marching regiments
of foot, and which have been ufually allowed, fhall, for
the future, be inferted in the general half-yearly contingent
bill, ordered to be tranfmitted to Our Secretary at War,
by his letters bearing date the 26th day of November, 1765 :
Our

Our farther will and pleafure is, that in the keeping and making up the non-effective accounts of each of Our faid regiments, the following directions be for the future ftrictly obferved.

" That no more than   fhall be allowed to any Recruiting-officer for each man recruited by him; out of which fum no more than   fhall be given to each recruit, according to Our directions, fignified by Our Secretary at War, bearing date the 17th of December, 1765; but no charge whatever is to be admitted on account of recruits who may defert before they join the regiment.

" No Recruiting-officer fhall be allowed credit for the levy-money of any fuch recruits as fhall not be approved of by the Commanding Officer of each regiment refpectively; but their fubfiftence he fhall be allowed.

" The non-effective fund fhall be charged with the real expence of all the recruits who may die before they join the regiment, provided the day of their death, and the exact bounty-money given them, be certified by the Recruiting-officer on the back of the atteftation.

" All fubfiftence given to recruits, before they join the regiment, fhall be charged feparately from the levy-money. The accounts of all Recruiting-officers are to be ftated and fettled on or before the 24th of June. In regiments ftationed in Great-Britain, the recruiting accounts are to be figned by the Recruiting-officer, and by the Field-officer commanding at quarters; in regiments ftationed abroad, the faid accounts are to be figned by the Recruiting-officer, and by the Colonel, or one of the Field-officers, if either of them fhall be in Great-Britain.

" And Our pleafure is, that the above accounts, fo figned, fhall be good and fufficient vouchers to the Agent, for the credit given by him to each Recruiting-officer on the head of recruiting.

" That in all future ftates of the regimental accounts given in to the Reviewing-general, the number of recruits for which levy-money and fubfiftence are charged, fhall be particularly and feparately fpecified.

" And whereas it has been the practice in fome of Our marching regiments of foot, to allow the Captains, without accounts, the fubfiftence of the vacant men, in their refpective companies, arifing from vacancies which happen between the days whereon each Captain ufually receives the

fubfiftence

subsistence of his company ; it is Our express order, that, for the future, the Captains shall account for the vacant subsistence of each man, who shall die, desert, or be discharged, between the abovementioned periods, from the date of such death, desertion, or discharge ; and that the non-effective fund shall have credit for the vacant subsistence of every man from the day on which he is no longer entitled to subsistence.

" We are farther pleased to direct, that every Colonel shall himself carefully examine the non-effective account, previous to its being laid before the Reviewing-general. He is likewise to certify under his hand, that he believes it to be fair and exact ; and the Reviewing-general shall report to Us any articles which shall appear to him to be charged contrary to these Our orders; as likewise whether proper credit be given to the non-effective fund, for the whole vacant subsistence.

" All the aforesaid orders, regulations, and directions, We strictly charge and command all Reviewing-generals, Colonels, Commanding Officers, and Agents, of Our regiments of infantry, and all others whom they may concern, to follow and obey, under pain of Our highest displeasure.

" Given at Our court at St. James's, this 19 February, 1766, in the sixth year of Our reign.

" *By his Majesty's Command,*

BARRINGTON."

" *Warrant for regulating the Attendance of Officers belonging to the several Regiments of Infantry.*

" GEORGE R.

" WHEREAS We were pleased by Our warrant, 27th July, 1764, to establish certain rules and regulations for the attendance of the several Officers of Our regiments of foot within Our kingdom of Great Britain, with their respective corps ; And whereas We have since found it necessary, for the good of Our service, to establish some farther regulations for the attendance of the said Officers ; We have therefore judged it proper to revoke and annul Our Warrant above-mentioned, and we do hereby revoke and annul the same. And Our farther will and pleasure is, that,

that, in lieu thereof, and for the more effectual maintenance of good order and difcipline in Our faid regiments of
foot, the following rules be ftrictly obferved; for the exact
execution of which the Colonel and Field officer commanding each regiment are to be refponfible.

" 1ft. That with each battalion of infantry there be always prefent 1 Field-officer, 3 Captains; and 1 Subaltern
with each company.

" 2d. That the Colonel or Field-officer commanding
each regiment may grant leave of abfence to fuch other Officers whofe private affairs may require it, taking care
always to detain, or from time to time to call in, a fufficient
number of Officers to do the duty of the regiment, in cafe
it fhould be fo fituated as to require the attendance of more
Officers than We have hereby directed to be conftantly
prefent.

" 3d. That the Officers appointed to carry on the recruiting fervice fhall not be included in the number hereby fixed
for the conftant duty of the regiment, or in the number of
thofe who fhall be further called in by the Commanding-
officer for that duty.

" 4th. That the monthly return of each regiment be
made up and tranfmitted as ufual to Our Secretary at War,
and to the Adjutant-general of Our forces; and that the
return of the abfent Officers, which We have directed to
be made on the 14th of each month, fhall, in like manner,
be made up, and tranfmitted from the head-quarters of
every regiment in England to Our Secretary at War, and
to the Adjutant-general of Our forces; and from the regiments in North-Britain; to the Officer commanding on
that ftation for the time being; and the Commanding Officer by whom the faid returns fhall be figned, is carefully to
examine the fame, as he is to be refponfible that they are in
every refpect conformable to Our Regulations.

" 5th. That the number of Officers hereby ordered to
be prefent, fhall remain with their commands until they
fhall be relieved; and, notwithftanding the returns are
ordered to be tranfmitted on the 1ft and 14th of each
month, yet the Officers are to continue at quarters during
all the intermediate time, and the Commanding Officer is
hereby enjoined not to permit them to abfent themfelves
from the duty they are employed on, except in cafes of great
emergency, and then but for two days only: and all leaves
fo

fo granted are to be fpecified in the next return, with the reafons for granting them.

" 6th. That no application fhall be made either to Us, or to the Commander in Chief of Our forces, for a leave of abfence for any Officer of Our faid Regiments, except through the Colonel or Field-officer commanding the regiment ; and that all fuch applications fhall be fo regulated, that no particular Officer fhall be abfent from his duty too long at one time. The fame caution is to be obferved in limiting the leaves granted by the Colonel or Officer commanding each regiment.

" 7th. That every Officer, whether taken from the half-pay or otherwife, on being appointed to the regiment, fhall join it within 4 months at fartheft from the date of his commiffion, unlefs he fhall have obtained a particular leave of abfence, which is not to be granted except on very cogent reafons.

" 8th. That if any Officer, fo appointed, fhall exceed the time hereby limited, without a leave obtained for that purpofe, he fhall be returned *abfent without leave* ; and the date of his commiffion is to be fpecified in the return, it being Our firm intention immediately to fuperfede any Officer who fhall neglect to pay due obedience to this Our order.

" 9th. That every Officer newly appointed, and who has never before been in Our fervice, fhall, upon joining his regiment, remain in quarters until he fhall be perfected in all regimental duty.

" 10th. That no Officer belonging to any of Our faid regiments ftationed in Great-Britain, fhall go out of the kingdom without leave obtained of Us, the warrant for which is to exprefs the time for which the leave is granted, and is to be entered in the office of Our Secretary at War.

" 11th. All Officers, while prefent with their corps, are conftantly to wear their uniforms.

" 12th. Every Officer is to be prefent with his regiment annually in England by the 10th of March, and in Scotland by the 10th of April, and remain with it till after the fpring review : And this Our order is upon no account to be difpenfed with, except a particular leave fhall be obtained for that purpofe from Us, or the Commander in Chief of Our forces ; and no fuch leave fhall be applied for, except in cafes of abfolute and unavoidable neceffity.

" 13th. All

" 13th. All Recruiting-officers and recruits are to join their respective corps in England by the 10th of March, and in Scotland by the 10th of April ; as We do expect that Our regiments on each station shall be compleat annually by those respective days.

" And We do hereby direct, that all and several the rules and regulations hereby established be punctually observed, upon pain of Our highest displeasure. Given at Our court at St. James's the eleventh day of February, 1767, in the seventh year of Our reign.

" *By his Majesty's Command,*

" War-Office.   " BARRINGTON."
A true Copy.

Description of Recruits entertained for the following Companies at   this   Regiment of   Day of   and drawn to the   17

By whom entertained.	Recruits Names.	Years of Age.	Size.		Trade.	Where born			Where Inlisted		Dates of their attestations.	Where attested		By whom attested.	By whom certified.	Hair.	Complexion.	When joined the Regiment.	Company drawn to.
			Feet.	Inches.		Kingdom	Town.	County.	Town.	County.		Parish.	Town.						

Roll of   Company, with their Age, Size, Service, County, &c.

Names.	Country.				Age	Size.		Service.		Where born.		Their Debts.	Casualties.
	English	Scotch	Irish	Foreign		Feet	Inches	Years	Months	Town	County	l. s. d.	

Roll of Serjeants, Corporals, Pioneers, Drummers, and Fifers, as they are posted to Companies.

Companies.	Serjeants.	Corporals.	Pioneers.	Drummers.	Fifers.
Colonel Lieut. Col. Major					
Captains					

Roll to be kept in each Company of the Non-commissioned Officers and Private Men of the Regiment of 17 Foot, commanded by

Name.	Rank.	When made non-commissi- oned.	Confin- ed by	Crime.	President.	Day of fitting.	Sentence.	Reduced.	Pardoned or part remitted.	Discharged.	Deferred.	Dead.	Observations.

A Roll of the Officers of the ——— Regiment of Foot, as they are posted to Companies, with the Dates of their Commissions.

Field Officers and Captains.	Dates.	Lieutenants.	Dates.	2d Lieutenants.	Dates.	Ensigns.	Dates.	Staff.	Dates.
Colonel Lieut. Colonel Major ⎫ ⎬ Captains ⎭									

General Return of the Names, County, Age, and Service of the Officers of ⸻ Regiment of Foot, commanded by ⸻ to the ⸻ Day of ⸻ 17⸻

with the Dates of the several Commissions each Officer has had in the regiment.

Officers ranks and names, according to their seniority in the regiment. [Names.]	English	Scotch	Irish	Foreigners	Years of: Age	Years of: Service	Dates of their several Commissions in the Army. Ensign, or Cornet, Mon. Yr.	Second Lieut, Mon. Yr.	Lieutenant, Mon. Yr.	Captain Lieut. Mon. Yr.	Captain. Mon. Yr.	Major. Mon. Yr.	Lieut.Col Mon. Yr.	Colonel. Mon. Yr.
Colonel														
Lieut. Col.														
Major														
Capts.														
Capt. Lieut. & Capt.														
Ensigns. 2d Lieuts. Lieuts.														

Staff Officers.

Chaplain
Adjutant
Quarter-Master
Surgeon
Mate

General Return of the Country, Size, Age, and Time of Service of the Men of   Regiment of Foot, commanded by   including Serjeants, Corporals, Drummers, and Fifers.

Number of Men of each Country in the several Companies.												Ages of the Men, from 18 and upwards, to 55 Years and upwards.											
	COMPANIES.													COMPANIES.									
Countries	Colonel	Lieut. Colonel	Major	Captain	Captain	Captain	Captain	Captain	Captain	Captain	Total of countries.	Years of Age.	Colonel	Lieut. Colonel	Major	Captain	Captain	Captain	Captain	Captain	Captain	Captain	Totals of each Age.
English												55 50											
Scotch												45 40											
Irish												30 25											
Foreign												20 18											
Totals												Tot.											

Size of the Men in each Company, from 5 Feet 6 Inches and under, to 6 Feet 2 Inches and upwards.			Service from 1 Year and under to 35 Years and upwards.		
Size. Ft. Inch.	Companies as above.	Total of each Size.	Years.	Companies as above.	Total Years.
6 2			35		
6 1½			30		
6 1			25		
6 0½			20		
6 0			15		
5 11½			10		
5 11			9		
5 10½			8		
5 10			7		
5 9½			6		
5 9			5		
5 8½			4		
5 8			3		
5 7½			2		
5 7			1		
5 6½					
5 6					
Under 5 6					
Total			Tot.		

Abstract of the Respites of each Company of the ———— Regiment of 17——

from ———— to ————

	COMPANIES.										Total in each muster.	Amounting to		
	Colonel	Lieutenant Colonel	Major	Captain	Captain	Captain	Captain	Captain	Captain	Captain		L.	s.	d.
Muster ending } }														
Total														

1st of Officers present.

17

COMPANIES.

		Colonel, Lieut. Col. Major, Captains,	Total

Commission.
- Colonel
- Lieut. Colonel
- Major
- Captains
- Lieutenants
- Enfigns

Staff.
- Chaplain
- Adjutant
- Quarter-Master
- Surgeon
- Mate

- Serjeants present.
- Drummers and Fifers prefent

Effective Rank and File.
- Prefent and fit for Duty.
- Sick in Quarters.
- Sick in Hofpitals
- On Command
- Recruiting
- On Furlough
- Total

Wanting to compleat to the Allowance.
- Serjeants
- Drummers and Fifers
- Rank and File

Alterations fince laft return.
- Inlifted
- Dead
- Difcharged and recommended.
- Difcharged and not recommended.
- Deferted

ABSENT OFFICERS.
- Names and Rank
- Since what Time
- By whofe Leave
- For what Time.

Names and Rank of Officers on Duty, and on what Duty.

Vacant Officers, and by what Means.

No. of Serjeants recruiting
No. of Drummers recruiting
No. of Recruits not joined

A RETURN OF ARMS, ACCOUTREMENTS, COLOURS, DRUMS, &c. OF A REGIMENT OF FOOT.

ARMS AND ACCOUTREMENTS.

Halberts			Serjeants Sashes			Fire-locks			Bayo-nets			Ram-rods			Swords			Car-touch Boxes			Pouches			Shoul-der Belts			Waist Belts			Slings		
Good	Bad	Waning	Good	Bad	Waning	Good	Bad	Waning	Good	Bad	Waning	Good	Bad	Waning	Good	Bad	Waning	Good	Bad	Waning	Good	Bad	Waning	Good	Bad	Waning	Good	Bad	Waning	Good	Bad	Waning

PIONEERS ACCOUTREMENTS

Axes			Saws			Aprons			Caps		
Good	Bad	Waning	Good	Bad	Waning	Good	Bad	Waning	Good	Bad	Waning

DRUMS.

Rims & Mounting			Cafes			Pairs of Sticks			Carri-ages			Sword-Belts		
Good	Bad	Waning	Good	Bad	Waning	Good	Bad	Waning	Good	Bad	Waning	Good	Bad	Waning

FIFERS.

Fifes			Fife Cafes			Carri-ages			Slings			Sword-Belts		
Good	Bad	Waning	Good	Bad	Waning	Good	Bad	Waning	Good	Bad	Waning	Good	Bad	Waning

LIGHT COMPANY.

Light Arms			Powder Horns		
Good	Bad	Waning	Good	Bad	Waning

COLOURS, &c.

GRENADIRS Match Cafes.			1ft.		Taffels.		
Good	Bad	Waning	Good	Bad	Good	Bad	Waning
			2d.				
			Good	Bad			

Return of the Officers, prefent and abfent, of his Majefty's _____ Regiment of Foot, commanded by _____   14   17

Number of Officers prefent.

Quarters of the Regiment.	Refpective Companies at each Quarter.	Colonel.	Lt. Col.	Major.	Captains.	Lieutenants.	Enfigns.	Chaplain.	Adjutant.	Qr.-Maftr.	Surgeon.	Mate.
								Staff.				
	Total											

Names and Rank of Officers on Duty, and on what Duty.				Vacant Officers, and by what Means.

Abfent Officers.

Names and Rank.	Since what Time.	By whofe Leave.	For what Time.

The preceding Monthly Return is to be thus backed.

MONTHLY RETURN.

Of

1ft, 177

No. of   at each quarter.

_____

{   Head quarters.

_____

Detachments, and Number of Officers, &c. at each place.

{

_____

The regiment muſt keep conſtantly to all regulations, orders, forms of diſcipline and exerciſe, now uſed (and the before-mentioned regulations, &c. be read to the regiment on
the firſt Monday in every ſecond month) and on no account
whatever change or let fall any part of them without orders:
when the regiment is divided, the ſame muſt be duly obſerved, and exactly followed, as far as ſituation and circumſtances will admit of.

the   17

[*The Colonel of the regiment
is to ſign his name.*]

On the delivery of theſe orders, forms and regulations,
the Field-officers, whoſe buſineſs it is to ſee them punctually
obſerved, ſhould alſo give a general admonition to young
Officers; by pointing out to them ſuch farther inſtructions
as they may think needful, and inciting all to the harmonious
diſcharge of their duty.

PRINCE FERDINAND OF BRUNSWICK'S DISPOSITION.

*To be obſerved on all Marches of the Army during the Cam-
paign; and which are to be exactly followed in every particular unleſs otherwiſe ordered.*

1ft. THE army will march either by columns or lines:
in the firſt caſe it will form 7 columns, and 4 in
the ſecond.

2. If

2. If the army marches by columns, the British cavalry will form the column on the right, and the German cavalry that on the left; the infantry will march in 4 columns between thefe 2 of cavalry; the British infantry, with 12 cannon, 6 pounders, from the British park of artillery, will form the columns on the right; the Brunfwick infantry, with 12 cannon, 6 pounders, from the British park, will form the fecond column; the Heffian infantry, with 12 fix pounders, from the Hanoverian park of artillery, will form the third column; and the Hanoverian infantry, with 12 fix pounders, from their own park of artillery, will form the fourth column of infantry.

The battalion of Buckeburg, with the heavy artillery, both Englifh and German, viz. twelve pounders and hawitzers, will form the column of the centre or the fourth column of the army: in this manner, when the army marches forward, the British cavalry forms the firft column; the British infantry the fecond; the Brunfwick infantry the third; the heavy artillery the fourth; the Heffian infantry the fifth; the Hanoverian infantry the fixth; and the German cavalry the feventh.

If the army marches by the rear, this order is reverfed, and the German cavalry forms the firft column on the right.

3. When the army marches by lines, the firft column will be compofed of infantry of the firft line, according to the order of battle, with 12 cannon, 6 pounders, from the British park, which will march with the brigades of British infantry; and 12 fix pounders, from the Hanoverian park, which will march with the brigades of Hanoverian infantry: the fecond column will be compofed of infantry of the fecond line, with 12 fix pounders, from the British park, which will march with the brigades of Brunfwick infantry: 12 fix pounders from the Hanoverian park, which will march with the Heffian infantry, and the battalion of Buckeburg, with the heavy artillery, will form the third column: the fourth will be compofed of the whole cavalry.

4. The eldeft General Officer of each nation will lead the column or troops of that nation when the army is to march by lines; General Sporken will lead the firft column; the eldeft Lieutenant-general of the fecond line will lead the fecond column; Major-general Brown of the Hanoverian artillery will lead the third; and the eldeft General Officer of cavalry will lead the fourth.

5. Neither

5. Neither chaifes, bread or ammunition-waggons, or any kind of carriages, are to march in the columns between the battalions and fquadrons; the baa-horfes only will be fuffered to march with their battalions and fquadrons, keeping on their flanks, without mixing with, advancing before or remaining behind them; the field-pieces are to march at the head of their refpective battalions; the battalions are to keep well clofed, without intervals, and to march by fub-divifions: the 12 fix pounders, attached to each nation, are to march between the firft and fecond brigades of that nation, in the rear of the battalions, which clofe the column, are to follow the ammunition-waggons of all the regiments, according to the order of march of the battalions and brigades: 2dly, the ammunition-waggons of the 6 pounders, attached to the column, by brigades, and according to the order of march.

The columns of cavalry having neither cannon or ammunition-waggons, the equipages will immediately follow the fquadron that clofes the column in the order prefcribed.

The equipage belonging to the column formed by the heavy artillery, will follow the laft ammunition-waggons, and other carriages of the artillery.

The order for marching will for the future be given in the following manner:

The army will march the   exactly at

This order for the march will be fent to each nation; it muft be received by the eldeft General Officer, Colonel, or Lieutenant-colonel, prefent, and executed as follows:

Half an hour before the time fixed for the march, the General Officer commanding each nation will give the fignal for that purpofe; the tents muft be ftruck, and the baggage loaded immediately; each brigade formed at the time appointed, and the baggage remain in the rear ready to file off.

The Commanding Officer of each brigade will order a Subaltern to conduct the carriages with regularity.

Befides this notice of march, the eldeft General Officer, Colonel, or Lieutenant-colonel, prefent, of each nation, will receive a fealed order, on the outfide of which will be marked the time for opening it; this order will contain the difpofition of the march.

When the army is to march in columns, the brigades which are already formed in order of battle, muft begin their march the moment prefcribed to form in column, in the rear of each other; the infantry by battalions, and the
cavalry

cavalry by regiments; the baa-horfes forming and remaining on the flank of their brigades; the carriages, following each other in clofe order, march as before prefcribed; the 12 pieces of cannon attached to each column will file off between the laft battalions of the firft brigade and the firft battalion of the fecond brigade; the ammunition-waggons of thefe pieces will remain in file, oppofite the intervals; the columns be formed in half an hour from the time the brigade leaves the camp. Upon the fignal being given, the whole army is to move at once; and fo foon as the column has quitted the ground upon which they were formed, the ammunition-waggons and carriages will follow in the order above prefcribed.

When the army marches by lines, it will form in column by fub-divifions; in the firft line, 12 fix pounders from the Britifh park of artillery will draw up between the firft and fecond brigades of Britifh infantry; and 12 fix pounders from the Hanoverian park, between the firft and fecond brigade of Hanoverian infantry, in the fecond line; 12 fix pounders from the Britifh park will draw up between the 2 brigades of Brunfwick infantry, and twelve other pieces from the Hanoverian park between the 2 Heffian brigades; the heavy artillery, parked in the centre of the army, will file off, and the cavalry form in columns by quarter ranks; the baggage of each line will draw up on the flanks of their refpective brigades: when the fignal is given, all the columns will begin their march together; and, as they quit their ground, the ammunition-waggons and carriages belonging to the infantry will follow in the order prefcribed (namely, by brigades) according to the order of march, in the rear of the laft battalion of the column; the equipage of the cavalry will follow the laft fquadron of that column, and the baa-horfes march on the flanks of their refpective battalions and fquadrons, without advancing before or remaining behind them.

7. The Commanding Officers of battalions, fquadrons, and brigades of artillery, will be refponfible that they are formed, that the tents are ftruck, and the baggage loaded in half an hour from the time that the fignal for the march was given them; and for this purpofe it is neceffary that they fhould exercife their men to it while they remain in fettled camps.

The General Officers commanding brigades, will be refponfible that the columns are formed in half an hour from

the

the time the battalions are drawn up; and the Generals who lead columns are to be anfwerable that they move together exactly at the hour appointed.

8. The Aid-de-camps, and Majors of brigades, before they carry the orders for marching to camp, are to fet their watches together; and the General Officers who receive the orders are to regulate their watches by them, in order that the inequality of watches may not occafion any in the movement of the troops, and that every brigade may move at the fame time.

9. The guides will be always ordered for the brigades, which form the head of the columns, and prefent themfelves to the Commanding Officers of the battalion or fquadron which leads.

10. The Commanding Officer of each battalion and fquadron will pay the greateft attention during the march, and be anfwerable that the battalions march always by fubdivifions, and the fquadrons by quarter ranks; if the defiles oblige them to file off, they muft double up again immediately as foon as they are paft: fecondly, that every Officer remains with his divifion and never leaves it on any account: thirdly, that no foldier is permitted to quit his rank under any pretence: fourthly, that the baa-horfes are not fuffered to interrupt the marches of the column, but obliged to keep on the flanks: fifthly, that the diftance between each divifion be properly obferved.

The Generals, or Commanding Officers of brigades, are to take care, firft, that the brigades and fquadrons march well clofed, and keep their proper diftance: fecondly, that the Commanding Officers of battalions and fquadrons punctually obferve the orders prefcribed; and, in cafe of difobedience, the Generals, or Commanding Officer of brigades, are to put in arreft, or to correct the diforders of thofe Commanding Officers of battalions or fquadrons, if neceffary, and acquaint me with it: thirdly, when the army halts, it may be permitted to fend for water; but the foldiers muft not be fuffered to ftraggle: as many Officers and Non-commiffioned Officers as are neceffary muft conduct them regularly, and be anfwerable that no diforders are committed: fourthly, no carriages, except the cannon, to be permitted to march between the battalions in the order as above: and, fhould any of them ftick faft, a proper number of men muft be ordered immediately to draw them out: if a carriage breaks, it muft be drawn afide, the road cleared, and a proper

per

per efcort left with it, that the march of the column may not be interrupted : the Officer under whofe care it is left, muft get it repaired, and follow the column as foon as poffible : the General Officers commanding brigades fhall remain with them, and punctually obferve the order of march, and the execution of every article prefcribed.

The Generals who lead the columns are to inforce the obedience of them with the utmoft feverity : fecondly, they are carefully to begin their march precifely at the hour appointed, to keep an equal pace, and to regulate it fo that the troops march, at moft, 3 miles in an hour and a quarter : thirdly, the guides ferve only to fhew the way for the columns ; they muft be preceded by pioneers to make the neceffary overtures, lay bridges, and repair the roads ; the Generals muft not truft entirely to thefe precautions, but gain the moft exact knowledge of the route they are to march, and reflect on the moft proper means to avoid all difficulties that might embarrafs the march : fourthly, there is no manœuvre in the Art of War by which a General has greater opportunity to fhew his fkill, activity, and experience, than in conducting the columns which he leads in fuch a manner, that the Commander in Chief of the army may depend on the exact march of thefe columns, and make his calculations accordingly. The more a General endeavours to excel in this important point, the greater fhare he will have in the great and advantageous events, which may be expected from order and exactnefs. On the contrary, a General who does not diftinguifh himfelf in this article, will not only have a fmaller fhare in thefe events, but will likewife have to reproach himfelf with the difadvantages which is ever to be apprehended when columns do not march with exactnefs, and arrive punctually at their deftination. Though troops do not always march immediately before an enemy, it is of infinite confequence that they fhould always march as if in the enemy's prefence : equal and well ordered marches contribute not only to the prefervation of the army, but likewife accuftom the troops to be always ready to attack or repulfe the enemy.

11. The Quarter-mafters General of each nation, or thofe who act as fuch, will always go forward with the Quarter-mafters and camp-colour men. Lieutenant-colonel Bower, or fome engineer whom I employ to reconnoitre the new camp, will direct, in general, the ground that the brigades of each nation are to occupy ; after which, the Quarter-mafters General will order their refpective encampments.

Each

Each nation is to take care to park the brigade of 6 pounders attached to them.

The heavy artillery muft detach an Officer, with their camp-colour men, who is to do the duty of Quarter-mafter General ; to whom Lieutenant-colonel Bower will fhew the ground appointed for the heavy artillery to fix their camp.

12. Whenever the baggage is ordered to be fent away, every carriage, without exception, is comprehended in this order, except fuch as are otherwife particularly fpecified : the equipages of each battalion and fquadron are to affemble in the rear of the camp, exactly at the hour appointed ; thofe of each brigade, on the fignal being given, are to file off to the rendezvous of the nation to which they belong, from whence they will be conducted to the place appointed for them ; the guides ordered to fhew the way will come to the Commanding Officer of the laft battalion, or laft fquadron of the laft brigade of each nation, where the Officer who is to conduct the baggage ; the eldeft of whom of each nation fhall take the charge of the whole of that nation, and fhall be anfwerable for the departure of it at the proper time, and of the neceffary order during the march.

13. The chaffeurs and light troops always form the advanced and rear-guards, or march on the flanks of the army.

The General Officer who commands them will likewife have under his orders thofe battalions and fquadrons which may at any time be ordered to re-inforce the advanced or guards; this General Officer will always be particularly named.

14. Lord Granby's referve will obferve, in every thing which relates to it, the above orders : with regard to the march of the army, it will march conftantly in 2 columns ; 1 of which will be compofed of the infantry and artillery ; and the other of cavalry.

[*Dated Corvey, the 8th of June, and forwarded the 11th of June; figned Ferdinand, Duc de Brunfwick and de Lunenburg.*]

" GEORGE R.

" Our Will and Pleafure is, that the following Regulations for the Standards, Guidons, Clothing, &c. of Our Regiments of Dragoon Guards, Horfe, Dragoons, and Light Dragoons, be duly obferved and put in Execution, at fuch Times as the Particulars are or fhall be furnifhed.

R

" NO Colonel is to put his arms, creft, device, or livery, on any part of the appointments of the regiment under his command.

Standards and Guidons.

" THE ftandards and guidons of the dragoon guards, and
the ftandards of the regiments of horfe, to be of filk damafk
embroidered, and fringed with gold or filver. The guidons
of the regiments of dragoons, and of the light dragoons, to
be of filk. The taffels, and cords of the whole, to be of
crimfon filk and gold mixed. The lance of the ftandards
and guidons (except thofe of the light dragoons) to be nine
feet long (fpear and ferril included.) The flag of the ftandard to be two feet five inches wide without the fringe, and
two feet three inches on the lance. That of the guidons to
be three feet five inches, to the end of the flit of the fwal-
low-tail, and two feet three inches on the lance. Thofe of
the light dragoons to be of a fmaller fize.

" The King's, or firft ftandard, or guidon, of each regiment, to be crimfon, with the rofe and thiftle conjoined,
and crown over them in the centre. His Majefty's motto,
Dieu et mon droit, underneath. The white horfe, in a com-
partment, in the firft and fourth corner; and the rank of the
regiment, in gold or filver characters, on a ground of the
fame colour as the facing of the regiment, in a compart-
ment, in the fecond and third corners.

" The fecond and third ftandard, or guidon, of each
corps, to be of the colour of the facing of the regiment,
with the badge of the regiment in the centre, or the rank of
the regiment, in gold or filver Roman characters, on a
crimfon ground, within a wreath of rofes and thiftles on the
fame ftalk. The motto of the regiment underneath. The
white horfe, on a red ground, to be in the firft and fourth
compartments, and the rofe and thiftle conjoined upon a red
ground, in the fecond and third compartments. The diftinction of the third ftandard, or guidon, to be a figure 3 on
a circular ground of red, underneath the motto.

" Thofe corps who have any particular badge, are to
carry it in the centre of their fecond and third ftandard, or
guidon, with the rank of the regiment on a red ground,
within a fmall wreath of rofes and thiftles, in the fecond
and third corners; except thofe of the Prince of Wales's
dragoon guards, and light dragoons. The rank of thofe 2
regiments to be under the plume of feathers.

Banners

Banners of the Regiments of Horse.

" The banners of the kettle-drums and trumpets to be of the colour of the facing of the regiment. The badge of the regiment, or its rank, to be in the centre of the banner of the kettle drums, as on the second standard. The King's cypher and crown to be on the banner of the trumpets, with the rank of the regiment in figures underneath. The depth of the kettle-drum banners to be 3 feet 6 inches ; the length 4 feet 8 inches, exclusive of the fringe. Those of the trumpets to be 12 inches in depth, and 18 inches in length.

Trumpets.

" The trumpets to be of brass. The cords to be crimson, mixed with the colour of the facing of the regiment. The King's own regiment of dragoons, and the Royal Irish, are permitted to continue their kettle-drums, and to which they are to have banners of the same dimensions as those which are ordered for the regiments of horse.

Bells of Arms.

" The bells of arms to be painted with the colour of the facing of the regiment, upon which is to be the badge or rank of the regiment, as in the second guidon.

Camp Colours.

" The camp colours to be of the colour of the facing of the regiment, with the rank of the regiment in the centre. Those of the horse, to be eighteen inches square. Those of the dragoon guards, dragoons, and light dragoons, to be swallow-tailed, and to be 18 inches long on the part affixed to the pole. The poles of the whole to be 7 feet 6 inches long, except those for the standard and rear guards, which are to be 9 feet.

Uniform of Officers.

" The number of each regiment to be on the buttons of the uniforms of the Officers and men ; except the 3 regiments of dragoon guards. The initial letters of the title of those corps are to be on the buttons, instead of the number.

" The uniforms to be made up in the same manner as those of the men. The buttons on the sleeve to be set on length-ways, up the arm, but the sleeves not to be slit.

The

The waiftcoats, breeches, and lining of the coats, to be of the fame colour as what is ordered for the men.

Coats of the Officers of Dragoon Guards, Horfe, and Light Dragoons.

" The coats of the Officers of the dragoon guards, horfe, and light dragoons, may be without lace or embroidery ; but if the Colonel thinks proper, either gold or filver embroidered, or laced button-holes are permitted.

Coats of the Officers of Dragoons.

" The coats of the Officers of the regiments of dragoons, to have either gold or filver embroidered, or laced button-holes.

Waiftcoats of the Whole.

" The waiftcoats of the whole to be without lace or embroidery, and to have crofs pockets.

Epaulettes.

" The Officers of the dragoon guards, horfe, and dragoons, to have a gold or filver embroidered or laced epaulette, with fringe, on the left fhoulder.
" Thofe of the light dragoons to have one on each fhoulder.

Lappels.

" The breadth of the lappels to be 3 inches, and to be no wider at the top than at the bottom.

Houfings and Caps.

" The houfings and caps, except thofe of the Queen's, and Prince of Wales's light dragoons, to be laced with gold or filver lace, and a ftripe of cloth in the middle, of the colour of that on the mens. A taffel to be on the corners of the houfings, and one on the middle of the caps. To have black or white bear-fkin to cover the piftols. Thofe of the Queen's light dragoons to be of leopard fkin, with filver fringe ; and thofe of the Prince of Wales's, to be black cloth, with ftripes of white goat fkin and filver lace.

Saddles, Girths, Surcingles, Piftols, Bits, Gloves, Boots, and Spurs.

" The faddles, girths, furcingles, piftols, bits, gloves,
boots,

boots, and fpurs, to be uniform. The boots of the whole to be round-toed, and not of a heavy fort.

Standard Belts.

" The ftandard belts to be of the colour of the facing of the regiment, and laced as the houfings.

Safhes.

" The fafhes to be of crimfon filk, and worn round the waift.

Swords, Sword-Knots, and Sword-Belts.

" The fwords, fword-knots, and fword-belts, of the Officers of each regiment, to be uniform. The fword-knots and fword-belts to be plain, either of buff colour or white, according to the colour of the waiftcoat; and to have yellow or white buckles or clafps, according to the colour of the buttons of the uniform. The fword-belts of the Officers of regiments of horfe, and of the light dragoons, to be worn over the right fhoulder. Thofe of the Officers of dragoon-guards, and dragoons, to be worn round the waift.

Hats and Helmets.

" The hats to be cocked uniformly, and in the fame manner as thofe of the men. The Officers of the light dragoons to have helmets.

Gaiters.

" The Officers and men of the dragoon guards, horfe, and dragoons, to have black linen gaiters, with black buttons, with a fmall ftiff top, black garters, and uniform buckles. Thofe of the light dragoons to have black half-gaiters.

Uniform of the Quarter-Mafters.

" The uniform of the Quarter-mafters to be without lace or embroidery, but to have a gold or filver button on the coat and waiftcoat, and an epaulette. Thofe of the light dragoons to have two epaulettes. The hats to be laced and cocked in the fame manner as thofe of the Officers. To wear crimfon fafhes of fpun filk round the waift. The faddles, girths, furcingles, piftols, bits, houfings and caps, fwords, fword-belts, gloves. boots, and fpurs, to be uniform. The furniture to be made like thofe of the Officers, but the lace not to be fo broad; and to have no taffels on the houfings and caps.

R 3

Serjeants

Serjeants Coats of Dragoon Guards, Dragoons, and Light Dragoons.

" The Serjeants of the dragoon guards, dragoons, and light dragoons, to be diftinguifhed by a gold or filver button-hole, a narrow lace round the cape, and to have epaulettes, The cloth of the epaulettes to be of the colour of the facing, with a narrow gold or filver lace round it, and a gold or filver fringe. To wear pouches as the men do, and a fafh round the waift, of crimfon fpun filk, with a ftripe of the colour of the facing of the regiment.

Coats of the Corporals of Horfe.

" The Corporals of horfe to be diftinguifhed by a gold or filver button-hole, and a narrow lace round the cape, and to have gold or filver lace round the edge of the fhoulder-ftraps.

Coats of the Corporals of Dragoon Guards, Dragoons, and Light-Dragoons.

" The Corporals of dragoon guards, dragoons, and light dragoons, to have a narrow filver or gold lace round the turn-up of the fleeves, and to have epaulettes. The cloth of the epaulettes to be of the colour of the facing, with a narrow yellow or white filk tape round it, and a filk fringe.

Coats of the Private Men of the Dragoon Guards.

" The coats of the dragoon guards to be lapelled to the waift. The fleeves to be turned up with the colour of the lappel. An epaulette on the left fhoulder.

Coats of the Private Men of the Horfe.

" The coats of the horfe to be lappelled to the waift. The fleeves to be turned up with the colour of the lappel. No epaulette.

Coats of the Private Men of the Dragoons.

" The coats of the dragoons to be without lappels. One row of buttons, but to have button-holes on each fide. The fleeves to be turned up with the colour of the facing.

Coats of the Private Men of the Light Dragoons.

" The coats of the light dragoons to be lapelled to the waift.

waist. The sleeves to be turned up with the colour of the lappel. An epaulette on each shoulder.

Sleeves of the Whole.

" The buttons on the sleeves of the whole to be set on length-ways up the arm ; but the sleeves not to be slit.

Epaulettes of the Private Men of the Dragoon Guards, Dragoons, and Light Dragoons.

" The cloth of the epaulettes to be of the colour of the facing, with a narrow yellow or white tape round it, and worsted fringe.

Shoulder-Straps of the Horse.

" The private men of the horse to have red shoulder-straps.

Pockets, Capes, and Button-Holes of the Coats of the Whole.

" The coats of the whole to have long pockets, and turn-down capes, of the colour of the facing. The capes to be made in such manner, that they may occasionally be buttoned up round the neck. The button-holes of the coats of the dragoon guards, dragoons, and light dragoons, to be of a very narrow yellow, buff, or white braid, and set on as hereafter specified. Those of the horse to be of plain twist.

Pockets and Button-Holes of the Waistcoats.

" The waistcoats to have cross pockets, without flaps. The button-holes to be without the braid.

Coats of the Kettle-Drummers, Trumpeters, and Hautboys.

" The coats of the kettle-drummers, trumpeters, and hautboys, are not to have long hanging sleeves, and are to be conformable to the particulars hereafter specified.

Caps and Hats of the Kettle-Drummers and Trumpeters.

" The kettle-drummers of the regiments of horse to have black bear-skin caps. On the front, the King's arms ; also trophies of colours and kettle-drums. The number of the regiment to be on the back part.

" All trumpeters to have hats, with feathers of the colour of the facing of their lappels, except those of the fourth regiment of dragoons, who are to have Moorish turbans. Those regiments who have black kettle-drummers, may

also

alſo have the turbans, inſtead of the bear-ſkin caps. All kettle-drummers and trumpeters to have ſwords with a ſci-mitar blade.

Farriers.

" The farriers of the dragoon guards, horſe, dragoons, and light dragoons, to have blue coats with blue lining, and blue waiſtcoats and breeches. The lappels of the dragoon guards, horſe, and light dragoons, to be blue. The capes and cuffs of the ſleeves to be of the colour of the facing of the regiment, except thoſe of the royal regi-ments, which are faced with blue, whoſe capes and cuffs are to be red. The button-holes to be the ſame as thoſe which are ordered for the men. To wear a ſmall black bear-ſkin cap, with a horſe-ſhoe on the fore part, of ſilver plated metal on a black ground, and to have churns and an apron.

Hats, Caps, and Helmets.

" The hats to be laced with gold or ſilver lace; the breadth to be one inch and a half, a quarter of an inch of which is to be on the inſide of the brim. To have black cockades. The royal North-Britiſh dragoons, only, to wear black bear-ſkin caps, inſtead of hats. On the front of the cap, the thiſtle within the circle of St. Andrew; and the motto, *Nemo me impunè laceſſit.* All the light dra-goons to have helmets.

Watering Caps.

" The watering or forage caps to be red, turned up with the colour of the facing, and the rank of the regiment on the little flap.

Cloaks.

" The cloaks to be red, lined with the ſame colour as the mens coats, and claſps ſet on at top, upon loops of the ſame colour as the lace on the houſings. The capes to be of the colour of the facing.

Shoulder-Belts and Waiſt-Belts.

" The breadth of the ſhoulder-belts of the dragoon guards, horſe, and dragoons, to be four inches and a half. Thoſe of the light dragoons to be two inches and a half. Thoſe regiments which have buff waiſtcoats, are to have buff-coloured accoutrements. Thoſe which have white waiſtcoats, are to have white. The breadth of the waiſt-belts to be 2 inches and 3-4ths, except thoſe of the light

dragoons,

dragoons, which are to be one inch and 3-4ths. To have yellow buckles or clasps. The horse to have cross belts. The dragoon guards and dragoons to have only one shoulder-belt, except the eighth regiment, which is permitted to wear cross belts.

Housings and Holster Caps.

" The housings and holster caps to be of the colour of the facing of the regiment, except the King's dragoon guards, the royal dragoons, the 4th regiment of horse, the King's, Queen's, and Prince of Wales's light dragoons. Those of the King's dragoon guards, and of the royal dragoons, to be red. Those of the 4th regiment of horse, to be buff. Those of the King's and Queen's light dragoons, to be white. The housings and caps to be laced with one broad white or yellow worsted or mohair lace, with a stripe in the middle, of 1-3d of the whole breadth, as hereafter specified. The rank of the regiment to be embroidered on the housings, upon a red ground, within a wreath of roses and thistles, or the particular badge of the regiment, as on the second guidon or standard. The King's cypher, with the crown over it, to be embroidered on the holster-caps; and under the cypher, the number or rank of the regiment. The housings and caps of the Prince of Wales's regiment of light dragoons, to be of black cloth, with stripes of white goat-skin.

Bridons.

" The Officers and men of all the regiments of dragoon guards, horse, dragoons, and light dragoons, to have black bridons; and they are to be made in such manner, that the horses may be linked with them when the regiments are dismounted.

" GEORGE R.

" Our will and pleasure is, that the following regulations for the colours, clothing, &c. of Our marching regiments of foot, be duly observed and put in execution, at such times as the particulars are or shall be furnished.

" NO Colonel is to put his arms, crest, device, or livery, on any part of the appointments of the regiment under his command.

Colours.

Colours.

" The King's, or firſt colour of every regiment, is to be the Great Union throughout.

" The ſecond colour to be the colour of the facing of the regiment, with the Union in the upper canton; except thoſe regiments which are faced with red, white, or black. The ſecond colour of thoſe regiments which are faced with red or white, is to be the red croſs of St. George in a white field, and the Union in the upper canton. The ſecond colour of thoſe which are faced with black, is to be St. George's croſs throughout; Union in the upper canton; the 3 other cantons, black.

" In the centre of each colour is to be painted, or embroidered, in gold Roman characters, the number of the rank of the regiment, within the wreath of roſes and thiſtles on the ſame ſtalk; except thoſe regiments which are allowed to wear any royal devices, or antient badges; on whoſe colours the rank of the regiment is to be painted, or embroidered, towards the upper corner. The ſize of the colours to be 6 feet 6 inches flying, and 6 feet deep on the pike. The length of the pike (ſpear and ferril included) to be 9 feet 10 inches. The cords and taſſels of the whole to be crimſon and gold mixed.

Drums.

" The drums to be wood.

" The front to be painted with the colour of the facing of the regiment, with the King's cypher and crown, and the number of the regiment under it.

Bells of Arms.

" The bells of arms to be painted in the ſame manner.

Camp Colours.

" The camp colours to be 18 inches ſquare, and of the colour of the facing of the regiment, with the number of the regiment upon them. The poles to be 7 feet 6 inches long, except thoſe of the quarter and rear guards, which are to be 9 feet.

Uniform of Officers.

" The number of each regiment to be on the buttons of the uniforms of the Officers and men. The coats to be lapelled to the waiſt with the colour of the facing of the regiment, and the colour not to be varied from what is par-

ticularly

ticularly fpecified hereafter. They may be without embroidery or lace; but, if the Colonel thinks proper, either gold or filver embroidered or laced button-holes are permitted. To have crofs pockets, and fleeves with round cuffs, and no flits. The lappels and cuffs to be of the fame breadth as is ordered for the men.

Epaulettes.

" The Officers of grenadiers to wear an epaulette on each fhoulder. Thofe of the battalion to wear one on the right fhoulder. They are to be either of embroidery or lace, with gold or filver fringe.

Waiftcoats.

" The waiftcoats to be plain, without either embroidery or lace.

Swords and Sword-Knots.

" The fwords of each regiment to be uniform, and the fword-knots of the whole to be crimfon and gold in ftripes. The hilts of the fwords to be either gilt or filver, according to the colour of the buttons on the uniforms.

Hats.

" The hats to be laced either with gold or filver, as hereafter fpecified, and to be cocked uniformly.

Safhes and Gorgets.

" The fafhes to be of crimfon filk, and worn round the waift. The King's arms to be engraved on the gorgets; alfo the number of the regiment. They are to be either gilt or filver, according to the colour of the buttons on the uniforms. The badges of thofe regiments which are entitled to any, are alfo to be engraved.

Caps, Fuzils, and Pouches, for Grenadier Officers.

" The Officers of the grenadiers to wear black bearfkin caps; and to have fuzils, fhoulder-belts, and pouches. The fhoulder-belts to be white or buff, according to the colour of their waiftcoats.

Efpontoons.

" The battalion Officers to have efpontoons.

Gaiters.

Gaiters.

" The whole to have black linen gaiters, with black buttons, and small stiff tops, black garters, and uniform buckles.

Serjeants Coats.

" The coats of the Serjeants to be lapelled to the waist, with the colour of the facing of the regiment. The button-holes of the coat to be of white braid. Those on the waistcoats to be plain. The Serjeants of grenadiers to have fuzils, pouches, and caps. Those of the battalion to have halberts, and no pouches.

Serjeants Sashes.

" The sashes to be of crimson worsted, with a stripe of the colour of the facing of the regiment, and worn round the waist. Those of the regiments which are faced with red, to have a stripe of white.

Corporals Coats.

" The coats of the Corporals to have a silk epaulette on the right shoulder.

Grenadiers Coats.

" The coats of the grenadiers to have the usual round wings of red cloth on the point of the shoulder, with six loops of the same sort of lace as on the button-holes, and a border round the bottom.

Private Mens Coats.

" The mens coats to be looped with worsted lace, but no border. The ground of the lace to be white, with coloured stripes. To have white buttons. The breadth of the lace which is to make the loop round the button-hole, to be about half an inch. Four loops to be on the sleeves, and 4 on the pockets, with 2 on each side of the slit behind.

Lappels, Sleeves, and Pockets.

" The breadth of all the lappels to be 3 inches, to reach down to the waist, and not to be wider at top than at the bottom. The sleeves of the coats to have a small round cuff, without any slit, and to be made so that they may be unbuttoned and let down. The whole to have cross pockets, but no flaps to those of the waistcoat. The cuffs of the sleeve

which

which turns up, to be 3 inches and a half deep. The flap on the pocket of the coat to be fewed down, and the pocket to be cut in the lining of the coat.

Shoulder-Belts and Waift-Belts.

" The breadth of the fhoulder-belts to be 2 inches and 3-4ths; that of the waift-belt to be 2 inches and 3-4ths; and thofe regiments which have buff waiftcoats, are to have buff-coloured accoutrements. Thofe which have white waiftcoats, are to have white.

Drummers, and Fifers Coats.

" The coats of the drummers and fifers of all the royal regiments are to be red, faced and lappelled with blue, and laced with royal lace. The waiftcoats, breeches, and lining of the coats, to be of the fame colour as that which is ordered for their refpective regiments. The coats of the drummers and fifers of thofe regiments which are faced with red, are to be white, faced, lappelled, and lined with red ; red waiftcoats and breeches. Thofe of all the other regiments are to be of the colour of the facing of their regiments ; faced and lappelled with red. The waiftcoats, breeches, and lining of thofe which have buff or white coats, are to be red. Thofe of all the others are to be of the fame colour as that which is ordered for the men. To be laced in fuch manner as the Colonel fhall think fit. The lace to be of the colour of that on the foldiers coats. The coats to have no hanging fleeves behind.

Drummers and Fifers Caps.

" The drummers and fifers to have black bear-fkin caps. On the front, the King's creft, of filver plated metal, on a black ground, with trophies of colours and drums. The number of the regiment on the back part ; as alfo the badge, if entitled to any, as ordered for the grenadiers.

Grenadiers Caps.

" The caps of the grenadiers to be of black bear-fkin. On the front, the King's creft, of filver plated metal, on a black ground, with the motto, *Nec afpera terrent.* A grenade on the back part, with the number of the regiment on it. The royal regiments, and the 6 old corps, are to have the creft and grenade, and alfo the other particulars as hereafter fpecified. The badge of the royal regiments is

to

to be white, and set on near the top of the back part of the cap. The heighth of the cap (without the bear-skin, which reaches beyond the top) to be 12 inches.

Hats of the Whole.

" The hats of the Serjeants to be laced with silver. Those of the Corporals and private men to have a white-tape binding. The breadth of the whole to be 1 inch 1-4th; and no more to be on the back part of the brim, than what is necessary to sew it down. To have black cockades.

Caps for the Officers and Men of the Regiments of Fuzileers.

" The regiments of fuzileers to have black bear-skin caps. They are to be made in the same manner as those which are ordered for the grenadiers, but not so high; and not to have the grenade on the back part.

Swords.

" All the Serjeants of the regiment, and the whole grenadier company, to have swords. The Corporals and private men of the battalion companies (except the regiment of royal highlanders) to have no swords.

" All the drummers and fifers to have a short sword with a scimitar blade.

Gaiters.

" The Serjeants, Corporals, drummers, fifers, and private men, to have black gaiters of the same sort as is ordered for the Officers; also black garters and uniform buckles.

Pioneers.

" Each pioneer to have an axe, a saw, and an apron; a cap with a leather crown, and a black bear-skin front, on which is to be the King's crest in white, on a red ground; also an axe and a saw. The number of the regiment to be on the back part of the cap.

" *Devices and Badges of the Royal Regiments, and of the Six Old Corps.*

" FIRST, or ROYAL REGIMENT. In the centre of their colours, the King's cypher within the circle of St. Andrew, and crown over it. In the 3 corners of the
second

fecond colour, the thiftle and crown. The diftinction of the colours of the fecond battalion, is a flaming ray of gold defcending from the upper corner of each colour towards the centre.

" On the grenadiers caps, the King's creft; alfo, the King's cypher within the circle of St. Andrew, and crown over it, as in the colours.

" The drums, and bells of arms, to have the fame device painted on them, with the number or rank of the regiment under it.

" IId, or QUEEN's ROYAL REGIMENT. In the centre of each colour, the Queen's cypher on a red ground, within the garter, and crown over it. In the 3 corners of the fecond colour, the lamb, being the ancient badge of the regiment.

" On the grenadiers caps, the King's creft; alfo, the King's cypher and crown, as in the colours.

" The drums, and bells of arms, to have the Queen's cypher painted on them in the fame manner, and the rank of the regiment underneath.

" IIId, or BUFFS. In the centre of their colours, the dragon, being their ancient badge; and the rofe and crown in the 3 corners of their fecond colour.

" On the grenadiers caps, the King's creft; alfo, the dragon.

" The fame badge of the dragon to be painted on their drums, and bells of arms, with the rank of the regiment underneath.

" IVth, or KING's OWN ROYAL REGIMENT. In the centre of their colours, the King's cypher on a red ground within the garter, and crown over it. In the 3 corners of their fecond colour, the lion of England being their antient badge.

" On the grenadiers caps, the King's creft; alfo, the King's cypher and crown, as in the colours.

" The drums, and bells of arms, to have the King's cypher painted on them, in the fame manner, and the rank of the regiment underneath.

" Vth. In the centre of their colours, St. George killing the dragon, being their antient badge; and in the 3 corners of their fecond colour, the rofe and crown.

" On

" On the grenadiers caps, the King's creft ; alfo, St. George killing the dragon.

" The fame badge of St. George and the dragon, to be painted on the drums, and bells of arms, with the rank of the regiment underneath.

" VIth. In the centre of their colours, the antelope, being their ancient badge ; and in the 3 corners of their fecond colour, the rofe and crown.

" On the grenadiers caps, the King's creft ; alfo, the antelope.

" The fame badge of the antelope to be painted on their drums, and bells of arms, with the rank of the regiment underneath.

" VIIth, or ROYAL FUZILEERS. In the centre of their colours, the rofe within the garter, and the crown over it. The white horfe in the corners of the fecond colour.

" On the grenadiers caps, the King's creft ; alfo, the rofe within the garter and crown, as in the colours.

" The fame device of the rofe, within the garter and crown, on their drums, and bells of arms. Rank of the regiment underneath.

" VIIIth, or KING'S REGIMENT. In the centre of their colours, the white horfe on a red ground within the garter, and crown over it. In the 3 corners of the fecond colour, the King's cypher and crown.

" On the grenadiers caps, the King's creft ; alfo, the white horfe, as in the colours.

" The fame device of the white horfe within the garter, on the drums, and bells of arms. Rank of the regiment underneath.

" XVIIIth, or ROYAL IRISH. In the centre of their colours, the harp in a blue field, and the crown over it ; and in the 3 corners of their fecond colour, the lion of Naf-fau, King William the Third's arms.

" On the grenadiers caps, the King's creft ; alfo, the harp and crown, as in the colours.

" The harp and crown to be painted, in the fame manner, on their drums, and bells of arms, with the rank of the regiment underneath.

" XXIft,

" XXIft, or ROYAL NORTH-BRITISH FUZILEERS. In the centre of their colours, the thiftle within the circle of St. Andrew, and crown over it; and in the 3 corners of the fecond colour, the King's cypher and crown.

" On the grenadiers caps, the King's creft; alfo, the thiftle, as in the colours.

" On the drums, and bells of arms, the thiftle and crown to be painted, as in the colours. Rank of the regiment underneath.

" XXIIId, or ROYAL WELCH FUZILEERS. In the centre of their colours, the device of the Prince of Wales, viz. Three feathers iffuing out of the Prince's coronet. In the 3 corners of the fecond colour, the badges of Edward the Black Prince, viz. rifing fun, red dragon, and the 3 feathers in the coronet. Motto, *Ich dien.*

" On the grenadiers caps, the King's creft; alfo, the feathers, as in the colours.

" The fame badge of the 3 feathers, and motto, *Ich dien,* on the drums, and bells of arms. Rank of the regiment underneath.

" XXVIIth, or INNISKILLING REGIMENT. Allowed to wear, in the centre of their colours, a caftle with 3 turrets; St. George's colours flying, in a blue field; and the name Innifkilling over it.

" On the grenadiers caps, the King's creft; alfo, the caftle and name, as in the colours.

" The fame badge of the caftle and name, on the drums, and bells of arms. Rank of the regiment underneath.

" XLIft, or INVALIDS. In the centre of their colours, the rofe and thiftle on a red ground, within the garter, and crown over it. In the 3 corners of their fecond colour, the King's cypher and crown.

" On the grenadiers caps, the King's creft; alfo, the rofe and thiftle, as in the colours.

" On the drums, and bells of arms, the fame device of the rofe and thiftle conjoined, within the garter and crown, as in the colours.

" XLIId, or ROYAL HIGHLANDERS. In the centre of their colours, the King's cypher within the garter, and crown over it. Under it, St. Andrew, with the motto,

S   *Ne na*

Nemo me impunè lacessit. In the 3 corners of the second colour, the King's cypher and crown.

" On the grenadiers caps, the King's crest ; also, St.
Andrew, as in the colours.

" On the drums, and bells of arms, the same device,
with the rank of the regiment underneath.

" LXth, or ROYAL AMERICANS. In the centre of
their colours, the King's cypher within the garter, and
crown over it. In the 3 corners of the second colour, the
King's cypher and crown. The colours of the second battalion to be distinguished by a flaming ray of gold, descend-
ing from the upper corner of each colour, towards the
centre.

" On the grenadiers caps, the King's crest ; also, the
King's cypher and crown, as in the colours.

" On the drums, and bells of arms, the King's cypher
painted in the same manner, and the rank of the regiment
underneath."

N. B. Since these regulations have been issued, a light
company has been added to each corps of infantry, and,
I am informed, have the following appointments :

Jackets ; black leather caps, with 3 chains round them,
and a piece of plate upon the centre of the crown ; in the
front, G. R. a crown, and the number of the regiment ;
small cartouch boxes, powder-horns, and bags for ball ;
short pieces, and hatchets.

" *Warrant for regulating the Attendance of Officers belonging
to the several Regiments of Cavalry.*

" GEORGE R.

" WHEREAS We were pleased by Our warrant, bearing date the 27th day of July, 1764, to establish
certain rules and regulations for the attendance of the several Officers of Our regiments of horse and dragoons within
Our kingdom of Great Britain, with their respective corps ;
And whereas We have since found it necessary, for the good
of Our service, to establish some farther regulations for the
attendance of the said Officers ; We have therefore judged
it proper to revoke and annul Our warrant above-mentioned,
and We do hereby revoke and annul the same. And Our
farther will and pleasure is, that, in lieu thereof, and for
the

the more effectual maintenance of good order and difcipline in Our royal regiment of horfe guards, and in Our regiments of dragoon guards and dragoons, the following rules be ftrictly obferved; for the exact execution of which the Colonel and Field-officer commanding each regiment are to be refponfible.

" 1ft. That with each of Our faid regiments one Field-officer fhall be always prefent with the regiment; that one Captain fhall be prefent with each fquadron; and one Subaltern with each troop.

" 2d. That the Colonel or Field-officer commanding each regiment may grant leave of abfence to fuch other Officers whofe private affairs may require it, taking care always to detain, or from time to time to call in, a fufficient number of Officers to do the duty of the regiment, if fo fituated as to require the attendance of more Officers than We have hereby directed to be conftantly prefent.

" 3d. That the Officers appointed to carry on the recruiting fervice fhall not be included in the number hereby fixed for the conftant duty of the regiment, or in the number of thofe who fhall be further called in by the Commanding-officer for that duty.

" 4th. That the monthly return of each regiment be made up and tranfmitted as ufual on the firft of each month to Our Secretary at War, and to the Adjutant-General of Our forces; and that the return of the abfent Officers, which We have directed to be made on the 14th of each month, fhall, in like manner, be made up and tranfmitted from the head-quarters of every regiment in England to Our Secretary at War, and to the Adjutant-General of Our forces; and from the regiments in North-Britain, to the Officer commanding on that ftation for the time being; and the Commanding Officer by whom the faid returns fhall be figned, is carefully to examine the fame, as he is to be refponfible that they are in every refpect conformable to Our regulations.

" 5th. That the number of Officers hereby ordered to be prefent, fhall remain with their commands until they fhall be relieved; and, notwithftanding the returns are ordered to be tranfmitted on the 1ft and 14th of each month, yet the Officers are to continue at quarters during all the intermediate time, and the Commanding Officer is hereby enjoined not to permit them to abfent themfelves from the duty they are employed on, except in cafes of great emer-

gency,'

gency, and then but for two days only: and all leaves fo granted are to be fpecified in the next return, with the reafons for granting them.

" 6th. That no application fhall be made either to Us, or to the Commander in Chief of Our forces, for a leave of abfence for any Officer of Our faid regiments, except through the Colonel or Field-officer commanding the regiment ; and that all fuch applications fhall be fo regulated, that no particular Officer fhall be abfent from his duty too long at one time. The fame caution is to be obferved in limiting the leaves granted by the Colonel or Officer commanding each regiment.

" 7th. That every Officer, whether taken from the halfpay or otherwife, on being appointed to a regiment, fhall join it within 4 months at fartheft from the date of his commiffion, unlefs he fhall have obtained a particular leave of abfence, which is not to be granted except on very cogent reafons.

" 8th. That if any Officer, fo appointed, fhall exceed the time hereby limited, without a leave obtained for that purpofe, he fhall be returned *abfent without leave* ; and the date of his commiffion is to be fpecified in the return, it being Our firm intention immediately to fuperfede any Officer who fhall neglect to pay due obedience to this Our order.

" 9th. That every Officer newly appointed, and who has never before ferved in any of Our regiments of cavalry, fhall upon joining his regiment, remain in quarters until he be perfected in riding and all regimental duty.

" 10th. That no officer belonging to any of Our regiments of cavalry ftationed in Great-Britain, fhall go out of the kingdom without leave obtained from Us, the warrant for which is to exprefs the time for which the leave is granted, and is to be entered in the office of Our Secretary at War.

" 11th. All Officers, while prefent with their corps, are conftantly to wear their uniforms.

" 12th. Every Officer is to be prefent with his regiment annually in England by the 10th of March, and in Scotland by the 10th of April, and remain with it till after the fpring review: And this Our order is upon no account to be difpenfed with, except a particular leave fhall be obtained for that purpofe from Us, or the Commander in Chief of Our forces ; and no fuch leave fhall be applied for, except in cafes of abfolute unavoidable neceffity.

" 13th.

" 13th. All Recruiting-officers and recruits are to join their refpective corps in England by the 10th of March, and in Scotland by the 10th of April ; as We do expect that Our regiments on each ftation fhall be compleat annually in men by thofe refpective days.

" And We do hereby direct, that all and feveral the rules and regulations hereby eftablifhed be punctually obferved, upon pain of Our higheft difpleafure. Given at Our court at St. James's the 11th of February, 1767, in the feventh year of Our reign.

" By His Majefty's Command,

" War-Office.   " BARRINGTON."
A true Copy.

" Warrant for regulating the Stock-purfe Fund of the Regiments of Dragoon-Guards and Dragoons.

" GEORGE R.

" WHEREAS We have judged it neceffary for Our fervice, to afcertain the articles which may be charged againft the ftock-purfe fund of Our regiments of dragoonguards, and dragoons, excluding at the fame time all other articles whatever, in order that the faid fund may be kept apart for the purpofe of recruiting, and that the balance which fhall remain (after fatisfying the charges hereby admitted) may be applied to other public military ufes. We have therefore thought fit to order and direct, that, for the future, no charge fhall be made againft the faid ftock-purfe fund, but what comes fairly and evidently under the following heads, viz.

" The levy-money and expence of each recruit, and alfo his fubfiftence till he joins the regiment.

" Bounty - money to difcharged men, to carry them home.

" The fubfiftence of invalids difcharged and recommended to Our royal bounty of Chelfea hofpital, from the day to which they are fubfifted by the regiment, to that on which they are admitted on the penfion, or rejected by the Board.

" Expences of beating-orders, and attefted copies thereof,

" Expences of debenture warrants.

" Expences relating to deferters.

" And whereas our late Royal Grandfather, of glorious memory, was pleafed to direct, during the laft peace, that

S 3   each

each of the Captains of Our regiments of dragoons fhould be allowed £.25 yearly, to enable them to bear the contingent expences of their refpective troops; which fum was, during the late war, encreafed to £.35 : And whereas it is highly proper that the faid allowances fhould be now fixed by Us : We taking into Our royal confideration, various expences which have, from different circumftances, become an additional charge on the Captains of dragoons, fince the aforefaid regulation of Our late Royal Grandfather, at £.25 *per annum*, are pleafed to direct, that, for the future, the ftock-purfe account of Our regiments of dragoons fhall be fettled annually to the 24th of June, when £.5 fhall be fet apart for each man, and twenty guineas for each horfe, wanting to compleat on the 1ft of February, and be carried to the credit of the fucceeding account; after which the fum of £.30 fhall be given out of the faid fund to each of the Captains. And We are pleafed to direct that the fums fo paid to the Captains fhall be entered as the laft charge in the ftock-purfe account of each regiment of dragoons.

" And Our farther will and pleafure is, that in cafe any furplus fhall remain on balance of the ftock-purfe fund, annually ftated on the 24th day of June, (after deducting the aforefaid fums for recruiting and remounting, which muft be carried to the credit of the fucceeding account, and after paying to each Captain their entire allowance of £.30) that balance fhall be carried to the credit of the fucceeding year's account. And the feveral Agents are hereby directed to acquaint Our Secretary at War, upon the fettling of each year's accounts, with the amount of this furplus or balance, for Our information.

" And We do hereby direct, that all other charges and expences whatever, incurred by Our regiments of dragoon-guards and dragoons, and which have been ufually allowed, fhall for the future be inferted in the general half-yearly contingent bill, ordered to be tranfmitted to Our Secretary at War, by his letter bearing date the 26th day of November, 1765.

" Our farther will and pleafure is, that in the keeping and making up the ftock-purfe accounts of each of Our faid regiments, the following directions be for the future ftrictly obferved.

" That no more than three pounds eight fhillings fhall be allowed to any recruiting Officer for each man recruited by him; out of which fum no more than one guinea and

a crown

a crown fhall be given to the recruit, according to Our
directions fignified by Our Secretary at War bearing date
the 24th day of December, 1765; but no charge whatever
is to be admitted on account of recruits who may defert before they join the regiment.

" That no recruiting Officer fhall be allowed credit for
the levy-money of any fuch recruits as fhall not be approved
of by the Commanding Officer of each regiment refpectively; but their fubfiftence fhall be allowed. The ftock-
purfe fund fhall be charged with the real expence of all the
recruits who may die before they join the regiment; provided the day of their death, and the exact bounty-money
given them, be certified by the Commanding Officer, on
the back of the atteftation.

" That all fubfiftence iffued to the recruits before they
join the regiment, fhall be charged feparately from the levy
money.

" The accounts of all the recruiting Officers are to be
ftated and fettled on or before the 24th day of June.

" The recruiting accounts are to be figned by the recruiting Officer himfelf, and by the Field-officer commanding at quarters; and Our pleafure is, that thofe accounts,
fo figned, fhall be good and fufficient vouchers to the Agent
for the credit given by him to each recruiting Officer, on
the head of recruiting.

" That in all future ftates of the regimental accounts
given in to the reviewing Generals, the number of recruits,
for which levy-money and fubfiftence are charged, fhall be
particularly and feparately fpecified.

" That no more than twenty guineas fhall be given for
each horfe.

" That the travelling expences incurred until the horfes
join the regiment, fhall be charged in a feparate article,
and the charges on that account particularly fpecified and
vouched.

" That the Captains fhall account for the fubfiftence of
the vacant men and horfes in their refpective troops, arifing
from vacancies which happen between the days whereon
each Captain ufually receives the fubfiftence of his troop;
and that the ftock-purfe fund fhall have credit for the vacant fubfiftence of every man who fhall die, defert, or be
difcharged, and of every horfe that fhall die, or be caft between the above-mentioned periods, from the day on which
they are no longer entitled to fubfiftence.

" That

" That the ſtock-purſe fund ſhall alſo have credit for the ſums for which the horſes that ſhall be caſt from time to time, ſhall be ſold.

" We are farther pleaſed to direct, that every Colonel ſhall himſelf carefully examine the ſtock-purſe account, previous to its being laid before the reviewing General : he is likewiſe to certify under his hand, that he believes it to be fair and exact. And the reviewing General ſhall report to Us any articles which ſhall appear to him to be charged contrary to theſe Our orders ; as likewiſe whether proper credit be given to the ſtock-purſe fund for the whole vacant ſubſiſtence of men and horſes, and for the price of the caſt horſes.

" All the aforeſaid orders, regulations, and directions, We ſtrictly charge and command all reviewing Generals, Colonels, Commanding Officers, and Agents of Our regiments of dragoon-guards and dragoons, and all others whom they may concern, to follow and obey, under pain of Our higheſt diſpleaſure.

" Given at Our court at St. James's, this 19th of February, 1766, in the 6th year of Our reign.

" By His Majeſty's Command,

" War-Office.
A true Copy.

BARRINGTON."

" *Warrant for regulating the Recruiting and Reviewing of the
ſeveral Regiments of Foot upon Foreign Stations.*

GEORGE R.

WHEREAS it hath been humbly repreſented unto Us, that it would greatly tend to the preſervation of good order and diſcipline in Our ſeveral marching regiments of foot, which are or may be upon foreign ſtations, to have ſome certain regulations laid down by Us, for reviewing and recruiting thoſe regiments, as well as keeping them compleat in arms, accoutrements, and cloathing ; Our will and pleaſure is, that the following rules and regulations be, for this purpoſe, ſtrictly obſerved for the future, by Our Commander in Chief in North America, and by all Our Governors and Officers commanding Our regiments abroad, and by all other military Officers whom it may concern.

1ſt. That all the old and unſerviceable men, who are now in any of Our regiments above-mentioned, be diſcharged

charged as foon as poffible, and fuch as are proper objects recommended to Our bounty of Chelfea; care being however taken at the fame time not to diminifh the numbers of any regiment, fo far as to prejudice the fervice on which it may be employed; and, it is Our will and pleafure, that this duty, which We efteem to be indifpenfible, fhould be obferved, not only now, but conftantly; as we expect that Our faid regiments fhall at all times be maintained, in fuch a ftate of compleatnefs, ftrength, and difcipline, as always to be prepared for immediate fervice.

2d. That conftant care be taken to keep as many parties employed upon the recruiting fervice, as the number of vacancies, and the ftate of the regiment may require.

3d. That pofitive orders be given to all Officers, who fhall be fent with the command of recruiting parties, that they do not inlift any men but fuch as are in every refpect fit for Our fervice; and, that they may be informed that a moft ftrict examination will be regularly made of their recruits, and that fuch of them, who do not anfwer the inftructions, fhall be rejected.

4th. That for the future, the following refpective fums fhall be allowed to Officers fent upon the recruiting fervice, from the feveral ftations abroad, towards bearing the expence of paffage: viz.

	l.	s.	d.
From North-America, the Weft-Indies, and Africa	12	10	0
From Minorca	7	17	6
From Gibraltar	5	5	0

and that thofe fums be advanced to each Officer, when he fhall be fent on the recruiting fervice, by the Pay-mafter of the regiment, and fhall be placed as a charge againft the non-effective fund.

5th. And, whereas it is effential to the good of the fervice, that the arms, accoutrements, and cloathing of Our faid regiments, fhould be always kept complete, and in proper ferviceable order; and, that the ftricteft attention fhould be had, not only to the difcipline, but to the interior œconomy of each corps; for this purpofe Our will and pleafure is, that each of Our faid regiments (provided it may not be inconfiftent with the fervice on which they may be feverally employed) fhall be affembled annually, at the moft convenient feafon, and reviewed and infpected by the Commander in Chief, Governor, Brigadier,

or

or any other Officer, under whofe command it may happen to be, by whom the following returns are to be made up, and fent as foon as may be practicable, after the review and infpection hereby directed, to Our fecretary at War, and Adjutant General of Our forces refpectively, according to the form herewith tranfmitted, in order to their being laid before Us : viz.

A return of Officers prefent and abfent.
A return of Non-commiffioned Officers and private men.
A general return of the regiment.
A field return.
A return of the ftate of the arms, accoutrements, and clothing. ,

6th. That the Officer, who fhall refpectively review, and infpect each regiment, do add fuch farther remarks and obfervations of his own, as may, in every refpect, tend to give Us a full information of the actual ftate and condition of each regiment.

7th. That, if, from the circumftances of Our fervice, any regiment fhall be fo fituated that it cannot be affembled, the different parts of it fhall be infpected in fuch a manner as the Commander in Chief, Governor, Brigadier, or other Officer, under whofe command it may happen to be, fhall think moft convenient for the fervice, and that the returns, according to the forms which are now ordered, fhall be made up, and tranfmitted by the earlieft opportunity ; and We do hereby direct, that all, and feveral the rules and regulations hereby eftablifhed, be punctually obferved, upon pain of Our higheft difpleafure. Given at Our court at St. James's the 8th of January, 1768, in the 8th year of Our reign.

By His Majefty's command,
War-Office.   BARRINGTON.

Warrant for regulating the Attendance of Officers belonging to Regiments on Foreign Stations.

G E O R G E R.

WHEREAS We have thought it neceffary for the good order and difcipline of Our forces ftationed in Our garrifons and other Our dominions beyond the feas, to eftablifh certain rules and regulations for the due attendance of
           the

the Officers belonging to, or who fhall be appointed to commiffions in Our faid forces, Our will and pleafure is, that
the fame be obferved ftrictly as follows.

1ft. That when any Officer who may be in Britain or
Ireland fhall be appointed to a commiffion in any of Our
regiments ftationed abroad, he fhall fet out to join his
regiment within four months at fartheft from the date of his
commiffion, unlefs he fhall have obtained Our leave of abfence for a longer time; it being Our firm intention to fuperfede any Officer who fhall difobey this Our order.

2d. Application fhall not be made to Us for farther leave
except on very extraordinary occafions; and it fhall then
be made through the Colonel of the regiment, if he is in
Britain.

3d. All leaves granted by Us, for any term beyond the
four months above-mentioned, fhall exprefs the particular
time for which they are granted, and fhall be entered in the
office of Our Secretary at War; and all Colonels are hereby
required to take care that all Officers when newly appointed
to their refpective regiments, be apprized of thefe Our orders; and report to Us if they fhall find that they are not
ftrictly complied with.

4th. The Officer commanding on each ftation fhall be
made acquainted with the leaves fo granted, and fhall tranfmit the fame to the refpective regiments, in order that they
may be inferted in the monthly returns.

5th. A lift of all Officers newly appointed fhall be tranfmitted by our Secretary at War, by the earlieft opportunity,
to the Colonel of the regiment, if he be in Britain; as alfo
to the Commander or Governor where the refpective regiments are ftationed, with the dates of their commiffions.

6th. The faid lift fhall be tranfmitted by the faid Commander or Governor to each regiment under his command;
and when any Officer fhall be returned not joined, the date
of his commiffion fhall be inferted in the return; to the ecd
that We may be fatisfied of the due performance of Our
commands herein.

7th. When any Officer belonging to a regiment ftationed
abroad, fhall obtain leave of abfence from the Commander
in Chief, Governor or Commanding Officer, it fhall be for
a limited time only; which time fhall be fpecified in the
returns; and before the expiration thereof, he fhall join his
regiment.

8th.

8th. But as from the uncertainty of a fea paſſage, it may fometimes happen that an Officer may not return exactly to the day prefcribed by his leave, the Commanding Officer is in that cafe to enquire, and make proper allowances; the whole of which is to be explained in the next return.

9th. And whereas it may be neceſſary in fome particular cafes to prolong the leaves fo granted, the Colonel of the regiment is upon fuch occafions to make the application, in order that it may be properly laid before Us, and if granted, the fame is to be fignified by Our Secretary at War to the refpective Commander or Governor, with the particular time for which each leave is prolonged; in order that the Officer commanding the regiment may be acquainted therewith.

10th. But in order to prevent the neceſſity of frequent applications to Us upon this head, it is Our pleafure that fuch leave fhall in the firſt inſtance be granted, as is reafonable and fufficient; it not being Our intention to prolong the fame, except in very particular cafes and circumſtances which could not have been forefeen by Our faid Governors or Commanders.

11th. The refpective Commanders in Chief, Governors, and Field Officers, are to be refponfible that, according to the fituation and circumſtances of each regiment, there are always a fufficient number of Officers prefent to do duty.

And we do hereby direct that all and feveral the rules and regulations hereby eſtabliſhed be punctually obferved, upon pain of Our higheſt difpleafure. Given at Our court of St. James's, the 11th of February, 1767, in the 7th year of Our Reign.

By His Majeſty's command,

War-Office.   BARRINGTON.

Form of a Warrant for holding a General Court-martial for the trial of A. B.

GEORGE R.

WHEREAS We were pleafed, by our commiſſion dated on the   Day of   to appoint ————, commonly called ————, then a Lieutenant General in Our fervice, to be Commander in Chief of all Our Britiſh forces, as well horfe as foot, then ferving on the Lower Rhine, in our army aſſembled, or to be aſſembled there under

under the command of Our good Coufin Prince Ferdinand of Brunfwick, Commander in Chief of Our faid army, enjoining and requiring him the faid ————, to obey fuch orders and directions as fhould be given him by the faid Prince Ferdinand, or fuch other perfon as might hereafter be Commander in Chief of our faid army, according to the Rules of War : and whereas We were pleafed by Our inftructions, under Our fign manual, bearing date the fame   Day of   to direct the faid ——, conftantly to put in execution fuch orders as he might receive from Our faid good Coufin Prince Ferdinand of Brunfwick, or fuch other perfon as might hereafter be Commander in Chief of Our faid army, according to the Rules of War, with regard to marching, counter-marching, attacking the enemy, and all operations whatfoever to be undertaken by Our faid troops; and whereas We are informed that the faid ————, hath difobeyed the orders of the faid Prince Ferdinand, which charge We thinking fit fhould be enquired into by a General Court-martial, did, by Our warrrant, bearing date the   Day of   order that a General Court-martial fhould be forthwith held upon that occafion, which was to confift of Our trufty and well beloved ————, Lieutenant-General of Our forces, whom he did appoint to be Prefident thereof, and of Our trufty and well-beloved ————, Sir ————, Knight of the Bath, ————, ————, Our right trufty and well beloved Counfellor ————————, Our trufty and well beloved ————, Our right trufty and well beloved Coufin ——, Earl of ——, Our trufty and well beloved ————, commonly called Earl of ——, Our right trufty and well beloved Coufin ——, Earl of ———, Our trufty and well beloved ————————, Our right trufty and well beloved Coufin ——, Earl of ———, Our trufty and well beloved ————————, Lieutenant Generals, Our trufty and well beloved ————————, Our right trufty and well beloved Coufin ——, Earl of ———, Our trufty and well beloved ————, and ————, Major Generals of Our forces; and of whom, or the faid Prefident, together with any twelve or more of the faid Officers, might conftitute the faid General Court-martial ; which faid General Court-martial hath met, but hath not yet examined any witneffes : and whereas it hath been fince reprefented that the faid Prefident Lieutenant General ————, hath been taken fuddenly ill, and is unable to attend : and
whereas,

whereas, if others of the said members should by unavoidable accidents be prevented from attending, there may not be a sufficient number to compose a General Court-martial, Our will and pleasure is, and We do hereby direct, the General Court martial for the trial of the said ———— ——,
do consist of Our trusty and well beloved Sir ———, Knt. of the Bath, whom We do hereby appoint to be President thereof, and of Our trusty and well beloved ———— ——;
———— ——, Our right trusty and well beloved Counsellor ——, Lord ———, Our trusty and well beloved ————.
——, ———— ——, Our right trusty and well beloved Cousin ——, Earl of ———, Our trusty and well beloved ———— ——, commonly called Earl of ———, Our right trusty and well beloved Cousin ——, Earl of ———— ——,
Our trusty and well beloved ———— ——, ———— ——, Esquire, commonly called Lord ———— ——, Lieutenant Generals, Our trusty and well beloved ———— ——, Our right trusty and well beloved Cousin ——, Earl of ———;
Our trusty and well beloved ———— ——, Esquire, commonly called Lord ———— ——, and ———— ——, Major Generals of Our forces; all of whom, or the said Lieutenant General Sir ———— ——, President, together with any twelve or more of the said last mentioned Officers, may constitute the said General Court-martial: and you are to order the Provost Martial General, or his Deputy, to give notice to the said President and Officers, and all others whom it may concern, when and where the said Court-martial hereby appointed is to be held, and to summon such witnesses as shall be able to give testimony in this matter, the said Provost Master General and his Deputy being hereby directed to obey your orders, and give attendance where it shall be requisite. And We do further authorize and empower the said Court-martial hereby appointed, to hear and examine all such matters and informations, as shall be brought before them, touching the charge aforesaid, and proceed in the trial of the said ———— ——, and in giving of sentence according to the rules of military discipline, which said sentence you are to return to Our Secretary at War, to be laid before Us for Our consideration: and for so doing this shall be as well to you, as to the said Court-martial hereby appointed, and all others concerned, a sufficient warrant. Given at our Court at *St. James's*, this   Day of in the   year of Our reign.

BY HIS MAJESTY's COMMAND.

To

To
Our trusty and well beloved
——————, Esquire, Judge-
Advocate-General of Our forces,
or his Deputy.

A Description of a General Court-martial.

AT a General Court-martial held at the Judge Advocate
General's Office at the Horse Guards, on   the
and continued by several adjournments to   the
   of   by virtue of his Majesty's special warrant,
bearing date the   day of the same month.

LIEUTENANT GENERAL, SIR ——————————,
—————.

Lieutenant General.
{
J—— C————.
J—— LORD D————.
J—— C————.
J—— S————.
W—— EARL OF P————.
W—— K——, EARL OF A————.
W—— EARL OF H————,
J—— A————.
G—— EARL OF A————.
F—— L————.
LORD R—— M————.

Maj. Gen.
{
E—— C————.
T—— EARL OF E.
LORD R—— B————.
J—— C————.

——————————, DEPUTY JUDGE ADVOCATE GENERAL.

The members being met, and duly sworn (the Judge
Advocate being also sworn, and prosecuting in his Majesty's
Name,)
The right honourable ——————, Esquire, commonly
called ——————, came prisoner before the Court, and
the following charge was exhibited against him : viz.
" Whereas his Majesty was pleased, by his commission
dated the   day of   to appoint him, being then a
Lieutenant General in his Majesty's service, to be Commander in Chief of all his British forces, as well horse as
oot, then serving on the Lower Rhine, in his army assembled,

bled, or to be affembled there, under the command of
Prince Ferdinand of Brunfwick, Commander in Chief of
his Majefty's faid army, enjoining and requiring him to
obey fuch orders and directions as fhould be given him
by the faid Prince Ferdinand, or fuch other perfon as
might hereafter be Commander in Chief of his Majefty's
faid army, according to the Rules of War ; and whereas his
Majefty was alfo pleafed, by inftructions under his fign
manual bearing date the fame   day of   to direct
him conftantly to put in execution fuch orders, as he might
receive from the faid Prince Ferdinand, of Brunfwick, or
fuch other perfon as might thereafter be Commander in
Chief of his Majefty's faid army, according to the Rules of
War, with regard to marching, counter-marching, attacking the enemy, and all operations whatfoever to be undertaken by his Majefty's faid troops.

" That he the faid ——————, hath neverthelefs difobeyed the orders of the faid Prince Ferdinand of Brunfwick."

Which charge of difobedience was by the Judge Advocate declared to be confined to orders relative to the battle
of *M——*.

The following commiffion and inftructions being admitted by ——————————, to be true copies of thofe received
by his Lordfhip, were then read : viz.

" G E O R G E R.

" GEORGE the Second, by the grace of God, King of
Great-Britain, France and Ireland, Defender of the Faith,
&c. To Our trufty and well beloved ——————————,
Efq. commonly called ——————————, Lieutenant General
of Our forces, and Lieutenant General of Our ——————
greeting. We, repofing efpecial truft and confidence in your
prudence, courage, and loyalty, have appointed, and, by
thefe prefents, do appoint you to be Commander in Chief
of all our Britifh forces, as well horfe as foot, now ferving
on the Lower Rhine, in Our army affembled, or to be
affembled there under the command of Our good coufin
Prince Ferdinand of Brunfwick, Commander in Chief of
Our faid army ; and all Our Officers and foldiers of Our
faid Britifh forces ferving, or to ferve on the Lower Rhine,
as aforefaid, are hereby enjoined and required to obey you,
as Commander in Chief : and you, on your part, are hereby
enjoined and required to obey fuch orders and directions,

as

as fhall be given you by our faid good Coufin Prince Ferdinand of Brunfwick, or fuch other perfon as may hereafter be Commander in Chief of Our faid army, according to the rules of war ——And for the better government of our faid Britifh forces fo employed, or to be employed, in ferving on the Lower Rhine above-mentioned, we have thought fit to authorize and empower, and, by thefe prefents, do authorize and empower you to prepare and publifh fuch rules and ordinances, as are fit to be obferved by all Officers and foldiers under your command ; as alfo to punifh all offenders and tranfgreffors againft the fame, by death, or otherwife, according to the nature of their offences, as they fhall appear upon trial before a Court-martial, which we hereby give you power and authority to affemble, as often as you fhall fee occafion, agreeable to the rules and orders for the better government of our forces employed in foreign parts ; and, according to their judgment, you are to caufe fentence to be pronounced againft the perfon or perfons fo offending, either of pains of death, or of fuch other pains or penalties, as fhall be thought fit to be inflicted by the faid Court-martial ; which fentence, or fentences, you are to caufe to be put in execution, or to fufpend the fame, as, in your difcretion, you fhall fee caufe ; We giving you power to reprieve any perfon, under any fentence, till Our pleafure be known ; and for execution of juftice in Our faid Britifh forces, We give you authority to appoint a Provoft Marfhal, to ufe and execute that office, as is ufually practifed in the law martial. And whereas We have appointed a Judge Advocate to attend the faid Court-martial, for the more orderly proceedings of the fame, We do hereby give you power, in cafe of death, ficknefs, or neceffary abfence of the faid Judge Advocate, to depute another perfon, fuch as in your difcretion you fhall think fit, to execute the faid office. And We do further authorize you to caufe exact mufters to be taken of the refpective troops and companies of our faid forces, and to fign warrants for their pay, according to the faid mufters, in purfuance of an eftablifhment made for that purpofe. And whereas by the faid eftablifhment, there is a provifion made for fuch contingent charges as may arife for Our fervice, and the ufe of Our forces, you are hereby authorized to direct the payment of the faid money, in fuch proportions, as you fhall, in your difcretion, think neceffary for the purpofes aforefaid. And for executing the feveral powers and authorities herein ex

T.   preffed, preſſed, this ſhall be your warrant. Given at Our court at Kenſington, the   day of   in the 32d year of Our reign.   " By his Majeſty's command,

H————— ———.

GEORGE R.

" INSTRUCTIONS *for our Truſty and well-beloved ——— ——— Eſq. commonly called ——— ——— , Lieutenant General of Our Forces, and Lieutenant General of Our ——— ——— whom We have appointed to command our* Britiſh *Forces, now ſerving, or to ſerve on the Lower Rhine. Given at Our Court at Kenſington, the Day of   in the 32d Year of Our Reign.*

" 1.   WHEREAS We have thought fit to appoint you, by the commiſſion herewith tranſmitted to you, to be Commander in Chief of Our Britiſh forces employed on the Lower Rhine; you are, upon the receipt of theſe Our inſtructions and commiſſion, to give due notice thereof to Our good Couſin Prince Ferdinand of Brunſwick, Commander in Chief of our army now aſſembled upon the Lower Rhine.

" 2. With regard to marching, counter-marching, attacking the enemy, and all operations whatſoever, to be undertaken by Our ſaid troops, you are conſtantly to put in execution ſuch orders as you may receive from Our ſaid good Couſin Prince Ferdinand of Brunſwick, or ſuch other perſon as may hereafter be Commander in Chief of our ſaid army, according to the rules of war.

" 3. In caſe of the vacancy of any Commiſſion in Our ſaid Britiſh forces, you are to give Us immediate notice thereof, in order to your receiving Our further pleaſure thereupon, recommending to Our favour ſuch Officers as ſhall, in your opinion, beſt deſerve to be advanced.

" 4. During your continuance in this ſervice, you are to ſend, or cauſe to be ſent to Us, by one of Our principal Secretaries of State, conſtant accounts of all that paſſes ; and you are to follow all ſuch further orders and directions as We ſhall ſend you, either under Our ſign manual, or by one of Our Principal Secretaries of State.   G. R."

Then the ſeveral witneſſes were examined in ſupport of the charge, and all having been examined, the Court proceeded to the form of ſentence.

The

The Court, upon due confideration of the whole matter before them, is of opinion, that ――――――, is guilty of having difobeyed the orders of Prince F―――― of B――――――, whom he was, by his commiffion and inftruétions, direéted to obey as Commander in Chief, according to the rules of war : and it is the farther opinion of this Court, that the faid ――――――― is, and he is hereby adjudged unfit to ferve his Majefty in any military capacity.

Form of a Warrant for Refignation.

WHEREAS it hath been humbly reprefented unto Us, that Major A. of Our regiment of commanded by our trufty and well-beloved B. C. D. is now, after years fervice, rendered unable to do his duty ; We have, therefore, thought fit, at his own requeft, and for the good of Our fervice, by Our commiffion, bearing date the day of 17 laft, to promote Captain E. of Our faid regiment, to fucceed the faid A. as Major ; Captain Lieutenant F. of Our faid regiment, to fucceed the faid E. as Captain ; Lieutenant G. of Our faid regiment to fucceed the faid F. as Captain Lieutenant ; Enfign H. of Our faid regiment, to fucceed the faid G. as Lieutenant ; and I. Gentleman, to fucceed the faid H. as Enfign.

Notwithftanding which promotion, Our will and pleafure is, that the faid E. and the Major to Our faid regiment, without purchafe, for the time being, fhall continue to receive pay as Captain only ; that the faid F. and youngeft Captain, for the time being, in Our faid regiment, without purchafe, fhall continue to receive pay as Captain Lieutenant only ; the faid G. and the Captain Lieutenant of Our faid regiment, for the time being, without purchafe, fhall continue to receive pay as Lieutenant only ; and the faid H. and the youngeft Lieutenant in Our faid regiment, for the time being, without purchafe, fhall receive pay as Enfign only ; and the faid I. youngeft Enfign in our faid regiment for the time being, without purchafe, fhall receive no pay.

To the end that the faid A. may, for his future fupport and maintenance, hold and enjoy, during his life, the full pay of a day : the fame to commence from the faid day of 17 laft, inclufive, and to be iffued him or his affigns during his life ; and that upon the death of the faid A. the faid E. and the

T 2 Major

Major to Our faid regiment, for the time being, without purchafe, the faid F. and the youngeft Captain thereof, for the time being, without purchafe, the faid G. and the Captain Lieutenant in our faid regiment, for the time being, without purchafe, and the faid H. and the youngeft Lieutenant thereof, for the time being, without purchafe, and the faid I. and the youngeft Enfign thereof, for the time being, without purchafe, fhall receive pay conformable, to Our eftablifhment: and for fo doing, this, with the acquittance of the faid A. or his affigns, fhall be, as well to you as to all others whom it may concern, from time to time, a fufficient warrant, authority and difcharge. Given at Our Court at St. James's the   day of   17   in the   year of Our reign.

By his Majefty's command,

To   K. L.

The Agent of Our regiment of   commanded by Our trufty and well-beleved B. C. D. and to the Agent of Our regiment, for the time being, in Great Britain or Ireland, or to whom the payment thereof fhall or may concern.

B A C K E D.

Warrant for Major A. of the   regiment of
to retire upon   day.

Attorney General's Opinion concerning Soldiers making away with their Cloths or Neceffaries.

Captain A. B. of the   regiment, reprefents, in a letter of the   of June, from   that he has had feveral hearings before the Civil Magiftrates, with the inhabitants, for buying and taking in pledge from the foldiers, their fhirts, fhoes, and ftockings, particularly in regard to one   of Captain   company, who fold four fhirts, two pair of ftockings, and a pair of fhoes, leaving himfelf deftitute of linen, &c. &c.

By the objections made by the attorney, in behalf of the defendant, neither the expected penalty nor punifhment is inflicted, purfuant to the 45th claufe in the mutiny and defertion bill, which enacts, " That if any perfon fhall knowingly detain, buy, or exchange, or otherwife receive arms,
cloths,

cloths, caps, or any other furniture belonging to the King, from any soldier or deserter, upon any account or pretence whatever, or cause the colour of such cloths to be changed, the person so offending, shall forfeit for every such offence, the sum of five pounds, and, upon conviction of the oath of one or more credible witnesses, before any of his Majesty's Justices of the Peace, the penalty of five pounds be levied by warrant, under the hand of the said Justices of the Peace, by distress and sale of the goods and chattles of the offender.

OBJECTIONS.

The attorney in behalf of the defendant, will not admit the soldier who sells his linen, necessaries, or clothing, &c. to be an evidence against the person who buys or receives them ; neither will the attorney allow what a soldier is provided with to belong to the King, except his red cloths and hat; alledging, that shoes, linen, and stockings are the soldier's property, being bought out of his pay, so that he may do with them what he pleases.

ANSWER.

Every soldier is provided with a compleat clothing ; the fund whereof arising from his pay (in which is included his cloths, hat, shirts, shoes, and stockings) the three last species come within the denomination of small cloathing ; but these being of a more perishable kind, the soldier is to be provided with them from time to time, as necessity may require ; and for that end, there is a deduction of six-pence out of his pay, pursuant to the 14th clause in the mutiny act.

QUERIES.

Whether the soldier who sells, may not be admitted an evidence against the person who buys his clothing, linen, &c.

Whether linen, shoes, and stockings, are not as much a part of his clothing, and belonging to the King, as the cloths and hat; the whole being bought out of the soldier's pay?

As there is a criminal persecution, I am of opinion, that the soldier may be a witness against the person who buys and sells his clothing : the linen, shoes and stockings are, I conceive, within the intent of the recited clause ; the detaining, buying, or exchanging them knowingly, is an offence punishable in the manner therein directed.

D. RIDER.

T 3 ME-

MEMORANDUM.

If the afore-cited clause is not clear and exprefs, with regard to the perfon buying the feveral fpecies of fmall clothing before-mentioned, every foldier may embezzle them, or be feduced fo do to, by evil and defigning perfons.

Form of a Letter to the Poft-Mafter of ———— ————.

WAR-OFFICE.

SIR,

I AM directed by the Secretary at War, to defire you will be pleafed to deliver the enclofed order to the Officer commanding the regiment, troop, company, or any detachment, or recruiting parties, of his Majefty's forces, that are, or may arrive at   before or during the election of a Member of Parliament there : and you will be pleafed to acquaint me with the receipt of this for the information of the Secretary at War.

> I am,
>
> SIR,
>
> Your moft humble Servant.

Form of a Letter for the Removal of Troops, in Cafe of an Election.

IT is his Majefty's pleafure, that you caufe the regiment, troop, company, or any detachment, or recruiting parties, of his Majefty's forces at   to march from thence, three days before the day appointed for the election of a Member of Parliament there, to fome adjacent place or places not within a lefs diftance than three miles from in which place or places they are to be quartered, and remain for three days after the election fhall be over, and then return to   and it is his Majefty's farther pleafure, that you do take care, that the place, or places, chofen for fuch occafional quarters, be not within a lefs diftance than three miles from any town or city where the election for Members of Parliament fhall fall within the time of your being fo quartered; wherein the civil magiftrates, and all others concerned, are to be affifting in providing quarters, impreffing carriages, and otherwife, as there fhall be occafion. Given at the War-Office this day of

> By his Majefty's command.

To

To
The Officer commanding the
regiment, troop, company, or
any detachment or recruiting
parties of his Majefty's forces at

Form of Order for conveying Deferters from the Savoy.

IT is his Majefty's pleafure that you caufe a proper guard
to be made from the regiments of foot guards, and receive
from the keeper of the Savoy prifon,

and convey the faid deferter to the next regiment of horfe,
dragoons, or foot, quartered on the road to
And the faid regiment of horfe, dragoons, or foot, is hereby
required to convey the faid deferter to the next regiment,
and fo from regiment, to regiment, until he arrive at
where he   to be delivered to the Commanding-officer
                                                  and you are to caufe
the remainder of the fubfiftence which the keeper of the
Savoy prifon will advance with the faid deferter to carry him
to   to be delivered from regiment to regiment,
together with the M   Wherein the civil magiftrates and all others concerned, are to be affifting in providing quarters, impreffing carriages, and otherwife, as there
fhall be occafion.   Given at the War-office, the
day of
                              By his Majefty's command,
                   In the abfence of the Secretary at War.

    To
The Field Officer in ftaff
waiting, for the three regiments of foot guards.

Form of Leave of Abfence for Officers, granted in America,
in time of War.

BY   Efq. Colonel in the
or royal   regiment, Brigadier General and
Commander in Chief of his Majefty's Forces up the river
St. Lawrence.

    Leave of abfence is hereby granted to
of the   regiment of foot, commanded by
to go to   for the recovery of his health.
                         A. B. Brigadier General.
                 T 4   *Inftructions*

Inſtructions for making out Muſter-Rolls.

Article THE number of the ſeniority of the regiment,
I. (of horſe or foot) with the Colonel's name, to
be ſet down at the head of the roll, with a line of ſeparation:
(and the endorſement to expreſs the ſame.)

II. THE Commiſſion-officers (and ſtaff on the Colonel's
roll) to be ſet down in the middle of the page, immediately
under the ſaid line, and to be divided likewiſe by a line of
ſeparation.

III. THE Serjeants, Corporals, and drums, &c. to be
placed in three diſtinct columns, and to follow the Commiſſion Officers, with a third line of ſeparation.

IV. THE effective private men, for the whole time, to
follow alphabetically, on pencil'd lines, in three equal columns (or more, if neceſſary) and a diſtance of one line,
between every five names.

V. THE private men for the broken times, to be ſet down
after the effectives for the whole time, in ſuch order, that the
man who ſucceeds, ſhall immediately follow him who occaſioned the vacancy; whereby the intermediate time, if any,
will inſtantly appear: and all vacancies by death, diſcharges,
&c. between the end of the muſter, and time of taking it,
are, if certified, (as hereafter mentioned) to be allowed effective.

VI. THE ſeveral dates, and reaſons, of broken times, of
Commiſſion, Non-commiſſion-officers, and private men, to
be ſet down againſt their reſpective names, on the Commiſſary's (or call) roll; ſpecifying when, or whether appointed,
promoted, or transferred, (and to what corps) recruiting, on
party, on duty, abſent, or on furlough, (and by whoſe leave)
ſick, lame, in priſon, diſcharged, deſerted, or dead; which
are to be certified, by the Commanding-officer, on the back
of the ſaid roll; which roll is to be ſworn to, and ſigned by
the Commiſſary, (according to the act for puniſhing mutiny
and deſertion, &c.) under the ſaid certificate, and is afterwards
to remain on record in the Commiſſary General's office.

VII. THE Officer of the troop, or company, is to have
a return roll, except the certificate, and oath on the back.

VIII. WHERE the men are drawn up according to their
ſizes, they cannot be muſtered alphabetically; the Officer's
return-roll muſt then be made out conformable thereto, and
ſerve for the call-roll, which muſt afterwards be compared
with the certified-roll, and with two other alphabetical rolls,
one on parchment, for the Pay Maſter General, and one on
paper

paper for the Comptrollers of the Accompts of the army, (according to the aforesaid act) which are to be exact copies of each other.

IX. No reasons to be given, nor any remarks to be made, on the parchment, and Comptrollers rolls, except specifying the dates of the broken times against the respective names, with the words to—day of the month, (implying inclusive, and the date from whence the muster is taken,) and from ——————day of the month, (implying inclusive, and the date to which time the muster is taken.)

X. The above being completed by a ruled line, the absent, as well as present effectives, are to be comprised in one article, and to be closed thus, in

The Docquet of the Parchment and Comptroller's Rolls.

(Name of Place) Day of *(Month)* 17—

1. MUSTERED then in his Majesty's (Nº. of seniority) regiment of (horse or foot) commanded by (the Colonel's name) and in (name troop, or) company, the

{ Colonel and
Lieut. Col. and } Captain, Lieutenant, (Cornet, Quarter-
Major, and

Master) Ensign, (Nº. of) Serjeants, Corporals, (trumpets, hautbois) drums, and —————— effective private men.

2. Allowing the Commission, Non-commission Officers and private men, to effective for the intermediate times, as set down against their respective names abovementioned, being certified on the back of the Commissary General's roll.

3. This muster is taken for $\frac{182}{183}$ days from the 25th of (month) 17— to the 24th of (month) following, both days inclusive.

The parchment, Comptrollers, and Commissary General's roll to be signed by two Commission Officers of the regiment, troop or company, under the close of the docquet, to the right-hand; the Commissary to sign on the left, and the Magistrate to sign in the space between the two Officers, and the Commissary's names: the return-roll is to be signed on the right-hand, by the Commissary only.

N. B. All garrison rolls are to be made out in like form as a regimental-roll, and may be signed by one Officer only, whose name is on the face of the roll, provided it appears, by proper certificates, that all the other Officers are absent with leave.

Commissary General's Office,
1st May, 1756.   THOMAS GORE.

FORM

FORM of the COMMISSARY's (or Call) ROLL, and the OFFICERS Return ROLL.

His MAJESTY's (N°ᵗʰ) Regiment of Foot, Commanded by Colonel *William Waterland.*

Prom. in the (th) Foot, 17th Sept. Commission dated 21st ditto

	Edward Blacket	} Captain
Sick,	*John Churchill*	Lieut.
	George Calcraft	Enſign.
Recruiting,	*William Earle*	

Drums.

Hugh Powel	Recruiting
Luke Nickol	Died, 15th December
Timothy Bangham	Appointed, 16th, ditto

Serjeants.

Died 21 Aug. *Joſeph Andrews* }	Prom.22 Aug.
App. 22 ditto *Peregrine Furye* }	
Recruiting, *George Abbott*	
Humphry Portman	

Corporals.

Prom.22Aug. *PeregrineFurye*	
Appoint.ditto *AnthonySawyer*	
Robert Randoll	
Frederic Heſſe	

Serjeants	Corporals		Drums
John Adair	*William Hogarth*		*Thomas Sadlier*
Thomas Aſhton	*Thomas Hudſon*		*Edward Sedgewick*
John Aſliffe	*William Johnſton* Party,		*Thomas Sherwin*
William Balderſton	*Chriſtopher Kilby*		*Philip Thickneſſe*
Thomas Barrow	*William Knapton*	Duty,	*John Upton*
Duty,			

	Corporals	Drums
Furlough } *Edward Bronſdon*	*Aaron Lamb*	*John Vardy*
Maj. Leave. } *Edmund Byron*	*Thomas Langford*	*Charles Vere*

Duty,	John Chapman	Prison,	Harman Leece	William Walmesley	
	Richard Cleveland		Peter Lebeup	James West	
	Ralph Culliford		Edward Lloyd	John Winter	
Sick,	Robert Dodsley	Party,	David Middleton	John Wiseman	Discharged, 12th July.
	George Durant		Charles Monson	John Lockman	Entertained, 14th ditto.
	Charles Dyson		Abraham Mortier	Thomas Tomkins	Died, 8th August.
	Thomas Elder		James Napier	Henry Bullock	Recd. fr. Capt. Gore's Co 9. d°
	Gilbert Elliot		Isaac Newton	Edward Scarlett	Transfer. to Col's Co. 6 Sept.
Lame,	Henry Fome	Duty,	Wentworth Odiarn	John Millan	Entertained, 7th ditto.
	Thomas Fisher		Arthur Onslow	Philip Sharpe	Discharged, 18th October.
	James Fitter		John Page	Peter Blacow	Entertained, 20th ditto.
	Richard Ford		William Pitt	Robert Sambie	Desert. 5th Nov. Ret. 9th d°
	Peter Fowler		James Pitcher	John Bowers	Discharged, 27th ditto.
Recruiting,	George Garnier	Sick,	Robert Quarme	Edward Compton	Entertained, 28th ditto.
	David Garrick		John Quin	Samuel Jeake	Transf. to Major's Co. 3d Dec.
	Maynard Guerin		James Rivers	Simon Mill	Received from ditto, ditto.
	Philip Hardwicke		Baynton Rolt	James Shuttleworth	Discharged, 14th Dec.
	Cæsar Hawkins		David Ross	Gillery Pigott	Entertained, 15th ditto.
		Recruiting,		Nicholas Rowe	Ent. 18th d° Desert. 22d d°
				Lewis Castelfranc	Died, 6th January.

Reading, 14th January, 1756.

1. MUSTERED then in his Majefty's (Nº   ) regiment of foot, commanded by Colonel William Waterland, and in Captain John Churchill's company, the Lieutenant, 2 Serjeants, 3 Corporals, 1 drum, and 54 effective private men.

2. ALLOWING the Commiffion, Non-commiffion Officers, and private men to be effective for the intermediate times, as fet down againft their refpective names above-mentioned, being certified on the back of * this roll.

3. ALSO allowing the Captain, and Enfign, 1 Serjeant, 1 drum, and 14 private men that are abfent, to pafs unrefpited, being certified effective on the back of * this roll.

4. THIS Mufter is taken for 100 and 83 days, from the 25th of June, 1755, to the 24th of December following, both days inclufive.

Robert Seymour,	James Pope,	George Calcraft, Lieut.
Comry. of Mufters.	Mayor.	Edward Patten, Enfign.

The Officer's Certificate, on the back of the Commiffary General's Roll.

I DO hereby certify, that the Commiffion, Non-commiffion Officers, and private men of this (troop, with their horfes, or) company, were effective for the intermediate times, as fet down againft their refpective names within-mentioned; and thofe that are abfent, (except the † refpited) have proper leave, and the reafon affigned againft their names on the face of this roll, and are effective at the time of taking the within mufter: and that Lewis Caftelfranc, who died the 6th of January, was effective the whole time for which this mufter is taken.

George Calcraft, Lieut.

The Commiffary's Oath, on the back of his Office-Roll.

I DO fwear, that I faw at the time of taking this mufter, fuch Commiffion, Non-commiffion Officers, and private men, (with their horfes) as are borne (and not refpited) upon the within roll, for which, a figned certificate is not indorfed as above.

Robert Seymour, Comry. of Mufters.

Sworn before me, at Reading, this
14th Day of January, 1756.
James Pope, Mayor.

* In the return-roll, inftead of——on the back of this roll, write——on the back of the Commiffary General's roll.
† Where there are no refpites, thefe words are to be omitted.

Proof

Proof of the Effectives on the Commiſſary's Roll.

Effectives	Capt.	Lieut.	Enfign.	Serj.	Corp.	Drums.	Pr. Men.
Preſent	0	1	0	2	3	1	54
Abſent	1	0	1	1	0	1	14
Total	1	1	1	3	3	2	68

The Endorſement.

(N°) Regiment of Foot, Commanded by Colonel WILLIAM WATERLAND.

Captain JOHN CHURCHILL's company, for 100 and 83 days, ending the 24th of December, 1755.

Proportion of Ammunition for the following Troops, being the Extra Allowance for one Year, commencing the 25th of March 1760, agreeable to the King's Warrant.

		Powder Barrels	Ball Muſq C.	Ball Carbine C.	Ball Piſtol C.	Flints Muſq No.	Flints Carbine No.	Flints Piſtol No.
A regiment of foot of 900 men for	Service	13½	35			2700		
	Exercife	19	11			1800		
A regiment of dragoons of 360 men for	Service	5	9		2	1134		2268
	Exercife	7	1			756		1512
A light troop of 121 men for	Service	2½		7			363	393
	Exercife	1½					242	262

N. B. The proportion of ammunition for a regiment of foot is 64 rounds for each man for ſervice, at 6 drachms each cartridge, and 100 and 35 rounds each man for exerciſe, at 1-4th of an ounce.

Muſquet flints, 3 to each man for ſervice, and 2 for exerciſe.

Muſquet balls, 20 to each man for exerciſe.

The proportion for a regiment of dragoons is, 1 pound of powder for ſervice, and 2 pounds for exerciſe, to each man; each cartridge to contain the ſame as thoſe of the foot.

The proportion for the light dragoons is, 64 rounds for each man for ſervice, at half an ounce each cartridge, and

400 and 5 rounds each man, for exercife, at 3 drachms each cartridge.

The battalions of militia embodied are to have the fame proportion of ammunition as a regiment of foot, according to their numbers.

Office of Ordnance,
  May 14, 1760.

Form of a Certificate for Ammunition, to be addreffed to the Right Honourable and Honourable the Board of Ordnance, whenever a Supply of Ammunition is wanted.

THESE are to certify the Right honourable and honourable the Board of Ordnance, that the laft fupply of ammunition received for ufe of   regiment of or company of   under the command of   is nearly expended in the duty and exercife of the faid

    Witnefs my hand, this   day of
To the Right Honourable and Honourable
    the Board of Ordnance.

Of Forage and the Ration.

A Compleat ration of forage, in Germany, confifts of

	lb.
Old Hay	14
Oats	8
Straw	6

A compleat ration of forage, in Flanders, confifts of

Old Hay	12
Oats	10
Straw	6

When double rations of corn, in lieu of hay, were delivered, they were reckoned a compleat ration.

Each time the army forages, five or fix rations are to be weighed in the prefence of the Field-officer commanding the foragers: and, if any are found to be fhort of weight or meafure, the proportion of that deficiency is to be demanded upon the allowance, which each regiment is entitled to by regulation.

No more than 1 ration is to be given to a horfe.

No more than 16 facks of corn muft be put into any waggon.

Double rations of hay are to be reckoned as hay and corn.

One hundred rations of grafs or clover, weighing 40 pounds, are allowed each regiment of foot *per diem.*

The

The Quarter-masters of regiments are to pick out five of the largest, and the country Commissaries five of the smallest bundles of hay or grass; which are to be weighed together, and divided by ten : every bundle they receive afterwards is to be given as weighing the aforesaid tenth part.

200 faggots are allowed for each battalion, *per diem:* and, every 8 days, every battalion, including Officers, servants, and baa men, is also to receive 400 bundles of straw; each bundle to weigh 12 pounds and an half.

American *Weekly Allowance of Provisions for one Person.*

Seven 〕pounds of〔 bread or flour.
Seven 〔pounds of〕 beef or pork.
Half a 〔pound of〕 rice.
Three 〕pounds of〔 peas; and
Six ounces of butter.

When they receive fresh meat, each person is to have 1 pound of beef a day, and 1 pound of flour; a bullock's head is to be used for 8 pounds; a tongue for 3 pounds; and a heart for its weight.

Proportion of Rations.

Brigadier-general - - -	12
Colonel - - - - - -	6
Lieut. Col. - - - - -	5
Major - - - - - -	4
Captain - - - - - -	3
Subaltern - - - - -	2
Staff - - - - - - -	2

Allowance of Straw and Firing in Ireland, 1759, *judged necessary for each Tent.*

The first delivery of straw for each tent is to be 6 bundles, each bundle 20 pounds of wheat straw; two bundles of the like weight to be delivered to each tent every 7 days afterwards during their encampment. Where wood firing is made use of, 20 pounds weight is allowed to each tent a day, provided the wood has been some time cut; and every day, if green, 40 pounds weight, adding 1 faggot of furze. If furze be made use of without wood, 2 faggots a day to each tent, provided each faggot weighs 20 pounds; but, if the custom of the country is to make their faggots of 16 pounds weight, 2 faggots and a half should be allowed each day. This com-
putation

putation is to fhew, that double the weight fhould be allowed where only furze is burnt.

If turf is made ufe of inftead of wood or furze, 44 turf fhould be allowed to each tent a day.

10 pounds is allowed for each baa-horfe. Sunks and fods to be furnifhed out of the above allowance.

Order to empower the Colonels and Commanding Officers of every Regiment in his Majefty's Service, to poft the Subaltern Officers in fuch Manner as they fhall think may beft conduce to the Good of his Majefty's Service.

GEORGE R.

WHEREAS it has been humbly prefented to Us, that difputes have frequently arifen amongft Our forces concerning the pofting Subaltern Officers to troops and companies, whereby Our fervice hath fuffered, or may fuffer: We have therefore taken the fame into our Royal confideration, and have thought fit, in order to remedy the faid inconveniences for the future, hereby to authorize and give full power to the Colonels and Commanding Officers of every regiment in Our fervice, to poft the Subaltern Officers in fuch manner as he or they fhall think may beft conduce to the good of Our fervice, and the regular difciplining and due government of the troops and companies under their command, having regard always to the feniority of fuch Subaltern Officers, as far as may be, to the end that no prejudice may happen to Our fervice, or to them: and this Our pleafure, the Colonels, Field-officers, and every other Commiffion-officers, in Our fervice, are to obferve and pay due obedience to accordingly.

Given at Our Court at St. James's, this 23d day of April 1736, in the ninth year of our reign.

By his Majefty's command,

WILLIAM YONGE.

Points of Command.

ALL commands fall to the eldeft in the fame circumftance, whether of horfe, dragoons, artillery, foot, or marines. Among the Officers of the corps of the Britifh troops, entire or in parts, in cafe 2 of the fame date interfere, a retrofpection of former commiffions, or length of fervice, is to be examined and ended by the judgment of the rules of war.

American

American *Troops.*

THE Officers and foldiers of any troops which are or fhall be raifed in America, being muftered and in pay, fhall, at all times, and in all places, when joined, or acting in conjunction with Our Britifh forces, be governed by thefe rules or articles of war, and fhall be fubject to be tried by Courts-martial in like manner with the Officers and foldiers of our Britifh troops.

Whereas, notwithftanding the regulations which We were pleafed to make for fettling the rank of Provincial General and Field-officers in North America, difficulties have arifen with regard to the rank of thefe Officers when acting in conjunction with Our regular forces; and We being willing to give due encouragement to Officers ferving in Our provincial troops, it is Our will and pleafure, that, for the future, all General Officers and Colonels ferving by commiffion from any of the Governors, Lieutenant or Deputy-governors, or Prefidents of the Council for the time being, of Our provinces and Colonies in North America, fhall, on all detachments, Courts-martial, or other duty, wherein they may be employed in conjunction with Our regular forces, take rank next after all Colonels ferving by commiffion figned by Us, though the Commiffions of fuch provincial Generals and Colonels fhould be of elder date; and, in like manner, the Lieutenant-Colonels, Majors, Captains, and other inferior Officers ferving by commiffion from the Governors, Lieutenant or Deputy-governors, or Prefidents of the Council for the time being of Our faid provinces and colonies in North America, fhall, on all detachments, Courts-martial, or other duty, wherein they may be employed in conjunction with Our regular forces, have rank next after all Officers of the like rank ferving by commiffions figned by Us, or by Our General commanding in chief in North America, though the commiffions of fuch Lieutenant-colonels, Majors, Captains, and other inferior Officers, fhould be of elder date to thofe of the like rank figned by Us, or by Our faid General.

ARTILLERY.

OFFICERS, Conductors, Gunners, Matroffes, Drivers, or any other perfons, receiving pay or hire in the fervice of Our artillery, fhall be governed by the aforefaid rules and articles, and be fubject to be tried by Courts-martial, in like manner with the Officers and foldiers of Our other troops.

U

For differences arising amongst themselves, or in matters relating solely to their own corps, the Courts-martial may be composed of their own Officers; but where a sufficient number of such Officers cannot be assembled, or in matters wherein other corps are interested, the Officers of artillery shall sit in Courts-martial with the Officers of our other corps, taking their rank according to the dates of their respective commissions, and no otherwise.

Engineers Rank.

Chief, as Colonel.
Director, as Lieutenant-colonel.
Sub-director, as Major.
Engineer in ordinary, as Captain.
Engineer extraordinary, as Captain-Lieutenant.
Sub-engineer, as Lieutenant.
Practitioner-engineer, as Ensign.

Rank and Precedence between Land and Sea Officers.

1. THAT the Admiral, or Commander in Chief of his Majesty's fleet, have the rank of a Field-martial of the army.

2. That the Admirals, with their flags on the main-topmast-head, have rank with Generals of horse and foot.

3. The Vice-admirals have rank with Lieutenant-generals.

4. That Rear-admirals have rank as Major-generals.

5. That Commodores, with broad pendants, have rank as Brigadiers-general.

6. That Captains commanding post-ships, after three years from the date of the first commission, for a post-ship, have rank as Colonel.

7. That all other Captains commanding post-ships have rank as Lieutenant-colonels.

8. That Captains of his Majesty's ships or vessels, not taken post, have rank as Majors.

9. That Lieutenants of his Majesty's ships have rank as Captains.

10. That the Rank and precedence of Sea-officers in the classes above-mentioned, do take place according to the seniority of their respective commissions as Sea-officers.

11. That Post-captains commanding ships or vessels that do not give post, rank only as Majors during their commanding such vessel.

12. That nothing in this regulation shall give any pretence

tence to any Land-officer to command any of his Majefty's fquadrons or fhips, nor to any Sea-officer to command at land, nor fhall either have a right to demand the military honours due to their refpective ranks, unlefs fuch Officers are upon actual fervice.

BREVETS.

War-Office.

I AM commanded to fignify the King's pleafure, on the 2 following points, to the Officers of the regiment under your command: this I cannot do more properly than through you, who I am perfuaded will take the moft effectual care that his Majefty's intentions fhall be fully known and underftood in the   regiment of

Any Officer, who by the King's leave fhall quit a commiffion which he has in any regiment or corps, and who at that time alfo enjoys a rank in the army fuperior to his faid regimental commiffion, fhall not be confidered as entitled to any rank whatever in the army, unlefs his Majefty fhall exprefsly fignify his pleafure to be otherwife.

Officers (not being General-officers) having a rank in the army fuperior to that of the commiffion which they bear in any regiment or corps, are not thereby to be exempted from their attendance at quarters, and doing regimental duty, according to their rank in the corps to which they belong.

War-Office, October 3, 1755.

SIR,

CERTAIN commiffions in the army are fometimes allowed to be fold, though the King is in general very much averfe to a practice fo injurious to Officers of merit who have no money; but it is highly proper, when any commiffions are fold, that their price fhould be fixed, determined, and known: without fome regulation of that kind, a practice exceptionable at beft, may be rendered very hurtful to the army.

Before the King declares his pleafure on this fubject, he wifhes to know the opinion of his General Officers, what fum is proper to be given for each of the following commiffions.

War-Office, February 9, 1773.

PRICES OF COMMISSIONS.

First and Second Troops of HORSE-GUARDS.

Commissions.	Prices.	Difference in value between the several commissions in Succession.
	£.	£.
First Lieutenant-colonel	- 5,500	- - 400
Second Lieutenant-colonel	- 5,100	- - 800
Cornet and Major -	- 4,300	- - 200
Guidon and Major -	- 4,100	- 1,400
Exempt and Captain -	- 2,700	- 1,200
Brigadier and Lieutenant or ⎫ Adjutant and Lieutenant ⎭	1,500	- - 300
Sub-brigadier and Cornet	- 1,200	- 1,200
		£.5,500

First and Second Troops of HORSE GRENADIER GUARDS.

Lieutenant-colonel -	- 5,400	- 1,200
Major - - -	- 4,200	- 1,100
Lieutenant and Captain	- 3,100	- - 100
Guidon and Captain -	- 3,000	- 1,300
Sub-lieutenant -	- 1,700	- - 300
Adjutant - - -	- 1,400	- 1,400
		£.5,400

HORSE.

Lieutenant-colonel -	- 5,200	- - 950
Major - - -	- 4,250	- 1,150
Captain - - -	- 3,100	- - 650
Captain-lieutenant, with ⎫ rank of Captain -⎭	2,450	- - 700
Lieutenant - -	- 1,750	- - 150
Cornet - - -	- 1,600	- 1,600
		£.5,200

GEORGE

GEORGE R.

OUR Will and Pleasure is, that in all cases where We shall permit any of the commissions in our regiments of dragoon guards, and dragoons, to be sold, the sum to be paid for the said commissions respectively, shall not exceed the prices under-mentioned, viz.

DRAGOON GUARDS and DRAGOONS.

Commissions.	Prices.	Difference, &c.
	£.	£.
Lieutenant-colonel - -	5,350	- 1,100
Major - - -	4,250	- 1,100
Captain - - -	3,150	- 1,050
Captain-lieutenant, with rank of Captain }	2,100	- 735
Lieutenant - -	1,365	- 262 10s.
Cornet - - -	1,102 10s.	- 1,102 10s.
		£5,350

FOOT GUARDS,

Lieutenant-colonel - -	6,700	- 400
First Major Second Major } with rank of Colonel Third Major	6,300	- 2,800
Captain - - -	3,500	- 900
Captain-lieutenant, with rank of Lieutenant-colonel }	2,600	- 1,100
Lieutenant, with rank of Captain	1,500	- 600
Ensign - - -	900	- 900
		£6,700

MARCHING REGIMENTS of FOOT.

Lieutenant-colonel -	3,500	- 900
Major - - -	2,600	- 1,100
Captain - - -	1,500	- 550
Captain-lieutenant, with rank of Captain }	950	- 400
Lieutenant - -	550	- 150
Ensign - - -	400	- 400
		£3,500

U 3

In

In the regiments of Fuzileers which have 1st and 2d Lieutenants.

1st Lieut.	550	- -	100
2d Lieut.	450	- -	450

And all Colonels, Agents, and other our military Officers are hereby required and directed to conform strictly and carefully to the regulation hereby laid down and established, upon pain of Our highest displeasure; given at Our Court at St. James's, this 22d day of Feb. 1773, in the thirteenth year of Our reign.

By his Majesty's command.

BARRINGTON.

War-Office, Feb. 2, 1766.

S I R,

I Have received your letter containing the report of the Board of General Officers, on a matter referred to them by the King touching the price which should for the future be given for commissions in the army. I will lay it before his Majesty the first opportunity; but, as you were present during the settling of these prices, I must desire you will acquaint me, for the King's information, what were the general grounds on which the Board went, in fixing the different rates.

I am, S I R,

Your most obedient

Humble Servant,

Charles Gould, Esq.   BARRINGTON.

Horse-Guards, Feb. 3, 1766.

M Y L O R D,

A GREEABLE to your Lordship's letter, desiring me to acquaint you, for his Majesty's information, what were the general grounds upon which the Board of General Officers has proceeded in fixing the prices of the several commissions; I have the honour to inform your Lordship, that the Board considered the value of the pay and of the rank distinctly; and, after fixing what appeared to them a reasonable price for the commissions of Cornet and Ensign in the respective corps, and which they might probably be sold for in time of war as well as peace; proceeded to estimate every increase of pay, after the rate of £100 for each shilling *per diem*, in a general view, not attending minutely to fractional sums;

and

and in the next place endeavoured to fix a certain propor-
tionate value upon each advancement in rank, fuch as might,
if poffible, be extended to all the different corps. Accordingly, your Lordfhip will obferve the valuation of rank to be
uniformnly the fame throughout the cavalry ; (allowing only
for fome fractions occafioned by the difference in pay aforementioned) viz. for gaining the rank of Lieutenant £.50 ;
for a Captain-lieutenancy, £.250 ; for the rank of Captain,
£.450 ; (or in corps where there is no Captain-lieutenant,
and the promotion from Lieutenant to Captain is made in
one ftep £.700) for a majority, £. 600 ; and for the rank of
Lieutenant-colonel, £.700 : and the fame valuation of rank
is extended alfo to the foot fervice, except in the fingle
commiffion of Captain ; wherein the Board has, in fome
degree, conformed to the difference which has ever prevailed
in the price, and reputed value, between a troop in the cavalry and a company of foot, and has valued the advancement from Lieutenant to Captain, including the Captain-
lieutenancy, nearly at £.400.

I believe thefe few obfervations will fhew the principles
upon which the prefent report is founded, concerning which,
I am perfuaded, the board would wifh me to give your Lordfhip every explanation in my power.

I am, with refpect,
My Lord,
Your Lordship's moft humble
and moft obedient Servant,

Lord Vifcount Barrington. CHARES GOULD.

War-Office, February 8, 1766.

Sir,

I Have laid before the King your letter of the 31ft day of
January, containing a report of the Board of General Officers, on a matter referred to them by his Majefty in my
letter of the 3d day of October laft, touching the different
prices to be given for commiffions in the army, in cafes
where he fhall pleafe to allow them to be fold. The King
entirely approves the faid report, and every particular therein
contained. His Majefty commands me to exprefs his perfect
fatisfaction to the Officers who have figned it ; and to acquaint them, that he will order what they recommend to be
invariably obferved for the future, under pain of his higheft
difpleafure.

U 4 Having

Having now finifhed what I am commanded by the King to communicate to the Board, I take this opportunity of conveying through you, Sir, to the Generals who compofe it, fome thoughts on a matter of great importance to the regiments they command, and indeed to the whole army.

Colonels frequently recommend, that Officers in their refpective corps fhould fell commiffions which they did not buy: long and faithful fervice has worn them out; they have families; the eldeft in each rank are able and willing to purchafe; they all deferve preferment, which in time of peace can fcarcely be obtained any other way; in fhort, the good of the corps, merit and humanity, all ftrongly plead for the indulgence which is recommended. It is no wonder that thefe arguments have fo frequently fucceeded, when any one of them would be fufficient inducement, if there were not another fide of the queftion.

' Officers who buy are permitted to fell: men who find themfelves growing old or infirm difpofe of their commiffions, which are purchafed by the young and the healthy; and thus what has been once bought continues for ever at fale, efpecially in time of peace, except now and then in a cafe of fudden or unexpected death. The confequence often is, that men who come into the army with the warmeft difpofitions to the fervice, whofe bufinefs becomes their pleafure, who diftinguifh themfelves on every occafion that offers, are kept all their lives in the loweft rank becaufe they are poor. Thefe meritorious Officers have often the cruel mortification of feeing themfelves commanded by young men of opulent families, who came much later into the fervice; and whofe fortunes have enabled them to amufe themfelves frequently elfewhere, while the others continually at quarters, have done the duty of thofe gentlemen, and have learnt their own.

' Flagrant abufes feldom grow up at once, but arife from circumftances whofe confequences were not forefeen. The firft time a commiffion is fold, it is almoft always bought by a good Officer, the next in fucceffion: he afterwards afks to fell; the corps is changed, the Senior Officers have merit and long fervice, but they have no money; this circumftance does not prevent the tranfaction; and the commiffion is purchafed, perhaps by the youngeft, leaft fteady, and leaft experienced of that corps, or of fome other, to the infinite diftrefs of many deferving men, and to the great fcandal and detriment of the fervice. Like circumftances happen more or lefs every change, and bring with them the
                                                                    fame

fame diftrefs and mifchief : each frefh commiffion brought
to market multiplies both ; and therefore, inftead of encrea-
fing purchafes, they cannot be too much leffened, fo far as
is confiftent with the invariable practice of the army.

That Colonels of regiments fhould not attend to thefe
confequences, is not matter either of wonder or blame :
their care is extended no farther than to their own corps,
and while they command it ; but the Officer of the Crown,
who is entrufted with the important charge of the whole
army, a body whofe probable duration infinitely exceeds the
fhort fpace allotted to individuals, cannot be too vigilant,
left confined temporary convenience or compaffion, fhould
produce general permanent mifchief or diftrefs. To be firm
in preventing future evil by immediate refufal, is not the
leaft difficult part of his duty : he muft withftand the feel-
ings of humanity, and the defire to pleafe : he muft expect
the uncandid interpretation of the prejudiced, the hafty
judgment of the ignorant, and the malignant conclufion of
the difappointed : he muft often contradict the paffions
and interefts of the powerful ; and even difappoint the wifhes
and expectations of the deferving : he muft acquire a great
many enemies, and lofe a great many friends ; and yet he
had better fuffer all this than do wrong.

It is of confequence that the army fhould know the rules
of the fervice, and fee the reafon of them. That Officers
fhould fell what they bought, and no more, has long been
a rule ; and perhaps this letter will tend to explain the
grounds on which it was eftablifhed. If that rule be good,
can it be too invariably obferved ? Specious diftinctions will
be made ; they fhould never be admitted, for every devia-
tion tends to difufe. Nothing can be more fatal for the
army in general, than occafional exceptions from good regulations ; or give more advantage to the unjuft attempts of
the importunate and of the great.

It is frequently afked, what can be done with an Officer
who is become ufelefs to his corps through age, wounds, or
infirmities ? It muft be owned there are too few comfortable
retreats, from active fervice in this country ; however, our
eftablifhment affords fome. The commiffions in the invalids,
fmall governments, and other garrifon employments, always
properly beftowed, would go a great way ; till there can be
a more ample provifion, the young and healthy muft do the
duty of the old and infirm ; and they can fufficiently do it
in time of peace ; hereafter, in their turn, they may receive
the like benefit themfelves ; and in the mean time, efcape
a thoufand

a thoufand mortifications to which indigent merit is too often expofed. It frequently happens in the army, as elfewhere, that want of money is alfo accompanied by a want
of affifting friends : but the poor, though deferving Officer,
fhould always find at the War-Office, a conftant affertor of
his rights, and faithful guardian of his interefts.

   I am,
     S I R,
       Your moft obedient humble Servant,
Charles Gould, Efq.   BARRINGTON.

  GEORGE R.

WHEREAS We were pleafed to fignify Our pleafure
   by a letter from Our Secretary at War, bearing date
the 3d of October, 1765, to the Judge Advocate General of
Our forces or his Deputy, that he fhould fummon the Board
of Our General Officers, in order that they might confider and
report their opinion to Us, what fum might be proper to be
given for each of the commiffions in Our army particularly
fpecified in the above-mentioned letter, in cafes where We
fhould be pleafed to permit the fame to be fold ; and alfo,
that they fhould confider and report their opinion to Us,
whether any difference fhould be made between the price of
commiffions of regiments ferving in and out of Europe ; and
if any, that they fhould fpecify what difference : and the
faid Board of Our General Officers having accordingly taken
the faid matters into confideration, and having fubmitted to
Us their opinion thereupon, by their report, bearing date
the 31ft of January, 1766, a copy of which report is here-
unto annexed ; and We having been pleafed to approve of
the fame ; Our will and pleafure is, that in all cafes where
we fhall permit any of the commiffions fpecified therein to
be fold, the fum to be paid for the fame, fhall not exceed the
prices fet down in the faid report. And all Colonels,
Agents, and other Our military Officers are hereby required
and directed to conform ftrictly and carefully to the regulation hereby laid down and eftablifhed, upon pain of Our
higheft difpleafure.

  Given at Our court at St. James's, this 10th day of Fe-
bruary, 1766, in the fixth year of Our reign.
      By his MAJESTY's command,
 War-Office.   BARRINGTON.
True Copies.

                Price

Price of Commiſſions, with the Difference between Full and Half-pay upon the Iriſh Eſtabliſhment.

RANK OF OFFICERS.	Daily Pay.			Full Price of the Commiſſions.	Total Difference in Value between each Commiſſion in Succeſſion.	Daily half-pay.		Difference between full and half-pay when all Commiſſions were purchaſed.		
	l.	s.	d.	l.	l.	s.	d.	l.	s.	d.
Horſe. Lieut. Col.-	1	5	0	4940	1009	11	0	2932	10	0
Major - -	1	2	6	3931	1200	9	9	2151	12	6
Captain -	0	17	0	2731	1138	7	0	1453	10	0
Capt. Lieut.	0	10	6	1593	271	4	6	500	15	0
Lieut. - -	0	10	6	1322	255	4	6	500	15	0
Cornet - -	0	8	6	1067	1067	3	6	428	5	0
Total - -					4940					
Dragoons. Lieut. Col.-	0	19	4	4365	959	8	6	2813	15	0
Major - -	0	17	4	3406	1150	7	6	2037	5	0
Captain - -	0	12	4	2256	1013	5	0	1343	10	0
Capt. Lieut.	0	7	2	1243	271	3	0	424	10	0
Lieut. - - -	0	7	2	972	155	3	0	424	10	0
Cornet - -	0	6	2	817	817	2	6	360	15	0
Total - -					4365					
Foot. Lieut. Col.-	0	17	0	3657	959	8	6	2105	15	0
Major - -	0	15	0	2698	1150	7	6	1329	5	0
Captain - -	0	10	0	1548	717	5	0	726	15	0
Capt. Lieut.	0	4	8	831	271	2	4	176	15	0
Lieut. - -	0	4	8	560	155	2	4	176	15	0
Enſign - -	0	3	8	405	405	1	10	103	17	6
Total - - -					3657					

The

The Value of Half-pay in Ireland to be received or deducted in each Rank, according to the Commiffions which the Officer who exchanges from Full to Half-Pay, did or did not purchafe.

RANK OF OFFICERS.	l.	s.	d.
Horfe. Cornet - - - - -	428	5	0
Lieutenant - - - - -	72	10	0
Captain - - - - -	952	15	0
Major - - - - -	698	2	6
Lieutenant Colonel - - -	780	17	6
Dragoons. Cornet - - - - -	360	15	0
Lieutenant - - - - -	63	5	0
Captain - - - - -	919	0	0
Major - - - - -	693	15	0
Lieutenant Colonel - - -	776	10	0
Foot. Enfign - - - - -	103	17	6
Lieutenant - - - - -	72	17	6
Captain - - - - -	550	0	0
Major - - - - -	602	10	0
Lieutenant Colonel - - -	776	10	0

Articles of Agreement.

AGREEMENT between   of the
regiment, and   of the faid regiment, whereby the faid   doth confent and
agree to refign his commiffion in favour of
for and in confideration of the fum of   to be
lodged in the hands of   and as foon as his
Majefty's approbation and royal confent fhall be obtained,
and the commiffion made out, the faid fum of
is to be paid to the faid

To

GENERAL VIEW OF THE DIFFERENCES AND DISTINCTIONS

OF THE SEVERAL CORPS OF CAVALRY, IN THE CLOTHING,

HORSE-FURNITURE, AND STANDARDS.

Given at Our Court, at St. JAMES's, this 19th Day of December, 1768, in the Ninth Year of Our Reign.

By His MAJESTY's Command,

BARRINGTON.

CLOTHING of the SERJEANTS, CORPORALS, and PRIVATE MEN.

Colour of the several Facings	REGIMENTS. Rank and Titles of the several Corps of Dragoon Guards, Horse, Dragoons, and Light Dragoons.	Colour of the Facings and Lappets.	Colour of Buttons, and how set on. Lappets.	Colour of Waistcoats, Breeches, and Lining of Coats and Cloaks.	Hat Lace.
Blue	1ſt, or King's reg. of drag. guards	Blue with half lappels	Yellow 2 and 2	Buff	Gold
	1ſt horſe	Blue with half lappels	White 2 and 2	White	Silver
	1ſt, or royal dragoons	Blue without lappels	Yellow 2 and 2	White	Gold
	2d, or royal North-Britiſh dragoons	Blue without lappels	White 2 and 2	White	None
	3d, or King's own reg. of dragoons	Blue without lappels	Yellow 3 and 3	Buff	Gold
	5th, or royal Iriſh dragoons	Blue without lappels	White 3 and 3	White	Silver
	15th, or King's light dragoons	Blue with half lappels	White 2 and 2	White	None
	16th, or Queen's light dragoons	Blue with half lappels	White 2 and 2	White	None
Yellow	6th, or the Inniſkilling dragoons	Full yellow without laps.	White 2 and 2	White	Silver
	8th regiment of dragoons	Yellow without lappels	White 3 and 3	White	Silver
	10th regiment of dragoons	Deep yel. without laps.	White 3, 4, and 5	White	Silver
	14th regiment of dragoons	Lemon without lappels	White 3 and 3	White	Silver
Buff	2d, or Queen's reg. of drag. guards	Buff with half lappels	Yellow 3 and 3	Buff	Gold
	9th regiment of dragoons	Buff without lappels	White 2 and 2	Buff	Silver
	11th regiment of dragoons	Buff without lappels	White 3 and 3	Buff	Silver
White	3d, or P. of Wales's reg. of drag. gds.	White with half lappels	Yellow 2 and 2	White	Gold
	5d reg. of horſe, or the carabineers	White with half lappels	White 2 and 2	White	Silver
	7th, or the Queen's reg. of dragoons	White without lappels	White 3 and 3	White	Silver
	17th regiment of light dragoons	White with half lappels	White 2 and 2	White	None
	18th regiment of light dragoons	White with half lappels	White 2 and 2	White	None
Green	2d regiment of horſe	Full green with half lap.	Yellow 2 and 2	White	Gold
	4th regiment of dragoons	Full green without laps.	White 2 and 2	White	Silver
	13th regiment of dragoons	Deep green without laps.	Yellow 3 and 3	Buff	Gold
Black	4th regiment of horſe	Black with half lappels	Yellow 2 and 2	Buff	Gold
	12th reg. or P. of Wales's light drag.	Black with half lappels	White 2 and 2	White	None

Colour of the Coat, and of the Facing.	Colour of Waist-coat, Breeches, and Lining of the Cloaths.	Colour of the Lace on the Cloaths of the Trumpeters, &c.	Colour of the Housings and Holster Caps.	Colour of the Lace on the Housings & Holster-Caps.	Badge, or Device, on the Housings and Holster-Caps.
Red with blue	Buff	Royal lace, blue and yellow	Red	Royal lace	King's cypher within garter and crown
Blue with red	White	White with a red stripe	Blue	White with a red stripe	Rank of the regiment - I. H.
Red with blue	White	Royal lace	Red	Royal lace	Crest of England within the garter
Red with blue	White	Royal lace	Blue	Royal lace	Thistle within circle of St. Andrew
Red with blue	Buff	Royal lace	Blue	Royal lace	White horse within the garter
Red with blue	White	Royal lace	Blue	Royal lace	Harp and crown
Red with blue	White	Royal lace	White	Royal lace	King's crest within the garter
Red with blue	White	Royal lace	White	Royal lace	Queen's cypher within the garter
Full yel. with red	Red	White with a blue stripe	Full yellow	White and blue stripe	Castle of Inniskilling within a wreath
Yellow with red	Red	White with a yellow stripe	Yellow	White and yel. stripe	Rank of the regiment - VIII. D.
Deep yel. with red	Red	White with a green stripe	Deep yellow	White with a green str.	Rank of the regiment - X. D.
Lemon with red	Red	White with red&green strip.	Lemon col.	White, red, and gr. str.	Rank of the regiment - XIV. D.
Red with blue	Buff	Royal lace	Buff	Royal lace	Queen's cypher within the garter
Buff with red	Red	White with a blue stripe	Buff	White with a blue str.	Rank of the regiment - IX. D.
Buff with red	Red	White with a green stripe	Buff	White with a green str.	Rank of the regiment - XI. D.
White with red	Red	Royal lace	White	Royal lace	The feathers issuing out of the coronet
White with red	Red	Yellow with black stripes	White	Yellow with black str.	Rank of the regiment - III. H.
Red with blue	White	Royal lace	White	Royal lace	Queen's cypher within the garter
White with red	White	Royal lace	White	White with black edge	Rank of the regiment XVII. L. D.
White with red	Red	Red and white	White	Red and white	Rank of the regiment XVIII. L. D.
Full green with red	White	White with a red stripe	Full green	White with a red stripe	Rank of the regiment - II. H.
Full green with red	White	White with a red stripe.	Green.	White with a red stripe	Rank of the regiment - IV. D.
Deep green with red	White	White with a yellow stripe	Deep green	White with a yel. str.	Rank of the regiment - XIII. D.
Buff with red	Red	White with a black stripe	Buff	White and black stripe	Rank of the regiment - IV. H.
Red with blue	White	Royal lace	Black with ftr. of white goat skin	None	The feathers issuing out of the coronet

STANDARDS and GUIDONS.

Colour of the Second and Third Standard, or Guidon.	Embroidery on the three Standards.	Fringe on the three Standard, or Guidon.	Badge, or Device, on the Second and Third Standard or Guidon.	Mottos on the Second and Third Standard or Guidon.
Blue	Gold	Gold	King's cypher within the garter	
Blue	Gold and silver	Gold & silv.	Rank of the regiment - I. H.	
Blue	Gold	Gold	Crest of England within the garter	
Blue	Gold and silver	Gold & silv.	Thistle within circle of St. Andrew	Nemo me impune lacessit.
Blue	Gold	Gold	White horse within the garter	Nec aspera terrent.
Blue	Gold and silver	Gold & silv.	Harp and Crown	
Blue	Gold painted	Gold	King's crest within the garter	Emsdorff.
Blue	Gold & silv. painted	Gold	Queen's cypher within the garter	Aut cursu, aut cominus armis.
Full yellow	Silver	Silv. & blue	Castle of Inniskilling	
Yellow	Silver	Silv. & yell.	Rank of the regiment - VIII. D.	
Deepyellow	Silver	Silv.& green	Rank of the regiment - X. D.	
Lemon	Silver	Silv. & red	Rank of the regiment - XIV. D.	
Buff	Gold	Gold	Queen's cypher within the garter	
Buff	Silver	Silv. & blue	Rank of the regiment - IX. D.	
Buff	Silver	Silv.& green	Rank of the regiment - XI. D.	
White	Gold and silver	Gold & silv.	Feathers issuing out of the coronet, a ris. sun & red-dragon.	In Diem.
White	Gold	Gold	Rank of the regiment - III. H.	
White	Gold	Gold	Queen's cypher within the garter	
White	Gold & silv. painted	Silv. & red	Death's head	Or Glory.
White	Gold & silv. painted	Silver	Rank of the regiment XVIII. L. D.	
Full green	Gold	Gold	Rank of the regiment - II. H.	Veffigia nulla retrorfum.
Full green	Silver	Silv. & blue	Rank of the regiment - IV. D.	
Deep green	Silver	Silv. & yell.	Rank of the regiment - XIII. D.	
Black	Gold	Gold & silv.	Rank of the regiment - IV. H.	In Diem.
Black	Silver painted	Silver	The feathers issuing out of the coronet; also, the rising sun, and red dragon	

General View of the Facings, &c. of the several Marching Regiments of Foot, as fixed by his Majesty, December 19, 1768.

Colour of Facing.	Rank and Title of the Regiment.		Distinctions in the Lace, same Colour. If Gold or Silver Hair... Colour for the Officers.	Colour of the Waistcoats, Breeches, and Lining of the Coats.	Colour of the Lace.
Blue.	1st, or the royal regiment		Gold	White	White, with a blue double worm
	2d, or the Queen's royal regiment		Silver	White	White, with a blue stripe
	4th, or the King's own regiment		Silver	White	White, with a blue stripe
	7th, or royal fuzileers		Gold	White	White, with a blue stripe
	8th, or King's regiment		Gold	White	White, with a blue and yellow stripe
	18th, or royal Irish		Gold	White	White, with a blue stripe
	21st, or royal North-British fuzileers		Gold	White	White, with a blue stripe
	23d, or royal Welch fuzileers		Gold	White	White, with red, blue, and yellow stripes.
	41st, or invalids		Gold	Red	Plain button-hole
	42d, or royal Highlanders		Gold	White waistcoats and lining of coats. No breeches.	White, with a red stripe
	60th, or royal Americans		Silver	White	White, with two blue stripes
Yellow	6th regiment	Deep yellow	Silver	White	White, with yellow and red stripes
	9th regiment	Bright yellow	Silver	White	White, with two black stripes
	10th regiment		Silver	White	White, with a blue stripe
	12th regiment		Gold	White	White, with yellow, crimson, and black stripes
	13th regiment	Philemot yel.	Silver	White	White, with a yellow stripe
	15th regiment		Silver	White	White, with a yellow and black worm, and red stripe
	16th regiment		Silver	White	White, with a crimson stripe
	20th regiment	Pale yellow	Silver	White	White, with a red and a black stripe
	25th regiment	Deep yellow	Gold	White	White, with a blue, yellow, and red stripe
	26th regiment	Pale yellow	Silver	White	White, with one blue, and two yellow stripes
	28th regiment	Bright yellow	Silver	White	White, with one yellow, and two black stripes
	29th regiment		Silver	White	White, with two blue, and one yellow stripe
	30th regiment		Silver	White	White, with a sky-blue stripe
	34th regiment	Pale yellow	Silver	White	White, with a blue and yellow worm, and red stripe
	37th regiment	Bright yellow	Silver	White	White, with a red and a yellow stripe
	38th regiment		Silver	White	White, with two red, and one yellow stripe
	44th regiment		Silver	White	White, with blue, yellow, and black stripe

Group	Regiment	Facing colour	Lace	Ground	Lace pattern
Green	5th regiment	Goslin green	Silver	White	White, with two red stripes
	11th regiment	Full green	Gold	White	White, with two red, and two green stripes
	19th regiment	Deep green	Gold	White	White, with two stripes, red and green
	24th regiment	Willow green	Silver	White	White, with one red, and one green stripe
	36th regiment		Gold	White	White, with one red, and one green stripe
	39th regiment		Gold	White	White, with a light green stripe
	45th regiment	Deep green	Silver	White	White, with a green stripe
	49th regiment	Full green	Gold	White	White, with two red, and one green stripe
	51st regiment	Deep green	Gold	White	White, with a green worm stripe
	54th regiment	Popinjay green	Silver	White	White, with a green stripe
	55th regiment	Dark green	Gold	White	White, with two green stripes
	63d regiment	Very deep green	Silver	White	White, with a very small green stripe
	66th regiment	Yellowish green	Gold	White	White, with one crimson and green, and one green stripe
	68th regiment	Deep green	Silver	White	White, with yellow and black stripes
	69th regiment	Willow green	Gold	White	White, with one red and two green stripes
Buff	3d reg. or the Buffs		Silver	Buff	White, with yellow, black, and red stripes
	14th regiment		Silver	Buff	White, with a blue and red worm, and buff stripe
	22d regiment	Pale Buff	Gold	Pale Buff	White, with one blue, and one red stripe
	27th, or Inniskil. reg.		Gold	Buff	White, with one blue, and one red stripe
	31st regiment		Silver	Buff	White, with a blue and yellow worm, and small red stripe
	40th regiment		Gold	Buff	White, with a red and a black stripe
	48th regiment		Gold	Buff	White, with a black and a red stripe
	52d regiment		Silver	Buff	White, with a red worm, and one orange stripe
	61st regiment		Silver	Buff	White, with a blue stripe
	62d regiment	Yellowish buff	Silver	Yellowish buff	White, with two blue, and one straw-coloured stripe
White	17th regiment	Greyish white	Silver	Greyish white	White, with two blue, and one yellow stripe
	32d regiment		Gold	White	White, with a black worm, and a black stripe
	43d regiment		Silver	White	White, with a red and a black stripe
	47th regiment		Silver	White	White, with one red, and two black stripes
	65th regiment		Silver	White	White, with a red and black worm, and a black stripe
Red	33d regiment		Silver	White	White, with a red stripe in the middle
	53d regiment		Gold	White	White, with a red stripe
	56th regiment	Purple	Silver	White	White, with a pink-colour stripe
	59th regiment	Purple	Silver	White	White, with a red and yellow stripe
Black	50th regiment		Silver	White	White, with a red stripe
	58th regiment		Silver	White	White, with a red stripe
	64th regiment		Gold	White	White, with a red and a black stripe
	70th regiment		Gold	White	White, with a narrow black worm stripe
Orange	35th regiment		Silver	White	White, with one yellow stripe

To all which, the faid parties have interchangeably fet their hands and feals, this   day of   17

A. B.

Witnefs, C. D.
          E. F.

N. B Previous to the above agreement, the Commanding Officer of the regiment at quarters is to be confulted ; and if it is approved of by him, the articles are then to be laid before the Colonel of the regiment for his approbation.

.*. There is no order for the above form.

Entry of Commiffions.

ALL commiffions granted by Us, or by any of Our Ge-nerals having authority from Us, fhall be entered in the books of Our Secretary at War, and Commiffary General, otherwife they will not be allowed of at the Mufters.

Of Military Burials, from the Field-Marfhal's to a common Soldier's.

THE funeral of a Field-marfhal fhall be faluted with 3 round of 15 cannon, attended by 6 battalions, and 8 fquadrons.

That of a General, with 3 rounds of 11 cannon, 4 bat-talions, and 6 fquadrons.

That of a Lieutenant-general, with 3 rounds of 9 can-non, 3 battalions, and 4 fquadrons.

That of a Major-general, with 3 rounds of 7 cannon, 2 battalions, and 3 fquadrons.

That of a Brigadier-general, with 3 rounds of 5 cannon, 1 battalion, and 2 fquadrons.

That of a Colonel, by his own battalion, (or an equal number by detachment) with 3 rounds of fmall arms.

That of a Lieutenant-colonel, by 300 men and Officers, with 3 rounds of fmall arms.

That of a Major, by 200 men and Officers, with 3 rounds of fmall arms.

That of a Captain, by his own company, or 70 rank and file, with 3 rounds of fmall arms.

That of a Lieutenant, by a Lieutenant, 1 Serjeant, 1 drummer, 1 fifer, and 36 rank and file, with 3 rounds of fmall arms.

That

That of an Enfign, by an Enfign, 1 Serjeant, 1 drummer, and 27 rank and file, with 3 rounds of fmall arms.

That of a Serjeant, by 1 Serjeant, and 19 rank and file, with 3 rounds of fmall arms.

That of a Corporal, mufician, private man, drummer, or fifer, by 1 Serjeant and 13 rank and file, with 3 rounds of fmall arms.

All Officers attending the funerals, of even their neareft relations, fhall notwithftanding wear their regimentals, and only have a piece of black crape round their left arms.

The pall fhould be fupported by Officers of the fame rank with that of the deceafed ; if that number cannot be had, Officers next in feniority are to fupply their place.

A non-commiffioned Officer's corps fhould be attended to the grave by the non-commiffioned Officers of the regiment, and private men of the troop or company to which he did belong.

N. B. As the Editor has never feen any form or order for the burial of a Field-marfhal, &c. he does not lay down the before-recited regulations as ordered to be ftrictly adhered to.

Directions for a funeral Party.

THE party (according to the rank of the deceafed) appointed to efcort the corpfe to the grave, is to draw up 3 deep, with open ranks, facing the houfe, or marquée, where it is lodged ; and when the corpfe is brought out of the houfe, or marquée, the Officer commanding the party will order

Reft your firelocks.
Reverfe your firelocks.
Rear ranks clofe to the front.
March.

On which the ranks clofe.

To the right wheel by divifion.
March.

They wheel into 2 or more divifions, according to their ftrength. The Officer or Officers will then reverfe their efpontoons, and the eldeft poft himfelf in the rear. The Serjeants reverfe their halberts.

Halt.

The party ftands faft, till all is ready ; when the Officer will order

March.

The

The party then marches off, led by the youngeſt Officer, and opens ranks; the corpſe following the party; and the drums being muffled, beating the dead march, and fifers playing a ſolemn tune. When it comes to the burial-ground, the Officer orders

> *Halt.*

And the party ſtands faſt.

> *Ranks to the right and left, wheel backwards.*
> *March.*

Each Rank being told off, wheels back; one half to the right, the other to the left; and form a lane.

> *Reſt on your arms reverſed.*

They come to the funeral poſture. The corpſe, &c. then paſs through the lane, and he orders

> *Reſt your firelocks.*
> *Shoulder your firelocks.*
> *To the right and left, wheel and form your ranks.*
> *March.*

They wheel up, and form as before.

> *Rear ranks cloſe to the front.*
> *March.*

The rear rank of each diviſion cloſe up.

> *Diviſions to the right, or left, wheel.*
> *March.*

They wheel.

> *Halt.*

They ſtand faſt.

> *March.*

They march till they come to the grave.

> *Halt.*

They ſtand faſt.

> *Rear ranks, to your proper diſtance.*

They go to the right about.

> *March.*

They march five or ten paces.

> *Front.*

They come to their front.

When the Adjutant gives the Officer commanding the party a ſignal, he orders

> *Make ready.*
> *Preſent.*

They preſent in the air.

> *Fire.*

They

They fire a volley, which is to be repeated three times. After the third time, they stand recovered. He then orders

> *Half cock.*
> *Shoulder.*
> *Shut your pans.*
> *Rear ranks close to the front.*
> *March.*

They close.

> *To the right, wheel by division.*
> *March.*

They wheel again in two or more divisions.

> *Halt.*

They stand fast.

> *March.*

The Commanding Officer leads the first division, the rest following in their usual posts. They open their ranks, the drums beat, and fifers play. When drawn up on the regimental parade, he orders

> *Recover your arms.*
> *To the right about.*
> *March.*

And the men go to their quarters.

N. B. The party load before they march off.

Estimate of Funeral Expences for a Soldier.

To the parson	2	6
To the sexton	1	0
To the grave digger	1	0
For the pall	1	6
For a coffin	8	6
Total	14	6

" *Effects of the Dead.*

"WHEN any Commissioned-officer shall happen to die, or be killed in Our service, the Major of the regiment, or the Officer doing the Major's duty in his absence, shall immediately secure all his effects or equipage then in camp or quarters; and shall, before the next Regimental Court-martial make an inventory thereof, and forthwith transmit the same to the office of Our Secretary at War, to the end that his executors may, after payment of his debts in quarters, and interment, receive the overplus, if any be, to his or their use.

" When

" When any Non-commiffioned-officer or private foldier
fhall happen to die, or be killed in Our fervice, the then
Commanding-Officer of the troop or company fhall, in the
prefence of 2 other commiffioned-officers, take an account
of whatever effects he dies poffeffed of, above his regimental
clothing, arms, and accoutrements, and tranfmit the fame
to the office of Our Secretary at War; which faid effects are
to be accounted for, and paid to, the reprefentative of fuch
deceafed Non-commiffioned Officer or foldier. And in cafe
any of the Officers, fo authorifed to take care of the effects
of dead Officers and foldiers, fhould, before they fhall have
accounted to their reprefentatives for the fame, have occafion to leave the regiment, by preferment or otherwife, they
fhall, before they be permitted to quit the fame, depofit in
the hand of the Commanding Officer, or of the Agent of the
regiment, all the effects of fuch deceafed Non-commiffion-
ed-officers and foldiers, in order that the fame may be fecured for, and paid to, their refpective reprefentatives."

" *Orders for mounting the Cavalry.*

War-Office, July 27th, 1764.

" HIS MAJESTY having been pleafed to order, that all
his regiments of horfe and dragoons, except the
light-dragoons, fhall be mounted only on fuch horfes as fhall
have their full tails, without the leaft part taken from them;
all breeders and dealers in horfes, for the fervice of the army,
are defired to take notice, that, for the future, no horfes but
fuch as fhall have their full tails, without the leaft part
taken from them, will be bought for any of the regiments of
horfe and dragoons, except the light-dragoons.

Return of Quarters through which the   Regiment of   has marched from
to   with the Number of Men and Horses they are capable of containing as a Marching Quarter.

Date.	Regiment.	County.	Town.	Quarters.		Contiguous Towns, &c. for enlarging Quarters.				Total of Troops in the Quarters and Enlargements.		Greatest Extent of Quarters.		remarks on the road, where good or bad.
				Men.	Horses.	Towns, &c.	Men.	Horses.	Miles from headquarters.	Men.	Horses.	From	To	Miles.

Private Orders for the Security of a Poſt.

Montreal, April 12, 1764.

PRIVATE orders for Lieutenant Dow, of the 28th regiment of foot, going to take poſt at the Cedars.

Any paſs produced to you, and ſigned by me, that has not the ſame ſeal to it, as what is at the bottom of this, you are to look upon as counterfeit; you are therefore to keep ſuch paſs, ſeize the boat or canoe, with what is in it, and ſend the conductors down to me.

R. BURTON.

[Seal.]

Form of a Paſs.

By the Right Honourable William, *Lord Viſcount* Barrington, *His Majeſty's Secretary at War.*

PERMIT the bearer hereof
of the regiment commanded by
without any lett, hindrance, or moleſtation whatſoever, to
paſs to   provided   continue
in the poſt-road; and do not remain above 24 hours in one place, except in caſe of ſickneſs,   behaving
as becometh. This paſs to continue in force for
            from the date hereof, and no longer. Given under my hand and ſeal, at the War-Office, this   day
of   177
            In the abſence of the Secretary at War.
    To all His Majeſty's Officers,
civil and military, and others,
whom it may concern.

Form of a Paſs for the Out Penſioners of Chelſea.

IN order to prevent any of the out-penſioners of Chelſea-Hoſpital, from being taken up as deſerters or vagrants, we the Commiſſioners appointed to examine the ſaid out-penſioners, by virtue of   us, do certify that the bearer hereof   now reſiding at
in or near the market-town of   in the County
of   aged about   years,   feet,
        inches high,   complexion,
                    X 2   haired,

haired, formerly a   in   regiment of
was admitted upon the out-penfion of the faid Hofpital, the
day   17   on account of

This certificate is to be fhewn, and a duplicate of the
ufual affidavit, from time to time given to the perfon by
whom he is paid his out-penfion, according to the late act
of parliament. Given under our hands at   this
day of   17

Form of a Difcharge, by the Secretary at War.

By the Right Honourable Welbore Ellis, his Majefty's Secretary at War.

HAVING received his Majefty's commands to difcharge, I do hereby difcharge

from any further fervice in the faid corps. Given under
my hand and feal at the War-Office, this   day of
176
          To
All His Majefty's Officers,
civil or military, and others,
whom it may concern.

Return

Return of Slops, &c. from on Board his Majesty's Ship under the Command of A. B. of the ⸺ stationed in ⸺ Division.

Name.	Rank.	When last clothed.	When embarked.	When accounted to.	Balance due.	Debtor.	Jackets.	Trowsers.	Shirts.	Stocks Black.	Stocks White.	Stockings.	Spatterdashes.	Caps.	Names of Places where they received Slops, &c.	By whom supplied.	Time when Debtor. Month.	Yr.	Charge. L. s. D.	observations

Nett Arrears for the 365 Days, for the following Ranks in the Dragoons.

Colonel.			Lieut. Col			Major.			Captain.			Lieute.			Cornet.			Chaplain.			Adjutant.			Surgeon.			Q. Master.		
l.	s.	d.	l.	s.	d.	l.	s.	d.	l.	s.	d.	l.	s.	d.	l.	s.	d.	l.	s.	d.	l.	s.	d.	l.	s.	d.	l.	s.	d.
112	13	3	79	14	9	66	7	0	54	3	5	25	11	4	26	15	8	22	6	4	3	1	0	20	1	9	20	13	10

MARCHING REGIMENTS.

Colonel.			Lieut. Col			Major.			Captain.			Lieute.			Ensign.			Chaplain.			Adjutant.			Q. Master			Surgeon.			S. Mate.		
l.	s.	d.	l.	s.	d.	l.	s.	d.	l.	s.	d.	l.	s.	d.	l.	s.	d.	l.	s.	d.	l.	s.	d.	l.	s.	d.	l.	s.	d.	l.	s.	d.
80	7	0	52	7	0	45	13	1	33	9	7	15	12	5	14	7	3	22	6	4	13	7	10	15	12	5	13	7	10	4	17	5

Scheme of a Mess for Dinner and Supper, in Camp.

No. of Officers	Rank.	Each per Day. s. d.	Total per Day. l. s. d.	ESTIMATE.	l. s. d.
1	Colonel -	3 0	0 3 0	A dining Tent - - - - -	21 0 0
1	Lieut. Colonel -	2 6	0 2 6	A Kitchen Tent - - - -	10 0 0
1	Major - -	2 0	0 2 0	A Cart and two Horses - -	23 3 0
7	Captains -	1 6	0 10 6	Linen, Utensils, &c. - -	14 0 0
11	Lieutenants -	1 0	0 11 0	Total	68 3 8
9	Ensigns -	0 9	0 6 9	Field Officers and Captains, six Guineas each -	63 0 0
1	Chaplain -	3 0	0 3 0	Eleven Lieutenants, at 4s. 8d. each -	2 11 4
1	Surgeon -	1 0	0 1 0	Nine Ensigns, at 3s. 8d. each -	1 13 0
1	Adjutant -	1 0	0 1 0	One Chaplain, at 6s. 8d. -	0 6 8
1	Quarter Master.	1 0	0 1 0	One Surgeon, at 4s. -	0 4 0
				One Adjutant, at 4s. -	0 4 0
				One Quarter Master, at 4s. 8d. -	0 4 8
34	Total		2 0 0	Total	68 3 8

By this fcheme each Field-Officer and Captain is to contribute fix guineas, and each Subaltern and Staff-Officer 1
day's pay each, towards the purchafing of a dining tent,
kitchen tent, and alfo to enable a futler to buy a cart and 2
horfes, table linen, kitchen furniture, &c. Wine, punch,
ale, cyder, &c. being diftinct articles, muft be paid for by
thofe only who chufe to call for them ; and for each ftran-
ger's dinner, 1 fhilling is to be paid by the inviter.

No gentleman can have his dinner fent him from the
mefs, except in cafe of ficknefs, duty, or when under an
arreft.

If this be difapproved of, upon a fuppofition that the
futler will be too great a gainer, a bill of his expences may
be delivered by him, to any Officer accepting that trouble,
who, with the confent of the reft, may appropriate the furplus to whatever purpofe is moft agreeable to the mefs.

And if the futler be a lofer, fuch fum muft be made good
by the mefs in general, as well as a gratuity to him for his
trouble.

*Things neceffary for a Gentleman to be furnifhed with, upon
obtaining his firft Commiffion in the Infantry.*

A Full fuit of cloths ; 2 frock fuits ; 2 hats ; 2 cockades ;
1 pair of leather gloves ; fafh, and gorget ; fuzee, or
efpontoon ; fword, fword-knot and belt ; 2 pair of white
fpatterdafhes (if in the foot guards) ; 1 pair of black, and
tops ; 1 pair of fhort ; 1 pair of garters ; 1 pair of boots,
(all regimentals) ; a cafe of piftols ; a blue furtout coat ;
a Portugal cloak ; 6 white waiftcoats ; 12 white, and 2
black ftocks ; 18 pair of ftockings ; 10 handkerchiefs ; 1
pair of leather breeches ; 6 pair of fhoes ; 24 fhirts ; 8
towels ; 3 pair of fheets ; 3 pillow cafes ; 6 linen night
caps, and 2 yarn ; a field bedftead, and a painted canvas
bag to hold it ; bed-curtains, quilt, three blankets, bolfter,
pillow, 1 mattrafs, and a pailace. Thofe articles fhould
be carried in a leather valife ; a travelling letter-cafe, to
contain pens, ink, paper, wax, and wafers ; a cafe of inftruments for drawing, and Muller's Works on Fortification, &c. It is alfo effential that he fhould have a watch,
that he may mark the hour exactly when he fends any
report, or what he may have difcovered that is of confequence.

If

If he is to provide a tent, the ornaments muſt be uniform, according to the facing of his corps.

Common Dimenſions of the Tent, for a Captain or Subaltern.

	Ft.	Ins.
Length of the ridge pole ———	7	0
Height of the ſtandard pole —— ——	8	0
Length from the front to rear of the marquée between half walls — — — —	14	0
Breadth of the marquée between the half walls -	10	6
Height of the half walls of the marquée — —	4	0

Scheme

Scheme of an Ensign's constant Expence, &c.

	A Day.			A Week.			4 Weeks.			52 Weeks.		
	l.	s.	d.	l.	s.	d.	l.	s.	d.	l.	s.	d.
Breakfast	0	0	6	0	3	6	0	14	0	9	2	0
Dinner	0	1	0	0	7	0	1	8	0	18	4	0
Supper	0	0	6	0	3	6	0	14	0	9	2	0
Wine and Beer	0	0	6	0	3	6	0	14	8	9	2	8
Four Shirts, 4 Stocks, and 4 Handkerchiefs a Week	0	0	2	0	1	2	0	4	8	3	0	8
Four Pair of Stockings, and 2 Night-caps a Week	0	0	1	0	0	7	0	2	4	1	10	4
Hair Powder, Pomatum, Soap, Black-Ball, Pens, Ink, Wax and Wafers	0	0	2	0	1	2	0	4	8	3	0	8
Soldier to drefs Hair, fhave, &c.	0	0	1 6/27	0	1	0	0	4	0	2	12	0
Total	0	3	0 6/27	1	1	5	4	5	8	55	13	8
Yearly Subfiftence										54	15	0
Ballance										0	18	8
Yearly Arreurs										7	14	3
Total Ballance										8	12	11

In barracks there will be an additional expence for wafhing of bed-curtains, fheets, pillow-cafes, and towels. From hence you fee how neceffary it is to be an œconomift, and what a fmall balance you have to fupport the charaɗer of an Officer; and that upon a fuppofition of the arrears being paid yearly.

From this moderate calculation, it appears that 8 pounds, 12 fhillings, and 11 pence, is the whole that an Enfign has to find himfelf in regimentals, fhirts, fhoes, ftockings, boots, fpatterdafhes, and all other neceffaries, to appear as an Officer and a Gentleman. Should not common humanity therefore prompt the Parliament to fupport thofe Gentlemen, who had fo great a fhare in adding that vaft extent of territory to this Kingdom, fo much glory to its annals, and wealth to its individuals? What greater objeɗs of compaffion to relieve; or where is gratitude more due!

N. B. I muft alfo remark, that the prefent pay of an Enfign was eftablifhed near a century ago, and at that time was worth thrice its prefent value.

Form of an Arbitration to fix the Price of Tents.

WE the following Officers of the   regiment of foot, commanded by   being ordered to afcertain in what thofe who have been appointed Officers fince   fhould pay the predeceffors for their tents, or fhares of tents; it is Our opinion, that thofe Officers who have fucceeded to a tent, fhould pay   l. and thofe who have fucceeded to half a tent, fhould pay   l. Dated   17

A. B. Captain.   C. D. Captain.   E. F. Captain.

State of Britifh Half-Pay.

	Horfe		Dragn.		Foot.	
	s.	d.	s.	d.	s.	d.
Colonel ⎱	16	6	13	0	12	0
Lt. Col. ⎬ and Captain per day	12	0	10	0	8	6
Major. ⎰	11	6	8	0	7	6
Captain - - - - - - - -	7	0	5	6	5	0
Lieutenants - - - - - - -	5	0	3	0	2	4
Cornet, Enfign and 2d. Lieut. Marines	4	6	2	6	1	10
Quarter-mafter - - - - - -	3	0	2	0	2	0
Adjutant - - - - - - -	2	0	2	0	2	0
Surgeon - - - - - - - -	2	0	2	0	2	0
Chaplain - - - - - - - -	3	4	3	4	3	4

Phyſician

Phyſician Hoſp. - - -⎫
Apothecary - - - -⎬ Forces. ⎰ 10s.
Dep. Commiſſary - -⎭   ⎱ 5
                                             5

Form of an Affidavit for receiving Britiſh Half-Pay.

County of ⎱

                                             maketh oath
that he has not, between the   of   17   and the
   of   17   any other place or employment of
profit, civil or military, under his Majeſty, beſides his allowance of half-pay ; as a reduced   in Colonel A—'s
late regiment of

Sworn before me
this   day of   17

N. B. The proper periods for ſwearing the above, are, the
25th of June and 25th of December ; immediately after
which, they ſhall be delivered or tranſmitted to the Agent
for half-pay.

State of Iriſh Half-Pay.

	Horſe		Dragn.		Foot	
	s.	d.	s.	d.	s.	d.
Colonel ⎫	19	0	15	8	12	3
Lt. Col. ⎬ and Captain - - -	12	6	9	8	8	3
Major ⎭	11	3	8	8	6	9
Captain - - - - - - - - -	8	6	6	2	4	9
Lieutenants - - - - - - -	5	3	3	1	2	9
Cornet, 2d. Lieut. and Enſign - -	4	3	2	7	1	9
Quarter-maſter - - - - - - -	1	6	1	6	2	0
Chaplain - - - - - - - - -	3	4	3	4	3	4
Adjutant - - - - - - - - -	2	0	2	0	2	0
Surgeon - - - - - - - - -	2	0	2	0	2	0

Remarks, with the State of the Deductions.

IT too frequently happens that the brave and deſerving
Officer, through age, wounds, or other infirmities, is rendered incapable of doing his duty, and therefore obliged to
quit the ſervice, though, perhaps, at that very time, the eldeſt
of his rank in the corps : but, not having purchaſed his commiſſion, exchanges upon half-pay, with the uſual difference,
from

from whence the following deductions are made; which will, it is hoped, reach the ear of our gracious Sovereign.

Stopped at the Treasury - - -$\left\{\begin{array}{l}\text{Poundage 6}\\\text{Hospital 6}\\\text{Pells - - }1\frac{1}{3}\end{array}\right\}$ s.   d.

                                                             1   1

At the Half-pay Office, for Agency, &c. - - - - o 6¾
And if not on the spot, he must also allow his Agent $\left.\right\}$ o 6
for receiving it - - - - - - - - - -

Total per pound 2 2

Form of the Certificate to receive Irish Half-Pay.

County of $\left.\right\}$

                                                          came this
day before me, and maketh oath, that he is no otherwise provided for, by any commission or employment, civil or military, in his Majesty's service, than by half-pay on the establishment of Ireland, and is not on any other establishment of half-pay.

                         Sworn before me
this   day of   17

N. B. The certificates should be dated and delivered into the Half-pay office immediately after the 31st of March, 30th of June, 30th of September, and 31st of December.

Widows Pensions, British and Irish.

Colonel	50l.	Lieutenant	20l.	Q. Master	16l.
Lt. Colonel	40	Ensign	16	Surgeon	16
Major	30	Cornet	16	Chaplain	16
Captain	26	Adjutant	16		

Gun-Smiths.

IT would be of infinite service, if a Gun-smith, with an assistant, was appointed to each corps, and a carriage provided on a march, at the Government's expence, to carry the impliments for that business. Vegetius had carpenters, smiths, and other workmen to each corps. Perhaps it will be said, that the battalions of artillery have them : but that is of no consequence, as they are not always quartered with the rest of the army; besides, their own business will sufficiently employ them.

                                                          How

How to extract Saltpetre from damaged Gun-powder.

YOU muſt have filtring bags, hung on a rack, with glazed earthen pans under them: then take any quantity of damaged powder, and put it into a copper, with as much clean water as will juſt cover it; and, when it begins to boil, take off the ſcum, and, after it has boiled a little, ſtir it up; take it out of the copper with a ſmall hand-kettle, and then put ſome into each bag, beginning at one end of the rack, ſo that by the time you have got to the laſt bag, the firſt will be ready for more; continue thus, till all the bags are full; then take the liquor out of the pans, which boil and filter, as before, 2 or 3 times, till the water runs quite clear, which you muſt let ſtand in the pans for ſome time, and the ſaltpetre will appear at top. To get all the ſaltpetre entirely out of the powder, take the water from the ſaltpetre already extracted, to which add ſome freſh water and the dregs of the powder that remain in the bags, and put them together in a veſſel, to ſtand as long as you pleaſe; and, when you want to extract the nitre, you muſt proceed with this mixture as with the powder at firſt, by which means you will extract all the ſaltpetre; but this proceſs muſt be boiled longer than the firſt.

To reſtore damaged Gun-powder.

IF powder be long in a damp place, it will become damaged, and formed into hard lumps; when thus cemented, you will ſee, at the bottom of the barrel, ſome ſaltpetre, which, by being wet, will ſeparate from the ſaltpetre and coal, and always fall to the bottom, and ſettle there in the form of a white downy matter; to prevent this, move the barrels as oft as convenient, and place them on their contrary ſides or ends, to which they before ſtood; though great care be taken of powder, and kept as dry as poſſible, yet length of time will greatly leſſen its former ſtrength.

When any of the above-mentioned accidents happen to your powder, you may recover it by applying to the directions here given: viz. if the powder has not received much damage, proceed thus. Spread it on canvas cloth, or dry boards, and expoſe it to the ſun; then add to it an equal quantity of good powder, mix them well, and, when quite dry, barrel it up. If gun-powder be quite bad, the method to reſtore it is, firſt to know what it weighed when good; then,

then, by weighing it again, you will find how much it has loft by the feparation and evaporation of the faltpetre; then add to it as much refined faltpetre as it has loft in weight; but, as a large quantity would be difficult to mix, it will be neceffary to add a proportion of nitre to every 20 pounds of powder; when done, put 1 of thefe proportions into your mealing table, and grind it therein, till you have brought it to an impalpable powder; then fearch it with a fine fieve; if any remain in the fieve that will not pafs through, return it to the table, and grind it again, till you have made it all fine enough to go through the fieve; being well ground and fifted, it muft be made into grains thus: firft, you muft have fome copper wire fieves made according to what fize you in-tend the grains to be; thefe are called corning fieves, or grainers; fill them with the powder compofition, then fhake them about, and the powder will pafs through the fieve form-ed into grains. Having thus corned your powder, fet it in the fun; and when quite dry, fearch it with a fine hair fieve, to feparate the duft from the grains. This duft may be worked up again with another mixture; fo that none of the powder will be wafted: fometimes it may happen, that the weight of the powder when good cannot be known; in which cafe, add to each pound an ounce, or an ounce and an half, of faltpetre, according as the powder is decayed; then grind, fift, and granulate it, as before directed.

N. B. If a large quantity of powder is quite fpoiled, the only way is to extract the faltpetre from it, as powder thus circumftanced would be difficult to recover.

A few neceffary Extracts from the moft material military Acts of Parliament.

LODGINGS. Officers to pay for no lodgings, but in the fuburbs of Edinburgh.

GUARDS. Foot-guards may be quartered in Weftminfter and liberties, and places adjacent, excepting the city of London.

BILLETS. No more to be ordered than there are effective foldiers prefent to be quartered.

Petty conftables, &c. are to billet foldiers in their refpective divifions.

None to be quartered on private houfes without confent.

Officers quartering foldiers contrary to the act, or mena-cing or compelling any magiftrate, are *ipfo facto* cafhiered, and difabled from employments.

Military

Military Officers, being Juftices of the peace, are not to be concerned in quartering of foldiers under their own commands.

Officers taking money for excufing people quartering foldiers, are to be cafhiered, and rendered incapable of military employments.

In quartering horfe and dragoons, not lefs than 1 man fhall be quartered with one or two horfes, two men with four horfes, and fo on.

Quartering in Scotland, to be in fuch houfes as were liable to quarter foldiers at the time of the Union; and fuch houfes to furnifh Officers and foldiers according to the fame law.

Men and horfes may be fhifted in their quarters, for the benefit of the fervice.

Juftices of the peace to redrefs grievances relating to quartering foldiers.

Officers, who pay companies, not giving notice within 4 days to the landlords where Officers and foldiers are quartered, of their having received pay for them, or not clearing quarters according to the daily rates therein mentioned, are *ipfo facto* cafhiered.

Daily rates are fixed for all under the degree of a Captain, for diet, fmall beer, and horfes.

Paymafters not ftopping out of Officers arrears, who neglect to clear quarters, as much as will pay them, forfeit their employments, or out of Officers fubfiftence, in cafe no arrears are due.

Officers, upon not receiving money for clearing quarters, neglecting to make up accounts, are to be cafhiered *ipfo facto*.

Paymafter-general, to pay the quarters on fight of a certificate figned by the Officer.

Officers quartering their wives, children, men, or maid-fervants, on any houfe without confent, are *ipfo facto* cafhiered.

Civil magiftrates doing it, to forfeit 20s.

Conftables, or other Civil Magiftrates, taking money to excufe any perfon from quartering foldiers, forfeit from 40 fhillings to 5£. to the poor.

Victuallers refufing to quarter men, or to furnifh them with fuch neceffaries as the act directs, forfeit the fame.

Juftices may demand of the conftables the number of the Officers and foldiers by them billeted, with the names of the houfe-keepers, the ftreet, and fign.

GAME

GAME. Any Officer, or foldier, in or near quarters, without leave of the Lord of the Manor, killing any hare, coney, pheafant, partridge, pigeon, or any other fort of fowls, poultry, or fifh, or his Majefty's game, within the kingdom of Great Britain, if an Officer, he forfeits 5 £.

The Commanding-officer to pay 20 fhillings for every fuch offence committed by a foldier under his command.

Officers refufing or neglecting to pay the above penalties within 2 days, after conviction before a Juftice, and demand made by the conftable or overfeers of the poor, fhall forfeit, and are hereby declared to have forfeited their commiffions, and their commiffions are hereby declared to be null and void.

ARRESTS. No volunteer to be arrefted, or taken out of the fervice, except for fome criminal matter, or a real debt of 10 £. Oath of the debt to be firft made before a Judge of the Court of Record, or other Court, or before a perfon authorized to take affidavits in fuch courts.

The oath to be marked on the back of the writ.

Perfons arrefted contrary to the intent of the act, upon complaint, to be difcharged by one or more Judges of fuch court, without fees. Judge to award cofts.

Perfons perfuading foldiers, or endeavouring to perfuade them to defert, forfeit 40 £. by an act of the firft year of the reign of King George the Firft.

Perfons fufpected of defertion to be carried by the conftable before a Juftice of Peace, who is to examine them; and, if it appears they are deferters, they are to be fent to goal, and the Juftice to give notice to the Secretary at War.

Collector of the land-tax to pay 20 s. to the perfon that takes, or caufes to be taken, any deferter, upon a warrant from a Juftice of Peace being fhewn to fuch Collector.

Perfons, harbouring, concealing, or affifting deferters, forfeit 5 £.

Officers breaking open any houfe, or out-houfe, to fearch for deferters, without warrant from a Juftice, forfeit 20 £.

Perfons buying, exchanging, or receiving arms, cloths, caps, or other furniture belonging to the King, from any foldier or deferter, or any other perfon, upon any account whatever, or changing the colour of cloths, forfeit 5 £. Penalty in Ireland. Part of the 5 £. for the informer, part for the Captain.

Offenders herein not having 5 £. or goods of that value, or not paying within 4 days to be fent to goal for 3 months,

Y   or

or to be whipped publickly, at the difcretion of a Juftice of Peace. Penalty in Ireland and other places.

For further particulars, fee page 327.

CARRIAGES. Juftices in England, Wales, or Berwick, by order of his Majefty, or General, fhall grant a warrant for carriages, with able men to drive them. The Officer to pay into the conftable's hands the rates as regulated.

Officers forcing carriages to travel more than one day's journey, or detaining them too long, or fuffering foldiers or fervants (except the fick) or women, to ride, or forcing con-ftables to provide faddle-horfes for themfelves or fervants, or forcing horfes from the owners, forfeit 5 £.

Conftables neglecting or refufing to execute the Juftice's warrant for carriages ; and perfons neglecting or refufing to provide carriages, when appointed by the conftable ; and per-fons hindering others from providing them ; forfeit from 20 to 40 s.

Treafurers of the county to pay the conftables extraordina-ry charges.

No waggons, &c. to carry above 3000 weight. Carriages in Scotland to be had in like manner, and at the fame rates as directed by the laws in force in Scotland at the Union.

FERRIES. Officers paffing regular ferries in Scotland, may hire the boat for themfelves and party only, paying but half the ufual rate for each.

Or they may all pafs as common paffengers, paying but half the ufual rate for each.

But where there are no regular ferries, they muft hire boats at the rates other perfons give.

CRIMES CAPITAL. Officers or foldiers guilty of any ca-pital crime, or of any violence or offence againft the perfon, eftate, or property of any fubject, which is punifhable by law, to be delivered over to the Civil Magiftrate.

The Commanding-officer refufing or neglecting to deliver fuch perfon, or to affift the Civil Magiftrate in apprehending him, is *ipfo facto* cafhiered, and difabled to hold any Office, civil or military.

Soldiers liable to be proceeded againft by the ordinary courfe of law.

LISTING. Perfons lifted, to be carried within 4 days, but not fooner than 24 hours after, before the next Juftice of Peace of any county, riding, city, or place, or Chief Magif-trate of any city or town-corporate, (not being an Officer in the army) and if they before fuch Juftice, or Magiftrate, dif-

fent

sent to such inlisting, and return the inlisting-money, and also 20 shillings in lue of all charges expended on them, they are to be discharged.

But such persons refusing or neglecting to return and pay such money within 24 hours, shall be deemed as duly listed as if they had assented thereto before the proper Magistrate; and they shall, in that case, be obliged to take the oath, or, upon refusal, they shall be confined by the officer who listed them, till they do take it.

Persons owning before the proper Magistrate, that they voluntarily listed, are obliged to take the oath, or suffer confinement by the Officer who listed them, till they do take it.

The Magistrate is obliged in both cases to certify, that such persons are duly listed; setting forth their birth, age, and calling, if known, and that the second and sixth sections of the Articles of War against mutiny and desertion were read to them, and that they had taken the oath.

Officers offending herein are to be cashiered, and displaced from their office, and disabled to have any office, civil or military, and forfeit 100 £.

Persons receiving inlisting-money from any Officer, knowing him to be such, and afterwards absconding, and refusing to go before a proper Magistrate, to declare their assent or dissent, are deemed to be inlisted to all intents and purposes, and may be proceeded against as if they had taken the oath.

POSTSCRIPT.

P O S T S C R I P T.

ON revifing this work, I was concerned to find nothing had been faid in its proper place on recruiting the army; as fo many plans have been propofed, to facilitate that moſt effential fervice, by methods more honourable and effectual than the prefent, it may be prefumed that fuch plans have appeared exceptionable.

In the beſt that I have feen it was propofed to inliſt men for 7, 8, or 10 years; at the expiration of which, they ſhould either be permitted to receive another bounty and enter into a fimilar engagement, or claim a difcharge. From this motive, I confefs, many may be induced to inliſt; another bounty, with the common attachment to their corps, may impel them to engage again; and their refpect for thofe banners under which they have been victorious, with the expectation of a penfion, may incline them to voluntary fervice. But to this I muſt object, firſt, That thofe who quit, would be difciplined foldiers, whofe vacancies muſt be replaced with recruits: fecondly, that evil and defigning men would be enabled to work upon credulity, and occafion the men to leave their corps at fuch critical junctures as might be attended with pernicious confequences.———I therefore would form regiments into brigades, and call each by the name of a county in Great Britain wherein the men who compofe it were natives. This points out many advantages to the fervice, particularly thefe; viz. the fhires would probably contend who foonest and beſt could compleat the brigade of its name: they would more refolutely combine to protect their native country: as they would be piqued in honour to deliver up the offenders to juſtice, defertions would feldom occur; and laſtly, by this fcheme, fo ſtrong an emulation would be raifed between (for inſtance) Yorkſhire, Nottinghamſhire, and Cumberland Brigades, that each would fooner fuffer itfelf to be deſtroyed, than yield a laurel to its neighbour.

Much might be faid on the utility of fuch a plan: if the idea is tolerably perfect, this will be fufficient; if erroneous, too much has been urged.

A MAP of
AFRICA.

ADDITIONS to the EDITION of 1776.
CAMP DUTIES and REGULATIONS.

Orders given out to the Army during the War in Germany, the Netherlands and Scotland, on Account of the Rebellion, by his Majesty King George the Second and his Royal Highness the Duke of Cumberland.

G. R.

WHEREAS it is our Royal intention that an exact discipline should be kept amongst our forces, and due care taken for preventing all violences, excesses, disorders, outrages and robberies being committed upon the inhabitants of this country, which if not timely prevented will hinder our army from being duly supplied with necessary provisions, We do therefore command, and enjoin all our General Officers, Colonels of Our regiments and others, forthwith to signify our will and pleasure, that whosoever shall be guilty of such crimes and offences shall suffer immediate death for the same, without being tried by a Court-martial; or, whosoever shall be found straggling beyond the limits of their respective camps, unless he, or they shall produce a proper pass from his or their Commanding-Officers, shall be deemed delinquents, and likewise suffer immediate death : and We do hereby further command and direct the Provost Martial-general of Our forces, to take care that due obedience be paid to these Our express orders and commands.

Given at our head quarters at Aschaffenburgh, the 11th day of June, O. S. 1743, in the seventeenth year of our reign.   By his Majesty's command,
CARTERET.

K. August 5th, 1743. No Officer or any other person to wear a white feather, least they should be taken for French by the Hussars.

9th. No man under pain of the severest punishment is to set fire to the straw or wood at decamping.

No huts or tents to be placed in the front or intervals of regiments.

K. September 7th. No soldier to sell his wood, or suttler to buy it, on pain of severe punishment to both.

K. 14th. The following method is to be constantly observed by the British horse, foot, and dragoons, when his Majesty passes along the line.

Y 3   1st.

1ft. The private men are to turn out with their fide-arms, and draw up in ranks between their bells of arms, and drefs in a line with them; the Serjeants to draw up in the front of their refpective companies, a pace advanced before the men, the whole dreffing in a line.

2d. The Commiffioned Officers to draw up before their colours or ftandards in three ranks; the Captains in the front, the Lieutenants in the centre, and the Enfigns in the rear, leaving but one pace diftance between each rank; and the rear rank to be but one pace from the colours.

3d. The Field-officers to draw up in the front, the Lieutenant-colonel on the right, the Major on the left, and the Colonel in the centre, who is to be advanced before them.

4th. The colours and ftandards are to be unfurled, and an Enfign or Cornet to ftand by and take hold of them.

5th. If the King fhould pafs along the line after the taptoe is beat, they are not then to turn out, only the quarter and ftandard guards.

6th. The regiments of horfe, who have not bells of arms, muft turn out their men at the head of the ftreets, and drefs in a line with the Quarter-mafters tents.

7th. The Camp-colours on the flanks muft always be removed, when the King goes along the line, that his Majefty may approach nearer the men.

K. September 16. The horfe and dragoons to draw up their ftandard guards behind their ftandards and kettle-drums.

D. June 14th, 1747. When the line turns out, the regiments are to regulate their turning out, or returning into their tents, by the right or left, as H. R. H. fhall come.

N. B. The King's colour is the firft with the foot-guards, as a particular diftinction, but with all the marching regiments, royal or not, the union is the 1ft ftand of colours.

A centinel with bayonet fixed, to be pofted on each of the colours in camp.

K. September 14th, 1743. It is his Majefty's orders, that all the Officers of foot have Efpontoons, inftead of half pikes.

W. 1744. The regiments of foot in camp, to place their Efpontoons to the colours, the broad part of the fpear to the front.

K. September 19th, 1743. Gaming of all kinds among
the

the foldiers to be difcountenanced, and when any are found difobeying thefe orders, they are to be made prifoners and punifhed.

K. Sept. 22, 1743. Men that come from the Hofpital, not to be put upon duty till they are perfectly recovered.

K. 29th, The Officers to take particular care, to prevent all quarrels between the different nations that compofe the army.

W. June 27, 1744. No man to draw his fword againft his fellow foldier, or to ufe any infulting words or geftures, on the penalty of being punifhed with the utmoft feverity.

Oct. 2, 1744. The Commanding-Officers of the regiments of foot, may allow the Men to go out for roots, fending with them a fubaltern and thirty men with arms, and an Officer, to poft fuch centries as fhall be neceffary, to prevent the men from ftraggling, or doing any damage, and to take care to bring all men back to camp.

N. B. Great care fhould be alfo taken to direct the Officer where to go if near the enemy, or in an enemy's country. In the year 1744, when Marfhal Wade commanded the Britifh troops, an Officer of Brags regiment by miftake, and want of the French language to acquire knowledge of the fituation of the country, conducted his party and a man of a tent to gather roots under the cannon of Lifle, and clofe to an out-guard of the enemy. A Captain and 80 men, who having intelligence from the country people, that there were only fome men without arms marauding, fent a Non-commiffioned Officer and 12 men with arms to reconnoitre the Britifh: this party feeing ours without arms fired upon them, and endeavoured to take prifoners; but the Officer and his party who were pofted on the outfide of the garden and village, and whom the enemy had not difcovered, fuftained the routers, killed 1 of the enemy's party, and made another a Swifs prifoner, and brought off two of their firelocks.

W. June 10, 1744. The Officers next upon duty never to ftir any further out of camp, than their own Brigades, leaving word where they are to be found.

W. 27th, The regiments that are in Brigades that have no Brigadiers appointed to them, are to report to the eldeft field Officer of the Brigade, who is to make it to the Major-General appointed to infpect the Brigade.

The Brigadier or field Officer commanding the Brigade of foot guards, is, to report to the General commanding the foot.

D, April

D. April 27th, 1745. The guards to be relieved at eight every morning; the reports of the Cavalry to the eldest General of Cavalry; the reports of the Infantry to the eldest General of Infantry.

The Officers to wear their regimental cloaths in camp.

D. May 1st, Orderly guards, viz. Train-guard, Provost, Magazine-guard, and others, within the limits of the camp to be relieved every forty-eight hours.

D. July 1st, The several regiments to send to the train for tools, to make openings and communications; the Quarter-master giving receipts for the number of tools they take, and if any are lost they are to pay for them.

D. June 3, 1747. When regiments encamp on highways and roads, they are to make an overture in the most convenient places for carriages to pass.

D. 18th, At the arrival at every camp, lines to be made in the front and perches for the arms and drums, as also chevaux de frise between the camp colours.

D. July 3, 1745. So soon as the army comes into a new camp, the Commanding Officers of regiments are immediately to order an Officer and such a number of men as they shall judge necessary, to make communications between their respective corps, as also openings to the front if possible. This to be constantly done, and such as neglect to be put in arrest and reported to H. R. H.

D. May 3, 1745. The communications to be made between the intervals of regiments, to be sufficient for a carriage to pass safely, whether over ditches or boggy ground, in order to facilitate the moving of the ground for the troops and baggage, whether marching by the right or left.

D. June 7, 1747. All holes in the front of the camp to be filled up, and none to be made for the future on pain of punishment for disobeying of orders.

D. April 29, 1745. No Officer below the rank of a Brigadier to lie out of camp.

D. May 2d, If any country waggon is found with any corps, unless it is allowed them, the Commanding Officer of it will incur H. R. H's displeasure.

D. May 3d, All orders relating to the men, to be read constantly to them by an Officer of each troop and company.

D. July 16th, No person belonging to the army, to go a hunting, or fowling, or to fire in camp.

D. July 17th—22d, All the men to be acquainted, that

whoever

whoever is taken either fifhing of ponds, drawing them, or cutting the dykes, fhall be punifhed with death, or with the utmoſt feverity.

D. May 13th, No French deferters to be taken as fervants.

D. Aug. 12th, No deferters horfes to be bought before they have been at head quarters.

D. June 3, 1745. The cartridges for common ufe to be fifty out of a pound of powder.

D. May 20, 1745. All Serjeants of horfe grenadiers, dragoons, and foot, are to wear their fafhes round their wafte.

D. June 1ft, All returns to be figned by the Commanding Officers of regiments.

2d, The men to go for water twice or thrice a day, with a Serjeant at the head of them to keep them together, and to bring them back to camp, but none to go after gun firing.

No man to lay in the tents or huts in the rear.

Ap il 26, 1746. When a regiment fends for bread, coals, ftraw, or forage, the men are to be regularly paraded, and marched by a Subaltern Officer of each Brigade, and a Serjeant of each regiment to the place of delivery, befides the Quarter-mafter or the Quarter-mafter Serjeant, the Officers to take care that the men receive it regularly, and in their turns, and then to march them back in order to camp.

D. July 2, 1745. When foldiers go to market, a Serjeant or more is to go with them, who are to keep them together and conduct them back to camp, and to be anfwerable for their behaviour in the town and villages they go to, on pain of being broke; and when returned to report to the Commanding Officer, giving in a lift of the names of the men with him at the fame time, that he may be fure all the men are returned; Commanding Officers to be anfwerable that this is obferved during the campaign.

D. May 23, 1747. None of the Britifh Infantry to go for provifions, ftraw, or wood, even to the neareft towns or villages, or for water without having a Subaltern Officer with them, who is to march them regularly, and bring them back to camp in the fame order, the Officer to be anfwerable for all diforders: the Commanding Officers to fee this done.

D. June 30, 1745. No foldier to go from his camp without leave; all foldiers who are found beyond the grand guard fhall be deemed deferters.

D. July 28, 1745. All men who are found gathering beans, peafe, or under pretence of rooting, to be hanged as marauders

marauders without tryal; this order to be read to every man.
H. R. H. expects that the Commanding Officers of each
corps fhall be anfwerable to him for every one he fhall fee
out of camp, without a Non-commiffion Officer or Paffport
with him.

D. May 26, 1747. If any Officers meet foldiers ftrolling
after retreat beating, they are to fend them prifoners to the
next quarter-guard, and the Officer of that guard is to fend
them immediately on to the regiment they belong to, in order to their being punifhed with the utmoft feverity.

D. July 3, 1748. No foldier of the Britifh to appear
out of camp, particularly near head-quarters without fide-
arms.

July 13, 1745. It is H. R. H's orders, that the Officers
ftay in camp, and unlefs they have bufinefs that calls them
from it, they are not to ftir without firft having leave from
the Commanding Officer of their corps, who is to take care
to let but few be abfent at the fame time, and no Officer to
lye out of camp without H. R. H's leave.

D. April 23, 1747. If any foldier is found taking ftraw,
wood, or any thing elfe out of any houfe without an Officer
is prefent, he is to be punifhed immediately and feverely
at the head of his corps.

Auguft 6, 1745. On the firing of three cannon, all Officers and foldiers to repair to their colours.

All quarter-guards to be loaded with a running ball.

D. Aug. 13th, The men to be obliged to mefs regularly,
and an Officer of a Company to infpect into the meffes
daily, and to take care that the men drefs bacon, or other
flefh meat, with their roots and greens, and that every man
puts his proportion of pay towards it twice every week, viz.
each pay day.

D. June 15, 1747. The Commanding Officers to fee
that their captains account regularly with their men, for
their weekly ftoppages, at the end of every four months,
they are to pay them the balance of the firft two months
that may be then in their hands and the Commanding
Officers of Companies are ftrictly forbid to make any other
ftoppage or deduction from their men than the regulated
ftoppage, except by order of a court-martial; and H. R. H.
expects that with the affiftance of thefe ftoppages, the Officers will provide them conftantly with fhoes, gaiters, linnen,
their arms, accoutrements, and ammunition compleat, and

in

in good order, and that their cloaths will be kept tight and in good repair.

D. Aug. 14, 1745. All foldiers who fire their pieces in camp, or any where elfe off duty, to be feverely punifhed.

D. Feb. 9, 1745-6. When pieces cannot be drawn, an Officer to affemble the men, and fee them fired together in a fafe place.

Aug. 17, 1745. Soldiers who take your arms out of the bell tents after retreat to fuffer death, and the Officers of quarter-guards to be anfwerable.

The men on piquet to carry their arms into their tents.

N. B. Every regiment fhould allow the tents next to the Serjeants for the men on piquet.

D. Sept. 4th, Men who give falfe alarms to be feverely punifhed.

D. Jan. 29, 174⅚. Any man that is convicted of felling his powder, ball, or ammunition bread, to be punifhed with the utmoft feverity.

D. Feb. 11th, All men confined for crimes cognizable by regimental court-martial, to be tryed within twenty-four hours after their confinement, and the Commanding Officers to take care that this order be conftantly complied with.

D. Aug. 25, 1745. It is recommended to the Commanding Officers, that the men appear always well dreffed, and when on duty with fkirts hooked back, and with marching gaiters.

D. Sept. 6th, The Captains to infpect into their Companies arms, cloths, accoutrements, and ammunition on the pay days twice a week, and a Subaltern Officer of each Company to examine the men every morning before they leave camp, and to be anfwerable that they appear clean and well dreffed.

The tents to be opened and aired every day, the Officers to fee this done.

N. B. The Commanding Officers of every regiment fhould once every fortnight make the men dry the beft of their ftraw in the fun before their tents, which fhould be alfo ftruck, then the bad ftraw and litter burnt on the fpot where the tents ftood; the floor which the tent covered fhould be dug, and the upper fpit turned in, and frefh earth thrown upon the faid floor or place where each tent ftood; a fun fhine day fhould be chofe if poffible, as alfo the day the regiment receives frefh ftraw. This is very neceffary for the mens healths,

healths, and towards keeping the camp wholefome and fweet, as it deftroys vermin and other dirt, that are to be met with too frequently in the mens tents, if not well looked after.

June 8, 1745. All the men to be acquainted that from this day inclufive, if any deferts he is to expect no mercy or pardon, though he fhould return again of his own accord.

D. Aug. 30th, Commanding Officers to fee that their men have twenty four rounds each, and that the cartridges are well made and fit the pieces.

D. Sept. 1ft, All green fruit brought to camp to be deftroyed.

D. June 3d, The recruits of the fift line to be exercifed in the front, and thofe of the fecond line in the rear.

A Corporal of horfe, or Serjeant of dragoons, to go with the men who go to water their horfes, and no man to gallop his horfe.

D. April 1ft, 1746. It is recommended to the Commanding Officers of regiments, to order their new Officers to attend the parade every morning.

D. 2d, When recruits and aukward men exercife, H. R. H. expects that Officers attend at the fame time.

D. May 30, 1748. The recruits to exercife and fire as early in the morning as the Commanding Officers pleafe, but the drummers not to practice, except two hours in the morning after the relief of the quarter-guards, and two hours in the afternoon before the retreat.

D. June 6, 1748. Whenever a Commanding Officer intends to exercife, and fire his whole Battalion, he is to acquaint the Adjutant General with it in writing the evening before.

D. May 28, 1745. Straw being fcarce, Commanding Officers were ordered to fee that all huts were pulled down, and not permit any to be erected for the future.

D. June 2d, When H. R. H. or any General Officer goes into the rear of a quarter-guard, the Officer is only to make his men ftand fhouldered, and not to face his guard about, or beat a drum.

D. 14th, Commanding Officers of regiments to review their refpective regiments horfes, futtlers included, and if any are found glandered, to have them put to death immediately.

D. 18th, June 3, 1747. Commanding Officers to be anfwerable, that all butchers bury their garbage; and cleanlinefs in camp, in every refpect, recommended to them.

D. July

D. July 10th, The Commanding Officers to send and acquaint the Provost General when they have any dead horses, that they may be buried, for which they are to pay four shillings for each horse.

N. B. A man is looked upon as infamous by all the Germans, who touches any animal carcase that dies a natural death.

D. May 6th, Divine service to be constantly performed on Sundays, and the Commanding Officers to suffer no exercise or firing those mornings.

D. June 24, 1745. Prayers to be read every morning at nine, at the head of each Brigade; the Chaplains of which are to take it by turns beginning with the eldest.

D. June 12, 1747. The Chaplains to take it by turns to visit the wounded in the hospitals. N. B. After a battle.

D. June, 1745. All Surgeons to keep a book, and to enter into it each man's name that goes into the hospital, the Company he belongs to the day he was sent, and that of his discharge from the hospital.

March 3, 174⅚. The Surgeons of each regiment to visit their sick twice a day, and make a report to the Commanding Officers every morning.

D. July 13, 1745. No young trees to be cut down.

D. Sept. 30th, No avenues to be cut down, on pain of death.

D. 30th, All Officers to wear gloves when they have a fuzil or espontoon in their hands.

W. Aug. 6, 1744. No regiment to interfere with the front or rear of any other, in cutting wood, corn, or any thing else.

D. May 27, 1747. Whenever any Engineers call for carpenters from any regiment, that regiment is to furnish all the carpenters they have immediately.

D. June 2d, No regiment to demand a tour of duty, unless it has marched off the place of parade.

April 24, 1746. The beating in camp to be taken regularly by signals, beginning from the right of the first line, and continued from the left of the second line; the quarter-guard to march off, and to be trooped back at the same time, and no regimental punishment to intercept the marching off or relieving those guards.

N. B. The army when this order was given consisted entirely of British troops, and being small was not divided into right and left wings, as it was in the Netherlands,

when

when joined with the imperialifts and other foreign troops, the Britifh being then encamped on the left of the left wing, the fignals begun on the left of the firft line, and when anfwered by the laft regiment of Britifh in the firft line, it was returned by the regiment that covered it in the fecond line, and continued till it reached the regiment of Britifh foot upon the left of the fecond line.

D. April 23, 1747. The Commanding Officers to encourage their butchers to buy, kill, and fell meat to their regiments.

D. June 13th, No Pay-mafter to pay the troops in any other coin, but that they receive from the Pay-mafter General, under the penalty of making up the deficiency, and of being cafhiered for it, and the Commanding Officers of corps to be anfwerable that this order be obeyed.

June 14, 1747. All Jews found in camp without pafsports, to be ordered out of it, and if they return to be fent to the Provoft.

Feb. 22, 174$\frac{5}{6}$. No drum to be beat for orders after the retreat.

D. July 3d, All horfes, accoutrements, arms or baggage, which one nation or regiment may have belonging to any other in the army, are to be returned immediately to the nation or corps they belong to, for which the Commanding Officers fhall be anfwerable; and if it fhall appear that any foldier fhall offer to fell any horfes, arms, &c. of any other corps in the army, he fhall be hanged.

5th, Each nation to pay one another according to the following rates fettled by H. R. H.

	Ducats.	Sh.
For a horfe	3	0
Firelock, with or without bayonet	0	8
Sword, or fabre	0	4
Each fingle bayonet	0	1
Pair of piftols	0	4
Sword belt	0	1
Shoulder-belt and pouch	0	4
Copper kettle	0	4
Tin kettle	0	1

N. B. The above-mentioned was made after a battle, and here it is proper to caution Commanding Officers of corps, that when any man of another corps brings them a firelock belonging to the regiment they command, in order

to

to receive the reward as above, they acquaint his Commanding Officer of it, that he may enquire whether he brought off his own firelock or not, as well as that for which he demands a reward, it being a common trick with Soldiers, who have been often in action, to throw away their own firelock, and take up another on pretence that theirs did burst or break; every man, therefore, after an action should be punished that does not bring back his own firelock, unless he is severely wounded, or makes it appear that it burst or broke in the action, and that he shewed it to the Officer Commanding the Platoon he was in; or to the Major Adjutant, or to one of the Officers appointed to take care of the rear; neither should any man, unless wounded, be permitted to throw away his knapsack during the action.

The tent-poles should not be parted with, until a Battalion is absolutely sure of engaging, and when they do it, they should, if possible, lay them up in a heap, in a place where they are not liable to be broke by the train or other wheel-carriages, or by the cavalry; a stanch old soldier might also be left to take care of them till he sees the success of the day, which must determine him either to remain or leave them. The loss of the tent-poles is attended with great inconveniencies to a Battalion for several days, but particularly the night of the action; several wounded, which remain with a regiment, being exposed to the air, for want of poles to pitch a tent, and for some days before the poles can be made; the sticks the men cut, or standards to support the ridge-pole, being forked for want of iron spikes, wear and do more damage to the tents than can be repaired that campaign.

Breda, March 22, 1748. It is H. R. H. the Duke's orders, that whatever arms have been lost by neglect should be replaced by the regiments themselves, who may purchase them at the train at a regulated price; but those lost in action, or by any other unavoidable way, will be replaced at the expence of the government.

D. April 21st, It is H. R. H. the Duke's positive orders, that the Commanding Officers of regiments do not allow upon any account whatsoever more bat-men than three per Company, except the foot-guards which are allowed four, and these to be such of the aukward and new men, as can be best trusted with the baggage. H. R. H. expects that no General Officers, or others, take any men as bat-men or fervants out of the regiments, more than the above three or four men per company allowed, and the Commanding Officers of corps will be anfwerable that this order be ftrictly complied with.

D. May 19th, The Commanding Officers of Regiments to provide their hatchet-men with three fpades, three faws, and three axes.

D. 25th, No recruit, or any foldier, to take off the lock of his firelock, on any pretence; when they want to clean them, they are to apply to their Corporals, who are to inftruct them how it is to be done.

D. June 7th, Whenever the men appear in brown gaiters, the Officers are to be in boots, the Piquets to obferve this order.

D. July 3, 1747. The Adjutants of regiments which are detached from the army, are to be made acquainted with all general orders during their abfence.

N. B. When a regiment returns again to the army, the Adjutant fhould borrow an orderly book, and examine whether all material orders have been fent to him while abfent, and enter fuch as have not.

D. 26th, No trees, or forage, to be cut near any of the General Officers quarters by the troops of any nation, on any account whatfoever.

D. 28th, No Officer, or foldier, to fwim in the Maefe, the fentries having orders to fire at them that difobey this order; and no Officer, or other, to pafs betwixt the fentries and the river, except General Officers and Officers upon duty, and no converfing with the enemy.

N. B. This is a general order, though it only queftions the Maefe to be obferved, whenever two oppofite armies are to be encamped clofe to, or near, the oppofite banks of a river.

D. 30th, No woman to go to the French hofpital without a pafs from H. R. H. which the Commanding Officer of the regiment her hufband belongs to, is to apply for, and not to return till her hufband comes back.

D. Aug. 2d, The Britifh are not to thrafh their corn in order to grind or fell it.

D. July 22d, Prices and rates for work fettled by H. R. H. each Non-commiffioned Officer at a working party to receive 12 pence per day.

A private foldier or drummer, 6d.

For a fafcine, 7 feet long, with its picket, 3d.

A battery

A battery fafcine, 12 feet long, with its piquet, 6d.

A mallet, 6d.

A battery picket 3 inches thick, 1d.

A gabion with piquet, 14d.

The whole to be paid in Barabants money, the ducats at 17 permifcie fkillings, and each fkilling at 7 pence.

S. June 1743. An Officer of the train to receive orders daily with the Majors of Brigade.

K. 23d, An Engineer to be appointed for the day.

K. July 5th, No foldiers to pluck up fticks out of the vineyards, they being of little ufe to them, and great hurt or ruin to the country.

K. 16th, The Adjutants themfelves to attend the Majors of Brigade for orders, and not to prefume to appoint any one under the rank of a commiffioned Officer to attend, when they cannot themfelves.

K. 24th, When the Adjutants of the Cavalry cannot attend, they muft fend Quarter-mafters in their places to the Majors of Brigade.

May 18, 1747. If the bread is deficient in weight, the Commiffaries are to change it, or make up the deficiency, of which the Quarter-mafters are to keep an account.

N. B. The Major of every regiment fhould take care that the encampment of his corps is kept clean, and every morning fee that the men have fwept their ftreets, and that the camp colour-men have done the fame in the front of the regiment and the Officers ftreets, and that the men do not heap up earth or fods againft the tents to fhelter them from the wind, and alfo that they do not bury the loops that go round the tent pins into the ground, or lay their wood or other things againft their tents, all which wear, or rot them before half the campaign is over, and the Officers are to infpect every day very minutely within and without the tents, that no damage is done to them, and if any happens, to make the men repair it immediately; he fhould alfo examine the quarter and rear guard tents daily, and not permit the guard to be relieved till they have made good all damages. They are very foon tore to pieces if not narrowly looked into.

The Major fhould alfo take care of the detail of duty done by the regiment, and fee that no more men per Company are warned for duty than what is required, and that

Z the

the Adjutant keeps his rosters and returns in an exact and methodical manner.

The Major should also both in camp and garrison inspect into every thing received for the regiment by the Quarter-master, or delivered by him, and see that he neither imposes, nor has been imposed upon, either in number, weight, or measure, and that he enters into a book copies of all receipts he gives on the regiment's account, whether for arms, slope geldt, bedding, utensils, particularly such as are to be returned, or may be demanded from the regiment again ; he should also himself enter every thing received by the regiment, not only to be able to answer such questions as may be asked by any general Officer, but also to have it in his power to settle the regiment's accounts of forage, straw, or fire, in case the Quarter-master should die, be killed, or lose his books, columns ruled as follows will take up very little time to fill up.

Explanation of the ORDERS.

The date in the margin is, that of the order; and the letter before the date, is the initial of the person who gave the order, viz.

K. The King.
D. H. R. H. the Duke.
S. Earl of Stair.
W. Marshal Wade.
A. Earl of Albemarle.
L. Sir John Ligonier.

Account

Account of Bread, Forage, Fire and Ammunition, received for the King's Regiment, 1748.

1748. Day, Receiv'd.	Bread.			Straw for Tents.		Firing.		Forage.				Powder.		Ammunition.	
	Rations per Man.	To what Day inclusive.	Total Loaves receiv'd.	No. of Bundles.	To what Day inclusive.	No. of Faggots.	To what Day inclusive.	Rations of Hay.	To what Day inclusive.	Rations of Oats.	To what Day inclusive.	For Exercise.	For Duty.	No. of Ball.	No. of Flints.
March 29th	4	Apr. 1st	581	—	—	150	May 29	178	May 30	89	May 29				
April 4th	4	5th	656	350	Apr. 10	600	April 5	267	April 6	356	April 6				
5th	4	9th	640	—	—	300	6th	267	9th	267	9th				
7th	—	—	—	250	17th	600	9th	267	—	—	—	4 Bar.	2 Bar.	6300	1400
18th	2	20th	220	200	24th	200	18th	178	19th	—	9th				

THE Quarter-mafter is alfo to keep an account of what he delivers to each Company, and to enter what forage each Officer or Sutler receives, and on the back of the receipts he gives for bread he fhould fet down the number of loaves each Company receives, and on the back of the receipts for forage, the number of rations delivered to each Company; by this method if all regimental entries fhould be loft, any one may fettle the bread and forage accounts as foon as the receipts are produced.

A ration of bread is the weight of one pound and a half, each loaf to contain four rations, being fix pounds weight, the bread in the Netherlands was brown, but that delivered to the army in England and Scotland was white ; for which each Non-commiffioned Officer and foldier paid one penny and one farthing per day per ration, or five-pence Englifh for every loaf of fix pounds: this was paid to the contractors by the corps as often as they were required to do it, which was fignified in publick orders ; but the government made the contract, the ammunition bread for the Englifh was entirely made of wheat.

Hall Camp, May 1, 1745. Seventy-five faggots were ordered to be delivered to each fquadron, and two hundred per battalion per day.

One hundred and fifty boles or bundles of ftraw to be delivered per fquadron, and four hundred per battalion, Officers fervants and bat-men included ; each bole or bundle to weigh twelve pounds, and half that quantity to be delivered every eight days after, until the army changed camp, then each fquadron and battalion to receive the firft delivery 150 and 400 bundles as above.

H. R. H. will give a gratuity of one hundred crowns for every ftandard or colour taken from the enemy. Query, whether German crowns, fix perpifcie fkillings.

Colours or ftandards taken, to be fent to H. R. H's quarters, guarded by an Officer and twelve grenadiers, carried by the men who took them betwixt the front and center ranks.

To make colouring for accoutrements, to four pounds of whiting put one pound of the beft yellow oaker.

GUARDS, DETACHMENTS, PIQUETS, DUTIES OF FA-
TIGUE, AND GENERAL COURTS-MARTIAL.

*Regulations for doing Duty, Hilenraet Camp, April 25, 1748,
by H. R. H.*

IN all duties, whether, with or without arms, Piquets,
or Courts-martial, the tour of duties fhall be from the
eldeft downwards.

Ift. Of duties of honour ; the firft is the King's guard ;
the Queen's guard ; the Prince of Wales's ; the Captain-
General, or Field-Marfhal commanding the army.

IId. Detachments of the army and out-pofts.

IIId. General Officers guards.

IVth. The Ordinary, either in camp or garrifon.

Vth. The piquets.

VIth. General Courts Martial.

VIIth. Laft duties without arms or of fatigue.

An Officer who is upon duty cannot be ordered for any
other before that duty is finifhed, except he be on the piquet.

If an Officer's tour of duty happens when he is on the
piquet, he fhall immediately be relieved and go upon that
duty, the tour of the piquet fhall pafs him, though he
fhould not have been on it a quarter of an hour.

If any Officer's tour for the piquet General Courts-Martial, or duty of fatigue, happens when he is on any other
duty, he fhall not make good that piquet, Court-Martial,
or duty of fatigue when he comes off; but his tour fhall pafs,
and the fame if he fhould be on a General Court-Martial,
or duty of fatigue, his guard or detachment fhall pafs, and
he fhall not be obliged to make it up.

The Officers and men of the grenadier Companies fhall
not be put on any but camp duties, except when the grenadiers are to be detached.

No Major of Brigade to be detached but with his Brigade.

No Adjutant to be detached but with his regiment or
battalion.

Guards or detachments which have not marched off from
the place of parade or rendezvous, are not to be reckoned
as a duty done ; but if they fhould have marched off from
the place of parade, it fhall be reckoned a duty done, though
they fhould be difmiffed immediately after.

General

General Courts-Martial that have affembled, and the members fworn in fhall be reckoned, though they fhould be difmiffed without trying any perfon.

The King's ftandard in the guards can never be carried to any guard but that of His Majefty.

The firft colours of regiments is not to be carried to any guard, but that on the King, Queen, Prince of Wales, or Captain General being of the Royal Family, and except in thofe cafes it fhall always remain with the regiments.

N. B. The Union is the firft ftand of colours in all regiments, Royal or not, except the foot guards, with whom the King's colour is the firft as a particular diftinction.

The Field-Officers when ill to fend word to the Adjutant-General, that they may not be ordered for duty, they are alfo to fend word when recovered.

D. May 19, 1745. All detachments that are ordered to march immediately, to be taken from the piquet, and replaced immediately.

D. May 21t. All guards ordered at orderly time to remain for that duty, and a new detachment to be made for all ordered after, except when they are to march immediately, then they are to be taken from the piquets.

D. June 14, 1745. When any Officer is given out for one duty in orders, he is not to be taken off to be put on another duty.

N. B. This does not relate to regimental details, but to the Field-Officers and other commiffioned ones, given out in order at head-quarters; for in the field it frequently happens, that moft of the Subalterns are given out in regimental orders for one duty or other, with or without arms.

D. May 5th, When a detachment above two hundred men is ordered out, a furgeon or mate to be fent with them, and the cavalry to fend a farrier.

D. Auguft 8th, When any piquet or other detachment marches with a Field-Officer, he is to take a furgeon or mate of his own corps with it.

N. B. When all the piquets are ordered to affemble and parade together, thofe on the front line are to draw up on the right, and thofe of the fecond line on the left, and to march off in that order.

D. June 7th, All detachments ordered to affemble at a general parade at the national one an hour before.

S. No out-guards to march to or from the camp with drums beating or trumpets founding.

K. July

K. July 26, 1743. All horfe and dragoon guards are to found trumpets and beat drums at marching from the parade and relieving.

K. Sept. 9th, A Captain's command to have always two Subalterns.

K. Aug. 24th, The Officers upon all out-guards are to fend guides to conduct the new guards, and upon marches they are to fend notice to the Majors of Brigade of the Day, where they are as foon as they arrive at their quarters or pofts.

K. June 24th, One rank of the grand-guard to be mounted all night, from Taptoe to Reveille.

K. June 25th, All foldiers who fire dropping fhot, to be made prifoners, and to be immediately tried and punifhed.

The grand-guard and advanced pofts not to fuffer any deferter to fell his horfe, or any thing elfe, till he has been examined at the King's quarters. (Head quarters.)

Servants deferting from the French, viz. from the enemy, to be brought to head quarters; and if it be found that they have robbed their mafters, they are to be fent back to the French camp.

S. That no guards or fentries prefume to ftop any perfons coming to camp with provifions, nor take any thing for their free paffage.

D. May 4, 1745. The grand-guard to patrole and take up all men ftrolling beyond the grand-guard, and carry them prifoners to their regiments, a Court-Martial to be held immediately at the head of the colours or ftandards, and the punifhment adjudged to be immediately inflicted.

D. May 8th, All Officers upon grand-guards or detachments out of camp that have fentries or vedettes out, are to order them to ftop all paffengers at night, and detain them till the Commanding Officer of the faid guard or detachment has examined them.

K. July 8th, 1743. Any Officer or other perfon that comes from the enemy's camp, to be fecured by the firft guard he comes to, till His Majefty's (viz. the Commanders in Chief's) pleafure be known.

W. Aug. 27, 1744. When any detachment goes out, no perfon of whatfoever rank to go that way a fhooting on pain of being made prifoner.

D. May

D. May 2ϛ, 1747. None of the cavalry to advance the advanced poſts on any pretence, not even to water their horſes.

D. May 26, 1745. All Officers and Non-commiſſioned Officers commanding guards, as well cavalry as foot, are to confine all perſons of whatſoever nation they meet with plunder, and are to make a report of it to the Generals of the day for the army, and alſo to give notice to the regiments the offenders belong to.

D. May 6th, All out-poſts of the foot are to join their regiments at beating the General.

D. April 1, 1746. Officers that mount guard to wear their faſhes tucked up ſhort.

D. Auguſt 1, 1745. All the cavalry that go upon out-poſts, to take forage with them for the time they are to be there.

D. June 1ſt, Officers of magazine guards to be anſwerable for all forage their ſentries ſuffer to be ſtolen or embezzled.

Officers who give receipts for bread and forage delivered to detachments, to put on the back the names of the ſeveral regiments that compoſe it, and the quantity delivered to each corps ; they are alſo to put down their own rank, and the corps they belong to under their names.

D. Aug. 30th, Majors to viſit the men that are to go upon the out-poſts, and ſee that they are provided with ammunition, pay, and bread, and arms in good order.

D. July 20th, All ſentries to be alert, and not to ſit down on their poſts on any pretence.

Any Serjeant or Corporal that negleᴄts to make the ſentries he poſts to take off their thumb-ſtalls, ſhall not only be broke but ſeverely puniſhed.

D. Aug. 18th, When a pontoon-bridge is to be taken up, the guard that attends upon it is to aſſiſt in taking up the pontoons out of the water, and placing them on the carriages.

June 2, 1747. All out-poſts are to receive General Officers, even H. R. H. with ſhouldered arms.

D. April 23d, The Cavalry on the grand-guard to advance their fire-arms when viſited by the Generals.

D. Aug. 23, 1745. Officers of out-poſts never to reſt their arms or ſalute any General Officer, but always face with their guards towards the enemy.

D. April

D. April 27th, 1747. When a General paſſes in the rear of a quarter-guard, the guard is to take no notice of him.

D. July 26th, The Officers of the quarter-guards to pay all compliments to the General Officers as they paſs by the line, as alſo at the time the guard is relieving.

N. B. The relieving guard to face to the right about, but the Officers of it to remain between the two guards with the Officer of the diſmounting guard.

W. June 1744. Honours due to General Officers to be punctually paid to thoſe of all nations, according to His Majeſty's regulations; and if Officers of guards do not know all General Officers, they are to ſend one of their guard or party to enquire the rank of any perſon they ſuſpect to be a General Officer, and who is advancing towards their poſt.

N. B. If a General Officer to whom a guard has paid his compliment remains at the head of the ſaid guard, and that another General Officer comes by it, and at that time, the ſaid guard is not to pay any compliment, unleſs it ſhould prove to be a General of a ſuperior rank, or of an elder date (if of the ſame rank) than the firſt.

W. The guards upon General Officers not to turn out to any but to the General Officer on whom they are poſted, or to ſuch as are of a ſuperior or equal rank with him.

The horſe and foot guards to pay the compliments due to the General Officers, according to His Majeſty's regulations of honours, excepting that they are to turn out all guards and detachments when ordered by the Generals of the day.

D. July 29, 1745. The Officers who have Cavalry under their command, to ſend all reports by one of them.

K. Nov. 29, 1743. Serjeants, Corporals, or private men that are ſent with reports, are to carry their proper arms with them.

D. Aug. 15, 1745. The daily reports of all guards to be ſent from poſt to poſt, when practicable, to head-quarters; when a report is brought to a poſt to be forwarded, the Officer of it is to write on the back at what hour he received it, and when he ſends it off to the next poſt.

D. Aug. 24th, The parole to be ſent from poſt to poſt in like manner, beginning with the poſt that is near the head-quarters.

D. June 13th, All Officers commanding out-poſts are upon their return to make their report immediately to the Major-General of the day at head-quarters, or in his abſence to leave the report with the Adjutant General.

D. Feb.

D. Feb. 16, 174⅘. When any Officer makes a report in writing, he is always to mention his rank and the regiment he belongs to.

June 20, 1745. All Officers on out-posts and detachments, to report to the General of the foot (or horse when there is none of the foot) when relieved, and likewise all Officers on duty in the line when any extraordinary happens.

The 17th Article of War, the 14th Section relates to Safe-guards, as follows:

" Whosoever of Our forces employed in foreign parts shall force a Safe-guard, shall suffer death.

July 8, 1743. Four permiscie skillings to be paid to each Safe-guard for 24 hours.

K. July 25th, All General Officers guards, except Brigadiers, to be allowed in the duty of the line.

N. B. At the time this order was given out, all the Brigadiers abroad had regiments in the field ; but as several had not their regiments abroad the campaign 1744 and 1745, or were colonels in the foot-guards, they had guards from any regiment they desired it, and it was allowed in the duty of the line.

All General Officers of Infantry take their guards from their own corps, or any that does not give a guard of the same sort to some other General Officer, and it is to be allowed to the regiment that gives it in the duty of the line for orderly guard; but no allowance is given to any corps for such guards out of the out-posts : the Generals kept the same guard, if they desired it, the whole campaign, otherwise it is to be relieved every 48 hours.

The Train-guard of Infantry was provided with tents by the Artillery, it consisted generally of one Captain, two Subaltern Officers, and 100 men.

D. Feb. 11, 174⅘. Whenever a guard or detachment which is marching by with arms passes by any guard, that guard is to be under arms ; and if the guard or detachment which is marcing by beat their drum, the other is to do the same with rested arms.

Directions for the more orderly forming and returning the Piquets of the Infantry.

D. Aug. 24, 1747. The Officers and men for the piquets being ready dressed and accoutered, as soon as the preparative for beating the retreat is made, the men take their arms, and form in their streets before their tents ; there the orderly

Serjeants

Serjeants and Corporals having their arms likewife, examine the men, and form thofe of their refpective Companies into their ranks within the lines of their tents ; when the retreat begins they march them forward, the front rank even with the bells of arms, each orderly Serjeant or Corporal being three paces advanced before the men of his Company ; the Officers, Serjeants, and Drummers, to go to the head of the colours, and taking their arms wait there.

As foon as the Retreat is ended, the Adjutant Orders, Advance to form the Piquet.

Upon this they march forward in their ranks to the lines of parade, the Officers, Serjeants, and drummers of the piquet, as well as the orderly Serjeants, or Corporals, advancing 12 paces towards the line of parade, and as foon as they are all at their ground the Adjutant orders

Halt.

Upon this the Officers, Serjeants, and drummers, face to the right about.

Form the Piquet.

At the word of command the whole, except the Officers, Serjeants, and drummers of the piquet, faces to the right and left inwards.

March.

They march together clofing to the center, and the Officers, Serjeants, and drummers of the piquet take there pofts, the orderly Serjeants or Corporals clofe likewife, but fo as to be oppofite to the men of their Companies to anfwer for what may be wanting or amifs.

Halt.

The piquet faces to the front, and the orderly Serjeants or Corporals to the piquet.

The Adjutant then goes through the ranks, and after examining the whole, orders the orderly Serjeants or Corporals to their Companies to call their rolls, they are to march regularly facing to the right and left outwards, he then is to acquaint the Captain that his piquet is compleat.

The Captain and his Officers are then to examine the mens ammunition, and then orders

Prime.

Load.

Shoulder.

Which they are to do regularly and together : as foon as the Colonel or Field-Officer of the piquet has acquainted

the

the Captain that he may return his piquet, the Captain having firft cautioned them to be ready to turn out on the firft
notice, orders

Piquet to the right and left to your Companies.

Upon which the Officers, Serjeants, and drummers move
three paces to the front, and the men face to the right and
left outwards.

March.

They march till they come oppofite to their bells of arms,
waiting for the next words of command,

Halt.

Upon this they face to their bells of arms.

March and lodge your Arms.

They march together with an equal pace, and lodge their
arms carefully, the Officers, Serjeants, and drummers doing
the fame.

N. B. The piquet muft take their arms into their tents,
otherwife if ordered out, or that any alarm fhould be given
in the night when dark, they would not be able to diftinguifh their own arms (which are ready, being loaded) from the
reft of the arms in the bells; add to this that the piquet is to
patrole in the night round the flanks and rear, and accidents
would unavoidably happen by pieces going off if they were
to take them out of the bells of arms often in the dark; and
further, that probably under pretence of being of the piquet,
and of a patrole, marauders might flip out their pieces. I
mention the above, becaufe the laft part of the directions to
difmifs the piquet, might give room to think the men were
to lodge their arms in the bells, though a pofitive order was
given to the contrary the 17th of Auguft, 1745, and foldiers who took their arms out of the bells tents after retreat
were to fuffer death, and the Officers of the quarter-guard
were to be anfwerable for any arms taken out. This order
was occafioned by outrages committed in the country near
the army by marauders, who ftole out their arms.

When the line turns out without arms, the piquet is to
form on the right and left of the colours without arms.

N. B. The men on the piquet fhould not be fuffered to
pull off their accoutrements till that duty is done.

D. Sept. 1748. No fentry with a fixed bayonet is to reft
his firelock.

W. May 21, 1744. The foot-guards are not to be vifited
by the field Officers of the piquet, unlefs they belong to
their own body.

D. Aug.

D. Aug. 25, 1745. Advanced piquets to turn out to the Duke and Marfhals, &c. if ordered to the General's of the day, and to the General of foot.

D. Feb. 9, 174⅚. When the piquets is ordered out, the men are to have their ammunition, bread, knapfacks, and pay in the Officers hands.

W. Whenever the piquets are ordered to march to any parade, it is no duty unlefs they march off that grand parade.

S. That nobody prefume to turn out the piquets, but the General Officers of the day, unlefs by order of the Commander in Chief.

D. May 3, & June 3, 1745. A detachment of the piquet of every regiment to patrole in the front and rear of each line, and to take up all marauders and fend them to the Provoft.

Piquets alfo to patrole from 10 o'clock at night till day light, and to confine all men they find out of their tents.

D. June 13, The two Field Officers of the piquet to go to the rounds of the two lines, taking one line each, unlefs the Colonel of the piquet (when there is one) fends them word, that he will go the grand rounds himfelf. The Field Officer of the piquet of Cavalry to go the rounds of both lines of Cavalry. The three Field Officers are to report to the Colonel of the piquet; the Colonel to the Brigadier of the day, before nine o'clock in the morning at head-quarters.

D. June 18th, The Officer of the piquet of each regiment of horfe and dragoons to be at the ftandard guard, to give the parole to the Field Officer when he goes the rounds.

N. B. The Field Officers of the piquet went the grand-rounds, and vifited the quarter-guards of that line the regiment they belonged to was encamped in; but if they were both encamped in the fame line, or that one or both belonged to the foot-guards, the eldeft took his choice.

When the army encamped all in one line behind the canals of Vilvorden, in the year 1745, H. R. H. the Duke gave out an order Auguft 3d, viz. The Field Officers of the piquet to vifit the right and left, according as it be nearest to where they are encamped.

When the Field Officers goes the grand-rounds, it is generally about midnight, they commonly take a Serjeant and four men of the piquet of their own regiment, or from the firft quarter-guard they vifit, and may be in upon the right or left of the line as they find moft convenient.

D. Aberden,

D. Aberdęn, March 21, 1746. As foon as any centinel challenges Who comes there ? the Serjeant is to anfwer, *Rounds*; and all centinels (except thofe who have orders to make rounds ftand) are to reply, *Pafs rounds, keep clear of my arms, all is well.*

When the centinel of the quarter-guard, or any other guard or poft that is to be vifited has challenged, and been anfwered *Rounds*, he may reply *Stand rounds*, and immedi · ately to call out to the Serjeant of the guard to turn it out, and he is not to fuffer the rounds to advance in the mean time.

The Officer of the guard is to make the men take their arms, and is to fend off a Serjeant and the firft four men that turn out to meet and examine the rounds; the Serjeant of the guard is to challenge, *Who comes there?* anfwer, *Rounds*; Serjeant of the guard, *What rounds ?* anfwer, *Grand rounds;* the Serjeant of the guard is to reply *Stand grand rounds, advance one with the word,* upon which the Serjeant of the grand is to order his men to reft their firelocks, then go up to the other Serjeant who is to make his men reft their firelocks; then ftepping three or four paces towards the Serjeant of the rounds, that his men may not hear the parole or word, he is to receive it from the Serjeant of the grand, round, and go with it directly to the Officer of the guard, who, when he finds it right, is to call out, *Advance grand-rounds*; the Serjeant of his guard returning at the fame time to his four men, whom he is to open right and left, letting the Field Officer advance alone through them as far as the Officer of the guard, who is to order his men to reft their firelocks, then ftepping forward three or four paces towards the Field Officer for the reafon above-mentioned, he is to give him the parole; the Field Officer then paffes on with his attendance and guard, or orders them back, and demands a Serjeant and four men from the Officer, who is to give it to him to the next guard.

All rounds, except the grand-rounds, muft give the word or parole to the Officers of the guard they vifit.

One grand-round only is to go each night, and no Officer of any guard is obliged to receive any more as fuch, unlefs the General Officers of the day fhould vifit the guards or pofts; in which cafe, if in the night when a centinel challenges, and is anfwered, Lieutenant-General, Major-General, or Brigadier of the day, all guards are to examine and receive them as grand-rounds.

In

In going and receiving rounds nothing fhould be fpoke louder than juft to be heard diftinctly, except by the centinels who are at all times to challenge, *Who comes there*, with a loud and brifk voice.

The Officers of the guards which are vifited fhould not make the rounds wait any longer than the time neceffary for the Serjeant they fend to examine them, and if they and their guard are as alert as they fhould be, they will have fufficient time to turn them out, and put them in order, while their Serjeant is going for the parole and returning with it, and an Officer of a quarter-guard, or other poft, fhould be reported if he makes the rounds wait ; as it cannot be fuppofed, that if it was an enemy he would be ftopt by a centinel who bids him ftand, if he did not hear the guard hurrying out on the firft notice given by the centinel.

All the quarter-guards fhould mount at the fame time, and be ordered by the Commander in Chief to poft the fame number of centinels that they may be able to relieve at the fame time.

The quarter-guards that are to mount are to be drawn up in one rank on the line of parade, and are to be ready to march off as foon as the troop has been beat, but are not to begin their march till the fignals have been given, and till the regiments on the right, if of the right wing, or on the left, if of the left wing, begins to march, and no regimental punifhment, or other reafon, is to prevent or interrupt any quarter-guard from marching off at the time with the reft.

While the centinels are relieving, the Officer that mounts is to mount his guard to the right and left, according to which wing he belongs to, in order to give room for the guard he relieves to march through his, which the difmounting guard is to do in a rank entire as foon as the centinels have joined them; and after the fignal for difmounting (which is a fhort preparative) has been given along the line, the Officer that comes off, or difmounts, are to march their men with clubbed firelocks to the firft line of parade, and there halt them, ftill facing to the bells of arms ; then make them firft *Reft*, then *Recover their firelocks*, next *Face to the right and left of your Companies*, on which the men face as their Companies are encamped ; laft word *March and lodge your arms*, upon which the men march along the line of parade regularly, with your arms recovered, till they come oppofite to the bells of arms of their refpective Companies towards which they are to face ; then march and lodge their

arms

arms carefully in the said bells; a Serjeant or Corporal of each Company should meet the men and the bells, to see that they rub their pieces clean before they lodge them, and that none are cocked, as also to prevent their damaging the bells.

Note, That the word *Halt* may be given to the men when they come opposite to their bells; then *March and lodge your arms*, by which means they will all be at the bells at the same time if that is judged necessary, by being more regular.

Of Countersigns and Centinels.

All guards and centinels should have a countersign even for the reliefs by the Corporals, but that is totally neglected among the British troops in time of peace, by which means they cannot be brought to it in time of war; and the paroles or words which are daily given to the army, being generally Saints and towns the British are strangers to, or not accustomed to pronounce: Our Officers who do not understand French rarely give the parole properly, and Our Serjeant or Corporal when they write it down (unless they copy it) make strange words of them, and not to be understood but by Chiefs, by one well versed in such things, and in the French language.

W. Aug. 16, 1744. The Saint is the parole, and the town is the countersign.

A few attempts were made to put this order in practice; and make our men understand what was meant; but some blunders committed soon discouraged it, and it was intirely laid aside; and yet all centinels upon out-posts, and advanced piquets, should always have the countersign given them; the Austrian troops, now Imperialists, never omit it, and no person can come in the night into their encampment without it, for they keep at all times the piquets of the front line advanced three or 400 yards in the front, and those of the second or rear line as far in the rear; to prevent desertion, which is always great among them, they advance their piquets at retreat, beating and return them at reveille.

Beside the security of the camp, any persons or spies sent out by the General or Commander in Chief, may have the town that is the countersign of the parole given him for some days, by which he will be admitted quicker and easier, and without being obliged to make himself known to so many people as he must if he came in the day-time;

and

and it is of no more confequence, in cafe an enemy fhould difcover it, than if they did any other counterfign; for if any more than two perfons fhould prefent themfelves to an out-poft, all centinels are to ftop them and call out to the guard, who are to examine them as rounds, and make them prifoners if they have not the whole parole, that is, the Saint as well as the counterfign, all perfons by day or night that comes from towards the enemy are to be examined by the Officer of the guard.

The centinels of all out-pofts or advanced piquets near an enemy fhould be pofted double in the night, and fhould be relieved every hour, and between each relief the Commanding Officer fhould fend a Subaltern to go rounds, or a Serjeant to patrole; the counterfign of an advanced poft fhould not be either a clap on the pouch, or any fign that may be eafily difcovered by the ear, by an enemy who may be pretty near, and yet concealed by the darknefs of the night. It fhould, therefore, be fome town or name as aforefaid which the centinel may be able to hear, without either danger of difcovery, or fuffering the perfon that gives it to come within his arms; and if any centinel is miffing upon an out-poft, or advanced piquet, the Commanding Officer is immediately to change the counterfign with all his centinels, and order them to call to the guard to examine any perfon that offers the counterfign that has been changed; the Officer fhould alfo fend notice of it to any pofts or perfons with whom he has any communication.

This part of military difcipline, and very important abroad for the fafety of all out-pofts, might, I think, be made familiar to Britifh foldiers, by ufing or accuftoming them to a counterfign in Great Britain, or Ireland, in any place or quarter where a guard is mounted, be it ever fo fmall, and not permitting a corporal to relieve without it; and it would prove of greater advantage ftill, if parole were given fuch as are and muft be when joined with foreign troops, the town to mode the counterfign for every relief; this, befide the ufe aforementioned in time of war abroad, would accuftom Officers and men to pronounce foreign paroles.

A centinel is to be very filent on his poft, and is not to fuffer any noife near it; nor is he to quit his arms at any time; nor to fmoak; and if any perfon or perfons approach him, he is to challenge; and if they do not anfwer when he has repeated the challenge, and keep advancing towards him, or do not ftand ftill when he has ordered them, he is

A a

to fire at them, and to retire to the next poſt or guard which is to turn out, and examine the occaſion or cauſe of the centinel's firing, and if they are not ſatisfied how it happened, they ſhould viſit all the centinels, and poſt and warn them to be alert.

If a centinel is taken ill on his poſt, he is not to quit it till he is relieved, but to call to the next centinel, and ſo on from one to another, till it reaches the guard ; the Corporal of which is to be immediately ſent with one or more men if they do not know what is the occaſion of calling.

A centinel is not to be ſtruck or puniſhed on his poſt ; but if he has done amiſs, he muſt be relieved by one of the Corporals of the guard he belongs to.

All Officers commanding guards, whether in camp, outpoſts, or garriſon, ſhould order their guards under arms at day-break or reveille where it is beat, and ſee that their men are properly accoutered, and have their arms in good order, and their hats well cocked, and that they are in every other part of their dreſs as well appointed as poſſible.

Provoſt Martial General.

D. May 6, 1745. The Provoſts of the right and left wings, with proper detachments, to aſſemble with the quarter-maſters and camp colour-men every time the army marches, and to march with them while the camp is ſettling.

D. April 22, 1747. A Subaltern and thirty men of the cavalry to be always ready to go out with the Provoſts General.

A Serjeant and eighteen of the Foot to mount the Provoſt's guard.

D. Aug. 5th, When the army forages, the Grand Provoſts of each nation ſhall parole with a detachment of cavalry, to puniſh with death all thoſe who ſhall be found plundering or marauding in the country or villages, that is to ſay, all ſuch perſons as belong to the corps he is appointed for. Perſons of all other corps or nations ſhall be made priſoners, and ſent to their reſpective Provoſts Martial.

D. April 28th, All men guilty of capital crimes to be immediately ſent to the Provoſts.

D. Sept. 25, 1745. When any men are ſent to the Provoſts, (viz. If thoſe who confine them are not of the ſame regiments the priſoners belong to) he is to ſend a report of them immediately to the regiment they belong to, and no
man

man to be received by the Provoſt except his crime be ſent with him in writing.

D. Sept. 22d, Whenever any man is executed, a label is to be fixed on his breaſt, ſetting forth the crime for which he is executed.

W. Aug. 26, 1744. The Provoſt to give in a liſt of his priſoners to the Generals of the day, (viz. of his own nation) at head quarters by nine in the morning.

July 10, 1747. The Commanding Officers to ſend and acquaint the Provoſt General when they have any dead horſes that they may be buried, for which they are to pay four permiſcie ſkillings for each horſe.

D. May 28, 1745. The Provoſt to bury all dead horſes and carrion ; notice to be given where there is any in or near the camp.

W. July 24, 1744. Liſts to be given to the Provoſt-Martial of the ſuttlers and butchers licenſed in every corps, that they may have all weights and meaſures of the ſame ſtandard, and to ſell by no others but thoſe ſtamped by the Provoſt, under pain of ſevere puniſhment.

N. B. The Provoſt is to inſpect and ſee that all the ſuttlers of his nation ſell by proper weights and meaſures, but the Provoſt General belonging to the Commander in Chief, beſides the ſuttlers of his own nation, takes cognizance of all ſuttlers that keep at head-quarters of all nations whatſoever, whether of the army or not, and is to examine whether they have proper paſſes or licences ; he is alſo to inſpect into thoſe who keep at the General Officers quarters of his, and ſtrictly to enquire into ſuttler's ſervants, and endeavour to watch them, and to find out by his emiſſaries, whether, under pretence of going to neighbouring towns or villages to market, they do not hold correſpondence with the enemy or their ſpies.

Though the Provoſt is to inſpect into the weights and meaſures of all ſuttlers, the Commanding Officers of corps and Majors, are to be anſwerable for all ſuttlers and their ſervants who encamp within the limits of the ground, belonging to the encampment of their regiments.

D. June 27, 1745. If ever the Provoſt is found giving ſafe-guards again, he is to be broke.

Grand and Petty Suttlers.

D. April 20, 1745, & June 20, 1747. No more than one

grand

grand futtler per regiment, one petty futtler per troop, and company to be allowed.

No Serjeant or Corporal to futtle on any account.

D. Sept. 16, 1745. Suttlers not to be allowed to keep more than fourteen horfes per battalion of foot-guards and foot; twelve to each regiment of dragoons ; fifteen to each regiment of horfe of three fquadrons ; eight per troop of horfe-guards, and ten to the train of Artillery.

D. May 23, & July 11, 1747. No futtlers tent or hutt to ftand in the front of a camp or any regiment.

D. Aug. 9, 1747. The Commanding Officers of corps are to infpect into the conduct of the futtlers and their fervants, in order to difcover whether they hold any correfpondence with the enemy.

D. Aug. 20th, All futtlers who do not belong to fome regiment, or have not H. R. H's pafs, to be turned away, and told that if they are found in camp they fhall be hanged.

S. May 26, 1743. No foldier or foldier's wife to be fuffered to futtle in any village ; all General Officers are defired to fee this obeyed in the feveral villages where they may happen to be quartered.

W. July 24, 1744. Lifts to be given to the Provoft-Martial of the futtlers and butchers licenfed in each corps, that they may all have weights and meafures of the fame ftandard, and to fell by no other but thofe ftamped by the Provoft, under pain of fevere punifhment.

K. Sept. 3, 1743. No futtler or other perfon belonging to the camp to buy any arms, clothing, or neceffaries belonging to a foldier, on pain of being obliged to return thofe things for nothing to the regiment the foldier belongs to, and of being feverely punifhed.

K. Sept. 7, 1743. No futtler to buy any foldier's wood on pain of fevere punifhment, and to have his tent or booth pulled down, and not to be permitted to futtle any more.

D. June 13, 1747. If any futtler or changer of money refufes to change for the men, demands a premium for doing it, or infifts upon the Serjeants or men fpending money in drink or other things before he will give them change, fuch futtler, or any other perfon fo offending, fhall be plundered and turned out of the army.

All light in the rear to be put out before ten o'clock every night.

N. B. As foon as regiments take the field abroad, the Commanding Officers fhould encourage butchers to follow

their

their refpective regiments, or fet up fome trufty foldier for that purpofe; they arc to take care that he is always provided with a good ftock of black cattle and fheep before-hand fit to kill; when the army marches without this precaution a regiment may want frefh meat along time, not only on marching, but often in fettled camps, as was experienced by moft of the regiments in the beginning of the late war, and was the occafion in a great meafure of the mens marauding, and their accuftoming themfelves to exceffive drinking of fpirits, having nothing elfe to lay out their pay upon.

Another very ufeful perfon in a regiment is a black-fmith that underftands fhewing horfes and mending of arms, &c. a regiment that is ordered abroad to take the field, fhould before they leave England provide a little forge, to be carried in a light cart, and fuch as can be drawn by any tolerable horfe; the forge confifts only of an iron plate to make the fire on, a pair of bellows, a fmall anvil, pinchers, and hammers of the lighteft fort; by keeping fhoes and nails ready made, and this little travelling forge, many a horfe will be preferved from being lamed; on a march he fhould alfo be provided with a fcrew plate for the arms.

It is a practice and cuftom of the army, that the Majors of regiments regulates the futtlers and examine into the provifions they fell, whether meat or drink, and take care that they are wholefome, and that they do not impofe upon the men in price, weight, or meafure; they are alfo to prevent gaming in the rear, whether in huts or tents, and fee that the futtlers do not harbour any perfons without their knowledge, or fuch as cannot give good accounts of themfelves, and fecurity for their good behaviour and honefty; the Major fhould take care, that the Adjutant or Quarter-mafter fignify all publick orders relating to futtlers and followers of the army, that is, to fuch as come under the denomination and belong to his corps.

IT is the King's pleafure, that, for the future, whenever any Officer in the army fhall defire to fell his commiffmiffion, he fhall fign a memorial, ftating the grounds on which he forms his expectations of being permitted to difpofe of his commiffion, and praying that he may be allowed to fell it at the regulated price to any perfon whom His Majefty fhall appoint.

If fuch Memorialift be with the Regiment, he fhall deliver his memorial to the Officer commanding at quarters, who fhall fend the fame to his Colonel (if within the realm)

who

who muſt approve thereof previous to it's being laid before His Majeſty. But in the abſence of the Colonel, if the Lieutenant Colonel be not at quarters, the memorial ſhall be ſent to him in order that he may tranſmit it to the War-Office, certifying under his hand the truth of the faćts therein contained, ſo far as his knowledge or belief may extend.

In North America theſe memorials ſhall be tranſmitted, certified as aforeſaid, to the Commander in Chief : in Gibraltar and Minorca, to the Governor or Commandant for the time being in theſe ſtations : but in the Weſt-Indies they may be ſent directly to the War-Office. It is, however, the King's pleaſure, that a duplicate ſhall at the ſame time be always ſent to the Colonel of the regiment. Given at the War-Office, this 23d day of December, 1775.

By His Majeſty's command,
BARRINGTON.

Stoppage for Camp Neceſſaries.

W. Oct. 16, 1744. Whereas it is His Majeſty's pleaſure, that the troops ſerving in the Low Countries ſhould be put upon the footing of the late war in regard to their payments and ſtoppages, and the King having empowered me to make ſuch regulations therein as I ſhall judge neceſſary for the ſupport and good of the ſervice.

I do hereby order, Firſt, That ſixpence per diem be ſtopt from every Serjeant or Corporal, kettle-drummer and private man, in the horſe-guards, horſe and dragoons, as well from the non-effectives as effectives, from the day the army takes the field to the day their returning to winter quarters, or are ſupplied from the horſe, provided for winter quarters, four-pence whereof to be kept in the pay-maſter's hands, to be applied by the Colonels as an addition to the ſtock-purſe, ariſing from the non-effectives for remounting regiments ; and the remaining two-pence to be applied by the Colonels for providing tents and camp neceſſaries for next year, as alſo one pair of black linnen gaiters for each man, for ſtandard-guards and other duties on foot, ſo that the regiments may be remounted, and tents, camp neceſſaries and gaiters may be provided on or before the firſt day of March next.

Secondly, That four-pence per week be ſtopped from every Serjeant, Corporal, drummer and private man of each battalion of foot-guards and marching regiments of foot, as well from the non-effectives and effectives from the day they go into winter quarters to the day they take the field, which

is

is to remain in the pay-mafters hands, to be applied by the Colonels for providing the battalions and regiments with tents, camp neceffaries, and one pair of grey gaiters for each man for marching and common duties.

Thirdly, That the Commanding Officers of the regiments of foot take particular care, that the men be accounted with conftantly every two months, for the weekly ftoppages made to provide them with neceffaries according to His Majefty's regulation.

Fourthly, That no man plead ignorance of thefe orders, they are to be read at the head of every regiment, troop, and company, and entered into the Majors of Brigade and Adjutants books to be a ftanding rule for the future, given at the head-quarters at the Chateau d'Huyffe, the 2d October, N. S. 1744.

W. May 15, 1744. All ftoppages for camp neceffaries to ceafe from the day the regiments March out of garrifon.

Sir J. L——r, Camp near Grave, Nov. 5, 1746. In Holland the ftoppages from a foot foldier were as follow: ten ftivers and three urkers were ordered to be ftopped in twelve weeks from each foldier for the furgeon and pay-mafter.

Three ftivers and half per week to be ftopped from each man for camp neceffaries.

A pound fterling being remitted from the Treafury in England to Holland for ten guilders fifteen ftivers Dutch money; the ducats to be paid at five guilders five ftivers; an Englifh fhilling to be paid for ten ftivers three urkers, or fix doits (four urkers or eight doits to a ftiver,) fo that a foot foldier's pay is five ftivers three doits per diem.

BAT-HORSES AND RATIONS OF FORAGE.

Allowance to enable the Officers of Infantry to purchafe Bat-Horfes.

FIRST, To enable the Captains to buy a horfe to carry the Companies tents, ten pounds was paid to the Captain or Officer commanding each Company, but no further allowance was made on that account to the Infantry but for the firft campaign, it being fuppofed that an overplus will remain after providing the men with camp furniture, tents, marching gaiters, &c. out of the ftoppage made for the fame from them in winter quarters; and this overplus is to be employed to make good the Company's horfe; but if a regiment was fent from the army to England, or to any other part or

A a 4 place

place which caufed the ftoppage for camp neceffaries to ceafe, and that they returned and joined the army the next or any other campaign, then ten pounds was paid per Company to provide a horfe.

The allowance to the Officers was every fpring feven pounds ten fhillings more between the Lieutenant and En-fign of each Company, the Field-Officers received nothing but as Captains.

Ten pounds was allowed alfo every fpring to the Sur-geon-major of each regiment, to purchafe a horfe to carry the medicine cheft inftruments for chirurgical operations and bandages at the head of the regiments on marches.

The allowance to purchafe bat-horfes continued the fame during the whole war as aforefaid, but the number of rations of forage allowed to each Officer during winter quarters, fuf-fered alterations under the different commands of Lord Stair, Marfhal Wade, and His Royal Highnefs the Duke of Cumberland.

The Forage Money for the Forces in the Netherlands granted by Warrants, dated September, 1742, by Lord Stair, were as follow :

	Rations.
To the General Commander in Chief - -	100
To 4 Aids de Camp at 10 horfes each - -	40
To each Lieutenant General - .. -	60
Two Aids de Camp, to each at 10 - -	20
To each Major General at - - -	40
One Aide de Camp to each at 10 - - -	10
To each Brigadier General - - - -	30
To each Major of Brigade - - - -	10
To the Quarter-mafter General - - -	10
To the Judge Advocate - - - -	6
To the Deputy Pay-mafter General - -	6
To the Provoft-martial - - -	3
To the Waggon-mafter General - - -	10
To the Colonels or Commanding Officers of the } 1ft. regiment of foot-guards - - }	150
To the Colonels, &c. of the 2d. Battalion ditto -	135
To the Colonel, &c. of the 3d. Battalion ditto -	135
To the refpective Colonels or Commanding Offi- } cers of each Battalion of foot for each Battalion }	100

Diftribution

Diſtribution of One Hundred Rations granted to each marching Regiment.

	Rations.
To a Colonel - - - -	20
Lieutenant Colonel - - - -	11
Major - - - -	11
Eight Captains, 4 each - -	32
Nineteen Subalterns at one each - -	19
Chaplain - - - -	1
Adjutant - - - -	2
Quarter-maſter - - -	1
Surgeon - - -	2
Surgeon's Mate - - -	1
Total	100

N. B. Each ration of forage paid in Flanders net money amourted to 5l. 6s. 3d. Engliſh, allowing a ducat to be equal to 9s. 11d. Engliſh, and a permiſcie ſkilling to 7d. Engliſh ; but a perquiſite of three ſtivers Dutch per pound ſterling made upon all money paid in Flanders to the army, at that time ſix ſtivers per day per horſe (or for each ration) were granted ten guilders, ten ſtivers only in Dutch currency were allowed for each pound ſterling, and two hundred days forage money were paid for the whole winter quarter to the Officers of Infantry in lieu of forage, which they provided themſelves every winter during the late war.

I judge it needleſs to mention the allowance for bat-horſes and forage, 1744, during Marſhal Wade's command ; the œconomy with which he ſettled it, having proved ſo hurtful to the Officers of Infantry, that numbers at the concluſion of his campaign ſold out of the army ; I ſhall therefore proceed to what was ſettled by H. R. H. the Duke, which I ſuppoſe will be a precedent for any future wars Britiſh troops may happen to be engaged in, though, I confeſs, I think it were to be wiſhed, that another ration was allowed to each Subal‧tern of the Britiſh Infantry, who are often ſent by themſelves at a conſiderable diſtance from the army, to bring to it recovered men from the hoſpital, and on many duties which they are generally obliged to perform on foot, nobody in a regiment being able to ſpare a horſe during the campaign, the Field-Officers themſelves being ſo ſtinted in their allowance of rations of forage, that they cannot keep one led or ſpare horſe to aſſiſt an Officer on a march, whoſe baggage is ſometimes loſt by an accident's happening to his bat-horſe ; and

when

when sent upon any command, they cannot carry provisions or liquor to refresh the Officers with them according to the customs of the army, and what is practised by the Field-Officers of other nations, who besides being allowed to keep a waggon (which the British are not) have about double the number of rations of forage allowed them, and the other rank of Officers more than double, by which means, when British Subalterns are mixed with those of other nations on detachments, they are on foot while every Subaltern of the foreigners is mounted; and what makes it still more remarkable, when an orderly Subaltern of Infantry is demanded by a foreign General, who commands either a party or corps de reserve as customary, if the said body or party marches, our Subalterns are obliged to steal off or trot before him on foot; this happened still in a more disagreeable light in Germany, when a Subaltern of Infantry of each nation attended the different Provosts, in order to see that a foreign Provost should not do injustice or accuse falsely any man of their respective nations, our Subalterns were the only Officers on foot on such occasions, for which reason Lord Dunmore procured an order, that a Subaltern of cavalry should do that duty for the British, and this continued to the end of the war.

Allowance to a Battalion of Infantry of ten Companies for Bat-horses, under H. R. H. the Duke.

To 10 Captains at 7*l.* 10*s.* each - - -	£.75	00
Twenty Subalterns at 3*l.* 15*s* each - -	75	00
Adjutant and Quarter-master at 3*l.* 15*s* each -	7	10
Surgeon to carry the medicine chest - -	10	00
Chaplain and Surgeon's Mate at 3*l.* 15*s.* each -	7	10

Total paid a Battalion of foot each campaign £.175 00

Paid to 10 Companies the first campaign
for horses, pack-saddles, &c. to carry } £.100
the tents at 10*l.* per Company.

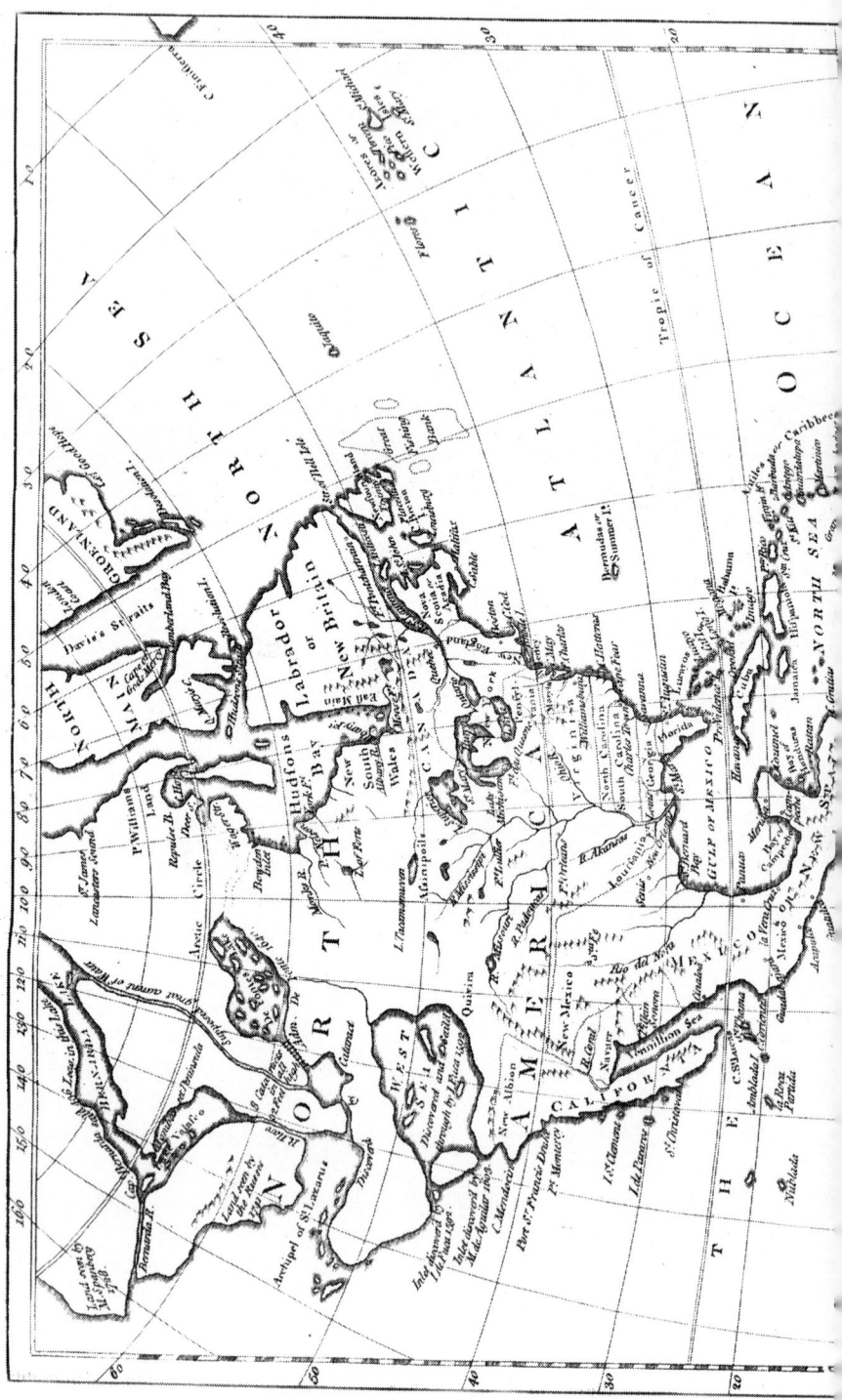

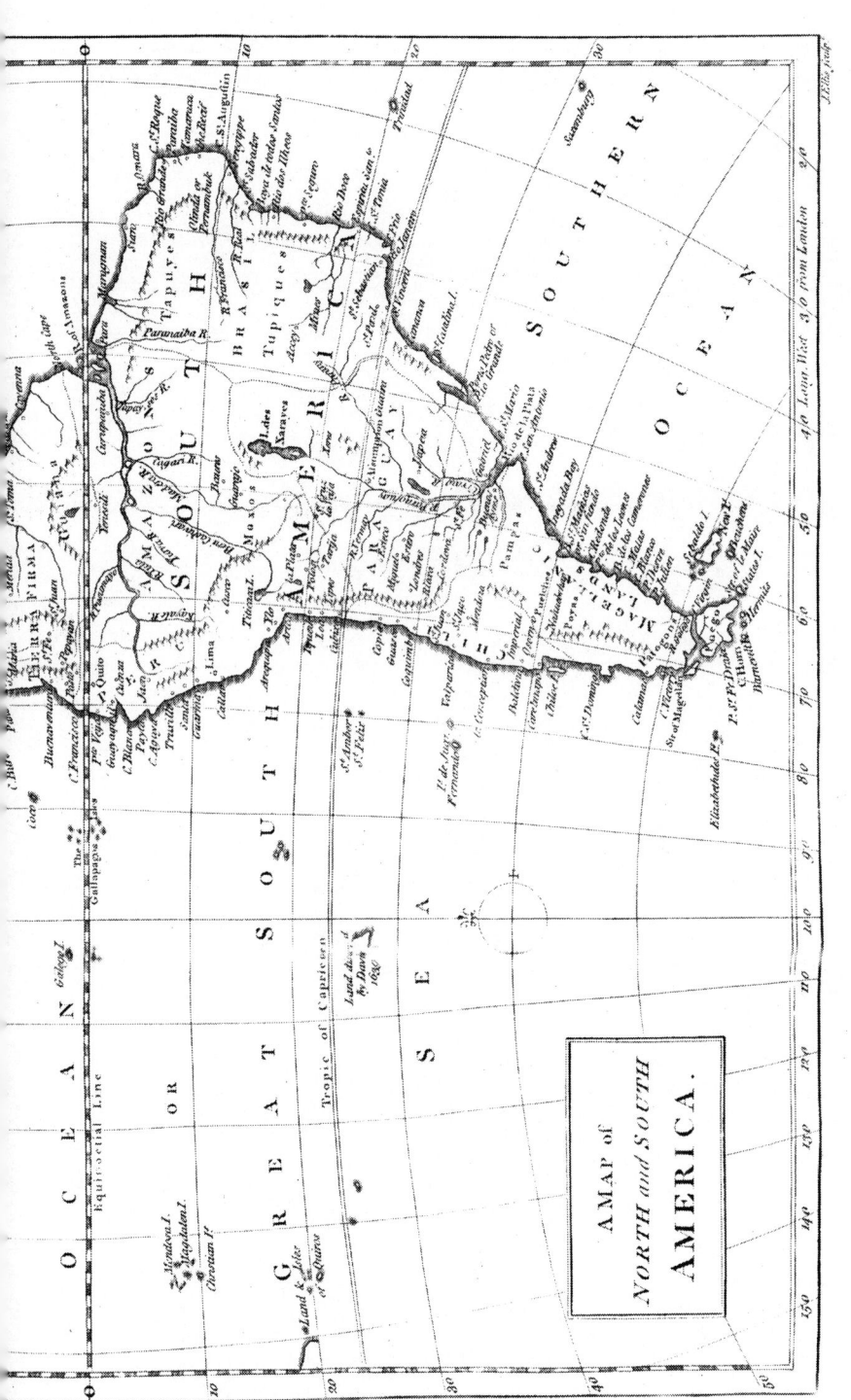

A MAP of
NORTH and SOUTH
AMERICA.

Rations of Forage allowed to each Battalion of Infantry.

Rations.

To the Colonel as such	-	6	} Total 10
To ditto as Captain	- -	2	
To carry the Company's tents	-	2	

To the Lieut. Colonel as such	-	4	} 8
To ditto as Captain	- - -	2	
To carry the Company's tents	-	2	

To the Major as such	- -	2	} 6
To ditto as Captain	- - -	2	
To carry the Company's tents	-	2	

To a Captain as such	-	2	} 4	} 28
To carry the Company's tents	2			
To 6 Capts. more ditto number each	24			

To 20 Subalterns one each - 20 - 20

To the Chaplain	- -	1	
Adjutant	- -	1	
Quarter-master	- -	1	
Surgeon	- - -	1	} 6
Medicine chest	- -	1	
Surgeon's Mate	- -	1	

Total Rations allowed per Battalion 78

30 Marine Fortification and Gunnery, with 16 large Plates, by Ardefoif, 5s.
31 Petiver's Natural Hiftory, with large Additions, 2 vols. Folio, 6l. 6s. od.
32 Coldbatch on Mifletoe, 1s.
33 Bradley's Survey of Hufbandry, 4s.
34 Bradley's Lectures, 3s.
35 Barrow's Medicinal Dictionary, 8s.
36 Sydenham's Compendium Medicinæ.
37 All Shell and other Fifh, both Salt and Frefh Water, brought to Market, with the Times of their being in Seafon, from the original Paintings of VANHAEKEN, engraved on 9 full Sheet Copper Plates, 10s. 6d.——1l. 1s. coloured.
38 Hill's Review of the Royal Society, 4to. 10s. 6d.
39 Palladio, finely engraved by Ware, 7s. 6d.
40 Langley's Gothic Architecture, 4to 15s.
41 Inigo Jones's Defigns for Cielings, Chimneys, Temples, &c. 10s. 6d.
42 Morris's Lectures on Architecture, 2 Parts, 6s.
43 Price's Carpentry, 4to. 7s. 6d.
44 Antiquities of Hereford Cathedral, 8vo.
45 Perrault's Architecture, Folio, 10s. 6d.
46 Pozzo's Perfpective, Folio, 15s.
47 Caftell's Villas of the Ancients, Folio.
48 Newton's Fluxions, 8vo.
49 Mead on Poifons, 8vo.
50 Orthopœdia, or the Art of correcting and preventing Deformities in Children, 2 vol. Cuts.
51 Dr. Sharpe's Englifh-Hebrew and Englifh-Latin Grammar.
52 Dr. Sharpe's Defence of Chriftianity, 2 Parts, 6s. Oligarchy, 1s.
53 Tandon's French Grammar to learn without a Mafter, 2s.
54 Pine's Horace, 2 vol. 2l. 2s.
55 Maafvicii Virgilius, 2 tom. 12mo. 2l. 6s.
56 Nollet's Compendium of the Bible, Fr. and Eng. 2 vol. 12mo. 6s.
57 Smith's Round Hand and Text Copies, beautifully engraved on 28 Plates, 2s. 6d.
58 Letters from a Perfian in England, 3s.
59 Prior's Pofthumous Works, 2 vol. 8vo. 12s.
60 Prior's Poems, 12mo. vol. ii. 3s.
61 Buckingham's Works, 2 vol. 8vo.
62 Vane's Letters.
63 Ozell's Telemachus, 2 vol. 8vo. 10s.
64 Atkins's Tracts, 8vo. 5s.
65 Malcolm's Tracts, 8vo. 5s.
66 Howell's Letters, 8vo. 5s.
67 Haywood's Love Letters, 4s.
68 Haywood's Cleomelia, 1s. 6d.
69 Pope's Works, vol. i. 4to. large Paper, 10s.
70 Love and Friendfhip, a Comedy, 1s. 6d.

A

Military, Historical, *and* Explanatory

DICTIONARY.

ABBATIS, a defence much used to defend a pass, entrance, &c. consists of trees hewn down, whose boughs are stripped of their leaves, and pointed. The method of planting these trees is to have their trunks buried in the ground, and the boughs fastened, by interweaving them with each other. A small ditch must be dug towards the enemy, and the earth thrown up properly against the lower part of the defence, which will add to its strength, and render it very difficult, nay, impassable, if defended by British troops.

ADVANCE-FOSS, a moat or ditch of water round the glacis or esplanade of a place of arms, to prevent surprize: being drained, serves for a trench to the besiegers, therefore is not now approved of.

AFFUT, the French name of a gun carriage. Its distinction from other carriages is, that it belongs to a gun.

AGINCOURT, about six miles north of Hesdin, remarkable only for the glorious victory obtained near it in 1415, by Henry V. of England, over a French army eight or ten times more numerous than his. According to writers, the king had not above 10,000 men, the French were near 100,000: the French historians confess that the English were not above 15 or 20,000 at most, and acknowledge that their own army was far superior in numbers. The odds were very great on the side of the French, and the English gained immortal honour by the action, of which the following is a short account.

King Henry, having landed near Harfleur, in the mouth of the Seine, about the middle of August, laid siege to that town, which was bravely defended, and did not capitulate till the latter end of September. The season being far advanced, and many of his men sick, he did not think proper to enter upon any farther action that campaign, but determined to march his army across Picardy, and take winter-quarters in the neighbourhood of Calais. In his march through Artois, he met with the French army, who having got between him and Calais, he found himself under a necessity of fighting. Accordingly the king drew up his little army on a very advantageous spot, where each wing was flanked with a wood, so that the French could not extend their front beyond that of the English; who had also planted sharp stakes before them, to defend them against the attack of the French cavalry. This precaution contributed very much to their victory; for the

squadrons

squadrons of horse, which were ordered to charge and break the English archers, falling upon the stakes, and being at the same time overwhelmed with a shower of arrows, immediately fled, broke through the lines that were drawn up in the rear, and put them into confusion. Another occasion of their defeat, as the French say, was the heavy armour of their horsemen; it being the custom of that time for the cavalry to dismount and fight on foot; and, except the first 2000 that charged the archers, all the French horse were dismounted. Now the ground, being at that time very wet and soft, the English, who had no armour on, and were much lighter, had a great advantage of the French gens d'armes, when they had discharged their arrows, and came to attack them with their clubs and axes. King Henry, observing the enemies confusion, ordered a body of horse he had in reserve to wheel about and attack them in the rear, by whom they were totally routed, several corps that were entire quitting the field without striking a blow. The loss on the side of the English was inconsiderable, and no persons of distinction killed, except the Duke of York the King's uncle, and the Earl of Suffolk; but the French had 10,000 men killed in the field of battle, of whom 8000 were gentlemen, and 14,000 prisoners. Among the slain were the Count of Nevers and the Duke of Brabant, two of the Duke of Burgundy's brothers; the Duke of Alençon, the Constable, the Count d'Albret, and 3 other French princes: among the prisoners were the Dukes of Orleans and Bourbon,

the Counts of Eau, Vendosme, and Richmont, and the Marshal de Boucicaut.

It is related of the Duke of Allençon, that seeing all was lost, he determined to die gloriously, and, with a troop of young gentlemen who attended him, broke through the English archers and the horse that were about King Henry, struck the Duke of York off his horse at one blow, and afterwards killed him; and the King stooping down to assist his uncle, the Duke of Alençon cleft the crown that was wrought on his Majesty's helmet in form of a crest; but being himself killed that very instant, the King's life was preserved, which otherwise would have been greatly endangered. After this battle his majesty continued his march to Calais without interruption.

AGNADELLA, a small place in Italy, in the duchy of Milan, in the territory of Crema, or the Cremasco, rendered famous by a memorable battle fought there August 16, 1705, between Prince Eugene and the Duke of Vendosme. The battle goes by the name of Cassano, but Agnadella was the hottest place of action. It lies upon a canal, between the river Adda and the Serio, 5 or 6 miles south east from Cassano, 10 north from Lodi, and 23 east by north from Milan. Longitude, 29. 43. latitude, 44. 58.

AIRE, a strong fortress of 8 bastions, and covered by fort St. Francis, which has 5 more. It lies upon the river Lys, 25 miles south of Dunkirk, and about 25 north-west of Arras.

ALARM, a sudden challenge to arms, upon apprehension of danger from an enemy, or of fire.

A fudden alarm is oft occafioned by the neglect of fentries; and fometimes it has been done to try the readinefs of the troops.

ALARM-POST, the place appointed for the affembling a regiment, troop, or company.

ALGIERS, the capital of a kingdom of the fame name, and a good fea-port, near the mouth of the river Saffran on the Mediterranean, oppofite to the ifland of Majorca, in lat. 36. 49. north; long. 3. 27. eaft. It ftands on the fide of a hill, which rifes gradually from the fhore, 300 miles weft of Tunis. It is defended by a pier or mole 500 paces long, reaching from the continent to a fmall ifland, where ftand a caftle and batteries of large guns, which however have not been able to defend the place from bombardments by Chriftian powers, whofe fubjects they have plundered and carried into flavery; the people fubfifting by the prizes made of fuch fhips as belong to Chriftians with whom they are at war.

ALICANT, a town of Spain, in the kingdom of Valencia, having a good harbour on the Mediterranean, defended by feveral baftions. Its caftle ftands very high; is fituated 60 fouth of Valencia, and about the fame diftance north of Carthagena.

ALMANZA, a fmall town in New Caftile, about 60 fouth-weft of Valencia, fubject to Spain, and remarkable for a battle fought there between the Duke of Berwick and the Earl of Galway, in April 1707, wherein the Allies were defeated.

ALMEIDA, a regular fortified town of Portugal, in the province of Beira, with a caftle on the river Coa. Lat. 40. 38. north; long. 6. 14. weft.

ALTENBURG OWAR, a pretty town of Hungary, in the county of Weifelburg, with a ftrong caftle, ftands on a fmall arm of the Danube, and on the Leitha; alfo furrounded with a deep and broad moat filled with water. It ftands 12 miles fouth of Prefburg, in lat. 48. 15. north; long. 17. 20. eaft.

AMBRAS, or *Amras*, a ftrong fort in the capital of Tyrol, fubject to the Emperor, ftands a mile fouth-eaft from Infpruck, in long. 31. 50; lat. 47. 11.

AMBUSCADE, or *ambufh*, is a lurking party in a wood, or other convenient place, to furprize an enemy.

AMERSFORT, a fmall town of the Low Countries, where fome feditious perfons mutinied againft the garrifon in 1703, but were foon after fuppreffed. It ftands 14 miles almoft eaft of Utrecht.

AMMUNITION, under this title is comprifed, not only cannon, mortars, cohorns, and all that is neceffary for them and the fervice, as bullets, cartridges, old iron, bombs, carcaffes, grenades, great and fmall; but all forts of offenfive and defenfive weapons; as wall-pieces, firelocks, bayonets, fwords, fine and coarfe powder, petards, quickmatch, and every thing that may add to the deftruction of the enemy, or your own prefervation.

Ammunition Bread, is carried with an army; each loaf generally weighs 6 pounds.

Ammunition Cart, a two-wheel carriage with fhafts; the fides of which, as well as the fore and hind parts, are inclofed with boards inftead of wicker-work.

Ammunition Waggon, a four-wheel carriage with shafts, the sides of it are railed in with raves and staves, and lined with wickerwork, serves to carry bread, and all sorts of tools.

AMIENS, a city of France, stands on the river Somme, is defended by a good citadel, lies in the road between Calais and Paris, 65 miles f. of the former, and 80 n. of the latter.

ANCLAM, a very strong city of Germany, stands on the river Pene, 24 miles almost f. of Gripswald, and 40 n. w. of Stetin, in long. 34. 28; and lat. 53. 58.

ANCONA, the capital of the marquisate of that name, situated on the sea, and between 2 mountains, on one of which stands the citadel, on the other the cathedral. It is a considerable place, but not so populous and large as the commodiousness of its situation and goodness of its harbour indicate. The latter was considerably enlarged by the Emperor Trajan, to whom for that reason, a triumphal arch of beautiful marble was erected on the mole, then built for its defence: the end of the mole is still fortified, and mounts between 8 and 12 cannon. The trade of this place is inconsiderable, and chiefly carried on by the Jews, the number of whom is said to be about 5000; these live together in a particular quarter of the city, where they have a synagogue. The Bishop of Ancona is immediately subject to the Pope. It lies 15 n. of Loretto, and 120 east of Rome, lat. 43. 20. n. and long. 15 east.

ANGERBURG, a well-built town in Prussia, surrounded with pallisades, has a strong castle,

built in 1335, on a lake of the name, from which rises the river Angerap. Lat. 54. 5. n. long. 23. 10. east.

ANGLE, is explained in the following definition.

1st, *Angle of the centre*, is that made by 3 lines, drawn from the centre of the extremes of any side of the polygon.

2d, *Angle of the polygon*, the angle made by the meeting of two sides of the polygon, and is the same with the angle of the gorge.

3d, *Angle of the curtain*, or of the flank, is the angle formed by the meeting of a flank and a curtain

4th, *Angle of the shoulder*; 2 is formed by 1 face and 1 flank.

5th. *Flank Angle*, the meeting of 2 faces.

6th, *Angle of the tenail*, or flanking angle, is composed of the lines of defence and the curtain.

7th, *Angle, forming the flank*, an angle composed of 1 flank and 1 demi gorge.

8th, *Angle, forming the face*, the inward angle, composed of 1 flank and 1 face.

9th, *Angle of the moat*, that which is formed before the centre of the curtain, by the exterior line of the foss or moat.

10th, *Angle-saillant*, or sally-angle, or what advances with its points towards the country; such is the angle of the counterscarp before the point of a bastion.

11th, *Angle-rentrant*, or re-entering angle, is what points inwards to the body of the place; such is the angle of the counterscarp before the centre of the curtain.

ANTESTATURE, a traverse or retrenchment, hastily made of gabions

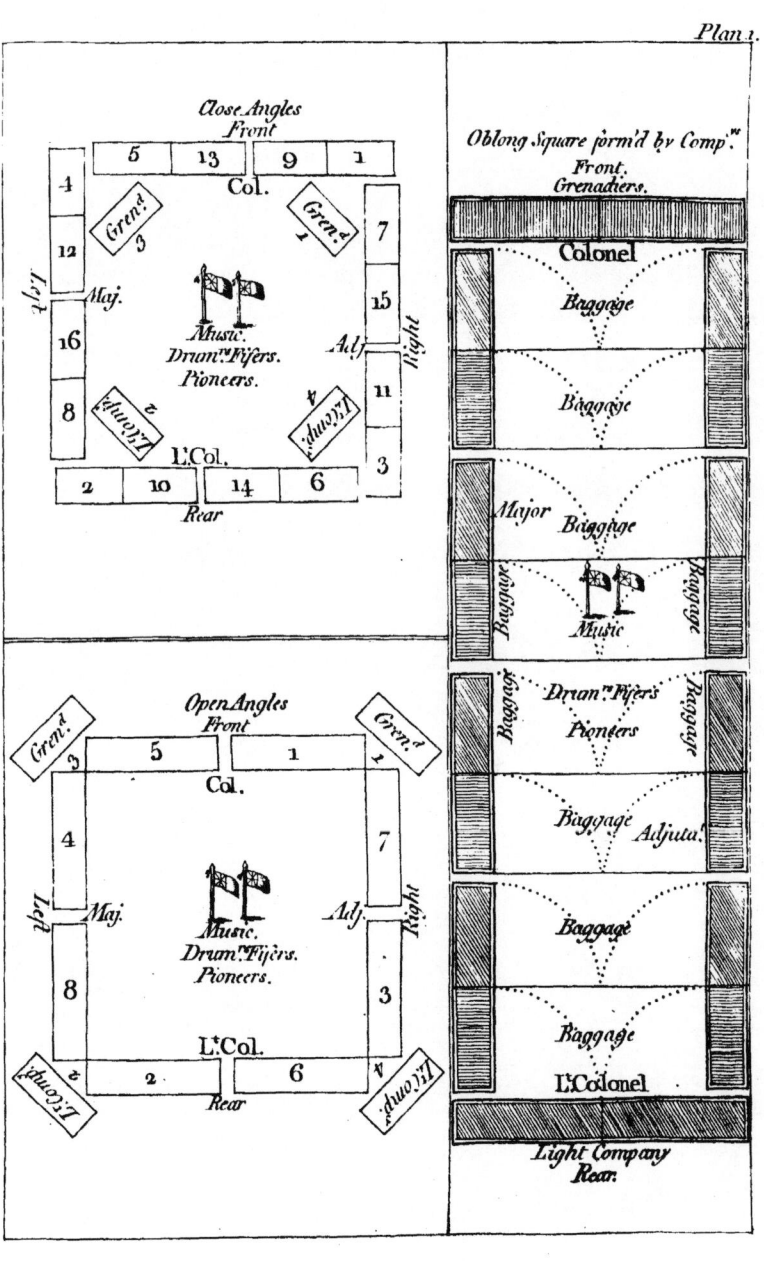

gabions or palifades, to ftop an enemy that is gaining ground. This is, to difpute ground, or lofe it inch by inch.

ANTWERP, fituated on the eaft fide of the river Scheld, about 25 miles north-eaft of Ghent, and as many n. from Bruffels. This city is built in the form of a crefcent, about 7 miles in circumference, and furrounded with a fine wall of a vaft thicknefs. It is delightful walking round the ramparts, which are planted with trees, from whence, at every turning, we have a fucceffion of agreeable objects. The citadel, built by the Duke of Alva, to keep the city in awe, is one of the ftrongeft and moft regular in the world, being a pentagon of 5 royal baftions, with only 1 gate to go in and out, and furrounded with double ditches. It ftands by the Scheld, on the fouth fide of the city, which it commands, as well as the river and the neighbouring country. Its circumference is about 2500 paces, having large repofitories for ammunition and provifions, and conveniencies for quartering 3 or 4000 foldiers. In the centre of this citadel the Duke of Alva caufed that famous ftatue to be erected, which reprefented him trampling upon the conquered ftates of the Netherlands, with a Latin infcription to this effect: To the honour of Ferdinand Alvarez de Toledo, Duke of Alva, and Governor of the Low Countries, for having appeafed fedition, extirpated rebellion, re-eftablifhed religion, and fecured the peace of thefe provinces. This gave great uneafinefs to the inhabitants of Antwerp, which increafed to fuch a degree, that the populace affembling on a holiday, forced their way into the citadel by furprize, and broke the ftatue to pieces.

APPROACHES, are the trenches, places of arms, lodgements, fap, gallery, and all works, whereby the befiegers advance towards a place befieged. This is the moft difficult part of a fiege, and where moft lives are loft. The ground is difputed inch by inch, and neither gained or maintained without the lofs of men: it is of the utmoft importance to make your approaches with great caution, and to fecure them as much as poffible, that you may not throw away the lives of your foldiers. The befieged neglect nothing to hinder the approaches; the befiegers do every thing to carry them on; and on this depends the taking or defence of the place.

The trenches being carried to their glacis, you attack and make yourfelf mafter of their covered way, make a lodgement on the counterfcarp, and a breach by the fap or by mines with feveral chambers, which blow up their intrenchments and fougades, or fmall mines, if they have any.

You cover yourfelves with barrels, facks, fafcines, or gabions; and, if thefe are wanting, you fink a trench.

You open the counterfcarp by faps to make yourfelf mafter of it; but, before you open it, you muft mine the flanks that defend it. The beft attack of the place is the face of the baftion, when by its regularity it permits a regular approach and attacks according to art: if the place be irregular, you muft not obferve regular approaches, but proceed

ac-

according to the irregularity of it; obferving to humour the ground, which permits you to attack it in fuch a manner at one place as would be ufelefs or dangerous in another; fo that the engineer who directs the attack fhould exactly know the part he would attack, its proportions, its force, and folidity, in the moft geometrical manner.

APRON, a little fheet of lead, which covers the touch-hole of a gun.

ARDRES, a fortified town of France, in the government of Picardy and Artois, built in the middle of a morafs. Here Francis I. the French King, and Henry VIII. King of England, had an interview in 1520. It lies 10 miles f. of Calais, in lat. 50. 45. n. long. 2. 2. eaft.

ARMS, a place of arms in a garrifon, at a fiege, are fmall redoubts bordered with a parapet, containing a fmall body of men, to make good the trenches againft the fallies of the befieged.

ARMY, a body of troops, confifting of horfe, foot, and dragoons, with artillery, provifion, baggage, &c. and fhould be divided into brigades, commanded by an able experienced officer.

Flying-army, a fmall body fent out to harrafs the enemy, intercept convoys, prevent the enemy's incurfions, cover its own army, or garrifon, and keep the enemy in continual motion.

Wings of an Army, the troops encamped on the flanks; they are chiefly horfe and dragoons, and are called the right wing and left.

ARONA, a town and caftle of confiderable ftrength in the territory of Anghiera, in the duchy of Milan, fubject to the King of

Spain; refcued from the hands of the ufurper, by the Imperialifts, in October 1706. It ftands a mile on the weft fide of a large lake, a mile and a half f. from Anghiera, 18 n. from Vercelle, in Piedmont, and 38 weft by north from Milan. Long. 28. 27. lat. 45. 12.

ARRAS, one of the moft ancient cities of the Low-Countries, being the Roman Atrebatum, a large populous town on the river Scarpe, upon a hill: it is divided into 2 parts, 1 of which is called the town, and is the largeft; the other, the city: they are both well fortified, furrounded with a ftrong wall, with high ramparts, 2 large ditches, and a citadel, repaired by the celebrated Vauban.

ARTILLERY, a magazine of all forts of arms and provifions for an army: fuch as cannon, mortars, bombs, balls, petards, grenades, fmall balls, powder, match, hand tools, planks, boards, ropes, coals, tallow, pitch, rofin, fulphur, faltpetre, quick match, all kinds of fireworks, pontoons, &c. The attendants are conductors, bombardiers, gunners, matroffes, pioneers, pontoon men, carpenters, wheel-wrights, fmiths, coopers, tin-men, collar-makers, &c.

Artillery-regiment, compofed of four battalions (and a Captain of Cadets, of which the Mafter-general is always Captain) each of them commanded by a Colonel, Lieutenant-colonel, and Major; the Mafter general of the Ordnance is Commander in chief; the Lieutenant-general, Commander en fecond; and the four Colonels are called Colonel-commandants each of his battalion; each company contains
commiffioned

commiffioned-officers, matroffes, gunners, and bombardiers.

Artillery-equipage, a quantity of guns, mortars, fhot, and fhells, with all neceffary ftores made for a campaign, or an expedition by land or fea.

Artillery-park, a place appointed in the rear of both lines of the army for encamping the artillery. The guns are in one line; the ammunition-waggons make two or three lines; the pontoon and tumbrils make the laft lines; and all is furrounded with a rope, which forms the park; the gunners and matroffes encamp on the flanks; bombardiers, pontoon-men, and artificers, in the rear.

ATTACK, the manner and difpofition made by an army, or a great party, to drive an enemy out of a fortified place, or any ftrong fituation.

Attacks. There are commonly two (each commanded by an experienced officer) and they have communication one with another, by lines or trenches, running parallel to the polygon of the place, that they may not be enfiladed, and are called *the parallel, the boyau, or the lines of communication.*

Falfe-attacks, are never carried on with fuch alacrity as the real; their defign being to favour the real by amufing the enemy, and obliging the garrifon to a greater duty.

BABUS, a ftrong town and caftle of Norway, taken by the Swedes in 1660. It ftands on the right of Trolet, 12 miles n. of Gottenburgh, and 120 miles n. of Copenhagen. Lon. 31, 40, lat. 58, 14.

BACULE, a gate like a pit-fall,

with a counterpoife before the corps-de guard, advanced near the gates, which is fupported by two great ftakes.

BALL, bullet, or fhot, is of iron or lead, to be fired out of piftol, firelock, carabine, or cannon, of different fizes.

Red-hot balls, are heated in a forge, ftanding near a gun. The gun being loaded with powder, and wadded with a green turf, is fpunged with a wet fpunge, and laid at a fmall elevation, that the ball, which is taken out of the forge with a long ladle, may flide down, and be inftantly difcharged by the gunner.

Fire-balls are made of a compofition of meal-powder, fulphur, falt-petre, pitch, and other combuftibles, for firing houfes.

BANDELIERS, fmall cafes of wood, covered with leather, holding cartridges of powder for the firelock.

BANQUETTE, a kind of ftep made in the rampart of a work near the parapet, for the troops to ftand upon, to fire over the parapet; it is generally 3 feet high, as many broad, and about $4\frac{1}{2}$ lower than the parapet.

BARBET: when the parapet of a work is but 3 feet high, or the breaft-work of a battery is only of fuch height, that the guns may fire over it without being obliged to make embrafures, it is faid *the guns fire en Barbet.*

BARCELONA, a ftrong and fpacious city, one of the chief of Spain. It was furrendered to the French in 1697, after a fmart fiege of 65 days, but reftored the fame year by the treaty of Ryfwick. King Charles III. and the Lord Peterborough took it in September 1703, after a fiege of 3 weeks, with a body of men

[a 4]   not

not more numerous than the garrison by which it was defended. In April, 1706, it was invested by the Duke of Anjou, with a large train and numerous army. The presence of the King greatly animated the city, and on the appearance of Sir John Leake, with a seasonable reinforcement, the siege was raised. It was taken, after a long siege by the French and Spaniards, and in 1713, by M. de Berwick.

BARREAUX, a town and strong fortress of Dauphiny, in France, on the river Isere, near the entrance of the valley of Graisivaudan, having Montmelion on the n. and Grenoble on the s. Lat. 45, 5. n. long. 5, 30. east.

BARRIER, a gate made of wooden bars 5 feet long, perpendicular to the horizon, which is kept together by 2 long bars going across, and another crossing diagonally: they are used to stop the cut that is made through the esplanade before the gate of a town.

BASE, or basis, the foundation of a work. The basis of a rampart joins to the ground on which it stands; and the basis of a parapet is that part of it which joins the top of a rampart.

Base of a gun, the same with the breech of a gun, and is that solid piece of metal behind the chase, towards the cascable: the great ring behind the touch-hole or vent, is called the base-ring; and the mouldings behind are, the base or breech-mouldings.

BASKETS. Small baskets are used in sieges, on the parapet of the trench, being filled with earth; they are about 1½ foot high, 1½ foot diameter at top, and 8 or ten inches at bottom; so that, when set together, there is a sort of embraiures to fire through, left at their bottom.

BASTIA, a city and strong castle, the metropolis of the Isle of Corsica, stands on the n. part of the isle by the sea, where there is a good harbour, 64 miles almost s. of Leghorn, and 134 s. east of Genoa, is remarkable for the defence it made under General Paoli, against the French General Marbœuf. Long. 30, 28. lat. 41. 56.

BASTION, a part of the inner inclosure of a fortification, making an angle towards the field, and consists of 2 faces, 2 flanks, and an opening towards the centre of the place called the gorge.

A bastion, is said to be full when the level ground within is even with the rampart; that is, when the inside is quite level, the parapet being only more elevated than the rest.

A bastion, is said to be empty, when the level ground within is much lower than the rampart, or that part next to the parapet, where the troops are placed to defend the bastion.

Bastion-detached, is that which separates or cuts off from the bastion of the place, and differs from a half-moon, whose rampart and parapet are lower, and not so thick as those of the place, because it has the same proportion with the works of the place.

Bastion-double, is a bastion, and sometimes in the nature of a cavalier.

Bastion-demi, composed of only one face, one flank, and one demi-gorge.

BATAVIA,

BATAVIA, in 6 degrees f. lat. on the n. of the Ifle of Java, is both beautiful and extenfive, almoft 2 miles in diameter, furrounded with ftrong walls and large foffes; has 5 gates defended by 6 forts and a caftle; the river Jacatra, which runs through the town, has 56 bridges, and opens into a fpacious harbour.

BATTALION, a body of foot compofed of feveral companies, armed with firelock and bayonet. In the late war, no particular number of companies was afcertained to compofe a battalion; but fince the laft reduction, 10 companies compofe a battalion; 8 companies, 1 grenadiers, and 1 light company.

Battalion difciplined, a term expreffive of a battalion when expert at their arms, firings, and manœuvres; which marches, wheels, and forms well, filent, fteady, and are folid under arms.

Angles of a battalion, are fuch as are made by the laft men, at the ends of the ranks and files.

BATTERY, a work made to place guns or mortars on. It confifts of an epaulment or breaftwork, about 8 feet high, and 18 or 20 thick. When it is made for guns, openings or embrafures are made in it, for the guns to fire through. The mafs of earth betwixt embrafures is called the *Merlin*; the platform of a battery is called a *floor of planks,* and hath fleepers to keep the wheels of the guns from finking in the earth,

Crofs-batteries, are fuch whofe fhot meet at the fame place and form an angle. The advantage of fuch batteries is, that the one beats down what the other fhakes.

Battery-de-enfilade, is what batters obliquely; *battery-de-reverfe*

is what plays upon the enemies back; *comrade-batteries* are thofe which play upon the fame place. To *raife a battery* is the bufinefs of an engineer; to *ruin a battery* is to blow it up, or nail the guns.

BATTLES, are of two kinds; *general* and *particular*; *general* where the whole army is engaged; *particular* where only a part is in action; but as they only differ in numbers, the methods are nearly alike. The caufe of general battles is either the hopes of victory, the neceffity you are under to relieve a place befieged, a want of provifions, an ardour and courage in troops that cannot be eafily reftrained, a confiderable reinforcement which the enemy may foon receive, and which may make them fuperior, or, laftly, fome happy conjuncture which the enemies motion may give you; fuch as the paffing of a river, or their forces being weakened or feparated.

The occafions which oblige you to avoid a battle, are, when there is little to be got, and much to be loft by it; when you are weaker than the enemy, or they are too ftrongly pofted; when your troops are divided, or any mifunderftanding prevails among the officers of high rank; when you perceive fear or confternation among the foldiers, or fufpect their fidelity; or when you can deftroy the enemy by delays.

You oblige the enemy to come to battle by laying fiege to fome important place; by attacking them on their march; by falling fuddenly upon them; by clofing them between two armies; by drawing them into an ambufcade; by making a feint as if you would retreat; by cutting off their provifions; by driving
into

into your ſtrong places all the cattle, forage, and grain of the country; by burning and laying waſte all the country they drew their forage, &c from, and taking poſſeſſion of all ſtrong poſts and paſſes near them.

The moſt remarkable on Engliſh record are the

Battle of Aſhdown, between Canute and Edmund, 1016.

—— of Haſtings, where King Harold was ſlain, Oct. 14, 1066.

—— of Bovines, July 25, 1214.

—— of Lincoln, May 19, 1217.

—— of Lewes, May 14, 1264.

—— of Eveſham, Aug. 4, 1265.

—— of Bannockburn, June 25, 1314.

—— of Haldon-hill near Berwick, where 30,000 of the Scotch were ſlain, and only 15 Engliſh, July 19, 1333.

—— of Creſſy, Aug. 26, 1346.

—— of Durham, when David, King of Scots, was taken priſoner, Oct. 17, 1346.

—— of Poictiers, Sept. 19, 1356, when the King of France and his ſon were taken.

—— of Otterburn, between Hotſpur and the Earl of Douglas, July 31, 1388.

—— of Shrewſbury, July 12, 1403.

—— of Agincourt, Oct. 25, 1415.

—— of Beaugè, where the Duke of Clarence was killed, April 3, 1421.

—— of Crevant, June, 1423.

—— of Verneuil, Aug. 27, 1424.

—— of Herrings, Feb, 12, 1429.

—— of St. Alban's, May 22, 1455.

—— of Bloreheath, Sept. 23, 1459.

—— of Northampton, July 10, 1460.

—— of Wakefield, Dec. 24, 1460.

Battle of Touton, Mar. 29, 1461.

—— of Hexham, May 15, 1464.

—— of Banbury, July 26, 1469.

—— of Stamford, March, 1470.

—— of Barnet, April 14, 1471.

—— of Tewkſbury, May 4, dit.

—— of Boſworth, Aug. 22. 1485.

—— of Stoke, June 6, 1487.

—— of Blackheath, June 22, 1497.

—— of Floudon, Sept. 9, 1513, when James IV. king of Scots, was killed.

—— of Solway, Nov. 24, 1542.

—— of Pinkey, Sept. 10, 1547.

—— of St. Quintin, Aug. 10, 1557.

—— of Edgehill, Oct 23, 1642.

—— of Shatton, May 16, 1643.

—— of Lanſdown, July 5, ditto.

—— of Round-away-down, July 13 ditto

—— of Newbury, Sept 20, ditto.

—— of Marſton-moor, July 2, 1644.

—— of Newbury, Oct. 27, ditto.

—— of Naſeby, June 1645.

—— of Dunbar, Sept. 3, 1650.

—— of Worceſter, Sept. 3, 1651.

—— of Bothwell-bridge, June 22, 1679.

—— of the Boyne, July 1, 1691.

—— of Aughrim, July 22, 1691.

—— of Steinkirk, 1692.

—— of Blenheim, Aug. 13, 1704.

—— of Ramilies, Whitſunday, 1706.

—— of Oudenard, June 30, 1708.

—— of Wynendale, Sept. 28, 1708.

—— of Malplaquet, Sept. 11, 1709.

—— of Blaregnies, Sept. 14, do.

—— of Dumblain, Nov. 12, 1715.

—— of Dettingen, June 26, 1743.

—— of Fontenoy, Ap. 30, 1744.

Battle

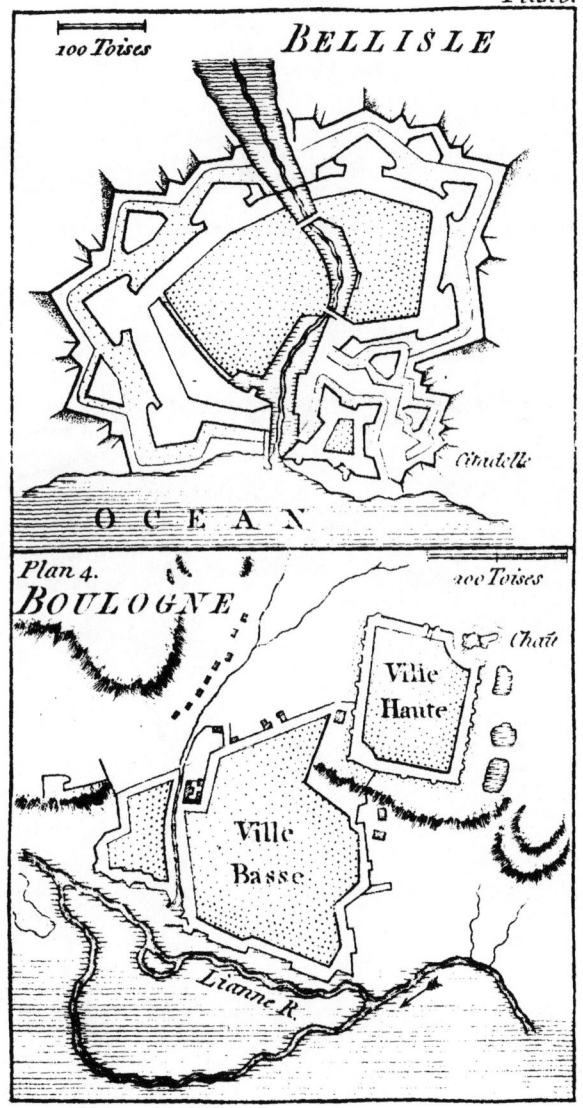

Plan 3.

100 Toises

BELLISLE

Citadelle

OCEAN

Plan 4.

BOULOGNE

100 Toises

Ville Haute

Chât

Ville Basse

Lianne R.

BAYONNE

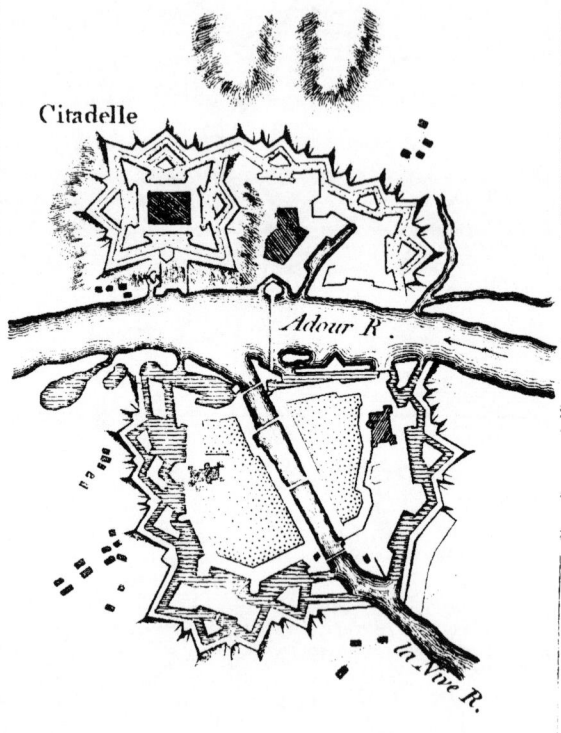

Citadelle

Adour R.

la Nive R.

100 Toises

Battle of Prefton-pans, Sept. 21, 1745.

—— of Falkirk, Jan. 17, 1746.

—— of Culloden, Ap. 16, 1746.

—— of Val or Laffeld, July 20, 1747.

—— of Rofbach, Nov. 5, 1757.

—— of Minden, Aug. 1, 1759.

—— on the plains of Abraham, Sept. 13, 1759.

—— near Quebec, April 28, 1760.

—— of Graebenftein, June 4, 1762.

BAYONNE, a ftrong city in France, 32 miles weft of Dax, 96 f. weft of Bourdeaux, 100 weft of Aux, and 370 f. weft of Paris. Long. 16. 18. lat. 43. 32. See plan 2.

BED, or *ftool, of a mortar,* a folid piece of oak, in form of a parallelopiped, bigger or lefs, according to the form of the mortar, hollowed a little in the middle to receive the breech and half the trunnions. On the fides of the bed the cheeks, or brackets, are fixed by 4 bolts of iron.

Bed of a Gun, a piece of a plank laid within the cheeks of the carriage, upon the middle tranfum, for the breech of the gun to reft on.

BEETLES, thick round pieces of wood, of a foot and a half long, and 8 or 10 inches diameter, having a handle of about 4 feet long : the ufe of them are for beating, or rather fetting the earth of a parapet, or about palifades, by lifting it up a foot or two, and letting it fall with its own weight. They are likewife called ftampers, and, by paviors, rammers.

BELLISLE, is a fmall ifland on the South coaft of Brittany in France, about 6 French miles from the continent; it is almoft entirely furrounded with fteep rocks, and acceffible only in 3 places, one of which is Palais, a fortified town, with a citadel. The road here is good. Lat. 47. 20. n. long. 3. 5. w. It made a gallant defence before it was taken by Lieut. General Hodgfon in 1761.

BERGEN-OP-ZOOM, fituated on an eminence, in the middle of a morafs, half a league from the eaftern branch of the Scheld, with which it has a communication by a navigable canal; and is fo ftrong by nature, as well as art, that this, if any, place may be deemed impregnable. By its advantageous fituation it not only fecures the communication between Holland and Zealand, but opens the Dutch a way into Brabant whenever they pleafe, and through which they have formerly made excurfions into the heart of that country.

Marfhal Saxe, finding that the Allies intended covering Maeftricht, fent a party of 8000 men to take poft near the mountain of St. Peter on the other fide, while Count Lowendhal advanced to Bergen-op-zoom with a large detachment, and a formidable train of artillery. He in his route poffeffed himfelf of Sanduliet on the Scheld, and blocked up fort Lillo, and on the 1ft of July 1747, appeared before Bergen-op-zoom, and on the 3d at night opened his trenches. On the 9th, 50 cannon and 24 mortars played furioufly on the town with red hot bullets and bombs, fo that the principal church, and a great part of the city, were in flames. The fiege continued very obftinate, the French making their advances with the greateft bravery,

very, and the garrison by frequent sallies often ruining their works and dislodging them, till the 5th of September, when a breach being made, the French entered and possessed themselves of the town. All that the Prince of Hesse Philipsdahl, who commanded the troops, could do, was with much difficulty to cover their retreat towards the lines of Steenbergen. General Cronstrom, the governor, was greatly censured on having that important fortress so shamefully surprized; for before he knew that the enemy were in the town, their colours were displayed in the market place. The fate of this ever before unconquerable town was the more surprizing, as the governor had an open communication with the lines of Steenbergen, from whence he had always fresh supplies, and seemed, till that time, resolute in opposing the enemy, and was in all appearance in a capacity of baffling their projects that campaign. He immediately retired with the troops in that neighbourhood to Oudenbosch, where he took the command, while Count Lowendahl detached part of his army to attack the forts of Lillo, Frederick-Henry, and Croix, which, by the 2d of October he possessed himself of, and made the garrison prisoners of war.

BERM, a little space, or path, of 6 or 8 feet broad, between the ditch and the parapet, made of turf, to prevent the earth from rolling into the ditch, and serves likewise to pass and repass from one to the other.

BETHUNE, a strong town situate on the river Biette, 8 miles n. west of Lens, and the capital

of a county of that name in the Low-Countries. It was taken from the Spaniards by the French in 1645, and confirmed to them. by the treaty of the Pyrenees M. Vauban fortified it with such works as were thought equal in regularity to Charleroy and Landau, two of his masterpieces. The Allies invested the place on the 15th of July 1710, the two different attacks being commanded by the Saxon General Schulemberg, and the Baron de Fagel, General of the Dutch infantry. M. du Puy Vauban, nephew to the engineer, was then governor of the town, which being strong by art and nature, and well garrisoned, a brave defence was expected. In effect, the siege was long, and the defence obstinate; but the attacks being vigorously carried on, and the counterscarp taken sword in hand, the governor beat a parley on the 28th of August, and desired to capitulate. On the 31st the garrison marched out with all the marks of honour, to the number of 1700 men, having lost near 2000 during the siege.

BIOVAC, a night guard performed by the whole army, when there is any danger from the enemy.

BLAREGNIES, a town of Hainault, in the Austrian Low Countries, where the Allies, under the Duke of Marlborough and Prince Eugene, obtained a victory over the French commanded by Marechals Villiars and Boufflers, 14th Sept. 1709. The French being encamped in the woods of Start and Sanfart, cut down trees and threw up a triple entrenchment, so that it cost the Confederates several thousand men before

fore they could drive them from thence. The armies on each fide confifted of 120,000 men, of which at leaft 20,000 were killed, and at laft the French made a regular retreat, though Villiars was wounded and difabled at the beginning of the engagement, called the battle of Malplaquet, Teniers, or Blaugies, from villages near the field of action. Blaregnies lies 7 miles f. of Mons. Lat. 50. 30, n. long. 3. 55. eaft.

BLENHEIM, a village of Germany, on the weft fide of the Danube, 3 miles north-eaft of Hochftet, and 25 north-weft of Augfberg. Lat. 48. 40; long. 10. 25. eaft. At this place the Duke of Marlborough obtained that great victory over the Elector of Bavaria, and the Marfhals Tallard and Marfin, 13th Aug. 1704.

Squads. Batt.

The enemy's whole } 158   85
army confifted of }

The confederates   181   66

The enemy had 90 cannon.
The Confederates 52.

French Army's difpofition.

On their right the Danube, and Blenheim village clofe on the bank of it; on their left a large thick wood, from whence runs a fmall rivulet, which empties in the Danube at Blenheim; this rivulet made the ground along their front in moft places very marfhy.

When Tallard found our general's refolution to attack them, he threw into the village of Blenheim 28 battalions, and 12 fquadrons of dragoons, commanded by the Marquis de Hautville, who had orders, that when he found our army pafs the marfhy ground to march out, and fall on

our rear; by which Tallard propofed to have us between two fires, and then he could not fail of what he propofed; he alfo ordered 2 more battalions, with 6 of thofe under Marfin, into the village of Oberclaw, which lay towards their centre; thefe were alfo to march out and join the troops from Blenheim; he alfo placed fome foot in the 2 mills that ftood on the rivulet between Blenheim and Oberclaw.

The reft of his troops he threw upon the height of the plain, near half a mile from the marfhy ground, to give our troops an opportunity to pafs over to him. This was the difpofition Tallard made of his 60 fquadrons and 40 battalions which he brought from the Rhine. But the Elector and Marfin made a quite different difpofition of their troops: they drew up clofe to the marfhy ground, and would not fuffer a man to come over to them. Thus was their whole army formed for receiving us, which confifted of 158 fquadrons, and 85 battalions, with 90 cannon and many mortars.

The Duke obferving the difpofition Tallard had made, faw immediately his defign; whereupon he ordered General Churchill, with 19 battalions, to attack the village of Blenheim; and Lieutenant General Wood, with 8 fquadrons, to fupport him in cafe of need. Here all our Britifh infantry were engaged. He alfo ordered Prince Holftein Beck, with 6 battalions, to attack the village of Oberclaw, and 2 battalions to attack the mills.

A little before one the fignal was given, at which time Brigadier Rowe, at the head of 2 Britifh

Britith brigades, led on the attack of Blenheim, but were repulſed with conſiderable loſs.
The Brigadier was killed, and
the brigades purſued by ſome
horſe that were on the flank of
the village; but upon the coming
up of the reſt of the cavalry the
horſe retreated, and the two brigades being ſoon rallied, came
again to the charge; ſo that we
drove the enemy from the ſkirts
of the village into the body of it,
which they had fortified after
the beſt manner they could in ſo
ſhort a time ; in which this great
body of troops were ſo crowded,
that they had not room to uſe
their arms. We made ſeveral attempts to force in upon them,
but could not, in which we
loſt many officers and ſoldiers,
whoſe lives might have been
ſaved, had General Churchill,
and ſome other of our warm
generals, been adviſed to halt
where we were forced to do at
laſt, which was about 100 paces
from them, where we drew up
in great order, ready to receive
them when they offered to come
out upon us ; by which they
were ſo hemmed in, that they
were of no farther uſe to their
army. They have been blamed
for not forcing through us, and
joining Tallard in the field : but
thoſe that were of that opinion
knew nothing of the matter; for,
conſidering the ſituation they
were in, it was impoſſible for
them to draw up in any order.
But ſuppoſe they could, they
muſt be put in great diſorder in
coming over the works ; ſo that
before they could put themſelves
into any order to attack us, they
would be mowed down by our
troops, which they found by experience ; for they made ſeveral

attempts to come out upon us,
but we cut them down as faſt as
they appeared.

Thus was this great body of
Tallard's army rendered incapable of doing him any ſervice
in the field, where he very much
wanted them.

The Duke having thus ſecured himſelf from any attack in the
rear, ordered Colonel Palmes,
with three Engliſh ſquadrons, to
paſs over before him ; who, not
meeting with the leaſt oppoſition,
drew up on the ſide at ſome diſtance from the marſhy ground, to
give room for our lines to form
behind him.

The Duke followed Palmes ;
the mills were attacked, but thoſe
that were in them ſet them on
fire, and made off. Both cavalry
and infantry, which the Duke
kept with him in the field, which
were not above 10 ſquadrons,
and 12 battalions, paſſed over as
well as they could, and formed
as faſt as poſſible. Tallard all
this while, as a man infatuated,
ſtood gazing, without ſuffering
either great or ſmall ſhot to be
fired at them; only when he ſaw
Palmes advanced towards him,
he ordered 5 ſquadrons to march
down and cut thoſe 3 ſquadrons
to pieces, and ſo return. The officer that commanded the French
ſquadrons ſo ſoon as he got clear
of the line, ordered the ſquadrons on his right and left to
edge outward, and then to wheel
in upon the flanks of Palmes ;
which Palmes perceiving, ordered Major Oldfield, who commanded the ſquadron on his
right, and Major Creed, who
commanded that on his left, to
wheel outwards and charge the
ſquadrons coming down upon
them ; and not doubting their
beating

beating them, ordered them, when they had done that, to wheel in upon the flanks of the others, and he at the fame time would charge them in the front; accordingly every thing fucceeded; fo that thefe 3 fquadrons drove their five back to their army. This was the firft action in the field, which took up fome time, and gave the Duke an opportunity to form his lines. And now there was a fair plain without hedge or ditch, for the cavalry on both fides to fhew their bravery, there being but few of the infantry to interpofe, and they drawn up feparately from the horfe.

Tallard feeing 5 of his fquadrons beat by 3, was confounded, yet advanced with all his cavalry to charge the Duke, at which time he expected the troops in the villages to have marched out and fallen on his rear; but the Duke having taken effectual means to prevent them, was now advancing with his fquadrons to meet him.

The gens d'armes (of which Tallard's horfe chiefly confifted) began the battle, giving a moft furious charge, and broke through part of our front line; but the fecond line coming up, made them retreat fafter than they came on; upon which our fquadrons advanced, and charged in their turn; and thus they charged each other for fome time with various fuccefs, till at length the French began to abate, and charged but faintly; fo that they gave ground as our fquadrons advanced, till they got on the height where they were firft drawn up, and where their 11 battalions had ftood while the horfe were engaged, but now ad-

vanced, and interpofed with their fire; which put a ftop to our fquadrons, till our foot and Colonel Blood's, with 9 field-pieces, laden with fmall fhct, came up, which kept them employed. This gave a refpite to the fquadrons on both fides to get into order, after the hurry and confufion that conftantly attend fuch actions. During which time Tallard fent to Blenheim for thofe troops to come out to join him; but they were neither able to help him nor themfelves; he alfo fent to Marfin; but he fent him word that he had too much work on his own hands.

The Duke, after this breathing, being freed from the fire of their foot, and finding their horfe had no great ftomach for renewing the battle, but rather feemed in a tottering condition, gave orders to all his cavalry to make a bold charge upon them; which they did with fuch refolution, that it decided the fate of the day, for they were not able to ftand this charge; and our fquadrons breaking through their very centre, put them to an entire rout: fo of their fquadrons fled towards their bridge on the Danube, between Blenheim and Hochftet; but by a crowd rufhing upon it, it broke, and our fquadrons purfuing with great fury, very few efcaped being killed or drowned. Tallard fled that way, but finding the bridge broke, he returned toward Hochftet, but was taken before he got thither; the reft of their horfe fled towards Lavingen, but were not purfued far; 13 battalions were cut to pieces, not one of them efcaping, but fuch as threw themfelves among the flain.

No general ever behaved with
more

more ferenity of temper and prefence of mind than the Duke
on this occafion; he was in all
places where his prefence was
requifite.

Now let us fee what was doing between Prince Eugene, the
Elector, and Marfin.

Thofe two generals ftood at
the very brink of the marfhy
ground; and all that Prince
Eugene could do, would not
force them to give an inch of
ground, till the Duke, having
difpatched Tallard, was drawing
fome fquadrons that way; which
the Elector and Marfin perceiving, and finding Tallard draw
out of the field, they immediately put themfelves on the retreat,
by readily forming their troops
into 3 columns, and marched off
with great expedition.

By this time the Duke was
drawing down to fall on them as
they marched off; but a body of
troops being obferved in their
rear, and their cavalry which
formed a column to cover the infantry, marching in great order,
he halted, believing thofe in the
rear to be a rear-guard they had
formed to cover their retreat; and
Prince Eugene, by this time, having got a good body of his troops
over, and juft ready to fall
on their rear, feeing the Duke's
fquadrons marching down, took
them to be fome of Tallard's
coming to join the Elector,
which occafioned him to halt, for
the reft of his troops to come
over; upon which our Generals
fent their Aids de Camps to
know how affairs ftood with
each other; in the mean time
the Elector and Marfin got over
the pafs of Nordlingen. Night
coming on, and the troops very
much fatigued, our generals

purfued no farther. The troops
in Blenheim, feeing their army
drove out of the field, furrendered at difcretion; but thofe in
Oberclaw made a fhift to get off
with Marfin.

The lofs of the enemy was
computed at 40,000 killed,
drowned, and taken, with 50
cannon, tents and baggage, befide a great booty. Our army
had near 6000 killed, and 8000
wounded: thofe under Prince
Eugene fuffered moft.

BLINDS, are properly all
things that cover the befiegers
from the enemy; fuch as wool-
packs, fafcines, chandeliers, mantelets, gabions, fand bags, and
earth bafkets.

BLOCKADE, is the blocking
up of a place, by pofting troops
at all the avenues, to keep fupplies of men or provifions from
getting into it; thereby pro-
pofing to ftarve it out, without
making any regular attacks. This
is called *forming a blockade*. To
raife a blockade, is to force the
troops that keep the place block-
aded up from their pofts. To
turn a fiege into a blockade, is
plain.

BLUNDERBUSS, is a fhort fire-
arm, with a large bore, very
wide at the mouth, carrying feveral piftol balls or flugs, proper
for the defence of a barrack,
ftair-cafe, or door. The fhorteft
fort of them are called mufque-
toons.

BODY, or main body of an
army, are the troops encamped
betwixt the two wings, and which
in general are infantry.

BOIS-LE-DUC is fituated at the
confluence of the rivers Aa and
Dommel, 20 miles eaft of Breda, and 43 north eaft of Antwerp. Both art and nature have
contri-

contributed to the ſtrength of this town: it is regularly fortified after the modern way; and ſtanding in the middle of a marſh, it can only be approached by cauſeways for a great part of the year.

BOLTS, are of ſeveral ſorts: thoſe that go betwixt the cheeks of a gun carriage to ſtrengthen the tranſums, are called the *tranſum bolts:* the large nobs of iron on the cheek of a carriage, which keep the hand-pike from ſliding, when it is poiſing up the breech of the piece, are called *the pricebolts:* the 2 ſhort bolts that, when put, one in each, and of an Engliſh mortar carriage, ſerve to traverſe her, are called *traverſebolts:* the bolts that go through the cheeks of a mortar, and by the help of coins keep her fixed at the elevation given her, are called *bracket bolts*; and the 4 bolts that faſten the brackets, or cheeks of a mortar, are called *bed-bolts.*

BOMB, is a great ſhell of caſt-iron, with a large vent to receive a fuſe. This fuſe is made of wood hollow at both ends, and filled with a compoſition of meal-powder, ſulphur, and ſaltpetre: when a bomb is filled with powder, the fuſe is drove into the vent, within an inch of the head, and pitched over to preſerve it: when the bomb is put into the mortar, the fuſe is untapped, and ſalted with meal-powder, which takes fire from the flaſh of the powder in the chamber, and burns all the while the bomb is in the air: when the compoſition is ſpent, it fires the powder in the bomb with a greater violence. Bombs are from 50 to 500 pounds weight.

BOMBARDIERS, are the men employed about mortars; they drive the fuſe, fix the ſhell, and load and fire the mortar; they work with the fire-workmen, and are the third rank of a private man in a company of artillery.

BOMBARDMENT, is when a great number of ſhells are thrown into a place, to ruin and deſtroy the buildings.

BONNET, is a ſmall work, conſiſting of 2 faces, having only 1 parapet, with 2 rows of paliſades, of about 10 or 12 feet diſtance; it is generally raiſed before the ſaliant angle of the counterſcarp, and has a communication with the covert-way, by a trench cut through the glacis, and is guarded on each ſide by paliſades.

BONIFACIO, a city on the ſouth of Corſica, founded on a rock, well fortified and ſurrounded by the ſea, with a caſtle that commands the entry of the port.

BOSTON, the capital of New England in North America, ſituated on a peninſula at the bottom of a fine bay, covered with little iſlands and rocks, and defended by a caſtle and platforms of guns, which make the approach of an enemy extremely difficult. It lies in the middle of a creſcent about the harbour.

BOUCHAIN, a fortified town of Hainault in French Flanders, 7 miles north of Cambray, divided by the Scheld into 2 parts. It was taken by the Allies in Queen Anne's wars, and afterwards retaken by the French. Lat. 50. 30. n. long. 3. 15. eaſt. It was inveſted on the ſide of the lower town by the Duke of Marlborough, 7th of Auguſt; and by the detachment made

[b]   from

from the fame army on the 9th, under the orders and command of his excellency General Baron de Fagel, on the fide of the upper town, the 11th, 12th, 13th, 14th, 15th, 16th, 17th, and 18th of the fame month, 1711; whereby the place was not only furrounded, but the fiege of it begun in fight of the army of Marfhal Villars, and of the intrenched camp, upon the height of Waurechain, commanded by Lieutenant General Abergotti. It beat the furrender on the 12th of September at 2 in the afternoon; the garrifon marched out the 14th prifoners of war, and was conducted to Tournay, and the fick and wounded fent to Cambray.

BOUILLON, a fortified city of a dukedom of the fame name in French Luxemberg, fituated on a rock near the river Semois, and has a ftrong caftle on the higheft peak, 10 miles north-eaft of Sedan. Lat. 45. 55. n. long. 5. 7. eaft.

BOULOGNE, or BOLOGNE, fometimes called BONONIA, a port-town on the Englifh channel, and the capital of the Boulognois, a territory of Picardy in France, near the mouth of the little river Liane. The entrance into the harbour is difficult, and defended by a fmall fort; fhips of war can come no farther than the road of St. Jean. Henry VIII. of England took it, but it was reftored to France in confideration 300,000 crowns. It lies 16 miles fouth-weft of Calais, and 130 north of Paris, in lat. 50. 40. long. 1. 30. See Plan 4.

BOURDEAUX, the capital of Bourdelois, Guienne, and Gafcony in France, the fee of an archbifhop, and the feat of a parliament. It lies on the Garonne, in the form of a crefcent. For the defence of the city and harbour are 3 forts; and during the reign of Lewis XIV. it was fortified in the modern tafte by the famous Vauban. Edward the Black Prince refided fome years in this city; and his fon, afterwards Richard II. King of England, was born here It is fituated 90 miles f. of Rochelle, and 260 fouth-weft of Paris. Lat. 44. 50. n. long. 40. See Plan 5.

BOYAU, or *branch of a trench*, is a line or particular trench, made parallel to the defence of the place, to avoid its being flanked or enfiladed. When 2 attacks are made upon a place, it forms a line of communication betwixt them; and the parapet of a boyau being ftill turned towards the place befieged, it ferves alfo for a line of contravallation, to hinder fallies and defend the workmen.

BREACH, an opening made in a wall or rampart, by cannon or mines, fufficiently wide for troops to enter the works and drive the befieged out of them.

You attack, at the fame time, at other places, to give a diverfion to the enemy, and leffen their refiftance at the real attack: and, if you cannot enter the place, you at leaft make a lodgement on the breach. To render the attack more difficult, the enemy fometimes plant the breach with crow-feet or *chevaux de frize*.

BREAK-GROUND, the firft opening of trenches againft a place; which is done in the night, by the advantage of fome rifing

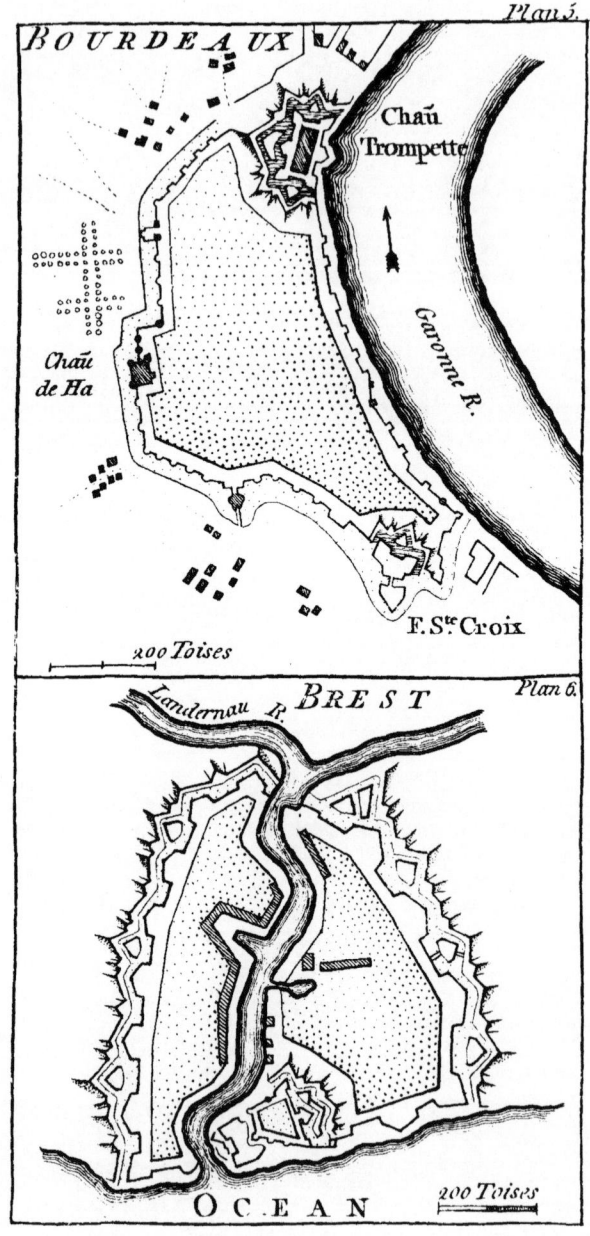

Plan 5.

BOURDEAUX

Chaũ
Trompette

Garonne R.

Chaũ
de Ha

F. Ste Croix

200 Toises

Landernau R. BREST Plan 6.

OCEAN 200 Toises

rifing ground, hollow way, or any thing that can cover the men from the enemy's fire.

BREDA, fituated in a flat country, on the banks of the river Merck, about 27 miles north-eaft of Antwerp, and as many to the f. of Rotterdam. It is a large city regularly fortified after the modern way, and one of the ftrongeft fortreffes on the Dutch frontiers, in which the ftates generally keep a numerous garrifon.

The Spaniards, having a correfpondence with fome papifts in the town, furprized it in 1581, but it was retaken by a ftratagem in 1590. It was befieged in 1624 by Spinola the Spanifh Admiral and General, with 30,000 men, who took fuch precautions, that Prince Maurice could not poffibly relieve it; fo that, after almoft a year's fiege, during which the garrifon defended themfelves with the greateft bravery and refolution, and raifed fuch fortifications as made it one of the ftrongeft cities in the world, it was forced to furrender for want of provifions, but obtained honourable conditions. It was retaken, after an obftinate defence, by Frederic Prince of Orange, in 1637.

BREST, a fmall fortified town of Lower Britanny in France, with a capacious fine road and harbour, the beft and fafeft in the whole kingdom, but of difficult entrance, by reafon of hidden rocks. It is defended by a ftrong caftle and tower. Here are naval ftores of all kinds, with a French academy: in this place the French lay up one of their largeft fquadrons of fhips of war. In 1694 the Englifh attempted to take the town, but

their defign tranfpired, and the avenues being defended by a numerous train of artillery, and a fuperior army to the invaders, General Talmafh, who commanded the Englifh, was mortally wounded in making the defcent, and the forces were obliged to retire with lofs. It lies 150 miles n. weft of Nantz, and 300 weft of Paris. Lat. 48. 25. n. long. 4. 30. weft. See Plan 6.

BRETON (CAPE) an ifland of North America, in the Atlantic Ocean, feparated from Acadia or New Scotland by the narrow ftreight of Canfo. It is about 100 miles in length, and 50 in breadth; fituated between 45 and 48 degrees n. lat. and between 61 and 62 w. long. It has feveral harbours, with an excellent fifhery on the coaft. In 1758 it was taken by the Englifh forces under General Amherft and Admiral Bofcawen.

BREVET-OFFICER, is one who, having a fuperior commiffion from his Majefty than that in his own corps, takes rank by it, when joined or doing duty with other corps, whether of horfe, foot, or dragoons.

BRIDGES, made ufe in military expeditions, are of various kinds Of late years, tin boats, called *pontons*, have been ufually carried in armies, for laying bridges over rivers upon occafion; which is done by joining thefe boats fide by fide till they reach acrofs the river, and laying planks over them for the men to march upon. A *flying bridge, pont volant*, is made of 2 fmall ones, laid one over the other in fuch manner that the uppermoft ftretches and runs out, by the help of certain cords, till the

the end of it joins the place it is
defigned to be fixed on. Both
thefe put together are not above
4 or 5 fathom long, and therefore are only of ufe to furprize
outworks, or pofts that have but
narrow moats. A *drawbridge* is
made faft only at one end, with
hinges, fo that the other may be
lifted up or let down at pleafure.
Bridges of *rufhes* are made of
great bundles of rufhes tied together, and planks faftened upon
them, to be laid over marfhes or
boggy places.

Bridge (in Gunnery) is a term
given to 2 pieces of timber,
which go between the 2 middle
tranfums of a gun-carriage, on
which refts the bed.

Bridges of communication, are
made over the river ; by which
2 armies, or 2 forts, which are
feparated by this river, have free
communication one with the
other.

Draw-bridges, are made of
feveral forms, but the moft
common are made with pliers,
twice the height of the gate,
and a foot diameter ; the inner
fquare is traverfed with a St.
Andrew's crofs, which ferves for
a counterpoife ; and the chains
which hang from the other extremities of the pliers to lift up,
or let down the bridge, are of
iron or brafs.

Floating, or *flying bridges*, are
made of 2 fmall bridges laid
one upon the other, fo that the
uppermoft, by the help of ropes
and pullies, is forced forwards,
till the end is joined to the place
defigned.

BRIGADE. An army is divided
into brigades of horfe, and brigades of foot. A brigade of
horfe is a body of 4 or 5 fquadrons : a brigade of foot con-

fifts of 4, 5, or 6 battalions :
the eldeft brigade has the right
of the firft line ; and the fecond,
the right of the fecond line ; the
2 next take the left of the 2
lines, and the youngeft hath the
centre. The battalions which
compofe a brigade obferve the
fame order.

Brigade of Infantry, confifts in
general of 4 battalions ; and
each brigade fhould take its
name from the eldeft regiment
of that brigade.

Brigade-major, an officer appointed to act to a particular
brigade. The moft ingenious
and expert captains fhould be
chofen for this poft : they are to
wait at orderly time to receive
the parole, and deliver the orders
which they carry, firft to their
proper general, and afterwards
to the adjutants of regiments,
at the head of the brigade, where
they regulate together the guards,
parties, detachments, and convoys, and appoint them the hour
and place of rendezvous, at the
head of the brigade, where the
brigade-major takes and marches
them to the place of the general
rendezvous. He fhould know
the ftate and condition of the
brigade, and keep a roll of the
Colonels, Lieutenant-colonels,
Majors, and Adjutants. When
a detachment is to be made, the
general of the day gives his
orders to the brigade-major,
how many men and officers each
brigade muft furnifh, and they
again to the adjutants of the
regiments, how many each battalion is to fend, which the
adjutants divide amongft the
companies. The complement
each regiment is to furnifh, are
taken by the adjutants, at the
head of each regiment, at the
hour

BROUAGE

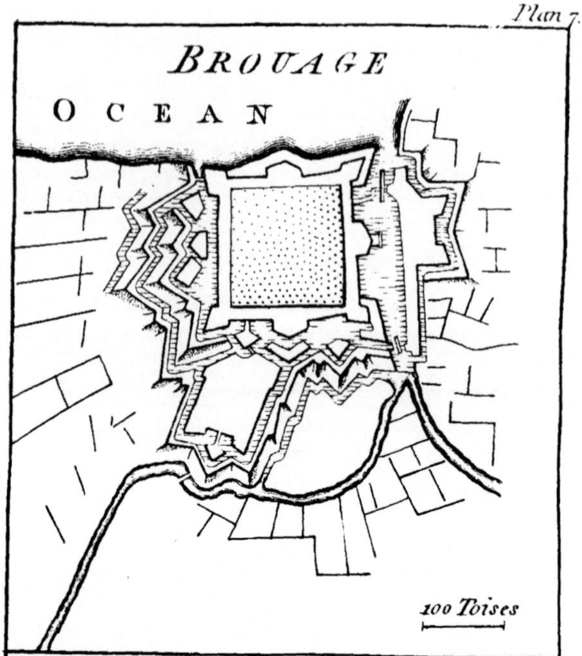

OCEAN

Plan 7.

100 Toises

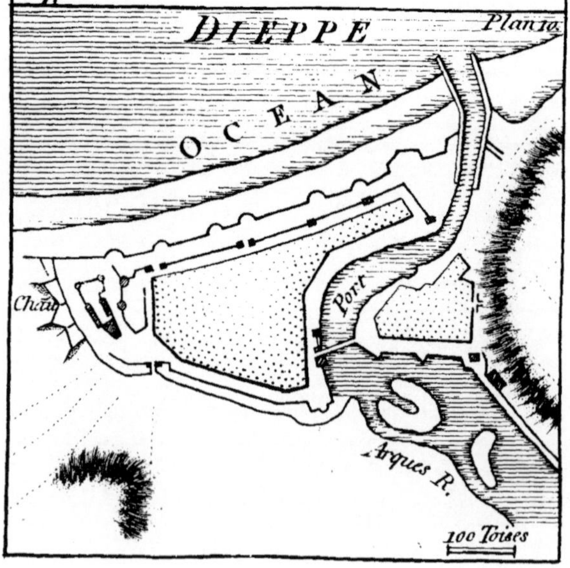

DIEPPE

Plan 10.

OCEAN

Chau

Port

Arques R.

100 Toises

hour appointed, who deliver them to the Brigade-major, at the head of the brigade.

BRIGADIER, a general officer, who has the command of a brigade. The eldeſt colonels are generally advanced to this poſt. He viſits all the out-guards and poſts of the army, and at night takes the orders from the Major-general of the day, and delivers it to the Majors of brigades, who attend at orderly time. They march at the head of their brigades, and are allowed a guard.

Brigadiers, and *Sub-brigadiers*, are poſts in the horſe-guards.

BRINGERS-UP. The whole laſt rank of a battalion, being the laſt men of each file, are called *Bringers-up*.

BRINN, a well-fortified city of Moravia, at the confluence of Schwarta and Switta, 40 miles north of Vienna, was unſuccesfully beſieged by the Swedes in 1646, and inveſted by the Saxons in 1742; but Prince Charles of Lorrain marching down at the head of his army obliged them to raiſe the ſiege, and evacuate Moravia with the utmoſt precipitation: they were greatly harraſſed in their rear by the Auſtrian huſſars. General Philibert, who was detached with 2000 Huſſars, and 1000 Croats, came up with the Saxon regiment of Hoſel, near Oſſow; which, after a bloody and obſtinate ſkirmiſh, they intirely defeated; having killed 340, and made priſoners 180, with an inconſiderable loſs.

BROUAGE, a fortified town in the territory of Brouageis, belonging to Aunis in France, 18 miles ſ. of Rochelle. Lat. 45. 58. n. long. 1. 5. weſt. See Plan 7.

BRUSSELS, a ſpacious, forti-

fied, and delightful city of the Low Countries, the metropolis of the Dukedom of Brabant, and ſeat of the Governors of the Auſtrian Netherlands. It was abandoned by the French in May, 1706, and poſſeſſed by the Duke of Marlborough; the Elector of Bavaria made ſeveral furious aſſaults on it in November 1708, but on the Duke of Marlborough's paſſing the Scheld, he was obliged to a precipitate retreat. It is ſweetly ſituated on the river Sennes, 24 miles ſouth of Antwerp, 20 ſouth eaſt of Ghent, and 190 eaſt of London.

BUDA (NEW) is a royal free town, the capital of Lower Hungary, and ſtands on a hill on the ſouth ſide of the Danube, being ſurrounded with walls and ditches, and ſtrongly fortified; near it lies a very conſiderable caſtle, the beſt in Hungary. This famous city was in the poſſeſſion of the Turks from 1629 to 1686, when the Germans, under the command of the Duke of Lorrain, after a ſiege of 10 weeks, took it by ſtorm. At this ſiege were many noble volunteers from all parts of Europe, who diſtinguiſhed themſelves by their valour, particularly the Duke of Berwick and Lord Cutts from England. It is ſituated 84 miles ſouth-eaſt of Preſburgh, and 136 of Vienna. Lat. 47. 40. n. long. 19. 20.

BUENOS-AYRES, one of the moſt conſiderable Spaniſh ports of the provin e of La Plata, on the eaſt coaſt of South America, lying on the ſouth ſhore of the river Plata, 50 leagues within its mouth, yet here it is 7 leagues in breadth. It is well fortified, and defended by a conſiderable number of guns. Hither is brought great part of the trea-

[b 3]   ſure

fure and merchandize of Peru and Chili by this and other rivers, and exported to Old Spain. Hither alfo the South Sea factors ufed to bring their negroes, when the Englifh had the benefit of the Affiento contract, and were bought up by the Spaniards, and fent to their fettlements in Peru and Chili. Lat. 36. 10. fouth ; long. 60, 5. weft.

CADET, is a young gentleman, who, to attain fome knowledge in the art of war, and who, in expectation of preferment, chufes at firft to carry arms as a private man.

CADIZ, a large city and feaport of Andalufia in Spain, on the north-weft extremity of a long neck of land in an ifland, extending from fouth-eaft to north-weft; the weft part of which is Cadiz; and the fouth-eaft the ifland of Leon, oppofite to port St. Mary's, being joined to the main land, from which it is feparated by a narrow channel of the fea, by the bridge Suaco, both extremities of which are defended by redoubts and other works. This ifland from fort St. Catalonia to the ifle St. Pedro is 5 miles long, and, from South-point near the latter, to the north near Suaco bridge, 2 miles broad. The neck of land extending from this ifland is at firft very fmall, afterwards it becomes broader, has feveral windings and angles, and terminates in 2 capes, the principal of which, namely, that to the weft, is called St. Sebaftiano. The ifland on which Cadiz ftands, and the oppofite fhore, form a bay 12 miles long, and about 6 in breadth ; but near the middle of the bay are 2 points of land,

1 on the continent, and the other on the ifland, 500 fathoms afunder, on which are the forts Puntal and Matagorda, commanding the paffage ; and within the points is a large and very good harbour, which no enemy can enter till thefe forts are taken ; for which reafon the Englifh landed in 1702 on the continent near St. Mary's, to attack the Puntal, which not being able to reduce, they were obliged to re-imbark without effecting any thing ; but the Earl of Effex landing on the ifland in 1596, took and burnt the town, having plundered it of immenfe treafure, and deftroyed the galleons in the harbour. Cadiz, which is of a pretty large circuit, is furrounded with walls and irregular baftions, and moftly inacceffible, by reafon of a fteep coaft, rocks, and fand banks. It is fituated 40 miles north-weft of Gibraltar. Lat. 36. 30. long. 6. 40. weft.

CAGLIARI, or CALARI, anciently CALARIS, the capital of the ifland of Sardinia, fituated on a large bay of the fame name, has a fecure harbour, and, befides other ftrong fortifications, a caftle. This place, with the whole ifland, was reduced by the Englifh in 1708, and given to the late Emperor Charles VI. then nominal King of Spain, and retaken by the Spaniards in 1717 ; but by a treaty 2 years afterwards it was ceded to the Duke of Savoy, with part of the Milanefe, in lieu of Sicily ; and the houfe of Savoy ftill retains this city and ifland, with the title of King of Sardinia. Cagliari is the feat of the viceroy, an univerfity, and the fee of an archbifhop. It lies 186 miles north-weft of Palermo in Sicily. Lat.

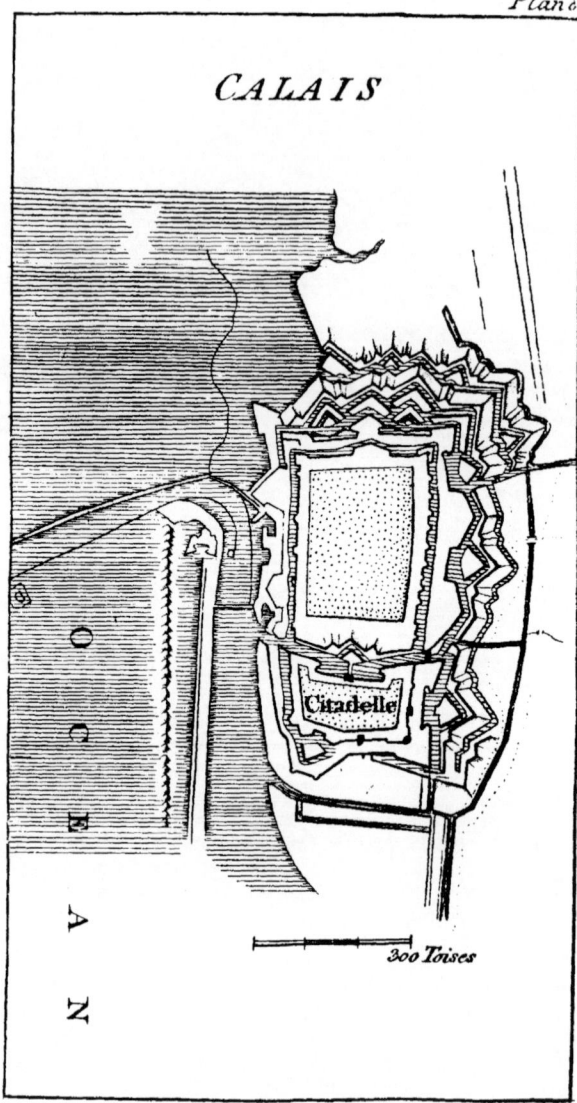

CALAIS

OCEAN

Citadelle

300 Toises

Lat. 39. 7. north; long. 9. 14. eaſt.

CAISSON, is a cheſt of wood, holding 4 or 6 bombs, ſometimes filled only with powder, and buried by the beſiegers under ground, to blow up a work which the beſiegers are like to be maſters of. After the bonnet is blown up by the mine, they lodge a caiſſon under its ruins; and the enemy being advanced to make a lodgement there, they fire the caiſſon by the help of a ſaucefs or pudding, and blow up that poſt a ſecond time.

CALAIS, the capital of the reconquered country in Picardy in France, a fortified town and harbour on the Engliſh channel. Its figure is a quadrangle, the two longer ſides being towards the ſea and land. Beſides its regular works, it has a citadel to the weſt, and the entrance into the harbour is defended by a fortreſs; but its greateſt ſtrength ariſes from its ſituation among the marſhes, as on the approach of an enemy it can be overflowed. For the conveniency of trade a canal runs from it to St. Omers, Graveline, Dunkirk, Bergues, and Ypres. Anciently the harbour was a good one, but is now ſo choaked up, that a ſhip of any burthen cannot ſafely enter it. It lies 22 miles ſouth-eaſt of Dover in England, and 143 north of Paris. Lat. 51. 2. north.; long. 2. 10. eaſt. See Plan 8.

CALIBER, is a term in gunnery, ſignifying the diameter or widenefs of a piece of ordnance.

Caliber-compaſſes, are compaſſes uſed by gunners, for taking the diameters of the ſeveral pieces of ordnance, or of bombs, bullets, &c. Their legs are therefore circular, on

an arch of braſs, whereon is marked the inches and half-inches, to ſhew how far the points of the compaſſes are opened aſunder.

CAMBRAY, a large city on the river Scheld. It ſtands about 20 miles to the eaſt of Arras, 15 ſouth weſt of Valenciennes, and 12 ſouth eaſt of Douay. It is regularly fortified, and has a very ſtrong citadel, its walls being all faced with free-ſtone; and as the neighbouring country may be laid under water, it is eſteemed one of the ſtrongeſt places in the Netherlands.

CAMP, is the ſpot of ground occupied by an army to pitch their tents.

CAMPAIGN, is that indeterminate portion of time expended by an army between taking the field, and returning to garriſon.

CAMPEACHY, ſtands open to the ſea; the houſes are not high, but the walls very ſtrong, the roofs flattiſh; when taken by the Spaniards, was a large town. There is a good dock, and a ſtrong citadel or fort, where a governor reſides with a garriſon, which commands both the town and harbour. The Engliſh, under the command of Sir Chriſtopher Mims, in 1659, ſtormed and took it with ſmall arms; and it was a ſecond time taken by the Engliſh and French Buccaniers, by ſurprize, in 1678. The port is large, but ſhallow.

CANDIA, probably the ancient Mutium, the preſent capital of an iſland of that name in the Mediterranean. It ſtands on the north ſide of an iſland near the ſea, in a plain at the foot of a mountain, and on the ſite of the ancient city of Heraclea; it is at preſent no more than the ſhadow of its former greatnefs, having been reduced by the fiege it underwent by the Turks from 1645 to 1669, when it was ftormed 56 times, and about 200,000 Turks killed under its walls. It is ftill in the poffeffion of the Turks. Lat. 35. 30. n. long. 35. 5. eaft.

CANNON. See GUN.

CANTEEN, is a tin veffel ufed by the foldiers to carry their drink or water in.

CAPITAL, *of a work*, is an imaginary line, which divides that work into 2 equal and fimilar parts.

CAPITULATION, is the agreement made by the befieged with the befiegers, on what condition the place is to furrender: the chamade being beat, all hoftilities ceafe on both fides; if the capitulation be agreed to and figned, hoftages on both fides are delivered, for the exact performance of the articles.

CAPONIER, is a paffage made from one work to another of 10 or 12 feet wide, covered on each fide by a parapet terminating in a flope or glacis: thus, when the ditch is dry, the paffage from the curtain to the ravelin, or that from the covert-way to the arrows or detached redoubts, are called *caponiers*.

They are often fingle parapets raifed on the entrance of a ditch, before the ravelin, for placing fmall cannons, and men behind them, to difpute the paffage over that ditch.

CAPTAIN *of battle-axe-guards*, generally obtains the rank of colonel: the 2 lieutenants have the rank of captains.

Captain-Lieutenant, the officer who commands the colonel's troop or company.

CARABINE, is a fire-arm,

fhorter than a firelock, hanging at the belt of a light-horfeman.

CARCASS, is an invention of an oval form, made of ribs of iron, afterwards filled with a compofition of meal-powder, faltpetre, fulphur, glafs, fhavings of horn, pitch, turpentine, tallow, and linfeed oil, and then coated over with a pitched cloth; it is primed with meal-powder and quick-match, and fired out of a mortar: the defign of it is to fet houfes on fire. Two fmall cords are fixed to the fides for lifting it into the mortar.

CARRIAGE, is a general term for waggons, carts, litters, &c.

Carriage of a cannon, is a long narrow cart, invented for marching of cannon; and for the more convenient ufing them in action, they are made of two planks of wood, commonly half as long again as the gun.

Carriage. See *Ammunition Cart*.

Block carriage, is a cart made on purpofe for carrying mortars and their beds from one place to another.

Truck-carriages, are 2 fhort planks of wood fupported on 2 axle-trees, having 4 trucks or wheels of folid wood, about a foot and a half, or 2 feet diameter, for carrying mortars or guns upon a battery, where their own carriages cannot go, and are drawn by men.

CARTEL, an agreement between princes, generals, governors, or commanding officers at war, for exchange of prifoners.

CARTAGENA-LA-NUEVA, or *New Carthagena*, fo called to diftinguifh it from *Carthagena* in *Old Spain*, lies fouth of Jamaica, on the Spanifh continent, to the eaft of the great gulf of Darien; in 10 degrees 26 miles n. lat. and

75.

75. long. weſt of London. It was begun in 1532, and about 8 years after became a wealthy, ſtately, and well inhabited city: it has one of the nobleſt baſons or harbours in the world, being ſome leagues in circumference; and is land-locked on all ſides; its entrance is defended by the ſtrong caſtle of Bocca-chica, and 3 leſſer forts. Between this harbour and the town are 2 necks of land, on which are the ſtrong fortreſs Caſtillo Grande, and fort Manzanella, which defend the leſſer harbour that runs cloſe to the town: there is likewiſe the fort St. Lazare, which defends the town on the land ſide; and though the ſea beats on the town walls, the ſurf runs ſo high, that there is no coming at it, but through theſe harbours. In 1583 it was plundered by Sir Francis Drake; who having burnt one half of it, the inhabitants ranſomed the other for 120,000 ducats. Before it was perfectly repaired, a diſguſted Spaniard again burnt it, and ſeized a great treaſure. In 1697, M. de Pointi, with a ſquadron of French ſhips, took the city after a formal ſiege, when the plunder amounted to about 8,000,000 of livres in ſilver, and one in jewels. Having recovered its trade and wealth, in ſo ſhort a time, it might well be accounted one of the principal cities in America. This place was unſucceſsfully attacked in 1741, under the commands of General Wentworth and Admiral Vernon. They injudiciouſly attempted this enterprize in a ſeaſon when the ſerena, or evening and night air, is deadly to all foreigners expoſed to it. The contagion in 6 days ſwept off above 500 men:

and out of the 10000 troops they landed, there were only 1650 fit for duty at re-imbarking.

CARTOUCH, a caſe of wood, about 3 inches thick at bottom, girt round with marlin, holding about 4000 muſquet balls, beſides 6 or 8 balls of iron, of a pound weight; it is fired out of a hobitz, a ſmall ſort of mortar, and is very proper for defending a paſs.

A new ſort is made, much better than the former, of a globular form, and filled with a ball of a pound weight; others were then made for the guns, being of ball of half or quarter pound weight, according to the nature of the gun, tied in form of a bunch of grapes, on a tompion of wood, and coated over: theſe were made in the room of the partridge-ſhot, and very much exceed them, as ſome of the French battalions experienced at the battle of Blenheim.

CARTRIDGE, is a caſe of brown paper, holding the exact charge of a fire-arm; thoſe for muſquets, carabines, or piſtols, hold both the powder and ball for the charge.

Cartridge-box, a caſe of wood or turned tin, covered with leather, holding 30 rounds of powder and ball, is wore upon a belt, and hangs a little higher than the pocket-hole.

CASCABAL, is the knob of metal behind the breech of a cannon; the diameter of it is equal to the diameter of the bore of the piece. The *neck of the caſcabal* is what joins it to the breech of the moulding.

CASEMENT, is a bomb-proof work made under the rampart, like a cellar or cave, with loopholes to place guns in.

CASKS.

CASKS, or *Barrels*, are ufed in the army, for carrying meal to be laid up in magazines, or along with the army, for bread.

CASTRAMETATION. By it we are literally to underftand the art of meafuring or tracing out the form of a camp on the ground; yet it fometimes has a more extenfive fignification, by including all the views and defigns of a general: the one requires a mathematician, the other an experienced officer.

CAVALIER, is a work raifed generally within the body of the place, 10 or 12 feet higher than its other works; their moft common fituation is within the baftion, and they are nearly made in the fame form; fometimes they are alfo placed in the gorges, or on the middle of the curtain; but then they are made in the form of an horfefhoe, and fomewhat flatter.

The ufe of Cavaliers is to command all the adjacent works and country about it; they are feldom or never made but when there is a hill or rifing ground, which overlooks fome of the works.

CAUDEBEC, a fmall but populous city in Upper Normandy in France, on the north fide of the Seine, 16 miles weft of Rouen. In 1419 it was taken by the Englifh; in 1562 by the Huguenots, and was retaken by the king's troops in 1592. Lat. 49. 32. n. long. 45 minutes eaft.

CAVIN, is a natural hollow, fit to lodge a body of troops: it is of great ufe to the befiegers; for by the help of fuch a place, they can open trenches, make places of arms, or keep guards of horfe, without great danger.

CAZERNS, or *Barracks*, are lodgings built in garrifoned towns.

CENTRE, is the middle point of a circle.

CESSATION *of arms*, is when a governor of a place befieged, finding himfelf reduced to fuch an extremity, that he muft either furrender, or facrifice himfelf, his garrifon, and inhabitants to the mercy of an enemy, plants a white flag on the breach, or beats the chamade to capitulate; at which both parties ceafe firing, and all other acts of hoftility, till the propofals be either agreed to or rejected.

CEUTA, a city of Fez in Africa, on the fouth fide of the Streights of Gibraltar, almoft oppofite to that place; it is a ftrong fortrefs, in the poffeffion of Spain, but frequently attacked by the Moors, and fituated 150 miles north of Fez. Lat. 35. 50. n. long. 6. 30. weft.

CHAGRE, is fituated on a fteep rock, at the mouth of the Rio de Chagre, 18 leagues diftant from Porto Bello, defended by the Caftillo de San Lorenzo, which commands the entrance of that river. On the weft fide of the harbour is Fuerto de la Punta. This fort is commanded by a commandant; the garrifon is detached from Panama. In 1669, Captain Morgan landed the Buccaniers a few miles to the eaft, and befieged Caftillo de San Lorenzo, which was defended with great refolution; for, after the Englifh had made a breach, defended by the governor with 25 men, feveral of the Spaniards threw themfelves from the top of the hill into the fea, choofing rather to die, than to afk quarter; the governor, though retreating, continued to defend himfelf, but at laft was killed; on on which the reft furrendered prifoners of war, being only 30 left out of 314, and moft of them wounded; all the officers being killed. The Englifh had upwards of 100 men killed, and 70 wounded. Captain Morgan having been refufed a ranfom by the governor of Porto Bello for this caftle, took all the cannon, demolifhed the walls, and burnt the buildings.

Admiral Vernon came before this place on the 20th of March 1740, and ordered Capt. Knowles clofe in with the ketches, who inceffantly bombarding the caftle for 2 days, it furrendered on the 22d to the Admiral; about 22 brafs cannon, with part of the garrifon, being embarked, on the 29th the mines were fprung, which entirely demolifhed the lower baftion, blew up fome of the upper works, and deftroyed by fire the inner buildings of the caftle of San Lorenzo.

CHAIN, a number of brafs or iron rings, linked in one another. An *engineer's chain*, for meafuring of ground, is of a certain number of links, of an equal length. *Chains of a gun* are of iron, and very ftrong, fixed on the draft-hooks, and going along the fhafts of the timber, to eafe them; but they are not ufed for fmall guns.

CHAMADE, a fignal made by beat of drum, for a conference with the enemy, when any thing is to be propofed; as a capitulation, or a ceffation of arms, to bring off the dead; or by the befieged, when they have a mind to deliver up a place upon articles of capitulation; then there is a fufpenfion of arms, and hoftages delivered on both fides.

CHAMBER, *of a mortar*, is that part of the chafe where the powder lies, and is much narrower than the reft of the cylinder; fome are like a reverfed cone, or fugar-loaf; others globical, with a neck for its communication with the cylinder, and are called *bottled chambers.* The *powder-chamber,* or *bomb-chamber,* on a battery, is a place funk under ground, for holding powder or bombs, where they may be out of danger, and preferved from the rain.

Chamber, is that place of a mine where the powder is lodged.

CHANDELIER, is a wooden frame, whereon are laid fafcines or faggots, to cover the workmen while carrying on the approaches.

CHARGED CYLINDER, is that part of the chafe of a gun where the powder and ball are contained.

CHARLEMONT, fituated on the top of a hill, under which runs the river Maefe, 25 miles f. of Namur, and 25 eaft of Charleroy. It was fortified in 1555 by the Emperor Charles V. to whom it was granted by the bifhop of Liege; but the French got poffeffion of it in 1680.

CHARLEROY, a ftrong fortified town of Namur in the Auftrian Low Countries, on the Sambre, 19 miles weft of Namur. Lat. 50. 30. n, long. 4. 20. eaft.

CHARLES-

CHARLES-FORT, in the county of Cork, and province of Munfter, ftands at the entrance of Kinfale harbour, is pretty ftrong towards the fea.

CHATEAU DAUPHINE, a fortified caftle in Piedmont in Upper Italy, ceded by France to Piedmont by the peace of U-trecht. Lat. 44. 30. n. long. 6. 40. eaft.

CHATHAM, a port-town of Kent, on the eaft of the river Medway; one of the principal ftations for the Britifh navy, and has a royal yard, well provided with timber, and all other ftores neceffary for building and fitting out the largeft fleet The mouth of the river is well defended by Sheernefs, and with other forts and caftles, yet the Dutch in 1667, through negleft, came up the river and burnt fome of the firft-rates and other fhips of war then lying there. It lies 30 miles from London. Lat. 51. 40. n. long. 3 min. eaft.

CHEEKS, *of a mortar*, or *brackets*, are made of ftrong planks of wood, of near a femi-circular form, bound with thick plates of iron, and are fixed to the bed by 4 bolts, called bed-bolts; they rife on each fide of the mortar, and ferve to keep her at what elevation is given her, by the help of ftrong bolts of iron which go thro' the cheeks, both under and behind the mortar, betwixt which are drove coins of wood. Thefe bolts are called bracket-bolts; and the bolts which are put one in each end of the bed, are the traverfe bolts; becaufe, with hand-fpikes the mortar is by thofe traverfed to the right or left.

CHERBOURG, a port-town of Normandy on the Englifh Chan-

nel, oppofite to Hampfhire, 50 miles weft of Caen. Off this place the confederate fleet under Admiral Ruffel obtained a fignal victory over the French, commanded by M. Tourville, in 1692, and afterwards burnt 20 of their fhips of war near Cape la Hogue. In 1758 the Englifh forces under General Blyth and Commodore now Lord Howe, took it from the French, deftroyed the fine bafon and works erected at a vaft expence, took 22 brafs cannon and mortars, and deftroyed 173 iron cannon, and 3 mortars. Lat. 49. 45. n. long. 1. 40. w. See Plan 9.

CHEVEAUX-DE-FRIZE, large joints or beams, ftuck full of wooden pins, armed with iron, to ftop breaches, or to fecure a paffage of a camp againft the enemy's cavalry.

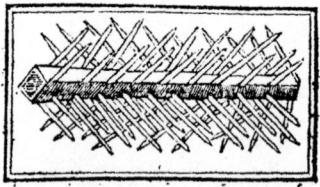

CHEVRETTE, among the many inventions for raifing of guns or mortars into their carriages, this engine is the moft ufeful; it is made of 2 pieces of wood of about 4 feet long, ftanding upright upon a third, which is fquare; they are about a foot afunder, and parallel, and pierced with holes exactly to one another, having a bolt of iron, which being put thro' thefe holes higher or lower at pleafure, ferves with a hand-fpike, which takes its poife over this bolt, to raife any thing by force.

CIRCLE, a plain figure, comprehended

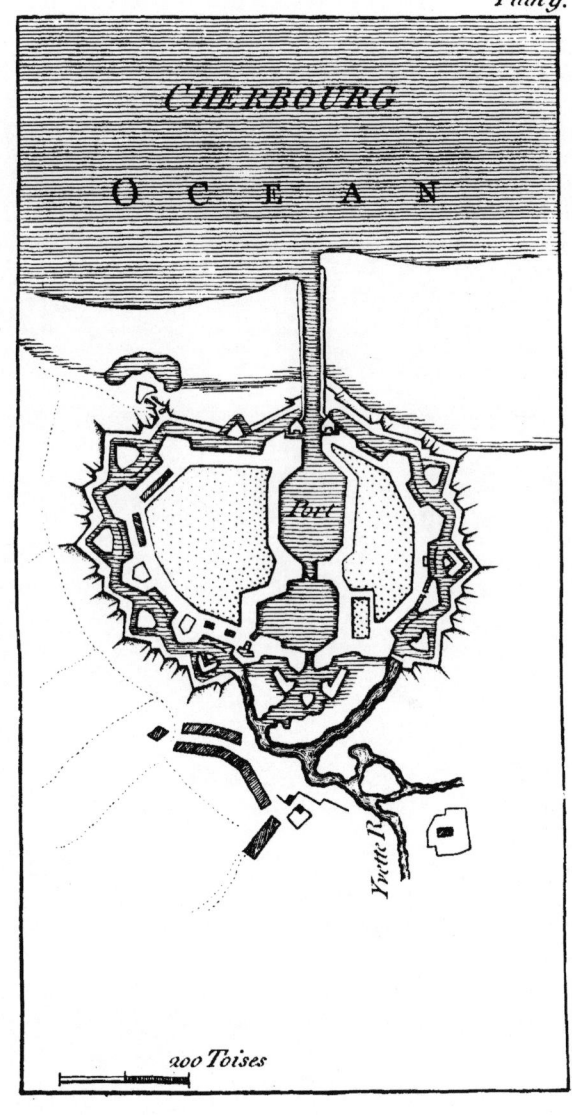

CHERBOURG

O C E A N

Port

Yvette R.

200 Toises

prehended within a crooked line, called the circumference, which has all its parts equally diſtant from a certain point, called the centre.

Arch of a Circle, an undetermined part of the circumference of a circle, being ſometimes larger, and ſometimes ſmaller.

Line of circumvallation, is a kind of fortification, conſiſting of a parapet, or breaſt-work, and a ditch before it, to cover the beſiegers againſt any attempt of the enemy in the field.

CITADEL, is a kind of a fort of 4, 5, or 6 baſtions, raiſed on the moſt advantageous ground about the city, the better to command it, by an open or eſplanade, to hinder the approach of an enemy; ſo that the citadel defends the inhabitants, and can puniſh their revolt. A citadel muſt not be too large, becauſe too ſpacious a circumference is difficult to fortify or defend, and ſhould therefore be ſo contrived, as to be eaſily defended, and ſpeedily ſuccoured, by having 2 of its baſtions within, and the reſt without. If the town be on a river, let the citadel not only command it, but likewiſe the place and country about it, without any fear of danger from the enemy's works on an eminence near it. Thus if the enemy ſhould ſeize the place, they may again be beaten out from the citadel.

CLOUTS, are thin plates of iron, nailed on that part of the axle-tree of a gun-carriage, that comes thro' the nave, and is ſecured by lins-pins.

COFFER, is a work ſunk in the bottom of a dry moat, about 6 or 7 feet wide, the length of it being from one ſide of the moat to the other, with a parapet of about 2 feet high, full of loopholes, covered overhead with joiſts, hurdles, and earth; they ſerve to fire on the beſiegers, when they endeavour to paſs the moat, and differ from the caponier, becauſe they are longer; for the caponier takes not the whole breadth of the moat; it differs likewiſe from the traverſe and the gallery, becauſe that is made by the beſieged, but this by the beſiegers.

COLOCZA, a fortified town of Hungary Proper on the Danube; it is the ſee of an archbiſhop, but has undergone ſeveral viciſſitudes from the Turks and Hungarians; it lies 50 miles ſouth-eaſt of Buda, and is ſubject to Auſtria. Lat. 46. 56. n. long. 19. 40. e.

COLUMN, *of an Army on a march*, is a long row of troops, following one another. Sometimes the army marches in 4, 10, or 8 columns, according to the convenience of the ground it occupies. All the parts ſhould be ſo ordered, that regularity may be preſerved by the officers, and no confuſion enſue, either by the form of the columns, the denſity of the body, the difficulty of communicating orders, or obſtacles to prevent the officers from having a continual eye on their men.

COMMANDING-GROUND, an eminence, or riſing-ground, overlooking a poſt.

COMMISSION, the authority granted by a prince, or his general, to officers, by which he inveſts them with commands agreeable to his pleaſure and their abilities.

COMPLEMENT, *of the curtain*, that part of it which makes the demi-gorge.

Comple-

Complement of the line of defence, the remainder of the line of defence, after the angle of the line is taken off.

COMPLIMENT, *of the line of an army, turning out,* is due to his Majesty, the Queen, or any of the Royal Family (Lord Lieutenant, if in Ireland) Captain-general, or Commander in Chief (being a general officer) of the encampment.

Compliment, from Guards, is due to his Majesty, the Queen, or any of the Royal Family, (Lord Lieutenant, if in Ireland) General Officers, &c.

COMPTROLLER *of the artillery,* is a post of great trust; he inspects the musters of the artillery, makes the pay list, takes the accompts, and the remains of stores, and is accountable to the ordnance.]

· CONDE, stands about 6 miles n. east of Valenciennes and Vail; and 10 or 12 westward of Mons, at the conflux of the rivers Schelde and Haine, in a low and marshy country. The town is small, but exceedingly well fortified, and strong by the nature of its situation. This town has oft been taken and retaken by the French and Spaniards. The last time the French took it was in 1676; and it was confirmed to them by the treaty of Nimeguen. After the victory gained over them at Ramillies, they cast up lines; which was from Mons along the Haipe to Condé, and from thence along the Scheld to Tournay.

CONDUCTORS, are assistants given to the commissary of the stores, to receive or deliver out stores to the army, to attend at the magazines by turns, when in garrison, and to look after the ammunition waggons in the field: they bring their accounts

every night to the commissary, and are immediately under his command.

CONE, a body made by turning a right angled triangle round a circle, the angular point of the right angle being fixed in the centre, which forms a pyramid, whose basis is a circle.

COINS, are wedges of wood under the breech of a gun, by which the gunner raises or falls the muzzle of his piece or mortar, till he points it exactly at the object; each gun has three coins.

CONTRAVALLATION, a trench, with a parapet, made by the besiegers, betwixt them and the place besieged, to secure them from the sallies of the garrison, so that the troops which form the siege, are encamped between the lines of circumvallation and contravallation: when the enemy has no army in the field, there is no occasion for lines of circumvallation; and when the garrison is weak, the lines of contravallation are seldom used.

CONTRIBUTION, an imposition, or tax, paid by frontier countries, to excuse them from being plundered by the enemy.

CONVOY, is a supply of men, money, ammunition, or provisions, conveyed into a town, or to an army. The body of men that guard this supply, are likewise called the convoy.

COPENHAGEN, the capital of Denmark, lies on the east shore of the island of Zealand on a fine bay of the Baltic, 5 miles from the streight called the Sound or Oresund, and not above 16 from the coast of Schoen in Sweden. It is opposite to the isle of Amack which forms the harbour. It stands in a marshy ground,

but

but is fortified in the modern manner, and has a citadel; the harbour is defended by forts and platforms, and the entrance to it so narrow as to admit only one ship. In certain places of the town are canals for large ships to come up to the very houses. It appears however that their fortifications are not a sufficient defence against a bombardment by sea, nor from the attacks of a land-army on that side; for the Baltic has been so firmly frozen over in some years, that the Swedes have brought their artillery over the ice, and besieged Copenhagen; and by its lying in a morass, it is more easily approached on that side in winter than summer. Lat. 55. 40. n. long. 12. 50. e.

CORDON, a round projection made of stone, in a semicircular form, whose diameter is about 8 inches, which ranges quite round the wall, within four feet from the upper part.

CORIDOR, a French term for covert way.

CORNET, the youngest officer of a troop, is a very honourable post; for one part of his duty is to carry the standard in the day of battle, though no greater dishonour can happen to a regiment than the loss of a standard.

CORNISH-RING, a small ring near the muzzle of the gun.

CORPORAL, an inferior officer to a serjeant, posts and relieves the sentries. While the guard is relieving, he gives the orders he received to the corporal of the new guard, and shews him all the posts. He carries a fire-lock advanced.

COVERT-WAY, is a space of ground, level with the country, about 3 or 4 fathoms wide, co-vered by a parapet, which goes quite round the place. The greatest effort in sieges is to make a lodgment on the covert-way, which the besiegers generally palisade and undermine: this parapet slopes insensibly towards the campaign; and the talus, or sloping, is called the glacis, which the besiegers are generally obliged to sap through to make a lodgement. The parapet of the covert-way is about 6 feet high, with a banquette, and forms a saliant angle before the curtain, which serves for a place of arms.

COUNCIL of War, is when a commander in chief of an army, or governor of a garrison, assembles the principal officers for their advice, upon some affairs of importance.

COUNTER-APPROACHES, are works made by the besiegers, when they come out, to hinder the approach of the enemy, when they design to attack them in form.

COUNTER-BATTERIES, such as are erected against each of the adverse batteries: and they should always be superior to those of the enemy. Cavaliers and platforms are sometimes erected to strengthen them.

COUNTER-GUARD, is a work placed before the bastions, to cover the opposite flanks from being seen from the covert-way; they are likewise made before the ravelins. When they are placed before the bastions, they are esteemed a very good defence.

COUNTER MARCH, an army's suddenly turning their march a contrary way, to prevent the enemy from getting between them and their garrison, to disappoint and amuse them. A
battalion

battalion is faid to countermarch, when the wings of a battalion interchange ground.

COUNTER-MINES, are uſed when the beſiegers have, notwithſtanding the oppoſition of the beſieged, paſſed the foſſe, and put the miner to the foot of the rampart. They are of 2 ſorts; being either made when the baſtion is raiſed; or afterwards, when it is attacked. Thoſe that are made when the baſtion is raiſed, are carried quite round the faces of a baſtion; their height is from 4 to 5 feet, and broad enough for a man to paſs eaſily: the others, which are made in time of neceſſity, when the beſiegers are undermining a baſtion, are pits ſunk deep in the ground, where the miner is ſuppoſed to be, from whence they run out branches, in ſearch of the enemy's mine, to fruſtrate the effect of it, by either taking away the powder, or cutting off the train.

COUNTERSCARP, is the outſide of a ditch, oppoſite to the parapet of the work, behind the ditch. It is often ſaid that the beſiegers have carried their lodgments upon the counterſcarp, when they are lodged on the covert-way.

Counterſcarps that are not walled, ſhould be as ſteep as poſſible, to hinder a deſcent into the foſſe, and yet they muſt be ſo contrived as to admit of ſuccours and afford a ſafe retreat to the town.

COUNTER-SIGN, is generally given out with the parole, is made uſe of in the ſame manner, and frequently exchanged by the guards and rounds.

COURT-MARTIAL, was inſtituted by the Legiſlature, not only to check all arbitrary proceedings that are contrary to good order and military diſcipline; but alſo to examine into the conduct of officers and ſoldiers; to paſs ſentence upon thoſe who ſhall be found guilty of a breach of the Articles of War; or, by their judgment, to remove any bad impreſſion, or miſrepreſentation, that may be made to the prejudice of an officer.

Court-martial, general, is compoſed of a preſident and 12 members, with a judge advocate. The preſident is of the rank of a field-officer, with 12 of the rank of captain, if they can conveniently be aſſembled: if to try any under the rank of a field-officer, a captain may ſit as preſident (when no field-officer can be had) with 12 commiſſioned officers, who are all ſworn: but in the garriſons of Goree and Senegal, or upon any detachments therefrom, they need only conſiſt of 5; but the preſident ſhould not be under the degree of a field-officer; though a captain may preſide, when a field-officer cannot attend.

Court-martial, regimental, is compoſed of 5 officers, the eldeſt whereof is preſident; but when that number cannot conveniently aſſemble, 3 are ſufficient. Neither the members or witneſſes are ſworn.

Court-martial, garriſon, is compoſed of the ſame number of officers, of horſe, dragoons, foot, or marines, as a Regimental Court. The approving officer is the governor, lieutenant-governor, or the officer commanding. Neither the members or witneſſes are ſworn.

Court of Inquiry, is of a very delicate nature: a number of officers

officers are aſſembled to enquire into au officer's *ſuppoſed* miſbeha-viour; and I have known them ordered to give their opinions in writing, to the perſon who or-dered them to aſſemble, that he may judge from their determi-nation, if there is a ſufficient matter to bring him to a General Court-martial.

There is no article of war for this kind of proceeding; and though it has frequently been complained of, becauſe the mem bers are not ſworn, and that its opinion may influence a General Court-martial by prejudging the cauſe; yet reaſon has hitherto been unſucceſsful in its endea-vours to aboliſh this inequitable *cuſtom of the army.*

CREMONA, a large city in the dukedom of Milan, defended by a ſtrong caſtle, is 5 miles in cir-cuit, lies cloſe to the Po, over which is a bridge of boats, co-vered by a fort. It ſtands on a fine plain, on the river Po, by the borders of Parma, 15 miles north-eaſt of Piacenza; 25 north-weſt of Parma; 28 ſouth of Breſcia; thirty almoſt weſt of Mantua; and 45 eaſt of Milan. Long. 30. 14. lat. 44. 42.

CRESCENTINO, a city of Italy, upon the borders of the princi-pality of Piedmont, ſubject to the Duke of Savoy, but taken by the French in 1704. In Septem-ber 1706, the Confederates re-took it after the glorious victory obtained in raiſing the ſiege of Turin. It ſtands 2 miles north of Venice, near the north ſide of the Po; 22 miles north-eaſt of Turin; and 18 north-weſt of Caſal. Long. 27. 53. lat. 49. 9.

CRONSIOT, *that is Crowncaſtle,* a caſtle with a harbour, in the

little iſle of the ſame name, at the mouth of the Neva and gulf of Finland, 14 miles weſt of Pe-terſburg; one of the ſtations for Ruſſian ſhips of war, and has magazines of all kinds of naval ſtores, with large docks and yards. Lat. 60. 20. n. long. 30. 15. e.

CROWN-POINT, a fortification of North America, built by the French in 1732, 120 miles ſouth of the river St. Lawrence, on the lake Champlain, where a bay and ſmall river form a point on which it ſtands. It is ſaid, that the proper name of this place is *Scalp-point,* from an In-dian battle which happened here, when many ſcalps were carried off. It is a regular fortification, defended on every ſide by re-doubts, particularly to the eaſt, where it is moſt likely to be ap-proached. From hence they ſupply their parties ſent upon the Engliſh frontiers with necef-faries: it ſtands 33 leagues north of Albany in New York, and 15 miles from Ticonderago. In his way to this fort, Governor Johnſon beat a party of French in 1755, and took their general priſoner. An unſucceſsful at-tempt was made on Ticonderago by the provincial and regular forces under General Abercrom-bie in July 1758; but in 1759, it fell into the hands of the Engliſh. Weſt long. 72. 45. lat. 44.

CROWN-WORK, a kind of work not unlike a crown, has 2 fronts and 2 branches; the fronts com-poſed of 2 half baſtions, and generally ſerve to incloſe ſome buildings, which cannot be brought within the body of the place, to cover the town-gates,

[c]   or

or occupy a spot of ground, which might be advantageous to an enemy.

CROWS-FEET, an iron of 4 points, about 6 inches long, used against cavalry; for 1 point will always be uppermost, let it fall as it will.

CUIRASSIERS, cavalry, armed with back, breast, and head-pieces.

CULLODEN, situated about 3 miles east of Inverness, remarkable for the intire defeat of the rebel army, which happened on the 16th of April 1746. His Royal Highness William Duke of Cumberland having given the necessary orders for the day, with great prudence and penetration, decamped from Nairn between 4 and 5 in the morning; and having disposed the army in 3 columns, covered on the flanks by the horse and dragoons, proceeded towards the enemy. After 8 miles march, the van-guard, under General Bland, perceived them in motion to the left; on which the Duke immediately formed the army: being at too great a distance, and the rebels not advancing, they again continued their march to the distance of a mile; when, after a short halt, they proceeded, and having passed the morass, had a full view of the enemy in line of battle, behind the huts and walls of Culloden House.

The young Pretender, on observing the order in which they advanced, asked one of the French officers his opinion of the day; who, after some pause, answered, " that he believed it lost, for he had narrowly observed the Duke's army, and never saw men drawn up with more conduct, nor advance in a more

cool and regular manner." The dispositions made by his Royal Highness would have done honour to the oldest and most experienced general, as may be seen by what follows. If any 1 battalion failed, there were 2 ready to supply its place; if any 2 pieces of cannon were taken, there were 3 to open upon them; which admirable situation was sufficient to support the army, on the offensive, to the last extremity, when headed by this soldier's friend, whose affable deportment reigned triumphant in the hearts of those under him. All things being in readiness to forward the attack, his Royal Highness addressed himself to the officers and soldiers to the following purport: " *Gentlemen, and fellow soldiers, it is incumbent on me to acquaint you, that you are instantly to engage in defence of your King and Country, your religion, liberties, properties, and all that is dear to you: through the justness of the cause, I make no doubt of leading you to victory; be firm, and your enemies will soon fly: if any amongst you are diffident of your courage or behaviour, which I have no reason to suspect; or any who, through conscience or inclination, cannot be zealous or alert in performing their duty; my desire is, that such would immediately retire; I assure them of my free pardon for so doing; as I had rather be at the head of 1000 brave and resolute men, than 10000, amongst whom, some, by cowardice or misbehaviour, might disorder or dispirit the troops, and bring dishonour on the command.*" This speech cemented the troops in the most heroic resolution, who unanimously exerted themselves with the greatest activity in the attack,

attack, to which they immediately advanced. Some time was spent by both armies in gaining the flank; but the Duke's army still advancing, they got clear of a morals that lay on their right. This gave his Royal Highness an opportunity of extending his front; for which end, Pultney's foot were ordered from the rear to take post on the right, and Kingston's horse, with a squadron of Cobham's dragoons, to cover that flank. Lord Bury was ordered forward to reconnoitre something that appeared like a battery; on which the Rebels began to fire their cannon; but being ill pointed, they did little execution. The first discharge of the artillery threw the enemy into a visible confusion, they being loaded with grape-shot, and their ranks so close, that avenues were fairly cut through them. The Rebels, disliking this manner of fighting, advanced; the Mac Donalds and Mac Intoshes on the right flank, who endeavoured several times to break in, were so warmly received by the Royal's and Pultney's, that they retired, closely pursued by the horse. Their attack at the same time on the left, though more furious, was equally unsuccessful; having out-flanked Barrel's foot, the Athol men, Camerons, and Frazers, rushed in sword-in-hand, with great resolution and intrepidity, seeming to carry all before them; but the King's troops being ordered to reserve their fire till they came close up, did great execution; yet their commanders, acting with great bravery, continued exhorting and forcing them down; on which the regiments of Barrel and Dejean opened for them to

pass; they then closing, brought them between the first and second line, where they so handled them with their bayonets, that their broad sword and target proved of little service, few escaping to their main body. In the mean time General Hawley, with Mark Krer's dragoons and the Highlanders, having advanced towards the enemy's right, broke the park-wall that covered them, and, surrounding their flank, met General Bland with Kingston's horse and Cobham's dragoons in the centre, which created a general dissolution and carnage; the foot pressing hard, brought them between several fires, which soon routed and destroyed their projects. The young Pretender seeing his hopes blasted, with several of the chiefs, fled from the field with great precipitation; and having forded the Ness almost to the neck, took up his quarters that night at the seat of Lord L————. The King's troops continued the pursuit with great bravery; the horse and dragoons made so continued a slaughter in the thickest of their ranks, that the roads from the field to Inverness, being 3 miles, were covered with killed and wounded, few of the Rebels submitting to take quarters; so that their loss, by their best accounts, exceeded 2500 in battle and pursuit; 450 were made prisoners; 30 pieces of cannon, 2320 firelocks, with their colours, ammunition, and swords, were taken; which determined that ever-memorable victory, with an inconsiderable loss to the King's troops.

CULVERIN, a cannon about $5\frac{1}{4}$ inches diameter in the bore, and from 9 to 12 feet long, carrying

rying a ball of 18 pounds: a good battering gun, but too heavy for a field-piece.

CUMANA, built about 14 leagues to the f. of Margarita, on the continent, by the Spaniards, in 1520, and called at firft Nueva Corduba, is defended by a very ftrong caftle, and the town ftands near the entrance of a great gulph, known by the name of Golfo de Carrico, or Cumana.

CUNETTE, or *Cuvette*, a deep trench about 3 or 4 fathom wide, funk along the centre of a a dry moat, to make the paffage more difficult to the enemy; it is generally funk deep enough to find water to fill it, and neceffary to prevent the befiegers mining.

CURTAIN, that part of the rampart of a place, which is between the flanks of 2 baftions, and is the beft defended of any part of the rampart; wherefore befiegers never make their attacks in the curtains, but on the faces of the baftions, becaufe of their being defended but by one flank.

Curtains, the fpace between the 2 baftions, or that which joins them. They ferve to cover the houfes, and the infide of the place. To be good, they fhould be in a ftraight line: the others are defective, as they hinder the flanking from feeing and defending each other.

The curtains fhould therefore be defended with 2 flanks; but, if neceffity admits only of one, you muft plant palifades before it, and an advanced foffe; let your line of defence go from the flanking angle, or from fome part of the curtain, to the point of the oppofite baftion: and let it not exceed 240 yards, which

is the ordinary range of a firelock.

There are *fimple* and *prolonged curtains*; the latter are beft, as they leffen the number of baftions, and enlarge the place: fuppofing them to be fhort enough for the defence of the place, according to the rules of fortification.

The fimple curtain, has generally 140, or 160 yards in length; fhould never exceed 170, nor be lefs than 80 yards, to be within the rule of defence.

The prolonged curtain, never more than 260 or 270 yards in length.

CYLINDER, or *Chafe of a gun*, the bore or concavity of a piece, whereof that part which receives the powder and ball, is called the *Charged Cylinder*; that which remains empty after the gun is charged, is called *the Vacant Cylinder*.

DAMME, a fmall but ftrong fortrefs, 3 miles north-eaft of Bruges, fubmitted to the Duke of Marlborough, in 1706, after the battle of Ramilies.

DANTZIC, a fortified city, the capital of Little Pomerania in Polifh Pruffia, fituated on the weft fhore of the Weifchel or Viftula, having the little rivers Radaune and Motlau running through the town, and about a mile from the Baltic, has a fine harbour. This was formerly one of the principal towns of the Hanfeatic union; and ftill maintains a garrifon of its own, the fortifications being confiderable, particularly towards the fouth and weft, where the city is furrounded with hills. They coin their own money, and are under the protection of Poland. In 1703,

1703, the Englifh, Dutch, and Pruffians entered into an alliance to protect them againft Charles XII. of Sweden; as alfo in 1706, when that prince threatened them with a vifit, upon his fuccefs againft King Auguftus II. if they refufed to acknowledge Staniflaus for their king. But in 1734, having received Staniflaus, they held out a fmart fiege and bombardment from the Ruffians and Saxons; but after lofing all hopes of affiftance from the French, whofe money had corrupted them, they were obliged to furrender on the 9th of July, fubmit to Auguftus III. and purchafe their peace with feveral thoufand pounds for letting Saniflaus make his efcape during the fiege. It is fituated 72 miles fouth-weft of Konigfburg, and 136 north of Warfaw. Lat. 53. 38. n. long. 18. 35. eaft.

DARDANELLES, 120 miles fouth-weft of Conftantinople, are 2 two famous caftles defending the gulf of Lapanto and the narrow ftreight called the Hellefpont, which is here 2 miles over, and the key as it were to Conftantinople; one on one fide of Europe, and the other on that of Afia; the former was antiently called Seftos, and the latter Abidos. In 1656, the Venetians paffed through with their fleets between thefe forts, and drove that of the Turks on fhore. Here all veffels coming from the Archipelago are examined. Not far from hence, namely off Lepanto, the Venetians gained a confiderable victory over the Turkifh fleet in 1571.

DECAGONS, polygons, or fortifications of ten fides.

DECAMP, to break up from a place where the army has been encamped.

DEFENCES, of a place, the parts of a wall, or rampart, which flank and defend the reft; as the flanks, cafements, parapets, and faufebrays. The face of a baftion, though it has the fimpleft defence of any part of the fortification, yet it cannot be formed till the oppofite flank be ruined. To be in a pofture of defence, it is to be in a condition to refift or oppofe an enemy.

DEFILE, a narrow pafs, which obliges an army to defile off: it is one of the greateft obftacles that can occur in the march of an army, efpecially if it happen between woods or marfhes; as it not only gives an enemy an extraordinary advantage, of either attacking the front or rear, when they cannot come to relieve one another, becaufe of the ftraitnefs of the paffage; but it alfo much impedes the march: a retreating army always puts a defile between them and the enemy to fecure its retreat.

To defile, to reduce an army, &c. to a fmall front; to march through a narrow paffage.

DEGREES, properly a term in geometry, ufed in fortification, to meafure the angles, being the 360th part of the circumference of a circle; a degree is divided into 60 equal parts, called minutes; and each minute into 60 feconds.

DEMI-CANNON, a gun carrying a ball of 32 pounds; the diameter of its bore is 6¼ inches, and its length from 12 to 14 feet. It is feldom ufed at fieges, becaufe of its extraordinary charge.

DEMI-CIRCLE the half of a circle, cut by a line paffing thro' the centre, called the diameter.

DEMI-CULVERIN, a cannon of about 9 feet long: the diameter of the bore is 4¼ inches, carrying a ball of 9 pounds. It is a very good field piece.

DEMI-GORGE, that part of the polygon which remains after the flank is raifed, and goes from the curtain to the angle of the polygon: it is half of the vacant entrance into a baſtion.

DENDERMOND, a fortified town of Flanders, in the Auſtrian Low-Countries, ſituated in a marſhy ground, at the junction of the Scheld with the Dender, 14 miles eaſt of Ghent. It was taken by the Allies in 1706, and is now ſubject to the houſe of Auſtria. Lat. 51. 16. eaſt; long. 3. 56 north.

DESCENT into a moat, a deep trench, or ſap, through the eſplanade, and under the covert-way, covered over head with planks and hurdles, and loaded with earth againſt artificial fires to ſecure the deſcent; which, in ditches that are wet, is made to the brink of the water; but in dry moats, the ſap is carried to the bottom of the moat, where the traverſes are made, to lodge and cover the beſiegers.

DESERTER, the officer or ſoldier who deſerts from his majeſty's ſervice. A ſoldier, who, after having inliſted into one corps, again inliſts into another, without having previouſly obtained a diſcharge from the firſt, ſhall ſuffer death, or ſuch other puniſhment as a court-martial ſhall inflict. If the offence ſhall be thought not deſerving capital puniſhment, the court may adjudge the offender to ſerve in any of the corps ſtationed in foreign

parts, either for life, or a term of years according to the degree of the offence: but, if afterwards convicted of returning without leave before the expiration of ſuch term, he ſhall ſuffer death.

This clauſe extends to all the forces in Great Britain, Ireland, Minorca, Gibraltar, and his majeſty's dominions beyond ſea.

DETACHMENT, a certain number of officers, non-commiſſioned officers, and ſoldiers, drawn out from ſeveral regiments or companies, equally to be employed, whether on an attack at a ſiege, or in parties to ſcour the country, &c.

DETTINGEN, a village in the territory of Hanau and Upper Rhine in Germany, ſtands on an open plain, 6 miles weſt of the city of Aſchaffenburg, and 12 of Hanau, in lat. 50. 12. long. 7. 9. eaſt; is remarkable for a battle fought there, in June 1743, between the Allies, headed by King George II. the Duke of Cumberland, &c. and the French, commanded by Marſhal Noailles, who intended to ſurround the confederate Allies, and reduce them, by cutting them off from all the common paſſes, to ſurrender or ſtarve. This ſcheme was ſoon ſurmounted by the intrepidity of the Allies, animated by the preſence of his Majeſty and the Duke, who forced the French to repaſs the Maine with the greateſt precipitancy, leaving 31 officers of note killed or wounded, 34 taken priſoners, and about 4000 killed or wounded; 6 ſtandards taken, and ſeveral hundred men drowned in repaſſing the Maine. The Allies loſt above 2000. The principal officers killed were, Lieutenant-general Clayton, and Major-general

neral Murray, who died of his wounds. The Duke was shot in the leg; Duke Aremberg, the Earl of Albemarle, General Huske, the Colonels Ligonier and Peers, &c. were wounded. Our generals behaved with the greatest conduct and intrepidity. The Duke gave early proofs of a transcendant bravery, and a generosity inherent only in the truly great, by ordering a French officer, whom he observed to behave bravely, and weltering on the field, to be taken care of before himself.

DIAMETER *of a circle*, a right line, which passes through the centre and touches the circumference in two points, dividing the circle into two equal parts.

DIEPPE, a town of Upper Normandy in France, strong, but very irregularly fortified, has a good harbour, and is generally a station for privateers, but has not water enough for large ships. It lies on the English channel opposite to Rye, and 36 miles north of Rouen. In 1694, it was almost entirely destroyed by a bombardment of the English; and in the late Queen's wars roughly treated in the same manner. Lat. 49. 55. n. long. 1. 9. east. See Plan 10.

DODECAGON, a figure, bounded by 12 sides, forming as many angles, capable of being fortified with the same number of bastions.

DOLCIGNO, or DULCIGNO, a town of Albina, in European Turky, 46 miles south-east of Ragusa, has a good harbour on the Adriatic, and a strong castle. Its inhabitants are famous corsairs, and subject to the Turks, who took the place in 1571. Lat. 42..12. n. long. 19. 15. east.

DOMINGO, ST. situate on the

south side of the island of Hispaniola, in North America, on the north-east, is a fruitful country; improved by art, and the approaches to it so difficult, that the natives baffled a most formidable force, sent to America by the English, though commanded by experienced generals, in 1655. This city was built by Columbus. Lat. 18. 25. long. 69. 30. west.

DONJON, a place of retreat, to capitulate with more advantage, in case of necessity.

DOSSIR, a kind of basket, in form of a sugar-loaf reversed, to be carried on the shoulders, and is used to carry the overplus earth from one part of a fortification to another where it is wanted. There are also small carts and wheel-barrows for the same use.

DOVER, by the Romans called *Portis Dubris*, a sea-port and borough-town of Kent, on the east extremity of the county, opposite to Calais in France. It was formerly looked upon as a strong fortress, and the key of the kingdom. The castle stands on a very high hill; 15 miles southeast of Canterbury, and 71 of London.

DRAIN, a trench made to draw the water out of a moat, which is afterwards filled with hurdles and earth, or with fascines, or bundles of rushes and planks, to facilitate the passage over the mud.

DRAUGHT-HOOKS, large hooks of iron, fixed on the cheeks of a cannon-carriage, 2 on each side; 1 near the trunnion hole, and the other at the train; and are called *the fore and hind draught hooks*. Large guns have draught hooks near the middle transum, to which are fixed the chains, and serve to ease the shafts of the limbers on a march; the fore and hind hooks are used for drawing a gun backwards or forwards by men, with strong ropes, called *draught-ropes*, fixed to these hooks.

DRESDEN, the capital of the electorate of Saxony, situated on the Elbe, is one of the largest and strongest cities in the empire, and the only place which Charles XII. of Sweden did not reduce, when he laid the whole country of Saxony under contribution, in 1706; for Augustus II. Elector, and then King of Poland, residing there, determined to hold it out to the last extremity; and hither Charles XII. after exhausting Saxony of its treasure, came to take his leave of that king, who did not think proper to detain his person, but let him depart quietly to his camp. It lies 70 miles northwest of Prague, and 90 south of Berlin, in lat. 51. 12. long. 13. 40.

This place was taken from the king of Prussia by the French, who garrisoned it with 4000 men, and cut off the communication between it and the mouth of the river: but he besieged it again when defended by General Maguire. To form an idea of this siege, imagine the most determined attack upon one side, and the ruin of the finest buildings in the world on the other, by an incessant fire from 3 batteries of cannon and mortars, while each commander practised every art usual in such cases. The approach of Count Daun to its relief redoubled the fury of the Prussians, and at the same time confirmed and encreased the resolute intrepidity of the besieged; especially when Daun found means, as he did, to throw into it 16 battalions. After such a reinforcement, and while 3 armies were in the neighbourhood (for the army of the empire, and that under Lacy, had by this time returned) it then would have been madness for his majesty to continue the siege: he therefore raised it, but without molestation from the enemy.

DRUM, a martial instrument used by the foot. To beat the *general*, is a signal for the whole army to make ready to march; the *assemble* is the next beat, which is an order for the soldiers to repair to their colours; and the *march* is to command them to move. To beat the *reveille* at day-break, is to warn the soldiers to rise, and the sentries to cease challenging; the *troop* is to assemble them together for the inspection of an officer, and to mount the guards; and *retreat* beating is at sun-set, when the rolls are called, the men warned for duty, and the orders of the day lead to them. *Tatoo-beating* is generally at nine in summer, and eight in winter; by which hour it is expected, that the men are at their quarters, to answer roll-calling, and go to rest. *Alarm* is to call the regiment under arms to their alarm-posts, on some sudden danger, fire, or other occasion. To beat a *parly*, or *chamade*, is to desire a conference with the enemy: and to beat to *arms*, is to advertise the corps to stand to their arms. The adjutant's call, is the first part of the *tatoo*. The drummer's call, is a particular beat, and called the *drummer's call*. Two *rolls* and 6 *flams*, is for 1 serjeant and 1 corporal of a company. Three *rolls* and 9 *flams*, is for all the serjeants **and**

and corporals to attend for orders, &c.

DUNCANNON, a fort fituated on the harbour of Waterford, in the county of Wexford, and province of Leinfter, in Ireland. All fhips bound up that harbour muft fail within piftol-fhot of the place. It was taken by King William's army in 1690. It ftands 7 miles eaft of Waterford, and 60 fouth of Dublin. From this place King James fled into France. It is ftrong towards the fea, but commanded by rifing grounds towards the land. Weft long. 6. 50. lat. 52. 10.

DUNKIRK, a town of Flanders, in the French Low Countries, and a government of the fame name, fituated on the river Coln, which here falls into the German ocean. After having had feveral mafters, the French, in conjunction with the Englifh, took it from the Spaniards in 1646, and in 1658 it was given the Englifh in confideration of their fervices againft Spain; in 1662, Charles II. of England fold it to France for 5000000 of livres: after which its fortifications were confiderably improved and enlarged; alfo canals, fluices, and dams were added; fo that in fucceeding wars, it became a ftation for privateers, which did confiderable damage to the Englifh, who, at the treaty of Utrecht, in 1713, infifted on the demolition of the harbour and its fortifications, which coft Louis XIV. immenfe fums. The arfenal, magazines, and the caferns are well worthy infpection. It lies 26 miles eaft of Calais, 55 of Dover, and 26 fouth weft of Oftend. Lat 51. 2. long. 2. 27. eaft

DUTY, the exercife of thofe functions that belong to a foldier, with this diftinction; that mounting guard, and the like, where there is not an enemy to be directly engaged, is called *duty*; but their marching to meet or fight an enemy, or being fent on party, or detachment, is termed *going upon fervice*.

ECHARPE. To batter an echarpe is to batter obliquely or fideways: the flanks of Count Pagan's conftruction may be battered on an echarpe, becaufe the angles of the curtain, being too obtufe, are too much difcovered.

EDINBURGH, the capital of Scotland, a large and populous city of Midlothian, is fituated on an eminence; it has, befides feveral other ftreets, one very remarkable, called the High-ftreet, about a mile long, and pretty broad, with handfome ftone houfes; at the weft end of it is a ftrong caftle on a rock, inacceffible but at one avenue opening to that ftreet, and at the other is the Nether-bow, one of the gates which leads to the Cannongate; 320 miles from London, in lat. 55. 58. n. long. 3. weft. During the rebellion, on the 29th of September, the communication between the city and caftle was cut off. Till this time, the brave governor, General Gueft, forbore firing on the rebels, being unwilling to damage the town, or involve the innocent in deftruction with the guilty; but as hoftilities were unavoidable, a battery from the caftle was opened upon them, when feveral houfes were beat down, and about 20 killed. One Taylor, a refolute fellow, that had a captain's commiffion in the rebels fervice, engaged to make himfelf mafter of the caftle with

30 men; but in the attempt he was taken prisoner with moft of his party, which fate his prefumption juftly merited. General Gueft finding that, if the blockade continued, the garrifon would foon want provifions, as all communication was cut off, on the 4th of October ordered a fally to be made under favour of the half-moon battery; by which means they threw up a trench between the town and caftle; and having pofted a body of men behind the parapet, cleared the ftreet; on the 5th he got in fome provifions, and that evening a party of the rebels marched up the hill to attack the entrenchment; but that detachment cautioufly retreating into the garrifon, expofed the enemy to a fmart cannonade, which obliged them to retire with a confiderable lofs: from that time a communication was opened, and the garrifon plentifully fupplied.

EFFE DING, a place of ftrength, defended by two caftles, ftands nine miles weft of Lintz.

EGRA, a ftrong town in Bohemia, upon a river of the fame name, a few miles weft from Prague, near the borders of Franconia and the Upper Palatinate; to which laft it formerly belonged. Fortified with a double wall, in fome parts with a treble, and has a ftrong caftle. In March 1742, the allied army, confifting of French, Pruffians, and Saxons, laid fiege to this place; and on the 8th of April, the garrifon furrendered the place by capitulation; the fubftance of which was, that the troops fhould march out with the honours of war, 4 cannon, 2 covered waggons, be conducted to Paffau, and not ferve againft the Emperor or his allies

for a certain term. The beginning of 1743, the Auftrians began to blockade Egra, the only place then poffeffed by the French in Bohemia. They afterwards befieged it in form, and the garrifon made a long and vigorous defence; but at laft they agreed to the terms of capitulation infifted on by her Hungarian Majefty; they furrendered the place to her army on the 27th of Auguft; and on the 31ft the place was entirely evacuated.

ELVAS, a well fortified city of Alentejo in Portugal, has a caftle on an eminence, reckoned one of the ftrongeft fortreffes in the kingdom, and another on the Guadiana, whereon the city is fituated, near the borders of Spanifh Eftramadura. It contains about 2500 inhabitants, is the fee of a Bifhop, and has a very remarkable aqueduct near a mile long. In 1580 it was taken by the Spaniards, who were defeated by the Portuguefe in 1659, near this place; which lies about 17 miles weft of Bajadox, in lat. 38. 39. n. long. 7. 28. weft.

EMBRASURES, openings made in the flanks of a fortification, or in the breaft-work of a battery, about 2 feet and a half within, 8 or 9 without, and 3 feet from the bottom. for part of each gun to enter and fire through.

EMBDEN, an imperial city of Weftphalia, in Germany, and capital of a county of the fame name, ftands in lat. 53. 5. n. long. 7. 26. eaft.

EMINENCE, a high or rifing ground, which overlooks and commands the low places about it. Such places within cannonfhot of a fortification are a great difadvantage; for if the befiegers
become

become masters of them, they can from thence fire into it.

ENCAMP, pitching of tents, when the army, after a march, is come to a place where it is designed to halt. The bells of arms are in the front; serjeants tents immediately behind them; and the soldiers following: the officers encamp in the rear, the subalterns in 1 line next the company, fronting from it; the captains in another line, at some distance, each behind his own company, fronting the subalterns; and the field-officer's behind them: the colonel's is in the centre, the lieutenant-colonel's on his right, the major's on his left, the surgeon's and chaplain's behind them, and the sutler's behind all.

ENCEINTE, the wall or rampart which surrounds a place: it is, properly, composed of bastions and curtains, either faced or lined with brick or stone; but sometimes made only of earth. When flanked by round or square towers, it is called a Roman wall.

ENFANS PERDUS, in English called the Forlorn or Forlorn Hope, a body of men appointed to give the first onset in battle, to begin the assault upon a place besieged, or go upon any other desperate service.

ENFILADE. A work is said to be enfiladed, when a gun can be fired into it, so that the shot may go all along the inside of the parapet.

ENGHEIN, a town of Hainalt in the Austrian Low Countries, 20 miles south-west of Brussels. Near this place King William III. attacked Marshal Luxemburg in 1692, who lay fortified in the village of Steinkirk,

whence the battle has its name, but was repulsed by the French with considerable loss, and General Mackey killed on the spot, who in 1689 dispersed the Highlanders under Viscount Dundee, at the pass of Killicranky in Athol in Scotland. Lat. 50. 36. long. 3. 52. east.

ENGINEER, an officer of the military branch, who, assisted by geometry, delineates upon paper, or marks upon the ground, all sorts of forts, and other works proper for offence or defence; who understands the art of fortification; can discover the defects of a place, find proper remedies, and knows how to make an attack on a place, or defend it when attacked.

Engineers are necessary for both these purposes, and should not only be ingenious, but brave in proportion to their knowledge; that employ requiring both expert and bold men. At a siege, when the engineers have observed and narrowly inspected the place, they are to acquaint the general which they judge the weakest part, and where the approaches may be made with most ease. Their business is to take all advantages of ground; delineate the lines of circumvallation and contravallation; mark out the trenches, places of arms, batteries, and lodgments; taking great care that none of their works be flanked, or discovered from the place; to make a faithful report to the general of what is doing; demand a sufficient number of workmen and utensils, and foresee whatever is necessary.

An Engineer should be an adept in arithmetic, to project the plots of places, and calculate

late the expences of the fiege;
in geometry, to meafure his work
and raife plans ; in military architecture, to diftinguifh himfelf
in his profeffion; in civil architecture, to know how to conduct
buildings, and works of places;
in mechanics, to make fluices,
march cannon, and ufe all forts
of machines; in perfpective, to
exprefs his works on paper in
their juft proportion; for without defign, he can neither make
charts or plans. Thefe fciences
are called the genius, in which
confifts the whole fpirit of war
and fortification.

ENNEAGON, a nine-fided figure
in fortification.

EN SECOND, an officer whofe
troop or company is broke,
though he continues on whole pay,
and, upon a vacancy, is appointed to a troop or company.

ENVELOPE, a work of earth,
made fometimes in the ditch of a
place, fometimes without the
ditch, fometimes in the form of
a fimple parapet, and at other
times like a fmall rampart with
a parapet. Envelopes are often
made to enclofe a weak ground;
when it is to be done with fimple
lines, to avoid the great charge
of horn-works, tenailles, or the
like; or when they have not
ground for fuch large works.
The caftle of Namure has 2 envelopes on the fouth-weft fide of
the donjon ; one before the other,
compofed of 2 demibaftions and a
curtain, called the *firft* and *fecond*
envelopes. When made without
both thefe, a large work extending
itfelf on the top of a hill, with
2 demi-baftions, is called the
Terre-Neuve, or Newland.

The citadel of Benfanfon, fituated on a high fteep rock, has
three envelopes, one before an-

other, towards the campaign,
which ferve as fo many covert-
ways before the moat.

The fort Nuerburg, in Holland,
is famous for its envelope, which
goes quite round the fort, and is
fraifed and palifaded with ftakes
as thick as a man's body.

EPAULE, or *fhoulder of a baftion,* the place where the face
and flank meet, and form the
angle, called the angle of the
fhoulder.

EPAULEMENT, a work raifed
either of earth, gabions, or fafcines, loaded with earth to cover
fide-ways. The epaulements of
the places of arms for the cavalry,
at the entering of the trenches
are generally of fafcines mixed
with earth.

Epaulement, a kind of breaft-
work, to cover the troops in front,
and fometimes in flank.

Epaulement, or *fquare orillon,* a
mafs of earth.

EPTAGON, or *Heptagon,* a figure of 7 fides and 7 angles.

ESCALADE. To efcalade a
place, is to approach it fecretly,
and to place ladders againft the
wall or rampart, for the troops to
mount and get into the place.

ESPLANADE, an open fpace,
between the citadel and town, to
prevent an enemy from making
approaches under cover, after he
is mafter of the place.

ESPONTOON, an offenfive and
defenfive weapon, ufed by the officers of battalion companies, except in fuzileer regiments, where
the officers carry fuzees.

ESSECK, a town of Sclavonia
in Hungary, on the Drau, which
near it falls into the Danube. It
is pretty large, and ftrongly fortified; has a remarkable wooden-
bridge over the former river and
the marfhes here, 5 miles long,
built

built by the emperor Solyman in 1566, who employed 20000 men in the undertaking. This difficult pass has been several times taken and retaken, and several battles fought between Christians and Turks for the possession of it. The bridge has also been oft burned; particularly in 1686, by the Hungarians, though they could not take the town; however, after the battle of Mohatz, they drove the Turks from it; so that this place with all Hungary is now subject to Austria. It lies 75 miles north-west of Belgrade, in lat. 46. 20. long. 20. 22. There is also a strong fortification of the same name in the district of Sclavonia in Hungary:

EVOLUTION, a movement made by troops, when they are obliged to change their form and disposition, to preserve one post, or occupy another; to attack an enemy with advantage, or strengthen their defence against superior numbers.

EXACTITUDE, the general's care of the parole, countersign, rounds, patroles, spies, and parties; the preservation of the ammunition and provisions; to try the waters, lest they should be bad or poisoned; and to prevent them from being cut away; to see that no fortified towns, garrisons, forts, or ports, are in the front, rear, or flanks, to form an ambuscade, or cut off the convoys.

EXAGON, a figure bounded by 6 sides, or polygons, making as many angles capable of bastions.

EXERCISE, the practice of all those motions, actions, and management of arms, whereby a soldier is taught the different postures he is to be in under arms, and the different motions he is to make to resist an enemy;

4

which he must be perfect in, before he is fit for service.

EXILES, a small town on the confines of Dauphiny and Piedmont, in Italy, defended by bulwarks, and a strong castle on a mountain; situated in the valley of Oulx, and on the north shore of the Doria; 14 miles west of Susa. Taken from the French by the Duke of Savoy, in 1711; confirmed to him by the treaty of Utrecht in 1713; and now subject to the King of Sardinia. Lat. 45. 12. n. long. 7. 10. e.

EXTERIOR *side of a fortification*, the distance or imaginary line drawn from one point of a bastion to that of the next.

FACE, *of a work*, that part where the rampart is made, forming an angle, and pointing outwards.

Faces of the bastions, 2 sides, which meet in an angle, projecting towards the field.

Face of a gun, the superficies of the metal, at the extremity of the muzzle of the piece.

Face prolonged, that part of the line of defence razant, betwixt the angle of the shoulder and the curtain, or the line of defence razant, diminished by the length of a face.

FACING, a particular turning of the aspect, from one part to another, whereby the front proper becomes front accidental; and a front accidental may be reduced to its proper front.

FANION, small flags, carried with the baggage of artillery.

FARO, a sea port town of Algarve, in Portugal, tolerably fortified, dividing it from Cabo de Santa Marca, or Baretta, situated in a bay, and defended by a castle, 24 miles east of Lagos,

gos, in lat. 36. 48. long. 9. 12. weſt.

FASCINE, a kind of faggot, made of branches, tied in 2 or more places, about 6 inches diameter. They ſerve to keep up the earth in trenches, and are alſo uſed in batteries, inſtead of ſtone or brick walls. When uſed in raiſing batteries, they are generally 16 feet long, and are then called ſauciſſons.

FAUSS-BRAY, a low rampart, going quite round the body of the place, about 3 feet at moſt, above the level of the ground; and its parapet about 4 or 5 toiſes diſtance from that of the body of the place.

FELLOWS, 6 pieces of wood, each whereof forms a piece of an arch of a circle, of 60 degrees, and, joined both together by duledges, make an entire circle; which, with the addition of a nave and 12 ſpokes, make a wheel.

FENISTRELLE, a fortified town of Piedmont, in Italy, ſituate on the Cluſon; taken by the duke of Savoy in 1708, one of the ſtrongeſt frontiers againſt France belonging to the king of Sardinia. Lat. 45. 10. n. long. 7. 26.

FERRARA, an old city of the dutchy of that name, in the Pope's dominions, ſituated on the Po, and defended by a citadel of 5 whole and 5 half baſtions; 30 miles n-eaſt of Bologna, in lat. 44. 36. n. long. 12. 14. eaſt.

FERROL, a town in Gallacia, in the gulph of the Groyne, n. of the river Java; the harbour is the ſtrongeſt in Spain, and affords an entry but of one ſhip at a time, having the land high on both ſides, and a paſſage defend-

ed by ſeveral ſmall batteries. 24 miles north-eaſt of the Groyne, and 54 north of Compoſtella. Lat. 43. 26. n. long. 8. 46. weſt.

FIELD-OFFICERS, are Colonel, Lieutenant-colonel, and Major.

FIELD-PIECES, ſmall cannon: each battalion has 2.

FILE, the line of ſoldiers ſtanding behind one another. 3 make a file.

To file off, the ſame as to defile, or to file off from a large front to march in length. An army is ſaid to file off from the right or from the left, when they move from the right or left, marching one after another, and ſo reducing the lines of an army.

FINALE, the capital of the marquiſate of that name, in the dominions of Genoa, in Italy; it has a good harbour, defended by 4 forts and a ſtrong caſtle. In 1745, the Engliſh fleet threw ſeveral bombs into the town with little damage; taken by the king of Sardinia in 1746; 36 miles n. eaſt of Eneglia. Lat. 44. 30. n. long. 9. 12. eaſt.

FIRE-BALL, a compoſition of meal-powder, ſulphur, ſaltpetre, pitch, &c. about the ſize of a hand-grenade.

FIRE-MASTER, an officer who gives the directions and proportions of ingredients for each compoſition required in fire works.

FIRE-WORKERS, the youngeſt commiſſioned officers in a company of artillery.

FLANK, in general, that part of a work which defends another work, along the outſide of its parapet.

Flank, alſo the ſide of an army, battalion, company, &c. from the front to the rear.

Te

To flank, to attack and fire upon the flank of an enemy.

Flank, direct or *grafing,* that which is perpendicular to the oppofite face produced, and oblique, or *fifhant,* when it makes an acute angle with that face.

Flank, concave, that made in the area of a circle.

Flank of the baftion, that part between the face and curtain. The flank of one baftion ferves to defend the ditch before the curtain, and face of the oppofite baftion.

Flank, retired, that made behind the line, which joins the extremity of the face and the curtain towards the capital of the baftion.—M. Vauban makes his 5 toifes from that line; others, more or lefs, occafionally.

Flank, fecond. When the face of a baftion produced does not meet the curtain at its extremity, but in fome other point, this flank is called *the fecond flank.*

Flanks of a battalion, are the right and left of it.

Flanks of an army, the troops encamped on the right and left flanks of it.

F L Y I N G C A M P, a body of light horfe, or foot, who are always in motion, either to cover an army or garrifon, and to keep the enemy in continual alarm.

F O R G E, an engine carried with the artillery for the fmiths; as a travelling fmith's forge; a forge for hot balls, &c.

F O R L O R N - H O P E. See *Enfans Perdus.*

F O R M E R S, are of feveral forts, but chiefly for making cannon cartridges : they are round pieces of wood, fitted to the diameter of the bore of a gun, on which the paper, parchment, or cotton,

which is to make the cartridge, is to be rolled before it is fewed.

F O N T A R A B I A, or F U E N T A-R A B I A, a fmall genteel and well fortified town of Guipuzcoa, in Bifcay, properly in Spain, with a pretty good harbour and fortrefs, at the mouth of the Bidaffoa, here very broad, and the boundary between France and Spain. It lies 18 miles weft of Bayonne. In 1638, it held out a fiege againft the French; in 1718, they took it, but reftored it the following year. Lat. 43. 27. n. long. 1. 38. weft.

F O N T E N O Y, a town of Hainalt, in the Auftrian Low-countries, on the borders of Flanders, 3 miles fouth-eaft of Tournay, and 16 north-weft of Mons. This place is particularly remarkable for a battle on the 30th of April 1744, between 20000 of the Britifh allies, commanded by the Duke of Cumberland, and 120000 French, under the command of Marfhal Saxe.

At 4 in the morning, Prince Waldeck, with the Dutch, on the left wing, was ordered to attack Fontenoy, and Brigadier Ingoldfby to deftroy a mafked battery, while Earl Ligonier attacked the French, with the Britifh and Hanoverian infantry, covered by the cavalry under Sir James Campbell : but this brave general was carried off by a cannon-ball, and his poft left defective for fome time, till the Duke ordered up 7 cannon at the head of the foot guards, that foon filenced the enemy's guns. The army, obliged to pafs by 3 narrow defiles, took from 4 to 9 to form in order of battle as they advanced. Here the Duke's intrepid refolution and prefence of mind,

mind, though expofed to a moft terrible inceffant cannonade, pofted himfelf at the head of the Britifh troops.

The brave generals, Earls Ligonier, Albemarle, and Count Zaftraw, took poffeffion of the French trenches, and bore all before them. But the timid Dutch were repulfed, and remained idle fpectators, though fupported by 2 Britifh battalions. The Duke and Britifh troops were expofed, on his left flank, to an inceffant fhower of cannon; the battery to be attacked by General Ingoldfby poured on his right flank; and about 200 cannon, rending the very air, in his front. In this fituation, at the head of the few remains of 20000 to attack 120000 French, defended by 260 trenches, mafked batteries, &c. to avoid this infernal poft or circle of cannon, he retired from the trenches to rally the troops. By this movement, the ungenerous Dutch, as expected, made a fecond attack, or rather feint, and were eafily repulfed. The Britifh and Hanoverian troops drove the French from the trenches with great flaughter; and in all probability had obtained a moft glorious victory, if the two flank attacks had been carried on with the fame alacrity, conduct, and bravery; as Earl Ligonier, with his troops, had twice repulfed the French from their works. To redrefs the mifconduct of the two wings, the Duke at the head of Ligonier's (the fourth regiment) horfe, advanced, through the fevereft fire, to the right flank; which the French Irifh brigades attacked before he could come up, having poured down legions

on the right, fupported by their whole army.

Our moft intrepid, ever-undaunted young hero, after acting the part of the moft fage experienced general, deferted by his allies, his own troops greatly decreafed, was reduced to form a retreat about 3 at noon: but fuch difpofitions were made, that, Noaille's regiment being entirely broke, with the lofs of 32 officers, in making an attempt on our rear, the French declined the purfuit. The allies marched in order from the field, having pofted the highland regiment, fome battalions of foot, and feveral fquadrons of horfe, to fecure our retreat, which that night encamped under the cannon of Aeth.

The Britifh and Hanoverians were truly heroic, ftanding 10 hours and an half the moft furious cannonading. Lieutenant-general Sir James Campbell, and Major-general Ponfonby, were killed; the Earls of Albemarle and Ancram, Lord Cathcart, Major-general Howard, Brigadiers-general Churchill and Ingoldfby, wounded; feveral Hanoverians, and even two Brigadier-generals of the Dutch fpectators, with 7370 men, killed, wounded, and miffing. We had 81 cannon, 3 pounders, and 8 mortars, half of them with the Dutch.

The French had above 300 (chiefly large) ordnance, well plied. They had 40 general officers, and 20 colonels, killed or wounded, with 6000 men killed, and as many wounded.

The French had the advantages of a well-chofen fituation, and a numerous artillery; to this,

this, add the fcandalous behaviour of the Dutch, the enemy's
great fuperiority in numbers,
and pofterity will be amazed at
the glorious pufh the Englifh,
&c. made for victory.

A fine victory to boaft of!
120,000 French, covered and defended by all that art could add
to nature, trenches, woods, fixed
batteries, and redoubts, with
300 large ordnance, &c. againft
20,000 Englifh, and 12 cannon.
The Englifh pierced beyond
Fontenoy and the redoubt.

Such was the refolution of our
young hero, and his brave generals, with their handful of men, fo
equipped, and feconded, that the
brave Saxe, at the head of a
moving world, fent to the King
and Dauphin to fly, imagining
all loft, and frequently repeated
the fame requeft.

The battle feemed irretrievably loft; they even began to
fend off the train; fays Voltaire,
" They the Englifh, were mafters of the field of battle." Had
the timid Dutch in the leaft feconded, we had gained the moft
glorious victory upon record.

Saxe fent orders to evacuate
Antone, and fecure Cologne
bridge, to favour a retreat; nay,
fent a fecond and a third time,
defpairing of the victory. Voltaire faid, " the French had no
title to or expectation of it, a
great part of the day:" he took
every means to obtain a true
ftate of that day's action: a day
of immortal honour to the Duke
and the Britifh arms; who, from
the perfidy of their daftardly allies, were forced to yield the
laurels they had won with fo
much glory and flaughter, where
every Englifh foldier behaved
like a Cæfar.

FORT, a fmall fortification,
made in a pafs near a river, or
at fome diftance from a fortified
town, to guard the pafs, and
prevent an enemy's approach,
either by fea or by land, is of
different figures and fize.

Field Fort,
with a *Crown,*
is fo well de-
fcribed in this
figure, as to
require no-
thing farther.

FORTIFICATION, a name for
any work made to oppofe an
enemy, is put into fuch a pofture
of defence, that every one of its
parts defend, and is defended
by another.

Fortifications artificial, the
works raifed by an engineer, to
ftrengthen the natural fituation
of a place, by repairing and fupplying its defects.

Fortification natural, a place
ftrong by nature.

Fortification defenfive, regards
the precaution and induftry, by
which a weak party oppofes a
ftronger.

Fortification regular, confifts
in a place being regularly fortified, and defended by baftions.

Fortification irregular, is when
a town has fuch an irregular fituation, as renders it incapable
of being regularly fortified.

It is ufual in fortification to
make a diftinction between regular and irregular places. The
firft are thofe whofe fituation
will permit every part of the
work to be made according to
the rules of art, and in juft geometrical proportions. The fecond, where the ground is fo
irregular and ill difpofed, that
it will not admit of thofe geometrical proportions being given to

the

the different parts of the work?
Thofe irregular which come the
neareft to the regular fortifications, are the beft. Places
commanded by high grounds
are lefs ftrong than thofe that
are not, and cannot make a
long defence againft an enemy,
who has fkill to make ufe of the
advantage.

That place which has moft
ground inclofed with feweft baftions is the beft: thus the greateft baftions are the ftrongeft.

In fortifications the body of
the place is to be confidered, as
well as the out-works; upon
which you are to obferve that
a place, though ftrong by its
out-works, is worth little, and
cannot hold out a long fiege in
form, if the body of the place is
not likewife fortified as well as
the ground will admit of; let each
part of the place be fufficiently ftrong to refift the force
of the enemies cannon; and
every part of the wall feen
from top to bottom, at one or more
places of the town: this is what
is called flanking, and is not
to be out of mufket-fhot; for in
cafe of an attack, it is of great advantage to the fuftainers, to keep
as good a fire on it as poffible.

Let your ramparts be fo wide
as to afford you a good cannon-
proof parapet, a good banquet,
and room fufficient for your artillery.

FORTRESS, a term for all places
that are fortified by nature or
art.

FORT DU QUESNE, fituated
on the river Ohio, 250 miles
weft by north of Philadelphia.
On account of its fituation, it bids
fair to be the moft important place
in all North America. The Englifh troops, under the command

3

of General Forbes, compelled the
French to abandon this important place in 1758. Lat. 40. 28.
n. long. 80. weft.

FORT GEORGE, near Inver-
nefs in Scotland, upon the fea
fide, is a place of confiderable
ftrength, and remarkable for
having fine barracks.

FORT-LEWIS, an excellent
fortrefs of Alface in Germany, on
an ifland in the Rhine, confifting
of a long and regular quadrangle,
with 4 baftions and 4 half-moons,
was ceded to France by the trea-
ties of Ryfwick and Baden. Lat.
48. 51. long. 8. 12.

FORT-WILLIAM, in the
Highlands and county of Loch-
aber, at the mouth of a bay or
lough, on the Caledonian fea,
28 miles fouth-weft of Loughnefs,
40 from Invernefs, and 100 north
weft of Edinburgh. It was in
vain befieged by the rebels in
1745. The village of Maryburgh,
which lies near it, being previoufly deftroyed by the governor,
prevented the enemy taking
fhelter in it.

FOSSE, or Ditch, fhould be at
leaft 40 yards wide, and as deep
as poffible. The deep foffes, when
moderately wide, are preferable
to thofe which are wide and
fhallow; as they are not fo liable to be filled up with the
ruins of your breach, nor do
they give the enemy fo eafy an
efcalade or mounting; and the
foot of the wall is not fo readily difcovered, which obliges
the enemy to raife their batteries higher.

For citadels and forts the foffe
fhould be very deep, but may
be narrower; and if there be
water in them, they will the
better prevent your being furprized.

In

In great towns, the dry foſſe is beſt; you more eaſily defend yourſelf by making intrenchments, caſe-mates, coffers, and mines; and may diſpute it inch by inch; your ſallies may be quicker made, and your ſuccours leſs impeded.

Though the wet foſſes prevent eſcalading and ſurprize, and if they ſhould be filled up, it is only in one part, againſt which you provide a proper defence; yet they have great inconveniencies: they are unwholeſome, frozen in winter, render your ſallies difficult, your ſuccours doubtful, and your retreat dangerous; you cannot make new defences when the enemy is maſter of your counterſcarp. In a word, the foſſes full of water are leſs advantageous than thoſe totally dry; but the beſt are ſuch as have ſluices, to keep them wet or dry at pleaſure.

The little foſſes, or cuvets, which you make in the centre of the large one, ſhould be 12 or 15 feet deep, and as many broad.

FOUDAGE, *foucade*, or *foucaſſe*, a ſmall mine under a poſt which is in danger of falling into the enemy's hands, to blow it up.

FORNEAU, the place of a mine, where the powder is lodged, and only another name for the chamber of a mine.

FRAGA, anciently *Flavea Gallica*, an old town of Arragon in Spain on the Cinca, has a good garriſon, 58 miles eaſt of Saragoſſa. Lat. 41. 21. long. five. m.

FRAISE, a kind of ſtakes or paliſades, placed horizontally on the outward ſlope of a rampart of turf, to prevent the work being taken by ſurprize. When an army retrenches, they frequently fraiſe the parapets of their retrenchments in the parts moſt expoſed to an attack.

FRANCFORT UPON THE MAINE, an imperial and ſovereign city, on the borders of Heſſe and Franconia in Germany, on both ſides the river Maine; it is large, regularly fortified, and commodiouſly ſituated for trade. Lies 21 miles eaſt of Mentz, and 17 weſt of Hainalt. Lat. 50. 16. long. 7. 36.

FRAUENBERG, a few miles to the north of Budweis, a place of ſome ſtrength, and remarkable for a battle, or rather ſkirmiſh, near it on the 14th of May 1742, between the French under the Marſhals Broglio and Belliſle, and the Hungarian army commanded by Prince Lobkowitz. The Prince was then employed in the ſiege of Frauenberg, which he left on hearing the French were marching towards him, having firſt ſent his heavy cannon to Budweis. When the French were come up, and entered the camp which the Hungarians had quitted, the latter attacked them about 6 in the evening, and were every where ſucceſsful till night parted the 2 armies: but the Prince being jealous that the French deſigned to get between him and Budweis, to cut off his retreat,

marched

marched towards that place the same night to prevent them. On this account the French boasted of their having obtain'd a complete victory and killed a great number of the enemy, though the Hungarians say they did not lose above 200 men.

An end was soon put to this boasting, for Prince Charles and Prince Lobkowitz having joined their armies, and for several days vainly endeavoured to bring the French to a battle: at last, upon the 27th of May in the evening, Prince Charles was informed that Marshal Broglio had detached a body of 4 or 5000 men, most of them horse and dragoons, under the command of the Duke of Boufflers, to seize Lomnitz and some other posts in the neighbourhood of Budweiss. Upon this, his Highness, who was then with the united armies encamped at Weseli, decamped that very evening, and advanced towards the enemy. Next morning he marched with 4 battalions and 15 squadrons of Cuirassiers and Hussars to attack them, and found them drawn up in order of battle, advantageously posted, having their infantry and some field pieces in the centre. His Highness attacked them at the head of the Cuirassiers with such fury, that he soon put their infantry and part of their cavalry in disorder. At length the French carabineers, sustained by their dragoons, repulsed Prince Charles's cavalry; but these rallying and returning to the charge, the shock was so great, that not only the French carabineers and dragoons, but the whole corps was broke, and fled with precipitation, leaving behind them their cannon, ammunition, and the greatest part of their baggage. Several regiments of horse and Hussars, with large bodies of Croats, Waradins, &c. were immediately sent to pursue them; and when Marshal Broglio, who was encamped at Frauenburg, heard of what had passed, he decamped in such haste, that the military chest, with a great part of the baggage, were left in the camp, and became a prey to the Hungarian army.

FREDERICA, a town of Georgia in North America, on the island of St. Simon, at the mouth of Alatamaha, built and fortified by General Oglethorpe. In 1742, the Spaniards having invaded the island, took Fort St. Simon; but upon marching to besiege Frederica, were repulsed by the said general, and obliged to quit the attempt. This island is about 13 miles in length, and 3 or 4 in breadth, 20 leagues n. of St. Augustine. The fort taken by the Spaniards, and again abandoned, is 7 miles from the town. Besides this, there are several other small islands in the mouth of the river, which have been fortified by the English. Lat. 31. 12. n. long. 81. 42. west.

FRIBURG, a city of Suabia, and the capital of Brisgau in Germany, 30 miles s. of Strasburg and the same n. of Brasil, subject to Austria, taken by the French in 1677, but restored by the peace of Ryswic in 1697; also taken again by them, but restored by the peace of Baden in 1714. Lat. 48. 21. long. 7. 46.

FRONTIGNIAC, a fort of Canada, in N. America, on the river St. Laurence, taken by the English

Englifh forces, under the command of Colonel Bradftreet, from the French in 1758. Lat. 43. 18. long. 77. 18.

Fuse, a piece of hollowed wood, filled with meal-powder, and drove into grenades, or fhells to fire them.

GABION, a cylinder bafket, open at both ends, about 3 feet wide, and as much in height. They ferve in fieges to carry on the approaches under  cover, when they come pretty near the fortification.

Gabion, ſtuffed, made in the fame manner as the former, filled with all forts of branches and fmall wood, 5 or 6 feet long. They ferve to roll before the workmen in the trenches, to cover them in front againſt muſquet-ſhot.

GAETA, a well fortified city of Lavora, in Naples, fituate on a mountain, furrounded by the fea, except a narrow neck of land which joins it to the continent. It was the only town that held out any time againſt the Auſtrians in 1707, but taken at laſt by ſtorm, and its two caſtles furrendered at difcretion. It alfo made a good defence in 1734, when the Spaniards recovered Naples from the Auſtrians. In one of thefe caſtles is the unburied body of the famous Charles of Bourbon. Lat. 41. 32. long. 14. 36.

GALLERY, the paſſage made under ground, leading to the mines, from 4 and a half to 5

feet high, and about 4 broad. The earth above it is fupported by wooden frames, with boards over them.

Gallery of a mine, the fame as a branch of a mine, is a paſſage under ground, of 3 or 4 feet wide, under the works, where a mine or counter-mine is carried on. Both befieged and befiegers carry branches under ground, in fearch of each other's mines, which oft meet and deſtroy both.

GAZONS, triangular fods, or pieces of freſh earth, covered with grafs, about a foot long, and half a foot broad, to line the parapet: if the earth be fat and full of herbs, it is the better; that being mixed, and beat with the reſt of the earth of the rampart, they may eaſily fettle together, and incorporate in a mafs with the reſt of the rampart.

The firſt bed of gazons is fixed with pegs of wood; the fecond bed binds the former, and fo on till the rampart is finiſhed. If no fods can be had with herbage on them, they generally fow fome between each layer to bind them together.

GENERAL, *Maſter-general of the ordnance*, an employment of the greateſt truſt: he has the management of all the ordnance, and fhould know, and provide, whatever can be ferviceable or ufeful in the artillery; and fill the vacancies with fuch only as are equal to the truſt.

General, alfo a beat of the drum. See *Drum*.

GENEVA, a city of Savoy, and the capital of the territory of that name, fituate near the borders of France and Switzerland, on the Rhone, at the weſt

extre-

extremity of the Leman, or Geneva lake; 48 miles n. of Chamberry, and 60 weſt of Lyons, is well fortified, and about 2 miles in circuit. Lat. 46. 31. long. 6. 12.

GENOA, the capital of the republic of that name, in Riviera di Levante, in Italy, ſituate on the ſea. On the land ſide ſurrounded with 2 walls, the outermoſt of which reaches beyond the mountain, beginning at the light-houſe on the ſhore, and ending at the mouth of the Biſagno; the whole circuit being about 10 Italian mile; but this ſerves only to keep off the incurſions of the banditti, it having but here and there only a few baſtions. The number of cannon mounted on all the out-works is computed at 500. The harbour is large and deep, but lies expoſed to the ſouth and weſt wind, though it has a mole on the right and left ſide of its entrance, for the ſecurity of their gallies and ſmall veſſels. Their land forces are generally about 4 or 5000, which may be increaſed to 20000.

The celebrated Andrew Doria, one of the moſt eminent admirals and generals of his time, delivered his country from the oppreſſion of the French and Spaniards, and ſettled their preſent form of government in 1528. In 1713. the Emperor. Charles the VI. granted the marquiſate of Final to the republic of Genoa, for a large ſum; and in 1743, the queen of Hungary, by the treaty of Worms, making over to the king of Sardinia, all the right ſhe had to Final; upon his demanding it, the republic entered into an alliance with France, Spain, and

Naples, and, in 1745, declared war againſt Sardinia; but, being hard preſſed by Great Britain and the queen of Hungary, in 1746, the king of Sardinia took the whole Riviera de Ponente; the Engliſh fleet bombarded ſeveral places belonging to the republic, and the Imperialiſts made themſelves maſters of the city of Genoa. But by the treaty of Aix-la-Chapelle, in 1748, its peace was reſtored. Lat. 44. 25. long. 8. 41.

GEORGE. (St.) the capital of the Engliſh ſettlements on the Coromandel coaſt, and hither province of India in Aſia, lying 4 miles n. of the city of St. Thomas, is divided into the White and Black town. The fort, and the White town contiguous to it, inhabited only by Engliſh, are not above half a mile in circuit, and ſurrounded with a ſtone wall; the Outer or Black town, called Madrates, has been lately ſurrounded by a ſtone wall and baſtions cannon proof, and is about a mile and a half in circuit; the whole almoſt encompaſed by a river and the ſea. Its garriſon conſiſts of between 3 and 400 men, beſides blacks. Lat. 13. 15. long. 80. 50.

GHENT, the capital city of Flanders, in the Auſtrian Low-countries, lying on 4 rivers, is a large and well fortified city, but not eaſily defended, on account of its vaſt circumference, which is about 12 Engliſh miles. This was the winter-quarters of a great part of the Engliſh forces. Taken by the French in 1678, but reſtored by the treaty of Nimeguen. On the death of Charles II. king of Spain, they poſſeſſed them-

themselves of it, with the rest of the towns in Flanders; but it surrendered to the Allies after the battle of Ramillies in 1706. In 1708, the French retook it by surprize and treachery, and threw an army into the place to defend it; but the confederates, having taken the castle of Lisle, invested Ghent in the latter end of the same year, when the town surrendered soon after the trenches were opened, though the French had a garrison of 20000 men. The French, on the morning of the 30th of June 1745, surprized and took the town; and in 5 days after the citadel surrendered. 35 miles n. west of Brussels. Lat. 51. 12. long. 3. 36.

GIBRALTAR, a strong fortified town and garrison, in Andalusia, Spain, on the streight between the Atlantic and Mediterranean. On account of its strength by nature and art, esteemed the key of Spain; is situated on a rock, in a peninsula, and accessible only on the land side, by a narrow passage between the rock and the bay; across the widest part, the Spaniards have fortified lines, which they keep constantly garrisoned. In 1704, a confederate fleet of the English and Dutch, commanded by Sir George Rooke, after bombarding the town 2 days, obliged the Marquis de Salinas to surrender. The Spaniards attempted to recover it the same year, when it stood out a very remarkable siege, under the Prince of Hesse Darmstadt; 4 or 500 of the enemy creeping up the rock, which covers the back of the town, were driven down headlong next morning: neither siege nor negotiations availing the Spaniards, they

ceded it to the English by the peace of Utrecht in 1713. They made another attempt in 1727, but were obliged to raise the siege, after laying before it several months. At this time they endeavoured to blow up the rock, but it was found impracticable, so that it remains in the hands of the English, and is now so strong as to render a siege only an amusement to the garrison. I apprehend it never can be taken but by bribery or famine. It lies 40 miles south-west of Cadiz, and 80 south of Seville. Lat. 36. 21. n. long. 6. 15. west.

GIN, or *Crab*, an engine for mounting guns on their carriages.

GLACIS, that part of a fortification beyond the covert-way, to which it serves as a parapet, and terminates towards the field in an easy slope.

GLATZ, 36 miles n. east of Koningratz, a strong town, with a good castle, on the river Niefs. Laudohn took one part of the place by storm, and the other by capitulation in 1760, though defended by 2000 men, and 100 brass cannon; which, perhaps, was not the greatest loss. The important situation of the place, and the great magazines it contained, were irretrievable, and Silesia thus opened to the Austrians.

GORGE, that part of a work next the body of the place, where there is no rampart or parapet.

Gorge of a bastion, the interval between the extremity of one flank and that of the next.

GRENADE, an iron orbicular case of about 3 inches diameter, filled with powder, to be thrown by the grenadiers amongst the enemy in an attack.

GROUND. *To give ground*, to retire or quit a poft, when attacked by an enemy : *to get* or *gain ground*, is to have the advantage of the enemy, and to force them from a poft.

GUADELOUPE, the largeft of all the Caribbee iflands, fituate on the Atlantic ocean, 85 miles north of Martinico, 22 leagues in length and 11 in breadth. The French, fenfible of its importance, fortified it with feveral forts and redoubts, which refifted the attack made on it by Admiral Bembow in 1702, but could not withftand the valour of the Britifh forces under General Barrington and Commodore Moore in 1759, who after feverely cannonading Baffeterre, the metropolis of the ifland, for nine hours, reduced it. Lat. 16. 36. long. 61. 22.

GUARD, duty or fervice, which fhould be performed with the utmoft vigilance, to prevent the efforts and furprizes of an enemy.

Guards, denotes in general, the horfe and foot guards.

Guards in the lines, are generally commanded by a captain; the *main-guard*, by the eldeft fubaltern that mounts; the *poft-guards* and *magazine-guards*, by fubalterns, who draw lots for their guards on the parade, the youngeft fubaltern excepted, who always mounts guard under the command of a captain.

Guards ordinary, fuch as are fixed during the campaign, and relieved daily. The *grand-guards* of the cavalry, the *ftand-dard* and *quarter guards*, *picquet-guards* of each regiment, *guards* for the general-officers, train of artillery, bread-waggons, quarter mafter general, majors of brigade, judge advocate, and provoft marfhal, are alfo called *guards ordinary*.

Advanced guard, the party of either horfe or foot, which marches 4 or 500 yards before the body, to give notice of any danger.

Advanced guard, a fmall body of horfe, under a ferjeant or corporal, pofted before the *grand guard* of the camp

Rear-guard, that part of the army which brings up the rear.

Grand-guard, compofed of 2, 3, or 4 fquadrons of cavalry, commanded by a field-officer, and pofted before the camp, on the right and left wings, towards the enemy, for its fecurity.

Picquet guard, a certain number of horfe and foot, which are to keep in readinefs, in cafe of an alarm. The cavalry keep their horfes faddled, and themfelves booted, that they may mount in a minute. The foot draw up at the head of the battalion when the retreat beats, but are returned to their tents, where they hold in readinefs, upon the fhorteft notice.

Forage guard, a detachment fent out to fecure the foragers, and pofted at all places, where the enemy's party can come to difturb the foragers, alfo called the *covering party*, confifts fometimes of foot, and often of both.

Corps-de garde, folders intrufted with the guard of a poft, under the command of one or more officers.

Artillery guard, a detachment from the army, to fecure the artillery. Their corps-de-garde is in the front, and their fentries round the park. Upon a march they go in the front and rear of the artillery.

GUAS-

GUASTALLA, a small fortified town in a dukedom of that name in Italy, situate on the river Croftoblo, 20 miles south of the city of Mantua, famous for a battle between the Imperialists and Spaniards, in 1734, when the former were defeated. It was ceded to Don Philip, Duke of Parma, by the treaty of Aix-la-Chapelle, in 1748. Lat. 45. 12. n. long. 11. 15. east.

GUERRITTE, a fort, o small tower of stone or wood, on the point of a bastion, or  on the angles of the shoulder, to hold a sentry.

GUIDON, an officer in the horse-guards, who ranks as major.

GUIDES. *Captain of the Guides,* an officer appointed for providing guides for the army, of which he should have always a sufficient number with him, who know the country, to send out as occasion requires; to guide the army on a march, conduct convoys, parties, baggage, artillery, and detachment. To furnish himself with these, he should send a party of horse to adjacent villages, castles, or forts, there demand boors, bring them to his quarters, and set a guard over them, lest they escape before the army comes to another ground where he in like manner can obtain fresh guides. He should understand several languages, especially that of the country in which the army is.

GUN. The length is distinguished by three parts; the first reinforce, the second reinforce, and the chace; the first reinforce is two sevenths, and the second one-seventh and half a diameter of the shot: the inside hollow, wherein the powder and shot are lodged. The bore, and the diameter of the bore, is called *the diameter of the caliber:* the part between the hind end and the bore, *the breech;* and the fore part of the bore, *the mouth.* The cascable is the part terminated by the hind part of the breech, and the extremity of the button. The trunnions are the cylindric parts of metal which project on both sides of the gun, and rest in the grooves made in the side-pieces of a carriage. The mouldings are those behind the breech, and reckoned to belong to the cascable, the first and second reinforce rings, ogees, astragals, and fillets. Those of the first reinforce are a ring ogee joining to it, and an astragal with fillets; the part of the gun between the ogee and astragal is called *the vent field,* because the vent is placed there; the ogee of the second, *a ring and ogee;* and those of the chace, *a ring ogee;* the astragal with fillets, *the muzzle astragal;* the swelling of the muzzle, *an ogee,* or *cimaise and two fillets:* the part between the ogee and chace astragal, *the chace girdle;* and the part from the muzzle, astragal, and the mouth, *the muzzle.* Formerly guns were distinguished by the names of sakers, culvrins, cannon, demi cannon, &c. at present their names are taken from the weight of their shot; as, for example, a twelve or twenty-four pounder carries a ball of twelve or twenty-four pounds.

Guns are made of brafs or caft iron; the brafs is a mixture of copper and tin; fometimes yellow brafs is added, but it is reckoned to make the metal brittle. The moft common proportion is to 100 pounds of copper, 12 pounds of tin: copper requires a red heat to melt, and tin melts in a common fire; when a gun is much heated by firing, the tin melts or foftens fo much that the copper alone fupports the force of explofion, whereby they generally bend at the muzzle, and the vent widens fo much as to render the gun ufelefs. If fuch a compofition of metal could be found that required an equal degree of heat to melt, it would anfwer the intent; but as no fuch thing has been hitherto difcovered, I look upon good iron to make better and more durable guns than any other compofition whatever, as experiments and practice have fhewn. All our brafs battering guns made ufe of this laft war were too foon rendered unferviceable.

The necefiary tools for loading and firing guns are rammers, fponges, ladles, worms, handfpikes, wedges, or fcrews. The rammer is a cylinder of wood, whofe diameter and axis is equal to that of the fhot, and ferves to ram home the wads put upon the powder and fhot; the fponge is the fame, only covered with lamb-fkin, and ferves to clean the gun when fired: the rammer and fponge are fixed to the fame handle. The ladle ferves to load the gun with loofe powder; the worm, to draw out the wads

when a gun is to be unloaded; the hand-fpikes, to move and lay the guns; and the coins, or wedges, to lay under the breech of the gun, or to raife or deprefs it. In field-pieces, a fcrew is ufed inftead of coins, by which the gun is kept to the fame elevation. The tools necefiary to prove guns, befides thofe mentioned for loading, are, a priming-iron, a fearcher with a reliever, and a fearcher with one point. The firft fearcher is an iron, hollow at one end to receive a wooden handle; and having on the other, from four to eight flat fprings of about fix inches long, pointed and turned outwards at the ends. The reliever is an iron flat ring, with a wooden handle at right angles to it. When a gun is to be fearched after it has been fired, this fearcher is introduced, and turned every way from one end to the other; and if there is any hole, the point of one or the other fpring gets into it, and remains till the reliever, pafling round the handle of the fearcher, prefies the fprings together and relieves it; if any of the points catch in the vent, the priming-iron is introduced to relieve it. When there is any hole or roughnefs in the gun, the diftance from the mouth is marked on the outfide with chalk. The other fearcher has alfo a wooden handle and a point at the fore end of about an inch long: at right angles to the length about this point is fome wax mixed with tallow, and when introduced into the hole or cavity, is prefied in, and drawn forwards and backwards; then the impreffion upon the wax gives the depth, and the length is known by the motion

motion of the fearcher: if the hole is a quarter of an inch deep, and downwards, the gun is rejected.

A gun, when pointed to hit the mark, will carry the ball about 700 yards: the culverin about the fame diftance; but the baftard lefs. The ordinary force of a gun, fired at 200 yards from the mark, drives the ball into the folid earth about 10 or 12 feet; and into fand, or loofe earth, from 22 to 24 feet.

HAGENAU, a fmall fortified town of Alface, in a territory of that name in Germany, on the Motter, 16 miles n. of Strafburg, is defended by a wall and ditch only, was frequently taken and retaken in the wars between the Imperialifts and French, in the laft century and beginning of this. There is alfo a foreft bearing this name, 5 German miles long, and 4 broad, belonging partly to the French king and partly to this town. Lat. 48. 46. n. long. 7. 48. eaft.

HAIR-CLOTHS, cover powder in waggons, batteries, fixed bombs, hand grenades, &c.

HALF-MOON, properly an outwork, compofed of 2 faces, making a faliant angle, whofe gorge is turned like a crefcent, or forming an arch of a circle. The ravelins built before the curtains are now called Halfmoons; the name of ravelin being almoft laid afide by the foldier.

HANAU, the metropolis of a county of that name, well fortified, in the circle of the Upper Rhine, on the rivers Kintz and Main, 11 miles eaft of Franckfort.

HAND-BARROW, made of light wood, and of great ufe in fortification, for carrying earth from one place to another; or in a fiege, for carrying bombs or cannon-balls along the trenches, &c.

HANOVER, a city of Lower Saxony, the capital of the electorate of that name, in Germany, on the Leina, and furrounded by a wall and other works, of no confiderable ftrength. The Elector, like all the German Princes and States, is abfolute in his own territories, and ftiles himfelf Arch-treafurer of the empire. He can raife 60000 men in his German dominions, which, befides Hanover, confifts of Lunenburg and Zel, Bremen, Verden, and Lawenberg, 40 miles weft of Brunfwic, in lat. 52. 29. n. lon. 51. eaft. The French had poffeffed themfelves of this electorate and its capital, with fome of the neighbouring territories, in 1757, but by the intrepidity of the inhabitants, under the command of the Prince of Brunfwic, they were entirely driven out; and the King of Pruffia defeated, broke, and took moft of their army prifoners, in the engagement at Rofbach.

HAVANNAH, built by Diego de Velafquez, who conquered the ifland of Cuba, and formed a little town here in 1511, named originally the Port of Carenas, but afterwards, when the city by its increafe of wealth grew confiderable, it was called San Chriftopher of the Havannah. In 1536 it was fo inconfiderable, that, being taken by a French pirate, he accepted of fo fmall a fum as 700 pieces of eight for its ranfom. Some time after it was taken by the Englifh, and a second

second time by the French; nor was it, till the reign of Philip II. of Spain, that the importance of it was known, or care taken to strengthen it: what was then done, proved insufficient, and most of the fortifications were in very bad condition; but since the accession of the house of Bourbon to the throne of Spain, many more works have been erected. The city of Havannah lies in lat. 23. 12. n. long. 82. 13. west from London, in the most fruitful part of the island, on the west side of the harbour. The port is the best in the West Indies, and so capacious, that the largest fleet of ships may ride in it commodiously; there being generally six fathom of water in the bay. At the entrance of the channel, which is narrow, and difficult of access to an enemy, being well flanked by forts and platforms of guns, there are 2 strong castles, which were supposed to be capable of defending the place against any number of ships. The chief of these is Ell Morro, on the east side of the channel, and is a kind of triangle, fortified with bastions, whereon are mounted now upwards of 100 cannon. A little to the south of this is a battery, called the Twelve Apostles, almost level with the water, of 36 pounders. On the other side of the channel stands a strong fort called the Puntal, a regular square, with bastions, mounted with cannon. The third is stiled *the forts*, which is a small, but strong work, on the west side, towards the end of the narrow channel, with 4 bastions and a platform, mounted with 38 heavy cannon.

The city is walled round, and fortified with bastions on the land side; beside which there are 2 forts on the sea coast, to prevent an enemy from landing; one a league from the entrance of the harbour, on the east side, called the Cojimar; the other on the west, called the Fort of Chorea, of about 12 guns each.

But, however secure this port may appear to ships within, it is of no great security to those without, the entrance being too narrow to give quick admittance to a fleet. The galleons have been often insulted, and some taken in sight of this port, without being able to get in, or receive any succour from its castles; as was the case of the Flota, in its return from La Vera Cruz, in 1629, mentioned by Gage, &c At Cape Saint Antonio, the most western point of Cuba, they met with the famous Dutchman, Pie de Pelo, as much dreaded by them as Sir Francis Drake, who waited there for them; after he had given them a broadside or 2 the Admiral Don Juan de Guzman y Torres called a council of war, wherein it was resolved to fly from the enemy, as the surest way to save the king's treasure, which amounted to some millions, and to make directly for the bay of Matanzes, imagining that the Dutch would not venture in after them. The misfortune however was, that they could not get in far enough, the bay being very much too shallow for their heavy great bellied galleons; this obliged them to run their ships aground, after which the rich endeavoured to escape to land with what wealth they could in cabinets and bags: but the Dutch coming

coming suddenly upon them, retarded their flight by the cannon from their ships; so that except a few cabinets that were secreted, the rest of the treasure became the Hollanders. Two friars, who had fleeced their sheep of 30000 ducats, were now fleeced themselves. Thus lightened of their treasure, the fleet proceeded to Spain, where the Admiral was imprisoned, lost his senses for a time, and on recovery was beheaded.

The first attempt made upon this city, after the Spaniards settled here, was in 1536, by a French pirate, who took the place, which then consisted only of wooden houses thatched, and made the Spaniards redeem it from fire, by 700 ducats, as before-mentioned. It happened, that 3 ships arriving from New Spain, the day after he set sail with the ransom, unloaded their goods with expedition, and pursued the pirate; but the commanders behaved so cowardly, that he took them all 3, though one was an admiral's ship; which so encouraged the pirate, that he returned to the Havannah, and made the inhabitants pay him 700 ducats more. After this the Spaniards built their houses of stone, and a fort at the mouth of the harbour; but the city being still open on the land-side, some English cruizers landed not far from the town, and having entered it before day-break, the Spaniards fled into the woods, and left the place to be plundered. During the war between Henry II. of France, and the Emperor Charles V. a French ship with 90 men, after having plun-

dered St. Jago, came there in the night; but to their disappointment found all the houses empty, they having been so often plundered, that the Spaniards had removed their goods to houses in the country. While they were searching, 2 persons came to them, pretending to agree for ransom, but in reality to observe their number. The French demanding 6000 ducats, the spies pretended their effects would not amount to the sum, and therefore that they would return to consult their countrymen. A consultation was accordingly held, when the majority despising the enemy's number, were for disputing it by the sword; and marching secretly with 150 men, they surprized the enemy at midnight; but the French, upon firing an alarm gun, immediately recovered their arms, put them to flight, and being enraged at this design of the Spaniards, set fire to the town, after having daubed the doors and windows, &c. with pitch and tar, which soon consumed it to ashes. A Spaniard desiring that they would spare the churches, erected for the worship of God, the French answered. That people who had no faith, had no occasion for churches. They then pulled down the walls, and entirely demolished the fort. After this, the town was rebuilt, and Philip II. appointed Juan de Texeda his camp-master, and Baptista Antonelli, a celebrated architect, to fortify the place, and put it in a posture of the strongest defence. Yet in 1762, it was taken under the command of the Earl of Albemarle, and

Sir

Sir George Pocock, the loss of which gave such a blow to the interest of Spain, as was inconceivable even to themselves.

N. B. The Cavanas from Cojimar are now well fortified by strong forts.

HAVRE-DE-GRACE, a strong sea-port town, the capital of a government of that name, in France, situated at the mouth of the Sein, on the English Channel, has an excellent harbour, lying between the town, and a small, but regular citadel. In 1562, it was surprized by the Huguenots and delivered up to the English, but recovered the following year; 45 miles west of Rouen. Lat. 49. 30. n. long. 17 minutes east. See Plan 11.

HEAD *of a work*, the front of it next the enemy.

Head of a double tenaille, the saliant angle in the middle, and the 2 other sides which form the re-entering angle.

Head-piece, armour for the head, an helmet, such as the light dragoons wear.

Head of a camp, the ground before which the army is drawn out.

HEIDELBERG, a city with a strong castle, betrayed to the French in 1693, who burnt it, 22 miles on the Nechar, south-east of Worms.

HELENA (ST.) a small island, subject to the East-India company of England, situate in the Atlantic Ocean, consists of one steep and lofty rock, resembling a castle in the sea, accessible only in one place, defended by a platform of 40 guns, beyond which is a fort where the governor resides; and near it a pretty little town. This island is 27 miles in circuit, and the rock has only a foot of vegetable.

HENDECAGON, a figure having 11 sides, and as many angles.

HEPTAGON, a figure, capable of being fortified with several regular bastions.

HERISON, a barrier of one strong beam, or plank of wood, stuck full of iron spikes; supported in the middle, and turning upon a pivot or axis.

HERSE, or *Port-cullice*, made of strong pieces of wood, jointed cross-ways, like a lattice, or harrow. Before it can be broke open, the besieged have time to rally. A herse is also an engine, like a harrow, stuck with iron spikes; and used in the place of a cheveaux-de-frise, to throw in the ways where horse or foot are to pass.

HAXAGON, a figure of 6 sides, capable of being fortified with 6 bastions.

HIDES, *tanned*, are always carried along with an army, especially in the fire-workers stores, to protect powder or bombs from rain; they are also useful upon batteries, or in laboratories.

HISPANIOLA, an island of America, in the Atlantic Ocean, lying between 18 and 20 degrees n. lat. and between 67 and 74 degrees w. long. about 476 miles in length from east to west, and 124 in breadth from north to south: it lies about 46 miles east of Cuba. Is often called St. Domingo from its capital of that name. In 1586, Sir Francis Drake took St. Domingo; but this and several other places were quitted in the reign of Queen Elizabeth, it being judged impolitic to keep them. Cromwell, however, thought otherwise; for

he

he sent his generals, Penn and Venables, with the greatest force the English ever had in these seas, to possess St. Domingo ; of which being disappointed, they subdued Jamaica in 1654.

Hobits, small mortars, of about 6, 7, or 8 inches diameter, resembling a mortar in every thing but their carriage, which is made in the form of that belonging to a gun, only shorter : they march with the guns, and are good for annoying an enemy at a distance, with small bombs, or in keeping a pass, being loaded with cartouches.

Horizontal, a superficies parallel with the horizon.

Horizontal Range, the level range of a piece of ordnance, being the line which it describes parallel to the horizon.

Horizontal Superficies, the plain field, which lies upon a level, without sinking or raising.

Honey-combs, flaws and defects in the charged cylinder of a cannon : a fault in casting the piece.

Horn-beam, a wood much used for making the fuses of shells.

Horn-work, is composed of a front and two branches. The front is made into two half bastions and a curtain : this work is of the nature of a crown work, only smaller, and serves for the same purpose.

Howitz, a mortar, mounted upon a field carriage, like a gun. The difference between a mortar and howitz is, that the trunnions are at the end of the first, but in the middle of the last.

Hull, or *Kingston upon Hull,* a large and populous borough of the east riding of Yorkshire, with an harbour situate at the mouth of the Humber; is naturally strong, as the neighbouring country can be overflowed ; and has a garrison and some old fortifications; 36 miles from York, and 169 from London. Near this town the river Hull discharges itself into the Humber.

Hurdles, or *clays,* made of branches or twigs closely interwoven, about 5 or 6 feet long, and 3 or 3½ broad. Their use is to cover traverses, lodgments, caponeers, coffers, &c. and are covered over with earth, to secure them from the enemy's artificial fire-works, or stones which might be thrown upon them; they are also frequently used to cover marshy ground, or pass a fosse.

Hussars, Hungarian light horse, and such troopers as are now common among other European nations, lately introduced in the English army under the title of Light Dragoons.

Huy, a town of strength, with a castle, each fortified in the modern way, stands 12 miles north-east of Namur, upon the river Maese. The French invested in 1662 with 18,000 men, but the garrison made such a brave defence that they were
obliged

obliged to retire. In 1693, it was again befieged by the Duke of Luxemburg and Count Harcourt: after two days attack, the garrifon mutinied againft the governor, and obliged him to furrender it. In 1664, the Confederates befieged it, when the French immediately furrendered the town, on condition that the garrifon fhould retire into the caftle, and neither fire upon the town nor the town upon them ; but, on fome frefh difputes arifing between them, the attacks were carried on againft the caftle with fo much fury, that the governor in 18 days beat a parley, and capitulated on honourable terms. The French put a garrifon into Huy; but in Auguft 1703, the Duke of Marlborough came before it, and took both town and citadel in 9 days, making the garrifon of 900 hundred men prifoners of war. The French befieged it again in May 1705, and in 2 days the town furrendered upon honourable conditions. The caftle held out a week longer, but was then taken by affault, and the garrifon made prifoners. 9th July, the fame year, the Allies befieged it, and having taken Fort Picard and the Red Fort by ftorm, the garrifon of the caftle, being 600 men, furrendered prifoners at difcretion. By the treaty of Utrecht it was agreed, that it fhould be garrifoned by the Dutch; but in 1718, the out-works were demolifhed, and it was given up to the Elector of Cologne.

JACK, an engine much ufed about guns or mortars, and always carried with the artillery, for raifing the carriages, &c.

JAMAICA, an ifland of America in the Atlantic ocean, fituated between 27 and 18 degrees, 27 minutes n. lat. and between 76 and 79 w. lon. The ifland is about 140 miles in length, from eaft to weft, and 60 in breadth from north to fouth. Columbus firft difcovered this ifland in 1493, and the Spaniards continued in poffeffion of it above 150 years, during which time they deftroyed the greateft part of the natives. The Englifh, under Penn and Venables, made themfelves mafters of it in 1656, with very little oppofition, after they had failed in the attempt on Hifpaniola. It is now well fortified.

JASSY, the capital of the Lower Moldau, in European Turky, a large ftrong town fituated on the river Pruth, 128 miles fouth-eaft of Homenec, was taken by the Ruffians in 1711 and 1739; and greatly damaged by a fire in 1753. Lat. 47. 22. long. 28. 56.

IGLAW, on the river Igla, near the mountains which feparate Moravia from Pohemia, about 40 miles weft of Brin, 60 fouth-weft of Olmutz, and much the fame diftance fouth-eaft of Prague, is a large, well-built, ftrong town, and ftands in the chief road between Bohemia and Hungary.

IMOLA, antiently Forum Cornelli, a fine city of Romagna in the ecclefiaftical ftate in Italy, furrounded with walls, towers, and ditches; has alfo an old ftrong caftle, and lies 19 miles eaft of Bologna, in lat. 44. 38. long. 12. 21.

INDENTED-LINE, a line running out and in, like the teeth of a faw, forming feveral angles, fo that one fide defends another. They are ufed on the banks of rivers, where they enter the town.

INDE-

INDEPENDENT-TROOP, or *company*, is a troop not incorporated into any regiment.

INGOLSTADT, a ftrong confiderable city, on the north of the Danube; it furrendered to the Emperor in 1704, and has been taken and retaken feveral times. Lat. 46. 6. long. 11. 45.

INVESTING *a place*, the firft operation of a fiege, is to furround it with troops, fo as to prevent any thing entering into, or being carried out of it.

INSULT, a work is faid to be infulted when it is attacked fuddenly and openly.

INTERIOR *fide of a fortification*, is the imaginary line drawn from the centre of one baftion to that of the next ; or, rather, the curtain produced to the centre of the baftions.

INTRENCHED, an army is faid to be intrenched, when they have raifed works before, to fortify a poft againft the enemy. A poft is intrenched, when it is covered with a foffe and parapets.

JOHN (ST.) an ifland in the bay of St. Lawrence, in North America, having Nova Scotia on the fouth and weft, and Cape Breton on the eaft, taken by the Englifh from the French, July 27th, 1758.

JOINT-BOLTS, iron bolts which fix one end of a cap fquare to the carriage.

ISABELLA (FORT) a fortrefs in the Auftrian Netherlands, on the weft fide of the Scheld, and oppofite to Antwerp, rebuilt by the French in 1701, contrary to the peace of Munfter: attempted in vain by General Cohorn in 1702.

ISLAND OF BRICHAT (BRITANY) in 1408, the Earl of Kent attacked the town of that name, in which the privateers had taken fhelter ; he took it by ftorm, and put them all to the fword; but in this action he received a mortal wound.

ISLAND OF JERSEY, in the Englifh channel, 18 miles weft of Normandy in France, and 84 miles f. of Portland in Dorfetfhire, fubject to Great Britain, has a good harbour, and a caftle to defend it. It is well fituated for trade, and for annoying the French with privateers in time of war. Lat. 49. 7. n. long. 2. 26. north-weft.

In 1549-50, the French, tho' there was no war, attacked the iflands of Jerfey and Guernfey, which they invaded with a ftrong fquadron of men of war, and 2000 land forces. The Englifh court having notice of this attempt, and knowing thofe iflands to be but indifferently provided, fent thither a fmall fquadron, under the command of Commodore Winter, with 800 men, as a reinforcement, on board a few tranfports. At his arrival, he found the ports blocked up, and himfelf under the neceffity either of defifting from his enterprize, or attacking the French ; he therefore, notwithftanding their fuperiority, like a brave man chofe the latter ; and executed his defign with fuch courage and conduct, that having killed near 1000, he obliged the enemy to embark the reft on board fome light veffels, and abandon their fhips of force ; all of which he caufed to be fet on fire.

KALISH, a large town furrounded by moraffes, and fortified with walls and towers, fituated on the Pofna, in a diftrict of the fame name in Great Poland.

Poland. Taken by the Swedes in 1655: in 1706 the Swedish troops were defeated by the Confederates under the command of King Augustus II. and Maderfeld their General was taken prisoner. 18 miles west of Warsaw, in lat. 52. 36. long. 17. 56.

KAMINEC, the capital of Podolia in Little Poland, defended by a strong castle on a rock, under which runs the river Semetricz; was besieged in vain by the Cossacs in 1651, but in 1672 the Turks took the town, which was restored by the peace of Carlowitz in 1699. It lies on the borders of Moldavia 24 miles n. of Choczin, and 130 south-east of Limburg, in lat. 47. 51. n. long. 26. 42. east.

KARSTEIN, near Beraun in Bohemia, is a strong town, with a good castle.

KEXHOLM, the capital of a province of that name in Finland, full of lakes, &c. yielded by Russia to Sweden in 1646; but reconquered by Peter I. is situated on the Lake Ladoga; 84 miles n. of Petersburg.

KEYS, *forelock*, serve to pass through the lower ends of bolts to fasten them.

Keys, with chains and staples, fixed on the side pieces of a carriage, or mortar-beds, fasten the cap-squares, by passing through the eyes of the eye-bolts.

Keys, spring, serve for the same purposes as the former; but, instead of being a single piece, they are of 2, like 2 springs laid one over another. When they are put into the eye-bolts they are pinched together at the ends; and when in, open again, so as not to be shaken out by the motion of the carriages. They are also used in travelling carriages.

KIOF, or KIOW, the capital of the Russian Ukrain, in the circle of that name, is fortified, and lies on the Nieper, and frontiers of Poland, in lat. 51. 12. n. long. 30. 47. east.

KIOGE, or KOGE, a town of Seeland in Denmark, situated on the little river Koagen, in the bay of Copenhagen, 21 miles south of the city, was much damaged by a fire in 1633. Gustavus Adolphus fortified it with walls and ditches in 1659; and in 1677 the Danish Admiral, Niels Juel, defeated the Swedish fleet in the bay near this place. Lat. 55. 46. n. long. 12. 31. east.

KLINKETS, a sort of small gate, made through palisades for sallies.

KRAINSLAW, a town in the palatinate of Chelm, in Red or Little Russia in Poland, where the Archduke Maximilian was prisoner in 1588, after being defeated by Zamoyski at Byczyn, on the frontiers of Silesia, and next year released on renouncing his right to the crown of Poland; lies 115 miles south-east of Warsaw, in lat. 51. 27. n. long. 23. 17. east.

LABORATORY, in gunnery, signifies the place where fire-workers and bombardiers prepare their stores. There is sometimes a large tent carried along with the artillery to the field for this use, with all sorts of tools and materials, and is called *the laboratory tent*.

LAGOS, a city of Algarve in Portugal, irregularly fortified on the south coast, on a bay navigable for large ships; has a harbour defended by forts: it stands on the side of the Lacobriege, 30 miles west of Faro. Lat. 36. 51. n. long. 9. 36. west.

LANDEN,

LANDEN, a small town of Brabant in the Austrian Low-Countries, on the Becke, 22 miles south-east of Louvain. Here Marshal Luxemburgh defeated the confederate army commanded by King William III. when the Duke of Ormond was taken prisoner by the French, and the Duke of Berwick by the Allies; 20,000 men were said to be killed on both sides in this battle, which was fought July 10, 1693.

LANDRECY, a small fortified town of Hainault in the French Netherlands, on the Sambre; taken by the French in 1655, and besieged by Prince Eugene in 1712, after separating from the English forces; but the French defeating part of his army at Denain, and possessing his magazines, he was obliged to raise the siege. It lies 20 miles south-east of Valenciennes, and 22 east of Cambray. Lat. 50. 29. n. long. 3. 26. east.

LANSCROON, a strong town of Schonen and South Gothland in Sweden, situated on the Sound, with a safe harbour and well fortified castle; taken by the Danes in 1678; 26 miles north-east of Copenhagen. Lat. 55. 56. n. long. 14. 36. east.

LAON, a well built city of Laonnois, in the Isle of France, on a steep eminence, surrounded by a large plain, defended by an old castle; and 27 miles north-west of Rheims. The neighbouring country produces excellent wine. Lat. 49. 56. n. long. 3. 52. east.

LANDAU, a well fortified city of Germany, in the circle and palatinate of the Rhine, subject to France, since the treaty of Munster, till taken in 1702, by the Germans. The French retook it in 1703, and in 1704, it was retaken, after the glorious battle of Blenheim. Afterwards taken and retaken; but left to the French by the treaty of Baden in 1714. On the Queich, 16 miles south-west of Spire.

LAWINGEN, a town of Suabia in Germany, situated on the Danube, where the Duke of Bavaria fortified his camp to defend his country against the British forces, and their allies under the Duke of Marlborough in 1704. 12 miles south-west of Hockstet, 35 north-east of Ulm. Lat. 48. 41. n. long. 10. 40. east.

LEDESMA, a fortified town of Leon in Spain, very old, and formerly called Bletisa, on the river Tormes. 18 miles west of Salamanca, in lat. 41. 15. long. 6. 35. west.

LEFFINGEN, an inconsiderable village in the neighbourhood of Ostend, in the Netherlands, where General Earl posted some troops in the campaign of 1708, to keep a communication open to the besiegers of Lisle with the grand army of the Conf derates, from whence the Duke of Vendosme could not drive them without attacking them in form.

LEGHORN, a city in the territory of Pisano, and great dukedom of Tuscany in Italy, not remarkably large, but regularly built in the modern taste, is well fortified; has 2 small fortresses on the sea side, and on that of the land a citadel. For the conveniency of navigation, there is a light-house lanthern, with 30 lamps erected on a rock without the harbour, and on the shore a lazaretto, where suspected persons, or goods, perform quarantine. Leghorn lies 46 miles west

of

of Florence, and 154 north-weſt of Rome. Lat. 43. 33. n. long. 10. 25. eaſt.

LENCICIA, or LENCZICZ, a city of Great Poland, the capital of the palatinate of that name, lying in a moraſs on the Bſura, with a wall, ditch, and caſtle: in 1294 was laid in aſhes by the Lithuanians, and in 1656 underwent the ſame fate from the Poles, when the Swedes were in poſſeſſion of it; and all the inhabitants, eſpecially Jews, were put to the ſword 74 miles weſt of Warſaw. Lat. 52. 21. lon. 18. 49.

LENS, formerly ELENE, a ſmall inconſiderable town of Artois in French Flanders, on the Souchet, formerly fortified, and held out ſeveral ſieges. In its neighbourhood the Spaniards were defeated by the French in 1648: 9 miles north of Arras. Lat. 50. 31. n. long. 2. 36. eaſt.

LEON, a city of Spain, the capital of the province of that name, built by the Romans in the reign of Galba, and called Legio Septima Germanica, whence its preſent name. It lies between the two ſprings of the Elſa, and immediately ſubject to the Pope. In the cathedral, famed for its beauty, lie buried ſeveral ſaints, 37 kings, and one emperor. It was the firſt conſiderable city taken from the Moors, who were defeated by Pelago in 722, and fortified by him; from which time it became the royal reſidence of the firſt Chriſtian King of Spain, and preſerved that dignity till the year 1029. It lies 160 miles north-weſt of Madrid, in lat. 43. 10. n. long. 6. 20. weſt.

LEOPOLDSTADT, a regular fortification in Upper Hungary, on the Wag, in a moraſs, built in 1663, by the Emperor Leopold, inſtead of the diſmantled Neuhauſel, for the defence of the country againſt an invaſion. Dexterouſly relieved by Count Starenberg in March 1707, when ready to fall into the hands of the Hungarian male-contents. 42 miles north-eaſt of Preſburg, and ſubject to Auſtria. Lat. 48. 46. long. 18. 41.

LEPANTO, antiently NAUPACTUS, a city of Livadia in European Turky, having an harbour on the north ſide, and a gulf of that name, formerly called the Corinthian Bay. On the uppermoſt peak of the mountain, on the declivity of which the place is ſituated, ſtands a ſmall caſtle. It lies 14 miles eaſt of the ſtreight or entrance of Lepanto Bay, and 26 miles n. of the oppoſite ſhore of the Morea. Near this place, off the Cape of Lepanto, the Venetians obtained a ſignal victory at ſea over the Turks in 1571. Many of the inhabitants are Greek Chriſtians, and the place is the ſee of a biſhop, but ſubject to Turky. Lat. 38. 20. n. long. 23. 15. eaſt.

LERIDA, a well built and fortified city of Catalonia in Spain, on the river Segre, has a good citadel. This city declared for King Charles III. on the reduction of Barcelona in 1705; but the Duke of Orleans took it by ſtorm after the unfortunate battle of Almanza in 1707; the garriſon, conſiſting chiefly of Britiſh troops, retired into the caſtle, and ſurrendered on honourable terms, 12 of November following. It lies 114 miles weſt of Barcelona, in lat. 41. 43. long. 3 minutes.

LERINS,

LERINS, 2 iflands called *St. Margarette* and *St. Honorat*, on the coaft of Provence in France, taken by the Spaniards in 1625, and retaken by the French in 1637. The firft was antiently called Lero, and the other Lerin; the former has 3 ports, and the latter a ftrong caftle, for its defence. 6 miles fouth of Antibes.

LIEGE, a city in the bifhopric of that name in Germany, on the Maefe, 14 miles fouth of Maeftricht, and 28 miles northeaft of Namur, is about 4 miles in circuit. The fortifications are inconfiderable, being overlooked and commanded by hills; but the citadel is ftrong, and capable of making a good defence. In the beginning of the confederate war in the reign of Queen Anne, the then bifhop, who was Elector of Cologne, put it into the hands of the French, from whom the Duke of Marlborough took it in 1702; and the French, invefting it in 1705, were, by the fame general, obliged to raife the fiege, upon his expeditious return from the Mofelle. Lat. 50. 46. long. 5. 28.

LIERE, a town of Brabant, in the Auftrian Low Countries, on the Nethe, 8 miles north of Mechlin or Malines, and 14 fouth-eaft of Antwerp, abandoned by the French, May 26, 1706, 3 days after their defeat at Ramillies. Lat. 51. 20. long. 4. 35.

LILLO, ftands 3 or 4 miles fouth of Santvliet, near the river Scheld, a little ftrong fortrefs.

LIMA, the metropolis of the whole empire of Peru, fituate on the banks of a river bearing its name, 7 miles eaft of the South Sea, and of the port town of Callao, furrounded with a brick wall flanked with 34 baftions, but without platforms or embrafures, the intention of it being to inclofe the city, and render it capable of refifting any fudden attack from the Indians. It has in its whole circumference 7 gates and 3 pofterns. On the fide of the river oppofite to the city is a fuburb called St. Lazaro, which has within thefe few years greatly increafed. Lat. 12. 2. f. long. 75. 52. weft.

LIMBER, a two-wheel carriage with fhafts to faften the trail of travelling carriages by means of the pintle or iron pin, when travelling, and taken off from the battery, or in the park of artillery, which is called *unlimbering the guns.*

LIMBURGH, fituated on a fteep hill, near the river Vefe, about 20 miles fouth-eaft of Liege, and 15 to the fouthward of Aix-la-Chapelle, is fmall, but its fituation renders it exceeding ftrong, there being but one paffage to it, and that almoft inacceffible: This town, notwithftanding the ftrength of its fituation, has often changed its mafters. The Dutch took it in 1633 from the Spanifh Dukes of Brabant; but fome time after it was retaken by the Spaniards. In 1675 the French took it, and in 1677 deftroyed the caftle; but reftored it to the Spaniards by the treaty of Nimeguen. After the death of King Charles II. of Spain, the French feized and kept it till 1703, when it was befieged and taken by the Confederates. The Hanoverian General Bulau invefted it on the 9th of September, and the artillery and other neceffaries coming up on the 20th, the befiegers foon made themfelves

masters

masters of the Lower Town, the defendants retiring on the firſt aſſault. On the 25th and 26th, they battered the place with ſucc"eſs, the cannon playing all day, and the mortars all night: info much that on the 27 h they were preparing for a general ſtorm, when the garriſon, conſiſting of 1400 men, beat a parley, but could obtain no other conditions than to ſurrender priſoners of war The officers and ſoldiers, however, were allowed to keep what belonged to them, and the officers had 12 waggons to carry off their baggage.

Line, the name of the works made by an army from one town or ſtrong poſt to another, behind which it is encamped, to guard a part of the country.

Line of the baſe, a right line, which joins the points of the 2 neareſt baſtions.

Line capital, that which is drawn from the angle of the gorge to the angle of the baſtion.

Line of circumvallation, the work or retrenchment made about an army beſieging a place to ſecure it againſt any inſult from without. It is made of a parapet, with a ditch before it at every 120 toiſes, or thereabout. The parapet projects outwards in an angle; which projection is called a redan, and ſerves to flank or defend the other parts.

Line of counter approach, a kind of trench made by the garriſon when beſieged, going from the covert-way, in a right line, ſo as that part of the enemy's approaches may be enfiladed from thence.

Line of countervallation, the work made by an army which beſieges a place between their

camp and the town, to cover it againſt an enterprize of the garriſon; made much after the ſame manner as the line of circumvallation, only in a contrary diſpoſition.

Line of defence, the diſtance between the ſaliant angle of the baſtion and the oppoſite flank; that is, the face produced to the flank.

When lines are deſigned to be attacked, always make a falſe one with a ſmall body of men, in order to favour the true attacks, and let them all begin at the ſame moment, and, if poſſible, in the night, that your enemy may not ſee your diſpoſition, or know where the ſtorm will fall. For the above purpoſe, carry plenty of faſcines and hurdles with you; let your cavalry, as well as infantry, be loaded with them, to fill up all advanced or other foſſes; and direct your men, ſo ſoon as they have entered the lines, to open the barriers, and level the line for the cavalry to enter.

Reconnoitre well the enemy's lines, that you may know their ſituation, and the approaches to them, before you attack. March briſkly up to them, with the infantry in 2 lines: keep your fire regular, and to each battalion of the front line appoint 4 or 5 ſquadrons to carry faſcines and hurdles: ſeem to reſolve to attack the intrenchments in the part you leaſt intend: let faſcines be cut, and other glazing preparations made; and whilſt the enemy is intent on the defence of that part, ſlip into their lines where they leaſt expect.

It generally happens, that an army which attacks intrenchments or troops in the field with vigour,

vigour, and is well suftained, reaps great advantages over thofe who defend them. If you apprehend the enemy will attack your lines, keep out fmall parties, especially in the night, to give the earlieft intelligence of their movements, that you may be prepared to receive them.

This was practifed with great fuccefs by the Duke of Marlborough, to the great faving of lives, when he paffed the Geet, to the lines at Helifhem, and after that at Arlieux.

LINSPINS, fmall pins of iron which keep the wheel of a cannon or waggon on the axletree; when the end of the axletree is put through the nave, the linfpin is put in to keep the wheel from falling off.

LINSTOCK, a ftaff of wood about three feet long, upon one end of which is a piece of iron that divides in 2 turnings from each other, having each a place to receive a match and a fcrew to keep it faft; the other end pointed and fhod with iron to ftick in the ground.

LINTZ, the capital of Upper Auftria, is pleafantly fituated on the fouth fide of the Danube, over which there is a wooden bridge, about 100 miles weft of Vienna. It is not a large city, but ftrong, neat, populous, and wealthy, the inhabitants carrying on a confiderable trade, efpecially in the linen manufacture. Many of the Auftrian nobility, as well as the regency of the province, refide at Lintz, particularly in the fummer; the queen has a palace here, a handfome and commodious ftructure, fituated upon an eminence, commanding the city. Hither the Emperor Leopold retired during the laft fiege of Vienna by the Turks: but not thinking himfelf fafe, he afterwards removed to Paffau. As to the buildings of Lintz, the houfes are generally of ftone, the churches beautiful and magnificent, and the monaftery of the Capuchins an elegant and ftately edifice.

In 1741, the confederate army of French and Bavarians not only took Lintz and all the Upper Auftria, but advanced within 10 leagues of Vienna. Their fuccefs, however, was not long without interruption; for in December, the fame year, Marfhal Khevenhuller, with a part of the Auftrian army under his command, drove the Confederates from Ens and Steyr; upon which all the French and Bavarian troops in that neighbourhood retired into Lintz, where they were immediately furrounded and blocked up by the Auftrians. They were foon reduced to great ftraits for want of provifions, and being unfuccefsful in all their fallies, they furrendered on the twelfth of January 1742, upon capitulation, whereby all the troops inclofed in the place, to the number of 6 or 7000, were obliged not to bear arms for the fpace of a twelvemonth againft her Hungarian Majefty.

LISBON, a city of Eftramadura, the capital of Portugal, and the royal refidence, fituated on the north fhore of the Tagus, about 10 miles from its mouth, 78 miles weft of the borders of Spain, 300 weft of Madrid, and 850 fouth weft of London, is commanded by a citadel, or caftle, and furrounded with a wall.

LISLE,

LISLE, the capital of French Flanders, stands on the river Deule, about 11 miles weft of Tournay, and almoft 9 fouth of Menin; is large, populous, and fo ftrongly fortified, that it coft the Allies more men to take it than any other town in Flanders, and was very near baffling their united forces. Its citadel is efteemed a mafter-piece in fortification, and not inferior to Antwerp. This city was built in 1007, and foon after walled round. It fuffered much in the thirteenth century, being difmantled by Philip Auguftus of France in 1213, retaken the next year by Count Ferrand, and almoft ruined in 1297, by Philip the Fair. It had formerly lords of its own, who had the title of Caftelans, from the 11th century to 1234, when it came to the family of Perone, afterwards to Luxembourg, then to Vendofme, next to Burgundy, and from them to the Houfe of Auftria, who kept it till 1667, when Lewis XIV. took it, built the citadel, enlarged the city, as well as its fortifications, and made it extremely ftrong. It was confirmed to the French by the treaty of Aix-la-chapelle, but taken by the Confederates in 1708, after a tedious and bloody fiege.

The firft parallel at this fiege was made between the 22d and 24th of Auguft inclufive; batteries were erected from the 24th to the 27th; a chapel and houfes cannonaded by 2 batteries, and both attacked together in the night, between the 24th and 25th, by grenadiers. Two guts were made the fame night after the attack, with a battery of 4 cannons at the end, to

prevent fallies of the enemy; and 2 batteries for bombs, on the 26th and 27th. The fecond parallel was made on the 27th and 28th; batteries were erected from the 30th to September the 1ft; and another battery for bombs on the fecond; batteries were made from the 3d to the 5th, and lines from the 4th to the 7th, with 2 batteries for bombs. On the 7th began the affault at the counterfcarps, which lafted till midnight, by 2000 grenadiers; and, though the enemy was driven from thence, the affailants became mafters of moft of them. Lines were made from the 8th to the 12th, between the horn-works, and againft the detached ravelin and the lunettes, as alfo againft the batteries; the befiegers advanced their works from the 13th to the 14th, made galleries againft the 2 lunettes from the 15th to the 20th and the 21ft, and attacked them both on the 21ft; that on the right hand was carried, and that on the left hand abandoned, but attacked again the fame day, and a lodgement effected in both. On the 3d of October, at noon, the ravelin was affaulted, and a lodgement effected; the lines were alfo advanced, to arrive behind the ravellin, at the glacis, to which they were conducted between the 4th and 9th inclufive. From the 10th to the 18th, all the works were finifhed upon the glacis behind the ravelin. On the 20th, at 10 in the morning, the befiegers began to fire from the faid batteries, to make new breaches, and to widen the old. During this fire, galleries were erected upon the main ditches, and advanced. On the

22d,

22d, the enemy feeing the 2 galleries finifhed, and that the 2 others would likewife be fo the next night, and the breaches rendered eafy, began to capitulate, after great breaches. The enemies had entrenchments and mines, a place by which the main ditch was drained, and a half gallery againft the hornwork. Redoubt twice attacked. New work made by the enemy immediately before the fiege; and the covert-way towards the redoubt; which, after the town was taken on the 22d of October, began likewife to be attacked under the command of his ferene Highnefs Prince Eugene of Savoy, the 29th of that month, and continued fo to be till the 8th of December 1708, when the enemy beat a furrender at 8 in the morning, and marched out of it 3 days after, drums beating, and colours flying. The firft parallel made during the ceffation of arms was between the 25th and 29th of October; batteries of cannon and of bombs were put in condition from the 29th to the 31ft; and the guts, with a battery of cannon and one of bombs, between the 31ft and 3d of November. The fecond parallel and other fmall lines and batteries were finifhed between the 3d and 10th. The third parallel upon the firft counterfcarp, with the batteries and lodgements, was made between the 10th and 16th; and 6 bridges thrown over the ditches between the 2 counterfcarps, between the 16th and 20th. The 4th parallel upon the border of the glacis of the fecond counterfcarp was put in condition between the 20th and 27th. The fifth parallel, with all the batteries of cannon and mortars,

was made between that time and the 8th of December, or day of furrender; a canal to draw off the waters between the 2 counterfcarps and the place where the wall on the right hand was pierced; rows of trees were cut down; a new work erected; inundation and cuts made; the cavalier marked in the profile; cuts in the places d'armes; and the batteries projected. Ceded to the French in 1713, in lat. 50. 46. n. long. 3. 12. eaft.

LIZILERE, *Berm, Forland,* or *Relais,* a fpace of ground left at the foot of the rampart, on the next fide the country, defigned to receive the ruins of the rampart, to prevent its filling up the foffe; it is fometimes palifaded, and in Holland generally planted with a quickfet hedge. When this fpace is covered with a parapet, it is called a faufs-bray, or low-wall.

LOCHES, an inconfiderable town of Tourain in France, fituate on the Judre, over which is a bridge, and near it a caftle on a fteep rock, formerly an important fortrefs, where Lewis Sforza, Duke of Milan, was kept prifoner above 10 years. In a large tower are 2 cafes, or removeable repofitories, made of very ftrong pieces of oak, plated over with iron, in one of which Cardinal Balve, bifhop of Angers, was fhut up by Lewis XII. 29 miles fouth eaft of Tours, in lat. 47. 26. n. long. 1. 21. eaft.

LOCKING-PLATES, thin, flat pieces of iron, nailed on the fides of a field carriage, where the wheels touch it, in turning, to prevent the wearing of the wood in thofe places.

LOCKSPIT, a fmall cut or trench made with a fpade, about a foot a foot wide, to mark out the firſt lines of a work.

LODGEMENT, the work made by the beſiegers in ſome part of a fortification to maintain it after the beſiegers are drove out.

LOOP-HOLES, ſquare or oblong-holes made in the wall to fire through with muſkets.

LOUVAIN, a city of Brabant, in the Auſtrian Low Countries, ſituated on the Dyle, 14 miles ſouth eaſt of Mechlin, and 15 north-eaſt of Bruſſels. The walls are between 6 and 7 miles in circuit, but of inconſiderable ſtrength, being generally obliged to ſubmit to that army which is maſter of the field, without any formal ſiege. The French abandoned it on the 20th of May 1706, the day after the battle of Ramillies, and the Duke of Marlborough took poſſeſſion of it May 25. It lies 14 miles ſouth-eaſt of Mechlin. Lat. 51. 12. n. long. 4. 40. eaſt.

LOVENDEGEN, a fortreſs of Flanders, in the Auſtrian Low Countries, ſituated on the canal between Ghent and Bruges, 7 miles weſt of the former. Here Baron Spar, in 1705, forced the French lines, though defended by ſeveral forts, and advanced within a league of Bruges. Lat. 51. 31. n. long. 3. 43. eaſt.

LOWOSCHUTZ, in Bohemia, is only remarkable as a place where the King of Pruſſia attacked Marſhal Brown in his camp, on the 1ſt of October 1756, with 25000 men; though his enemy amounted to no leſs than 60000 Auſtrians. His Majeſty began the attack, and defeated their cavalry; while his infantry took this town, and put the whole Auſtrian army to flight. The battle began at 7 in the morning, and ended at 3 in the afternoon. The Auſtrians loſt between 6 and 7000 men killed or wounded, and about 500 priſoners, with 5 cannon and 3 pair of colours. The Pruſſians had 2000 killed or wounded.

LOZANCE, or *rhombe*, a figure of 4 equal ſides, whoſe angles are too acute and too obtuſe.

LUELIN, a trading city and capital of a palatinate of that name in Little Poland; pretty large, ſurrounded with a wall and ditch, and defended by a caſtle on a high rock, on the banks of the little river Byllzna. In 1240 the town was deſtroyed by the Tartars, and afterwards long in the poſſeſſion of the Ruſſians; in 1447 and 1606 it was greatly damaged by an accidental fire, and burnt down by the Swedes in 1656. In 1703, an extraordinary diet was held here. It lies 121 miles north-eaſt of Cracow, in lat. 51. 26. long. 22. 36. eaſt.

LUCAR, ST. DE GUADIANA, a town of Andaluſia in Spain, on the weſt ſide of the river Guadiana, defended by 3 towers, and on the other ſide by a fort of two baſtions. Lat. 37. 32. long. 8. 18. weſt.

LUCAR, ST. DE BARAMEDA, a well built city of Andaluſia, in Spain, with a good harbour at the mouth of the Guadalquiver, defended by 2 batteries. Before the place is an excellent road, where a whole fleet may ride in ſafety. It lies 26 miles north of Cadiz, and 44 ſouth-weſt of Seville.

LUNETTE, a ſmall work raiſed ſometimes in the middle of the foſſe before the curtain, forming an angle, its terreplein riſing but a little above the ſurface of the water, about 12 feet broad, with a parapet of 18 feet. There is another ſort of lunette which is larger,

and

and raifed to cover the faces of the half-moon; and this alfo is compofed of 2 faces; a longer and a fhorter.

LUTZEN, a town of Upper Saxony, 10 miles weft of Leipfic. Here the Swedes obtained a victory over the Germans in 1632, but loft their King Guftavus Adolphus, who was killed in the field of battle Lat. 51. 31. n. long. 12. 34. eaft.

LUXEMBURG, fituated partly on the eafy way of a rocky hill, and partly on a plain, through which runs the river Elfe or Olzet, is about 24 miles fouthweft of Triers or Treves, 52 fouth of Limburg, and 100 fouth-eaft of Bruffels. The town is ftrong by art and nature.

This city was taken from the Houfe of Auftria by the Duke of Orleans in 1542, but retaken 2 years after by the Emperor Charles the Fifth. In 1684 it was taken by the French, who made great additions to its fortifications while in their poffeffion; but was reftored to the Spaniards in 1697, by the treaty of Ryfwick. The French feized it again in 1701, after the death of King Charles II. of Spain; but by the treaty of Utrech in 1713, the town and fortrefs, together with the duchy, was yielded to the States General in favour of the houfe of Auftria, on condition that the Elector of Bavaria fhould have the fovereignty and revenues thereof till he was reftored to his electorate, and fatisfied as to fome other pretenfions; during which time he was allowed to keep troops in the duchy, not exceeding 7000 men; but the town and fortrefs were to be garrifoned by the troops of the States, at the expence of the town and duchy. Lat. 49. 52. n. long. 6. 10. eaft.

LUZZARA, a town of the Mantuan in Upper Italy, not far from the influx of the Coftrollo into the Po, 14 miles fouth of Mantua, belonging to the houfe of Auftria. Here an obftinate and bloody battle was fought between the Germans, commanded by Prince Eugene, and the French and Spaniards, under Lewis Duke of Vendofme, on the 4th of Auguft 1702, in which feveral 1000 were killed on both fides, each claiming the victory. Here alfo was fought another battle in 1734. Lat. 45. 10. long. 11. 16.

MACHIAN, an ifland in the Moluccas, in Afia, has 3 forts on inacceffible rocks for maintaining their poffeffion. Lies under the equator, and in 125. 10. eaft long.

MADRASS, or _Fort George_, the capital of the Englifh fettlements on the Coromandel coaft, and hither Province of India in Afia, ftands 4 miles north of the city of St. Thomas, in lat. 13. 15. and long. 80. 50. It is a mile and a half in circuit, and has lately been furrounded by a ftone wall, and baftions cannon proof, the whole being almoft encompaffed by a river and the fea; but while in a far more defencelefs ftate than at prefent, it was defended by Sir William Draper, in 1758, with fuch fpirit and courage, as obliged Count Lally to raife the fiege, after laying two months before the place.

MADRIERS, long planks of broad wood ufed for fupporting the earth in mining, carrying on

a fap

a fap, making coffers, caponeers, galleries, and various
ufes at a fiege; alfo to cover
the mouth of petards after they
are loaded, and are fixed with
the petards to the gates or other
places defigned to be forced
open. When the planks are not
ftrong enough, they are doubled
with plates of iron.

MAESTRICHT, a city on the
borders of the duchy of Limburg,
and bifhoprick of Liege, about
four miles in circumference;
and its fortifications, which are
in the modern way, may be
reckoned amongft the beft in
Europe. It revolted from Spain
in 1570, but was befieged by
the Duke of Parma in 1579,
when after a brave defence, the
garrifon having repulfed the
Spaniards in two bloody attacks,
it was at laft furprized in the
night. Retaken by the Prince
of Orange in 1632, after an obftinate fiege of 2 months; and
from that time continued in the
hands of the Dutch till 1673,
when it was taken by the French
King in perfon, after 13 days
open trenches.

The fiege of Maeftricht, in
1676, by William Prince of
Orange, afterwards king of England, is very memorable. The
garrifon confifted of 8000 men
under M. Calvo, an experienced
and daring commander (and the
befiegers were 30000) who carried on their attacks with fuch
bravery for 3 weeks, that it was
fuppofed the place would at laft
be taken. During this fiege the
Englifh gave fignal proofs of
their valour, and many of the
out-works were taken with
great flaughter on both fides:
but the befieged continually
fupplying them with new re-

trenchments, and the Prince
finding his troops much dimi-
nifhed by ficknefs, and hearing
that M. Schomberg was ad-
vancing to the relief of the
town with a fuperior army,
whilft he waited in vain for the
reinforcements which the Germans had promifed to fend him,
obliged the Prince to raife the
fiege, after 52 days open trenches, and the lofs of 8000 men.
This city, however, did not
long continue in the hands of
the French, being reftored to
the States of Holland by the
treaty of Nimeguen in 1678.
In 1703 the French had formed
a defign againft Maeftricht,
but were prevented from putting
it in execution by General Aver-
querque, who commanded part
of the confederate army in the
neighbourhood.

Marfhal Saxe, in 1748, ordered
the troops to hold themfelves in
readinefs to take the field, and
immediately affembled his army
near Antwerp. The firft ftep
he took was to fend Marfhal
Lowendahl towards Maeftricht,
who in his rout poffeffed himfelf of Limburg, while Marfhal
Saxe proceeded on the other fide
the Maes to Tongre, feizing
the Auftrian magazines. On
the firft of April they invefted
the important city of Maeftricht,
began their lines of circumvallation, foon broke ground before it in four different points;
by the 17th they carried on
their approaches almoft to the
covert way, and that night attacked and carried it with the
lofs of 900 grenadiers; at
which time the Baron d'Ayl-
va, the governor, made a fally,
in which he killed above
1000 men, and nailed up 14
can-

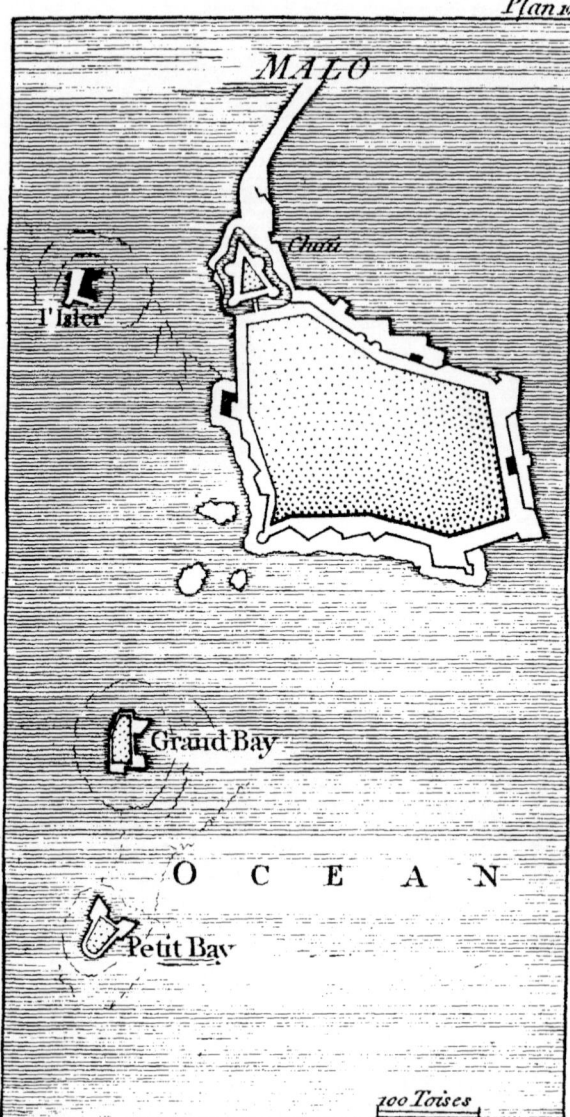

Plan 19.

MALO

l'Inter

Chata

Grand Bay

O C E A N

Petit Bay

100 Toises

14 cannon. Thus they conti nued at bay with each other, till the ceffation of arms concluded 19 April, O. S. was notified; when, purfuant to the aiticles therein, his Royal Highnefs the Duke of Cumberland, who was preparing the allies to relieve the town, fent an officer to the governor to deliver it up to the French; on which a capitulation was agreed to, and the garrifon marched out with all the honours of war.

MAGAZINE, or *arfenal*, where all ftores are kept, guns founded, and carpenters, wheelwrights, fmiths, turners, and other handicrafts, conftantly employed in making all things for the artillery.

MAJORCA, fituated on a bay between 2 capes, on the fouthweft of the ifland, fortified after the modern manner, and large. Lat. 39. 36. n. long. 2. 36. eaft.

MAIN-BODY *of the army*, the body of troops that marches between the advance and rear guard. In a camp, that part of the army encamped between the right and left wing.

MAIN-GUARD, or *grandguard*, a body of horfe pofted before a camp for the fecurity of an army. In garrifon, it is a guard generally mounted by the eldeft fubaltern-officer upon the parade the morning of mounting.

MALACCA, the moft fouth part of the further peninfula of India in Afia; its walls and fortifications are founded on a rock, and carried up to a confiderable height; the lower part is wafhed by the tide, and on the landfide is a wide canal, or large ditch, cut from the fea to the river, whereby it is made an ifland. In 1604 the Dutch took it from the Portuguefe. Lat. 2. 12. long. 102. 2.

MALAGA, an antient fortified city of Granada, in Spain, on the Mediterranean, at the foot of a fteep mountain, with a large harbour, and defended by 2 caftles, one on the top, and the other at the foot of the mountain. Off the Cape Malaga, near this city, the Englifh, with their Allies, the Dutch, under the command of Sir George Rooke, obtained a fignal victory over the French fleet, commanded by the Count de Thouloufe, in Auguft 1704. Lat. 36. 51. long. 4. 56. weft.

MALO (ST.) a fmall but populous town of Britany in France, on a rocky ifland in the Englifh channel, joined to the main land by a caufe-way, at the beginning of which is a ftrong caftle. The harbour is large, and one of the beft on the coaft, but of difficult entrance, being furrounded with feveral rocks, and at tide of ebb almoft left dry; fo that it will not admit large veffels. On the neighbouring rocks are 10 different forts. They fitted out many privateers, who made feveral prizes in the war with England during the reign of King William, which brought a bombardment upon the town, but did it little damage. In 1758, a body of Britifh troops, under the Duke of Marlborough, and a fquadron commanded by commodore, now Lord Howe, having landed at Cancalle bay, between the 6th and 7th of June, burnt all the fhipping in St. Malo's harbour, to the number of 100 great and fmall; after which, finding the town impracticable,

practicable, they re-imbarked, and returned to Spithead. Lat. 48. 36. n. long. z. 15. weſt. See Plan 12.

MALPLAQUET, a village of Hainault, n the neighbourhood of Bavay, Mons, and Maubeuge, near which a memorable and bloody battle was fought, 11th of September 1709, between the Allies commanded by the Duke of Marlborough and Prince Eugene on one ſide, and the French under the command of the Marſhals Villars and Boufflers on the other; each army conſiſting of above 100000. The left wing of the French, commanded by Marſhal Villars, was poſted near Blangies, having before them the woods of Blangies and Sart. Their centre was before Erquennes and Taniers; and the right wing, under Marſhal Boufflers, had in flank the wood of Janſart. The open ground between the 2 woods was about 3000 yards, acroſs which was thrown up a triple entrenchment, and before that entrenchment was a village, covered ſtrongly by ditches and hedges. The woods on both wings were felled and entrenched, and 100 cannon planted in the avenues.

The French having made this diſpoſition, the whole army of the Allies moved towards them in the morning. General Schulemberg, with the Britiſh and other troops from Tournay, was drawn up to the right of the wood of Sart; the infantry of Prince Eugene's army along the great road which paſſes through that wood; and General Lottum, with part of the foot of the right wing, to the left of the ſame wood. The reſt of the

infantry of that wing, conſiſting chiefly of Hanoverians, had in front the lines in the opening between that wood and the village; and the infantry of the States, commanded by the Prince of Naſſau, ſome battalions excepted, had in front the lines between the village and the wood of Janſart. The horſe of the whole army were poſted behind the foot, to ſupport and ſecond them where the ground would permit.

The ſignal being given by the diſcharge of 50 cannon, the whole confederate army moved together, and began the attack with incredible bravery, and with ſuch ſucceſs at the wood of Sart, that, after an hour's reſiſtance, the enemy were driven out of the wood, and out of their entrenchments. On the left, between the village and the wood of Janſart, the Dutch having 3 entrenchments before them, forced the 2 firſt; but, in the attack of the third, were repulſed by the great fire of the enemy, and loſt a great number. They rallied again, and the right wing having made themſelves maſters of the wood of Sart, and coming to flank the entrenchments between the 2 woods, gave the horſe an opportunity of breaking in upon them; and though the firſt ſquadrons that entered were repulſed, yet all broke through at laſt, and advanced into the plain to charge the cavalry of the enemy. The left wing of the Confederates alſo drove the French from their entrenchments in the wood of Janſart.

The Engliſh foot in the right wing, with thoſe of Prince Eugene, having marched through the

the wood of Sart with much difficulty, forcing the enemy to retire as they advanced, began to form upon the plain. This being done, the Duke of Marlborough ordered a halt, and rode to obſerve what had paſſed on the left, where the troops of the States had attacked the French between the two woods : the Duke ſeeing how much the Dutch had ſuffered, ordered Lieutenant-general Withers to march with the body under his immediate direction to ſuſtain them. Upon farther deliberation and notice that the Lieutenant-general had been attacked, and was actually engaged with the enemy, and all things going well on the right, the Duke thought fit rather to preſs on the advantages there, than to hazard a new motion towards the left in the heat of the action. Soon after, the enemy's left began to retire towards Attiche, and draw off their cannon from the plain of Bleron. Their foot alſo began to break in the centre ; upon which the Duke of Marlborough commanded the Earl of Orkney to attack them in their entrenchments on the plain before Bleron, with orders, if he ſucceeded there, to poſt himſelf in thoſe entrenchments, and cover the horſe as they ſhould file off through the woods into the plain, to charge the enemy's cavalry. This was executed with great reſolution and ſucceſs ; and though the firſt ſquadrons, as before obſerved, were repulſed, yet before the horſe of the Allies were marched into the plain, and while they were forming in order of battle, the French horſe retired by the way of Bavay ; and the right of their foot, which

were entrenched on the plain of Bleron, alſo marched off with precipitation. The whole army retreated by different ways, leaving the field and 16 cannon to the Confederates.

Prince Eugene was ſlightly wounded in the head ; Lieutenant-general Count Oxenſtiern, and the Pruſſian General Tettau, were killed ; Lieutenant-general Spar, Brigadier May, and M. Demys, Adjutant of the Prince of Naſſau, wounded, and the Prince had two horſes killed under him. On the ſide of the French, Marſhal Villars was ſhot in the knee, the Duke de Guiche in the leg, M. Albergotti in the thigh ; and at leaſt 25 other officers of diſtinction killed, and 20 wounded. Indeed, officers and ſoldiers ſhewed in this bloody battle as much reſolution and intrepidity as were ever ſeen ; being very obſtinate from half paſt 8 in the morning till 3 in the afternoon. The French were ſo advantageouſly poſted, that when the battle was over, the Allies wondered how they had ſurmounted ſuch difficulties. About 20,000 were left dead on the field ; nor muſt it be wondered at if half of thoſe were loſt by the conquerors. Thoſe troops that were in the open plain gave way ; thoſe that were ſtrongly poſted maintained their ground for a long time, and made the Allies horſe ſuffer conſiderably.

Though the French fought ſo well at Malplaquet, that it was ſaid they retrieved their nation's honour, yet, an intercepted letter from one of their officers, ſpeaking of Eugene and Marlborough, ſays, What can withſtand the rapid force of theſe 2 famous heroes ! If an army of
100,000

100,000 of the beſt troops, poſt-ed between 2 woods, trebly in-trenched, and performing their duty as well as brave men could do, were not able to ſtop them one day, will you not own with me that they ſurpaſs all the he-roes of former ages ?

MALTA, ſtands on a hill, in the centre of an iſland, and con-ſiſts of 3 towns ſeparated by channels, forming ſo many pe-ninſulas of ſolid rock : the har-bours are deep and good ; the ſituation naturally ſtrong ; and no efforts of art are wanting to render the fortifications impreg-nable. Lat. 35. 54. n. long. 14. 34. eaſt.

MALVASIA, or *Napodi de Mal-veſia*, antiently *Epidaurus*, a city of the Morea in European Tur-ky, on the gulf de Neopoli, in the Archipelago, is the ſtrongeſt fortreſs in all the Morea; it has a good harbour, 34 miles eaſt of Lacedemon, and 75 ſouth-weſt of Athens, in lat. 36. 40. north; long. 23. 40. eaſt.

MANILLA, or *Leuconia*, the principal of the Philippine Iſlands in Aſia, is ſubjeƈt to the king of Spain, 410 miles long, and in ſome places 217 broad, but in others not above 97. Admiral Corniſh, with a ſmall ſquadron, Sir William Draper, and the Hon. Colonel Monſon, at the head of 2300 men, thro' an un-remitting heavy, dreadful perio-dical monſoon deluge of rain, and the moſt terrible tempeſtuous ſurfs at ſea, between the 24th of September, and the 6th of Oƈtober 1762, reduced a ſtrong fort and 10,800 men, ſpurred with the jeſuitical fury of an ever erring religion, to a capitu-lation in ten days, and to ſur-render priſoners at diſcretion ;

to give up the town and fort of Cavite, with all the iſlands and forts dependent on Manilla ; and for the preſervation of the town, to pay 4,000,000 of dol-lars. The Archbiſhop, their Go-vernor, the Marquis de Villa Medina, and other officers, were favoured on their parole, and their Indian ſoldiers were diſ-miſſed in ſafety. Our loſs was 36 killed, and 105 wounded : the Spaniards had about 1000 killed and wounded.

MANOEUVRE, *of troops*, con-ſiſts ſolely in diſtributing equal motion to every part, to enable the whole to form, or change their poſition, in the moſt expe-ditious and beſt method to an-ſwer the purpoſes required of a battalion, brigade, or line of ca-valry or infantry.

MANTELETS, either *ſingle* or *double*, are great planks of wood, of about 5 feet high and 3 inches thick; which, by being puſhed forward on ſmall trucks, ſerve at a ſiege to cover the men from the hand-grenades and fire works of the place. *Single mantelets* are made by joining 2 or 3 ſuch planks together with bars of iron, to cover thoſe that carry them. *Double mantelets* are made by putting earth between two ſuch rows of planks, and are uſed in making approaches and batteries near the place, as the others are in making lodgments on the counterſcarp. They are covered with letten, and made ſmall at bottom and top, that they may more eaſily be joined together, to cover the ſoldiers from fire in front or in flank.

MANTUA, ſtands in the mid-dle of a lake 24 Italian miles in circuit and 2 in breadth, formed by the river Mincio. One of the

2 prin-

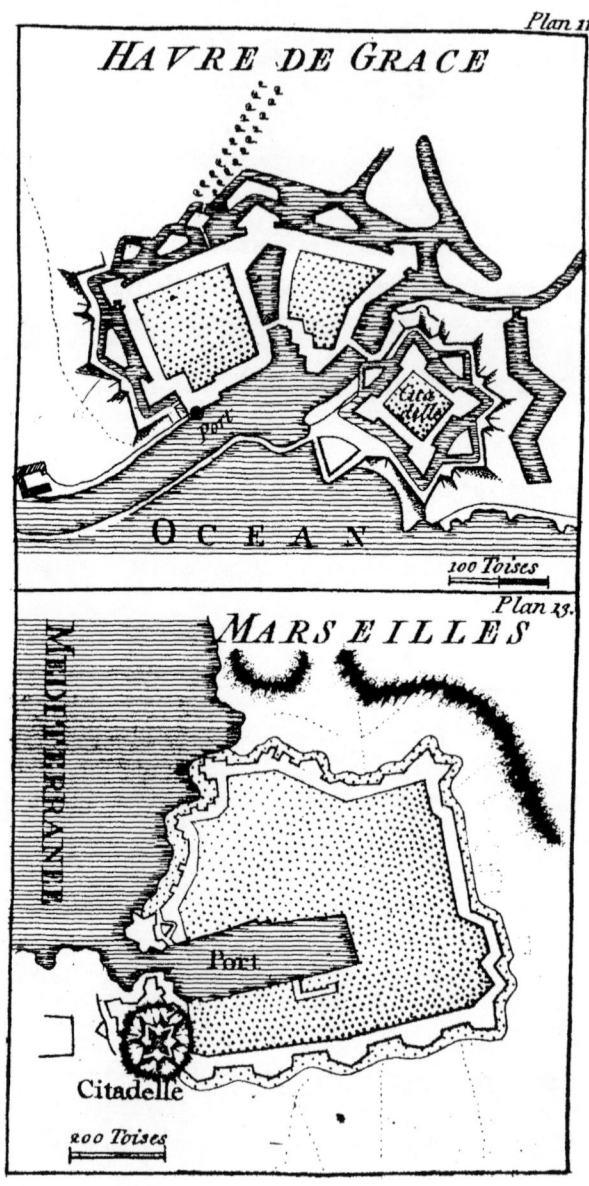

Plan 11.

HAVRE DE GRACE

port

O C E A N

100 Toises

Plan 23.

MARSEILLES

MEDITERRANÉE

Port

Citadelle

200 Toises

2 principal bridges which lead to this city is defended by 2 citadels : the other, by bulwarks at each end. The river divides the town into two parts, but thefe are joined by fix bridges. Here is a good citadel, fortified more by nature than art. The city is 5 miles in circuit. The antient ducal palace is neither modern nor regular, but large and fpacious; its famous gallery and cabinet of curiofities were entirely plundered in 1630, by the Imperialifts, when they took the city by ftorm. It lies 75 miles weft of Milan, and 84 fouth-weft of Venice. Lat. 45. 31. long. 11. 20.

MARCHES. *Secret marches,* are made with a defign to reconnoitre an enemy, furprize their camp, fecure a poft, or feize a place. It is in this fervice that a commander has occafion for his utmoft fagacity and penetration, to prevent his being difcovered or betrayed; and to enfure fuccefs, it is neceffary that the perfon who conducts the march has certain information concerning the different roads, fituation of the enemy's pofts, and the nature of the country through which he is to march.

MARDIKE, a village of French Flanders, having a harbour on the fea, 4 miles weft of Dunkirk; famous for a fort on the fea, about 1 mile from Dunkirk, oft befieged and taken, but at laft difmantled. La Blanc, after the peace of Utrecht, by order of Lewis XIV. made a famous canal here, which, with Mardike, the French began to fortify; but were obliged to defift upon remonftrances made by the Britifh Court. Lat. 51. 12. long. 2. 26.

MARSALQUIVER, a town of Algiers, fituate on the Barbary coaft, in Africa, with an harbour on a bay lying oppofite to Oran, and taken with that city by the Spaniards in 1732. Lat. 36. 28. n. long. 10 minutes weft.

MARSEILLES, the fecond city of Provence, in France, is large, rich, well fortified, and faid to have been built 500 years before Chrift. It ftands at the foot of a high rocky mountain, on a fine bay of the Mediterranean, which forms a fecure, capacious, oblong harbour, where the royal galleys are ftationed, but is not fufficiently deep to admit large men of war. Its arfenal is richly provided with all forts of ftores for the royal galleys; and the armory, which is reckoned the fineft in the kingdom, has arms for 40,000 men. It lies 27 miles fouth-weft of Toulon, and 356 fouth eaft of Paris, in lat. 43. 18. long. 5. 27. eaft. See Plan 13.

MARSTRAND, a very old ftaple town of Bohus lehen, in Gothland, in Sweden, with an excellent harbour, to which is an entrance on the fouth and north fide, defended by the impregnable citadel of Carlftein. So reduced, partly by war and partly by fire, that in 1745 there remained but 20 poor burghers.

MARTIGUES, a fmall town of Provence, in France, ftanding on an ifland at the mouth of a falt lake, near the fea, built out of the ruins of the old city of Genes, was formerly very ftrong; in 1591 taken by Duke Charles Emanuel of Savoy after a long fiege. Lat. 43. 36. n. long. 5. 15. eaft.

MARTINICO, the principal of all the French Caribbee iflands, and the feat of the governor-

[f]   general,

general, is about 58 miles in length, but hardly 20 in breadth. The inland parts of the ifland are mountainous, from which iffue numerous fmall ftreams. On the coaft are feveral commodious and fecure harbours.

It was taken under the commands of General Monckton and Sir George Rodney, February 14, 1762. Lat. 14. 33. n. long. 60 54. weft.

MARTINS. St. a fmall forttrefs on the ifle of Ree, and coaft of France, 12 miles weft of Rochelle. Lat. 45. 20. n. long. 23. 8. weft. See Plan 14.

MASULIPATAN, a city of Golconda and the Hither India, in Afia, with a harbour on the weft fide of the Bay of Bengal, 212 miles north of Fort St. George. Here are feveral Englifh and Dutch factories, from whence the moft beautiful callicoes are exported. This place was ftormed and taken by Colonel Forde in 1759. Lat. 16. 21. long. 81. 12.

MAULEON, a town of Gafcony, in the valley of Soule, in France, with a caftle on the Gave, 18 miles fouth-eaft of Bayonne. Lat. 43. 26. n. long. 1. 51. weft.

MAXIMS, in fortification, are general rules eftablifhed by engineers, founded on reafon and experience, which being exactly obferved, a place fortified according as they direct, will be in a good pofture of defence. The chief are fuch as follow;

1. There fhould be no part in the fortification of a place, but what is difcovered and flanked by the befieged: if there be any part of a place which is not well flanked, the enemy being thus under cover, will more readily attack in that place, and carry it.

2. A fortrefs fhould command all the country round it, that the befiegers may neither cover, find places to favour their approaches or attacks, or overlook the works of the place, to batter them with more advantage.

3. The works fartheft diftant from the centre of the place muft be ftill loweft, and commanded by thofe that are nearer; fo that they may be defended by the higher works and thofe nearer the place; that the enemy by being expofed may be obliged to quit them, even after poffeffion; for the enemy, by being mafters of fuch works, cannot overlook the works of the place.

4. The flanked angle, or point of the baftion, fhould be at leaft 70 degrees, that it may better refift the force of an enemy's battery, if they fhould form a defign to beat it down and lodge there.

5. The acute flanked angle near to a right angle is preferable to all other: it is certain, if the flanked angle be a right angle, it has all the ftrength that can be given it, having folidity enough to withftand the enemy's batteries; but an angle near the right makes the tenaille of the place more compact, by the angle of the fhoulder fhortening and battering the defence, and by not expofing the face fo much to the enemy. Thus an obtufe angle is very deficient.

6. The fhorteft faces are beft; becaufe the enemy attack them with a front in proportion to their length.

7. The flank muft have fome part under cover: viz. it muft be covered by an orillon, otherwife the defence is foon ruined, and the lodgement no fooner made on the counterfcarp, but the

the place is obliged to capitulate; as has oft been seen.

8. There must be an accord between these maxims to render the fortification perfect. If the gorge be too large, the face suffers; the more the flank is covered the less it is subject to be ruined; but then the defence is more oblique. In making a second flank, the flanked angle is made too weak; and by discovering the face the defence is more easy, though more exposed to the enemy's batteries. There are advantages and disadvantages in all, and the secret consists in judging whether conforming with one maxim be more advantageous than disagreeing with another.

MEADIA, a fortress, sconce, or citadel of Walachia, in European Turky, on the river Czerna, near which a battle was fought between the Imperialists and Turks in 1738.

MEASURE-ANGLE, a brass instrument to measure angles, either saliant or rentrant, for exactly ascertaining the number of degrees and minutes, to delineate them on paper.

MECHLIN, a large city on the Dyle and Demer, 12 miles northwest of Lovain, 14 north-east of Brussels, and 16 south-east of Antwerp. It is large, and fortified all round, but of inconsiderable strength. Lat. 51. 20. long. 4. 31.

MELINDA, a town of Zanguebar, in Africa, with a good harbour defended by a citadel, on the Indian ocean, 74 miles north of Mombaze, the capital of a province bearing its name, and of all the Portuguese settlements on the coast. Lat. 3. 12. south; long. 30. 10. east.

MEMEL, a populous town of Prussia, in Poland, with a harbour on the Baltic, that has a good and deep entrance, fortified with 3 whole and 2 half bastions, and other modern works. It formerly belonged to the Hanseatic union. The citadel consists of 4 bastions, chiefly regular, with the necessary ravelines and half-moons. This place surrendered to the Russians 5th July 1757, 68 miles north of Koningsberg. Lat. 56. 12. long. 21. 36.

MENIN, a small town of Flanders, in the Low-Countries, consisting of one street, but remarkable for the strength of its fortifications, which are reckoned a master-piece; but it was taken by the Allies on the 22d of August 1706, after 18 days opening the trenches, the garrison being allowed to march out with the usual marks of honour. The storming of the counterscarp, which was taken on the 18th, proved a very bloody action, it being computed that the French had not less than 1000 killed and wounded in that attack: yet some say that the place was ill defended, and that the French commandant, when he surrendered it to the Duke of Marlborough, having demanded leave to march out of the breach, was answered, "That it was not adviseable for him to do it unless he had ladders;" upon which he chose, with his garrison, to march out at the gate. During the whole siege, the French lost about 1300 men, and the Confederates about 517, who found in the place 55 brass cannon, 16 of iron, 6 mortars, a great quantity of powder and ball, and all sorts of ammunition. The French made themselves masters of it at

[f 2]   the

the opening of the campaign, 1744. It ſtands 5 or 6 miles ſouth-weſt of Courtray, 9 almoſt north of Liſle, and about 10 ſouth-eaſt of Vipres.

Menin capitulated on honourable terms 6th Auguſt, with about 4300 men, 55 braſs cannon, 16 iron cannon, 6 mortars, 810 double barrels of powder, 387 double barrels of muſket balls, 1300 French killed and wounded; 583 killed of the Allies, 2045 wounded.

MENTZ, a large and populous city, in an electorate of that name, in Germany; its public buildings are magnificent, but the private ones mean, and its fortifications of no conſiderable ſtrength. It was beſieged by the Imperialiſts in July 1689, under the command of Prince Charles of Lorrain, and the Electors of Bavaria and Saxony, who joined their forces with the others. This place was the year before, when the Elector of the ſame name received a French garriſon into the town, ſo inconſiderable in its fortifications, that though a great number of men were employed during the winter, to put them in a ſtate of defence, they could ſcarce bring the out-works to perfection. Its chiefeſt ſtrength at that time conſiſted in a garriſon of 10,000 men, who reſolved to hold out till the laſt extremity. It was vigorouſly attacked; and there has not been a place defended with more bravery. In 48 days after opening the trenches, the beſiegers had only made one lodgement upon the utmoſt point of the counterſcarp. The beſieged made frequent ſallies at noon, with their colours flying and drums beating, ſometimes 3

or 4 times in a day. They marched out ſometimes with a body of 2 or 3000, in order of battle, engaged the enemy, cut in pieces thoſe that guarded the trenches, nailed up their cannons, filled up their works, and once drove the enemies back at ſuch a diſtance from the place, that their main horſe guard took poſt at the head of their trenches. The Confederates having oft felt the effects of the intrepidity of the beſieged, reſolved to attack and carry the counterſcarp, whatever might be the event. With this reſolution, all their batteries played furiouſly by break of day, and thus continued till ſignal was given for the aſſault. In a few moments the ground was covered with dead carcaſſes, cannon, &c. their ſwords eſpecially made ſuch havock among the enemy, as is rather to be conceived than expreſſed. The aſſault laſted 5 hours, when the beſieged being overpowered by numbers, who without intermiſſion, ſeconded their men with freſh troops, were forced to yield, and leave them maſters of the counterſcarp, with the loſs of 4000 men on the Confederate ſide. The beſieged having, beſides this, loſt, during the aſſault, all their ammunition, by a bomb which blew up their magazine, the next day eſſayed to regain the counterſcarp with their ſwords in hand; but the Marquis d'Uxelles, their governor, unwilling to ſacrifice ſo many brave fellows in the attempt, beat a parley, and the Allies granting him honourable conditions, the garriſon marched out with colours flying, and 6 cannon. It lies 24 miles weſt of Francfort. Lat. 49. 16. long. 8. 16.

MERLAN,

MERLAN, that part of the parapet which is terminated by 2 embrasures of a battery, so that its height and thickness is the same with that of the parapet. It serves to cover those on the battery from the enemy, and is better when made of earth well beat and close, than of stone, because these fly about, and wound those it should defend.

MESSINA, antiently *Zancle*, afterwards *Messana*, a large and well built city of Val di Demona in Sicily, with an harbour on the Streight of Faro of Messina; besides an irregular fortification, has a citadel of 5 large and regular bastions, with several forts on the neighbouring eminences. The harbour is of an oval form and large, being well secured, the city lying between it and the mountains, though this last is not strong. It lies 115 miles west of Reggio, in Calabria. Lat. 38. 41. long. 15. 39.

METZ, the capital of a government of that name, in Germany, between the Moselle and Seille, which unite here; is a large well fortified place, lies 28 miles north of Nancy, subject to France. Lat. 49. 32. long. 5. 49.

MEZIERES, a small fortified town of Upper Champagne, on an island formerly by the Meuse, over which it has 2 bridges, was taken by the Emperor Charles V. in 1521, 12 miles north west of Sedan. Lat. 49. 46. long. 4. 38.

MILAN, the capital of the Milanese, situate on the rivers Olana and Lombros, 10 Italian miles in circuit, including several gardens, and surrounded only with a wall and rampart. At some distance is a citadel consisting of 6 bastions well fortified.

The city was built in the year of Rome 39; since that æra it has been 40 times besieged, 20 times taken, and 4 times almost entirely destroyed, but has always recovered itself; stands 116 miles north-east of Turin, and 248 north-west of Rome. Lat. 45. 31. north; long. 9. 42. east.

MILLAND, the capital of the territory of Rouvergne in Guienne, in France, situate on the Tarn, 64 miles north-west of Montpelier, was formerly fortified by the Reformed, but dismantled by Lewis XIII. in 1629. In 1744 the maintenance of 2 troops of dragoons quartered on the protestant inhabitants, cost them 30000 livres for 3 months, by which the town was totally ruined. Lat. 44. 12. n. long. 2. 51. east.

MINDEN, a city of Westphalia, and a capital of a duchy of that name, in Germany, 38 miles west of Hanover, is subject to the King of Prussia. On the 31st July, 1757, it was taken by the French. March 8, 1758, it surrendered to the Hanoverians, when 3516 men were also made prisoners. July 9, 1759, the French retook it by assault, when 1500 men of the Allies were made prisoners, with many pieces of artillery and large magazines; but, on the 2d of August 1759, it again surrendered to the Allies at discretion, with 1533 men prisoners, and considerable magazines. Lat. 52. 31. n. long. 8. 38. east. Near this place, the allied army, commanded by Prince Ferdinand of Brunswick, obtained a glorious victory over the French army, commanded by Marshal de Contades, on the 1st of August 1759.

Contades was encamped before Minden, and Prince Ferdinand's camp extended from Thornhufen to Hille. The prince, on the 31ft July, refolved to attack the French early the next morning, and Contades prepared to do the fame by the Allies. The French were 110000 men, including 12000 Saxons: the Allies 80000. The French cavalry was placed in the centre confifting of 60 fquadrons, their infantry on the wings. On the contrary, the cavalry of the Allies was on the wings, and the infantry in the centre. The French began the attack about 5 in the morning, and about 8 the Britifh infantry routed the French cavalry. The cavalry of the Allies did not come up in time to complete the victory, which gave the French cavalry time to rally and return to the charge, fupported by the Saxon infantry, and a very brifk cannonade, which took the infantry of the Allies obliquely in front, and directly in flank ; and the Duke de Broglio brought up the right to fupport the centre, but the Britifh infantry performed wonders, and the French were totally routed about noon. The Allies loft about 2000, killed and wounded, of which 1200 were Englifh. The French loft 6000, killed and wounded : 154 officers, and 79 non commiffioned officers were taken, befides 1533 left fick in Minden ; 80 cannon, 10 pair of colours, and 7 ftandards. The fame day the Hereditary Prince of Brunfwick defeated a body of 10000 French, under the Duke de Brifac, at Creveldt, which obliged Contades to quit his camp, and evacuate Minden. By this fighal victory, Prince Ferdinand

preferved Hanover a fecond time from the French, who were obliged to abandon all Weftphalia, and retire 200 miles back to the Rhine. Caffel, Zeigenhayn, Weller, and Marpurgh, were retaken from the French, who alfo furrendered Munfter on the 30th of November.

MINE, a lodgement made under ground to place powder in, which is fet on fire to blow up the works above it. The difference between mines and counter-mines is, that the firft are made by the befiegers, and the latter by the befieged.

Two ounces of powder will blow up 2 cubic feet of earth : and confequently 200, viz. 12½ pounds, will raife 200 feet of earth, which is near 200 yards cube.

The Miner fhould obferve, that his powder exerts its force againft the weakeft part : therefore, no hollows fhould be near the chamber of his mine, but at leaft one and a half of folidity more than is above the mine he would blow up.

N. B. Powder has the fame force on walls, &c. as it has on earth ; viz. it raifes with equal quantities the meafure of wall or earth. The art of mining requires the fkill of an able engineer, to know the height, breadth, depth, thicknefs, and flopes, by a plumb-line ; what is parallel to the horizon, and what is not. He fhould alfo take the exact levels of all earths, and have a perfect knowledge of rocks, earths, fands, and the ftrength of all forts of powders.

To counter-mine, or blow up the enemy's mines, you petard them, bury their powder, faufages, and fometimes the miners,

or

or drive them out by fmoak of fulphur, or other fuffocation, if they are above you.

MINORCA, one of the Balearean iflands, in the Mediterranean, about 24 miles eaft of Majorca; is 32 miles in length, and 14 in breadth, covered with barren hills, only valuable for its fecure and capacious harbour of Port-Mahon. The only towns of any confequence are Citadella, at the weft extremity of the ifland, and Port Mahon at the eaft. In 1708 the Englifh took it from Spain. and it was confirmed to them by the peace of Utrecht in 1713, which they kept poffeffion of till 1756, when the French, with 13000 troops under Marfhal Richelieu, invaded the ifland, and in about 2 months made themfelves mafters of St. Philip's caftle, &c. Long. 4. 6. lat. 39. 50.

MINSK, or MINSKI, a city of Ruffian Lithuania, in Poland, the capital of a territory of that name on the Swiflocz, was taken by the Ruffians in 1656, and is 72 miles fouth eaft of Wilna. Lat. 54. 41. n. long. 27. 41. eaft.

MIRANDA DE DOURO, a city of Tralos Montes, in Portugal, being a frontier againft Spain, near Leon, and fituated in a mountainous rugged country, on the Douro; befides its fortifications it is defended by a caftle and fort, and lies 26 miles fouth of Braganza, in lat. 41. 31. n. long. 6. 39 weft.

May 1762, while the commander of the Spanifh forces was preparing to befieg: it, a powder magazine blew up, and killed 800 men; they furrendered prifoners of war. Lat. 45. 10. long 11. 31.

MIRANDOLA, a fortified city in a dukedom of that name, in Modena, in Italy, 18 miles north of Modena; befieged in 1702 by the Imperialifts, and taken by the French in 1705, but reftored in 1707.

MOAT, ditch, or foffe, a depth or trench round the rampart of a place to defend it and prevent furprizes. The brink of the moat next the rampart is called the fcarp; and that oppofite, on the other fide, the counter-fcarp, which forms a re entering angle before the centre of the curtain. A dry moat round a place that is large and has a ftrong garrifon, is preferable to one full of water, becaufe the paffage may be difputed inch by inch; and the befiegers, when lodged in the moat, are continually expofed to the bombs, grenades, and other fire-works, which are thrown inceffantly over the ramparts on their works. In the middle of a dry moat is fometimes made another fmall moat called the cunette, which is generally dug fo deep as to obtain a fpring for filling it. The deepeft and broadeft foffes are efteemed the beft; but a deep foffe is preferable to a broad one. The ordinary breadth is about 20 fathoms; the depth 16 feet.

To drain a moat or foffe full of water, is, to dig a trench deeper than the level of the water to let it out. When it is drained, there are hurdles thrown upon the mud and flime, and covered with earth, or bundles of rufhes, to make a firm paffage.

MOBILE, Movile, or Fort Conde, a ftrong fort on a river of the fame name near the gulph of Mexico, 140 miles north eaft of New Orleans. Lon. 88. la;

31. un'er the government of Louifiana.

MODENA (CITY of) the capital of a dukedom of that name, in Upper Italy, is fortified, has a ftrong citadel, and lies 24 miles north weft of Bologna. and 38 fouth of Mantua. Lat. 45. 3. long 11. 36.

MODON, a city of the Morea, in European Turky, has a good harbour, defended by a caftle, 18 miles weft of Coran, of the Morea. Lat. 36 42. long. 21. 27.

MOGULSTAN, an inconfiderable town of Hungary Proper, on the Danube; famous for the unfortunate defeat of Lewis II. by the Turkifh Emperor Solyman in 1526, and alfo for a fignal victory obtained here over the Turks in 1687; 18 miles north-weft of Effeck, belongs to the Houfe of Auftria. Lat, 46. 21. long. 20. 15.

MOINEAU, a French term for a little flat baftion, raifed upon a re-entering angle, before a curtain, which is too long, between two other baftions. Commonly joined to the curtain, but fometimes feparated by a fofie, and then called a detached baftion. They are not raifed fo high as the works of the place, becaufe they would then be expofed to the fire of the befieged. Left the enemy fhould lodge themfelves, their parapet, as well as the parapet of all out-works, fhould be cannon-proof, viz. 18 feet thick.

MONACA, the capital of a principality of that name, in the territory of Genoa, in Upper Italy, a fmall fortified city, has a good harbour. Lat. 43. 56. long. 7. 21.

MOLWITZ, a town of Grotfka in Silefia, and the kingdom of Bohemia, 38 miles fouth of Breflaw, in the neighbourhood of Neifs. Lat. 50. 31. long. 16. 51 It is remarkable for an engagement that happened near it between the Auftrians and Pruffians, 30th March 1741; when the latter having received intelligence that Count Neuperg had orders to hazard a battle, that he might cover the fortreffes of Neifs and Brieg, they marched directly towards him, and made the neceffary difpofitions for engaging. The battle was bloody, the Auftrians having drove back and put into diforder the left wing of the Pruffians, commanded by Lieutenant-general Count Schulemberg, who was killed on the firft onfet: but the confufion was foon redreffed by fome regiments of infantry, and by the grenadiers, intermixed with the Pruffian horfe. The attack on the right wing proved as warm as that on the left; five fquadrons of Schulemberg's dragoons being almoft cut to pieces; but the Pruffians foon gained advantages in their turn, and after an engagement of 4 hours, obliged the Auftrians to retreat, who marched off in pretty good order, and encamped under the cannon of Neifs. General Schulemburg, Colonel Burke, Lieutenant-colonel Fitzgerald, the Margrave Frederick of Brandenburg, &c. were killed. The Veldt Marfhal Schwerin, the Lieutenant-generals Marcwits and Kleift; General Margrave, Charles of Brandenburgh; the Colonels, Prince William, the Margrave's brother, &c. wounded, and between 2 and 3000 killed. The Auftrians loft 4000, killed, wounded, and taken; among which were the Generals Romer

Romer and Galdi, and the Count de la Nais killed : Generals Brown, Kahil, Lentulus, &c. wounded.

MONJUICH, or *Montjoy*, a castle standing a mile west of Barcelona, taken by the English in 1705.

MONSANTO, a fortified frontier of Spanish Estramadura, invested by the Confederates under the Marquis de los Minas in 1704, who on that occasion gained a considerable victory over the Spaniards ; 18 miles west of Valverde.

MONS, or *Bergen*, a large, strong, and rich city of the Austrian Low-Countries, and the capital of Hainault, on a hill, near the junction of the Haine and Trouille. The country round it may be so overflowed, as to render an enemy's approaches very difficult. The French took it in 1691, but ceded it to Spain by the treaty of Ryswick in 1697. The Duke of Marlborough having, in its neighbourhood, gained the memorable victory of Malplaquet over the French in 1709, it was followed by the reduction of this city, and all the province of Hainault, which was confirmed to the House of Austria by the peace of Utrecht in 1713, and made part of the barrier. The French, under Count Saxe, took this city, but restored it by the treaty of Aix-la-Chapelle in 1748, after demolishing its fortifications. 24 miles south-east of Tournay, and 30 south-west of Brussels, in lat. 50. 30. long. 3 36.

MONTAUBAN, a well built city of Lower Quercy, in Guienne, in France, 20 miles n. of Thouloule. In 1562, the inhabitants embraced the reformed religion, and fortified the town, so that Lewis XIII. besieged it without success in 1621, and did not take it till 1629, when it was dismantled. Lat. 44. 10. n. long. 1. 4 east.

MONTMEDY, a town of considerable strength, on a hill near the river Chiers, about 30 miles west of Luxemberg, and 20 south of Boreillou, taken by the French in 1657.

MONT-PAG NOTE, *or post of the invulnerable*, an eminence chosen out of cannon-shot of the place besieged.

MONTREAL, a town of Canada, in North America, in an island of the same name, formed by the river St. Lawrence, 170 miles south-west of Quebec. Surrendered to Sir Jeffery Amherst, Sept. 1760, and was ceded to the English in 1763. Lat. 45. 18. long. 74. 15.

MONTREUIL, a fortified town of Picardy in France, on the river Canche, 4 miles from the sea, and 32 south of Calais. Lat. 50. 27. long. 1. 50.

MORELLA, a small town of Valencia in Spain, on the frontiers of Arragon, among high mountains, and encompassed with steep rocks. Almost destroyed by Philip V. in 1705, now in a very declining condition.

MORLAIX, properly *Montrelais*, a small trading town of Lower Bretagne in France, on a river which has water for ships to come up with the tide, on the English channel, has a harbour defended by the castle of Toureau, on an opposite island, 26 miles n. east of Prest. Lat. 48. 41. long. 3. 58. west.

MOROCCO, the capital of a kingdom of that name in Africa,

is fortified; but the works, as well as the city, are at present in a declining condition, the seat of the empire having been removed from thence to Fez, 216 miles south-west of it. Lat. 31. 56. n. long. 9. 12. west.

MORTARS, are made of brass or iron, used both in the land and sea service for throwing shells and carcasses; but those for land are shortest and lightest, and their chambers hold the least powder. They are distinguished by the diameter of their bores; as a 13, 10, or 8 inch mortar; the royal and coehorn. The royal carries a shell whose diameter is 5. 5. inches; the coehorn, 4. 6.

MOSAMBIQUE, the capital of a province of that name in Africa, on an island, has a good harbour, defended by a citadel, and the fortifications of the town, which is regularly fortified. Lat. 15. long. 41. 10.

MOTION, *of an army,* the several marches and countermarches it makes, or the changing of its post for an advantageous encampment, either with a design to engage the enemy, or shun fighting.

Motion of a bomb or *ball,* the progress it makes in the air, after delivered, is of 3 sorts: the *violent motion,* or first explosion, when the powder has worked its effect upon the ball, so far as the bomb or ball may be supposed to go in a right line; the *mixed motion* denotes when the weight of the ball begins to overcome the force which was given by the powder; and the *natural motion,* when the ball or bomb is falling.

MOULDINGS, *of a gun* or *mortar,* are all the eminent parts;

as squares or rounds, which serve generally for ornaments; such as the *breech moulding.* The rings of a gun are likewise mouldings.

MOUNT GUARD, to go upon duty: *to mount a breach,* is to run up to attack; *to mount the trenches,* to go upon guard in the trenches.

MOUNT (ST. MICHAEL) a little town, abbey, and fortress in the territory of Avranche in Normandy in France, on a rock called Tumba in the English channel. The town lies lower than the abbey, and is fortified. Not far from hence is the rock Tumbella, on which formerly stood a castle, 18 miles east of St. Malo, in lat. 48 37. long. 1. 40.

MUNDE, FORT, at the entrance of the river Persante, taken Nov. 15, 1761, by General Romanzow, by which all communication by water was cut off between Stetin and Colberg.

MUNDEN, long. 9. 32. east; lat 51. 25. a town of Brunswick, in Germany, which has oft been evacuated since 1758, and in August 1762, the French abandoned it.

MUNICH, the capital of Bavaria, a large and elegant city, on the Iser, is surrounded with a wall and fortifications, but of so little strength, that it has always surrendered to those who were masters of the field, and been frequently plundered, particularly by the Austrians, in 1742, 64 miles south west of Ratisbon, and 205 west of Vienna. Lat. 48. 22. long. 11. 41.

MUNSTER, a city, the capital of a bishoprick of that name

on the Aa, in the moſt fruitful plain of the country. The city is well built of free-ſtone. Here the famous treaty was concluded in 1648, which put an end to the civil commotions of Germany on account of religion, after a 30 years war, in which Guſtavus Adolphus, King of Sweden, made ſo great a figure; the claims were ſettled of the German, and ſeveral other Princes and States of Europe, with regard to the limits of their territories; particularly the Spaniards acknowledged the Dutch to be a free independent ſtate at this treaty, which from the city was ſometimes called the peace of Munſter; ſometimes the treaty of Weſtphalia, from the province in which it was concluded; and at other times, the religious peace, from the diſſentions on this ſcore between the Germans being ſettled in it. 38 miles ſouth-weſt of Oſnaburg, and 68 n. of Cologne. Lat. 52. 18. long. 7. 14. eaſt.

MURCIA, the capital of a province of that name in Spain, on the Segura, is large and populous, has ſtrait ſtreets, a caſtle on an eminence without the city, 26 miles n. of Carthagena, in lat. 38. 12, long. 1. 14. weſt.

MUSQUET, the moſt commodious and uſeful fire-arm uſed by an army; they carry a ball of 29 to 2 pounds of lead.

MUTINY, " Any officer or ſoldier who ſhall preſume to uſe traiterous or diſreſpeⱦtful words againſt the ſacred perſon of his Majeſty, or any of the Royal Family, is guilty of mutiny.

" Any officer or ſoldier who ſhall behavé with contempt or diſreſpeⱦt towards the general, or other commander of our forces, or ſhall ſpeak words tend-

ing to their hurt or diſhonour, is guilty of mutiny.

" Any officer or ſoldier who ſhall begin, excite, cauſe, or join in, any mutiny or ſedition, in the troop, company, or regiment to which he belongs, or in any other troop, or company, in our ſervice, or on any party, poſt, detachment, or guard, on any pretence whatever, is guilty of mutiny.

" Any officer or ſoldier, who, being preſent at any mutiny, or ſedition, does not uſe his utmoſt endeavours to ſuppreſs the ſame, or coming to the knowledge of any mutiny, or intended mutiny, does not, without delay, give information to his commanding-officer, is guilty of mutiny.

" Any officer or ſoldier, who ſhall ſtrike his ſuperior officer, or draw, or offer to draw, or ſhall lift up any weapon, or offer any violence againſt him, being in the execution of his office, on any pretence whatſoever, or ſhall diſobey any lawful command of his ſuperior officer, is guilty of mutiny."

NAJARA a ſmall town of Old Biſcay, in Spain, 48 miles ſouth of Bilboa, famous for a battle in 1639. Lat. 51. 22. long. 56.

NAILING OF CANNON, driving a large nail or iron ſpike into the touch-hole of a piece of artillery, to render it unſerviceable. The remedy is to drill a new touch-hole, for if the ſpike be taken out, the hole is left ſo large that the piece cannot be fired.

NAMUR, city, is between two hills, at the conflux of the Maeſe and the Sambre, 36 miles eaſt of Mons, 28 ſouth-weſt of Liege, and 32 ſouth-eaſt of Bruſſels. The chief part of the town

town stands on the north side of the Sambre; on the other side stands the citadel, upon a rocky mountain, being a magnificent structure, and esteemed the strongest fortress in Europe; the rock on which it is, is not only very steep, but the approaches to it are fortified with the greatest art; and on the top of the rock are several good springs of water.

In May 1692, the French King, with 45000 men, covered by the Duke of Luxemburg with 60000, besieged and took Namur, King William not being able to come to its relief, on account of the great rains which had rendered the rivers impassible. The city surrendered in 11 days on good terms, after having sustained 3 assaults; and the castle, which held out near a month longer, also obtained honourable conditions. The governors of the town and citadel were the Prince of Brabançon and the Dutch General Coehorn; which last made a brave defence, and was dangerously wounded.

Third July 1695, King William invested this city, at which time the French garrison consisted of 8 regiments of dragoons, 1 of horse, 20 battalions, a company of volunteers, 1 of cannoneers, another of miners, and a brigade of engineers. Since their last conquest of it, they had omitted nothing that art could invent to render it impregnable by new fortifications and additional out-works. It was furnished with 120 cannon, 8 mortars, 12000 grenadoes, bullets and bombs; 13000 and 30000 weight of powder, 16000 muskets, and great store of other arms, 100000 crowns in specie, and 6 months provisions. But notwithstanding all this, with the brave defence of the garrison, the Confederates carried on their attacks so vigorously, that the town capitulated 4th of August.

During the siege of the citadel, Marshal Villeroy advanced as if he would attempt to relieve it; and passing by Brussels, he threw near 2000 bombs into that city, with a great number of red-hot bullets; whereby whole streets were laid in ashes, there being about 1500 houses ruined or much damaged, besides several publick edifices. This the French pretended was done by way of reprisal for the Confederate fleets bombarding Dunkirk; but their real intention was to retard the siege of the castle of Namur; which, after a most resolute defence, made by Marshal Boufflers, capitulated on the first of September, in view of Marshal Villeroy's army. The French King so much depended on the strength of this place, that he put up over the gates, *It may be surrendered, but cannot be conquered.*

After the death of Charles II. of Spain, the French seized Namur, with the rest of the Netherlands. In 1704, the Dutch army, under M. d'Auverquerque, bombarded it from the 26th to the 29th of July, and destroyed great part of the city: but the French kept possession of it till the treaty of Utrecht, when the country, town, and castle, were yielded to the States General, to serve as a barrier against France: the Elector of Bavaria was to enjoy the sovereignty and revenues, and the town to contribute its quota to the maintenance of the Dutch troops and the fortifications.

NANCY, the capital of Lorrain

rain in Germany, near the Meurte, is situated in a delightful plain. It is divided into the old and new town. In the collegiate Church of St. George is the monument of Charles the Bold, Duke of Burgundy, who was killed before this place in 1746. By the peace of Ryswic, the out-works of the old and new town, with the fortifications of the latter, were demolished; but those of the former suffered to remain. It lies 68 miles south of Triers, 68 north-west of Strasburg, and 143 east of Paris. Lat. 48. 41. n. long. 6. 5. east.

NANT, a town of considerable strength, on the river Maese, about 12 miles from Namur, and 6 from Charlemont.

NAPLES, the capital of a kingdom of that name: the island lying before it forms a secure harbour, and ships of great burthen may lie close to the quays: to the east is a large plain, terminated by Mount Vesuvius; to the west stands the castle of St. Elmo, or St. Eramo, on a hill, having bomb-proof subterraneous vaults; there are also 4 castles to defend the town. Their militia is numerous, the lands being held by military tenures: but it is seldom called out, and but little depended on. The King generally maintains a body of 15000 regular troops in time of peace, and can raise an equal number in time of war. This city has alternately been governed by Spanish and German Viceroys, till Don Carlos was, in 1734, placed on the throne by the united powers of France, Spain, and Sardinia; while the British fleet under Sir Charles Wager

conveyed him safely thither. As this prince obtained the crown by force, he must maintain his possession by the same means, unless, by a wise and prudent administration, he should gain the affections of the people. In the arsenal, are said to be continually lodged arms for 50000 men. 146 miles south east of Rome. Lat. 41. 51. long. 14. 45.

NAPOLI DI ROMANIA, a town and fortress on a peninsula of the Morea in European Turky, extending into the bay called Golfo de Napoli, has a good harbour, is one of the strongest towns in the Morea, 64 miles south-west of Setines, or Athens. Lat. 37. 36. n. long. 23. 31. east.

NARBONNE, a large fortified city of Languedoc in France, in a deep valley between mountains, on a canal running through it, which joins the river Ande, and the great royal canal, with the lake Robine, also with the Mediterranean sea. In the time of the Romans, it was the capital of this part of France, and called Gallia Narbonensis. 64 miles west of Montpelier. Lat. 43. 22. long. 2. 51.

NARENZA, formerly *Naro,* or *Narbona,* a town of Venetian Dalmatia in European Turky, having an harbour on a bay of the Adriatic; was in ancient times a considerable city, the capital of Dalmatia, and one of its best fortresses. In succeeding ages the Sclavonians settled here, and by their piracies rendered the coasts unsafe for navigation, till the Venetians took it in 987. It had its own governors, till it fell under the Turkish yoke in 1749; and lies 28 miles north of Ragusa, in lat. 42. 56. long. 18. 26.

NARVA,

NARVA, a port town of Livonia, on the frontiers of Ingermanland, on the rapid river of that name, issuing from the Peipus lake, and falling into the gulf of Finland, 2 miles below the town, is well fortified, has a strong garrison; besieged by the Russians in 1700, but relieved by Charles XII. King of Sweden, who gained a signal victory over them with 20000 men, though the Russians were 100000. But the Czar Peter the Great afterwards took Narva by storm, and transplanted the inhabitants to Astracan; and the Russians have been in possession of Narva, and all Livonia, ever since, making it one of the stations of their fleet. Lat. 59. 21. n. long. 27. 41. east.

NASEBY, a village near Rothwell in Northamptonshire, 10 miles north of Northampton, famous for a victory gained by the Parliament's forces over the Royalists, June 14, 1645: Long. 50 min. lat. 52. 20.

NAXICA, south-east of Micone, and east of Paros, 100 miles in circuit. On the south side of the island is a town defended by a castle. At about a gun-shot distance is a fine marble tower, on a rock. Lat. 36. 41. n. long. 26. 10. east.

NEGAPATAN, a town of the Hither India, with a harbour, on the Coromandel coast, 20 miles south of Trincumbar or Frankebar, where is a Dutch fort with a factory. Lat. 11. 12. n. long. 79. 12. east.

NEGROPONT, or *Egripos city*, the capital of the island, bearing its name, in the Archipelago, or Egæan sea, lying on the Euripus, and probably on the site of its ancient capital Chalcis, and on the west of the island, 34 miles n. of Sentines or Athens, and 70 north of Corinth. The walls of the town where the Turks reside, are 2 miles in circuit; but the suburbs where the Christians dwell, are much larger. The Turkish Admiral, who is Beglerbeg or governor of this island, and the neighbouring parts of Greece, has his seat here; and this port is commonly a station of Turkish gallies. It is also the see of a Greek metropolitan. This is by much the largest of all the islands in the Archipelago, and with the others subject to Turky. Lat. 38. 36. n. long. 24. 36. east.

NEIDENBURG, a fine town in the county of that name, and Ortelsburgh circle, in Regal Prussia, with a mountain and castle, in a very delightful country.

NEISS, a town of Silesia, in Bohemia, on the river bearing its name, 46 miles south of Breslaw. On the 5th and 6th of November 1758, General Harsh raised the siege of this place, with precipitation, on the approach of the King of Prussia, abandoning a large quantity of ammunition. Lat. 50. 31. n. long. 16. 10. east.

NELSON, FORT, a settlement on the west side of Hudson's Bay, in Canada, North America, at the mouth of a river of that name, and on a bay of the sea, 250 miles south-east of Churchill Fort, and 600 northwest of Rupert Fort. Lat. 57. 12. n. long. 91. 12. west.

NERAC, a town of Gascony, capital of the duchy of Albret, in France, 12 miles west of Agen. It surrendered to Lewis XIII. in 1621. Lat. 44. 12. long. 14 m.

NERO, or *Fort Nassau*, a fortress

tress at the west extremity of one of the Banda islands, called by that name, in the India ocean, in Asia, 64 miles south of the island of Ceram, 131 south-east of Amboyna, is one of those forts by which the Dutch command the navigation of the neighbouring seas, and defend their usurped possession of the spice islands. Long 128 lat. 4.

NEUENBURG a small town of Little Pomerania, in Polish Prussia, having the Weichsel on one side, and morasses on the other.

NEUMARK, in the neighbourhood of Borne, Luthep, and Lissa, a village of Silesia, 16 miles from Breslaw, famous for a battle between the Austrians and Prussians, 5th Dec. 1757. The King of Prussia having determined to make himself master of Silesia, he resolved, at the head of 38000, to attack 80000 Austrians, commanded by Prince Charles of Lorrain. The battle began at 2 in the afternoon, and continued till night, when the Prussians carried the village of Luthep, which decided the victory in their favour. The Austrians sustained a loss of 6000 killed, and about 20,000 taken prisoners ; 3000 baggage and ammunition-waggons, 180 cannon, and 43 pair of colours ; the Prussians had only 2000 killed and wounded. The consequence of this victory was the retaking of Breslaw by his Prussian Majesty, where he made 14 generals and 14,000 men prisoners.

NEW ORLEANS, on the bank of the Mississippi, in 29 deg. 59 min. n. lat. On account of its vicinity to Mobille, vessels of 1000 tons may ride with their sides close to the banks at low water; has a good magazine and barracks. On the east of the Mississippi is Fort la Balise, which defends the entrance and channel.

NEWPORT, the capital of the colony of Rhode Island, in New England, 72 miles south of Boston. Lat. 41. 14. n. long. 74. 8. west.

Newport, a town of Flanders, in the Austrian Low-Countries, having a harbour 8 miles north-east of Furnes, and 10 south-west of Ostend. The French besieged this place in 1488, with 18000 men, and assaulted it 3 times, but were as often bravely repulsed. The Dutch, under Prince Maurice, intended to invest it in 1600; but the Archduke Albert coming up with them, a bloody battle ensued, and Maurice obtained a most glorious victory ; for which he was very much indebted to the English, under the conduct of Sir Francis Vere. The Archduke, who was wounded, and narrowly escaped being taken had 6000 killed, 600 made prisoners, and lost 30 colours. Prince Maurice, however, notwithstanding this success, returned to Holland without attempting any thing farther. Lat. 51. 15. lon. 2. 45.

NEWSTAT, a town of Hungary, situate 65 miles east of Tockay, subject to the Empress Queen. Lat. 47. 30. long. 22. 32.

On the 21st of September, 1759, General Wunch, with the Prussians, gained a considerable advantage near this place over the army of the Empire, commanded by Prince de Deux-Ponts, whilst General Rebentisch, with 5 battalions and 15 squadrons of the right wing, was

was engaged with the Auftrians, under General Haddick, near Stroifchen: the Pruffians were twice repulfed by the Auftrians; the infantry ftood with great firmnefs; but general Fink, having reafon to think that Prince de Deux Ponts intended to renew the engagement the next morning, ordered General Robentifch to retire at retreat-beating to the firft line. The Pruffians took 1 cannon and loft 5, when the cavalry were a fecond time repulfed.

General Fink remained in camp at Corbitz, on the 24th, when the army of the empire were retiring to Keffeldorf. The lofs of the Pruffians in both actions were about 1000; that of the Auftrians and Imperialifts, in killed, wounded, and prifoners, upwards of 4000.

NIAGARA, a fort in a province of that name, in America, at the influx into the Lake of Ontario. This important place was taken by Sir William Johnfon, 25th July 1759, when the garrifon of 617 men and officers furrendered with the honours of war.

NICE, the capital of the province of that name, in Piedmont, in Italy, fituate at the mouth of the Var, well fortified, has a good harbour on the Mediterranean, at the mouth of the river Paulon: but the only one capable of admitting fmall veffels, though endeavours have been for fome years ufed for improving it. It has alfo been declared a free port. Taken by the French in 1691, and reftored to Savoy in 1696. 12 miles north of Antibes, 38 fouth of Coni, is fouth of Turin, and fubject to the King of Sardinia. Lat. 43. 51. n. long. 7. 21. eaft.

NICOPOLIS, a large city of a province of that name, in Bulgaria, in European Turky, fituate on the Danube, defended by a caftle, famous for the firft unfortunate battle, fought here in 1396, between the Chriftians and the Turks. 96 miles north-weft of Adrianople. Lat. 42. 46. n. long. 24. 56. eaft.

NIMEGUEN, a city of Guelderland, in the United Provinces, on the river Waal. Here the famous treaty between the Dutch and their Allies with France, in 1679, was concluded, and thence called the treaty of Nimeguen. 12 miles f. of Arnheim, 54 f. eaft of Amfterdam. Lat. 51. 53. n. long. 5. 46. eaft.

NISMES, or *Nimes*, a large, elegant, and ancient city of Languedoc, in France, in a very pleafant country, has a citadel confifting of 4 baftions. 30 miles north-eaft of Montpelier. Lat. 43. 42. long. 4. 28.

NISSA, a city of Servia, in European Turky, on the river Moraw, furrounded with a wall and ramparts. 128 miles foutheaft of Belgrade. Lat. 43. 10. long. 22. 25.

NOLI, a fmall city of the Genoefe, has a good harbour defended by a ftrong caftle, 37 miles f. weft of Genoa. Lat. 44. 24. long. 8. 56.

NOTTEBURG, a ftrong fortrefs and fea-port of Ingria, in Ruffia, on an ifland formed by the river Nieva, near the weftern bank of the Ladoga, 26 miles to the eaft of that capital. Lat. 60. 15. long. 31. 46.

NOVI, a town in the Riviera di Ponente, belonging to Genoa, in

In Upper Italy, has a very ftrong city on the confines of the Milanefe, 27. miles north-weft of Genoa. Lat. 45. 16. n. long. 9. 20. eaft.

NOVIGRAD, a fmall town and caftle of Venetian Dalmatia, at the mouth of a bay of that name. In 1646 the Venetians loft the place, but recovered it in the following year. 38 miles n. eaft of Zara. Lat. 44. 27. long. 17. 33.

NOVOGOROD, the capital of the duchy of that name in Ruffia, a very old, large, and famous trading town, on the river Wolchow, where it iffues from the Ilmen lake; fortified with deep ditches and old walls. Lat. 58. 10. long. 34. 15.

NURENBERG, an imperial free city of Franconia, and capital of a territory of that name, 43 miles f. of Bamberg, 52 n. weft of Ratifbon, 7 miles in circuit, defended by a wall, caftle, and other works. Lat. 49. 41. long. 11. 22.

NYBORG, a fortified town on the eaft end of Tunen in Denmark on the Great Belt, 12 miles eaft of Odenfee. Lat. 55. 27. n. lon. 10. 15. eaft.

NYSLOT, a town of conquered Carelia in Sweden, the only one of Savolaxia, on the lake Saima, having a caftle on a rock in the river, and well fortified, fubject to the Ruffians. 58 miles n. of Wiborg. Lat. 62. 10. long. 29. 15.

OBLIQUE-DEFENCE, that which is under too great an angle, as is generally the defence of the fecond flank, which can never be fo good as a defence in front, nor approved of by engineers.

OBSLOW, a confiderable moun-tain caftle, in the Aggerfherred, a diftrict in the diocefe of Aggerhuus in Norway on the weft fide of the bay, under which lies the town of Chriftiana, 30 miles north-weft of Frederickfhad, fubject to the King of Denmark. Lat. 59. 25. long. 10. 30.

OCTAGON, an 8 fided figure of a fortification.

OCZAKOW, anciently *Ordeffus*, a ftrong fortrefs of Oczakow Tartary, having a harbour near the mouth of the Dnieper, on the fide of a hill, on which is a ftrong caftle, 123 miles n. eaft of the northern branch of the Danube, and 151 weft of Precop. Lat. 46. 12 n. long. 35. 17. eaft.

ODENSEE, the capital of a diftrict of that name, and of Funen in Denmark, the largeft Danifh ifland in the Baltic. Here, in 1538, a diet was held, in which the reformation of the whole kingdom was fettled. 75 miles weft of Copenhagen. Lat. 55. 25. n. long. 10. 30. eaft.

OFFA'S DYKE, an intrenchment thrown up by Offa, King of Mercia, to defend the Englifh Saxons from the incurfions of the antient Britons, who had retired into Wales, extends 90 miles from the mouth of the Wye to that of the Dee.

OFFICERS, are of 3 claffes. Thofe having commiffions from the king, are *Commiffioned Officers*. Such as have no commiffion, only warrants from their colonels, *Warrant Officers*: and thofe who have no commiffions or warrants, *Non-commiffioned Officers*; fuch as ferjeant majors, quartermafter-ferjeants, ferjeants, corporals, drum-majors, and fifemajors, who can be reduced by the colonel of a corps without a court-

court-martial; but that is seldom done.

OHM, river, at the foot of the
mountain of Amoenburgh, ftands
a ftrong redoubt and a mill,
which the French attacked and
took September 20, 1762.

OLDENBURG, the capital of
the county of that name, in Weftphalia, on the Honta, fortified
with walls and ditches, 26 miles
weft of Bremen. Lat. 53. 32. n.
long. 7. 20. eaft.

OLDENDORP, a fmall ftrong
town of Holftein and Lower
Saxony, on the river Brockaw,
near the Baltic, 25 miles n. eaft
of Ploen, fubject to the Duke of
Holftein Gothorp. Lat. 54. 34.
n. long. 10. 43. eaft.

OLERON, anciently *Uliarus*, an
ifland of France, in the Bay of
Bifcay, on the coaft of Aunis
and Saintogne, has on its eaft
fide a very ftrong caftle. Lat.
46. 10. n. long. 26. weft.

OLERON, a fmall well fortified city of Bearn, in France, and
in a diftrict of that name, on the
river Gave d'Oleron, 28 miles
f. of Dax. Lat. 43. 20. n. long.
40 min. weft.

OLIVENZA, one of the beft
fortreffes of Alentejo, in Portugal, on a fine plain, with 9 baf-
fions, 8 ravelins, a caftle, and
other works, containing about
5300 fouls, taken by the Spaniards in 1657. On the eaft fide
of the river Guadiana, 10 miles
f. of Elvas. Lat. 40. 38. n. long.
7. 38. eaft.

OLMUTZ, the metropolis of
Moravia, on the river Morau,
100 miles fouth-eaft of Prague,
90 f. of Breflaw, and 80 n. of
Vienna, a ftrong city; its fortifications are none of the meaneft.
15th December 1741, it was furrendered to the Pruffians by ca-

pitulation, but foon fell into the
hands of its former mafters. July
1, 1758, the General, Laudfhu
and Zifkowitz having in 2 attacks, on the 28th and 29th of
June, defeated and deftroyed the
greateft part of a large convoy
coming from Troppau, and made
General Puthhammer, with feveral 100 men prifoners, in the
defiles of Domftadt, the King of
Pruffia found himfelf, after near
5 weeks open trenches, obliged
to raife the fiege of Olmutz,
which he effected with little lofs.
32 miles f. weft of Troppau, 76
n. of Vienna. Lat. 49. 38. long.
16. 51.

OMERS, ST. a town on the
river Aa, one of the beft fortreffes in French Flanders, the
fecond city of Artois, lies partly
on a hill, and partly in a morafs,
well fortified in the modern manner, and has a communication
with the fea, by means of a navigable canal, cut from the Aa
to Gravelines. 19 miles f. eaft of
Calais, and 23 f. of Dunkirk.
Lat. 50. 51. long. 2. 24. See
Plan 15.

ONDECAGON, an 11 fided fortification.

ONEGLIA, a well built and
fortified fea port town, in a principality of that name, in the
middle of the Genoefe dominions
in Italy, fubject to the King of
Sardinia, 47 miles f. eaft of
Coni, and 74 f. weft of Genoa.
Lat. 44. 10. long. 20. 27.

ONOTH, or *Onod*, a town and
caftle of Hungary, on the river
Sajo, 56 miles n. eaft of Buda,
fubject to the Houfe of Auftria.
Lat. 48. 16. long. 20. 27.

OPENING FLANK, that part of
the flank covered by the orillon.

OPENING OF TRENCHES, the
firft breaking of ground by the
befiegers,

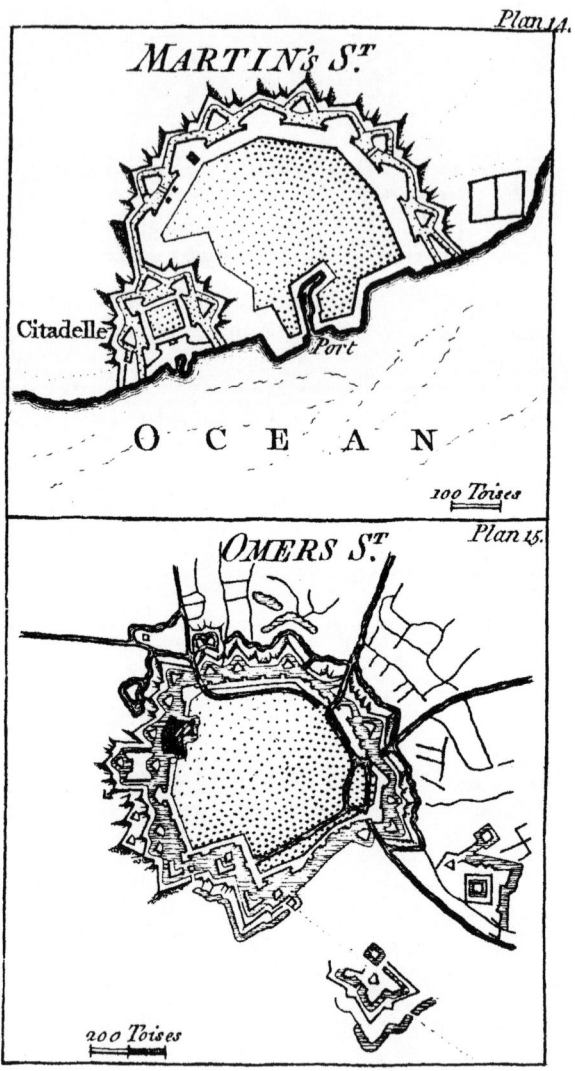

Plan 14.

MARTIN'S S.^T

Citadelle

Port

O C E A N

100 Toises

OMERS S.^T

Plan 15.

200 Toises

befiegers, to carry on their approaches.

OPPEREN, a town of Silefia, in Bohemia, fortified with very thick walls and ftrong gates, on the north bank of the Oder, over which is a bridge, 34 miles f. eaft of Breflaw. Lat. 50. 45. long. 17. 26.

ORAN, a city and port town of Barbary, in a province of that name, in Algiers, near the fea, oppofite Carthagena, in Spain, partly on a plain, and partly on the declivity of a craggy hill, about a mile and a half in circuit, and well fortified, but commanded by the adjacent hills and eminences. Oran having become a neft of pirates, who infefted the coaft of Spain, Cardinal Ximenes refolved to take it from the Moors, and after a fhort fiege made himfelf mafter of it in 1509; the Spaniards kept it till 1708, when it fell into the hands of the Infidels after a long fiege; but they loft it in 1732. Lat. 36. 41. n. long. 5. min. eaft.

ORANGE, a very old city, and the capital of a principality of that name, on the eaft banks of the Rhone; formerly governed by its own fovereigns, among whom was William III. King of England, whofe heir, Frederic William, ceded it to the Houfe of Bourbon by the treaty of Utrecht, in 1713. Maurice of Naffau, prince of Orange, ftrongly fortified its caftle, which ftood on an eminence, in 1622; Lewis XIV. demolifhed the works in 1660, and the caftle in 1673. 18 miles n. of Avignon, 74 f. weft of Grenoble. Lat. 44. 21. long. 4. 51.

ORDERS, all that is lawfully commanded by fuperior officers.

ORDNANCE, a term given to whatever concerns the artillery. The commander in chief is called Mafter-general of the Ordnance, inftead of artillery; the fecond in command Lieutenant general.

Ordnance, Board of, confifts of 4 officers; the Surveyor-general, Clerk of the Ordnance, Storekeeper, and Clerk of the Deliveries; over which prefides the Mafter, or, in his abfence, the Lieutenant-general. This board regulates every thing relative to the artillery.

OREBRO, an old inland town of Niricia, in Sweden Proper, well known in hiftory; fituate on the lake Hielmar, has a caftle entirely furrounded with water, and a harbour to go by water to Stockholm, by means of the river and canal of Arboga, reaching to the Maler fea, 68 miles weft of Stockholm. Lat. 59. 25. long. 14. 6.

OREGRUND, a port-town of Upland, in Sweden Proper, thrice deftroyed and burnt by the Ruffians, now pretty well rebuilt, on the Bothnic gulf, 58 miles n. of Stockholm. Lat. 60. 27. long. 18. 18.

ORGNES, thick long pieces of wood, pointed and fhod with iron, clear one of another, hanging perpendicularly each by a particular rope or cord, over the gate of a ftrong place, to be dropped in cafe of emergency.

ORIGUELA,

ORIGUELA, a city of Valencia, in Spain, furrounded with mountains, defended by a good caftle, 14 miles n. eaft of Murica. Lat. 38. 22 long. 56 min. weft.

ORILLON, part of a baftion, near the fhoulder, ferves to cover the retired flank from being feen obliquely.

Orillon, a mafs of earth, faced with ftone, built on the fhoulder of a cafement baftion, to cover the cannon of the retired flank, and prevent its being difmounted by the enemy's cannon; fome are round, fome fquare; but thofe which refemble the fquare *orillon* are beft, as they can be made at lefs expence, and contain more men to fire directly on the face of the oppofite baftion, than the round can. *Orillon*, is alfo the *fhould.r* and *epaulment*.

ORISTAGNI, a fortified city, having a harbour on a bay of the Mediterranean, on the weft fide of the ifland of Sardjnia in Upper Italy, 47 miles noith weft of Cagliari, fubject to the King of Sardinia. Lat. 39. 27. long. 8. 36.

ORNE, upon the banks of a river of that name, in Lower Normandy, guarded by two batt.ries.

Five hundred marines from Admiral Young's fquadron made a defcent upon it, to deftroy 13 veffels: they fucceeded in nailing up the cannon of the batt.ries, but were obliged to reimbark, without deftroying or taking the veffels, July 11th, 1762.

ORSA, a town of Lithuania in Poland, having a caftle on the Nieper, 26 miles from Mohilow, and 70 weft of Mifciflaw. Lat. 55. 27. long. 30. 46.

ORSOWA, *Old* and *New*. The former is a middling town of Walachia, in European Turky; the latter, a fortrefs on the Danube almoft oppofite to Belgrade, 63 miles f. weft of Temefwaer; fubject to the Turks. Lat. 45. 36. long. 22. 10.

ORSOY, a fmall ftrong town of the duchy of Cleve in Weftphalia, 24 miles f nth of Cleve. Lat. 51. 36. long. 6. 5.

ORTHOGRAPHY, *or* profile, the reprefentation of a work, fhewing its breadth, thicknefs, heighth, and depth, as it would appear cut perpendicularly on the horizontal line, from the uppermoft to the loweft of its parts: as ichnography fuppofes an edifice or work cut horizontally, fo orthography fuppofes it cut vertically, and never fhews the length or any of its parts as a plan does: a plan fhews nothing of the heighth or depth of a work.

OSNABRUCK. M. de Schlieffen, under the orders of General Dreves, made himfelf mafter of it, July 28, 1759, where the Volunteers de Clermont loft fome men and 2 pieces of cannon.

OSNABRUG, anciently an imperial city, and one of the Hanstowns, in the bifhopric of that name, in Weftphalia. It is well built, encompaffed with walls and ditches, but commanded by a mountain within cannon fhct. This bifhopric, the territories of which are 40 miles long, and 30 broad, is held alternately by a proteftant and papift, the former of which is always of the houfe of Hanover. Here was concluded the treaty betwixt the Emperor and the King of Sweden, in 1648; wherein all the affairs of the proteftants were previoufly fettled, and was a confiderable

2

derable branch of the famous treaty of Weſtphalia. As the exercife of both religions is equally free in this diocefe, proteſtants are not moleſted when there is a Roman Catholic biſhop. 78 miles weſt of Hanover. Lat. 52. 42. long. 7. 38.

OSTEND, a well fortified town, on the coaſt of Flanders, in a mooriſh foil, has a good harbour, famous for a ſiege begun in 1601, under the Arch-duke Albert, continued unfuccefsful till reinforced by the Spaniſh General Spinola, who undertook the ſiege, and obliged it to furrender, according to calculation, after 3 years, 3 months, 3 weeks, 3 days, and 3 hours, the befieged having no room left to form retrenchments. It coſt 100,000 men on both fides. Taken by the French in 1745, reſtored to the Houfe of Auſtria 1748, and on the 19th or 20th of July 1757, admitted a French garrifon, under the command of Lieutenant-general de la Motte. 14 miles weſt of Bruges. Lat. 51. 14. long. 2. 59.

OSWEGO, an Engliſh fort and trading-houfe with the Indians in N. America, on the eaſt fide of the lake Ontario, 225 miles weſt of Albany, and in the government of New York. A fmall garrifon is always kept here. It was taken and demoliſhed by the French, 14th of Auguſt 1756; but foon after recovered; built much ſtronger than before in the year 1759. Lat. 43. 10. long. 76. 27.

OSWESTRY, a very ancient town of Shropſhire, furrounded with a wall and ditch, and defended by a caſtle; 15 miles from Shrewſbury, and 157 from London.

OTRANTO, anciently *Hydruntham*, a city of a province of that name, in Naples, at the mouth of the Adriatic, on the eaſt coaſt of the peninfula; a commodious port, till deſtroyed by the Venetians; ſtill furrounded with walls, bulwarks, and defended by a caſtle. In 1480, taken by Mahomet II. who ordered the archbiſhop that came to meet him, at the head of his clergy, to be fawed afunder, and the latter maſſacred at the foot of the altar. 43 miles eaſt of Tarento, and 200 of the city of Naples. Lat. 40. 22. lon. 19 31.

OVAL, a plain figure bounded by its own circumference, within which no point can be taken, and from which all right lines drawn to the circumference, can be equal.

OUDENARD, 14 miles f. of Ghent, 18 n. of Tournay, a large and well fortified town, divided by the river Scheld, in 2 parts, and almoſt furrounded by meadows, in 1706 furrendered to the Confederates. The French inveſted it in 1708, which gave occaſion to the famous battle of Oudenard, between the allied army, under the Duke of Marlborough and Prince Eugene, and that of the French by the Dukes of Burgundy and Vendofme, wherein the former obtained a glorious victory. The French having quitted Oudenard, and paffed the Scheld, fuffered the Allies to pafs it with little oppoſition, who had made a long quick march to attack them. About 3 at noon the action began, when Generals Cadogan and Sabine, with 12 battalions, attacked the village of Heaurne, where the French had 7 battalions, 3 of which were taken priſoners, prifoners, and a great part of the other 4. General Rantzau with 8 fquadrons fell upon the French horfe, between the villages of Rotz and Mullen, and entirely defeated them, driving them into inclofures and the highway that led into the march of their own army. Here the Elector of Hanover, afterwards King of Great Britain, gave early proofs of his valour, charging the enemy at the head of a fquadron of dragoons, had a horfe fhot under him, and Colonel Lufcky killed while fighting near him with the utmoft bravery. Several volunteers, amongft whom was General Schulemberg, diftinguifhed themfelves upon this occafion, charging in the van of the horfe with great fpirit, and animating the private men by their example. Here the French regiment of La Bertofche, and feveral others, were entirely broke; Colonel La Bertofche, being dangeroufly wounded, was taken prifoner; as were many others, with 12 ftandards and kettle-drums.

During this the French attacked the battalions of Major-general Collier and Brigadier Grumchon with great fury, who maintained their poft with furprizing bravery for a long time, till the Duke of Arg, le came to their fupport with 20 battalions. Thefe no fooner pofted, than the French falling furioufly upon them, drove fome Pruffian battalions from their poft, which they recovered fword in hand, notwithftanding the inequality of numbers. At length, Count Lot um coming up with the reft of the foot, they formed in 2 lines before the horfe, and attacked in good order the inclo-

fures and villages in their front, where the French were pofted; about 7 the fire grew univerfal, At firft the French gave way in moft places; but being fuftained with frefh troops, they maintained the action a confiderable time with great obftinacy. The Prince of Frize, who commanded the Dutch infantry, and Count d'Oxerftiern, attacked the French houfhold troops under the hedges of a large field; at the fame time M. d'Auverquerque and Count Tilley bore down upon them with the Danifh horfe, and forced them back into the inclofures in diforder; when it grew dark, many battalions and fquadrons flung themfelves out defperately, fome being cut to pieces as they attempted to make their way, others driven back, fome paffed through unperceived, and fome capitulated with their whole regiments. Had there been 2 hours more light, the whole body of French foot, and their right wing of horfe, which was near furrounded, had probably been cut off; but growing dark, and the fire directed various ways at once, it was impoffible to know friends from foes; orders were therefore given to ceafe firing till morning, and rather let the enemy efcape than run the hazard of killing each other. During the night, a great part of the French army retired to Ghent; early in the morning, the Lieutenant-generals Bulau and Lumley, with 40 fquadrons and a confiderable body of foot, were ordered to attack their rear-guard; when a fmart action enfued, in which many were killed and wounded on both fides, till at length the French were worfted, having

ing one regiment entirely ruined and many taken prisoners. The Allies pushed them within two leagues of Ghent; but their foot being much fatigued, it was judged improper to pursue them farther.

In this famous battle the French had above 4000 killed upon the spot, 5000 wounded, and about 7000 prisoners. Among the slain were the Marquis de Ximenes, Major-general Count de Dreux, Chevalier de Luxemburg, and Prince de Egmont. Their wounded were carried to Ghent and Bruges, where the Chevalier de Longueville, and fifteen other officers, died of their wounds. On the side of the Allies near 2000 slain, and about the same number wounded. Major-general Berensdorf, the Danish General Rantzau, the Dutch Lieutenant-colonel Hop, Captain Dean of the English guards, and Sir John Matthews, among the former; among the latter, Lieutenant-general Watsmore, Major-generals Meredith and Lauden, Colonels Groves and Pennyfeather. Lat. 50. 58. long, 3. 41. east.

OVERSLAGH, a term originally derived from the Dutch, to *skip over*.

For instance, suppose 4 battalions, each consisting of 8 captains, are doing duty together, and that a captain's guard is daily mounted: if, in the buffs, the second captain is doing duty of Deputy-adjutant-general; and the 4th. and 7th captain in the King's are acting, one as aid-de-camp, the other as brigade-major, the common duty of these 3 captains must be overslaghed; that is, equally divided among the other captains.

This table explains the term *overslagh*.

Regiments.	Nᵒ of Captains.	Heads of each Column.							
		1	2	3	4	5	6	7	8
Royal,	8	1		8		15	19	23	26
Queen's Royal	8	2	5	9	12	16	20	24	27
Old Buffs,	8	3	6	10	13	17	21	25	28
King's own,	8	4	7	11	14	18	22		29
Total	32								

N. B. The three blanks shew where the *overslaghs* take effect.

OVERYSCHE, a small town of Brabant, in the Austrian Low Countries, on the river Yscyhe, where the Duke of Bavaria and Marshal Villeroy lay encamped, when the Duke of Marlborough and the Allies attacked them in 1705. 10 miles n. east of Brussels, 12 s. west of Lovain. Lat. 40. 57. long. 4. 35.

OVIEDO, anciently *Brigetum*, the capital of Austria, in Spain, betwixt the rivers Ove and Deva, is well fortified. Here the Gothic Prince Pelayo fixed his residence. 50 miles n. of Leon. Lat. 43. 39. n. lon. 6. 42. west.

[g 4]   OUT.

OUT-POSTS, a body of men posted beyond the grand-guard, called out-posts, being without the rounds or limits of the camp.

OUT-WORKS, *advanced works, detached*, and *exterior works*; works of several kinds, which cover the body of the place: as, ravelins, half-moons, tenailles, horn-works, crown works, counter-guards, envellopes, swallows, tails, lunettes, &c.

These out-works, not only cover the place, but likewise keep an enemy at distance, and hinder his gaining any advantage of hollow or rising grounds, that may be near the counterscarp of the place; as such cavities and eminences may serve for lodgments to the besiegers, facilitate the carrying on approaches, and raising their batteries against the town. When out-works are placed one before another, you will find a ravelin before the curtain, a horn work before the ravelin, and a small ravelin before the curtain of the horn-work; then the nearest to the body of the place must be the highest, though lower than the works of the place, that they may gradually command those without them, and oblige the enemy to dislodge, if in possession of them.

PADANG, a town on the west coast of the island of Sumatra, in the Indian sea, in Asia, with a harbour belonging to the Dutch, who have a fort and settlement there. Lat. 1. 10. s. long. 99. 5. east.

PADERBORN, a large and fortified city, in the bishopric of that name, in Germany, the capital of that district, and a Hans-

town, 40 miles n. west of Cassel, Lat. 51. 47. n. long. 8. 25. east.

In March 1758, was evacuated by the French. June 8, 1759, the French entered it, and magazines fell into their hands. August 9, 1759, the Allies made 400 prisoners and took another magazine. July 18, 1760, the Allies evacuated it, the French took possession. June 28, 1761, Marshal Broglio took possession of it: Lieutenant-general Sporcken lost a few men in the retreat from it.

PADIS, or *Badis*, a fortress of Livonia, 25 miles west of Revel, and subject to Russia. Lat. 50. 15. long. 23. 10.

PADUA, a city, the capital of Il Paduana, in Italy, on a fine plain, on the river Brenta, surrounded with walls, ramparts, and other works, is about 7 miles in compass, and 27 miles west of Venice. Lat. 45. 36. long. 12. 29.

PAITA, a small Spanish seaport of Quito, in Peru, in South America, in a small bay, under a high hill, defended by a little fort, which with only muskets will prevent any boat from landing. On the top of the hill is another, which commands the town and the lower fort. It has frequently been plundered by the Bucaneers, and was burnt by Lord Anson in 1741, the governor refusing to ransom it. Lat. 5. 5. s. long. 80. 5. west.

PALAMOS, a small well fortified town, on the coast of Catalonia, 70 miles n. east of Barcelona, has a good harbour. Taken by the French in 1694, but restored to Spain by the treaty of Ryswick, 1697.

PALANCA, a town of Hungary Proper,

Proper, fortified by the Turks, but now subject to the House of Austria, 34 miles n. of Buda. Lat. 48. 20. north. long. 21. 1. east.

PALERMO, the capital of Sicily, on the north coast of that island, has a commodious harbour on the bay in the Mediterranean, the entrance defended by a strong citadels, fortified with a wall and other works of inconsiderable strength, 154 miles west of Meffina. Lat. 38. 28. long. 13. 10.

PALISADES, stakes made of strong split wood, about 9 feet long, 3 feet deep in the ground, in rows about 6 inches asunder, placed in the covert-way, at 3 feet from, and parallel to the parapet or side of the glacis, to secure it from surprize.

PALMA, or *Palamoda*, for *Palma Nova*, a populous town and strong frontier of Friuli, on the canal of Roia. The fortifications consist of 9 regular bastions, with strong ramparts and a deep ditch, to cover this state from the insult of the Turks, as well as Austrians, it being situated in that pass through which the Hunns and other northern barbarians poured their hosts into Italy; 20 miles north of Aquilea. Lat. 46. 15. long 13. 35.

PALOTA, a town of Lower Hungary, near the Bakoni Forest; surrounded with a broad ditch and high wall, being a frontier against the Turks. 46 miles s. west of Buda, subject to the House of Austria. Lat. 47. 34. n. long 18. 16. east.

PAMPELUNA, anciently *Pompejopolis*, or *Pampelo*, as having been built by Pompey, a pretty large city, capital of Navarre, in Spain, in the Pyrænean moun-

tains, defended by 2 castles, one of which built upon a rock. 34 miles s. of St. Sebastian, in lat. 43. 12. u. long. 1. 26. west.

PANAMA, a city of New Spain, on the South Sea, capital of a government of that name, ransacked and burnt by Sir Henry Morgan in 1670, but since rebuilt and fortified.

PARA, a captainship, or government of Brafil, bounded on the west by a large bay formed by the Atlantic, at the mouth of the river of Amazons; on the east by the captainship of Maranhoa, from which it is divided by the river Maracu; on the s. by the unconquered nations of the Pacaos and Paranaybas; and on the n. by the Atlantic ocean. It has its river Para, which runs through it, and falls into the bay above-mentioned. At the mouth of the river is a fortress of a square form situated on a high rock, commanding all the adjacent country; the side towards the river is fortified only with a number of gabions and large cannon; but the other side is defended by a stone wall, about 2 fathoms in height, and a dry ditch; on the s. of this fort to the bottom of the bay is another small fortification, called Commota, intended to keep the savage nations in awe, and protect the Portuguese plantations.

PARAIBA, the capital of a country of that name, in South America, about 3 leagues from the ocean, on the river of that name; surrounded with ramparts; the mouth of the river guarded by 3 forts. Lat. 6. 58. n. long. 55. 20. west.

PARALLELS, *at a siege*, the trenches or lines made parallel to the defence of the place besieged:

fieged : they are alfo called lines of communication and boyau's.

Parallels, or *places of arms*, deep trenches, 15 or 18 feet wide, joining the feveral attacks together, ferve to place the guard of the trenches in readinefs to fupport the workmen when attacked. There are ufually 3 in an attack : the firft about 300 toifes from the covert-way; the fecond and third nearer on the glacis.

PARAPET, an elevation of earth, defigned for covering the foldiers from the enemy's cannon, or fmall fhot; its thicknefs is from 18 to 20 feet ; its height 6 on the infide, and 4 or 5 on the fide next the country ; it is raifed on the rampar', and has a flope, called the fuperior talus, or glacis of the parapets, on which the foldiers lay their mufquets to fire over. This pent, or flope, renders it eafy for the mufqueteers to fire into the ditch, or, at leaft, on the counterfcarp. To raze the glacis of the parapet, by firing, is called *firing-in-barbe*. The exterior talus of the parapet is the flope facing the country. The heighth of the parapet being 6 feet on the infide, has a banquet or 2 for the foldiers who defend it to mount on for better difcovering the country, the foffe and counterfcarp, to fire as they find occafion.

Parapet of the covert-way, or *coredor*, what covers that way from the fight of the enemy ; which renders it the moft dangerous place for the befiegers, becaufe of the neighbourhood of the faces, flanks, and curtains of the place: the fame with glacis, which fignifies that whole mafs of earth which ferves to cover the coredor, and flopes towards the country.

PARK, *of artillery*, the place appointed for the encampment of an artillery, generally the rear of both lines ; at a fiege, the park of artillery is a poft fortified out of cannon-fhot of the place befieged, where are kept all the arms and utenfils necefſary for a fiege ; as bombs, petards, carcaffes, hand grenades, powder, ball, &c. with all forts of inftruments and utenfils for erecting or deftroying any fort of fortification. Great precaution fhould be ufed about the park of artillery, for fear of fire.

Park of provifions, the place where the futlers pitch their tents, and fell provifions to the foldiers, in the rear of each corps. But I think the place where the bread waggons are drawn up, and where the foldiers receive their ammunition bread, being the ftore of the army, is moft properly the park of provifions.

PARLEY. See Chamade.

PARMA, the capital of a duchy of that name in Upper Italy, divided by the river Parma into two parts. Its fortifications are inconfiderable, but has a good citadel to the eaft, with which the ducal palace is joined by a bridge. In 1734, the French and Sardinian army having intrenched themfelves, were attacked by the imperial General Count Mercy, who loft his life in the attempt, upon which his troops were obliged to retire. 60 miles n. eaft of Genoa, 45 n. weft of Bologna, 65 f. eaft of Milan. Lat. 44. 45. lon. 11.

PARNAU, a city of Livonia, in Sweden, on the river of that name, clofe by the Baltic, is fortified, but owes its ftrength to its caftle, though of timber. Several times taken and retaken in the laft laſt century; became ſubject to the Swedes in 1617, and ſurrendered to the Muſcovites in 1710. 80 miles north of Riga. Lat. 58. 20. long. 24. 16.

PAROS, an iſland in the Archipelago, the ſmalleſt of the Cyclades, lying almoſt in the centre between the Morea and Aſia Minor. The town and caſtle Parichia, in all appearance, ſtands on the ſite of the ancient city of Paros, ſeveral valuable remains of marble being uſed in its walls and houſes, and in the neighbourhood we ſee many ancient monuments. The Panagia or Madonia, without the town, is the largeſt and moſt beautiful church of the Archipelago. On the iſland are ſeveral conſiderable villages, Greek churches and chapels. In the harbour of St. Mary, a whole fleet may lie at anchor with ſecurity; but the Turkiſh gallies commonly anchor in the port of Drio, or Treon, on the weſt ſide of the iſland. Lat. 36. 34. long. 25. 32.

PARTENAY, a town of Poictou in France, on the river Tone, 9 leagues weſt of Poictiers, has a conſiderable trade in cattle and corn. Lat. 45. 45. long. 20 min. weſt.

PARTIZAN, a perſon dexterous in commanding a party; who, knowing the country well, is employed in getting intelligence, or ſurprizing the enemy's convoy, &c.

PARTY, a ſmall number of horſe or foot, ſent into an enemy's country, to pillage, take priſoners, and oblige the country to come under contribution. Parties are often ſent out to view the ways and roads, get intelligence, ſeek forage, or amuſe the enemy upon a march. Alſo frequently ſent on the flanks of an army, or regiment, to diſcover the enemy if near, and prevent ſurprize or ambuſcade.

PASSAGE, a town of Guipuſcoa, in the province of Biſcay in Spain, having an excellent harbour with a narrow entrance, defended by mountains againſt all winds, very ſpacious; a little eaſt of St. Sebaſtian, and 60 of Bilboa; a ſtation of Spaniſh ſhips of war, ſeveral of which the French burnt in the laſt war between the 2 nations; they alſo ſeized upon it in 1710. Lat. 43. 20. n. lon. 4. 53. weſt.

PASSAU, an imperial city, ſeated on both ſides the Danube, into which the rivers Inn and Iltz have their courſe; ſtrongly defended by rocks and rivers, having both a citadel and caſtle. Taken by the Duke of Bavaria, 1704, but ſoon loſt. Is 30 miles from the borders of Auſtria, and 134 weſt of Vienna.

PATAN, a city of the Mogul, in Aſia, having a fortreſs and a moſque, reckoned the moſt ſumptuous of all the Eaſt, its roof being ſupported by 150 pillars, moſt of them marble; it has a conſiderable manufacture of ſilk ſtuffs, and coarſe callicoes, between Mangerol and Diu, 200 miles n. of Huegly, in Bengal. Lat. 27. 30. long. 80.

PATANA, a city of Malacca in Aſia, with a harbour 2 miles from it, fortified with wooden paliſadoes, as tall as a ſhip's maſt.

PATEE, a ſmall work reſembling a horſeſhoe, viz. an elevation of earth, of an irregular form; generally oval, with a parapet. It is frequently raiſed in marſhy grounds, to cover the gate

gate of a place, and has only a foreright defence, but nothing to flank it.

PATRAS, a city and port of the Morea, having a castle on a mountain, near a bay of the Mediterranean, 24 miles south of Lepanto, and 60 west of Corinth. Lat. 38. 5. n. lon. 31. 26 east.

PAVIA, a large, but old and thinly inhabited city of the Pavesan, in the duchy of Milan, on the river Ticino, inconsiderably fortified ; it has indeed an old fashioned citadel and castle, but no appearance now of its having been the ancient seat of the kingdom of Lombardy. Four miles n. of the Po, 16 s. of Milan, belongs to the King of Sardinia. Lat. 45. 18. long. 9. 44.

PEACE. See *War*.

PEARL, a fortress of Dutch Brabant, on the Scheld, by which the Dutch command the navigation of that river, 4 miles n. west of Antwerp. Lat. 51. 20. long. 4. 16.

PEINE, a small town of Lower Saxony, in the bishopric of Hildesheim, on the river Fuse ; famous for the battle fought near it in 1553, in which Maurice, Elector of Saxony, was defeated and killed by Albert, Marquis of Brandenburg. 18 miles west of Brunswick. Lat. 52. 41. long. 10. 20.

PEKING, the capital of the empire of China, in a province of the same name, which holds the first rank in the kingdom ; about 60 miles south of the Chinese wall, which separates China from Tartary ; the walls are about 40 feet high, and flanked with square towers, about 20 fathoms asunder : it is 20 miles in compass, consisting of 2 large cities ; namely, the

Tartarian and the Chinese, besides suburbs. The gates are 9 in number, and of marble ; of an extraordinary height, inclosing a large court, with 4 stout walls, over which are stately castles, both on the city and country side. The Emperor's palace, with the gardens, is in the middle of the Tartar city, 2 miles long, fronting the south, as all public buildings in this country do ; surrounded with 2 stout walls, the outward of a prodigious height and thickness. It stands on a fine, spacious, but sandy plain, near the foot of the mountains, and has a numerous garrison to defend it, as well in time of peace as war, besides the strong guard kept about the imperial palace. Lat. 40. 15. n. long. 111. 10. east.

PENDENNIS, a castle in the county of Cornwall, defending the harbour of Falmouth, and lying over against that of St. Maw's.

PENEMUNPER, a fortress of Pomerania, in Upper Saxony, on the isle of Usedom, at the mouth of the river Pene, subject to the King of Prussia. Lat. 54. long. 24. 16.

PENICHE, a fortified town of Estramadura, in Portugal, on a peninsula surrounded with rocks, separated from the main land by a canal, filled with water at high tide. It has a citadel and a fort for its defence ; 44 miles n. of Lisbon. Lat. 39. 26. n. long. 9. 28. west.

PENNAMUNDE, FORT, on the isle of Usedom. 13th of May 1758, garrisoned by the Swedes, it consisting of 8 officers and 180 men, who surrendered prisoners of war ; 27th of the same year the Swedes made themselves masters of it, when the garrison became

came prisoners of war; 10th of April 1759, it surrendered to General Manteuffel, and 200 were made prisoners, with 24 cannon, and 4 mortars. Lat. 54. 26. long. 14. 16.

PENSACOLA, in *Florida*, has a large harbour, well secured from winds, 4 fathom water at its entrance, deepening gradually to 7 or 8. On the west side of the harbour stands a town, lately much improved, defended by a stockaded fort.

PENTAGON, a figure bounded by 5 sides, or polygons, which form so many angles, capable of being fortified with an equal number of bastions.

PERGA, a town of Epirus, in European Turky; has a good harbour situate on a rock, opposite the east extremity of Porfu; it is fortified, belongs to the Venetians, and stands 26 miles s. of Batoints. Lat. 39. 26. long. 21. 5.

PERONNE, a small but very strong town of Santerre, in Picardy, in France, on the river Somme, between morasses. It is very ancient, and had formerly a palace, where the kings of the Merovidgian race resided; 23 miles n. east from Amiens. Lat. 50. 5. n. long. 3. 15. east.

PEROUSA, a small fortress in a valley of the same name, in Piedmont in Upper Italy, on the river Chefon, and in one of the vallies of the Vaudois, or Waldenses, so called from one Peter Vaud, or Veldo, a merchant of Lyons in France, who, in 1160, exposing the errors and superstitions of the Romish church, and having made a great many proselytes in that kingdom, was banished with his disciples, who took shelter in these vallies. 12 miles s. west of Turin; taken

by the French in 1651, but restored to Savoy in 1696, by the peace of Turin. Lat. 44. 48. lon. 7. 19.

PERPIGNAN, the present capital of Roussillon in France, on the river Tet, a little west of the Mediterranean: surrounded with high and thick walls and bastions, has a considerable citadel, besides the suburbs, defended by a small castle; 34 miles south of Narbonne, and 115 n. of Barcelona. Lat. 43. 5. long. 2. 36.

PERTH. The Rebels' chief place of arms and rendezvous in 1715, under the Earl of Mart. There they retired after the defeat at Dumblain, till the King's forces, commanded by the Duke of Argyle, marched against them, when they fled with the Pretender. In 1745 it was possessed alternately by the Rebels and the King's forces; 30 miles n. of Edinburgh. Lat. 56. 25. long. 3. 16.

PERUGIA, a very old city in Italy, famous in history for the cruel massacre of its inhabitants, by Augustus, when he blocked up L. Anthony, the Triumvir's brother. Between this city and Cortona lies the lake Thrasimenus, famous for the overthrow of the Consul Flaminius by Hannibal: 72 miles n. of Rome. Lat. 43. 5. long. 13. 20.

PEST, a royal free town of Lower Hungary, in a plain on the Danube, over which is a bridge of boats opposite to Buda, surrounded by a wall and ditch. Near it is the field Rakos, where the States of Hungary usually meet on horseback to chuse their king. 80 miles s. east of Presburg. Lat. 47. 39. long. 19. 22.

PETARD, a brass pot fixed upon a strong square plank, which

which has an iron hook to fix it against a gate or palisades. This pot is filled with powder; which, when fixed, breaks every thing about it; and thereby makes an opening to enter the place.

PETARDIER, he who loads, fixes, and fires the petard.

PETERSBURG, the capital of Ruffia, and the refidence of the Emprefs, is about 16 Englifh miles in circuit. The river is divided into 2 principal branches called the Large and Small Neva, with which the little rivers Fontanka and Mocka unite; and thefe form the different iflands on which Peterfburg is built. The citadel is a long and irregular hexagon with 6 parallel baftions; 1 of which oppofite to Carelia has 2 orillons or blinds; and that oppofite to the river, none; but each of the other 4 has one: all which was firft built with earth and turf, but is fince lined with ftrong walls. On the flanks are 2 rows of arched cafemates, one above another, bombproof. One of the curtains is a royal difpenfary, the fineft in Europe. In autumn a fouthweft wind ufually occafions inundations, which do confiderable damage. Lat. 50. 59. long. 30. 6.

PETERWARADEIN, a ftrong frontier town of Sclavonia, fuppofed to be the ancient Acuminium, fituated on the Danube. In its neighbourhood a memorable victory was obtained by

Prince Eugene over the Turks in 1716. It belongs to the Houfe of Auftria. Lat. 45. 24. long. 20. 15.

PETER-WARDEIN, a large town of the Ruffians, in Lower Hungary, furrounded with a rampart; on the Danube, oppofite to Sclavonia Peterwaradein.

PETRINA, a fortified town of the Bannat of Croatia in Hungarian Illyricum, between the rivers Culp and Petrina; fubject to Auftria. 40 miles eaft of Carlftadt. Lat. 46. 5. n. long. 17. 5. eaft.

PFIRT, or FORET, the capital of Sungow in Germany, defended by a ftrong caftle; 10 miles weft of Bafil. Lat. 47. 35. n. long. 7. 26. eaft.

PHARSA, a town of Theffaly in European Turky, famous for a battle fought in its plains between Pompey and Cæfar, and called the battle of Pharfalia; wherein the former was entirely defeated; on the banks of the river Enipeus, 10 miles f. of Lariffa. Lat. 39. long. 23.

PHILIP FORT, a fortrefs of Dutch Brabant, on the fide of the Scheld, commanding the navigation of that river, 5 miles n. weft of Antwerp.

PHILIPPEVILLE, a fmall well fortified town of Hainault, in the French Netherlands. Its works were much increafed by Lewis XIV. 22 miles fouth-weft of Namur. Lat. 50. 12. long. 4. 25.

PHILIPPI, a city of Macedonia, on the borders of Romania in European Turky; in its neighbouring fields Brutus and Caffius were defeated by Mark Antony and Octavius, afterwards ftyled the Emperor Auguftus; by which victory, Rome entirely loft

loft her liberty. It has a caftle on a mountain, and feveral fortreffes communicating with it, encompaffed with walls, which extend into the plain, 15 miles n. of the gulf of Conteffa. Lat. 41. 10. long. 25.

PHILIPSBURG, a city of the Palatinate in Germany, on the eaft of the Rhine, in a morafs, ftrongly fortified; has been often taken and retaken by the French and Imperialifts, having fuftained 7 memorable fieges in the fpace of 100 years. The laft time it was taken by the French in 1734, after a long fiege, in which the famous Duke of Berwick, natural fon of James II. King of England, was killed by a cannon-ball, when viewing the trenches: reftored to the Germans in 1735. 16 miles f. weft of Heidelburg. Lat. 49. 8. long. 8. 16,

PHOCEA, now *Foggia*, an ancient city of Afia Minor, on the borders of Æolis and Ionia. A neat place, with a good harbour and caftle.

PIACENZA, a large city of the dukedom bearing its name, in Upper Italy. Its fortifications are inconfiderable, but it has a good citadel. 30 miles n. weft of Parma. Lat. 45. long. 10 25.

PICIGHITONE, a fmall town of the Milanefe in Italy, having a caftle on the river Adda. Here King Francis was brought after being taken prifoner at the battle of Pavia. 35 miles f. eaft of Milan. Lat. 45. 10. long. 10. 12.

PICKET, a fmall pointed ftaff, fhod with iron, which ferves to mark out the angles and principal part of a fortification when the engineer is tracing a plan upon the ground with a line. There are alfo fmall pointed

ftakes, which ferve to drive thro' fafcines or gazons, to keep them faft, when the earth is bad, or the work raifed in hafte.

Pickets, ftakes which troopers drive before their tents, at about 2 yards diftance. From one to another of thefe pickets is ftretched a rope, called the picket rope, to which they tie their horfes; and alfo for feveral other ufes. Thofe for pinning the fafcines of a battery, are from 3 to 5 feet long; their heads 2 or 3 inches in diameter.

PIECE *of Ordnance*, includes all forts of great guns and mortars. *Battering pieces*, are large guns ufed at fieges for making the breaches; fuch as the 24 pounder and culverin; the one carrying a 24, and the other an 18 pound ball. *Field-pieces* are 12 pounders; and demi-culverins, 6 pounders; fakers, minions, and 3 pounders; which march with the army, and always encamp behind the fecond line, except in battle, when they are brought into the front. A foldier's firelock is alfo called his *piece*.

PILAW, a confiderable porttown of Ducal Pruffia, in Poland, at the mouth of the Frifche-haf; it has a regular citadel of 5 angles, being the key of Pruffia on the fea-fide; 50 miles weft of Koningfburg, fubject to the King of Pruffia. Lat. 54. 45. lon. 20. 5.

PILE, or *pyramid of bombs* or *balls*, fo termed from the form they ufe to ftore them up in magazines.

PILSEN, a large, well fortified city, at the conflux of 2 fmall rivers, in one of the moft fertile parts of Bohemia, 42 miles n. weft of Pileck, and the fame diftance weft of Prague.

PIRNA,

PIRNA, a fmall town of Mif-
ma, in Upper Saxony, on the
Elbe, over which is a fine ftone
bridge, defended by a ftrong
caftle. 4 miles f, eaft of Drefden.

PISA, a large city, belonging
to Tufcany, finely fituated on the
Arno, but fo poorly inhabited,
that the grafs grows in feveral
parts of its ftreets : it was once
a flourifhing republic, till fubdued by the Florentines in 1406.
It is furrounded with ditches and
old walls, and defended by a modern citadel, an ancient caftle,
and a confiderable fort. In this
city is the famous leaning tower.
5 miles eaft of the fea, 12 miles
n. of Leghorn, and 38 weft of
Florence. Lat. 45. 38. long.
11. 16.

PLACARD, or *Placart*, a term
ufed abroad for a proclamation,
edict, &c. fet up in all public
places, , by government authority, whereby their fubjects are
ordered to do, or forbear, fome-
thing expreffed therein.

PLACE, *in Fortification*, fignifies a fortified town.

Place of Arms, in a town, a
fpace left near its centre, where
a guard is generally pofted. In
towns regularly fortified, the
place of arms fhould be in the
centre, and refemble the figure
of a polygon.

Place of arms of an Attack, or
of a trench, a foffe, with a parapet, or an epaulment, to cover a
body of horfe or foot where they
may be ready to withftand the
fallies of the befieged. The
places moft convenient are fuch
as can eafily fuccour each other,
and out of view of the defences
of the place befieged ; as hollows or hollow ways, efpecially
if they crofs one another ; their
depth ferves as a parapet to co-

ver the infantry : if they have
not a fufficient depth, that defect may be fupplied with gabions, fand-bags, or whatever
can hinder the befiegers from
feeing into it. When a foffe is
cut round it, it is called a redoubt. In carrying on the
trenches, redoubts muft be raifed
at convenient diftances, to lodge
the infantry, who guard the
trenches.

Place of arms of a Camp, are
the bell tents at the head of each
company, where they lodge their
arms.

*Place of arms of the Covert-
way*, is a part of it oppofite to
the re-entering angle of the counterfcarp, projecting outwards in
an angle.

PLASSEY, near Cutwah, and
Coffimbuzar, in India, within
the Ganges, is remarkable for the
following battle.

On the 23d of June 1757,
Lord Clive, with 1000 Euro-
peans, 2000 feapoys, and fo
feamen, with 8 cannon, attacked, near this place, the army of
the Subah or Nabob of Bengal,
which confifted of 15000 cavalry,
and 25000 infantry, with 40
pieces of artillery, directed by
Frenchmen. A grove covered on
all fides by banks, fheltered the
Englifh from the cannonade, and
the falling of a fhower of rain,
the enemy drew their artillery
within their camp : Lord Clive
availed himfelf of this error ;
and from a well-placed detachment, prevented their artillery
appearing any more, and then
ftormed the eminences near their
camp, in which fome perfons of
diftinction fell ; which fo difpirited the Nabob's forces, that
their right wing and centre fled,
abandoning their camp and artillery

tillery: their lofs was upwards of 500 men; but their fhameful precipitate flight, and the number of cannon taken, anfwered all the purpofes of a bloody victory. The lofs of the Englifh was too inconfiderable to mention.

PLAN, a term in geometry, a fuperficies, whofe parts are all equally difpofed between its extremities, fo that one part is neither higher nor lower than another. A *horizontal plan*, is parallel to the horizon; a *vertical plan*, perpendicular to the horizon.

Plan, ground-plot, or *ichnography*, in fortification, is the reprefentation of the firft or fundamental tract of a work, fhewing the length of its lines, quantity of its angles, breadth of the ditches, thicknefs of the ramparts and parapets, the diftance of one part from another; fo that a plan reprefents a work, fuch as would appear if it were cut equal with the level of the horizon, or cut off at the foundation; it marks neither the heighths nor the depths of the feveral parts of the works; which is properly profile, and expreffes only the heighths, breadths, and depths, without taking notice of the lengths. As architects, before they lay the foundation of their edifice, make their defign upon paper, to difcover any errors in their plans; fo an engineer, before tracing his work on the ground, fhould make plans of his defigns upon paper, that he may do nothing without mature deliberation.

Plans are very ufeful for generals or governors, in either attacking or defending a place, in chufing a camp, determining attacks, conducting the approach-es, or examining the ftrength and weaknefs of a place; efpecially fuch plans as reprefent a place, with the country about it, and fhew the rivers, fountains, marfhes, ditches, vallies, mountains, woods, houfes, churches, and other particulars contiguous thereto.

PLANKS, or *madriers*, pieces of oak, very thick and broad.

PLASENDAL, a fortrefs of Flanders, in the Auftrian Low-Countries, 3 miles f. eaft of Oftend.

PLATES, *prife plates*, 2 plates of iron on the cheeks of a gun-carriage, from the cope-fquare to the centre, through which the prife-bolts go, and on which the hand-fpikes reft, when it poifes up the breech of the piece. *Breaft-plates*, the two plates on the face of the carriage on the other cheek. *Train-plates*, the 2 plates on the cheeks at the train of the carriage. *Dulidge-plates*, the 6 plates on the wheel of a gun-carriage, where the fellies are joined together, to ftrengthen the dulidges.

PLATFORM, a floor of ftrong planks, laid upon joints, on a battery, to place the guns or mortars upon, to prevent the wheels or mortar-beds from finking in the ground.

PLATOON, a few files of foldiers formed into a fmall body.

PLIMOUTH, anciently *Tamaræoftium*, a fea-port town of Devonfhire, with an excellent harbour at the mouth of the river Plim, ftrongly fortified. Here is a royal dock for building and fitting out fhips. 42 miles from Exeter, 215 from London. Lat. 50. 26. n. long. 4. 27. weft.

PLOCKSTOW, or *Plocxk*, a town of Great Poland, on the

[h]   high

high bank of the Viſtula, from which it has a pleaſant proſpect; a good trade, a caſtle for its defence; 50 miles n. weſt of Warſaw, in lat. 53. 10. long. 20. 15.

POICTIERS, or *Poitiers*, anciently *Lemnum*, the capital of Poictu, in France, on the river Clam, and one of the largeſt places in the kingdom, but thinly inhabited, and great part of it waſte, having been ruined by the civil wars. In the neighbourhood of this city, Edward the Black Prince obtained a ſignal victory over the French in 1356, and took John their king and Philip his ſon priſoners. 70 miles n. eaſt of Rochelle. Lat. 46. 48. long. 14 min.

POINT BLANK, the poſition of a gun when laid level.

Point blank range, that diſtance which the ſhot goes on a level plain.

POLYGON, a figure of many angles, regular or irregular, exterior or interior.

Regular Polygon, that whoſe angles and ſides are equal. It has an angle of the centre and of polygons. The centre of a regular polygon is the centre of a circle, which circumſcribes the polygon; that is, whoſe circumference paſſes through all the angles of the figure.

An irregular Polygon hath ſides whoſe angles are unequal.

Exterior Polygon, that whoſe lines touch the points of the flanked angles, when a place is fortified inwards.

An Interior Polygon, that outward fortification which makes the angles of the gorge; ſo that the whole baſtion is without the polygon.

POLOCK, a fortified town of the palatinate of that name, in Lithuanian Ruſſia, in Poland, ſituated on the river Dwina. It is the bulwark of Lithuania againſt the Ruſſians, 130 miles weſt of Smolenſko. Lat. 56. 39. long. 31.

PONDICHERRY, a ſtrong town, about 4 leagues in circumference, ſituate on the Coromandel coaſt, was taken by the Dutch from Batavia in 1690, but reſtored by the treaty of Ryſwic. In 1748 Admiral Boſcawen beſieged it, but was obliged by the periodical rains to abandon it.

In 1761 Major-general Sir Eyre Coote and Admiral Corniſh inveſted it; the firſt by land, the other by ſea. It was ſurrounded by adjacent fortreſſes, and yet eaſily reduced, as the neighbouring country was in the hands of the Engliſh. The approaching rainy ſeaſon, and Lally's known intrepidity, rendered a regular ſiege unadviſeable; therefore a blockade was reſolved upon, ſupported by batteries, which continually haraſſed the garriſon, and were daily, though inſenſibly, drawing near the place: but being incommoded by the heavy rains, theſe operations continued about ſeven months, the batteries oft ruined, and as frequently repaired. The Engliſh had the pleaſure to reflect, that, amidſt all their hardſhips and labours, the purpoſe of the blockade was ſtill advancing; and that the French within the place were reduced to live on dogs, cats, &c. and that even ſuch loathſome food muſt, if the blockade continued, fail them in a few days. The batteries being advanced within 450 yards of the rampart, and the garriſon having only 3 days of thoſe miſerable proviſions to ſubſiſt upon,

upon, at laſt a ſignal was made for a ceſſation of arms ; and the principals of the Jeſuits with 2 civilians, without any apparent authority from the governor, were ſent out to treat with the Engliſh : this deputation having no legal commiſſion, the Engliſh knew not how to act ; but underſtanding they would meet with no oppoſition from the governor, they took poſſeſſion of the place, with all its treaſure. 60 miles ſ. of Fort St. George. Lat. 12. 26. long. 80. 14.

PONT DE L'ARCHE, a town of Normandy, having a ſtone bridge over the Seine, and a ſtrong caſtle, 10 miles ſ. of Rouen. Lat. 49. 20. long. 1. 15. eaſt.

PONT DE SE, Cæſar's pons Ligeris, a ſmall town of Anjou, in France, on the Loire, over which is a bridge, partly of ſtone and partly of timber, 1000 paces in length; near it is a ſtrong caſtle. 8 miles ſ. of Angers. Lat. 47. 24. n. long. 36. min. weſt.

PONT KEMY, a conſiderable town of Picardy, in France, on the river Somme, over which it has a bridge leading to a caſtle, built on an iſland. 6 miles from Abbeville.

PONTOONS, form a floating bridge of great boats, with boards laid over them, and rails on the ſides for paſſing an army, &c. over a river.

PORTALARGRE, anciently *Portus Alacer*, a city of Alentejo, fortified with walls and towers in the old manner; 84 miles eaſt of Liſbon in lat. 39. 26. long. 8. 10. weſt.

PORT CULLICE, a ſtrong gate, or door, ſuſpended over the common gates of fortified places.

PORT FIRE, a compoſition of meal-powder, ſulphur, and ſalt-

petre, drove into a caſe of paper, but not very hard, about 9 or 10 inches long ; and when put into a linſtock, uſed to fire guns or mortars inſtead of a match.

PORTLAND, anciently an iſland, now a peninſula of Dorſetſhire, oppoſite Weymouth, has a good road for ſhips, defended by Portland and Sandford caſtles; 12 miles ſ. of Dorcheſter. Lat. 50. 30. long. 2. 18. weſt.

PORT L'ORIENT, a ſea-port town and fortreſs of Britany, at the mouth of the river Scorf, oppoſite to Port Louis. The chief ſtation of the French Eaſt-India ſhips, and hence called the Eaſt Port, or Port l'Orient ; and was unſucceſsfully attacked under the command of General Sinclair. 26 miles north-weſt of Vannes. Lat. 47. 45. n. long. 3. 18. eaſt.

PORT LOUIS, a town of Britany, defended by a citadel and other works, a ſtation for a part of the navy. Lat. 47. 46. long. 3. 8. weſt. See Plan 16.

Port Louis, a fortreſs on the ſouth-weſt coaſt of Hiſpaniola, belonging to France, taken and deſtroyed by Admiral Knowles in 1747, but ſince repaired.

PORTO-BELLO, a town well fortified with forts, lying on the north ſide of the iſthmus of Darien, joins the 2 vaſt continents of North and South America, at the bottom of a bay, about a mile deep and half a mile broad at the entry. There is a good harbour. It was taken by Admiral Vernon, with ſix ſhips only, in November 1739.

PORTO DI VENERE, a little town of Genoa, in Italy, defended by a caſtle, on the weſt ſide of the entrance of the gulf of Spezia; 45 miles f. east of Genoa. Lat. 44. 7. n. long. 10. 36. east.

PORTO LONGONE, a fortress and port town at the east end of the Isle of Elba, in the Tuscan sea, subject to the King of Naples. Lat. 42. 36. n. long. 21. 22. east.

PORTO PORT A PORT, a city of Entre Dourone Minho, of Douro, in Portugal, at the mouth of the Douro, defended by a castle, the town surrounded with walls and towers, o miles south of Braga. Lat. 40. 53. n. lon. 8. 35. west.

PORTO RICO, the capital of the island of that name, situated on its north side, and in a small island, joined to the continent by a causey, which runs across the harbour. The town is a mile and a half in circuit, and almost impregnable by sea. It is pleasantly situated on an eminence, commanding the ocean on one side, and the main island on the other. This city being the centre of the contraband trade, usually carried on by the English and French with the King of Spain's subjects, is better inhabited than most of the cities belonging to the crown in America.

PORT ROYAL, the south-east part of Jamaica, upon a neck of land, running out 10 or 12 miles west into the sea, defended by Fort Charles, and a line of near 100 cannon and a garrison; having the ocean on the south, and a bay on the north, 3 leagues in breadth, and a sufficient depth of water for vessels of 700 tons to lie close to the shore. Destroyed by an earthquake in 1692; by fire in 1702; and lastly by an inundation of the sea in 1722;

upon which the inhabitants removed to Kingston, on the opposite side of the harbour; but the convenient situation induced many to settle here again, it being better fortified against inundations. Lat. 17. 30. long. 77. 5. west.

PORTO VECCHIO, a small town in the Island of Corsica, in the Mediterranean, having a good harbour. In 1553 taken by the French; in 1736 by the mal content Corsicans, who improved its fortifications and harbour. 40 miles n. of Sardinia, according to M. de Chazell. In lat. 41. 39. long. 9. 30.

PORTSMOUTH, a borough-town of Hampshire, at the mouth of one of the largest and most secure harbours in England; the entrance as broad as the Thames at Westminster, well defended by forts and castles; the town strongly fortified in the modern way, and constantly kept neat and in good order. Here great part of the royal navy is built and laid up; here are docks, yards, and magazines filled with immense quantities of naval and military stores. 20 miles f. of Winchester, and 72 f. west of London. Lat. 50. 48. long. 1. 6. west.

PORTUGAL. Under this article, as the Spanish operations were confined to no particular place, I shall introduce the following, as what is the most remarkable during their invasion of this kingdom. 25th of August 1762, they were masters of Miranda, Braganza, Torre di Moncorvo, and Chaves. They demolished what fortifications the two former cities had, and left strong garrisons in the latter. They divided their forces which
were

were in the province of Trafof-mentes into 3 parts: the principal body was encamped near Miranda; the fecond, of 3000 men, at Torre di Moncorvo; the the third, of the fame number, near Chaves. Another corps of 80,000 men entered the Portuguefe frontier, near Almeida: this corps fuffered much by defertion, and its detached parties were oft repulfed by the militia. The fummer months are not favourable to military operations; and the Spaniards could do little more than chaftife the peafants of fmall villages, whofe natural averfion overcame the oath of obedience which they had taken, and who did every thing in their power to cut off the convoys of provifions defigned for their camp: thefe and the Portuguefe companies called auxiliaries, were eafily defeated. At laft, the Spaniards formed the fiege of Almeida; and on the 25th of Auguft it furrendered after a fiege of 9 days, and before a practicable breach had been made: 1500 regulars and 2000 peafants were permitted to retire with the honours of war, on condition of not ferving for 6 months againft the King of Spain or his allies: 83 brafs cannons, 11 iron, 9 brafs mortars for bombs, 31 brafs mortars and 1 iron for grenades, 700 quintals of powder, and a quantity of other ammunition and provifions were found in the place. Auguft 27, 1762, Colonel Burgoyne ordered a part of his light regiment to pufh into the town of Valenca d'Alcantra fword in hand. The guards in the fquare were all killed or made prifoners before they could ufe their arms; after the body of the Englifh was

come up and formed in the fquare, fome defperate parties attempted an attack, but all of them were killed or taken.

One major-general, with his aid-de-camp; one colonel, with his adjutant; 2 captains, 17 fubalterns, and 59 men, were made prifoners; the reft of the regiment of Saville were deftroyed.

Post, any fort of ground where a body of men can fortify themfelves, or be in a condition of refifting an enemy.

Advance Poft, a fpot of ground feized by a party to cover themfelves and fecure the pofts behind them.

Postern, now called *fally port*, a fmall door in the flank of a baftion, or other part of a garrifon, to march in and out unperceived by an enemy, either to relieve the works, or make fallies.

Powder, a compofition of fulphur, falt-petre, and charcoal. The fulphur and charcoal take fire, and the falt-petre makes the report.

Powder-magazine, a bomb-proof arched building to contain powder in fortified places.

Prague, the capital of Bohemia and ancient feat of its kings, fituate on the river Moldau, which divides it into two parts; it is one of the largeft cities in Europe, being 12 miles in circuit. It is divided into the old, new, and little city, and furrounded with a wall, baftions, and other works, rendering it as ftrong as its prodigious extent will admit of; but it is commanded by feveral of the neighbouring hills. It has been oft taken and plundered, and undergone great calamities. On the 6th of May 1757, between the

Pruffian

Pruffian army, commanded by the King and Marſhal Schwerin, and the Auſtrian army, commanded by Marſhal Brown. The Pruſſian army confiſted of 80,000 men, with which he attacked and defeated the whole combined Auſtrian force, amounting to 100,000 men, commanded by Marſhal Brown. This memorable battle was fought near Prague. The Auſtrians were poſted in a camp almoſt inacceſſible : the Pruſſians had moraſſes to paſs, precipices to climb, and batteries to face : but the preſence of the king animated his troops, who attacked the Auſtrian camp ; and after a long and obſtinate engagement, and many ſignal examples of valour, obtained a moſt glorious and deciſive victory. The Auſtrians abandoned the field of battle, leaving behind them 240 cannon, all their baggage and tents : they had 20,000 men killed and wounded, and 10,000 taken priſoners : the Pruſſians loſt only 4000 men, but Marſhal Schwerin fell among the ſlain. The left wing of the Auſtrian army fled into Prague, where Marſhal Brown died of his wounds, and the reſt of the Auſtrians retired towards Moravia. His Pruſſian Majeſty immediately inveſted and beſieged Prague, which was ſoon relieved by Marſhal Daun.

Bombardment on the night, between the 29th and 30th of May 1757, by the Pruſſian army, commanded by the King and Marſhal Keith.

After obtaining the victory of the 6th, the routed Auſtrians, to the number of 40,000, took protection within the walls of the capital, which was inveſted on the 11th and 12th at midnight,

The Pruſſian army, by the ſignal of a ſky-rocket thrown up for that purpoſe, by the king's battery, began to fire upon the town, from one battery on this ſide of the Moldau, and from 3 on the other ſide. Theſe batteries continued firing inceſſantly till the 8th of June, when the whole New Town was reduced to one great heap of ſmoaking rubbiſh, and only a few houſes left ſtanding in the Jews Quarter. Marſhal Daun brought an army from Arabia to the relief of Prague, which occaſioned his Pruſſian Majeſty to quit his camp on the 13th, and to put himſelf at the head of the army, commanded by the Prince of Bevern, with which he attacked Marſhal Daun in his ſtrong lines, at Collin, on the 18th, when the Auſtrians were victorious. Marſhal Keith had turned the ſiege of Prague into a blockade, and was rejoined by the King on the 19th, who raiſed the blockade the next day. In 1744 his Pruſſian Majeſty took Prague in a few days. He inveſted it on 2d of September, bombarded it on the 13th, and it was ſurrendered to him on the 18th. The garriſon then confiſted of 12,000.

PRAYE, a town on the iſland of Tercera, one of the Azores in the Atlantic ocean, in a plain on a large bay, ſurrounded with walls and 4 baſtions. There is alſo a town of the ſame name in the iſland of Gracioſa, another of the Azores, lying on a bay of the Atlantic ocean, and defended by a fortreſs.

PREMISLAW, or *Prezemyſi*, a well built populous town of Red Ruſſia, in Poland, on the river San, defended by ſtrong walls, and a caſtle on a rock, 112 miles ſouth-fouth eaft of Cracow. Lat. 49, 5. n. long. 22. 8. f. eaft.

PRESBURGH, a ftrong city and caftle, the capital of Upper Hungary on the n. of the Danube, 46 miles eaft of Vienna. Lat. 48. 26. long. 17. 36.

PROFILE. Engineers reprefent the heighths, depths, and thicknefs of a work with foffes, &c. by profile, or orthography; which fuppofes the work to be cut through perpendicularly from top to bottom.

PROPONTIS, or the fea of *Marmora*, a part of the Mediterranean, dividing Europe from Afia; it has the Hellefpont, or canal of the Dardanelles, to the f. well, whereby it communicates with the Archipelago, and the ancient Bofphoros of Thrace, or Streight of Conftantinople, to the north eaft communicating with the Black or Euxine Sea. It has 2 caftles: that on the Afia fide is on a cape, where formerly ftood a temple of Jupiter. The caftle of Europe is on an oppofite cape, and had anciently a temple of Serapis.

PROVIDENCE, one of the Bahama, or Lucaya iflands, in the American ocean, well planted and fortified by the Englifh. On the eaft fide of the gulf of Florida, and 206 miles from the continent of that name. Near this ifland are feveral others planted by the Englifh, but not fortified; fo that upon the approach of an enemy, the planters are obliged to withdraw to Providence, which lies in lat. 25. 16. n. long. 78. 5. weft.

PROVOST-MARSHAL, of an army, is an officer appointed to fecure deferters and all other criminals; he is often to go round the army, hinder the foldiers from pillaging, indict offenders, execute the fentence pronounced, and regulate the weights and meafures of the army, &c.

PUNISHMENT, in general, fignifies the execution of a fentence pronounced by a Court-martial upon any delinquent; but in particular means that one often ufed of inflicting a certain number of lafhes upon a non-commiffioned officer, or private man.

PUERTO CAVELLO, a fortified town on the coaft of Caraccas, 10 leagues from La Guaira; was but little known before the year 1743, when Admiral Knowles, after the repulfe at La Guaira, having refitted the fquadron under his command, came on the 15th of April before it, when it was fupplied with a garrifon of 1500 feamen and foldiers, 4000 Indians, blacks, &c. which the governor of the Caraccas had fent for the defence of the town. The Admiral having landed 1200 men, under the command of Major Lucas, they were attacked in the night from the fafcine battery, near Punta Brava, and being put into diforder, they retreated and re-imbarked. On the 24th the Admiral made a general attack upon the caftle and fafcine batteries, which lafted 10 hours. Some of the fhips having fpent their ammunition, and moft of them being fo fhattered in their mafts and rigging, as fcarce able to fet a fail, the Admiral made a fignal to cut, and failed for the keys of Burburata, to repair the damage they had fuftained.

PUERTO DE LA GUAIRA, is about 62 leagues from Cumana, and 15 from Cape Blanco to the weft. The town is fituated at

the

the foot of a high hill, and open to the land-side, but has 2 forts and batteries toward the sea. Taken in the last century by Captain Wright and his privateers; and attacked in 1743, when Don Mattheo Gaul defended it against a squadron of ships commanded by Admiral Knowles, who bombarded the town, made some breaches in the fortifications, demolished their churches, and blew up a magazine: there being only one landing place, they did not attempt to disembark; and most of the ships being so much damaged as to be entirely disabled from continuing the attack, they retired to Curasso to refit.

PURMEREN, a town of North Holland, well fortified with a rampart and ditch, at one end of the Purmer, and about 14 miles north of Amsterdam.

QUADRANT, or *quarter of a circle*, an instrument of brass or wood used by gunners in pointing their guns to an object, and by bombardiers in elevating their mortars.

QUADRAT. To quadrat a piece is to see it duly placed in its carriage, and that the wheels be of an equal height.

QUARTER, signifies the sparing of men's lives and giving good treatment to a vanquished enemy.

Quarter, at a siege, the encampment upon one of the most principal passages round a place besieged, to prevent relief and convoys.

When it is commanded by a general, it is called *the head quarters of the army*; when the camp is marked out about a place besieged, then *the quarters*

are said to be *disposed:* and when great detachments are made from a quarter for convoys, &c. such a *quarter* is said to be *weakened.*

Quarter of an assembly, the place where the troops meet to march from in a body, and the same as a place of rendezvous.

Head-quarters, the place where the general of an army has his quarters. The quarters of generals of horse are, if possible, in villages behind the right and left wings; and the generals of foot are often in the same village.

Quarter intrenched, a place fortified with a ditch and parapet to secure a body of troops.

Winter-quarters, sometimes means the space of time included between leaving the camp and taking the field; but more properly, the places where troops are lodged during the winter.

QUARTER MASTER of cavalry, except in the Blues, is a warrant-officer, appointed by the colonel. He takes up ground for the troop, divides it among them, and is constantly employed among the horse.

QUEBEC, the capital of Canada, in North America, at the confluence of the river St. Laurence, has a castle on the brow of a hill, about 40 fathoms above the town, but irregularly built and fortified, having only 2 bastions, without a ditch towards the city. Has also another fort on Cape Diamont, a solid rock, 400 fathoms high, with only some few works, and redoubts commanding both it and the town; but the place owes its strength more to nature than art; 300 miles north-west of Boston, in New England. Lat. 47. 35. long. 74. 10.

In 1759 the British army and navy

navy came before it, when the commanders made excellent dispositions for reducing it, but were baffled by the caution of General Montcalm, the strength of the place, and the insurmountable difficulty of the troops landing to attack it: so well was nature assisted by art, that even the undaunted Wolfe despaired of success, after being checked and repulsed by the enemy. However, by a train of stratagems, a landing was at last effected, but under greater disadvantages than any other upon record, by being obliged to drag their artillery up a steep and dangerous ascent; but having, by incessant labour, gained the top of the hill, September 13th, they immediately formed.

Montcalm was now compelled to risque a battle on the plains of Abraham, in which the English were victorious, but lost their brave Wolfe, who died on the field, and General Monckton was dangerously wounded. The honour of compleating the victory fell on Lord Townsend, who drove the enemy from every part, with the loss of only 500 men, though that of the French exceeded 1500. Five days after this, September 18, the city surrendered to the British troops. Though Wolfe has immortalized his name, whilst the glorious conquest of Canada illustrates English annals, yet all must allow, glorious as this victory was, and important in its consequences, that it was too dearly purchased by his death. Officers may be formed by attention and experience; but the loss of so great a general, Christian, and soldier, is irretrievable. He was an honour to his king,

a friend to his country, and an ornament to society and his profession. Montcalm was killed on the spot, and the next general in command so dangerously wounded that he died in a few days.

After this victory, General Murray was appointed governor of Quebec, and the garrison supplied with such stores and provisions as could be spared out of the fleet; which leaving Quebec, and the enemy knowing no ships of war were left to assist the garrison in case of danger, and sensible that they were greatly reduced in numbers, by sickness, &c. and the fortifications in a bad state of defence; with this striking appearance of success, Monsieur de Levi was encouraged to attempt its recovery; and therefore determined upon a regular siege, in the spring of 1760, before the place could receive succour from the English fleet.

Monsieur de Levi, having assembled an army of 13000, took the field on the 17th of April, being well provided for a siege. He sent his provisions, ammunition, and heavy baggage down the river St. Laurence, under the protection of six frigates, from 26 to 44 guns, by which he entirely mastered the river; and after 10 days march, his army appeared on the heights near Quebec.

General Murray had now only two things to determine on; to stand a siege within the ruined works of Quebec, or to march out and give battle to the enemy; he, therefore, with equal spirit and resolution to a variety of unpleasing circumstances which surrounded him, chose the latter;

latter; and marched out at the head of 3000 brave men, with about 20 field-pieces, refolved to attack the enemy, leaving a fufficient number to keep the inhabitants in awe, and the gates open. This daring fcheme ftruck the enemy with furprize: their troops were pofted beneath fome woody eminences; but before they could be in regular order of battle, their van, which was alfo pofted upon eminences, was fo furioufly attacked, as to be driven in the utmoft diforder, with great lofs, upon the main body, which was drawn up in the valley below, formed in columns, and received the troops with fo hot a fire, that they were ftaggered in the purfuit; and nothing but the intrepidity of the general, and that of thofe under him, could have preferved them and their garrifon, the enemy being above four times their number. Farther refiftance would have been imprudent, as they had loft fome hundreds of men, and the French upwards of 2000. General Murray, after retiring into his garrifon, was judged irretrievably undone, no fhips being near to affift him; yet his courage was unfhaken; his ardour redoubled by his difficulties; and by diligence and penetration, compenfated for the weaknefs of his fortifications and troops.

The French opened trenches that fame night againft the place; but it was the 11th of May before they could bring two batteries to bear; and their fire even then was ill plied: this gave the garrifon time to prepare for its defence, and upwards of 100 pieces of cannon were mounted on the ramparts.

On the 9th of May, two days before the batteries were opened, a veffel arrived in the bafon, with an account that Lord Colville, with a fmall fquadron, had entered the river St. Laurence, and would fail in a few days to their relief. On the 15th, a fhip of the line and two frigates arrived; which frigates were immediately fent againft the French fquadron, that lay above the town, and in a very few hours either took or deftroyed them; upon which Levi raifed the fiege with the greateft precipitation, abandoned all their immenfe ftores, their ftanding camp, baggage, &c. 34 battering cannon, 4 12 pounders, 10 field-pieces, 6 mortars, 4 petards, &c. Many prifoners were taken in the purfuit.

QUESNOY, a fmall town of French Hainault, in the Netherlands, irregularly built, but well fortified; taken by the Confederates 1711; but the French retook it next year, after the battle of Denain. 7 miles f. eaft of Valenciennes. Lat. 50. 29. long. 3. 36.

QUICK-MATCH, is beft made by putting cotton ftrands, drawn out to proper lengths, into a kettle juft covered with white wine vinegar, wherein a quantity of faltpetre and mealed powder has been boiled till well mixed: others put only faltpetre into water, take it out hot, and lay it in a trough with fome mealed powder, moiftened with fpirits of wine, and thoroughly wrought into the cotton, by rolling it backwards and forwards with the hands. But, when either is done, they are taken out feparately, drawn through mealed powder, and dried upon a line.

QUILLEBEUF,

QUILLEBEUF, a small city, the capital of Roumois, in Normandy, in France, on the Seine; its walls and fortifications have been demolished, but still defended by a little fort. 24 miles below Rouen, and 21 above Havre de Grace.

QUINTIN, ST. anciently Augusta Veromandorum, a fortified city of Picardy, in France, on the Somme. The church of St. Quintin is one of the finest of the kingdom. 35 miles east of Amiens. Lat. 49. 55. long. 3. 18.

QUITO, the capital of the province of that name, in Peru, well fortified, provided with every necessary for a good defence. 112 miles east of the Pacific ocean, 146 n. of Guagaquil, and 722 in the direction from Lima. Lat. 13. 13 f. long 78. 10. west.

RAAB, a royal free city in Lower Hungary, having an old but strong fortress at the confluence of the Danube, Raab and Rabnitz, by the waters of which it is surrounded. It is defended by 7 bastions, and provided with a strong garrison. Raab lies opposite to the isle of Schut, 57 miles west of Buda. Lat. 48. 10. long. 18. 18.

RABAT, an ancient city of Mauritania Tingitana, and the Oppidum of Ptolomy; it is a large strong place, esteemed the key of Barbary, on a rock at the mouth of the Gueron, and defended by a stout castle. The tower of the principal mosque is the highest in all Africa, and from its battlements a ship may be seen 20 leagues off.

RABINETT, a small eminence between a falconette and a base.

RACAUX, near Liege in Germany. On the 12th of October, 1747, was an attack of posts only, tho' there was a great plain.

The enemy made several furious attacks on Prince Waldeck, but were gallantly repulsed by his prudence, and the valour of his troops.

Lord Ligonier, having done all a great general could do, posted some English battalions behind the villages who formed a hollow square, secured their ground and the retreat of the army, half of which could not come to engage.

They retired to Maestricht; and the rear guard were brought up by the Imperialists in good order.

RACKELSBURG, a strong town of Stiria, in the circle of Austria, in Germany, situated on the Drave, 23 miles south east of Gratz. Lat. 47. 8. n. long. 16. 16. east.

RADOM, a town in the palatinate of Sandomir in Little Poland, encompassed with a wall, and other fortifications, in a fine plain on a rivulet that falls into the Weissel, 74 miles f. of Warsaw. Lat. 51. 41. long. 21. 9.

RAGUSA, the ancient *Epidaurus*, a town of Dalmatia, on a peninsula of the gulf of Venice. The old city was built long before the birth of Christ, and became afterwards a Roman colony; but in the third century destroyed by the Scythians. The new town, on the same spot, is not very large, but well built. Both the town and harbour, called Santa Croce, are defended by a fort, and secured by the small rocky island Chiroma, about half a mile distant in the sea on one side, and by the head-land of the peninsula on the other; the last is fortified, and,

and, were the first fortified also, it would be impregnable. It is 27 miles n. west of Cataro, and 68 f. east of Spalato. Lat. 42. 48. n. long. 18. 40. east.

RAIN, a well built and fortified town of Bavaria, one of the keys of this electorate, on the Loch, 20 miles west of Ingolstadt. Lat. 48. 51. long. 11. 12.

RAMEKINS, a fortress of the United Netherlands, on the south coast of the island of Wallchevin, in the province of Zeland. One of the cautionary towns given to Queen Elizabeth, for the repayment of the charges she had been at, for the defence of this republic in its infancy. 4 miles east of Flushing, in Lat. 51. 34. long. 4. 24.

RAMILLIES, a small village of Brabant, in the Austrian Low-countries, 12 miles n. of Namur, and 22 f. east of Bruffels. Lat. 50. 51. long. 4. 48. Famous for the battle fought by the Allies, commanded by the Duke of Marlborough and M. d'Auverquirque, against that of the two crowns, commanded by the Duke of Bavaria, and Marshal Villeroy, the 22d of May 1706. The troops destined to compose the army of the Allies, being joined at the camp of Borchloon, the 20th of May, halted the 21st: on the 22d the army marched from Borchloon in 4 columns, and posted itself the same day, with the right towards the Mill of Quorem, extending with the left towards Blehen: from this camp was discovered the army of the two crowns, which was encamped with the left at Over-Efpen, and the right towards the wood of Chapiavaux; Heyliffem in their front, and Tirlemont in their rear.

It was refolved the fame day

to march the next morning towards the plain of Meerdorp, or Mierdau, to view the posture of the enemies, and determine what would be the most proper means of attacking them according to the movement they should make.

To this end, an advanced guard of 600 horse. and all the quarter-masters of the army, were sent forward on the 23d at break of day.

The same morning, about 4, the army marched in 8 columns towards the aforefaid plain : the advanced guard and the quarter-masters arrived about 8, at the height of Meerdorp, or Mierdau, from whence the army of the enemy was seen in motion : a little after it was perceived that the enemy was marching through the plain of Mount St. Andrew, in 4 columns, of which information was given to the Duke of Marlborough and M. d'Auverquirque, who immediately repaired to the said height ; and by the time these generals were arrived there, the head of the enemy's army already appeared at the tomb of Ottomont, upon the caule-way, near the Mehaigne; whereupon the Duke of Marlborough and M. d'Auverquirque made the army advance with all expedition.

The enemy, as fast as they advanced, ranged in order of battle, with their right towards the tomb of Ottomont, upon the Mehaigne, extending with their left to Autr'Eglife, having Tranquiers in front of their right, into which they had thrown several battalions of infantry, and 14 squadrons of dragoons, who had dismounted their horses to support them.

They

They had placed many of their infantry, and a considerable part of their artillery, in the village of Ramillies, which fronted the right of their main body, as well as into the village of Offuz, which fronted the left of their infantry, and into the village of Autr' Eglife, quite on their left. The front between the village of Ramillies and Autr' Eglife, was covered by a fmall ftream of water, which rendered the meadows in fome places marfhy, and alfo by feveral roads covered with hedges, which difficulties prevented our cavalry of the right wing from coming to action.

As faft as the army of the Allies arrived, it was ranged in order of battle, with the left towards Bonnef, and the right toward Folz, and every thing was difpofed in order to attack.

To this end, four battalions were detached to attack the village of Franquenies, and twelve battalions to attack the village of Ramillies, which were to be fupported by the whole infantry.

Our artillery began to cannonade the enemy at one; at about two, the attack began with the poft of Franquenies, where our infantry had the good fortune to drive the enemy from the hedges, where they were advantageoufly pofted, and at the fame time all the cavalry of our left wing advanced to attack that of the enemy's right; foon after, all was in action: whilft the cavalry were engaged, the village of Ramillies was likewife attacked, and forced after a vigorous refiftance.

The battle lafted about two hours, and was pretty obftinate; but fo foon as our cavalry had gained ground enough to attack the enemy in flank, they began to give way; at the fame time, all their infantry were put in diforder, fo that the whole retreated in great confufion. The cavalry of their left wing formed a little upon the high ground, between Offuz and Mount St. Andrew, to favour their retreat: but after the infantry and cavalry of our right wing had filed off between the bottom of the village of Ramillies and Offuz, the whole army marched in feveral columns to attack the enemy anew; but they gave way before we could come up with them, and retired in great confufion, fome towards the defile of the Abbey de la Ramée and towards Dongelberge, others towards Judogne, and others again towards Hougarde.

They were purfued all night fo clofely, that they were obliged to abandon all their artillery and baggage, part of which was found at Judogne and at Hougarde, with their chefts of ammunition.

The enemy loft above 30000 men, 60 cannon, 8 mortars, ftandards, colours, baggage, &c. we about 3000. The reft of the campaign was fpent in the fieges of Oftend, Menin, and Aeth.

In fourteen days the Duke defeated and difperfed the beft appointed army the French ever had, and recovered all Spanifh Brabant, the marquifate of the holy Roman Empire.

The army of the enemy confifted of 76 battalions and 142 fquadrons, including the king's houfhould troops (*la Maifon du Roi*) and the army of the Allies was 74 battalions and 123 fquadrons.

Confider-

Considering the importance of the victory, the loss of the Allies was very small, not above 1100 being killed, and 2600 wounded.

RAMPART, an elevation of earth raised along the faces of any work of ten or fifteen feet high, to cover the inner part of that work against the fire of an enemy.

RANDERS, an antient city of Jutland, in Denmark, situated on the river Gude, within 12 miles lower falls into the Baltic. Its strong castle of Dronning-borg is well known in history, and the first mention we find made of the town itself was in 1247, when the enemy burnt it.

RANGE, the distance from the battery to the point where the shot or shell touches the ground.

Range, point blank, that when the piece lies in a horizontal direction, and upon a level plane.

Range, random, when the piece is elevated at an angle of elevation of forty-five degrees upon a level plane.

RASTADT, or *Raistadt*, a town of Baden, in Suabia. Here the preliminaries were settled for the peace concluded at Baden, between the Emperor and the King of France in 1714. It lies on the Rhine, 21 miles south west of Philipsburg, subject to the Margrave of Baden. Lat. 48. 42. n. long. 8. 8. east.

RASTENBURG, a fine city in Prussia, on the Guber, surrounded with a wall, and since 1629, also with a rampart.

RATISBON, the capital of Bavaria, and the only free imperial city and sovereign state in the electorate, is large and populous, fortified with a double wall, ditches, and ramparts. It is too large to be defended without an army, and therefore obliged to submit to the power which is master of the field. 65 miles n. east of Munich. Lat. 49. 10. long. 12. 10.

RATOLFZEL, a strong fortified town of Suabia, near the west extremity of the lake of Constance, that part of it called Cellersee; defended by the impregnable castle of Hohen Dwel, on an inaccessible hill, in the middle of a plain, the rock of which is flint, so that a few men may hold it out against an army. 12 miles n. west of the city of Constance, and belongs to Austria.

RATZEBURG, now a very strong city of Lawenburg, in Lower Saxony, surrounded by a lake of that name. The Duke of Lawenburg seized and fortified it in 1689, and the King of Denmark took it in 1693; but it was dismantled, and restored in 1700 to the Duke, who re-fortified it. This town has been frequently pillaged, particularly in 1552, by Francis Duke of Saxe Lawenburg, for the canons refusing to elect his son Magnus their bishop. It lies nine miles s. of Lubec Lat. 54. 10. n. long. 11. 3. east.

RAVELINS, works raised on the counterscarp before the curtain of a place, and serve to cover the gate and bridges of a town, consist of two faces, forming a saliant angle, and are defended by the faces of the neighbouring bastions. The half moons which cover the points of their bastions have their defence from the Ravelins, and are most in use of all out-works. They should be lower than the works of the place, that they may

may be under the fire of the befieged. Their parapets, as thofe
of all other out-works, fhould
be cannon proof.

RAVENSBERG, a town and
ftrong fort, on a hill, near the
river Heffel, in a country of the
fame name, in Weftphalia, fubject to the King of Pruffia. 28
miles f. weft of Minden, 30 n.
eaft of Munfter. Lat. 52. 20.
long. 8. 5.

RAUN, upon the river Miza,
a town of fome ftrength, remarkable for a bloody fkirmifh between the Pruffians and Auftrians,
in Auguft 1744. The King of
Pruffia intending to get poffeffion
of Beraun, fent thither 6 battalions, with 8 cannon, and 800
huffars; but General Feftititz
being there with a great party of
his corps, and M. Luchefi with
1000 horfe, they not only repulfed the Pruffians, but attacked
them in their turn, and, after a
warm difpute, obliged them to
retire with confiderable lofs.

REAR, fignifies, in general,
the hindmoft part of an army,
battalion, or regiment; alfo the
ground behind either.

RECKENHAUSEN, a ftrong
town of Cologne, in Germany,
in the middle territory of that
name. The Abbefs of its nun-
nery has power of punifhing offenders with death, and fhe alone
is obliged to the vow of chaf-
tity.

RECOIL, or *referve of a gun*,
its running back when fired, is
occafioned by the ftruggling of
the powder in the chamber, and
its feeking every way to fly out.
Guns whofe vents are a little
forward in the chace, recoil
moft. To leffen the recoil of a
gun, the platforms are generally

made floping towards the embrafures of the battery.

REDANS, or indented works,
are lines or faces forming faliant and re-entering angles
flanking one another, and generally ufed on the fide of a river which runs through a garrifoned town.

REDOUBT, a fquare work of
ftone, raifed without the glacis
of a place, about mufquet-fhot
from the town, having loop-
holes for the mufqueteers to fire
through, and furrounded by a
foffe; fometimes they are of
earth, having only a defence
in front furrounded with a parapet and foffe. Both the one and
the other ferve for detached
guards to interrupt the enemy's
works; and are fometimes made
on the angles of the trenches,
for covering the workmen a-
gainft the fallies of the garrifon.
The length of their fides may be
from 10 to 20 fathom; their parapet, having 2 or 3 banquets,
muft be 9 or 10 feet thick, and
their foffe the fame both in
breadth and depth. They contain a body of men for the guard
of the trenches, and are likewife
called places of arms.

Redoubt, a fmall work made
in a ravelin.

Redoubt, alfo a fquare work,
without any baftions, placed at
fome diftance from a fortification, to guard a pafs, or prevent an enemy from approaching that way.

Redoubt, *caftle*, or *donjon*, a
place more particularly intrenched, and feparated from the reft
by a foffe. There is generally
in each of them a high tower,
from whence the country round
the place may be difcovered.

REGGIO,

REGGIO, a well built town in the principality of that name, in the Modenese in Italy, having a strong citadel where the governor resides, and walls on which a cannon-ball can make little impression. 15 miles north-west of the city of Modena. Lat. 44. 45. long. 11 min.

REGULAR ATTACKS, are such as are made in form; that is, by regular approaches.

REICHENBERG, in Bohemia, 95 miles west of Prague, 205 n. west of Vienna. Lat. 50. 2. long. 12. 25. is only remarkable as the place where the Prussian army defeated the Austrians on the 21st of April 1757. The Austrian army, commanded by Count Konigseck, was posted near Reichenberg, and was attacked by the Prussians, under the command of the Prince of Brunswick Bevern. The Prussians were 20000, and the Austrians 28000: the action began at half after 6 in the morning, when the Prussian lines were formed, and attacked the Austrian cavalry, which was ranged in 3 lines of 30 squadrons, and their 2 wings sustained by the infantry, which was posted among felled trees and intrenchments. The Austrians had a village on their right, and a wood on their left, where they were intrenched. The Prussian dragoons and grenadiers cleared the intrenchment and wood, and entirely routed the Austrian cavalry: at the same time, the redoubts that covered Reichenberg were taken by General Lestewitz; and the Austrians were entirely defeated. The Prussians had 7 officers and 100 men killed; 14 officers and 150 men wounded. The Austrians had 1000 men killed and

wounded; 20 of their officers and 400 men taken prisoners. The action ended at eleven.

REINFORCEMENT, to an army, is an addition of fresh troops to strengthen an army, to enable them to go on an enterprize.

REINFORCED-RING of a gun, is that next the trunnions, between them and the vent; but the reinforced part of a gun, is from the base-ring to the reinforced-ring, which is much stronger at that place than any other part of the piece, from the great force of the powder.

RELIEVE. To relieve the guard, is to put fresh men upon the guard; and to relieve the trenches, is to relieve the guard of the trenches.

RELIEVER, an iron ring fixed to a handle by means of a socket, so as to be at right angles to it: it serves to disengage the searcher of a gun, when one of its points are retained in a hole and cannot be got out otherwise.

RENDEZVOUS, the place appointed by the general, where all the troops which compose the army are to meet at the time appointed.

RESERVE, a body of troops sometimes drawn out of the army, and encamped by themselves in a line behind the lines.

RESERVE-GUARD, the same as a picquet-guard, except that the one mounts at troop-beating, and the other at retreat-beating.

RETHEL, an ancient town, and capital of Retelois, in Champagne in France, situated on the river Aisne. Here Cæsar built a castle; and it is also famous for a victory obtained by the French, under Marshal du Plessis Praslin, over the Spaniards, in 1650. 16 miles

miles n. of Rheims. Lat. 49. 29. long. 4. 25.

RETIRADE, a trench with a parapet; but *retirade*, or *coupture*, is commonly taken for a retrenchment formed by the 2 faces of the re-entering angle in a body of a place, after the first defence is ruined, and the besieged obliged to abandon the head of the work without quitting it entirely; therefore, while some are making head against the enemy, others should be busy in making the *retirade*; which is only a simple barricade, or retrenchment, thrown up in haste, with a sort of fosse before it.

The *retirade* should be raised as high as possible, and some fourneaus, or fougades, made under it, to blow up the enemy's lodgements.

RETREAT. An army or body of men are said to retreat when they turn their backs upon the enemy, or are retiring from the ground they occupied.

A retreat is esteemed, by experienced officers, the masterpiece of a general: he should therefore be well acquainted with the situation of the country through which he intends to make it, and careful that nothing is omitted to make it safe and honourable.

Retreat. See *Drum.*

RETRENCHMENT, any work raised to cover a post, and fortify it against an enemy; viz. fascines loaded with earth, gabions, barrels of earth, sandbags, and all things that can cover the men, or impede the enemy: more particularly applicable to a fosse, bordered with a parapet; and the post fortified thus, is called post retrenched, or strong post. Re-

trenchments are either general or particular.

Retrenchments general, new fortifications, made in a place besieged, for to cover themselves when the enemy are masters of a lodgement on the fortification, that they may be in a condition of disputing the ground inch by inch, and putting a stop to the enemy's progress, in expectation of relief: as, if the besiegers attack a tenaille of the place, which they judge the weakest, either by its being ill flanked, or commanded by some neighbouring ground, then the besieged make a great retrenchment, inclosing all that part which they judge is most danger. These should be fortified with bastions and demi-bastions, surrounded by a good fosse, countermined, and higher than the works of the place, that they may command the old works, and put the besiegers to infinite trouble in covering themselves.

Retrenchments particular, such as are made in the bastions, when the enemy are masters of the breach. They can never be made but in full bastions; for in empty or hollow bastions, retirades only can be formed. These *particular retrenchments* are sometimes made at first, which certainly is best. Count Pagan always made a double parapet in all his bastions; and a retrenchment made before hand requires no more men for its defence, than if it were not made, because they never defend it till the principal work is lost: the parapet of such retrenchments should be five or six feet thick, and five feet high, with a large and deep fosse,

[i]   from

from whence fhould run out fmall fougades; and alfo be countermined.

RETURNS OF A TRENCH, the turnings and windings which form the lines of the trench, and are as near as they can be made parallel to the place attacked, to fhun being enfiladed. Thefe returns, when followed, make a long way from the end of the trench to the head, which going the ftrait way is very fhort, but then the men are expofed; yet, upon a fally, the courageous never confider the danger; but getting over the trench with fuch as will follow them, take the fhorteft way to repulfe the enemy, and cut off their retreat, if poffible.

REVEL, a fmall city of Languedoc, in France, fortified by the Reformed in the religious war, but difmantled in 1639. 6 miles from St. Papoul.

Revel, a port town and city of Efthonia, a fubdivifion of Livonia, at the fouth entrance of the gulf of Finland; not large, but a rich trading place, and furrounded with high walls, deep ditches, and ftrong baftions; is further defended by a caftle, with feveral towers ftanding on a rock. Has a fine harbour, where part of the Ruffian fleet is commonly laid up. The houfes are well built, and moftly of bricks. 100 miles weft of Narva, and 140 n. of Riga. Lat. 59. 10. long. 24. 10.

REVERSE, fignifies on the back, or behind; fo we fay, *Reverfe view, a reverfe commanding ground, a reverfe battery,* &c.

REVETEMENT, a ftrong wall, built on the outfide of the rampart and parapet, to fupport

the earth, and prevent its rolling into the ditch.

REUX, a fmall but fortified city of Hainault in the Auftrian Low-countries, in a very fruitful foil, one mile n. eaft of Mons.

RHENEN, a town of Utrecht, in the United Provinces of Holland, furrounded with walls and baftions, 7 miles eaft of Wychle Overftede.

RHINEFIELD, a town of the Upper Rhine in Germany, and capital of a county of the fame name, having a ftrong caftle on a very high rock, commanding the Rhine. 16 miles n. weft of Mentz; fubject to the Landgrave of Heffe-Rhinefield. Lat. 50. 20. long. 7. 28.

RHINFELDEN, a fmall but ftrong city of Suabia, on the fouth fide of the Rhine. In 1638 it was taken by the Swedes, under the Duke of Saxe-Weymar; it fuffered much from the French in 1678; but was reftored, by the treaty of Munfter, to the Houfe of Auftria. 16 miles eaft of Bafil. Lat. 47. 36. n. long. 7. 10. eaft.

RHODES, the capital of the ifland of that name; about 3 miles in circuit, furrounded with a treble wall, and the fame number of moats; the fortifications are not now in a good condition, but it has a convenient and fafe harbour. Lat. 36. 24. n. long. 20. eaft.

RHOMB, a four-fided figure, whofe fides are equal, but the angles unequal.

RHOMBOIDE, a four-fided figure, whofe angles and oppofite fides are equal, but all its 4 fides are not equal.

RICHELIEU, a town of Poictou in France, regularly built by Cardinal Richelieu, having a confi-

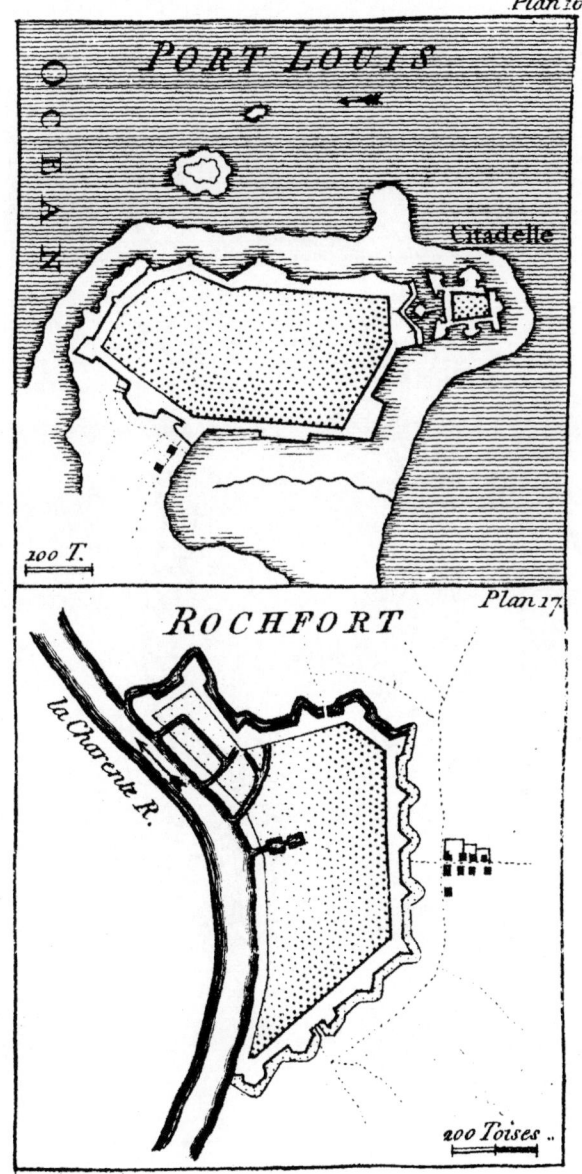

Plan 16.

PORT LOUIS

OCEAN

Citadelle

200 T.

Plan 17.

ROCHFORT

la Charente R.

200 Toises

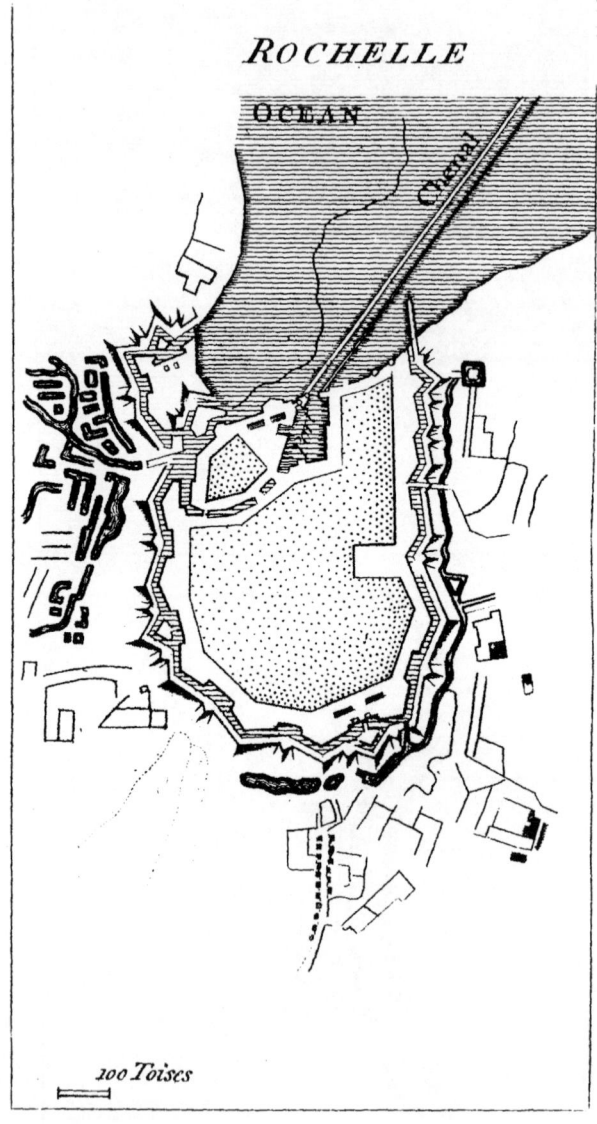

ROCHELLE

OCEAN

Chenal

100 Toises

confiderable caftle on the little rivers Amable and Vide. 27 miles n. of Poictiers. Lat. 47. 5. n. long. 28 mi. eaft.

RICOCHET. When guns are loaded with fmall charges, and elevated from 10 to 12 degrees, fo as to fire over the parapet, and the fhot rolls along the oppofite rampart, it is called ricochet-firing; and the batteries, ricochet-batteries.

RIDEAU, a rifing ground, or eminence, commanding a plain, fometimes near parallel to the works of a place. It is a great difadvantage to have rideaus near a fortification, efpecially when they fire from far, and terminate on the counterfcarp; they not only command the place, but alfo facilitate the enemy's approaches.

RIGA, a fmall, but populous port town in the divifion of Letten, and the capital of all Livonia, fituate at the mouth of the Dwina, in a bay of the Baltick; is furrounded with a wall; the houfes are moftly of ftone, has a ftrong citadel, and two arfenals, well provided with ftores. Taken in 1710, by the victorious arms of Peter the Great, and has ever fince been fubject to Ruffia. Lat. 57: 5. n. long. 24. 10. eaft.

RIO-DE-LÁ-HACHA, is the capital of a province of the fame name, about 40 leagues eaft of Santa Martha. The town has been feveral times taken by the Buccaneers, but is now fortified.

RIPATRANSONE, a fmall fortified city of Ancona, and the Pope's dominions in Italy; on the confines of Naples, 6 miles weft of the Adriatick. Lat. 42. 50. long. 15. 19.

RIPEN, an old town in New Jutland in Denmark, on a bay of the German ocean, with a ftrong caftle. 63 miles f. of Wiburg. Lat. 55. 36. long. 9. 10.

ROCELLA, a fortrefs of the further Calabria in Naples, near the Ionian fea, and commanding the cape of the fame name. Lat. 38. 26. long. 17. 10.

ROCHE, a fortified town of Luxemburg in the Auftrian Netherlands, furrounded with bulwarks, wet ditches, and a caftle on a rock, commanding the town.

ROCHELLE, a confiderable port and trading city of Aunis in France, in the Bay of Bifcay, 2 leagues from the Ifle of Rhé. The inhabitants embraced the reformed religion in the 16th century, fortified the city, and held out a long fiege againft Lewis XIII. who at laft obliged them to furrender, October 8, 1628, on which the place, except 2 towers defending the port, was demolifhed. Lewis XIV. raifed new fortifications. 70 miles fouth-weft of Poictiers. Lat. 46. 16. n. long. 1. 10. w. See Plan 18.

ROCHFORT, a city of Aunis in France, regularly built from a village by Lewis XIV. about a league and a half from the mouth of the Charante. It has a very commodious harbour; is one of the ftations for the royal navy, and has an excellent arfenal well furnifhed with naval ftores. 23 miles f. of Rochelle. Lat. 46. 5. n. long. 1. 10. weft. See Plan 17.

ROCROY, a fortified town of Remoies in France, on the borders of Hainault. Near it the Prince of Condé gained a complete victory over the Spaniards,

May

May 12, 1643. 34 miles f. of Namur. Lat. 50. 10. long. 4. 26.

ROLL, *to roll in duty*, when officers of the fame rank take their turns upon duty; as captains with captains, fubalterns with fubalterns, and command according to the feniority of their commiffions.

ROSBACH, a fmall town of Saxony, famous for a victory obtained November 5, 1757, between the Pruffian army, commanded by the King, and the combined army of Imperialifts and French, commanded by the Prince of Saxhilburghaufen, and the Prince of Soubife.

His Pruffian Majefty marched againft the combined army the 27th of October, and the 2 armies met, near the village of Rofbach, 5th of November. The combined army confifted of 60,000; but the Pruffians had only 25000: the Pruffians gained the rifing grounds, and began the attack at half paft two in the afternoon. The Pruffian cavalry foon intirely routed that of the enemy; whofe infantry were then attacked, and defeated by that of the Pruffians. The battle continued an hour and a half; the combined army fled, on all fides, before 5. The fugitives were favoured by the night, which gave them an opportunity of retiring towards Freyburg, and afterwards over the Unftrut to Erfert, where they were purfued till the 9th. The combined army had 3000 killed on the field, and upwards of 6000 taken prifoners; among whom were eight French Generals, and 250 officers of different ranks; they alfo loft 63

cannon, 15 ftandards, 7 pair of colours, and 300 baggage waggons. The Pruffians had only 100 men killed and 300 wounded. Pofterity will fcarce credit the account of this victory.

N. B. Juft before the battle, the king made the following fpeech to his army : " My dear friends, you know the hour is come in which all that is, and that fhould be dear to us, depends upon the fwords which are now drawn for battle; time permits me to fay but little; nor is there occafion to fay much : you know that there is no labour, hunger, cold, watching, or danger, that I have not hitherto fhared; you now fee me ready to lay down my life with you, and for you; all I afk, is the fame pledge of fidelity and affection as I give. Let me add, not as an incitement to your courage, but as a teftimony of my gratitude, that, from this hour, until you go into quarters, your pay fhall be doubled. *Acquit yourfelves like men, and put your confidence in God.*

ROSES, a fortified town of Catalonia in Spain, having a very good harbour on a bay of the Mediterranean, lies 64 miles n. eaft of Barcelona. Lat. 42. 30. long. 2. 43.

ROUEN, anciently *Rothomagus*, a city of France and the capital of Normandy, on the bank of the Seine, with a bridge of boats over it, rifing and falling with the tide. Is inclofed by an ancient wall flanked with baftions, has a caftle begun by Henry V. of England, and finifhed by his fon Henry VI. 46 miles foutheaft of Havre de Grace, and 67 n. weft of Paris, in lat. 49. 36. long. 1. 10.

ROVIGO,

Rovigo, a pretty fpacious but not well peopled city in the Venetian territories, in the Adigetto, fortified in the antient manner with a caftle; 22 miles fouth of Padua. Lat. 45. 10. long. 12. 28.

Route, an order to direct troops to march the road they are to take, and an authority to the magiftrates to provide quarters for the troops.

Ryswick, a fine village of Holland, between the Hague and Delft, with a grand palace of the Prince of Orange. Here the treaty of peace, called the treaty of Ryfwick, was concluded, between the Confederates and France, in 1697.

SABIONETTA, a ftrong town of the Mantuan in Italy, having a good caftle, 10 miles fouth of Mantua. Lat. 45. 10. n. long. 11. 5. eaft.

Safe-guard, a protection granted by a prince, or his general, for fome of the enemy's lands, &c. to preferve them from being infulted or plundered.

To force a fafe-guard, if upon fervice, by the articles of war, is death.

St. Gullian, 6 miles weftward of Mons, upon the river Haine, is a fortified town of little confequence. A day or two before the battle of Malplaquet, General Dedem, with a detachment from the blockade of Mons, took it fword in hand, and made the garrifon prifoners of war.

St. Omer. See Omer, St.

Saker, a piece of ordnance, carrying a ball of 5¼ pounds. The diameter of the bore is 3 inches and nine fixteenths; the

length of the gun about 8 or 9 feet.

Salankamen, a town of Sclavonia, near the Danube, memorable for a victory obtained in its neighbourhood over the Turks by Prince Lewis of Baden in 1691; and alfo another by Prince Eugene in 1716. It lies 23 miles north-weft of Belgrade. Lat. 45. 22. long. 21. 10.

Salerno, the capital of the hither Principate of Naples, on a bay of the Tufcan fea, having a pretty good harbour, but neglected. 28 miles f. of Naples. Lat. 40. 46. long. 15. 26.

Saliant-angle, that whofe points turn from the centre of the place.

Salins, a pretty confiderable city of the Franche Comté in France, fituated on the little river Furieufe; has 3 forts in its neighbourhood, 22 miles f. of Befançon. Lat. 47. 5. long. 6. 5.

Sally, when a part of the garrifon goes out privately, and falls fuddenly on the befiegers in their trenches, endeavouring to drive them out, and deftroy their works. If the garrifon is weak, fallies are feldom made; though they fatigue an enemy, obftruct their works, &c. Prudence is the beft guide: they fhould be always bold, daring, fecret, and at various times; equally concerted for the attack as the defence.

Saltsburg, the capital of an archbifhoprick of that name in Bavaria, on the river Saltz, well fortified; near it are fome rich mines of filver, copper, and iron. 71 miles eaft of Munich. Lat. 47. 45. long. 13. 5.

Saluzzo,

SALUZZO, antiently *Augusta Vagiennorum*, a city of Piedmont in Italy, on a mountain. In 1690 it was taken by the French, who demolished its walls; 17 miles f. of Turin, subject to the king of Sardinia. Lat. 44. 56. long. 7. 5.

SAND-BAGS, bags containing about a cubical foot of earth; used for raising parapets in haste, or to repair what is beaten down; they are of use when the ground is rocky, and affords no earth to carry on approaches, as they can be easily brought from afar, and removed at will. The smaller sand-bags contain about half a cubical foot of earth, and serve to be placed upon the superior talus of the parapet, to cover those that are behind, who fire through the embrasures or intervals left betwixt them.

SANDOMIR, a city, the capital of a palatinate of the same name, in Little Poland, on the Vistula. The Swedes blew up this castle in 1656; and here, in 1659, was a dreadful battle between the Tartars and Russians. 84 miles f. east of Cracow. Lat. 49. 26. long. 20. 10.

SAN FERNANDO, near the entrance of the Golfo Dolce, in 15 degrees 18 minutes n. latitude, and has lately been fortified by the Spaniards, with an intent to curb the Musquito-men, logwood-cutters, and bay-men. It is a very good harbour, with fafe anchorage from the n. and east winds, in 8 fathom water.

SAN JUAN DE PUERTO RICO. The harbour is so spacious, that the largest ships may lay with great safety. On the west side of this city is the Castillo del Morro, a strong citadel, which commands and defends it; while the mouth of the harbour is protected by the El Convelo, a large and well fortified castle. In 1595 Sir Francis Drake burnt all the ships in the harbour; but finding it impossible to keep the place, without abandoning his other designs, he declined it. A few years after the Earl of Cumberland reduced the island; but losing 4 or 500 men in a month, by a contagious disease, he was glad to depart. In 1615, the Dutch sent a strong fleet against it with little success; they only took and plundered the city, but were unable to reduce the castle with its forts.

SANTAREM, a city of Portuguese Estremadura, is situate on the Tagus, defended by a citadel, fortified in the modern manner, 56 miles n. east of Lisbon. Lat. 39. 18. long. 8. 45. west.

SANT AUGUSTINE, on the eastern coast of the peninsula of Florida, is 70 leagues from the Gulf of Florida, and 47 from the town and river of Savana, built along the shore, at the bottom of a hill, mounted with cannon. The castle, called St. John's, is built of soft stone, has four bastions, a curtain 60 yards long, a parapet about 9 feet thick, and a rampart 20 feet high, casemated, arched, and bomb-proof.

Sir Francis Drake attacked this fort in 1586, when the Spaniards

niards fled and left him 14 brafs guns, mounted on a platform of trees and earth, alfo a cheft of about 2000 pounds, &c. The town confifted of timber houfes; the fort of wood, and the walls of trunks of trees placed clofe together. In 1665, it was again attacked and plundered by Capt. Davis, at the head of the Buccaneers; at which time the fort is faid to have been an octagon, with a round tower at each angle. The next attack was in 1702, by the Englifh and Indians of Carolina, under Colonel Moor their governor; he deftroyed the villages and farms, and befieged this town 3 months; but on approach of fome Spanifh fhips to its relief, he raifed the fiege, and marched to Charles Town, leaving the fhip and ftores he brought with him to the enemy. The laft fiege of this place was by General Oglethorpe, in 1740, with 4 men of war and tranfports from Charles Town with troops. Having rendezvoufed near the mouth of Saint John's river, and being joined by the Cherokee Indians, on the 9th of May he marched 20 miles to Fort Diego, which he took, and made the garrifon prifoners of war: the Spaniards alfo abandoned Fort Moofa, or Negro Fort, to the general, who afterwards encamped his army on Sant Anaftafia ifland, having left a fmall part of his forces on the continent to garrifon Fort Negro, and alarm the Spaniards. June 15, the Spaniards made a fally from the caftle of Sant Auguftine, attacked and defeated the garrifon at Fort Negro, killed Colonel Palmer, and took many prifoners. After this, the Spaniards received a fupply of

provifions, &c. from Cuba, conveyed up the Matanzas, and landed to the fouth of the town, where the general had no battery to annoy, or force to intercept them. The befiegers bombarded both caftle and town; but their artillery was planted too diftant to effect any material execution, occafioned by the river, moraffes, and other obftructions; and the near approach of bad weather obliging the men of war to return to fea, the fiege was raifed the 4th of July; it appearing that 200 feamen, 400 foldiers, and 300 Indians, were too weak to fubdue 1000 Spaniards, fecured by a caftle. 7 leagues below Fort Sant Auguftine are two forts; the one on the north, the other on the fouth fide of a large lake. Oglethorpe deftroyed the laft, and took poffeffion of the firft, which is called Mauchicolis, furrounded with ftrong palifades, 8 feet high, with a parapet and loopholes about breaft high.

SAP, a trench, or an approach made under cover, of 10 or 12 feet broad, when the befiegers come near the place, and their fire grows fo dangerous; as not to be approached uncovered.

SARAGOSSA, a large city, the capital of Arragon, in Spain, furrounded with old walls, and other antique fortifications, at the confluence of the rivers Ebro, Galeyo, and Guerva, which run in a ferpentine manner through the neighbourhood. 156 miles weft of Barcelona, and 180 north-eaft of Madrid. This city fubmitted to Charles III. in 1706; but after the unfortunate battle of Almanza, in 1707, was obliged to furrender to his rival Philip. The former

mer of thefe princes obtaining a
victory over the latter in 1710,
entered this city in triumph the
fame evening; but a body of
Englifh forces being foon after
furprifed, and made prifoners at
Brihuega, King Charles was a-
gain obliged to quit Saragoffa,
and retire to Catalonia; on which
occafion Philip again entered it.
Lat. 41. 32. n. long. 1. 18. weft.

SARLOUIS, a fortrefs of Lorrain, fituate on the Sare, 10
miles n. weft of Sarbruck. Lat.
49. 28. long. 6. 4.

SARZANA, a fortrefs belonging to the Genoefe, on the confines of Italy and Tufcany, has
a caftle on a mountain, 12 miles
n. of Maffa. Lat. 44. 10. long.
10. 38.

SASH, a mark of diftinction,
generally made of crimfon filk,
and worn about an officer's
waift. The firft intention of
them were, if an officer received fo defperate a wound, as to
render him incapable of remaining at his poft, he might be put
into his fafh, and carried off by
the affiftance of 2 men; but
they are now ufed to diftinguifh
the officer upon duty.

SAUCISSE, a long train of
powder, fowed up in a roll of
pitched cloth, about 2 inches
diameter; its ufe is to fire mines
or caiffons; the length of it muft
reach from the mine to the place
where the engineer is to fire it, to
fpring the mine.

SAUCISSON a long pipe, or
bag of cloth or leather, about
an inch and a half diameter,
filled with powder, leading from
the chamber of a mine to the
entrance of the gallery. It ferves
to give fire to the mine.

Sauciffon, alfo a fafcine, longer than the common, ferves

to raife batteries, and repair
breaches.

SAVONA, a pretty ftrong city,
has a large harbour and caftle
next the fea, unfuccefsfully attacked by the French and Genoefe in 1748. 25 miles f. weft
of Genoa. Lat. 44. 31. long.
9. 10.

SCALADE, or efcalade, a furious attack, upon a wall or
rampart, carried on with various
forts of ladders, to infult by
open force.

SCALE, a right line divided
into equal parts, reprefenting
miles, fathoms, paces, inches,
&c. ufed in making plans upon
paper, giving each line its true
length, &c.

SCARP. The flope of the
lower part of the wall fhould be
as faliant as poffible at bottom,
without taking too much from
the breadth of the foffe: this
renders the efcalading more difficult, and the wall on battering
will not fo readily fall down as
one more erect.

SCHANTZ STERNEY, a for-
trefs of Carelia, in Ruffian Finland, is fituated on the Nieva, a
little eaft of St. Peterfburg, in
lat. 60. 15. n. long. 31, 20.
eaft.

SCHELLA, a town and fort of
Upper Hungary, fituated on the
Waag, 25 miles north-eaft of
Prefburg. Lat. 48. 32. long. 18. 15.

SCHELLENBERG, a fortified
mountain which ferves inftead
of a caftle, ftands on the Danube, about a quarter of a league
on the eaft fide of Donawert, in
Bavaria. Famous for the defeat
of the French and Bavarians,
in 1704, when the Confederates,
commanded by the Duke of Marlborough, forced the trenches,
and next day made themfelves
mafters

masters of Donawert. It lies 22 miles west of Ingolstadt. Lat. 48. 51. n. long. 11. 10. east.

SCHEMNITZ, the largest of all the mine towns in Upper Hungary; built upon a rocky hill, defended with 3 castles. 41 miles n. east of Presburg. Lat. 48. 46. long. 19. 10. east.

SCHENKEN SCHANTZ, a strong fort of Gelderland in the United Netherlands, 14 miles east of Nimeguen, subject to Prussia. Lat. 51. 54. n. long. 6. 16. east.

SCHENOGRAPHY, *profile*, or *view*, the natural representation of a place, as it appears when viewed from without: which shews its situation, the form of its walls, number and figure of its steeples, and tops of its public and private buildings.

SCHELESTADT, a town of Alsace and the Upper Rhine, in Germany, now belonging to France, the fortifications whereof have been very much increased since it has been in the possession of that crown. 9 miles s. of Strasburg, in lat. 48. 24. n. long. 7. 36. east.

SCHOONHOVEN, a town of Holland, situated on the n. bank of the river Leech, so well fortified, that the French were repulsed before it in 1672, with considerable loss. 14 miles east of Amsterdam, in lat. 52. 10. n. long. 4. 47. east.

SCHWEIDNITZ, the capital of a duchy of that name, in Silesia and kingdom of Bohemia, on the river Weistritz, strongly fortified in the modern manner, 26 miles s. of Breslaw, in lat. 50. 47. n. long. 16. 25. east.

This place was formally invested by his Prussian Majesty in 1758. The siege began on the 2d of April, and a brisk fire was

constantly sustained from 7 different batteries; but the garrison, under Count Thierhelm, made a brave resistance till the 16th, when he was obliged to surrender it. The King employed in this siege 5000 foot, 2 companies of miners, and 22 engineers. The prisoners taken in the town were 173 officers and 1739 men. The besiegers had 5 officers and 93 men killed, 24 officers and 233 men wounded.

1st Oct. 1761, the Austrians, under M. de Laudohn, became masters of it by a *coup de main*, when general Zastrow, the governor, and 3771 men were made prisoners of war, and a magazine of powder blew up in the attack, which did equal damage to both, and 181 pieces of cannon were found in the place. The loss of the Austrians was 279 killed, and 1150 wounded and missing; of the Russians engaged in this assault, 51 were killed and 45 wounded.

August 8th 1762. 8 battalions and 1000 Croats sallied out upon the Russians when before it, routed the battalion of Falkenhagen, made the colonel and some officers prisoners, and killed and wounded 100. But on the 9th October 1762, it capitulated with the King of Prussia, when the trenches had been opened before it for 2 months. General Guasco and his garrison surrendered prisoners of war. 8th of Oct. a grenade from the besiegers fell upon a magazine of powder, which did great damage to one of the forts, besides blowing up 205 officers and men. A mine took full effect in the night between the 8th and 9th, carried away a part of the rampart, made a breach in the

the covert-way, and filled up the ditch with rubbifh. The garrifon marched out of the fortrefs with military honours, laid down their arms, and were made prifoners of war. They had 32 officers and 1249 foldiers killed, 33 officers and 2223 foldiers wounded. The Pruffians loft 25 officers, 1084 fubalterns and private men killed, or dead of their wounds, befides 61 officers and 1845 fubalterns, or private men, wounded, in all 86 officers and 2929 foldiers. M. de Griboval acted as engineer to the garrifon; M. le Fevre to the befiegers.

SCHWEINFURT, an imperial and fortified city of Franconia, on the river Maine, 35 miles n. of Wurtzburg. Lat. 50.15. long. 10. 15.

SCOUR, To fcour a line, is to flank it, fo as to fee directly along it, that a mufquet-ball entering at one end may fire to the other, leaving no place of fecurity.

SCUTARI, by the Turks called Ifcodar, one of the moft confiderable cities, and the capital of Albania, in European Turky, on the river Boyana, is well fortified, defended by a ftrong citadel, 27 miles eaft of the Adriatic. Lat. 42. 36. n. long. 20. 4. eaft.

SEAFORD, a fmall borough of Suffex, having a harbour on the Englifh channel, defended by a fort, 7 miles from Lewes, and 54 from London.

SEBASTIAN, ST. a famous port of Guipufcoa, a territory of Bifcay, in Spain, at the mouth of the river Branco, inclofed with a triple wall, has a ftrong caftle, 25 miles f. weft of Bayonne. Lat. 43. 37. n. long. 1. 56. weft.

SEBENICO, a well fortified city of Venetian Dalmatia, on the Adriatic, has a fpacious port defended by the ifland of St. Nicholas. 42 miles n. of Spalatto. Lat. 43. 46. long. 17. 26.

SECOND COVERT WAY, that beyond the fecond ditch.

Second Ditch, that made on the out-fide of the glacis, when the ground is low and water plenty.

SEDAN, a very ftrong town of Champagne, in France, on the Maes, reckoned one of the keys of the kingdom, 38 miles weft of Luxemburg, in lat. 49. 34. n. long. 4. 50. eaft.

SEGEDIN, a city of Upper Hungary, on the weft fide of the river Theifs, belongs to the Houfe of Auftria; has undergone feveral fieges with various fuccefs, 20 miles n. eaft of Effeek. Lat. 46. 21. long. 21. 5.

SEGORBE, a city of Valencia, in Spain, on the banks of the Morviedro, defended by a ftrong wall and caftle, 30 miles n. weft of Valencia, in lat. 39. 56. long. 56. min. weft.

SEGOVIA, a city of Old Caftile, in Spain, on the river Frio, over which is a noble aqueduct, built by Trajan. The principal mint of Spain is fixed in this city, which is encompaffed with ftrong walls, adorned with lofty towers, 35 miles n. of Madrid, in lat. 41. 10. long. 4. 36. weft.

SELENGINSK, a town of Siberia, on the river Selenga, defended by a fortrefs of five brafs and as many iron cannon, on the road from Tobolfki to China, 215 miles fouth of the lake of Baikul. Lat. 50. 10. long. 95. 16.

SELINGENSTADT, a fmall town of Mentz, in Germany, on the weft bank of the Maine, 8 miles f. eaft of Hanau, and 14 eaft of Frankfort. Here the French army, under Marſhal de Noailles, paſſed the Maine to attack the Confederates, June 16th 1743, but were obliged to repaſs it after the battle of Dettingen. Lat. 50. 10. long. 8. 49. eaſt.

SEMUR, a town of Burgundy, in France, has a ſtrong citadel, 134 miles weſt of Dijon, in lat. 47. 24. long. 4. 15.

SENEGAMBIA, or *Gambia*, a large river, between the tropics, in Africa, ſurrounding James Iſland, where the company have a ſettlement, defended by a garriſon and fortreſs (under the command of a Lieutenant-governor) called James Fort.

SENLIS, a city of the Iſle of France, ſurrounded with walls and a dry deep ditch, has baſtions and half moons.

SENTRY, a private ſoldier placed in ſome poſt to prevent ſurprize from an ehemy. If placed in a very advanced and dangerous poſt, he is called, from the French, *Sentinel perdu.*

SESTOS, a ſtrong caſtle of Romania, in Turky, on the European ſide of the ſtreight of the Helleſpont, 24 miles ſouth-weſt of Gallipoli. Lat. 40. 10. long. 27. 36. eaſt.

SEVILLE, a very ancient city of Andaluſia, in Spain, in a fertile country, on the river Guadalquiver, over which it has a ſtout bridge of 17 boats, which joins the city to a large ſuburb on the other ſide. The compaſs of the city, including this ſuburb, is ſuppoſed to be near 14 miles, but the wall is only 8. It is very ſtrong, and adorned with 15 gates and 166 towers. Near the water-ſide is a ſtately tower, called the Golden Tower, com-

manding the whole river, city, and ſuburbs. It ſtands 50 miles north-eaſt of the port-town of St. Lucar, 70 north-eaſt of Cadiz, and upwards of 200 ſouth-weſt of Madrid. Lat. 37. 15. long. 6. 10. weſt.

SHELLS, hollow iron balls to throw out of mortars or howitzes, with a hole about an inch diameter, to load them with powder and receive the fuze. The bottom, or part oppoſite the fuze, is made heavier than the reſt, that the fuſee may fall uppermoſt; but in ſmall elevations that is not always the caſe; for when it falls firſt, it ſets fire to the powder in the ſhell. However, whether it breaks or not, it is proper to make the ſhell every where of the ſame thickneſs, as it would then burſt into a greater number of pieces than it does at preſent.

SHERBRO, a fort belonging to the Engliſh, at the mouth of a river of that name, on the coaſt of Guinea, in Africa, 100 miles ſouth-eaſt of Sierra Leone. Lat. 6. 5. n. long. 11. 10. weſt.

SHEERNESS, a regular fortification, on the north-weſt extremity of the iſle of Sheppey, in Kent, having a line of heavy cannon to defend the mouth of the Medway, 35 miles from London. Long. 50 min. eaſt; lat. 52. 25.

SHOT, all ſorts of ball, either for cannon, muſquets, carabines, or piſtols.

Chain ſhot, 2 whole or half bullets joined together, either by a bar or chain of iron, which allows them ſome liberty aſunder, ſo that they cut and deſtroy whatever they happen to ſtrike in their courſe.

Grape-ſhot, a certain number of

of small shots, of iron or lead, quilted together with canvas and ropes about a pin of iron or wood, fixed upon a bottom in the same manner, the whole together weighing nearly as much as the shot of that caliber.

SHOULDER, *of a bastion*, that part where the face and flank meet.

SIDES *of horn-works, tenailles, crown-works, &c.* those parts of the ramparts which reach from the borders of the fosse to the head of the works. Those in horn-works and tenailles are parallel. Sometimes these sides are no longer than the reach of a musquet-shot, and are then defended by the faces of the place; but when they are longer, they have either flanks in the long sides, which are then said to have shoulders; they are indented; or made with redans, traverses, or cross intrenchments in the ditch.

SIEGE. *To besiege a place*, is to surround it with an army, and approach it, by passages made in the ground, so as to be covered against the fire of the place.

When an army can approach so near the place as the covertway, without breaking ground, under favour of some hollow roads, rising grounds, or cavities, and there begin their work, it is called *accelerating the siege*: but when they can approach the town so near as to take it, without making any considerable works, the siege is called *an attack*.

To raise a Siege, to give over the attack of a place, quit the works thrown up against it, and the posts taken about it. If there be no reason to fear a sally from the place, the siege may be raised in the day-time. Artillery and ammunition must have a strong rear-guard and face the besiegers, lest they should attempt to charge the rear; if there be any fear of any enemy in front, this order must be altered discretionally, as safety, and the nature of the country, will allow.

To make, or *form a siege*, there must be an army sufficient to furnish 5 or 6 reliefs for the trenches; pioneers, guards, convoys, escorts, &c. an artillery, magazines furnished with a sufficient quantity of warlike stores, provisions of all sorts, and an infirmary, with physicians, surgeons, &c.

To turn a siege into a blockade, to give over the attack, and endeavour to take it by famine: for which purpose, all the avenues, gates, and streams leading into the place are so well guarded, that no succour can get to its relief.

SIEGEN, or *Sigen*, the capital of a country of that name in the landgravate of Hesse, defended by a strong wall, with regular fortifications, is subject to its own prince. 30 miles n. of the city of Nassau, in lat. 50. 46. long. 7. 54.

SIENNA, a very ancient city of the Sienese, in the great duchy of Tuscany, now subject to the Emperor. It was formerly a powerful republic, but after long and frequent struggles, it was forced in 1555 to submit to Florence. It is about 5 miles in circuit; its walls, towers, and castle, were formerly very strong, but are now decayed, so that there are no fortifications of consequence, except a citadel. 36 miles

miles f. of Florence, in lat. 43. 28. n. long. 12. 38.

SIERRA LEONE, a regular fort at the mouth of a river of that name, on the coaft of Guinea, or Negroland, in Africa, belonging to England. Lat. 2. 46. long. 14. 15. weft.

SIGETH, a fortified town of Lower Hungary, on the frontiers of Poland, taken by the Malcontents in 1703. 73 miles fouthweft of Buda, fubject to the Houfe of Auftria. Lat. 46. 35. long. 18. 38.

SIGISTAN, the capital of a province of the fame name in Perfia, on the river Senarond, a branch of the Hendmend, which falls into the lake Zaré, 231 miles fouth-weft of Candahor. Lat. 31. 10. long. 62. 18.

SILISTRIA, or *Doreftero*, a pretty large and ftrong town of Bulgaria in European Turky, defended by a good citadel. The capital of a fangiack, 90 miles eaft of Niffa, in lat. 42. 48. long. 27.

SILLON, or *envelope*, a work raifed in the middle of a foffe, to defend it when too wide. It has no particular form, but is promifcuoufly made, with little baftions, half-moons, or redans, which are lower than the works of the place, but higher than the covert way.

SINTSHEIM, a fmall city in the palatinate of the Rhine, where Marfhal Turenne obtained a fignal victory over the Imperialifts, under the Duke of Lorrain, in 1674. 18 miles fouth of Heidelberg, in lat. 49. 16. long. 8. 44. eaft.

SION, a city and fovereign ftate of Valais in Switzerland, is neat, well-built, defended by 2 caftles; 23 miles f. eaft of the Lake of Geneva, in lat. 46. 21. long. 7. 26.

SIRIK, or *Sirique*, a town of Metz in Lorrain, near the Mofelle, defended by a caftle, 12 miles fouth-eaft of the city of Luxemburg, in lat. 49. 41. long. 6. 15.

SIRADIA, the capital of a palatinate of that name in Great Poland, on the Warta, and defended by a ftrong wall and caftle. 22 miles fouth-eaft of Kalifch, in lat. 52. 10 long. 18. 15.

SIXIAN, an antient order of battle for 6 battalions, which, fuppofing them all in a line, is formed thus: the fecond and fifth battalions advance, and make the van; the firft and fixth, fall to the rear, leaving the third and fourth to form the body. Each battalion fhould have one fquadron on its right, and another on its left.

SLONIM, a town of Lithuania in Poland, built of wood; but has a caftle, and other regular fortifications on the Szura. 60 miles f. eaft of Grodno, in lat. 53. 10. long. 15. 25.

SLUYS, a pretty large town of Dutch Brabant, one of the 5 feaports of Flanders, on a fmall arm of the fea, which parts it from the ifland of Cadfand; very ftrong, even thought impregnable, becaufe of its fluices. 10 miles north-eaft of Bruges, in lat. 51. 24. long. 3. 21.

SMOLENSKO, the capital of a province of the fame name in Ruffia, on the Nieper, near the confines of Lithuania. It is a large city, fortified with good walls, and defended with a ftrong caftle. 200 miles w. of Mofcow, in lat. 56. 10. long. 33. 16.

SMYRNA, the capital of Ionia, in Afia Minor; one of the fineft ports

ports in the Levant, at the bottom of a bay of the Archipelago, in Afiatic Turky. The entrance of the haven is defended by forts and a caſtle, 100 miles north of Rhodes, and 200 ſouth-weſt of Conſtantinople, in lat. 38. 27. long. 26.

SNEEK, an antient, neat, and well fortified town of Friefland, in the United Provinces; on a lake of that name, 12 miles ſouth of Lecuwarden, in lat. 53. 15.

SOLMS, the capital of a county of the ſame name in the Wettera, and landgravate of Heſſe, ſubject to its own count, and defended by a caſtle. 35 miles n. of Francfort, in lat. 50. 41. long. 27. 12.

SOLOTHURN, the capital of a canton of that name in Switzerland, on the river Aar. This city is regularly fortified with baſtions, half móons, and ravelins, and encompaſſed with a deep ditch. 15 miles north of the city of Berne. Lat. 47. long. 7. 15.

SOLSONA, a thinly inhabited city of Catalonia in Spain, on the river Cardona. It is well walled, has 2 caſtles, 60 miles north-weſt of Barcelona.

SONDRIO, a pretty well fortified town of the Grifons, and capital of the middle Torzero, in Switzerland, on the right ſide of the Adda, 18 miles n. eaſt of Como. Lat. 36. 15. long. 9. 56.

SOPALA, the capital city of the king of that name in Monomotapa, in Africa, on the river Sofala. Here the Portuguefe have a ſtrong fort, are maſters of the town, and claim the ſovereignty of the country. Lat. 20. 5. long. 35. 10. eaſt.

SOUND, a paſſage or ſtreight, lying between the iſland of Zee-land, in Denmark, and the continent of Schonen, in Sweden, through which veſſels paſs from the ocean into the Baltic. On the Denmark ſide ſtands the town of Elſineur, and the ſtrong fortreſs of Cronenburg, near which is a tolefable good road; on the ſide of Sweden ſtands the town of Helſingburg, with only one old tower remaining of a demoliſhed caſtle.

SPALATTO, a pretty large and well fortified city of Dalmatia, having a very capacious and ſafe harbour on the Adriatic, 65 miles n. weſt of Ragufa, in lat. 43. 22. long. 17. 52.

SPOLETTO, the capital of a duchy of Ombria in the ecclefiaſtical ſtate in Italy, near the Teſſino, having near it a ſtrong old caſtle, and ſeveral grand ruins, lies 52 miles n. eaſt of Rome. Lat. 42. 46. n. long. 13. 38. eaſt.

SQUADRON, a body of cavalry, compoſed of 3 troops.

SQUARE, HOLLOW, a body of infantry drawn up with a ſpace in the centre (for the colonel, lieutenant colonel, major, adjutant, colours, pioneers, grenanadiers, light-company, muſic, drummers and fifers) to oppofe either cavalry or infantry, formed with cloſe and open files. See Plan 1.

Square, oblong, a figure of 4 faces; the front and rear of a ſmaller extent than the flanks; and the angles generally covered by the grenadiers and light-company. When that is not their ſituation, the former form the front face, and the latter the rear; fee Plan 1; where the baggage is ſuppoſed to be guarded by this, becaufe the country cannot admit of a larger front.

STAGNO,

STAGNO, or *Stagno Grande*, a small, but well fortified city, with a little, but commodious harbour, 15 miles n. of the city of Ragufa.

STAIN, or *Stein*, a small town of Auftria in Germany, defended by an ancient caftle on the n. fide of the Danube, over which is a wooden bridge ; oppofite to Mautern, 16 miles n. of Vienna. Lat. 48. 41. long. 15. 30.

STAR-FORT, a work with feveral faces, generally compofed of from 5 to 8 points, with faliant and re-entering angles flanking one another ; each fide containing from 12 to 25 fathoms.

STAVANGER, the capital of a diftrict of that name, on a peninfula in the province of Berghen in Norway. The harbour is not only large, but fafe, and the town is defended by a ftrong fortrefs. Lat. 59. 36. long. 6. 36.

STAVEREN, an antient town of Weft Friefland, in Holland, on the Zuyder-fea, has a bad entrance to the harbour, but is fortified with a good ditch and rampart, 16 miles fouth of Enchuyfen. Lat. 53. 5. long. 6. 36.

STEENKIRK, a village of Hainault, in the Auftrian Netherlands, famous for a battle, on the third of Auguft, 1692, between the army of the Allies, commanded by King William and Maximilian of Bavaria, who attacked the French, under Marefchal Luxemburg, in their fortified camp. 12 miles n. of Mons, and 16 f. weft of Bruffels.

STEENWYCK, a fmall but ftrong place in Overyffel, in the United Netherlands, on the Aa, near the borders of Friefland, 18 miles n. of Zwoll. Lat. 52. 54. long. 6. 15.

STENAY, formerly the capital of Bar, on the eaft fide of the river Maefe, ceded to France 1641, and its citadel and walls demolifhed by Lewis XIV. but the fortifications have been fince rebuilt. 14 miles weft of Montmedy, in lat. 49. 46. long. 5. 5.

STENDAL, the metropolis of the old March of Brandenburg, in Upper Saxony. A neat well built city and ftrongly fortified, on the river Ucht ; fubject to the King of Pruffia, 36 miles n. of Magdeburgh. Lat. 52. 47. long. 12. 12.

STERLING, the capital of a county of that name in Scotland, and a royal burgh, on the declivity of a fteep rock, at the foot of which runs the river Forth, has a ftrong caftle, inclofed by a wall, except towards the north, where it is bounded by the Forth, which is croffed by a bridge of hewn ftone. This caftle commands the paffes between the north and fouth of Scotland. The rebels, in 1716, endeavoured to poffefs themfelves of this caftle, but were prevented by the late John Duke of Argyle ; and in 1745, it held out againft all their efforts under Lord Blakeney. 30 miles n. weft of Edinburgh. Weft long. 3. 50. lat. 56. 52.

STETIN, the metropolis of Swedifh Pomerania, in Upper Saxony, having a fine caftle on the weft fide of the Oder, 40 miles from the fea, yet fhips of good burden come up to the walls, the river being navigable a great way above the town by fmaller veffels. It is fo ftrongly fortified as to be one of the moft formidable places in Europe ;

has

has a good trade, and is now very populous. 66 miles n. of Berlin. Lat. 53. 39. long. 14. 56.

STEVENSWART, a ftrong fortrefs of Gelderland, on an ifland of the Maes, has 7 baftions and a bridge of boats, the head of which is fortified with a halfmoon. 23 miles n. eaft of Maeftricht; fubject to the Dutch. Lat. 51. 20. long. 5. 49.

STOCKHOLM, the capital of Sweden. The harbour is capable of receiving 1000 fail of fhips, and has a quay near an Englifh mile in length. The only inconveniency is its being 10 miles from the fea; the entrance is defended by 2 forts. This city lies 300 miles n. eaft of Copenhaegn, 416 weft of Peterfburg, and 921 n. eaft of London. Lat. 59. 20. long. 19. 30.

STOLHOFFEN, a little town of Baden-baden, near a morafs in Swabia, on the eaft fide of the Rhine, famous for the lines thrown up here in the two laft wars, for the defence of the empire againft France. 15 miles n. eaft of Strafburg, in lat. 40. 38. long. 8. 18.

STRALSUND, a free imperial city in Upper Saxony, ftrongly fortified, has a good haven, 65 miles eaft of Wifmar. Lat. 54. 26. long. 13. 22.

STRAUBING, a well fortified town of Bavaria on the f. fide of the Danube, over which it has a bridge, 20 miles f. eaft of Ratifbon. Lat. 48. 50. long. 12. 41.

STURGATT, the capital of the Duke of Wirtemberg in Swabia, is a pretty large city, but moft of the houfes are of wood. The Duke's palace is a noble free-ftone fabric well fortified. 42 miles eaft of Baden, and 45 north-weft of Ulm. Lat. 48. 46. long. 8. 54.

SUB-BRIGADIER, an officer in the horfe-guards, who ranks as Cornet.

SUB-LIEUTENANT, an officer in the fufileers, where they have no enfigns, is the youngeft lieutenant in the company, and carries the colours.

SUCCOUR, the effort made to relieve a place; that is, raife the fiege, and force the enemy from it.

SUCCOURS, a general who marches to the relief of a place befieged fhould fend notice to the governors, by letters or otherwife: this renews the courage of the garrifon. He fhould be expeditious to prevent the enemy's fortifying their camp, or carrying on their approaches.

A place befieged may be retrieved by cutting off the enemy's provifion, feizing fome of their pofts, or attacking fome of their places, to oblige them by a diverfion to raife the fiege, or by throwing provifions into the place of powder, victuals, men, &c.

Thefe refrefhments are fent into the town by furprize, by attacking fome of their pofts, or the enemy in their camp.

To reduce a relief by furprize, you march in the night, through by-ways, and thofe leaft fortified and guarded; if you are difcovered, pufh on immediately, and force your way: thofe within make a *fortie* at the fame time, according as you have agreed with them, giving falfe alarms at other places,

to

to keep them in fufpence : reconnoitre well the relief before
they are admitted.

When you would relieve a
place befieged with open force,
as you draw nearer the town, you
fire fome cannon to acquaint the
garrifon of your approach.

A knowledge of the places
leaft fortified and moft neglected
gives you an eafy opportunity of
throwing in your fuccours : the
beft informed general has the
greateft advantage over his enemy.

When you march to the re-
lief of a place, let it be fpread
abroad that you have a numerous army : to make this appear
probable, your army on their
march fhould extend itfelf, by
enlarging their intervals ; the
enemy is intimidated, confternation fpreads through their
camp, and they often raife the
fiege precipitately.

SUNDERBURG, a town on the
fouth part of the ifland of Alfen,
in the Baltic, belonging to
Denmark ; it is a very ftrong
place, 104 miles weft of Copenhagen. Lat. 55. 24. long. 10.
4.

SURAT, a city and port of the
Eaft Indies, the capital of Cam-
baya, on the banks of the river
Tabtu, is defended by a flight
wall, with fome antique forts,
10 miles eaft of the Indian fea,
160 north of Bombay, and as
many fouth of the city of Cam-
baya. Lat. 21. 12. long. 72.
27.

SURFACE, or *fuperficies*, an extent, having length and breadth,
but no thicknefs : it is therefore
evident, that the extremities of
a furface are lines.

Surface, as a term in fortification, is that part of the fide

which is terminated by the flank
prolonged or extended, and the
angle of the neareft baftion :
the double of this line with the
curtain, is equal to the exterior
fide.

SURINAM, the chief fettle-
ment of the Dutch, in Guiana,
in South America. The French
and Englifh were fucceffively in
poffeffion of this place ; the former quitting it as unwholefome,
and the latter making no great
account of it, furrendered it
readily to the Dutch, who took
poffeffion of it in 1674. The
colony is now become very powerful, has feveral forts, and extended itfelf thirty leagues above
the river Surinam. Lat. 6. 34.
long. 56. 22. weft.

SURPRIZES. To fall on an
enemy by furprize, when they
march through narrow difficult
paffes, when one part has paffed,
fo as not eafily to come to the
fuccour of the other ; as in the
paffage of rivers, woods, or en-
clofures, in which lay an ambufcade, pofting alfo a body of
cavalry near the place they come
out at ; when part of the enemy
are come out, charge them in
front, rear, and flank.

A place is furprized by drains,
cafe-mates, or the iffues of rivers
or canals ; by encumbering the
bridge or gate, by waggons
meeting and ftopping each other ;
fending foldiers into the place,
under pretence of being deferters, who on entering furprize
the guard, being fuftained by
troops in ambufh near the place,
to whom they give entrance,
and feize it ; foldiers fometimes
dreffed like peafants, merchants,
Jews, priefts, or women. The
enemy fometimes fend in their
foldiers as if they were yours

coming from the hofpital, &c. they alfo drefs their foldiers in your regimentals, and prefenting themfelves at your gate as fuch, are immediately admitted, feize the guard and become mafters of the place; fometimes houfes are fet on fire, and whilft the garrifon comes out to extinguifh it, troops who lay in ambufh march in and furprize the place. Officers commanding guards at the principal gates are lured out under various pretences, fo contrived as to feize the gate in going in with them. Sometimes an alarm is given at one fide of the garrifon, whilft you enter fecretly at the other, at that time too often neglected.

SUSA, the capital of the marquifate of that name, in Piedmont in Italy, a fmall place, well fortified, and reckoned one of the keys of that country : on the Doria, furrounded with high mountains, 18 miles n. weft of Turin. Lat. 45. 5. long. 7. 10.

SUTLER, one who follows the army and provides provifions for the troops.

SWALLOW'S-TAIL, an outwork, differing from a fingle tenaille, as its fides are not parallel, like thofe of a tenaille ; but, if prolonged, would meet and form an angle on the middle of the curtain ; and its head or front compofed of 2 faces forming a re-entering angle. This work is extraordinarily well flanked, and defended by the works of the place, which difcover all the length of its long fide : they feldom fufficiently cover the flanks of the oppofite baftions

SWOLL, or *Zwoll*, a ftrong and regular city of Overyffel, in the United Provinces, with double ditches, filled by the Aa, 17 miles north of Deventer, in latitude 52. 37. north, long. 6. 5. eaft.

SYRACUSE, a famous ancient city and port of the Val di Noto, in a fine bay of the Mediterranean on the eaft coaft of the ifland of Sicily, and the capital of a once flourifhing ftate, is ftill confiderable on account of its harbour and ftrength of its walls. At the entry into the port is a ftrong but irregular caftle, in which is the celebrated fountain of Arethufa. 65 miles f. of Meffina, in latitude 37. 32. long, 15. 10.

TABARCA, a little ifland lying oppofite to a fmall town of that name, which divides the maritime coafts of Tunis and Algiers, in Africa, 2 miles from the land, in poffeffion of the noble family of the Lamellini of Genoa, who have here a governor and a garrifon of 200 men to protect the coral fifhery. Lat. 36. 36. long. 8. 10.

TABOR, a fmall town of Bohemia, having a caftle fortified with a double wall, flanked with towers and baftions, between Budweis and Prague, 45 miles f. of the latter. Lat. 49. 31. long. 14. 36.

TACTICKS. The art of difciplining armies, and ranging them into forms proper for fighting and manœuvring.

TAFALA, a city of Navarre, in Spain, pleafantly fituated on the banks of the Vidazo, and has an old caftle, with a royal palace, 22 miles f. of Pampelona. Lat. 42. 47. long. 1. 38.

TAFILET, a town of Biledulgerid, in Africa, near the river Tafilet,

Tafilet, is fortified with walls and a good castle. 200 miles f. east of Morocco. Lat. 29. 56. long. 4. 54. west.

TAILLEBOURG, a small town of Lower Saintogne, in France, stands on the Charante, is defended by a castle, 32 miles f. east of Rochelle, in lat. 45. 54. long. 38. m. west.

TALAUD, or *slope*, is made to the works of a fortification, both on the outside and inside, to prevent the earth from rolling down.

TALUS, or *epaulement*, the slope given to the rampart, or wall, that it may stand the faster; which is more or less sloped, according as the earth is looser or more binding. All ramparts should have a slope or talus on each side; that is, they should be broader at the basis than at the top. There are three sorts of this epaulement, which are distinguished by the terms *exterior*, *interior*, and *superior talus*.

Exterior Talus, is an outside slope of a work towards the country, and should be as small as possible, that the enemy may not find it easy to be mounted either by escalade or otherwise. But if the earth be not good, the talus must be large, that it may keep it up the better: then it is necessary to support the earth with a slight wall, which the French call *chemise*; or a strong one, if needful, they call a *revetement*, which signifies cloathing, or fencing it, to make the earth last, and save the expence of making too large a talus. This wall should have a small talus of a fifth or sixth part of its height; and, for a reinforcement, it is generally supported on the inside by counterforts, or a fort of buttresses.

Interior Talus, the inside slope of a work next the town, which is much larger than that of the outside, and has, at the angles of the gorge, and sometimes in the middle of the curtain, ramps, or sloping roads, to mount upon the terre-plain of the rampart. The interior talus of the parapet should be very small, that the men may with more ease fire over it.

Superior talus of the parapet, a slope on the top of the parapet, that allows of the soldiers defending the covert-way with small shot, which they could not do were it level.

TANGIER, the capital of Mauritania Tingitana, a port of Morocco, in the kingdom of Fez, in Africa, taken by Alphonso of Portugal in 1471, who fortified it with walls and other works: in 1662, it was given to Charles II. of England, upon his marriage with Catharine, Infanta of Spain; but he growing weary of the charges of defending it against the attempts of the Moors, caused it to be blown up and destroyed in 1684, but it is now repeopled by the Moors. At the entrance of the streights of Gibraltar. Lat. 35. 49. long. 7. 5. west.

TAPTOO. See *Drum*.

TARASCON, a very old town of Provence, on the Rhone, is large and well peopled, defended by a strong old castle, 7 miles n. of Arles. Lat. 43. 10. long. 47. 26.

TARBE, or *Tarbes*, a city of Bigorre, in the government of Gascony, on the Adour, defended by a castle, 58 miles f. east

of

of Bayonne. Lat. 43. 21. long. 5. minutes weft.

TARGAROD, a confiderable fortified town of Moldavia, in European Turky, at the confluence of the Moldaw and Sereth, 55 miles f. of Sochowa. Lat. 46. 52. long. 26. 36.

TARPAULINS, are pitched cloths, to throw over ftores in open boats, upon batteries, or in magazines.

TASIO, or *Thafus*, an ifland of the Archipelago, about 40 miles in compafs, near the coaft of Romania, in European Turky; its capital of the fame name has a good harbour and feveral caftles. Lat. 40. 37. long. 27. 12.

TAVASTUS, the capital of Taveftland, in the fouthern part of Finland, on a river, which a little below it falls into the Wana Lake. It is ftrong from its fituation. 86 miles eaft of Abo. Lat. 61. 24. long. 23. 56.

TAVIR, a city of Algarve, in Portugal, on the fmall river Gilaon, over which it has a ftately bridge; walled. 25 miles eaft of Faro, in lat. 37. 10. long. 8. 28.

TEFLIS, a fmall city of Carthuel, a kingdom of Georgia, in Afiatic Turky, fituate on the Kur, and defended by a large caftle or fortrefs. 300 miles n. of Tauris. Lat. 43. 10. long. 47. 26.

TEGAPATAN, a town of the Hither India, in Afia, with an harbour near Cape Comorin, 80 miles f. of Cochin. The Dutch have a factory and fmall fort here. Lat. 8. 5. long. 76. 7.

TELICHERRY, a fea port town of the Eaft Indies, on a bay of the Malabar coaft. Here the Englifh have a factory and fort.

28 miles n. of Calicut. Lat. 12. 10. long. 75. 11.

TEMESWAER, a large and ftrong city in the bannat of that name, in Sclavonia, 58 miles n. eaft of Belgrade. Lat. 45. 26. long. 22. 12. eaft.

TENAILLES, low works made in the ditch before the curtains, whereof there are 3 forts. The firft are the faces of the baftions produced till they meet much lower: the fecond have faces, flanks, and a curtain: but the third have only faces and flanks.

TENAILLONS, works made on each fide of the ravelin, much like the lunettes. They differ, in that one of the faces of a tenaillon is in the direction of the face of the ravelin; whereas that of the lunette is perpendicular to it.

TENT, a pavillion of ftrong ticking, to keep officers under cover night and day.

TERRE-PLAIN *of a rampart*, the horizontal fuperficies of it between the interior talus and banquette, ufed as a common paffage by the defendants. Trees on the terre-plain of a rampart ferve to bind it, but in a fiege are inconvenient: for the noife made by wind amongft the leaves hinders the befieged from hearing workmen in their approaches.

TERTIATE *a piece*, is to examine it, whether it has the due thicknefs of metal in every part, and whether it be true bored.

TESCHEN, a city of Bohemia, in the dukedom of Silefia, 27 miles fouth eaft of Troppau, is fubject to the Houfe of Auftria. The garrifon confifting of 200 men and officers, furrendered to the Pruffian General Werner on

3

on the 2d of June 1762; but it was ceded in 1765 by the Emprefs Queen, with the Emperor's confent, to Prince Albert of Saxony, fince called Duke of Saxa-Tefchen. Long. 18. lat. 49. 50.

TETUAN, a walled town of Habat, in the empire of Morocco, on the Cus, juft within the ftreights of Gibraltar, 5 miles from the fea, and 62 f. eaft of Tangier. Lat. 35. 26. long. 4. 50. weft.

TEXEL, a fmall ifland of Holland, in the United Provinces, at the mouth of the Zuyder-fea, divided from the continent by a narrow channel, through which moft fhips pafs to Amfterdam, has a ftrong caftle and good garrifon. Lat. 53. 10. long. 5. 57.

THERMOPYLE, a narrow pafs from Achaia to Theffaly, in European Turky, celebrated for the glorious ftand Leonidas, the Lacedemonian King, made here with 400 men againft Xerxes's formidable army till the former were all cut in pieces.

THIONVILLE, is 12 miles f. of Luxenburg, on the Mofelle, a well built town, and ftrongly fortified.

THURSO, a market town on the weft fide of Caithnefs, in Scotland, on the Caledonian ocean, has a fecure road for fhips of any burden, defended by Holborn Head. 15 miles f. weft of Dungfby-head. Lat. 59. long. 3. 14.

TICONDEROGA, a ftrong fort, fituate on the narrow paffage between Lake George and Champlain, in North America. It has all the advantages that nature and art can give it, being defended on 3 fides by water, which is furrounded by rocks,

and on the half of the 4th fide by a fwamp, and where that fails, by an entrenchment and breaft-work. This fort was built by the French in 1756; diftant from Crown Point 15 miles. In 1758, the Britifh troops, under General Abercrombie, attempted to take it, but were repulfed with lofs; and in 1759, the French abandoned their lines and fet fire to the fort, on the approach of Sir Jeffery Amherft.

TINIAN, one of the Ladrones or Marian iflands, in the Indian ocean. Here Commodore Anfon fupplied himfelf with provifions in his cruife towards the Philippines; a little north of the ifland of Guam, where the Spaniards have a fort and fmall garrifon. Lat. 15. 10. long. 100. 50.

TOBOLSKI, the capital of Siberia, in Afiatic Ruffia, at the confluence of the Tobo and Irtifk, well fortified, has a good garrifon. The Ruffian ftate prifoners are ufually banifhed to this place. 812 miles eaft of Mofcow, and 1015 in the fame direction from Peterfburg. Lat. 57. 30. long. 67. 13.

TOCKAY, a very ftrong town and citadel of Upper Hungary, in an ifland formed by the confluence of the Theifs and Bodrock; often taken by the Turks and Imperialifts. 74 miles n. eaft of Buda. Lat. 48. 16. n. long. 21. 14. eaft.

TOISE, a meafure of 6 feet, ufed by French engineers in all their fortifications. A fquare toife is 36 fquare feet; and a cubical toife is 216 cubical feet.

TOLEDO, the capital of New Caftile, antiently the royal feat of the Goths and Moors; on a ſteep craggy rock, encompaſſed by the Tagus, over which are two noble bridges. The land ſide is fortified by a ſtrong wall and 150 ſtately towers, formerly reckoned a place of ſtrength; but in the late wars has always ſubmitted to thoſe who were maſters of the field. Lat. 59. 46. long. 4. 20.

TORNA, a well fortified town of Upper Hungary, near the Save, 60 miles north-eaſt of Buda. Lat. 48. 41. long. 20. 9.

TORRES, a populous walled town of Portugueſe Eſtremadura, on the Almonda, three miles from the Tagus, and 60 n. eaſt from Liſbon

TOUL, a fortified city of Lorrain, on the Moſelle, 12 miles weſt of Nancy, ſubject to France. Lat. 48. 45. long. 5. 42.

TOULON, a ſtrong and noted port of France, in the Lower Provence, has a great naval magazine, and a fine harbour for ſhipping. It was unſucceſs-fully attacked by the Confederates in 1707, both by ſea and land, which greatly damaged the ſhipping. It is 400 miles f. of Paris. See Plan 19.

TOURNAY, a ſtrong and beautiful city, divided into 2 parts by that river, over which are ſeveral bridges. 30 miles f. of Ghent, 30 of Cambray, 11 eaſt of Liſle, and 13 f. eaſt of Menin. Henry the VIIIth beſieged and took it in 1513, and built a citadel; but it was delivered to the French again, upon a treaty of marriage between the Dauphin and the Princeſs Mary. The Spaniards took it in 1581; but the French ſurprized it again in 1667. Whilſt it was in their hands, its fortifications were

brought to as great perfection as any in the Netherlands. M. Vauban built a citadel there, which he called his maſter-piece. All the works belonging to this citadel are undermined; and in that conſiſts its chiefeſt ſtrength, as the Allies found, by dear-bought experience, when they beſieged it in 1709. After they had, with the utmoſt hazard and difficulty, made themſelves maſters of the ſtrongeſt works that ever were contrived, the French ſet fire to the mines, and frequently blew up hundreds, if not thouſands of the beſiegers at a blaſt; but ſuch was the bravery of the confederate troops, and the conduct and reſolution of their generals, that all difficulties were ſurmounted; the town was taken on the 28th of July, and the citadel on the 3d of September; the garriſon of the latter being obliged to ſurrender priſoners of war.

TOURNON, a ſmall, but ancient city of Vivarais, and government of Languedoc in France, on the Rhone, and built on the declivity of a hill, on the top of which is a caſtle. 56 miles f. of Lyons. Lat. 44. 56. long. 4. 46.

TOWER BASTIONS, ſmall towers made in the form of baſtions, with rooms and cellars underneath to place men and guns in.

TOWN, or FORT, ADJUTANT, is an aſſiſtant to the fort, or Town Major.

Town or *Fort Major of a garriſon,* is an officer conſtantly employed about the governor or officer commanding, iſſues their orders to the troops in garriſon, and reads its common orders to freſh troops when they arrive. He commands according to the rank

TOULON

Port

Rade

200 Toises

rank he had in the army; if he never had any other commiffion than that of *Town* or *Fort Major*, he is to command as youngeft captain.

TRAERSBACH, an important town of Spanheim, in the palatinate of the Rhine, in Germany, on the Mofelle, 20 miles north-eaft of Triers, and fubject to the Elector Palatine. Lat. 50. 10. long. 6. 46.

TRAIL, the end of the travelling carriage oppofite to the wheels, and upon which the carriage flides, when unlimbered, or upon the battery.

TRANI, a handfome well built city of Bari, in the kingdom of Naples, having an harbour on the Adriatic, and a noble caftle, 20 miles weft of Bari. Lat. 41. 21. long. 18. 16.

TRANSUM, a piece of wood, which goes acrofs between the cheeks of a gun-carriage, or a gin, to keep them fixed together. Each tranfum in a carriage is ftrengthened by a bolt of iron.

TRAPANO, a city in the Val de Mazaro, in the ifland of Sicily, on the peninfula facing the weft, is defended by a caftle to the fouth; its haven is large but expofed to fouth winds, and was one of the laft places taken by the Romans from the Carthaginians. 36 miles fouth-weft of Palermo. Lat. 38. 10. long. 12. 10.

TRAPEZOND, or *Trebizond*, a walled city, having a harbour on the eaftern part of Amafia, in Afiatic Turky, and on the fouth coaft of the Euxine fea; but ill built and worfe peopled. It was the metropolis of an empire of the fame name, founded by A-

lexis Commenus, a Frenchman, in 1209, which continued in the fame family till 1460; when David, the laft of that houfe, was fubdued and put to death by Mahomet II. fince which time it has continued in the poffeffion of the Turks. Its caftle, which ftands on a rock, is much neglected. Lat. 42. 26. long. 42. 20.

TRAVERSE, a parapet made acrofs the covert-way, oppofite to the faliant angles of the works, and near the places of arms, to prevent enfilades. They are 18 feet thick, and as high as the ridge of the glacis. There are alfo traverfes made in the caponiers, but then they are called *tambour traverfes*; and are likewife made within other works, when there are any hills or rifing grounds, from which may be feen the infide of thefe works.

To traverfe a gun or mortar, is to bring her about with handfpikes, to the right or left, till fhe is pointed exactly at the object.

TRAW, a fmall ftrong town of Dalmatia, built on an ifland of the Adriatic. 15 miles eaft of Spalatto. Lat. 43. 16. long. 17. 36.

TREMOINS, a French term for pieces of earth left ftanding, as marks in the toffes of places they are emptying, to know exactly how many cubical fathoms, or feet of earth, have been carried away, and thereby pay their workmen, who are fure to leave fome of the higheft fpots of ground for termoins, that they may have more depth to meafure. But the engineers are generally careful to mark out

[k 4]   indif-

indifferent places, some high, some low, to measure as exact as they can.

TRENCH, or *lines of approach and attack*, a way hollowed in the earth, in form of a fosse, having a parapet towards the place besieged, when the earth can be removed; or else it is an elevation of fascines, gabions, woolpacks, and such other things for covering the men as cannot fly into pieces or splinters. This is to be done when the ground is rocky; but when the earth is good, the trench is carried on with less trouble, and the engineers demand only a provision of spades, shovels, and pick-axes, to make it 2 fathoms wide. The greatest fault a trench can have, is to be enfiladed; to prevent which they are ordinarily carried on with turnings and elbows. As the trenches are never carried on but in the night-time, therefore the ground should be viewed and observed very nicely in the day. On the angles or sides of the trench there should be lodgements, or epaulements, in form of traverses, the better to hinder the sallies of the garrison, to favour the advancement of the trenches, and to sustain the workmen. These lodgements are small trenches fronting the places besieged, and joining the trench at one end.

The platforms for the batteries are made behind the trenches; the first at a good distance, to be used only against sallies of the garrison. As the approaches advance, the batteries are brought nearer, to ruin the defences of the place, and dismount the artillery of the besieged. The batteries for the breaches are made

when the trenches are advanced near the covert-way.

If 2 attacks, there must be lines of communication, or boyaus, between the 2 with places of arms, at convenient distances. The trenches should be 6 or 7 feet high, with the parapet, which should be 5 feet thick, and have banquettes for the soldiers to mount upon.

Returns of a Trench, are the elbows and turnings, which form the lines of the approach, and made as near as can be parallel to the defence of the place, to prevent their being enfiladed.

To mount the trenches, is to mount guard in the trenches; *to relieve the trenches*, is to relieve the guards of the trenches; *to dismount the trenches*, is to come off the guard from the trenches; *to cleanse or scour the trenches*, is to make a vigorous sally upon the guard of the trenches, force them to give way, and quit their ground, drive away the workmen, break down the parapet, fill up the trench, and nail their cannon.

Counter-trenches, are trenches made against the besiegers, which consequently have their parapet turned against the enemy's approaches, and are enfiladed from several parts of the place, on purpose to render them useless to the enemy, if they should chance to become masters of them; but they should not be enfiladed, or commanded by any height in the enemy's possession.

To open trenches, is the first breaking of ground by the besiegers, to carry on their approaches towards a place. The difference between opening and carrying on the trenches, is, that the first is only the beginning

ning of the trench; which is always turned towards the befiegers. It is begun by a fmall foffe, which the pioneers make in the night on their knees, generally a mufquet-fhot from the place, or half a cannon-fhot, and fometimes without the reach of cannon-ball, efpecially if there be no hollow or rifing grounds to favour them, or if the garrifon be ftrong, and their artillery well ferved. This fmall foffe is afterwards enlarged by the next pioneers which come behind them, who dig it deeper by degrees, till it be about 4 yards broad, and 4 or 5 feet deep, efpecially if they be near the place; to the end, the earth which is taken out of it, may be thrown before them, to form a parapet, and cover them from the fire of the befieged. The place where the trenches are opened, is called the end of the trench.

TRENT, the capital of the archbifhopric of that name, in Auftria, on the river Adige, encompaffed with fteep unpaffable hills, except from Tirol to the north, and Verona to the fouth. The city is about a mile in circuit, furrounded with a fingle wall, and defended by an old caftle. 74 miles fouth of Infpruc. Lat. 46. 10. long 11. 5.

TREPTOW, a town of Pomerania, in Upper Saxony, having a ftrong caftle on the Tollen lake, near the Baltic, fubject to the King of Pruffia, 43 miles north-eaft of Stetin. Lat. 54. 10. long. 15. 33. On the 24th of October 1761, the Ruffians, detached by General Romanzow from Colberg, made themfelves mafters of it, and obliged General Knoblock, with

3 battalions and a corps of cavalry, amounting to 4000 men, to furrender prifoners of war. The Pruffians alfo loft 6 colonels and 10 cannon.

TRESREVERE, a fortified town between Montreal and Quebec, ftands about 200 miles from Crown Point, on the north fide of the river St. Lawrence. Oppofite to this place was a village in which 300 armed Indians had taken up their refidence: thefe General Amherft was defirous to cut off, and therefore iffued the following order to that famous partizan Major Rogers; who accomplifhed his purpofe by means fo very different to common practice, that I cannot avoid paying a compliment to his abilities for carrying on a war againft this barbarous people; of which art we were totally ignorant when General Braddock, at the beginning of our late difpute with the French, led on his troops to unthought of deftruction.

Orders from Sir Jeffery Amherft to Major Rogers.

" You are this night to fet out with the detachment as ordered yefterday (viz. of 200 men) and proceed to Miffifquey Bay, from whence you will march and attack the enemy's fettlements on the fouthfide of the river St. Lawrence, in fuch a manner as you fhall judge moft effectual to difgrace the enemy, and for the fuccefs and honour of his Majefty's arms.

" Remember the barbarities that have been committed by the enemy's Indian fcoundrels, on every occafion where they had

an

an opportunity of shewing their infamous cruelties on the King's subjects; which they have done without mercy: take your revenge; but do not forget that though those villians have dastardly and promiscously murdered the women and children of all ages; it is my orders that no women or children be killed or hurt.

"When you have executed your intended service, you will return with your detachment to camp, or to join me wherever the army may be.

"Yours, &c.

"JEFF. AMHERST.

*Camp at Crown-Point,
September 13, 1759.*"

Pursuant to the above orders, the major set out with 200 men, in battoes, down Lake Champlain. The fifth day after his departure, when encamped on the eastern banks of Lake Champlain, a keg of gunpowder accidentally took fire, which wounded Capt. Williams of the Royal Regiment, and several of the men, who were sent back to Crown Point with some men to row them, which reduced the party to 142, officers included.

The Major proceeded on his journey, and landed on the 10th at Missisquey Bay. Here he concealed his boats with provisions sufficient to carry him back to Crown Point, and left 2 trusty rangers to lie concealed near the boats, with orders to stay till the return of his party, unless the enemy should discover the boats; in which case they were to pursue the track of the party with all possible speed, to give the Major the earliest intelligence. The second evening after this,

the two rangers overtook the party, and informed the Major that 400 French and Indians had discovered and taken possession of the boats, which they sent away with 50 men; and that the remainder were pursuing on the track of the party: but this intelligence was privately given him, so that none knew of what passed; and as the Major thought it necessary to keep this affair secret, he immediately ordered Lieutenant M'Mullen, with 8 men and these 2 rangers, to proceed to Crown Point, to inform the General of what happened, that he might send provisions to Cohoas, on Connecticut river, by which the Major proposed to return; so that the 2 rangers had not an opportunity to inform the party that they were pursued, it being believed that they were sent not to Crown Point, but to reconnoitre some place for an attack.

The Major resolved to outmarch his pursuers, and cut off the Indian town of St. Francois, before they should overtake him; and accordingly continued his march for several days, till, on the 4th of October at 8 in the evening, he came within sight of the town, and about 2 hours after he took 2 Indians, whom he had with him, who could speak the language of the inhabitants of St. Francois, and also dressed himself in the Indian manner, and went to reconnoitre the town. He found the inhabitants in a *high frolick*, or *dance*; and at 2 in the morning he returned to his detachment, which he marched in about an hour to the distance only of 500 yards from the town.

About 4 the Indians broke up
their

their *dance*, and retired to reft; but at break of day, when they were afleep, the Major fuprized them by a vigorous attack in feveral parts of the town; and this was fo well performed in every part, that the enemy had not time to recover, or make any confiderable refiftance. Out of 300 of the enemy, 200 were killed on the fpot, and 20 taken prifoners: the Major alfo retook 5 Englifhmen who were prifoners in the town; fecured what provifions were there, immediately fet it on fire, and thus reduced it to afhes. At 7 in the morning the affair was completely over, when the Major affembling his men, he found that one was killed, and 6 flightly wounded. After refrefhing the party for an hour, the Major began his march homeward, leaving the dead to be buried by his purfuers; but was harraffed on his march, and feveral times attacked in the rear, till, being favoured by the dufk of the evening, he formed an ambufcade upon his own track, and attacked the enemy when they leaft expected it: after this he was fuffered to continue his march without further annoyance from the enemy, and arrived fafe at No. 4, with the lofs of only a few men.

TREVIGIO, or *Trevifo*, the capital of the Marca Trevigiano, in the Venetian dominions, on the Sile, is reckoned impregnable, and lies 15 miles northweft of Venice, in lat. 45. 45. long. 12. 46.

TRIANGLE, a figure between three fides, either rectilineal or fpherical. A *rectilineal* or *plain triangle*, is a figure confifting of 3 ftraight fides: a *fpherical triangle* is a figure formed by 3 arches of 3 great circles, cutting one another at the furface of a fphere.

A *rectilineal triangle*, confidered according to the fides, may be either equilateral, ifofceles, or fcalene: and, confidered, according to its angles, may be either rectangle or oxigon.

Equilateral triangle, has 3 fides equal. It is evident the 3 angles muft be equal, each being 60 degrees triangle, and ifofceles is what hath 2 fides equal; fo that all *equilateral triangles* are ifofceles; though all ifofceles triangles are not equilateral.

Triangle fcalene, has 3 unequal fides.

Triangle rectangle, has one right angle.

Triangle ambligon, is what has one obtufe angle; and *triangle oxigon*, has angles all acute.

TRIESTE, the capital of Iftria in Carniola, and circle of Auftria, in Germany, a fmall but ftrong place, with a large harbour on the Adriatic. defended by 2 caftles. 58 miles n. eaft of Venice. Lat 46. 10. long. 14. 12.

TRIPOLI, a city of Phœnicia, a province of Syria, in Afia, commodioufly fituated at the foot of Mount Libanus, from whence a fmall river runs through the city; about a mile and a half from the Levant. and has a commodious harbour defended by 6 fquare caftles or towers built along the fhore, and 90 miles f. of Scanderoon. Lat. 34. 53. long. 36. 7.

TRINCUMBAR, or *Tranquebar*, a fortrefs and colony belonging to the Danes, in the Eaft Indies, on the coaft of Coromandel. The town is about 2 miles in circumference, 84 miles
south

fouth of Fort St. George. Lat. 11. 50. long. 80. 58.

TRINO, the capital of a territory of that name, in Montferrat, in Italy, a fmall but ftrong town, about a mile north of the Po, and 36 miles north-eaft of Turin, is fubject to the King of Sardinia. Lat. 45.16. long. 8. 13.

TRIPOLI, the metropolis of the republic of that name, in Africa, on the Mediterranean, is not very large, but populous, and furrounded with good walls and other works. 300 miles fouth-eaft of Tunis, in lat. 32. 54. long. 13. 13.

TROOP. See *Drum*.

TROOPER, a private man in a troop of horfe.

TROPPAU, a city of Upper Silefia, the capital of a duchy of that name, 70 miles fouth of Breflaw. The Pruffian General Werner, with a corps of cavalry, took poffeffion of it in 1757; but in 1758 the Marquis de Ville diflodged the Pruffians. In 1759 General Fouquet took it, and made 230 officers and men prifoners of war. In 1762, the Prince of Bevern and General Werner abandoned it.

TROY, the capital of Troas and Myfia, in Afia, near the Egean Sea, is rendered famous for a 10 years fiege it fuftained from the Greeks. 20 miles fouth of the Hellefpont and 100 north of Smyrna. Lat. 39. 36. long. 26. 36.

TROYES, a city of Champagne, in France, is a large fortified place, 70 miles fouth-eaft of Paris. Lat. 48. 21. long. 45 16.

TRUCKS, fmall wheels of one piece of wood, about a foot and a half, or 2 feet diameter, for truck carriages, and fometimes garrifon guns.

TRUMPET, made of brafs or filver, with a mouth-piece to take out and put in at pleafure. Each troop of cavalry has one.

The firft found of the trumpet before a march, is when the drum beats a general, at which the troopers boot, faddle, and get ready: when the affemble is beginning to beat, the trumpets found to horfe; on which the troopers mount, and at the third found march.

The trumpets likewife found a charge in day of battle, and the retreat at night, &c.

TRUNNIONS *of a gun*, are the 2 pieces of metal projecting from the fides of a piece, by which it fwings in its carriage.

Trunnion-ring, that ornament, or jutting out, a little before the trunnions.

TUNIS, the capital of the kingdom of that name in Barbary, on a plain, is about a league in circumference, walled, fortified, and defended by a ftout caftle, near a large lake, 3 miles fouth of the ruins of old Carthage, and 300 eaft of Algiers. Lat. 36. 26. long. 10. 15.

TURIN, the capital city of Piedmont, at the junction of the Po with the Doria, is finely fortified with 5 baftions, and other ftrong works. In 1706 it held out a very hard fiege of 10 weeks, when it was relieved by the army of the Allies, commanded by the late Duke of Savoy and Prince Eugene, who attacked the French before the place and gained a complete victory, having taken the enemy's cannon, with all their ammunition and baggage. In this action the Duke of Orleans and Marfhal Marfin were wounded, the latter mortally; and the fame

evening

evening the Duke entered his capital, which was reduced to a heap of ruins. It lies 100 miles south-west of Milan, and the same north-west of Genoa. Lat. 44. 56. north; long. 7. 16. east.

Tuy, a pleasant walled city of Galicia in Spain, near the mouth of a river of that name, is 14 miles east of Vigo, in lat. 42. 16. long. 9. 10. west.

VAL, 3 miles west of Mae-stricht, in the bishopric of Liege, in Westphalia, famous for a sharp battle fought near it, between the Allies, commanded by the Duke of Cumberland, and the French, under Marshal Count Saxe. 20th June 1744, our troops marched at day-break; about 4 the French were observed in motion in large columns to the right, with their flanks covered by the Hussars; on which a disposition was made to gain the hills of Herderen. Cannonading and forming were the work of this day.

The Allies continued under arms that night. 21st. The Duke observing the French dispositions, made some alterations in his; about 8 returned from viewing the line and reconnoitring the enemy to the grand commandery; when Earl Ligonier sent Colonel Forbes to acquaint him, that by their motions they seemed determined to attack the left wing; on which his Royal Highness repaired thither, and ordered M. Bathiani and Prince Waldeck to their posts. The French infantry advanced in a column of 10 battalions in front, and as many deep, and bent their whole force towards Val, where they were severely handled by the allied batteries raking them as they advanced; but the French gaining ground, brought their batteries to play on the village, and instantly attacked the troops posted there with their first brigades, who were soon repulsed with great loss; renewed the attack 3 times with fresh divisions, who were all forced to give way; but fresh divisions still advancing, those in Val were, in their turn, forced to retire, but soon rallied, as quickly to regain the village, and beat off the enemy with great slaughter; yet still fresh numbers crouding upon them, and the battalions ordered by the Duke to sustain them not all arriving, they they were obliged to evacuate the village, and form on the plain.

About 12, affairs went so well, that his Royal Highness ordered the wing to advance on the enemy, whose infantry gave way so fast, that they were obliged to post cavalry to keep them up. This attack was so well conducted, that M. Bathiani gained Elch village in the front of Herderen. But the misconduct of 5 Dutch squadrons, ordered to cover the infantry as the French advanced from Val, gave a sensible check to the whole affair; they being ordered to wheel to the right to make a front against the enemy, turned to the right-about, and broke and disordered 5 battalions that were advancing to reinforce the line; which confused that part of the army, and gave the French an opportunity of dividing them, so that they had 2 flanks to attack; that which the Duke headed were severely handled, and he near surrounded, as he remained with the greatest inflexibility animating the troops to renew the charge; which Earl Ligonier

Ligonier obferving, advanced, with great celerity, at the head of the Britifh cavalry, to his relief, and charged the enemy fo furioufly, that he bore down all before him, and purfued them with fuch fuccefs, that he routed a party of infantry pofted to attack him. But frefh fquadrons crouding on, his horfe was killed in the fecond charge, and he made prifoner, with feveral of his command. The army thus divided, and all efforts to repulfe the enemy fruitlefs, a retreat to Maeftricht was ordered with fuch conduct, that the enemy did not attempt a purfuit.

The generals, and their corps that were engaged did wonders; many French brigades were almoft cut to pieces; they loft 7 ftandards, 8 pair of colours, and 10000 killed, wounded, and prifoners: the Allies loft 4 ftandards, 1 pair of colours, and 16 field pieces. The prifoners were foon exchanged, and joined the army.

Thus ended an action that did honour to their generals and their royal Commander, though a defeat. No attacks were ever better concerted than thofe of the French; or with greater conduct and intrepidity fuftained, than they were by the Allies, till the cowardice of the 5 Dutch fquadrons difconcerted all their meafures.

VALENCIA, a city of Spain, and the capital of a province of that name on the river Turio. Its form is almoft round, and has a ftout wall with feveral towers. In 1705, after Catalonia had fubmitted to Charles of Auftria, this city opened her gates to the Earl of Peterborough and the Englifh forces;

but after the defeat of Almanza, 1707, the Duke of Orleans, at the head of the Spanifh forces recovered it. 180 miles fouth-eaft of Madrid. Lat. 39. 20. long. 35. m.

VALENCIENENS, a ftrong large well-buit city of Hainault, in the French Netherlands, on the Scheld, is defended by a citadel, with fluices that can lay the adjacent country under water, 15 miles f. of Tournay, in lat. 50. 25. long. 3. 24. On the 17th of March 1674. the French King took it by ftorm, after a fiege of 8 days, when he only defigned to have taken a horn work. He faved the town from plunder, but made the inhabitants pay 40000 crowns, which he laid out upon the citadel. This was the firft town in thefe parts that denied obedience to the Prince of Parma, and refufed to admit a garrifon.

VAN, a large and populous city of Turcomania, in Turky in Afia, on the north extremity of the lake bearing its name, and on the confines of Perfia, has a mountain caftle with a numerous garrifon of Turks, 100 miles north-weft of Tauris. Lat. 38. 30. long. 44. 30.

VAN, the front of an army, &c.

Van-guard, that part of the army which marches in the front.

VAUDREVANGE, a town of Lorrain, on the Sare, near which, fince it has come into the hands of the French, they have built the ftrong fort of St. Louis, 50 miles north-eaft of Nancy. Lat. 49. 28. long. 6. 36.

UBEDA, a well fortified city of Andalufia, in Spain, on a hill, with a ftrong caftle, 45 miles north-eaft of Grenada. Lat. 38. 40. north; long. 3. 6. weft.

UBES, St. corruptly for *Setubal,*

tubal, a confiderable fea-port of Eftremadura in Portugal, on a capacious bay of the ocean, and 21 miles fouth of Lifbon, is a walled ftrong town, but fuffered much by the late earthquake in the capital. Lat. 38. 36. long. 9. 30.

VEDETTE, a fentry on horfe-back with his horfe's head to-wards the place whence any dan-ger is to be feared, and his cara-bine advanced, with the but-end againft his right thigh. When the army lies encamped, there are *vedettes* pofted at all the avenues, and on all the rifing grounds, to watch for its fecurity.

UDINO, an ancient city and the capital of Friuli, in the Ve-netian territories in Italy, fur-rounded with a ftout wall, 25 miles north of Aquileia. Lat. 46. 30. long. 13. 20.

VENLO, a ftrong town of Dutch Guelderland, having a rampart and ditch, 3 miles in compafs, befides other works, is fituate on the Maes, 10 miles f. of Guelder. Lat. 51. 35. long. 6. 26.

VENT, of all fire arms, is a fmall hole at the end, or near it, of the bore or chamber, to prime the pieces with powder, to fet fire to the charge.

Vent-field, that part of a gun or howitz between the breech moulding and the aftragal; and *vent-aftragal*, is that which de-termines the *vent-field*.

VERA CRUZ, the grand port of New Spain in the province of Tlafcala, or Los Angelos in Mexico, having a fafe harbour protected by a fort, on a rock of a neighbouring ifland called St. John d'Ulva in the gulf of Mexico. Vera Cruz having been taken and plunderd feve-

ral times by the Buccaniers, the Spaniards have built forts and placed fentries along the coaft. Their ordinary garrifon confifts of 60 horfe and 2 companies of foot. At the old town, 15 or 16 miles further weft, Cortez landed on Good-friday, 1518, and being determined to conquer Mexico, or die, funk the fhips that tranfported his handful of men thither. 215 miles fouth-eaft of Mexico, in lat. 18. 41. north; long. 102. 15. weft.

VERCELLI, a city of Pied-mont in Italy, fituated at the confluence of the Sefia and Cer-va, defended by 14 regular baf-tions, a citadel and caftle, 42 miles north-eaft of Turin, is fub-ject to the King of Sardinia. Lat 45. 21. long. 8. 26.

VERDUN, a ftrong city of Lor-rain in Germany, on the Meufe, 38 miles north weft of Nancy, fubject to France. Lat. 45. 21. long. 5. 24.

VERONA, a fortified city, and capital of the Veronefe in the Venetian territories, in Italy, on the river Adge, 24 miles n. of Mantua. Lat. 45. 26. long. 11. 20.

VERRUA, a ftrong fortrefs of Afti, in Piedmont, built on a high rock on the Po, 24 miles north-eaft of Turin, held out a fiege of 6 months againft all the efforts the French could make in 1705; but expecting no re-lief, the governor was at length compelled to furrender. This and the reft of the towns of Piedmont were recovered by the Allies, and reftored to their old mafter the Duke of Savoy, in 1706. Lat. 45. 10. long. 8. 15.

VIANA DE FEZ DE LIMA, as ftanding on the mouth of the Lima, a confiderable fea port of
Entre

Entre Dours e Minho, in Portugal; it is walled, and defended with a caftle, 36 miles north of Oporto. Lat. 41. 46. long. 9. 10.

VIDIN, an important fortrefs of Servia, in European Turky, on the Danube, is 126 miles fouth-eaft of Belgrade. Lat. 43. 46. long. 24. 15.

VIENNA, the capital of the great duchy of Auftria, one of the ftrongeft cities in Chriftendom, was walled round in 1192, with the ranfom-money paid by Richard I. King of England, who was feized by the Duke of Auftria in his return from the Holy Land. It was unfuccefsfully befieged by Soliman the Magnificent in 1583; and in 1683 was reduced to great extremity by the Turks, but memorably relieved by John Sobiefki, King of Poland, who gained a fignal victory, and raifed the fiege.

VIEW, of a place, to befiege it, is faid to be taken when the general accompanied by the engineers, reconnoitres it; that is, rides round the place, obferving the fituation of it, with the nature of the country about it; as hills, valleys, rivers, marfhes, woods, hedges, &c. thereby to judge of the moft convenient place for opening the trenches, and carrying on the approaches; to find out proper places for encamping the army, for the lines of circumvallation and countervallation, and for the park of artillery.

To view, or reconnoitre an enemy, is to get as near their camp as poffible, to fee the nature of the ground, and the avenue to it; to find out the ftrength and weaknefs of their encampment, where they may be beft attacked; or whether it may be proper to hazard bringing them to action.

To view, or reconnoitre, is likewife when the quarter-mafter-general, with a ftrong party of horfe, goes to view the ways for the march of the army, or find the moft convenient place for an encampment: to wit, where there is water and forage; where the army may not be too much expofed to the infults of the enemy, but covered by rivers, marfhes, woods, or ftrong grounds, where they cannot eafily be forced.

Parties of light horfe are generally fent to view the enemy's march, to know if it tends to guefs at their defigns, and to regulate the motions of the army accordingly.

VIGEVANO, a city of the Vigevanefe, in the dukedom of Milan; it has a ftrong caftle on a rock, 16 miles fouth-weft of Milan. Lat. 45. 15. n. long. 9. 10. eaft.

VIGO, a fea-port, and walled town of Galicia, in Spain, in Bayonne bay, at the mouth of a fpacious harbour. Here, on October 12, 1702, Sir George Rooke, with the confederate fleet of Englifh and Dutch, attacked a French fquadron under Monfieur Chateau Renard, convoying 13 Spanifh galleons, whilft the Duke of Ormond drove the Spaniards from the caftles on fhore that defended the harbour; Admiral Hopfon at the fame time breaking the boom acrofs the the mouth of the harbour. The Confederates took 9 galleons, and 5 large men of war, having deftroyed 4 other galleons, with 14 men of war. 50 miles fouth of Compoftella, and 70 fouth-eaft of of Cape Finifterre. Lat. 42. 16. n. long. 9 14. weft.

VILLA FRANCA, a well fortified town, with a good harbour on the Nife, was taken by the French in 1691, and reftored in 1696; but again taken by the French in 1704; is fituated on the Mediterranean, 13 miles eaft of Nife.

VILLA VELHA, a Moorifh caftle, near the Tagus. In October 1762, the Spaniards made themfelves mafters of it, though fupported for fome time by Colonel Burgoyne acrofs the river. The garrifon confifted of about 300 officers and men, who furrendered prifoners of war.

VILLA VICIOSA, a town of New Caftile, 47 miles north-eaft of Madrid. Here Marefchal Staremberg, the 10th of December 1710, defeated the French and Spaniards the day after they had taken a great body of Englifh, commanded by General Stanhope, who furrendered prifoners of war for want of ammunition, in the town of Brihuega. Lat. 40. 56. long. 3. 27. weft.

VILLENA, a town of New Caftile in Spain, 40 miles north of Murcia. This place the Confederates were befieging in 1707, when, upon receiving advice that the French and Spaniards had advanced to Almanza, the Earl of Galway raifed the fiege, and fought the unfortunate battle of Almanza, in which he was entirely defeated, with the lofs of moft of the Englifh, who were either killed on the fpot, or taken prifoners. Lat. 38. 49. long. 4. 15. weft.

VILVORDE, a fmall but ftrong town of Brabant, in the Auftrian Low-countries, on the Seine, 7 miles fouth of Bruffels. Lat. 51. 10. long. 4. 26.

VISET, a fmall but fortified city of Liege, in the Auftrian Low-countries, fituated on the eaft bank of the Maefe, 7 miles north of Liege. Lat. 50. 56. north; long. 5. 47. eaft.

VISIAPOUR, a well fortified city, capital of the kingdom of Decan, in the Hither India, 136 miles north of Goa, is fubject to the Great Mogul. Lat. 16. 51. n. long 75. 54. eaft.

VITRI, a town of Champagne, and the capital of Perthe in France, on the Marne, which here begins to be navigable, is well built, furrounded with ramparts and ditches, 46 miles f. eaft of Rheims, in lat. 48. 51. long. 4. 50.

ULM, an imperial city, and fovereign ftate of Swabia, on the weft fide of the Danube. In 1702 bafely furprized by the Elector of Bavaria; but after the battle of Hochftet furrendered to the Imperialifts: it is a large city, with regular fortifications and deep ditches; but not able to fuftain a long fiege; 36 miles weft of Augfburg, in lat. 48. 30. long. 10. 5.

ULOVIESTEIN, the poft of, at the fource of the Hom, was taken by the Prince of Holftein, in April 1759; and in Auguft 1762, General d'Affry made himfelf mafter of the caftle of Ulrieftein, when the garrifon of 110 men and officers furrendered at difcretion.

VOLONA, a city of Albania, in European Turky, at the mouth of the gulf of Venice, having a capacious harbour, called the bay of Valona, and defended by a caftle; 55 miles f. of Durazzo. Lat. 42. 19. long. 20. 8.

[l]   VOLUN.

VOLUNTEERS, perfons who, of their own accord, either for the fervice of their prince, or out of the efteem they have for their general, ferve in the army without being inlifted, to gain honour and preferment, by expofing themfelves in the fervice.

UPSAL, a very ancient city of Uplandia in Sweden, on the river Sal, defended by a large ftrong caftle, 40 miles north of Stockholm. Lat. 60. 12. n. long. 17. 56. eaft.

UTICA, a city of Africa, famous for the death of Cato; it is now called Biferta; a confiderable town of Tunis, with a harbour on a fine bay of the Mediterranean, defended by 2 towers. 30 miles north-weft of the ruins of Old Carthage, in lat. 37. 10. long. 9. 36.

UTRECHT, an ancient place, capital of a province of that name in the United Low-countries, on the Rhine, is a fair, large, and populous city; the treaty of union between the confederate provinces was figned there in 1579, and the famous peace between the Allies and France concluded in 1713, about the clofe of Queen Anne's reign. Lat. 52. 10. long. 5. 7.

WAD, is a ftopper of hay, ftraw, or wadding, forced into a gun upon the powder, to keep it clofe in the chamber; when it is home at the powder, the gunner generally gives it 3 thumps with the rammer-head.

Wad-hook or worms, is a fmall iron turned ferpent-ways, like a fcrew, and put upon the end of a long ftaff, to draw out the wad of a gun, when fhe is to be unloaded,

Wad-mill, a hollow piece of wood to make the wads of proper form.

WAGGON-MASTER-GENERAL, has the ordering and marching of all the baggage of the army. On a day of march, he meets the baggage at the place appointed, and marfhals it according to the rank of the brigade, or regiment, each waggon belongs to; and marches it according to the route given him; which is fometimes in one column, at others in two; fometimes after the artillery, and at other times the baggage of each column follows that it belongs to.

WALDECK, a fmall city, and the capital of the principality of that name in Germany, fubject to its own prince, has a good caftle, and lies 18 miles fouthweft of Heffe-Caffel, Lat. 51. 20. long. 8. 46.

WALDSHUT, a fmall but ftrong town of Suabia, in Germany, fituate on the north fide of the Rhine, near the conflux of the Schult; fubject to Auftria, and lies 42 miles weft of Conftance. Lat. 47. 38. long. 8. 15.

WAR, is that important event for which all military education is defigned to prepare the foldier. It is for this that, in peace, he receives the indulgence of a fubfiftence from fociety; and by this that he is gratefully bound to fecure the repofe of that fociety from the outrage of barbarians, and to guard its poffeffions from the devaftations of banditti. But as I hope that every thing needful has already been faid about the means for attaining this defirable end, and as it would be equally needlefs as impoffible, to fhew how often this

this art of the foldier has accomplifhed the defign of its inftitution, I fhall only make ufe of the word, to diftinguifh thofe wars which are remarkable on our annals, for obtaining the bleffings of peace to this kingdom fince the

War with Scotland, 1068.
Peace with ditto, 1091.
Ditto with France, 1113.
War with France, 1116.
Peace with ditto, 1118.
—— with Scotland, 1139.
War with France, 1161.
Peace with ditto, 1186.
War again with France, with fuccefs, 1194.
Peace with ditto, 1195.
War with France, 1201.
—— civil war renewed, 1215.
—— ended, 1216.
—— with France, 1224.
—— ended, 1243.
—— civil, 1262.
—— ended, 1267.
—— with France, 1294.
—— with Scotland, 1296.
Peace with France, 1299.
—— with Scotland, Mar. 30, 1323.
War again with Scotland, 1327.
—— ended, 1328.
—— again with Scotland, 1333.
—— with France, 1339.
Peace with France, May 8, 1360.
War with France, 1368.
—— civil, 1400.
—— with Scotland, 1400.
Peace with France, May 31, 1420.
War with France, 1422.
—— civil, between York and Lancafter, 1452.
Peace with France, Oct. 1471.
War, civil, 1486.
—— with France, Oct. 6, 1492.
Peace with ditto, Nov. 3, following.
—— with Scotland, 1502.

War with France, Feb. 4, 1512.
—— with Scotland, 1513.
Peace with France, Aug. 7, 1514.
War with ditto, 1522.
—— with Scotland, 1522.
Peace with France, 1527.
—— with Scotland, 1542.
War with Scotland, directly after.
Peace with France and Scotland, June 7, 1546.
War with Scotland, 1547.
—— with France, 1549.
Peace with both, March 6, 1550.
War, civil, 1553.
—— with France, June 7, 1557.
—— with Scotland, 1557.
Peace with France, April 2, 1559.
—— with Scotland, 1560.
War with France, 1562.
Peace with ditto, 1564.
War with Scotland, 1570.
—— with Spain, 1588.
Peace with Spain, Aug. 18, 1604.
War with Spain, 1624.
—— with France, 1627.
Peace with Spain and France, April 14, 1629.
War, civil, 1642.
—— with the Dutch, 1651.
Peace with ditto, April 5, 1654.
War with Spain, 1655.
Peace with Spain, Sept. 10, 1660.
War with France, Jan. 26, 1666.
—— with Denmark, Oct. 19, following.
Peace with the French, Danes, and Dutch, Aug. 24, 1667.
Ditto with Spain, Feb. 13, 1668.
War with the Algerines, Sept. 6, 1669.
Peace with ditto, Nov. 19, 1671.
War with the Dutch, March 1672.

[I 2]   Peace

Peace with the Dutch, Feb. 28, 1674.
War with France, May 7, 1689.
Peace, General, Sept. 20, 1697.
War with France, May 4, 1702.
Peace of Utrecht, Mar. 13, 1713.
War with Spain, Dec. 1718.
Peace with ditto, 1721.
War with Spain, 1739.
——with France, Mar. 31, 1744.
Peace with France, &c. 1748.
War with France, 1756.
—— with Spain, Jan. 4, 1762.
Peace with France and Spain, Feb. 10, 1763.

WARADIN, GREAT, a town of Upper Hungary, on an island of the river Kewes, is subject to the House of Austria, and lies 98 miles east of Buda. Lat. 47. 21. n. long. 21. 46. east.

WARDHUYS, a small town on an island near the continent, in Norway, near the north-east point of that kingdom, has an harbour, is the residence of the governor, and lies 118 miles s. east of the north cape. Lat. 71. 10. n. long. 28. 5. east.

WARSAW, the capital of that province, and of the kingdom of Poland, is a large city, defended by a double wall and ditch; lies 38 miles south of Dantzic, and 148 n. of Cracow. Lat. 52. 21. n. long. 21. 10. east.

WEAPONS, all sorts of warlike instruments, except fire-arms.

WELL, is a depth sunk in the ground by the miner, from whence he runs out branches or galleries, in search of the enemy's mine, to prevent its effects, or make one for himself.

WESEL, or Nether Wesel, a well fortified town in the dukedom of Cleve and circuit of Westphalia, in Germany, situated on the east side of the Rhine near the mouth of the Lippe, 12 miles

south-east of the city of Cleves. Lat. 51. 28. n. long. 6. 12. east.

WERLE, a fortified town, subject to the elector of Cologne, in Westphalia in Germany, situated between the Rower and Lippe, is 32 miles south of the city of Munster. Lat. 51. 27. n. long. 7. 26. east.

WIBURN, the capital of Carelia in Russia Finland, having a convenient harbour on the Finnick gulf. It is well fortified, but was taken by the Czar Peter, and afterwards ceded to him. It lies 68 miles n. west of Petersburg. Lat. 61. 5. n. long. 29. 10. east.

WIGHT, a large and fertile island in the county of Southampton and diocese of Winchester, is separated from the continent of Britain by a small channel. It is of an oval form from east to west, 20 miles in length, and 12 broad, containing near 27000 souls. The forts and castles are garrisoned. But its principal strength consists in the royal navy being stationed at Portsmouth and Spithead, the channel between the island and Portsmouth. Its chief town is Newport.

WILLIAM HENRY FORT stands at the north end of the lake George, in America, at about 60 miles n. of Albany, and 40 south of Ticonderago. From this fort Major Rogers set out, on the 20th of May 1755, to reconnoitre the enemy's advanced guard at Ticonderago, the north end of the lake. The next day he viewed them, and found their numbers to be about 300, after which he went and reconnoitred the encampment at Ticonderago, and found they had

had about 1000 men encamped without the fort; he likewife difcovered there were about 200 men employed in carrying provifions from the fort to their advanced guard, which they did in batteaux, to the place called the Saw Mills, or the fall of lake George into lake Champlain; from thence they tranfported it by land to the advanced guard, where they landed the provifion. Here the ground rofe gradually for about 200 yards, and then ran on a level to their advanced guard. Both fides of the road were clofely covered with the wood. On the 22d in the morning about fix, the Major fixed an ambufcade upon the top of a rifing ground, at near 200 yards diftance from their boats; and within a quarter of an hour 42 men came along the road from the advanced guard, and paffing the Major defcended the hill; but juft as the foremoft reached their boats he attacked them in their rear, and killed 9 at the firft fire, which fo intimidated the reft, that they flung down their arms, fome taking to their boats, and others fwimming the river; the Major however continued his fire, took their commanding officer prifoner, deftroyed the whole party, and returned that fame evening to Fort William Henry, without one of his men having received any hurt, although the enemy were near four times his number.

WILMANSTRAND, a ftrong frontier fortrefs of Swedifh Finland, near Wyburg, is famous for the following battle. Count Lacy being difpatched to Carelia, the moft eaftern province of Finland, at the head of an army about

30000 men, he there received advice that the Swedifh rendezvous was at the fortrefs of Wilmanftrand; and on the 20th of Auguft 1741, he advanced from Wyburg to attack that poft. The Swedes were in a moft advantageous fituation, being covered by the fortrefs and an eminence on which their artillery was planted, while both flanks were fecured by lakes, fo that there was no acceffion but in the front, commanded by General Wrangel. But Lacy, regardlefs of their fituation, made forced marches to attack them; and after a fmart engagement of fix hours, the Swedes were totally routed, leaving their cannon, and about 4000 men killed, wounded, and taken prifoners. Among the latter were General Wrangel, Count Wafoburg, and feveral officers of diftinction.

The Ruffians immediately entered the fortrefs fword in hand, and got immenfe booty; the Swedes were defeated; and this fortrefs, with all its riches, became a prey to their enemy, whofe lofs was inconfiderable: only Major-general Uxbull being killed, Lieutenant-general Steffeln, and Major-general Abbrecht, wounded; and near 1900 inferior officers and private men.

WILMERDONCK, near Eecheren, in the Auftrian Low-countries, about 6 miles north of Antwerp, and 7 eaft of Lillo, is only remarkable for a battle between the French and Dutch in 1703, when fortune declared for the latter. Lat. 51. 42. n. long. 4. 18. eaft.

WINDAGE of a gun, is the difference between the diameter of the bore and the diameter of the ball; for the balls being

rough,

rough, if they were not fomewhat lefs than the bore, they might jam in the piece; fo the windage of a demi-culverin is a quarter of an inch.

WINDSOR, antiently a famous fortification in Berkfhire, where is ftill on an eminence a celebrated caftle, in which are inftalled the Knights of the Garter. It is 20 miles weft of London.

WINGS, *in fortification*, are the large fides of horn-works, crownworks, tenailles, and the like out-works; that is to fay, the ramparts and parapets, with which they are bounded on the right and left, from their gorge to the front.

WINLACE, a roller of wood, fquare at each end, through which is either holes for handfpikes, or ftaves acrofs, to turn it round. By a cord being faftened to this at one end, any thing very heavy, fecured at the other end, may be eafily raifed up to it.

WINSCHOTEN, a ftrong fortrefs of Groningen, in the United Provinces, 6 miles fouth-weft of the bay of Dallert. Near this place was fought the firft battle by the Dutch, under Count Lewis of Naffau, againft the Spaniards, in 1568; in which the latter were defeated, and their General Aremberg killed. Lat. 53. 20. n. long. 6. 56. eaft.

WINTER-QUARTERS, places where troops are quartered during the winter; and, likewife, the time comprehended between the end of one campaign and the beginning of another.

WITTENBERG, or *Wirtenberg*, the capital of the duchy of Saxony Proper, in Germany, on the eaft fide of the Elbe; it is well fortified by art and nature, and lies 54 miles n. of Drefden. Lat. 51. 56. n. long. 13. 10. eaft.

WORCUM, a well fortified town of Holland, fituated on the Waal, 24 miles eaft of Rotterdam. Lat. 51. 50. n. long. 4. 46. eaft.

WORD, in an army or garrifon is a token or mark of diftinction, by an ignorance of which, fpies or treacherous perfons are immediately known. It ferves likewife to prevent furprizes, and is given out by the general to the lieutenant-general or major-general of the day, who gives it to the adjutant-general, he to the majors of brigades, they to the adjutants, who give it firft to their own field-officers, and afterwards to the non-commiffioned officers, who write it in their orderly books, and then carry it to their own officers. In a garrifon it is given by the governor to the town or fort major; in their abfence, to the town or fort-adjutant, who fends it to the feveral guards fealed up, and alfo gives it to the adjutant at orderly time.

WORKS, generally denote all the fortifications about the body of a place; as by out-works are meant thofe without the firft inclofure. This word is alfo ufed to fignify the approaches of the befiegers, and the feveral lines, trenches, &c. made round a place, an army, &c. for its fecurity.

WOLFEMBUTTLE, a city of Brunfwic and Lower Saxony, in Germany, fituated on the river Ocker, the antient refidence of the Duke of Brunfwic-Wolfembuttle,

buttle, is ftrong by art and nature, and lies 12 miles fouth of
Brunfwic. Lat. 52. 26. n. long.
10. 41. eaft.

WORMS, an imperial city,
and the capital of the bifhopric
of that name, in the Palatine,
fituated on the weft fide of
the Rhine, was a fine place before deftroyed in 1689, by the
French, but has fince been rebuilt, and is mentioned in the
courfe of fome remarkable battles. It lies 27 miles f. of Mentz.
Lat. 44. 36. n. long. 8. 10. eaft.

WYNENDALE, a town of
Flanders, in the Auftrian Low-
countries, between Bruges and
Oftend, in lat. 51. 10. n. long.
3. 15. eaft; is rendered memorable by the following gallant
a 	ction on the 28th of Septem-
ber 1708, between a body of
the allied troops, commanded by
Major-general Webb, and the
French army, commanded by
Count de la Motte.

After the detachments fent to
cover the waggons of ammunition for the fiege of Lifle had
joined at Tourout, September
27th, Generals Webb and Cadogan received intelligence that
Major Savary, of the regiment
of Guethims, had poffeffed himfelf of the poft of Oudenbroughe;
whereupon 600 grenadiers, commanded by Colonel Prefton,
with a battalion of Orkney,
commanded by Colonel Hamilton, and that of Fune, commanded by Colonel Voogt, under
the orders of Brigadier Lanfberg,
were fent to reinforce that poft.

On the 28th at eight in the
morning, the cavalry was fent
to Hooglede, to wait there for
the convoy, excepting an hundred and fifty horfe, commanded
by Count de Lottum, who had
been fent the preceding night to
Oudenbroughe, to carry an order to the two battalions, and
600 grenadiers, to efcort the
convoy as far as Kokclaere, and
then to rejoin the infantry at
Tourout. At noon, Count de
Lottum returned to Tourout, and
reported, that having advanced
towards Ichtegem, he had found
an advanced guard of the enemy's; that he pufhed on as far
as the heath, where he difcovered 16 fquadrons, who mounted their horfes with great precipitation, upon the alarm given
by the advanced-guard; fo that
he had thought proper to return
with all fpeed, to bring information thereof. Upon this news,
all the infantry, to the number
of 22 battalions, and Count de
Lottum, with 150 horfe, who
compofed the advanced-guard,
with the quarter-mafters, and the
reft of the grenadiers, who had
not been commanded to endeavour to take Ichtegem, were ordered to march towards Wynendale. When the advanced-guard
arrived there, the enemies were
difcovered at the entrance of the
heath; whereupon the quarter-
mafter and the reft of the grenadiers were drawn up in order
of battle. Major-general Webb
and Count Naffau Loudenburg,
at the head of 150 horfe, advanced to reconnoitre the enemy, giving orders at the fame
time to the regiment to advance
with all fpeed upon the plain,
and to form: the 150 horfe under Count de Lottum were left
at the entrance of the heath, to
amufe the enemy; and to embarrafs them ftill more, the
quarter-mafters and grenadiers
were pofted among the bufhes,
which fkirted the ground where
the enemy were to pafs. As
faft as our regiments paffed the

defile,

defile, they were ranged in order of battle by General Webb and Count Naſſau, to occupy an opening between Wynendale-wood and the buſhes on the other ſide, which form a kind of little wood. Scarcely had 6 of our battalions paſſed, when the enemy began to cannonade with 10 pieces of cannon, and nine other pieces of 3 bores each, the 140 horſe which had been left at this advanced poſt, who, notwithſtanding the great fire of the enemy, did not ſtir. This produced the effect the general expected therefrom; which was to give him time to put the infantry in order of battle, to occupy the opening and form there two lines. The left wing extended far behind the buſhes above-mentioned, to hinder the enemy from paſſing that way, and to cover the flank. Upon the flank of the right in Wynendale-wood was placed the regiment of Heuklum; and upon the flank of the left, the regiment of Erf, Prince of Pruſſia, with orders to conceal themſelves, and not to fire till they could take the enemy in flank. Small parties of dragoons advanced 40 paces to the right and to the left with ſimilar orders: the quarter-maſters occupied on the left, which paſſes through the buſhes before mentioned. The enemy, after having cannonaded us during three hours, advanced towards us in order of battle in the plain, with four lines of infantry, and as many of cavalry; whereupon Count de Lottum was ordered to retreat, and poſt himſelf 300 paces behind the infantry; which he did in good order. The enemy, to the number of

40 battalions and 48 ſquadrons, continued to march ſtrait up to us.

The General obſerving that the enemy filed off from their right, into the buſhes, ſent thither Count Naſſau, to reconnoitre their motions; upon which, orders to march were given to the regiment of Grumbkow, commanded by Colonel Beſchefer. Brigadier Eltz arrived at the right with the regiments of the rear-guard, which he poſted in the wood of Wynendale. Half a quarter of an hour before the battle, the two battalions, and the 600 grenadiers detached with Brigadier Lanſberg, having joined us, formed a third line, having met by chance near Kokelaere ſome ſoldiers wives in great lamentation; upon which the Colonels Preſton, Hamilton, and Vooght, had adviſed Brigadier Lanſberg to advance to his aſſiſtance. A moment after, the enemy began to attack, and advanced to within 15 paces of the battalion poſted at the flank of the right, who had kept themſelves hid according to the general's order, and did not fire till the enemy's flank was juſt over againſt them; but they did it then with ſuch ſucceſs, that the enemy's left wing fell in great diſorder upon the right, which received from the regiment of Grumbkow, poſted at the flank of the left, and at about the ſame diſtance, ſo warm a ſalute as threw them quite into diſorder. They returned however to the charge, and puſhed hard two of our battalions; but the regiment of Albemarle Swifs, commanded by M. Hirtzet, advanced upon their

cavalry,

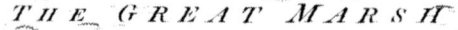

THE GREAT MARSH

B

C

M

A

A

O   F

Heath

H

G

A

D

E

L

PLAN
of the Action between the Corps of Troops of
the ALLIED ARMY
Commanded by Major General WEBB and the
FRENCH ARMY
Commanded by the Count de la MOTTE.

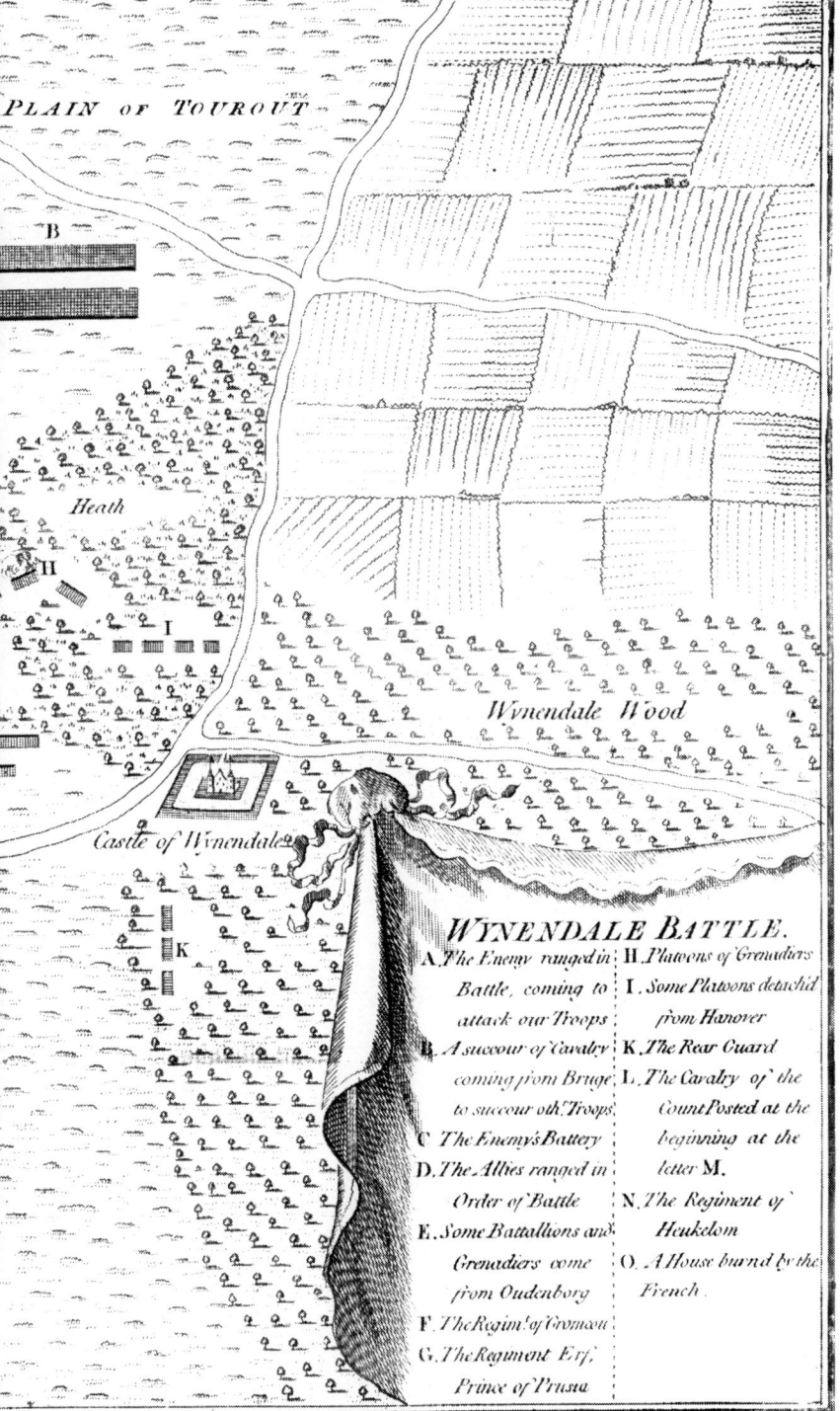

PLAIN of TOUROUT

B

Heath

H

I

Wynendale Wood

Castle of Wynendale

K

WYNENDALE BATTLE.

A . The Enemy ranged in
Battle, coming to
attack our Troops

B . A succour of Cavalry
coming from Bruge
to succour oth. Troops

C . The Enemy's Battery

D . The Allies ranged in
Order of Battle

E . Some Battalions and
Grenadiers come
from Oudenborg

F . The Regim.t of Cromou

G . The Regiment Erf.
Prince of Prusia

H . Platoons of Grenadiers

I . Some Platoons detach'd
from Hanover

K . The Rear Guard

L . The Cavalry of the
Count Posted at the
beginning at the
letter M.

N . The Regiment of
Heukelom

O . A House burn'd by the
French .

cavalry, who ſtrove to penetrate and engage with them, and by his vigorous reſiſtance gave the General and Count Naſſau time to bring up the regiments of Berndorf and Lindebom, in the place of thoſe that had been puſhed; which was done in a moment. In the mean time the enemy, ſupported by ſo many lines, made a ſecond effort to penetrate; but none of our battalions ſtirred, except to advance ſome ſteps; but the general prevented their purſuing, not to loſe the advantage of the two flanks. This penetration had the deſired ſucceſs; for the two regiments and the grenadiers making there a continual fire, obliged the two wings of the enemy to fall back upon their centre, and retreat in great confuſion: though their officers did every thing in their power to make them advance, they could not ſucceed: our ſoldiers fired by platoons, in the ſame order as if they had been performing at a review.

M. Cadogan, who arrived a moment after the engagement had begun, offered to charge the enemy in their confuſion at the head of two ſquadrons he then had; having already ſent orders for four ſquadrons to come and join us, which could not arrive till a little before ſeven o'clock; but it was not judged proper to expoſe ſo ſmall a number to charge an enemy ſo ſuperior, with all their cavalry advanced to favour their retreat.

The battle was ſevere, and laſted near two hours. We had 912 officers and ſoldiers killed or wounded. The enemy's loſs, according to the report of the priſoners, confirmed by the de-

ſerters, was between 3 and 4000; but they retired in ſuch confuſion, that they left their cannon in the wood, and did not return to look for it, till the next day at eleven, after having heard that our generals had continued their march at two in the morning, to conduct the convoy which was going to Rouſſelaer, after having cauſed all our wounded, and ſeveral of the enemy's, to be carried off. The advantage we gained is ſo much the more ſurprizing, as we had only between 6 and 7000 men, on account of the detachments which had been made, while that of the enemy amounted to no leſs than 23000. See Plan 20.

XATIVA, a walled town of Valencia in Spain, ſituated on a river of that name, and defended by a ſtrong caſtle, lies 28 miles ſ. of the city of Valencia. Lat. 39. 10. n. long. 52 minutes weſt.

YORK, New, the capital of the province of that name in North America, is ſituated on an iſland in the mouth of Hudſon's river, about 40 miles in length, and 3 in breadth. It is well built on an eminence, ſurrounded with a wall and other works. Here is alſo a ſpacious harbour, with commodious quays and warehouſes; great numbers of ſhips and veſſels being employed in its trade and fiſhery. Lat. 41. 5. n. long. 74. 15. weſt.

Younger regiment or officer. That regiment is youngeſt which was laſt raiſed; and that officer youngeſt whoſe commiſſion bears the lateſt date, of the

ſame

same rank, though he be aged, or has long served in other capacities.

YPRES, a city of the Austrian Low-countries, one of the barrier towns, and esteemed impregnable; but was shamefully delivered up by the Dutch garrison in 1744, almost as soon as the French came before it, together with the whole chatelary. Lat. 50. 57. north; long. 2. 51. east.

ZANT, an island of the Mediterranean, 10 miles south of the Morea, and near the south side of Chephalonia, from which it is divided by a channel of about 12 miles in breadth. The capital is well fortified and defended by a castle. This island is greatly exposed to the attempts of the Turks, since the Morea was taken from the Venetians in 1715.

ZARA, the capital of the city of Dalmatia, almost surrounded with the Adriatic sea, and joined to the continent by a bridge, is one of the best fortified places belonging to the Venetians; and it lies 58 miles north-west of Spalatto. Lat. 44. 10. n. long. 17. 21. east.

ZELL, the capital of a dukedom of that name, and Lunenberg, in Lower Saxony in Germany, is extremely well fortified, but not regularly; lies 32 miles n. of Hanover, and 37 s. of Lunenberg. It was the residence of the late Duke of Zell and Lunenberg; which dukedom, on the death of the last of that house, devolved on his nephew the elector of Hanover, George I. who also had married the heirefs of that duke, and

mother to George II. Lat. 52. 56. n. long. 10. 11. east.

ZIGZAG, is a line making several angles in approaching or erecting a work, to prevent the men being fired on in a straight line, or enfiladed.

ZIRICKSEE, a strong seaport town on the south side of the island of Schowen, and province of Zealand in the United Netherlands, is 18 miles n. east of Middleburg. Lat. 51. 52. n. long. 3. 56. east.

ZITTAW, a well fortified city of Upper Lufatia, in the circle of Upper Saxony in Germany, is situated on the Neisse, 58 miles east of Dresden. Lat. 51. 10. n. long. 14. 58. east.

ZNAIM, stands upon the river Teya, upon the borders of Austria. The town is fortified, and defended by a strong castle; but a neighbouring mountain overlooking it, renders it weak. It is 40 miles n. west of Vienna. Lat. 47. 47. n. long. 16. 12. east.

ZOLLERN, or HOHENZOLLERN, a city in the principality of the same name, in Suabia in Germany, having a castle on the river Zollern, lies 30 miles s. of Stutgard. Lat. 48. 21. n. long. 8. 50. east.

ZOLNOCK. a well fortified town of Upper Hungary, situated at the confluence of the Zaguya and Theifs. In 1552, it was shamefully surrendered by the soldiers to the Turks, who, at the governor's request, cut the garrison to pieces. It lies 52 miles east of Buda, lat. 47. 30. n. long. 20. 15. east.

ZORNDORFF, a village of New-Marche, in Brandenburg, is situated on the Oder; where a
bloody

bloody battle was fought between the King of Pruffia, and
Generals Fermor and Brown,
in 1758, when the latter was
defeated.

ZURICK, the capital of a
canton of that name, in Switzerland; is well fortified, has
wide ditches, and lies 40 miles
f. weft of Conftance. Lat. 47.
54. n. long. 8. 32. eaft.

ZUTPHEN, the capital of the
county of the fame name, in
Guelderland, fituated on the
eaft bank of the Yffel. It is
rich, populous, well fortified,
and lies 10 miles fouth of Deventer. Lat. 52. 20. n. long.
6. 10. eaft.

INDEX.

INDEX.

I N D E X.

ADDITIONS to the Edition of 1776.

F I N I S.

SUBSCRIBERS.

HENRY FREDERICK,

Duke of Cumberland and Strathern, Earl of
Dublin, Ranger of Windsor Great Park, and
Vice-Admiral of the White Squadron, K. G,

A,

RIGHT Honourable Earl Ailesbury
   Duke of Argyle, Lieut. General, Colonel of the Royal,
and Commander in Chief in Scotland, Two Books
Lieut. Charles Abbot, South Hants Militia
Second Lieut.   Ackroy, Marines.
Capt. Benjamin Adair, Marines
Mr. Patience Thomas Adams, Bushy, Herts
Ensign Francis Aiskell, 2d (or Queens Royal) Regiment
   of Foot
Col William Alcock, Militia, Waterford ✝
Capt. William Alcock, late of the 5;d Regiment of Foot ✤
Lieut. Richard Alcock, 66th Regiment of Foot
Lieut. John Fortescue Aland, Berkshire Militia
Second Lieut.   Alder, Marines
Major George Alexander, late of the 2d (or Queen's Royal)
   Regiment of Foot ✝
        Altham, Esq; of Chesfield, Hertfordshire
Lieut. and Adjut. Henry Anderson, Marines
Mr. Andrews, Stanmore, Middlesex
Lieut. Charles Arbuthnot, 66th Regiment of Foot
Lieut. Robert Arbuthnot, 31st Regiment of Foot
Lieut. and Adjut. Thomas Archbold, Marines ✤
Lieut. General Bigo Armstrong, Colonel of the 8th (or the
   King's) Regiment of Foot
Capt. Thomas Arnot, Marines
Capt. Robert Astle, Leicestershire Militia

B.

Cornet Lord Bamff, 6th (or Inniskilling) Regiment of Dragoons
Right Honourable William Wildman Lord Viscount Barrington, Secretary at War, and M. P. ✝

T   Lci 1

Lieut. Lord John Bellenden, 25th Regiment of Foot
Capt. Joseph Baddeley, 25th Regiment of Foot
Second Lieut.   Balfour, Marines
Lieut. John Balfour, the Royal
Second Lieut. George Ball, Marines
Second Lieut.   Baldwyn, Marines
Enfign Philip Bainbrigge, 2d (or Queen's Royal) Regiment of Foot
Capt. Henry Banks, Royal Navy †
Lieut. Col. James Barker, 2d (or Queen's Royal) Regiment †
Lieut. Edward Baynes, 2d (or Queen's Royal) Regiment of Foot
Mr. Becket, Adelphi, Strand, Twenty-five Books
Major General John Bell, Marines †
Lieut. James Berkeley, Marines
Capt. George Bernard, 6th (Innifkilling) Regiment of Dragoons
Lieut. Col. Albemarle Bertie, 1ft Regiment of Foot Guards †
Second Lieut.   Bidlake, Marines
Second Lieut.   Binks, Marines
Lieut. Col. Thomas Bisfhopp, Cold Stream of Guards, and Equerry to his Majefty †
Lieut. John Blagrave, Berkfhire Militia
Lieut. Peter Boiffieur, 11th Regiment of Dragoons
Cornelius Bolton, Efq; M. P. †
Lieut. Col. Mafon Bolton, 8th Regiment of Foot †
Cornet Bolton, Royal Regiment of Horfe Guards
Capt. Richard Bowls, late of the Second Troop of Horfe Guards †
Col. John Braithwaite, India Service
Cornet G. C. Braithwaite, 1ft (or the King's) Dragoon Guards
Major Arthur Hill Brice, 7th Regiment of Foot, or Royal Englifh Fuzileers †
Capt. Richard Bright, Marines
Lieut. Henry Bromley, Marines
Honourable Lieut. Col. Thomas Bruce, 65th Regiment of Foot
Lieut. Richard Bulkeley, 59th Regiment of Foot
Lieut. William Burd, Marines
Lieut. James Burn, late of the 52d Regiment of Foot
Lieut. and Adjut. James Burgefs, Hertfordfhire Militia
Mr. G. Burnett, Nº 134, Strand, Twenty-five Books
Mr. Peter Burrell, Pay Office, Whitehall
Lieut. Arthur Buttle, Marines
George Byng, Efq; M. P. †

C,

Right Honourable Capt. George Vifcount Chewton, 3d Regiment of Foot Guards and M. P.
Right Honourable Earl Cholmondeley, Lord Lieutenant and Cuftos Rotulorum of the County of Chefter, Two Books
Right Honourable John Smyth Deburgh, Earl of Glanricarde, Two Books †

Right

SUBSCRIBERS.

Right Honourable Lieut. Col. Lord Thomas Pelham Clinton, 1st Regiment of Foot Guards and M. P. Two Books

Right Honourable Col. Lord Viscount Cranborne, Hertford-shire Militia, Lord Lieutenant of the County, and M. P.

Lieut. Col. Sir Richard Chafe, Bart. Hertfordshire Militia

Major Sir Robert Salusbury Cotton, Bart. Royal Chefhire Militia

Lieut. General Sir Henry Clinton, K. B. 12th Regiment of Foot, Governor of Limerick, Groom of the Bedchamber to his Royal Highness the Duke of Gloucester, and M. P. Two Books †

Lieut. General Sir Eyre Coote, K. B. 37th Regiment of Foot, and M.P.

Lieut. Col. James Callander. 67th Regiment of Foot

Lieut. Campbell Callander, 67th Regiment of Foot

Capt. John Callow, 3d (or the King's own) Regiment of Dragoons

Lieut. General Henry Fletcher Campbell, 35th Regiment of Foot †

Lieut. Col. John Campbell, Half Pay †

Lieut. Col. John Campbell, 22d Regiment of Foot †

Capt. Duncan Campbell, Marines

Capt. John Campbell, Marines

Cornet John Campbell, 11th Regiment of Dragoons

Lieut. William Augustus Cane, 2d (or Queen's Royal) Regiment of Foot

Richard Capper, Esq; Bufhey, Herts

Col. James Capper, India Service, and Commiffary General at Madras

Lieut. William Cartwright, 10th Regiment of Dragoons

Cornet John Carnegie, 11th Regiment of Dragoons

Mr. George Carrol, Bookfeller, Catherine-ftreet, Six Books

Lieut. Col. Walter Carruthers, Marines †

Enfign William Carruthers, 23th Regiment of Foot

Second Lieut.   Caftell, Marines

Cornet   Chadwick, 3d (or King's own) Regiment of Dragoons

Anthony Chamier, Esq;

Capt. Lieut. and Quarter Mafter Bartholomew Chaundy, Marines †

Enfign Napier Chriftie, 3d Regiment of Foot Guards

Major General Thomas Clarke, Coldftream Regiment of Foot Guards

Capt. Thomas Clarke, 3d (or King's own) Regiment of Foot

Capt. Stephen Clarke, London Militia †

Second Lieut. Alexander Clarke, Marines

Second Lieut. Molesworth Cleiland, Royal Regiment of Artillery †

Lieut. William Clowes, 6th (or Inifkilling) Regiment of Dragoons

Lieut. William Colvill, Half Pay, Two Books †

Enfign James Alexander Colvill, 59th Regiment of Foot

T 3   Capt.

SUBSCRIBERS.

Capt. Conway
Col. George John Cooke, Weftern Battalion of Middlefex Militia, Two Books ✝
Second Lieut. John Coultherft, Marines
John Coutts, Banker, Strand
Enfign George Couffmaker, 1ft Regiment of Foot Guards
Lieut. Col. Michael Cox, 1ft Regiment of Foot Guards ✝
Lieut. General Francis Craig, 1ft Regiment of Foot Guards, and Groom of the Bedchamber to his Royal Highnefs the Duke of Cumberland
Lieut. General Robert Cuninghame, Colonel of the 14th Regiment of Foot, Governor of Kinfale, and M. P. ✝

D.

Otway, Lord Defart, late of the Royal ✝
Right Honourable Lord Dunkellin
Chevalier De Pinto, Envoy Extraordinary from his moft faithful Majefty to the Court of Great Britain, Two Books
Major Peter Damhon, 2d (or Queen's Royal) Regiment of Foot
Captain William Danfey, 33d Regiment of Foot ✝
Major William Dalrymple, 2d (or Queen's Royal) Regiment of Foot
Capt. Hugh Dalrymple, the Royal
Capt. James Dalrymple, 43d Regiment of Foot
Lieut. Thomas Dalton, 11th Regiment of Dragoons
Second Lieut. William Davids, Marines
Mr. John Davis, War Office
Lieut. William Dawfon, South Hants Militia
Col. John Deaken, 1ft Regiment of Foot Guards, and Groom of the Bedchamber to his Royal Highnefs the Duke of Cumberland ✝
Honourable Lieut. Col. J. T. Deburgh, 1ft Regiment of Foot Guards
Lieut. Governor of St. John's in the Gulph of St. Laurence, Thomas Defbriffay, Efq; ✝
Second Lieut. William Charles Dexter, Marines
Mr. James Dixwell, Printer and Bookfeller, St. Martin's-lane
Rev. Henry Dodwell, Chaplain, Berkfhire Militia
Lieut. Col. Robert Donkin, 23d Regiment of Foot, or Royal Welch Fuzileers ✝
Capt. William Anne Douglafs, 3d Regiment of Foot Guards
Lieut. George Douglafs, 25th Regiment of Foot
Capt. Douglas
Mr. John Dring
Capt. Francis D'Oyly, 1ft Regiment of Foot Guards
Capt. Alexander Duffee, 58th Regiment of Foot ✝
Capt. James Duffee, 1ft Regiment of Foot Guards
Enfign Thomas Dunckerley, Hants Militia
Lieut. Col. Ralph Dundafs, 11th Regiment of Dragoons
Capt. John Durour, Coldftream Regiment of Foot Guards
Capt. Thomas Duval, Marines

Right

SUBSCRIBERS.

E.

Right Honourable Lieut. General Archibald Montgomery, Earl of Eglington, 51ft Regiment of Foot, and Governor of Dumbarton, Three Books

Right Honourable Earl Erroll, High Conftable of Scotland ✝

Right Honourable Lieut. General G. Auguftus Elliot, 15th (or the King's) Regiment of Light Dragoons, and Governor of Gibraltar ✝

Capt. J. William Egerton, 7th (or Queen's) Regiment of Dragoons ✝

Capt. Thomas Edgar, 25th Regiment of Foot

Lieut. Bingham Ellifon, late of the 2d (or Queen's Royal) Regiment of Foot ✝

Capt. George Elives, Berkfhire Militia

Capt. Nathaniel Englifh, Marines

James Efdaile, Efq; Bunhill-row, London

Second Lieut.   Evelyn, Marines

Lieut. and Adjut. Henry Evens, Berkfhire Militia

Lieut. Hardy Euftace, 1ft Regiment of Horfe ✝

F.

Right Honourable General Lord Vifcount Falmouth, Capt. of the Yeomen of the Guard, &c. Two Books

Right Honourable Capt. Lord Vifcount Fairford, Hertfordfhire Militia, and M. P.

Right Honourable Lord Vifcount Fielding, Military Academy, Chelfea

Right Honourable Lord Forbes, Military Academy, Chelfea

Sir William Forbes, Baronet

Mr. William Faden, Two Books, Geographer, Charing-crofs

Second Lieut. Robert Hill Farmer, Marines

Major General William Faucitt, 3d Regiment of Foot Guards, Deputy Adjutant General of his Majefty's Forces, and Governor of Gravefend and Tilbury Forts ✝

Lieut. Everard Fawkener, 11th Regiment of Dragoons

Cornet George Fenwick, 6th (or Innifkilling) Regiment of Dragoons

Lieut. Col. Lewis Feyrac, late of the 18th Regiment of Foot ✝

Honourable Lieut. General Charles Fitzroy, Col. of the 5d (or King's own) Regiment of Dragoons, Vice-Chamberlain to the Queen, and M. P.

Honourable Lieut. General Fitzwilliam, 2d Regiment of Horfe ✝

Major General Hezekiah Fleming, Half Pay, late of 73d Regiment of Foot

Capt. John Fleming, South Hants Militia, and M.P.

Col. John Fletcher, 32d Regiment of Foot

Capt. Henry Fletcher, Marines

Capt. James Flint, 25th Regiment of Foot

Lieut.   Foley, Marines

Lieut. Gerrald Fortefcue, 25th Regiment of Foot

Lieut

SUBSCRIBERS.

Lieut. Col. Thomas Fowke, 3d Regiment of Foot Guards, and Equerry to his Royal Highnefs the Duke of Cumberland, Two Books ✝

Lieut. Col. Chriftopher French, 22d Regiment of Foot

Second Lieut.   Furzer, Marines

G.

Duke of Grafton, Lord Lieutenant and Cuftos Rotulorum of the County of Suffolk, High Steward of Dartmouth, K. G. &c. Three Books.

Moft Honourable Marquis of Granby, Col. of the Leicefter-fhire Militia, and M. P.

Right Honourable Lord Vifcount Grimfton, Three Books

Lieut. Col. Chriftopher Gauntlet, Marines

Richard Gale, Efq; Hackney

Capt. Samuel Gamble, Leicefterfhire Regiment of Militia

Lieut. William Glafcot, Half Pay, late of the 2d (or Queen's Royal) Regiment of Foot ✝

Honourable Lieut. Col. Cofmo Gordon, 3d Regiment of Foot Guards ✝

Major Charles Gordon, 11th Regiment of Foot

Capt. Archibald Kinlock Gordon, 65th Regiment of Foot

Quarter Mafter David Gordon, 59th Regiment of Foot

Lieut. Thomas Gore, 6th (or Innifkilling) Regiment of Dragoons

Charles Gould, Efq; Judge Advocate General

Abraham Gooding, Efq; London

Capt. Gregor Grant, 58th Regiment of Foot ✝

Major George Gray, 59th Regiment of Foot

Mr. Edward Gray, Queen-ftreet

Capt. and Adjut. Francis Grofe, Surry Militia

Major Thomas Groves, Marines ✝

Enfign Thomas Grove, Berkfhire Militia

Capt. William Gun, 6th (or Innifkilling) Regiment of Dragoons

Lieut. Thomas Gwyllyn, 59th Regiment of Foot

H.

Right Honourable Francis Haftings, Earl Huntingdon, F. R. S. Three Books;

Sir Thomas Heron, Bart. late of the 16th Regiment of Foot ✝

Thomas Hall, Efq;

Lieut. Col. Otho Hamilton, 59th Regiment of Foot ✝

Capt. Ifaac Hamon, Half Pay, late of the 2d (or Queen's Royal) Regiment of Foot ✝

Second Lieut. Leonard Hamon, Royal Artillery

Second Lieut. Frederick Hamon, Marines

Hugh Jofeph Hanfard, Efq; Gerard-ftreet

Lieut. Richard Hanfard, 60th Regiment of Foot

Lieut. John Harrifon, 59th Regiment of Foot

Enfign

SUBSCRIBERS.

Enfign Jofeph Hardy, 65th Regiment of Foot

Lieut. General Edward Harvey, 6th (or Innifkilling) Regiment of Dragoons, Adjut. General of his Majefty's Forces, Governor of Portfmouth, and M. P. Six Books ✝

Lieut. Col. Anthony Haflam, 5th Regiment of Foot

Capt. William Hawtayne, 3d Regiment of Foot Guards, Two Books

Capt. Adam Hay, 31ft Regiment of Foot

Capt. Alexander Hay, 7th Regiment of Foot, or Royal Englifh Fuzileers

Capt. Andrew Goater Haynes, South Hants Militia

Cornet James Roper Head, 6th (or Innifkilling) Regiment of Dragoons

Enfign George Headham, 59th Regiment of Foot

Lieut. William Heath, Efq; Hertfordfhire Militia

Enfign Jofeph Henegan, Independent Company at Tilbury Fort

Lieut. Col. Charles Hefilrige, Leicefterfhire Militia

Capt. Thomas Hewetfon, 59th Regiment of Foot

Lieut. Robert Hewetfon, 6th (or Innifkilling) Regiment of Dragoons

Lieut. Edward Hill, Marines

Mr. William Hinton, Copper Plate Printer, Racquet-court, Fleet-ftreet, Two Books

Second Lieut. Hobbs, Marines

Lieut. General Studholme Hodgfon, of the 4th Regiment of Foot, and Governor of Fort St. George and Fort Auguftus, Two Books ✝

Enfign William Hodgfon, Coldftream Regiment of Foot Guards

Mr. Chriftopher Holdfworth, Lyon's-inn

Mr. William Holdfworth, Park-ftreet

Capt. James Holwell, 2d (or Queen's Royal) Regiment of Foot

Lieut. Col. David Home, Lieut. Governor of Chefter ✝

Major Charles Home, 25th Regiment of Foot

Capt. Walter Home, 7th Regiment, or Royal Englifh Fuzileers

General Philip Honeywood, 4th Regiment of Horfe, Governor of Hull, and M.P.

Major Jacob Houblon, Hertfordfhire Militia

Capt. John Houblon, Hertfordfhire Militia

Second Lieut. Hunt, Marines

I.

Right Honourable Lieut. General Sir John Irwine, K. B. Col. of 57th Regiment of Foot, Commander in Chief in Ireland, and M. P. Three Books ✝

Capt. Lieut. John Jackfon, Half Pay, late of the 2d (or Queen's Royal) Regiment of Foot ✝

Lieut. and Adjut. John Jackfon, Marines

The

Lieut.

SUBSCRIBERS.

Lieut. Col. Robert Laurie, 7th (or Queen's) Regiment of Dragoons, M. P. ✝
James Lowther, Efq; M. P.
Major Henry Lyon, 11th Regiment of Dragoons

M.

Col. Sir Herbert Mackworth, Bart. Glamorganfhire Militia, and M P. Three Books ✝
Sir William Middleton, Bart. late of the Royal Regiment of Horfe Guards ✝
Major General John Mackenzie, Marines, Two Books ✝
Lieut John M'Combe, South Hants Militia
Capt. Hector M'Neal, Marines ✝
Lieut. William Madden, Marines
Capt. Samuel Malcher, late of the 2d, (or Queen's Royal) Regiment of Foot, Two Books ✝
Capt. Weftwang March, 32d Regiment of Foot
Capt. Benjamin Marlow, Royal Navy
Second Lieut. Benjamin Marlow, Royal Regiment of Artillery
Lieut. Col. Thomas Marriot, Marines ✝
Honourable Charles Marfham, L. L. D. one of the Vice-Prefidents to the Society for the Encouragement of Arts and Manufactures, and M. P. Three Books ✝
Lieut. Col. John Martin, Marines
Major General Maffey, 27th Regiment of Foot
Major General Edward Maxwell, 67th Regiment of Foot
Surgeon Mr. Thomas Mears, South Hants Militia
Second Lieut. Charles Menee, Marines
Capt. Henry Meredith, Merchant Service
Capt. William Mitford, South Hants Militia
Capt. Eyre Robert Mingay, 66th Regiment of Foot ✝
Cornet George Mitchell, 11th Regiment of Dragoons
Capt. John Mompeffon, 8th (or the King's) Regiment of Foot
Honourable Lieut. General Robert Monckton, 17th Regiment of Foot, and Governor of Berwick, Four Books ✝
Second Lieut. Monier, Marines
Second Lieut. Charles Moody, Marines
Lieut. Frank Moore, 11th Regiment of Dragoons
Lieut. Col. T. Afbert Mordaunt, 10th Regiment of Dragoons
Lieut. Col. George Morgan, Coldftream Regiment of Foot Guards
Lieut. Col. William Morrice, 10th Regiment of Dragoons
Lieut. Col. William Morris, Half Pay ✝
Major General George Morrifon, of the Corps of Engineers, and Quarter Mafter General of his Majefty's Forces ✝
Lieut. and Adjut. Edward Mortimer, Leicefterfhire Militia
Honourable Lieut. General Murray, 13th Regiment of Foot, and Lieut. Governor of Minorca ✝
Lieut. Charles Murray, Marines
Lieut. John Murray, 2d (or Queen's Royal) Regiment of Foot ✝

Duke

SUBSCRIBERS.

N.

Duke of Newcastle, Lord Lieutenant and Custos Rotulorum of Nottingham, Auditor of the Exchequer, K. G. L. L. D. and F. R. S. &c. Two Books

Duke of Northumberland, Lord Lieutenant and Custos Rotulorum of the Counties of Middlesex and Northumberland, Vice Admiral of all America, K. G. and F. R. S. Two Books ✠

Honourable Lieut. Col. Francis Napier, Marines

Lieut. Colebrook Nesbitt, 32d Regiment of Foot

Capt. Stephen Nevison, Marines

Lieut. Col. Michael Nickson, 2d (or Queen's Royal) Regiment of Foot ✠

Lieut. George Nugent, 7th, or Royal English Fuzileers

Capt. Clement Newsam, 6th (or Inniskilling) Regiment of Dragoons.

O.

Right Honourable Lord Onslow, one of the Lords Commissioners of the Treasury, Three Books

Lieut. General Sir J. Athol Oughton, K. B. 31st Regiment of Foot

Col. George Ogilvy, 3d Regiment of Foot Guards ✠

Capt. Thomas Osborne, late of the 58th Regiment of Foot ✠

Count O'Rourke, Maister General of Horse, Chamberlain to the late King of Poland, and Knight of the Order of St. Louis

Capt. Humphry Owen, 7th, (or Royal Fuzillers) Regiment of Foot

P.

Right Honourable Lieut. General Earl Pembroke, 1st (or Royal) Regiment of Dragoons, Lord Lieutenant and Custos Rotulorum of Wiltshire, and one of the Lords of the Bedchamber to his Majesty, Three Books ✠

Right Honourable Lieut. General Earl Percy, 5th Regiment of Foot, and Western Battalion of Middlesex Militia, Two Books ✠

Right Honourable Lord Algernoon Percy, Vice-President of the Middlesex Hospital, and M. P. Two Books

Sir Richard Perrot, Bart.

Capt. Peter Painter, Marines

Capt. Edward Parker, 31st Regiment of Foot

Mr. John Parker, Lyon's-inn

Ensign George Parkhurst, 25th Regiment of Foot

Ensign Hamps B. Palmer, 1st Regiment of Foot Guards

Second Lieut. James Parsons, Marines

Mr. Robert Parsons

Lieut.

SUBSCRIBERS.

Lieut. Charles Peckover, London Militia
Capt. Phillip Perry, Leicefterfhire Militia
Lieut. John Perry, Marines
Lieut. Jofeph Partridge, Half Pay
Lieut. Richard Phillips, Half Pay, late of the 2d (or Queen's Royal) Regiment of Foot †
Lieut. Pingfton, London Militia
William Plumer, Efq; M. P. Three Books
Capt. John Popple, 11th Regiment of Dragoons
Lieut. Richard Pottenger, Berkfhire Militia
Capt. Pennifton Powney, Berkfhire Militia
Meffrs. Pugh and Duncan, Panton-ftreet, Contractors for Army Neceffaries, Four Books
Capt. William Price, 7th (or Queen's) Regiment of Dragoons †
Capt. John Charles Price, Berkfhire Militia
Major George Prefton, Marines
Capt. Henry James Pye, Berkfhire Militia
Lieut. Walton Pye, ditto

R.

Right Honourable Earl Rochford, Vice-Admiral of the Coafts, and Lord Lieutenant and Cuftos Rotulorum of Effex, &c.
Col. Lord Robert Romney, Weftern Kentifh Militia, L. L. D. and F. R. S. and Prefident of the Society for Encouraging Arts and Manufactures, Three Books †
Major General Charles Rainsford, Coldftream Regiment of Guards, Equerry to his Royal Highnefs the Duke of Gloucefter, and Governor of Chefter, Two Books †
Lieut. Col. Robert Raitt, Half Pay, late of the 2d, (or Queen's Royal) Regiment of Foot
Cornet Edward Repington, 6th (or Innifkilling) Regiment of Dragoons
Mr. James Ryan, Germyn-ftreet
Mr. George Riley, Bookfeller, &c. Curzon-ftreet, Twelve Books
Enfign and Adjut. Francis Richardfon, 1ft Regiment of Guards
Cornet Jofeph Richardfon, 11th Regiment of Dragoons
Cornet John Richardfon, 3d (or King's own) Regiment of Dragoons
Lieut. George Poyntz Ricketts, South Hants Militia
Lieut. Col. Alexander Rigby, 25th Regiment of Foot
Lieut. John Roberts, London Militia
Major John Robins, 6th (or Innifkilling) Regiment of Dragoons
Lieut. General Robert Robinfon, Governor of Pendennis Caftle
Enfign George Rodney, 3d Regiment of Guards
Lieut. Henry Rooke, 3d (or King's own) Regiment of Dragoons

Col.

SUBSCRIBERS.

Capt. Richard Rofe, 25th Regiment of Foot
Lieut.   Rofe
Capt. Andrew Rofs, 31ft Regiment of Foot
Capt. William Rotheram, Marines, Two Books
Second Lieut. Rutford, Marines
Second Lieut. Edward Rufhworth, South Hants Militia
Capt. Rutt, Milkfham, near Bath
Cornet Rowley, 10th Regiment of Dragoons
Col. William Roy, of the Corps of Engineers, and Deputy
    Quarter Mafter General of his Majefty's Forces †

S.

Right Honourable Lord George Sutton, Col. of the Notting-
    hamfhire Militia, one of the Vice-Prefidents of the Lock
    Hofpital, and M. P. Two Books
Col. Sir Simeon Stuart, Bart. South Harts Militia, one of
    the Chamberlains of the Tally Court in the Exchequer,
    and M. P. †
Capt. Thomas Sadler, South Hants Militia
Capt. Samuel Salter, Hertfordfhire Militia
Lieut. General Edward Sandford, 10th Regiment of Foot †
Capt. George Sandford, 7th (or Queen's) Regiment of Dra-
    goons †
Lieut. Col. Clement Saxton, Berkfhire Militia
Capt. Edmund Seimure, Berkfhire Militia
Enfign Peter Serle, South Hants Militia
Lieut. Col. Henry Shawe, 11th Regiment of Foot †
Capt. Bernard Shawe, 2d, (or Queen's Royal) Regiment of
    Foot †
Col. Commandant Thomas Sheldon, Marines
Capt. Lieut. Edward Shephard, Berkfhire Militia
Lieut. Thomas Shephard, South Hants Militia
Honourable Lieut. General Philip Sherrard, 69th Regiment
    of Foot †
Lieut. Charles Simes, late of the 10th Regiment of Foot
Lieut. and Quarter Mafter Thomas Sims, Marines †
Lieut. Thomas Sims, Marines
Surgeon Mr. Thomas Stear, 7th, or Royal Englifh Fuzileers
Lieut. and Adjut. Ambrofe Simpfon, 59th Regiment of Foot
Major Jofeph Sirr, Deputy Advocate General in Ireland †
Lieut. Col. W. C. Farrell Sheffington, 1ft Regiment of Foot
    Guards
Major General Robert Skene, of 59th Regiment of Foot, and
    Adjut. General in North Britain
Lieut. Col. Boughey Skey, late of the 49th Regiment of Foot
Lieut. William Sladden, Berkfhire Militia
Brigadier General Francis Smith, 10th Regiment of Foot,
    Aid de Camp to the King, Three Books
Major General Henry Smith, Marines
Capt. Charles Smith, 25th Regiment of Foot
Lieut.   Smith, Marines

                                              Lieut.

Lieut. Walter Smith, Marines
Mr. Felix Smith, Watford, Herts
Capt. Edward Sparhawke, Hertfordshire Militia
Lieut. Nathan Spencer, Leicestershire Militia
Honourable Col. Henry St. John, 6th Regiment of Foot, Aid
    de Camp to his Majesty, one of the Grooms of his Majesty's
    Bedchamber, M. P. ✝
Col. Anthony St. Leger, H. P. ✝
Lieut. Col. Barry St. Leger, 34th Regiment of Foot ✝
Capt. William Sowle, late of the 70th Regiment of Foot
Capt. William St. Clair, 25th Regiment of Foot
Honourable Col. Edward Stopford, 66th Regiment of Foot,
    M. P. ✝
Lieut. J. Kennedy Strong, 64th Regiment of Foot
Capt. Richard Symes, 52d Regiment of Foot
Ensign Simeon Stuart, South Hants Militia
Major General William Style, 1st Regiment of Foot Guards

T.

Right Honourable Lieut. General Lord Viscount Townsend,
    2d (or Queen's) Regiment of Dragoon Guards, and Master
    General of the Ordnance, Four Books
Lieut. General William Taylor, 24th Regiment of Foot, Three
    Books ✝
Mr. William Thompson, Islington
Lieut. General John Thomas, Coldstream Regiment of
    Guards ✝
Capt. and Adjut. Edward Thornley, 2d (or Queen's Royal)
    Regiment of Foot ✝
Col. William Thornton, 1st Regiment of Foot Guards, Three
    Books ✝
Capt. Thomas Timmins, Marines
Capt. William Tomkins, Coldstream Regiment of Guards ✝
Mr. Francis Tomkins, Army Hospital ✝
Major General Cyrus Trapaud, 70th Regiment of Foot ✝
Mr. Roger Tremels, Northumberland-street
Major Alexander Trotter, Marines

V.

Lieut. Col. Charles Vallency, Engineer ✝
Charles Vane, Esq;
Col. Arthur Vanfittart, Berkshire Militia
Major John Vatals, 10th Regiment of Foot ✝

W.

Right Honourable General Earl Waldegrave, Coldstream
    Regiment of Foot Guards, Master of the Horse to her
    Majesty, and Governor of Plymouth, Two Books ✝
Right

SUBSCRIBERS.

Right Honourable Lord Vifcount Weymouth, Secretary of State for the Southern Department, and High Steward of Tamworth

Major Sir Richard Worfley, Bart. South Hants Militia, one of the Verdurers of the New Foreft, and M. P.

Francis Wadman, Efq; Gentleman Ufher to the Princefs of Amelia ✝

Lieut. General Hunt Wolfh, 56th Regiment of Foot ✝

Major John Walter, Berkfhire Militia

John Wallace, Efq;

Lieut. William Wardlaw, late of the 2d (or Queen's Royal) Regiment of Foot ✝

John Waters, Efq; Bufhey, Herts

Capt. Thomas Warbuton, 11th Regiment of Dragoons

Capt. Charles Watfon, 25th Regiment of Foot

Lieut. Alexander Watfon, Honourable Eaft India Company

Cornet Chriftopher Watfon, 3d (or the King's own) Regiment of Dragoons

John Wallis, N° 33, Ludgate-ftreet, Twenty-five Books

Lieut. Col. Richmond Webb, late of the 2d (or Queen's Royal) Regiment of Foot ✝

Capt. James Webber, 58th Regiment of Foot ✝

Capt. John Webber, Marines

John Wemys, Efq; Lieut. Governor of Edinburgh Caftle ✝

Capt. Maurice Wemys, Marines

Enfign John Wemyfs, 59th Regiment of Foot

Lieut. Col. Richard White, 3d (or the King's own) Regiment of Dragoons, Two Books ✝

Capt. William White, London Militia

Enfign Charles Williamfon, 25th Regiment of Foot

Lieut. Edward Winne, 6th (or Innifkilling) Regiment of Dragoons

John Wood, Efq; Governor and Captain General of the Ifle of Man ✝

Lieut. Thomas Wood, Marines

Lieut. Col. John Woodford, 1ft Regiment of Foot Guards

Capt. Thomas Worfley, South Hants Militia

Capt. Hale Young Worthern, Hertfordfhire Militia

Capt. John Wright, Leicefterfhire Regiment of Militia

Lieut. Col. Jofeph Wrightfon, Major of Chelfea College ✝

Lieut. William Wynne, Militia

Lieut. Col. Wadham Wyndham, Coldftream Regiment of Foot Guards

N. B. Thofe thus ✝ marked were Subfcribers to fome of my former Military Publications.